Second Workshop on Deep Learning Approaches for Low-Resource Natural Language Processing 2019

Hong Kong, China
3 November 2019

ISBN: 978-1-7138-0077-4

EMNLP-IJCNLP 2019

Deep Learning Approaches for Low-Resource Natural Language Processing (DeepLo)

Proceedings of the Second Workshop

November 3, 2019
Hong Kong, China

Introduction

The EMNLP-IJCNLP 2019 Workshop on Deep Learning Approaches for Low-Resource Natural Language Processing (DeepLo) takes place on Sunday, November 3rd, in Hong Kong, China, immediately before the main conference.

Natural Language Processing is being revolutionized by deep learning with neural networks. However, deep learning requires large amounts of annotated data, and its advantage over traditional statistical methods typically diminishes when such data is not available; for example, SMT continues to outperform NMT in many bilingually resource-poor scenarios. Large amounts of annotated data do not exist for many low-resource languages, and for high-resource languages it can be difficult to find linguistically annotated data of sufficient size and quality to allow neural methods to excel. Our workshop aimed to bring together researchers from the NLP and ML communities who work on learning with neural methods when there is not enough data for those methods to succeed out-of-the-box. Techniques of interest include self-training, paired training, distant supervision, semi-supervised and transfer learning, and human-in-the-loop algorithms such as active learning.

Our call for papers for this second workshop met with a strong response. We received 85 paper submissions, of which 10 were "extended abstracts" with non-archival status—work that will be presented at the workshop, but will not appear in the proceedings in order to allow it to be published elsewhere. We accepted 32 papers and 7 extended abstracts.

Our program covers a broad spectrum of applications and techniques. It is augmented by invited talks from Heng Ji, Barbara Plank, Dan Roth, Kristina Toutanova, and Luke Zettlemoyer.

We would like to thank the members of our Program Committee for their timely and thoughtful reviews.

Colin Cherry, Greg Durrett, George Foster, Reza Haffari, Shahram Khadivi, Nanyun Peng, Xiang Ren, and Swabha Swayamdipta

Organizers:

Colin Cherry, Google
Greg Durrett, University of Texas, Austin
George Foster, Google
Gholamreza (Reza) Haffari, Monash University
Shahram Khadivi, eBay
Nanyun Peng, University of Southern California
Xiang Ren, University of Southern California
Swabha Swayamdipta, Allen Institute for Artificial Intelligence

Invited Speakers:

Heng Ji, University of Illinois Urbana-Champaign
Barbara Plank, IT University of Copenhagen
Dan Roth, University of Pennsylvania
Kristina Toutanova, Google AI Language
Luke Zettlemoyer, University of Washington / Facebook AI Research

Program Committee:

Afshin Rahimi
Alexander Spangher
Ana Marasovic
Daniel Fried
Ekaterina Vylomova
Fei Liu
Gaurav Kumar
Hainan Xu
Jean-David Ruvini
Jiacheng Xu
Jifan Chen
Johnny Wei
Jonathan Kummerfeld
José G. C. de Souza
Julia Kreutzer
Ke Tran
Kenton Lee
Kevin Duh
Luheng He
Melvin Johnson
Mingyu Derek Ma
Nazneen Fatema Rajani
Orhan Firat
Parminder Bhatia
Parnia Bahar

Patrick Littell
Pavel Petrushkov
Peifeng Wang
Pengxiang Cheng
Poorya Zaremoodi
Robin Jia
Rujun Han
Sameen Maruf
Sanjika Hewavitharana
Sarvnaz Karimi
Selcuk Kopru
Shuoyang Ding
Suchin Gururangan
Te-Lin Wu
Tomer Lancewicki
Thamme Gowda
Vered Shwartz
Weiyue Wang
Xiaolei Huang
Xisen Jin
Yasumasa Onoe
Yi Luan
Yuchen Lin
Yunsu Kim

Table of Contents

Conference Program

Sunday, November 3, 2019

7:30–8:50   *Breakfast*

8:50–9:00   *Opening Remarks*

9:00–9:45   *Invited Talk 1: Heng Ji*

9:45–10:30   **Poster Session 1**

A Closer Look At Feature Space Data Augmentation For Few-Shot Intent Classification
Varun Kumar, Hadrien Glaude, Cyprien de Lichy and Wlliam Campbell

A Comparative Analysis of Unsupervised Language Adaptation Methods
Gil Rocha and Henrique Lopes Cardoso

A logical-based corpus for cross-lingual evaluation
Felipe Salvatore, Marcelo Finger and Roberto Hirata Jr

Adaptively Scheduled Multitask Learning: The Case of Low-Resource Neural Machine Translation
Poorya Zaremoodi and Gholamreza Haffari

Bad Form: Comparing Context-Based and Form-Based Few-Shot Learning in Distributional Semantic Models
Jeroen Van Hautte, Guy Emerson and Marek Rei

Bag-of-Words Transfer: Non-Contextual Techniques for Multi-Task Learning
Seth Ebner, Felicity Wang and Benjamin Van Durme

BERT is Not an Interlingua and the Bias of Tokenization
Jasdeep Singh, Bryan McCann, Richard Socher and Caiming Xiong

Building Bilingual Pre-trained Models In A Day
Ke Tran

Byte-Pair encoding for text-to-SQL generation
Samuel Müller and Andreas Vlachos

Cross-lingual Joint Entity and Word Embedding to Improve Entity Linking and Parallel Sentence Mining
Xiaoman Pan, Thamme Gowda, Heng Ji, Jonathan May and Scott Miller

Deep Bidirectional Transformers for Relation Extraction without Supervision
Yannis Papanikolaou, Ian Roberts and Andrea Pierleoni

Domain Adaptation with BERT-based Domain Classification and Data Selection
Xiaofei Ma, Peng Xu, Zhiguo Wang, Ramesh Nallapati and Bing Xiang

Empirical Evaluation of Active Learning Techniques for Neural MT
Xiangkai Zeng, Sarthak Garg, Rajen Chatterjee, Udhyakumar Nallasamy and Matthias Paulik

Fast Domain Adaptation of Semantic Parsers via Paraphrase Attention
Avik Ray, Yilin Shen and Hongxia Jin

Few-Shot and Zero-Shot Learning for Historical Text Normalization
Marcel Bollmann, Natalia Korchagina and Anders Søgaard

From Monolingual to Multilingual FAQ Assistant using Multilingual Co-training
Mayur Patidar, Surabhi Kumari, Manasi Patwardhan, Shirish Karande, Puneet Agarwal, Lovekesh Vig and Gautam Shroff

Generation-Distillation for Efficient Natural Language Understanding in Low-Data Settings
Luke Melas-Kyriazi, George Han and Celine Liang

H-FND: Hierarchical False-Negative Denoising for Robust Distantly-Supervised Relation Extraction
Tsu-Jui Fu and Wei-Yun Ma

10:30–11:00 *Break*

11:00–11:45 *Invited Talk 2: Barbara Plank*

Zero-shot Dependency Parsing with Pre-trained Multilingual Sentence Representations
Ke Tran and Arianna Bisazza

15:30–16:00   *Break*

16:00–16:45   *Invited Talk 4: Kristina Toutanova*

16:45–17:30   *Invited Talk 5: Luke Zettlemoyer*

17:30–17:40   *Closing Remarks*

A Closer Look At Feature Space Data Augmentation For Few-Shot Intent Classification

Varun Kumar, Hadrien Glaude, Cyprien de Lichy, Wlliam Campbell
Amazon Alexa
Cambridge, MA, USA
{kuvrun,hglaude,cllichy,cmpw}@amazon.com

Abstract

New conversation topics and functionalities are constantly being added to conversational AI agents like Amazon Alexa and Apple Siri. As data collection and annotation is not scalable and is often costly, only a handful of examples for the new functionalities are available, which results in poor generalization performance. We formulate it as a Few-Shot Integration (FSI) problem where a few examples are used to introduce a new intent. In this paper, we study six feature space data augmentation methods to improve classification performance in FSI setting in combination with both supervised and unsupervised representation learning methods such as BERT. Through realistic experiments on two public conversational datasets, SNIPS, and the Facebook Dialog corpus, we show that data augmentation in feature space provides an effective way to improve intent classification performance in few-shot setting beyond traditional transfer learning approaches. In particular, we show that (a) upsampling in latent space is a competitive baseline for feature space augmentation (b) adding the difference between two examples to a new example is a simple yet effective data augmentation method.

1 Introduction

Virtual artificial assistants with natural language understanding (NLU) support a variety of functionalities. Throughout the lifespan of the deployed NLU systems, new functionalities with new categories, are regularly introduced. While techniques such as active learning (Peshterliev et al., 2018), semi-supervised learning (Cho et al., 2019b) are used to improve the performance of existing functionalities, performance for new functionalities suffers from the data scarcity problem.

Recently, Few-Shot Learning has been explored to address the problem of generalizing from a few examples per category. While it has been extensively studied (Koch et al., 2015; Snell et al., 2017; Vinyals et al., 2016) for image recognition, a little attention has been paid to improve NLU performance in the low-data regime. Moreover, researchers have been mostly working on the unrealistic setting that considers tasks with few categories unseen during (pre)training, each with only a few examples, and introduces new categories during test time. We argue that a more realistic setting is Few-Shot Integration (FSI) where new categories with limited training data are introduced into an existing system with mature categories. FSI is well aligned with the goal of lifelong learning of conversational agents and measures the performance in a real-life system setting when only a few examples of a new class are added to the existing data from the old classes. To address the poor generalization in data scare scenarios, several pre-training methods such as ELMo (Peters et al., 2018), Generative pre-trained Transformer (Radford et al., 2018), BERT (Devlin et al., 2018), have been proposed which are trained on a large amount of unannotated text data. Such pre-trained models can be fine-tuned on a particular NLP task and have shown to greatly improve generalization. However, in FSI setting where only a handful of examples are provided, building accurate NLU model is still a challenging task.

In this paper, we focus on Feature space Data Augmentation (FDA) methods to improve the classification performance of the categories with limited data. We study six widely different feature space data augmentation methods: 1) upsampling in the feature space UPSAMPLE, 2) random perturbation PERTURB, 3) extrapolation (Devries and Taylor, 2017) EXTRA, 4) conditional variational auto-encoder (CVAE) (Kingma and Welling, 2013) CVAE, 5) delta encoder that have been especially designed to work in the few-shot

Proceedings of the 2nd Workshop on Deep Learning Approaches for Low-Resource NLP (DeepLo), pages 1–10
Hong Kong, China, November 3, 2019. ©2019 Association for Computational Linguistics
https://doi.org/10.18653/v1/P17

learning setting (Schwartz et al., 2018) DELTA, 6) linear delta which is a linear version of the delta encoder LINEAR. While UPSAMPLE, PERTURB, EXTRA and LINEAR doesn't require any training beyond hyper-parameter optimization, DELTA and CVAE are trained deep neural network generators.

We compare these six FDA techniques on two open datasets for Intent Classification (IC) : SNIPS (Coucke et al., 2018) and Facebook Dialog corpus (Gupta et al., 2018). We show that BERT combined with LINEAR data augmentation provides an effective method to bootstrap accurate intent classifiers with limited training data. We make the following contributions:

1. We propose the FSI evaluation, a relaxation of the few-shot learning setting that aims to better model the requirement of modern NLU systems. We provide a comprehensive evaluation of FSI for text classification and show that UPSAMPLE and PERTURB are simple yet efficient baselines that are often neglected in few-shot learning evaluations.

2. We provide an in-depth analysis of various FDA methods. We show that complex methods such as DELTA and CVAE do not always improve over simple methods like LINEAR, and the performance heavily depends on the feature extractor.

3. Finally, we provide guidance on when and how to apply FDA for FSI. We show that FDA consistently provides gains on top of the unsupervised pre-training methods such as BERT in FSI setting.

2 Related work

Few-shot learning has been studied extensively in the computer vision domain. In particular, several metric learning based methods (Koch et al., 2015; Vinyals et al., 2016; Snell et al., 2017; Rippel et al., 2015) has been proposed for few-shot classification where a model first learns an embedding space and then a simple metric is used to classify instances of new categories via proximity to the few labeled training examples embedded in the same space. In addition to metric-learning, several meta-learning based approaches (Ravi and Larochelle, 2016; Li et al., 2017; Finn et al., 2017) have been proposed for few-shot classification on unseen classes.

Recently, Few-Shot Learning on text data has been explored using metric learning (Yu et al., 2018; Jiang et al., 2018). In (Yu et al., 2018), authors propose to learn a weighted combination of metrics obtained from meta-training tasks for a newly seen few-shot task. Similarly, in (Cheng et al., 2019), authors propose to use meta-metric-learning to learn task-specific metric that can handle imbalanced datasets.

Generative models are also widely used to improve classification performance by data augmentation. For example, generative models are used for data augmentation in image classification (Mehrotra and Dukkipati, 2017; Antoniou et al., 2018; Zhang et al., 2018), text classification (Gupta, 2019), anomaly detection (Lim et al., 2018). Data augmentation through deformation of an image has been known to be very effective for image recognition. More advanced approaches rely on Auto-Encoders (AEs) or Generative Adversarial Networks (GANs). For example, in (Mehrotra and Dukkipati, 2017) the authors combine metric-learning with data augmentation using GANs for few-shot learning. However, classical generative approaches require a significant amount of training data to be able to generate good enough examples that will improve classification accuracy. To overcome this challenge, (Hariharan and Girshick, 2017) proposed to augment the training data in the feature space. This both eases the generation problem and enforces generation of discriminative examples. In addition, the authors propose to transfer deformations from base classes to new classes, which allows circumventing the data scarcity problem for new classes. Finally, in (Schwartz et al., 2018), authors used an Autoencoder to encode transformations between pairs of examples of the same class and apply them to an example of the new class.

Generative models are a good candidate for FSI tasks, as one can just combine the generated data for new classes with the old classes training data (Hariharan and Girshick, 2017; Wang et al., 2018). For text classification, several text generation based data augmentation techniques have also been explored (Hou et al., 2018; Zhao et al., 2019; Guu et al., 2018; Yoo et al., 2018; Cho et al., 2019a). However, generating discrete sequences, e.g. text, is known to be quite difficult and requires lots of training data. That is why, in this paper, we focus on generative models, which augment data

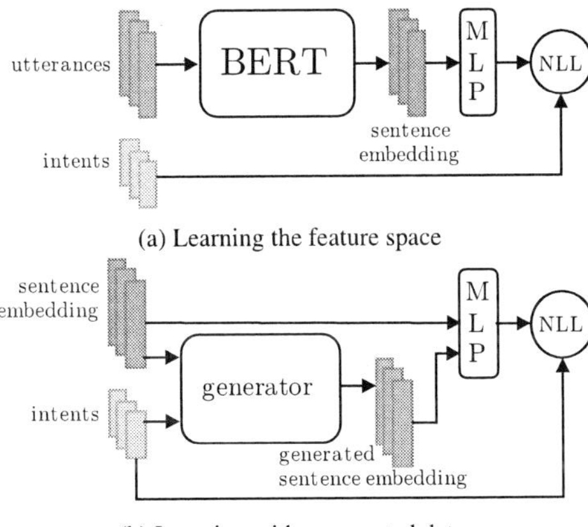

(a) Learning the feature space

(b) Learning with augmented data

Figure 1: Data augmentation in the feature space

in latent(feature) space to solve a few-shot integration problem for text classification.

3 Data Augmentation in Feature Space

Feature space data Augmentation (FDA) is an effective method to improve classification performance on different ML tasks (Chawla et al., 2002; Hariharan and Girshick, 2017; Devries and Taylor, 2017; Guo et al., 2019). As shown on Figure 1, FDA techniques usually work by first learning a data representation or feature extractor, and then generating new data for the low resource class in the feature space. After generating data, a classifier is trained with real and augmented data.

For IC, we finetune a pre-trained English BERT-Base uncased model [1] to build our feature extractor. The BERT model has 12 layers, 768 hidden states, and 12 heads. We use the pooled representation of the hidden state of the first special token ([CLS]) as the sentence representation. A dropout probability of 0.1 is applied to the sentence representation before passing it to the 1-layer Softmax classifier. BERT Encoder and MLP classifier are fine-tuned using cross-entropy loss for IC task. Adam (Kingma and Ba, 2014) is used for optimization with an initial learning rate of $5e - 5$.

For data augmentation, we apply six different FDA methods, described below, to generate new examples in the feature space. Finally, we train a 1- layer Softmax classifier as in the feature learning phase.

---

[1]https://github.com/huggingface/pytorch-transformers

3.1 Upsampling

The simplest method to augment training data for underrepresented categories is to duplicate the existing training data. Upsampling is a well studied technique to handle the class imbalance problem (Estabrooks et al., 2004). We show that for intents with limited labeled data, upsampling the existing data in latent space consistently improves model performance, and thus is a good baseline method for FDA techniques. We call this method UPSAMPLE.

3.2 Random Perturbation

Adding random noise to the existing training data is another simple yet effective data augmentation technique. Random perturbation data augmentation has been previously used to improve the performance of classification models as well as for sequence generation models. For example, (Kurata et al., 2016) applied additive and multiplicative perturbation to improve the text generation for data augmentation. In our experiments, we apply both additive and multiplicative perturbation to the existing training data. We sample noise from a uniform distribution [-1.0, 1.0]. We use PERTURB to refer to this method.

3.3 Conditional VAE

Conditional Variational Autoencoder (CVAE) is an extension of Variational Autoencoder (VAE) (Kingma and Welling, 2013) which can be used to generate examples for a given category. All components of the model are conditioned on the category. First, we train CVAE on the sentence representations and then generate new examples by sampling from the latent distribution. The encoder and decoder sub-networks are implemented as multi-layer perceptrons with a single hidden layer of 2048 units, where each layer is followed by a hyperbolic tangent activation. The encoder output Z is 128-dimensional. Mean Square Error (MSE) loss function is used for reconstruction. All models are trained with Adam optimizer with the learning rate set to $10 - 3$.

3.4 Linear Delta

A simple method to generate new examples is to first learn the difference between a pair of examples, and then add this difference to another example. In this case, we first compute the difference $X_i - X_j$ between two examples from the same class and then add it to a third example X_k also from the same class as shown in (1). We use LIN-EAR to refer to this method.

$$\hat{X} = (X_i - X_j) + X_k \qquad (1)$$

3.5 Extrapolation

In (Devries and Taylor, 2017), authors proposed to use extrapolation to synthesize new examples for a given class. They demonstrated that extrapolating between samples in feature space can be used to augment datasets. In extrapolation, a new example, $\hat{X}$ is generated according to (2). In our experiments, we use $\lambda = 0.5$. We call this method EXTRA.

$$\hat{X} = (X_i - X_j) * \lambda + X_i \qquad (2)$$

3.6 Delta-Encoder

Delta-Encoder (Schwartz et al., 2018) extends the idea of learning differences between two examples using an autoencoder-based model. It first extracts transferable intra-class deformations (deltas) between same-class pairs of training examples, then applies them to a few examples of a new class to synthesize samples from that class. Authors show that Delta-Encoder can learn transferable deformations from different source classes which can be used to generate examples for unseen classes. While the authors used Delta-Encoder to generate examples for unseen classes, in our experiments, for FSI, we also use the examples from the target class to the train both the feature extractor and the Delta-Encoder along with all other examples. Then we generate new examples for the target category using trained delta encoder. For data generation, we try two different approaches to select a source sentence pair.

1. **DeltaR**: Sample a pair of sentences (X_i, X_j) from a randomly selected class. DELTAR applies deltas from multiple source categories to synthesize new examples.

2. **DeltaS**: Sample a pair of sentences (X_i, X_j) from the target category. DELTAS applies deltas from the same target category.

The encoder and decoder sub-networks are implemented as multi-layer perceptrons with a single hidden layer of 512 units, where each layer is followed by a leaky ReLU activation ($max(x, 0.2 * x)$). The encoder output Z is 16-dimensional. L1 loss is used as reconstruction loss. Adam optimizer is used with a learning rate of $10 - 3$. A high dropout with a 50% rate is applied to all layers, to avoid the model memorizing examples.

4 Experiment

4.1 Datasets

We evaluate different FDA techniques on two public benchmark datasets, SNIPS (Coucke et al., 2018), and Facebook Dialog corpus (FBDialog) (Gupta et al., 2018). For SNIPS dataset, we use train, dev and test split provided by (Goo et al., 2018) [2].

SNIPS dataset contains 7 intents which are collected from the Snips personal voice assistant. The training, development and test sets contain $13,084$, 700 and 700 utterances, respectively. FB-Dialog has utterances that are focused on navigation, events, and navigation to events. FBDialog dataset also contains utterances with multiple intents as the root node. For our experiment, we exclude such utterances by removing utterances with *COMBINED intent* root node. This leads to $31,218$ training, $4,455$ development and $9,019$ testset utterances. Note that while SNIPS is a balanced dataset, FBDialog dataset is highly imbalanced with a maximum $8,860$ and a minimum of 4 training examples per intent.

4.2 Simulating Few-Shot Integration

In virtual assistants, often a new intent development starts with very limited training data. To simulate the integration of a new intent, we randomly sample k seed training examples from the new intent, referred to as target intent, and keep all the data from other intents. We also remove the target intent data from the development set. We train the feature extractor on the resulting training data, and then generate $100, 512$ examples using different augmentation methods for the target intent. To account for random fluctuations in the results, we repeat this process 10 times for a given target intent and report the average accuracy with the standard deviation. In all experiments, models are evaluated on the full test set.

---

[2] https://github.com/MiuLab/SlotGated-SLU

Size	Method	SNIPS	FBDialog
No Augmentation		98.14 (0.42)	94.99 (0.18)
5%	UPSAMPLE	98.14 (0.47)	95.01 (0.16)
	PERTURB	**98.26** (0.40)	94.98 (0.19)
	LINEAR	98.14 (0.45)	**95.02** (0.21)
	EXTRA	98.14 (0.45)	**95.02** (0.20)
	CVAE	98.14 (0.45)	94.98 (0.24)
	DELTAR	98.23 (0.46)	95.00 (0.22)
	DELTAS	**98.26** (0.42)	95.00 (0.20)
10%	UPSAMPLE	98.14 (0.47)	94.94 (0.18)
	PERTURB	98.23 (0.41)	94.98 (0.24)
	LINEAR	98.09 (0.50)	**95.02** (0.18)
	EXTRA	98.11 (0.49)	95.01 (0.19)
	CVAE	98.20 (0.42)	94.99 (0.26)
	DELTAR	**98.26** (0.42)	94.99 (0.21)
	DELTAS	98.23 (0.42)	94.97 (0.22)
20%	UPSAMPLE	98.14 (0.45)	95.02 (0.12)
	PERTURB	98.14 (0.44)	94.99 (0.20)
	LINEAR	98.17 (0.43)	95.05 (0.23)
	EXTRA	98.14 (0.45)	95.07 (0.11)
	CVAE	98.11 (0.44)	94.98 (0.23)
	DELTAR	**98.26** (0.40)	**95.08** (0.19)
	DELTAS	98.20 (0.46)	95.04 (0.22)

Table 1: IC accuracy on SNIPS and Facebook dataset with all training data, reported as *mean (SD)*.

5 Results and Discussion

5.1 FDA For Data-Rich Classification

For both datasets, we generate 5%, 10%, and 20% examples using different FDA methods. Then, we train a classifier using both generated as well as real data. Table 1 shows that augmenting data in feature space provides only minor improvements in classification accuracy. In particular, on SNIPS dataset, PERTUB and DELTAR improve accuracy from 98.14 to 98.26. On FBDialog dataset, DeltaR provides a minor gain, 95.02 to 95.08 over upsample baseline.

5.2 Impact Of The Number Of Seed Examples

To understand the impact of the number of seed examples, we vary it to 5, 10, 15, 20, 25, and 30 for SNIPS's AddToPlaylist. For each experiment, we generate 100 examples using different FDA methods. Figure 2 shows that as the number of seed examples increases, the accuracy of the model goes up. We also observe that for a few seed examples 5 - 15, LINEAR outperforms other FSA methods. Finally, gains are less significant after 30 seed examples.

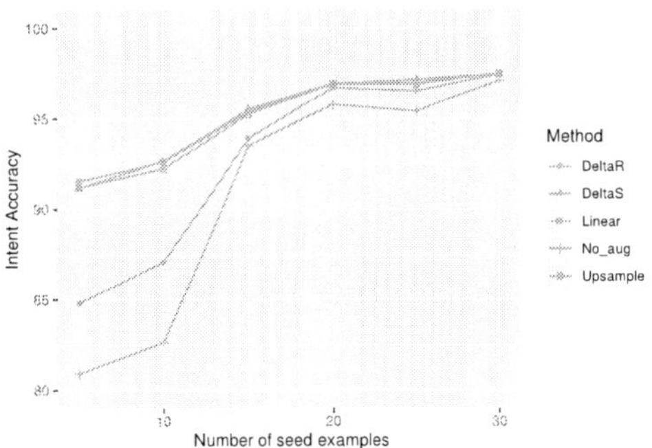

Figure 2: IC accuracy on SNIPS's AddToPlaylist intent with varying number of seed examples. 100 examples are generated using different FDA techniques. As indicated by the accuracy trend, increasing the seed examples leads to better performance.

5.3 Few-Shot Integration

We simulate FSI IC for all 7 intents of SNIPS dataset. For FBDialog dataset, we run simulations on the six largest intents, viz. GetDirections, GetDistance, GetEstimatedArrival, GetEstimatedDuration, GetInfoTraffic, and GetEvent. Since, BERT generalizes well with just 30 examples, to compare the effectiveness of different FDA methods, we use 10 seed examples in FSI simulations. For each intent, we select $k = 10$ seed training examples and use all training data for other intents.

Table 2 shows average accuracy for all intents' FSI simulations. Results on individual intent's FSI simulations can be found in Appendix's Table 5 and Table 6. On both datasets, all FDA methods improve classification accuracy over no augmentation baseline. Also, UPSAMPLE provides huge gains over no augmentation baseline. Additionally, on both datasets, with 512 augmented examples, LINEAR and DELTAS works better than PERTURB and UPSAMPLE.

5.4 Upsampling: Text Space vs Latent Space

In this section, we explore how upsampling in text space impacts performances as it is supposed to both improve the feature extractor and the linear classifier, compared to UPSAMPLE. To investigate whether upsampling in text space helps FDA, we upsampled the 10 seed examples to 100 and repeat the FSI experiments on all 7 intents of the SNIPS dataset. Table 3 shows the mean accuracy of all 7 intents FSI simulations results for different FDA techniques. FSI simulations scores for individual intents can be found in Appendix's Table 7. We

#	Method	SNIPS	FBDialog
No Augmentation		87.46(2.87)	81.29(0.11)
100	UPSAMPLE	94.26(1.66)	**84.34**(1.84)
	PERTURB	94.18(1.74)	84.04(1.95)
	CVAE	94.10(1.83)	84.10(1.94)
	LINEAR	**94.36**(1.69)	84.31(1.9)
	EXTRA	94.30(1.68)	84.13(1.83)
	DELTAR	91.32(3.12)	81.97(0.76)
	DELTAS	94.28(1.92)	83.50(1.92)
512	UPSAMPLE	95.68(0.86)	89.03(0.99)
	PERTURB	95.65(0.92)	89.02(0.99)
	CVAE	95.46(1.03)	88.71(1.09)
	LINEAR	**95.87**(0.87)	**89.30**(1.03)
	EXTRA	95.82(0.89)	89.21(0.99)
	DELTAR	95.33(1.56)	87.28(1.46)
	DELTAS	**95.88**(1.04)	89.15(1.12)

Table 2: Average IC accuracy for all intents' FSI simulations on SNIPS and FBDialog dataset. For each simulation, $k = 10$ seed examples are used for target intent. Scores are reported as *mean (SD)*. Refer to Appendix's Table 5 and Table 6 for individual intents' results.

#	Method	Overall Mean
No Augmentation		94.38(1.23)
100	UPSAMPLE	94.53(1.12)
	PERTURB	94.52(1.18)
	CVAE	94.53(1.18)
	LINEAR	94.53(1.12)
	EXTRA	94.53(1.13)
	DELTAR	**94.62**(1.16)
	DELTAS	94.57(1.14)
512	UPSAMPLE	94.67(1.11)
	PERTURB	94.68(1.14)
	CVAE	94.73(1.11)
	LINEAR	94.67(1.11)
	EXTRA	94.67(1.11)
	DELTAR	**94.88**(1.12)
	DELTAS	94.74(1.12)

Table 3: IC accuracy on SNIPS dataset in the FSI setting, reported as *mean (SD)*. The 10 seed examples are upsampled to 100 to train the feature extractor. Refer to Appendix's Table 7 for individual intents' results.

observe that upsampling in text space improves the no augmentation baseline for all intents. The mean accuracy score improves from 87.46 to 94.38. We also observe that different FDA techniques further improve model accuracy. Interestingly, upsampling in text space helps DELTAR the most. Surprisingly, upsampling in latent space provides better performance than upsampling in the text space. In particular, without upsampling the seed examples to learn the feature extractor, the best score is 95.88 for DELTAS, whereas with text space upsampling the best score decreases to 94.88. This decrease in performance is only seen with BERT and not with the Bi-LSTM feature extractor (see Table 4). We hypothesize that upsampling text data leads to BERT overfitting the target category which results in less generalized sentence representations. Overall, we found that augmentation in the latent space seems to work better with BERT, and is more effective than text space upsampling.

5.5 Effect Of The Pre-trained BERT Encoder

In FSI setting, Fine-Tuned BERT model provides very good generalization performance. For example, for SNIPS's RateBookIntent (column *Book* in Table 5), it yields 96.81% accuracy. Overall for BERT representations, LINEAR and DELTAS augmentation methods provide the best accuracy.

To investigate whether these augmentation improvements can be generalized to other sentence encoders, we experiment with a Bi-LSTM sentence encoder. For feature learning, we use a 1-layer Bi-LSTM encoder followed by a single layer softmax classifier. In our experiments, we use 128 as hidden units and 300 dimension Glove embeddings. For SNIPS dataset, we use 10 examples of AddToPlaylist intent and for FB Dialog dataset, we use 10 examples of GetDirections intent.

Table 4 shows intent accuracy for SNIPS and Facebook datasets. We find that, unlike BERT, in the FSI setting, the Bi-LSTM encoder provides a lower accuracy. In contrast to BERT FSI experiments, DELTAS performs worse than the UPSAMPLE and PERTURB baselines. The main reason is that Delta-Encoder's performance relies on a good feature extractor and with 10 seed examples, the Bi-LSTM encoder fails to learn good sentence representations. To improve representation learning, we upsample 10 utterances to 100 and then train the feature extractor. Upsampling in text space improves the performance of both delta encoder methods, DELTAS, and DELTAR. Moreover, for both SNIPS's AddToPlayList and FBDialog's GetDirections intent, DELTAR outperforms all other FDA methods.

Size	Method	SNIPS's AddToPlaylist		FBDialog's GetDirections	
seed examples (k)		10	100*	10	100*
No Augmentation		80.07 (2.08)	90.17 (1.39)	87.44 (0.12)	87.94 (0.32)
100	UPSAMPLE	**88.27** (1.74)	90.61 (1.52)	88.01 (0.26)	88.17 (0.32)
	PERTURB	88.03 (1.52)	90.86 (1.39)	88.01 (0.32)	88.25 (0.31)
	LINEAR	88.14 (1.62)	91.06 (1.58)	88.05 (0.25)	88.26 (0.32)
	EXTRA	88.09 (1.57)	90.74 (1.57)	**88.10** (0.29)	88.20 (0.3)
	CVAE	**88.27** (2.08)	90.90 (1.69)	88.04 (0.24)	88.17 (0.32)
	DELTAR	82.23 (2.21)	**91.46** (1.19)	87.60 (0.23)	**88.75** (0.43)
	DELTAS	84.4 (2.74)	91.07 (1.44)	88.02 (0.22)	88.57 (0.36)
512	UPSAMPLE	91.41 (1.03)	91.61 (1.4)	88.68 (0.49)	88.40 (0.35)
	PERTURB	**91.46** (0.99)	91.73 (1.32)	88.89 (0.57)	88.56 (0.39)
	LINEAR	91.20 (1.28)	91.41 (1.52)	88.97 (0.65)	88.47 (0.33)
	EXTRA	91.26 (1.22)	91.57 (1.55)	88.85 (0.61)	88.48 (0.37)
	CVAE	91.39 (0.94)	91.44 (1.2)	89.02 (0.52)	88.48 (0.4)
	DELTAR	87.09 (2.75)	**92.97** (1.2))	88.61 (0.35)	**89.70** (0.53)
	DELTAS	89.34 (1.48)	92.00 (1.25)	**89.34** (0.4)	89.09 (0.51)

Table 4: IC accuracy on SNIPS's AddToPlaylist and FBDialog's GetDirections in the FSI setting, reported as *mean (SD)*. A 1-layer Bi-LSTM model is used as a feature extractor. 100* represents 10 seed examples are upsampled to 100 to train the feature extractor.

5.6 Is Delta-Encoder Effective On Text?

While on few-shot image classification, Delta-Encoder provides excellent generalization performance (Schwartz et al., 2018) on unseen classes, on text classification, its performance is heavily dependent on the feature extractor. We observe that in most cases, DELTAR performs worse than DELTAS which suggests that unlike for few-shot image classification, Delta-Encoder fails to learn variations which can be applied to a different category. In addition, in FSI with BERT encoder, DELTAS performance is close to LINEAR. This indicates that in the low-data regime, simple subtraction between BERT sentence representations is a good proxy to learn intra-class variations. Upsampling data in text space improves Delta-Encoder performance for both BERT and Bi-LSTM encoders. As shown in Table 3, with upsampling in text space, DELTAR performs better than any other FDA method.

5.7 Qualitative Evaluation

We observe significant accuracy improvements in all FSI experiments for all FDA methods. Since UPSAMPLE and PERTURB also provide significant gains, it seems that most of the gains come from the fact that we are adding more data. However, in the FSI setting, LINEAR and DELTAS method consistently perform better than both UPSAMPLE and PERTURB, which indicates that these methods generate more relevant data than just noise, and redundancy. Here, we focus on visualizing generated examples from LINEAR, DELTAS and DELTAR methods using t-SNE.

Figure 3 shows visualizations for SNIPS's AddToPlaylist generated sentence representations using different FDA methods. We use 10 seed examples of AddToPlaylist and use BERT as sentence encoder. While data generated by LINEAR and EXTRA are close to the real examples, DELTAS and DELTAR generated examples form two different clusters. Since, Delta-Encoder performance improves when seed examples are upsampled in text space, we plot sentence examples from upsampled data.

Figure 4 shows that when 10 seed examples are upsampled to 100, DELTAS cluster moves closer to the seed examples, and while most of the DELTAR generated data forms a separate cluster, a few of the generated examples are close to the seed examples. Since, in experiments with upsampled text examples, DELTAR performs better than other FDA methods, we hypothesize that DELTAR increases the amount of variability within the dataset by generating diverse examples which leads to a more robust model.

6 Conclusion and Future Work

In this paper, we investigate six FDA methods including UPSAMPLE, PERTURB, CVAE, Delta-Encoder, EXTRA, and LINEAR to augment training data. We show that FDA works better when combined with transfer learning and provides an effective way of bootstrapping an intent classifier for new classes. As expected, all FDA methods become less effective when the number of seed examples increases and provides minor gains in the full-data regime. Through comparing methods on two public datasets, our results show that LINEAR is a competitive baseline for FDA in FSI setting, especially when combined with transfer learning (BERT).

Additionally, we provide empirical evidence that in few-shot integration setting, feature space augmentation combined with BERT provides better performance than widely used text space upsampling. Given that pre-trained language models provide state of the art performance on several NLP tasks, we find this result to be in particular encouraging, as it shows potential for applying FDA methods to other NLP tasks.

Our experiments on Delta-Encoder also shows that unlike few-shot image classification, Delta-Encoder fails to learn transferable intra-class variations. This result emphasizes that methods pro-

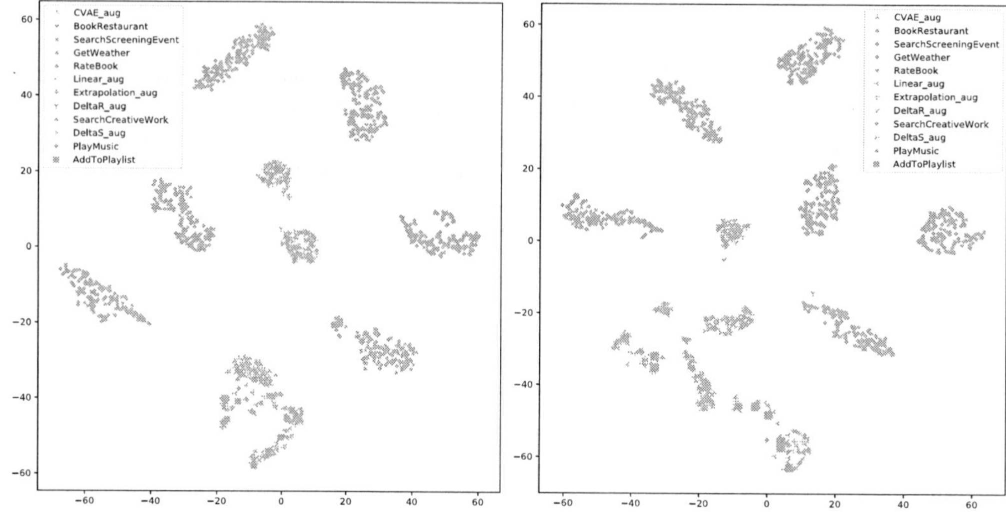

Figure 3: 10 seed examples

Figure 4: 10 seed examples are upsampled to 100

Figure 5: t-SNE visualization of different data augmentation methods for AddToPlaylist intent. BERT encoder is used to learn sentence representations.

viding improvements in computer vision domain might not produce similar gains on NLP tasks, thus underlining the need to develop data augmentation methods specific to NLP tasks.

References

Anthreas Antoniou, Amos Storkey, and Harrison Edwards. 2018. Data augmentation generative adversarial networks.

Nitesh V Chawla, Kevin W Bowyer, Lawrence O Hall, and W Philip Kegelmeyer. 2002. Smote: synthetic minority over-sampling technique. *Journal of artificial intelligence research*.

Yu Cheng, Mo Yu, Xiaoxiao Guo, and Bowen Zhou. 2019. Few-shot learning with meta metric learners.

Eunah Cho, He Xie, and William M Campbell. 2019a. Paraphrase generation for semi-supervised learning in nlu. In *Proceedings of the Workshop on Methods for Optimizing and Evaluating Neural Language Generation*.

Eunah Cho, He Xie, John Lalor, Varun Kumar, and William M Campbell. 2019b. Efficient semi-supervised learning for natural language understanding by optimizing diversity. In *IEEE Automatic Speech Recognition and Understanding Workshop*.

Alice Coucke, Alaa Saade, Adrien Ball, Théodore Bluche, Alexandre Caulier, David Leroy, Clément Doumouro, Thibault Gisselbrecht, Francesco Caltagirone, Thibaut Lavril, et al. 2018. Snips voice platform: an embedded spoken language understanding system for private-by-design voice interfaces. *arXiv preprint arXiv:1805.10190*.

Jacob Devlin, Ming-Wei Chang, Kenton Lee, and Kristina Toutanova. 2018. Bert: Pre-training of deep bidirectional transformers for language understanding. *arXiv preprint arXiv:1810.04805*.

Terrance Devries and Graham W. Taylor. 2017. Dataset augmentation in feature space. *ArXiv*, abs/1702.05538.

Andrew Estabrooks, Taeho Jo, and Nathalie Japkowicz. 2004. A multiple resampling method for learning from imbalanced data sets. *Computational intelligence*.

Chelsea Finn, Pieter Abbeel, and Sergey Levine. 2017. Model-agnostic meta-learning for fast adaptation of deep networks. In *Proceedings of the 34th International Conference on Machine Learning*. JMLR.org.

Chih-Wen Goo, Guang Gao, Yun-Kai Hsu, Chih-Li Huo, Tsung-Chieh Chen, Keng-Wei Hsu, and Yun-Nung Chen. 2018. Slot-gated modeling for joint slot filling and intent prediction. In *Proceedings of the North American Chapter of the Association for Computational Linguistics*.

Hongyu Guo, Yongyi Mao, and Richong Zhang. 2019. Augmenting data with mixup for sentence classification: An empirical study. *arXiv preprint arXiv:1905.08941*.

Rahul Gupta. 2019. Data augmentation for low resource sentiment analysis using generative adversarial networks. In *IEEE International Conference on Acoustics, Speech and Signal Processing*.

Sonal Gupta, Rushin Shah, Mrinal Mohit, Anuj Kumar, and Mike Lewis. 2018. Semantic parsing for task oriented dialog using hierarchical representations. *arXiv preprint arXiv:1810.07942*.

Kelvin Guu, Tatsunori B Hashimoto, Yonatan Oren, and Percy Liang. 2018. Generating sentences by editing prototypes. *Transactions of the Association of Computational Linguistics*.

Bharath Hariharan and Ross Girshick. 2017. Low-shot visual recognition by shrinking and hallucinating features. In *Proceedings of the International Conference on Computer Vision*.

Yutai Hou, Yijia Liu, Wanxiang Che, and Ting Liu. 2018. Sequence-to-sequence data augmentation for dialogue language understanding. *arXiv preprint arXiv:1807.01554*.

Xiang Jiang, Mohammad Havaei, Gabriel Chartrand, Hassan Chouaib, Thomas Vincent, Andrew Jesson, Nicolas Chapados, and Stan Matwin. 2018. Attentive task-agnostic meta-learning for few-shot text classification.

Diederik P Kingma and Jimmy Ba. 2014. Adam: A method for stochastic optimization. *arXiv preprint arXiv:1412.6980*.

Diederik P Kingma and Max Welling. 2013. Auto-encoding variational bayes. *arXiv preprint arXiv:1312.6114*.

Gregory Koch, Richard Zemel, and Ruslan Salakhutdinov. 2015. Siamese neural networks for one-shot image recognition. In *ICML Deep Learning Workshop*.

Gakuto Kurata, Bing Xiang, and Bowen Zhou. 2016. Labeled data generation with encoder-decoder lstm for semantic slot filling. In *INTERSPEECH*.

Zhenguo Li, Fengwei Zhou, Fei Chen, and Hang Li. 2017. Meta-sgd: Learning to learn quickly for few-shot learning. *arXiv preprint arXiv:1707.09835*.

Swee Kiat Lim, Yi Loo, Ngoc-Trung Tran, Ngai-Man Cheung, Gemma Roig, and Yuval Elovici. 2018. Doping: Generative data augmentation for unsupervised anomaly detection with gan. In *2018 IEEE International Conference on Data Mining*.

Akshay Mehrotra and Ambedkar Dukkipati. 2017. Generative adversarial residual pairwise networks for one shot learning.

Stanislav Peshterliev, John Kearney, Abhyuday Jagannatha, Imre Kiss, and Spyros Matsoukas. 2018. Active learning for new domains in natural language understanding. *arXiv preprint arXiv:1810.03450*.

Matthew E Peters, Mark Neumann, Mohit Iyyer, Matt Gardner, Christopher Clark, Kenton Lee, and Luke Zettlemoyer. 2018. Deep contextualized word representations. *arXiv preprint arXiv:1802.05365*.

Alec Radford, Karthik Narasimhan, Tim Salimans, and Ilya Sutskever. 2018. Improving language understanding by generative pre-training.

Sachin Ravi and Hugo Larochelle. 2016. Optimization as a model for few-shot learning.

Oren Rippel, Manohar Paluri, Piotr Dollar, and Lubomir Bourdev. 2015. Metric learning with adaptive density discrimination. *arXiv preprint arXiv:1511.05939*.

Eli Schwartz, Leonid Karlinsky, Joseph Shtok, Sivan Harary, Mattias Marder, Abhishek Kumar, Rogerio Feris, Raja Giryes, and Alex Bronstein. 2018. Delta-encoder: an effective sample synthesis method for few-shot object recognition. In *Advances in Neural Information Processing Systems*.

Jake Snell, Kevin Swersky, and Richard Zemel. 2017. Prototypical networks for few-shot learning. In I. Guyon, U. V. Luxburg, S. Bengio, H. Wallach, R. Fergus, S. Vishwanathan, and R. Garnett, editors, *Advances in Neural Information Processing Systems*.

Oriol Vinyals, Charles Blundell, Tim Lillicrap, Koray Kavukcuoglu, and Daan Wierstra. 2016. Matching networks for one shot learning. In D. D. Lee, M. Sugiyama, U. V. Luxburg, I. Guyon, and R. Garnett, editors, *Advances in Neural Information Processing Systems*.

Yu-Xiong Wang, Ross Girshick, Martial Hebert, and Bharath Hariharan. 2018. Low-shot learning from imaginary data. In *Proceedings of the IEEE Conference on Computer Vision and Pattern Recognition*.

Kang Min Yoo, Youhyun Shin, and Sang goo Lee. 2018. Data augmentation for spoken language understanding via joint variational generation.

Mo Yu, Xiaoxiao Guo, Jinfeng Yi, Shiyu Chang, Saloni Potdar, Yu Cheng, Gerald Tesauro, Haoyu Wang, and Bowen Zhou. 2018. Diverse few-shot text classification with multiple metrics. In *Proceedings of the North American Chapter of the Association for Computational Linguistics*.

Ruixiang Zhang, Tong Che, Zoubin Ghahramani, Yoshua Bengio, and Yangqiu Song. 2018. Metagan: An adversarial approach to few-shot learning. In *Advances in Neural Information Processing Systems*.

Zijian Zhao, Su Zhu, and Kai Yu. 2019. Data augmentation with atomic templates for spoken language understanding. *arXiv preprint arXiv:1908.10770*.

A FSI experiment results for all intents

In all tables, individual columns represent FSI results for an intent, and *Overall Mean* column, provides average accuracy for all intents' FSI simulations.

#	Method	Playlist	Restaurant	Weather	Music	Book	Work	Event	Overall Mean
No Augmentation		82.63(5.11)	87.86(3.53)	84.51(1.3)	88.07(2.37)	96.81(2.94)	85.14(1.53)	87.19(3.31)	87.46(2.87)
100	UPSAMPLE	92.24(2.96)	97.7(0.67)	96.44(0.75)	94.57(1.1)	97.96(0.82)	89.61(3.01)	91.26(2.35)	94.26(1.66)
	PERTURB	**93.09**(2.55)	97.41(0.92)	96.07(1.35)	94.39(1.13)	97.86(0.93)	89.36(2.76)	91.09(2.53)	94.18(1.74)
	CVAE	92.4(3.66)	97.47(0.67)	96.49(1.07)	94.36(1.26)	97.71(1.1)	89.1(2.79)	91.2(2.22)	94.1(1.83)
	LINEAR	92.61(3.02)	97.74(0.67)	96.44(0.77)	94.63(1.18)	**97.97**(0.78)	**89.61**(3.05)	91.53(2.34)	**94.36**(1.69)
	EXTRA	92.36(3.0)	97.74(0.66)	96.41(0.77)	94.6(1.18)	97.97(0.78)	89.47(3.11)	91.51(2.3)	94.3(1.68)
	DELTAR	87.07(4.67)	93.57(4.07)	91.0(4.23)	94.87(1.28)	97.66(1.42)	85.97(2.34)	89.11(3.84)	91.32(3.12)
	DELTAS	92.64(4.49)	**97.76**(0.7)	96.41(1.25)	**94.99**(0.92)	97.83(0.99)	88.69(2.69)	**91.64**(2.36)	94.28(1.92)
512	UPSAMPLE	95.3(1.09)	98.0(0.64)	97.63(0.34)	95.57(0.87)	98.03(0.55)	92.0(1.49)	93.26(1.05)	95.68(0.86)
	PERTURB	95.33(1.2)	97.94(0.6)	97.6(0.44)	95.5(0.91)	97.91(0.55)	92.03(1.78)	93.21(0.99)	95.65(0.92)
	CVAE	95.46(1.12)	97.89(0.62)	97.54(0.43)	95.36(1.02)	97.93(0.7)	91.34(2.17)	92.73(1.19)	95.46(1.03)
	LINEAR	95.39(1.1)	**98.0**(0.64)	97.67(0.36)	95.74(0.89)	**98.04**(0.5)	**92.61**(1.47)	93.66(1.13)	**95.87**(0.87)
	EXTRA	95.36(1.17)	98.0(0.64)	97.66(0.37)	95.74(0.88)	98.04(0.5)	92.29(1.52)	93.63(1.17)	95.82(0.89)
	DELTAR	95.36(1.74)	97.81(0.69)	97.6(0.44)	95.9(0.97)	97.74(1.02)	90.27(3.44)	92.61(2.64)	95.33(1.56)
	DELTAS	**95.66**(1.18)	97.96(0.59)	**97.8**(0.45)	**95.91**(0.88)	97.91(0.74)	92.26(2.57)	**93.66**(0.86)	**95.88**(1.04)

Table 5: IC accuracy on SNIPS dataset in the FSI setting ($k = 10$), reported as *mean (SD)*.

#	Method	Directions	Distance	Arrival	Duration	Traffic	Event	Overall Mean
No Augmentation		89.61(0.1)	89.94(0.09)	90.56(0.12)	81.74(0.13)	68.5(0.13)	67.39(0.11)	81.29(0.11)
100	UPSAMPLE	89.89(0.27)	93.64(0.87)	92.95(0.57)	84.28(3.45)	68.99(0.49)	**76.26**(5.41)	**84.34**(1.84)
	PERTURB	89.82(0.24)	93.58(0.84)	92.81(0.55)	**84.81**(3.77)	**69.15**(0.68)	74.07(5.6)	84.04(1.95)
	CVAE	89.91(0.32)	93.46(0.77)	92.7(0.67)	84.45(3.52)	69.11(0.9)	74.94(5.49)	84.1(1.94)
	LINEAR	**89.93**(0.24)	**93.65**(0.88)	**92.98**(0.57)	84.2(3.44)	68.96(0.51)	76.12(5.77)	84.31(1.9)
	EXTRA	89.88(0.27)	93.61(0.89)	92.96(0.59)	84.21(3.43)	68.94(0.46)	75.18(5.34)	84.13(1.83)
	DELTAR	89.64(0.11)	92.57(1.3)	90.79(0.37)	81.72(0.12)	68.48(0.08)	68.63(2.59)	81.97(0.76)
	DELTAS	89.88(0.34)	93.68(0.72)	92.6(0.76)	83.88(3.2)	68.93(0.67)	72.05(5.83)	83.5(1.92)
512	UPSAMPLE	91.93(0.48)	94.58(0.34)	93.99(0.31)	92.56(0.72)	75.84(2.19)	85.27(1.87)	89.03(0.99)
	PERTURB	91.78(0.49)	94.58(0.43)	94.02(0.25)	92.53(0.87)	**76.0**(2.27)	85.22(1.61)	89.02(0.99)
	CVAE	91.85(0.52)	94.57(0.39)	94.0(0.34)	92.45(0.92)	74.91(2.73)	84.5(1.61)	88.71(1.09)
	LINEAR	92.14(0.66)	94.6(0.35)	94.05(0.32)	**92.78**(0.67)	**76.0**(2.49)	86.22(1.7)	**89.3**(1.03)
	EXTRA	**92.11**(0.57)	94.61(0.35)	94.04(0.29)	92.72(0.7)	75.79(2.45)	85.98(1.58)	89.21(0.99)
	DELTAR	90.43(0.55)	94.54(0.35)	93.8(0.3)	86.64(4.38)	71.68(1.46)	**86.55**(1.75)	87.28(1.46)
	DELTAS	91.83(0.47)	**94.66**(0.4)	**94.08**(0.24)	92.31(1.45)	75.81(2.1)	86.23(2.08)	89.15(1.12)

Table 6: IC accuracy on FBDialog dataset in the FSI setting ($k = 10$), reported as *mean (SD)*.

#	Method	Playlist	Restaurant	Weather	Music	Book	Work	Event	Overall Mean
No Augmentation		96.0(1.69)	95.39(1.59)	96.41(1.18)	93.1(1.38)	97.79(0.77)	88.46(1.14)	93.49(0.87)	94.38(1.23)
100	UPSAMPLE	96.0(1.57)	95.87(1.26)	**96.51**(1.04)	93.19(1.25)	97.83(0.7)	88.63(1.21)	93.7(0.83)	94.53(1.12)
	PERTURB	96.1(1.64)	95.7(1.23)	96.43(1.28)	93.33(1.1)	97.8(0.77)	88.56(1.32)	93.7(0.9)	94.52(1.18)
	CVAE	96.07(1.46)	**95.91**(1.43)	96.43(1.31)	93.2(1.15)	97.83(0.78)	88.63(1.28)	93.66(0.86)	94.53(1.18)
	LINEAR	96.0(1.57)	95.89(1.26)	**96.51**(1.04)	93.19(1.25)	97.83(0.7)	88.63(1.21)	93.7(0.83)	94.53(1.12)
	EXTRA	96.0(1.57)	95.84(1.3)	**96.51**(1.04)	93.19(1.25)	97.83(0.7)	88.63(1.21)	93.7(0.83)	94.53(1.13)
	DELTAR	96.09(1.51)	95.74(1.46)	96.44(1.29)	**93.56**(0.95)	**97.86**(0.75)	**88.79**(1.25)	**93.86**(0.93)	**94.62**(1.16)
	DELTAS	**96.11**(1.52)	95.69(1.44)	96.46(1.29)	93.44(0.93)	**97.86**(0.75)	88.64(1.18)	93.76(0.89)	94.57(1.14)
512	UPSAMPLE	96.07(1.54)	96.09(1.2)	96.6(1.06)	93.5(1.14)	**97.87**(0.69)	88.73(1.23)	93.8(0.92)	94.67(1.11)
	PERTURB	96.23(1.6)	96.17(1.23)	96.63(1.13)	93.49(1.03)	97.84(0.72)	88.6(1.3)	93.79(0.98)	94.68(1.14)
	CVAE	96.14(1.46)	96.24(1.18)	96.63(1.06)	93.6(1.08)	97.87(0.75)	88.76(1.29)	93.87(0.98)	94.73(1.11)
	LINEAR	96.07(1.54)	96.11(1.21)	96.6(1.06)	93.49(1.13)	**97.87**(0.69)	88.76(1.25)	93.8(0.92)	94.67(1.11)
	EXTRA	96.07(1.54)	96.13(1.18)	96.6(1.06)	93.5(1.14)	**97.87**(0.69)	88.73(1.25)	93.8(0.92)	94.67(1.11)
	DELTAR	**96.29**(1.52)	**96.29**(1.34)	**96.71**(1.1)	**93.87**(1.04)	97.86(0.75)	**89.11**(1.22)	**94.03**(0.89)	**94.88**(1.12)
	DELTAS	96.19(1.61)	96.2(1.23)	96.69(1.07)	93.61(0.96)	97.86(0.75)	88.84(1.28)	93.83(0.94)	94.74(1.12)

Table 7: IC accuracy on SNIPS dataset in the FSI setting, reported as *mean (SD)*. The 10 seed examples are upsampled to 100 to train the feature extractor.

A Comparative Analysis of Unsupervised Language Adaptation Methods

Gil Rocha and **Henrique Lopes Cardoso**
Laboratório de Inteligência Artificial e Ciência de Computadores (LIACC)
Departamento de Engenharia Informática,
Faculdade de Engenharia da Universidade do Porto
Rua Dr. Roberto Frias, 4200-465 Porto, Portugal
{gil.rocha, hlc}@fe.up.pt

Abstract

To overcome the lack of annotated resources in less-resourced languages, recent approaches have been proposed to perform unsupervised language adaptation. In this paper, we explore three recent proposals: Adversarial Training, Sentence Encoder Alignment and Shared-Private Architecture. We highlight the differences of these approaches in terms of unlabeled data requirements and capability to overcome additional domain shift in the data. A comparative analysis in two different tasks is conducted, namely on Sentiment Classification and Natural Language Inference. We show that adversarial training methods are more suitable when the source and target language datasets contain other variations in content besides the language shift. Otherwise, sentence encoder alignment methods are very effective and can yield scores on the target language that are close to the source language scores.

1 Introduction

Recently proposed approaches for unsupervised adaptation have been explored in a variety of machine learning domains, including image recognition (Ganin and Lempitsky, 2015; Bousmalis et al., 2016) and natural language processing (Chen et al., 2018; Conneau et al., 2018).

In unsupervised language adaptation, annotated resources on a source language (S) are available, in the form $\langle X_S, Y_S \rangle$. For the target language (T), however, no annotations are assumed to exist for training machine learning models with. The goal is to learn representations that are useful to perform a given task on S while using representations useful to perform the same task in the target language T (or even across multiple languages).

Approaches to unsupervised language adaptation can be divided into those that (a) do not assume any particular kind of inter-language data (Chen et al., 2018), and those that (b) require sentences aligned for the source and target languages, obtained either manually or through machine translation systems (Banea et al., 2008; Zhou et al., 2016).

In this paper, we explore recent proposals from different domains for unsupervised adaptation and employ them to two natural language tasks. To do so without making use of aligned sentences, we explore Adversarial Training (Section 4.1) (Chen et al., 2018). Assuming the availability of parallel data, we also explore approaches that learn the similarities and differences between source and target language. We explore two different approaches that leverage parallel data: a Sentence Encoder Alignment (Section 4.2) (Conneau et al., 2018) and a Shared-Private Architecture (Section 4.3) (Bousmalis et al., 2016). We select these approaches from many recent proposals because they differ on the main axis of our analysis (assumptions made on the availability of unlabeled data resources), they approach the problem using conceptually different methods, and they correspond to state-of-the-art approaches.

To evaluate the proposed approaches, we explore two different cross-lingual tasks: Natural Language Inference (NLI) (also know as Recognizing Textual Entailment) (Dagan et al., 2013) and Sentiment Classification (Socher et al., 2013). Our source language is English, in both cases. For the target language, we constrain our work to Chinese and Arabic, the languages that the both tasks have in common. We believe that the linguistic differences between the source and target languages explored in this work are rich enough to demonstrate the quality of the proposed approaches, in particular in such a challenging setting as unsupervised language adaptation.

The main contributions of this work can be sum-

Proceedings of the 2nd Workshop on Deep Learning Approaches for Low-Resource NLP (DeepLo), pages 11–21
Hong Kong, China, November 3, 2019. ©2019 Association for Computational Linguistics
https://doi.org/10.18653/v1/P17

marised as follows: (a) we divide and analyse proposed approaches for unsupervised language adaptation by taking into account their assumptions on available resources; (b) for the natural language inference (NLI) task, we explore adversarial training approaches and provide a new baseline for sentence encoders without requiring parallel data. Moreover, we explore a shared-private architecture that leverages parallel sentences; (c) for the sentiment classification task, we explore recent approaches that use parallel data (sentence encoder alignment and shared-private architecture).

2   Related Work

The Natural Language Inference (NLI) task has emerged as one of the main tasks to evaluate NLP systems for sentence understanding. Given two text fragments, "Text" (T) and "Hypothesis" (H), NLI is the task of determining whether the meaning of H is in an *entailment*, *contradiction* or neither (*neutral*) relation to the text fragment T. Consequently, this task is framed in a 3-way classification setting (Dagan et al., 2013).

State-of-the-art systems explore complex sentence encoding techniques using a variety of approaches, such as recurrent (Bowman et al., 2015a) and recursive (Bowman et al., 2015b) neural networks. To capture the relations between the text and hypothesis, sentence aggregation functions (Chen et al., 2017; Peters et al., 2018) and attention mechanisms (Rocktäschel et al., 2016) have been successfully applied to address the task. On the cross-lingual setting, there has been work using parallel corpora (Mehdad et al., 2011) and lexical resources (Castillo, 2011), as well as shared tasks (Camacho-Collados et al., 2017). Most of these systems rely heavily on the availability of multilingual resources (e.g. bilingual dictionaries) and on machine translation systems to explore projection (Yarowsky et al., 2001) or direct transfer (McDonald et al., 2011) approaches. Recently, a large-scale corpus for NLI for 15 languages was released (details in Section 3) together with multilingual sentence encoders baselines (Conneau et al., 2018). More recently, new methods to train language models provided the ground basis for contextualized word embeddings (Peters et al., 2018), which constitute the new state-of-art in several tasks, including the NLI and XNLI tasks (Devlin et al., 2019; Lample and Conneau, 2019). In this paper, we constraint our

work to the conventional (cross-lingual) word embeddings (Ruder, 2017) that have been widely used and focus on a comparative analysis between different approaches for unsupervised language adaptation. We leave the study of the effects of this recent line of work on our analysis as future work.

For Sentiment Classification, several efforts have been made to address the task in a cross-lingual setting. Similarly to the NLI research focus, most of the approaches rely on projection or direct transfer approaches (Wan, 2008; Mihalcea et al., 2007; Banea et al., 2008; He et al., 2010). Some works explore parallel datasets to learn bilingual document representations (Zhou et al., 2016) or to perform cross-lingual distillation (Xu and Yang, 2017). Without requirements for parallel data resources and machine translation systems, Adversarial Deep Averaging Networks (ADAN) (Chen et al., 2018) employing adversarial training have been proposed to address the task in an unsupervised language adaption setting, which we follow in our work.

Crucial for our work is the existence of cross-lingual word embeddings (Ruder, 2017). Similarly to monolingual word embeddings, various approaches to learn cross-lingual word embeddings have been proposed in recent years, leading to existence of several pre-trained cross-lingual embeddings, including fastText embeddings (Joulin et al., 2018; Bojanowski et al., 2017), Multilingual Unsupervised and Supervised Embeddings (MUSE) (Lample et al., 2018), and bilingual word embeddings (BWE) (Zhou et al., 2016).

3   Corpora

In this section we detail on the corpora used to evaluate the unsupervised language adaptation approaches explored in this work.

3.1   Natural Language Inference

The Cross-Lingual Natural Language Inference corpus (XNLI) (Conneau et al., 2018) is a large-scale corpus for the task of NLI that contains annotations for 15 languages. Each pair of sentences is annotated with one of three labels: Entailment, Contradiction or Neutral.

The XNLI corpus is an extension for cross-lingual settings of the Multi-Genre Natural Language Inference (MultiNLI) corpus (Williams et al., 2018). This is a crowd-sourced collection of 433k sentence pairs annotated with textual entailment information. The corpus is modeled on the Stanford Natural Language Inference (SNLI) corpus (Bowman et al., 2015a), but differs in that it covers a range of genres of spoken and written text, and supports a distinctive cross-genre generalization evaluation. Given that the test portion of the MultiNLI data was kept private, they collect and validate 750 new test set examples from each of the ten text sources. To create the test set for the remaining languages, professional translators were asked to translate it into the ten target languages. The training set for the English portion is the same training data from the MultiNLI corpus. Additionally, in the official repository of the XNLI corpus, machine translations of the English data (including training, validation, and test set) to each of the 15 languages of XNLI are provided.

3.2 Sentiment Classification

For the Sentiment Classification task we follow the work of Chen et al. (2018), and replicate the dataset collection used by the authors.

For the English partition, we use a balanced dataset of $700k$ Yelp reviews from Zhang et al. (2015) with their ratings as labels (scale 1-5). We adopt the same training set of $650k$ reviews, but we randomly split the original $50k$ reviews validation set into $25k$ for the test set and the remaining for the validation set (keeping label distributions unchanged). For the Chinese dataset, $10k$ balanced Chinese hotel reviews from Lin et al. (2015) are used as validation set for model selection and parameter tuning. The results are reported on a separate test set of another $10k$ hotel reviews. Similarly to the English dataset, data is annotated with 5 labels (1-5). For the unlabeled target language data used during the training, we use another $150k$ unlabeled Chinese hotel reviews.

Regarding the Arabic dataset, we use the BBN Arabic Sentiment Analysis dataset (Mohammad et al., 2016) for Arabic sentiment classification. The dataset contains 1200 sentences (600 validation + 600 test) from social media posts annotated with 3 labels ($-$, 0, $+$). Since the label set does not match with the English dataset, we map the 4 and 5 English ratings to $+$ and the 1 and 2 ratings to $-$, while the 3 rating is converted to 0. For the unlabeled target language data used during the training, we use the text from the validation set (without labels) during training (similar to proce-

dure followed by Chen et al. (2018)).

3.3 Parallel Sentence Resources

We use publicly available parallel sentence resources to learn the alignment between English and target language sentence encoders, an approach that is used by Sentence Encoder Alignment (Section 4.2) and Shared-Private Architecture (Section 4.3). To retrieve and preprocess these parallel sentence datasets, we follow the description presented by Conneau et al. (2018). For the target languages addressed in this work, Arabic and Chinese, we use the United Nations (UN) corpus (Ziemski et al., 2016). This parallel corpus consists of manually translated UN documents from the last 25 years (1990 to 2014). In all the experiments reported in this paper, we set the maximum number of parallel sentences to 2 million.

4 Methods

To address the task of unsupervised language adaptation, we explore three approaches: Adversarial Training (Section 4.1), Sentence Encoder Alignment (Section 4.2), and Shared-Private Architecture (Section 4.3). By unsupervised language adaptation we consider that during the training phase the model is fed with labeled data (for the task at hand) on the source language and that no labeled data on target language is available. However, to train the model on a cross-lingual setting, unlabeled data on the source and target language are provided. We study on the assumptions that are made on the availability of unlabeled data for the source and target language.

The first, Adversarial Training, only requires the availability of unlabeled data in both languages, without requiring parallel sentences to perform the language adaptation. The remaining two approaches require parallel sentences for the source and target languages.

4.1 Adversarial Training

In a cross-lingual setting, the aim of adversarial training is to make the neural network agnostic to the input language while learning to address a specific task, following the intuition that if the network learns representations that are useful for the task and at the same time agnostic to language specificities, then such representations can be directly employed to address the task on a target language (unsupervised language adaptation).

A neural network with adversarial training is typically composed of three main components: a *Feature Extractor* $\mathcal{F}$ that maps the input sequence x to a feature space $\mathcal{F}(x)$, a *Task Classifier* $\mathcal{P}$ that given the feature representation $\mathcal{F}(x)$ predicts the labels for the task at hand, and a *Language Discriminator* $\mathcal{Q}$ that also receives $\mathcal{F}(x)$ as input and aims to discriminate the language of the input sequence. $\mathcal{F}$ and $\mathcal{P}$ correspond to the typical components employed to address a text classification task. $\mathcal{Q}$ corresponds to the second objective we want to optimise the neural network for, where the adversarial objective is defined.

The first formulation for an adversarial component following this setting was the Gradient Reversal Layer (GRL) (Ganin and Lempitsky, 2015), where $\mathcal{Q}$ is a binary classifier distinguishing whether the input sequence x comes from the source or target language.

However, training a neural network using the GRL is very unstable, and efforts need to be made to coordinate the adversarial training. To address this issue, Chen et al. (2018) propose to minimise the Wasserstein distance $\mathcal{W}$ between the distribution of the joint hidden features $\mathcal{F}$ for the source $P_{\mathcal{F}}^{src} \triangleq P(\mathcal{F}(x^{src}))$ and, similarly, for the target instances according to the Kantorovich-Rubinstein duality, and demonstrate that this improves the stability for hyperparameter selection. Following Chen et al. (2018), the adversarial component aims to maximize the following loss:

$$\mathcal{L}_{adv} \equiv \max_{\theta_q}(\mathbb{E}_{\mathcal{F}(x^{scr}) \sim P_{\mathcal{F}}^{src}} \left[\mathcal{Q}(\mathcal{F}(x^{src})) \right] - \quad (1)$$

$$\mathbb{E}_{\mathcal{F}(x^{tgt}) \sim P_{\mathcal{F}}^{tgt}} \left[\mathcal{Q}(\mathcal{F}(x^{tgt})) \right])$$

For the task classifier component $\mathcal{P}$, we want to minimize the negative log-likelihood of the target class for each source language example:

$$\mathcal{L}_{task} = - \sum_{i=0}^{N_{src}} y_i^{src} \cdot \log \hat{y}_i^{src}, \quad (2)$$

where y_i^{src} is the one-hot encoding of the class label for source input i and $\hat{y}_i^{src}$ are the softmax predictions of the model: $\hat{y}_i^{src} = \mathcal{P}(\mathcal{F}(x_i^{src}))$.

Finally, the goal of training the complete neural network is to minimize both the task classifier and adversarial component losses:

$$\mathcal{L}_{ADAN} = \mathcal{L}_{task} + \lambda \, \mathcal{L}_{adv} \quad (3)$$

where λ is a hyper-parameter that balances the importance of the adversarial component in the overall loss computation. Differently from Chen et al. (2018), who use a constant value $\lambda = 0.01$, we employ a λ schedule that increases with the number of epochs. The intuition is to make the adversarial component more important along time, while keeping a good performance on the task. Following Ganin and Lempitsky (2015), λ starts at 0 and is gradually increased up to 1:

$$\lambda_p = \frac{2}{1 + \exp(-\gamma \cdot p)} - 1 \quad (4)$$

where γ was set to 10 and p corresponds to the percentage of training completed given a predefined maximum number of epochs.

4.2 Sentence Encoder Alignment

The Sentence Encoder Alignment method aims to align the encoder for the target language based on a pre-trained encoder on the source language (Conneau et al., 2018). The key idea is that the target encoder learns to copy the source encoder representation based on parallel sentences in both languages. This method relies on the assumption that the representations captured by the source encoder (based solely on source language training for the task at hand) are useful for the target language as well. We hypothesise that in situations where the only variation between task and parallel data is the language shift, this approach can obtain promising results. However, in cases where the language shift is accompanied by other linguistic phenomena discrepancies (*e.g.* differences in domain), sentence encoder alignment might not yield competitive results.

This method includes three steps: (a) source language training using labeled data on the task at hand, (b) aligning sentence encoders with parallel data, and (c) inference on the target language. The architecture has three main components: a *Feature Extractor for the Source Language* $\mathcal{F}_S$ that maps input sequence x^{src} to a feature space $\mathcal{F}_S(x^{src})$, a *Feature Extractor for the Target Language* $\mathcal{F}_T$ that maps the input sequence x^{tgt} to a feature space $\mathcal{F}_T(x^{tgt})$, and a *Task Classifier* $\mathcal{P}$ that given the feature representation $\mathcal{F}(x)$ predicts the labels for the task at hand.

The first step, source language training, follows the typical training on monolingual settings. $\mathcal{F}_S$ and $\mathcal{P}$ are trained using labeled data in the source language. In the next step, the goal is to align a target encoder $\mathcal{F}_T$ based on the source encoder $\mathcal{F}_S$ learned in the previous step.

Given parallel sentences (from resources external to the task at hand) in the source and target language, z^{src} and z^{tgt}, we train $\mathcal{F}_{\mathcal{T}}$ to represent input sequence z^{tgt} as close as possible in the feature space to the representation produced by $\mathcal{F}_{\mathcal{S}}$ for the parallel sentence z^{src}. To this end, we follow the alignment loss $\mathcal{L}_{align}$ (Conneau et al., 2018):

$$\mathcal{L}_{align} = dist(\mathcal{F}_{\mathcal{S}}(z^{src}), \mathcal{F}_{\mathcal{T}}(z^{tgt})) - \tag{5}$$
$$\eta(dist(\mathcal{F}_{\mathcal{S}}(z^{src}_{neg}), \mathcal{F}_{\mathcal{T}}(z^{tgt})) +$$
$$dist(\mathcal{F}_{\mathcal{S}}(z^{src}), \mathcal{F}_{\mathcal{T}}(z^{tgt}_{neg})))$$

where $(z^{src}_{neg}, z^{tgt}_{neg})$ are contrastive terms obtained using negative sampling (*i.e.* z^{src}_{neg} was randomly sampled from the parallel sentences dataset and does not correspond to a parallel sentence of z^{tgt}; similarly between z^{tgt}_{neg} and z^{src}), and η controls the weight of the negative examples in the loss (we fix $\eta = 0.25$ has suggested by Conneau et al. (2018)). For the distance measure, we use the L2 norm $dist(x, y) = \|x - y\|_2$. During training, we only back-propagate through $\mathcal{F}_{\mathcal{T}}$ when optimizing $\mathcal{L}_{align}$ such that the target feature extractor is mapped to the source language feature space.

In the last step, the neural network is composed of $\mathcal{F}_{\mathcal{T}}$ obtained in the second step of this method and $\mathcal{P}$ obtained in the first step. Following this procedure we can directly make inferences on the target language, without requiring any kind of supervision on the target language.

4.3 Shared-Private Architecture

The key idea of a shared-private architecture is to obtain two different representations of the input. The shared representation aims to capture language agnostic features that can be shared across different languages. On the other hand, the private representation aims to capture language specific features. To prevent the shared and private spaces from interfering with each other, two strategies are typically used: adversarial training (Ganin and Lempitsky, 2015; Liu et al., 2017) and orthogonality constraints (Bousmalis et al., 2016).

A neural network following a shared-private architecture designed for a cross-lingual setting is composed of: a *Shared Feature Extractor* $\mathcal{F}_C$ that maps the input sequence x to a common/shared feature space $\mathcal{F}_C(x)$, a *Private Feature Extractor* $\mathcal{F}_P$ that maps the input sequence to a private feature space $\mathcal{F}_P(x)$, *Task Classifier* $\mathcal{P}$ that given $\mathcal{F}_C(x)$ predicts the labels for the task at hand, and a *Language Discriminator* $\mathcal{Q}$ that receives $\mathcal{F}_P(x)$

as input and aims to discriminate the language of the input sequence.

For the task classifier component $\mathcal{P}$, the goal is to minimize the negative log-likelihood of the ground truth class for each source language input sequence x^{src} given the representation obtained from $\mathcal{F}_C(x^{src})$. The loss used for this component is defined in Equation 2.

For the language discriminator component $\mathcal{Q}$ the main goal is to train the private feature extractor $\mathcal{F}_P$ to capture language specific phenomena. In the language discriminator component, we aim to minimize the negative log-likelihood of the ground truth language discrimination for each input sequence in x^{mix}, where x^{mix} corresponds to a balanced sample of sentences randomly taken from both source and target language datasets. $\mathcal{Q}$ receives the representation of the input sequence x^{mix} from the private feature extractor $\mathcal{F}_P(x^{mix})$. Again, we use the loss defined in Equation 2.

The difference loss, $\mathcal{L}_{diff}$, is applied to input sentences of both languages x^{mix} and encourages the shared and private feature extractors to encode different aspects of the input sequences. Following Bousmalis et al. (2016), we define the loss via a soft subspace orthogonality constraint between the private and shared representations, as follows:

$$L_{diff} = \left\| \mathcal{F}_C(x^{mix})^{\top} \mathcal{F}_P(x^{mix}) \right\|_F^2 \tag{6}$$

where $\| \cdot \|_F^2$ is the squared Frobenius norm.

The similarity loss, $\mathcal{L}_{sim}$, encourages the representations $\mathcal{F}_C(x^{src})$ and $\mathcal{F}_P(x^{tgt})$ to be as similar as possible irrespective of the language. We employ the same loss defined in Equation 5 as similarity loss, *i.e.*, $\mathcal{L}_{sim} = \mathcal{L}_{align}$. However, we emphasise that the training procedure is different. Here the alignment loss is one component of the total loss applied to the neural network, working concurrently with the other components.

Finally, the goal of training the complete neural network is to minimize the following loss:

$$\mathcal{L}_{SP} = \mathcal{L}_{task} + \lambda\, \mathcal{L}_{lang} + \tag{7}$$
$$\beta\, \mathcal{L}_{diff} + \gamma\, \mathcal{L}_{sim}$$

where λ, β and γ are hyper-parameters that balance the importance of each component in the overall loss computation. All these values are parameterized with the same schedule (Eq. 4). We leave for future work finding optimal values for these hyper-parameters.

5 Experiments

To evaluate the methods described in Section 4
for unsupervised cross-lingual settings, we report
on experiments performed on two different tasks:
Natural Language Inference and Sentiment Classification. On both tasks we consider English (en)
as source language and Chinese (zh) and Arabic
(ar) as target languages.

5.1 Implementation Details

For the NLI task, we kept most of the architecture details as similar as possible to the initial work
(Conneau et al., 2018). More specifically, the Sentence Encoder Alignment architecture is similar to
this work. However, some of the parameters were
changed to speedup computations on all architectures, so we expect the results to be worst than
those reported by Conneau et al. (2018). The main
goal of this work is not to provide a new state-of-
the-art system for the task, but instead we focus
on alternative architectures that explore different
assumptions about the data and that are backed up
by promising theoretical motivations.

The only pre-processing step required is the tokenization of the input sequence. We use MOSES
tokenizer (Koehn et al., 2007) for sentences in English and Arabic, and Stanford segmenter (Chang
et al., 2008) for Chinese. Each token is associated to the corresponding word embedding.
We use the fastText[1] pre-trained 300 dimensional
word vectors computed on Wikipedia, aligned on
several languages using the relaxed cross-domain
similarity local scaling (RCSLS) method (Joulin
et al., 2018; Bojanowski et al., 2017). For the
Feature Extractor component $\mathcal{F}$, we use a BiL-
STM (Hochreiter and Schmidhuber, 1997) with
128 hidden units, concatenating the initial and final hidden states (Sutskever et al., 2014). For
the Task Classifier $\mathcal{P}$ and Language Discriminator $\mathcal{Q}$ we employ a feed-forward neural network
with a 128 hidden units hidden layer, regularized
with dropout (Srivastava et al., 2014) at a rate
of 0.2. As suggested by Chen et al. (2018), the
weights of the adversarial component are clipped
to $[-0.01, 0.01]$. For optimization, we use Adam
(Kingma and Ba, 2014) with default parameters.

To compare the results of the different architectures described in Section 4 on the Sentiment
Classification task with existing work, we fol-

---

[1] https://fasttext.cc/docs/en/
aligned-vectors.html

low the experimental setup used by Chen et al.
(2018). The tokenization is performed using Stanford CoreNLP (Manning et al., 2014) for all languages. Regarding word embeddings, for Chinese we used the pre-trained 50 dimensional Bilingual Word Embeddings (BWE) by Zhou et al.
(2016). For Arabic, the 300 dimensional Bil-
BOWA BWE (Gouws et al., 2015) trained by Chen
et al. (2018) were not available. Instead, we used
the pre-trained 300 dimensional word vectors fast-
Text. For the Feature Extractor component $\mathcal{F}$, we
use the Deep Averaging Network (DAN) (Iyyer
et al., 2015). For each input sequence, DAN calculates the average of the word vectors in the input
sequence, then passes this tensor of average values
through a feed-forward network with ReLU (Glorot et al., 2011) non-linearities. The feature extractor $\mathcal{F}$ has three fully-connected layers, while
both $\mathcal{P}$ and $\mathcal{Q}$ have two. All hidden layers contain
900 hidden units. We also use Adam optimizer
for this task, but using a learning rate of 0.0005 as
employed by Chen et al. (2018).

For both tasks, to find the best model in each
experiment, we stop training once the accuracy on
the validation set does not improve for 3 epochs
(early-stop criterion) or when 30 epochs are completed. The batch size used in the experiments was
set to 96 learning instances.

5.2 Analysis

Experimental results for the NLI task are shown
in Table 1. The "Conneau et al. (2018) BiLSTM-
last" architecture corresponds to the *BiLSTM-last*
multilingual sentence encoders (in-domain) proposed by Conneau et al. (2018); the remaining architectures correspond to those described in sections 4.1, 4.2 and 4.3, respectively. The evaluation
metric used is accuracy given that all labels are
equally represented (balanced dataset).

Comparing our results with existing state-of-
the-art (*e.g.* Conneau et al. (2018)), we can observe that our scores are lower. We attribute this to
some parameter choices that were driven by computational efficiency concerns (described in Section 5.1). We focus our work on a comparison
between different architectures and, therefore, we
aim at a comparative analysis between those architecture in similar settings.

Comparing the architectures presented in Section 4, we can conclude that the Sentence Encoder
Alignment architecture yields better results in both

Architecture	en	zh	ar
Conneau et al. (2018) BiLSTM-last	71.00	63.70	62.7
Adversarial	68.62	47.29	45.59
Sent Enc Align	68.62	**58.24**	**57.33**
Shared-Private	68.62	49.14	48.80

Table 1: XNLI accuracy scores

	5 labels		3 labels	
Architecture	en	zh	en	ar
ADAN	-	42.49	-	54.54
Adversarial	60.40	**43.22**	77.68	**52.17**
Sent Enc Align	60.40	35.10	77.68	48.17
Shared-Private	60.40	29.13	77.68	43.50

Table 2: Sentiment Classification accuracy scores

languages. Against our intuition, the Shared-Private Architecture presents a considerable drop of performance when compared with the Sentence Encoder Alignment method even if the sentence encoder alignment procedure is also performed in the former (*i.e.* $\mathcal{L}_{sim} = \mathcal{L}_{align}$). We attribute this to the reduced number of updates that is performed for the alignment procedure in the Shared-Private Architecture (given that we compute a joint loss, the number of iterations is determined by the size of the labeled data for the task at hand). On the other hand, the Sentence Encoder Alignment method can make complete use of the 2 million parallel sentences. We also studied the capability of the shared and private feature extractors to predict the language of a given set of input sequences. After some epochs of training, we observe that the shared feature extractor is unable to distinguish the input sequence language (obtaining 50% of accuracy to distinguish the languages). On the other hand, the private feature extractor masters the task reaching an accuracy of approximately 100%.

Adversarial Training performed considerably worst in both target languages. We emphasise that this architecture relieves the assumption of the availability of parallel sentences in both languages, and therefore removes the expense of acquiring such data. This can be relevant for less-resourced languages, where the availability of such parallel datasets is scarce and where neural machine translation systems perform worst. To the best of our knowledge, this constitutes the first effort to obtain a NLI system in a cross-lingual setting employing adversarial training, and to address the task without making any requirement on the availability of parallel sentences. Therefore, we present here a baseline system in this setting.

The results of the experiments conducted for the Sentiment Classification task are shown in Table 2. The "ADAN" architecture corresponds to the ADAN model (Chen et al., 2018). In the 5 labels setting, the labels are distributed equally (bal-anced dataset). In the 3 labels setting, the classes are unbalanced in both target languages. We keep using the accuracy metric in order to compare with the current state-of-the-art in this task.

Since in this setting we follow the same component architectures and parameters used in Chen et al. (2018), the results of our implementation using Adversarial Training are close to the scores reported by Chen et al. (2018). From this we can conclude that the differences introduced in this work, namely the dynamic schedule for the λ value, did not influence the overall scores. Even if no substantial differences exist between the scores, we obtain a new state-of-the-art score for the Chinese language. We attribute the small drop of performance in Arabic to the different word embeddings used.

It is interesting to notice that in this task Adversarial Training works substantially better than the remaining architectures. We attribute this to the differences of domain between the source and the target language datasets (for both Chinese and Arabic). Using the Sentence Encoder Alignment in such a setting is not as promising, comparing with the NLI setting, where both source and target languages share the domain (even if the XNLI dataset is composed of different domains, they overlap between the languages). In fact, in the Sentiment Classification task we perform the alignment of the target language feature extractor to the source language feature extractor (i.e. for Yelp related reviews) and then ask the system to perform predictions on a different language and domain (*e.g.* Chinese and hotel reviews, respectively). On the other hand, Adversarial Training aims to obtain representations that are agnostic in respect to an auxiliary task, in our case related with language and domain shift. Consequently, despite the considerable drop of performance of Adversarial Training when compared to the source language, it might be a strong baseline for unsupervised adaption for datasets that differ not only

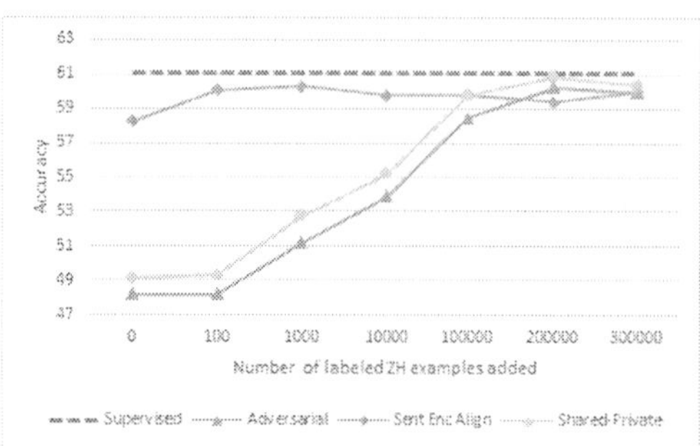

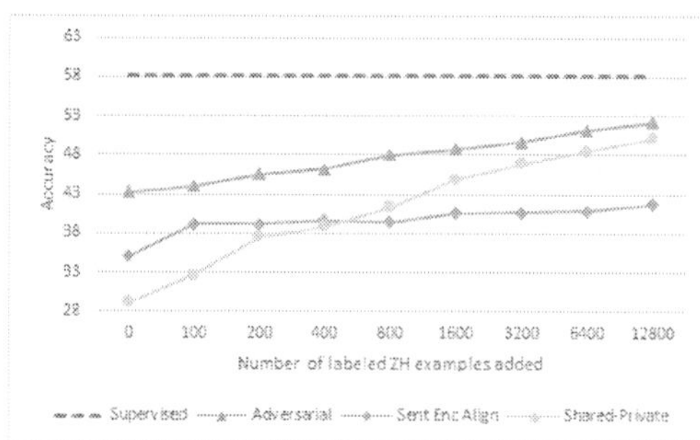

Figure 1: XNLI accuracy scores for Chinese in the semi-supervised setting.

Figure 2: Sentiment Classification accuracy scores for Chinese in the semi-supervised setting.

in language but also in other phenomena (such as domain, genre, style, etc).

5.3 Semi-Supervised Learning

In several scenarios, some annotated data in the target language is available. In this section we study how performance of the methods detailed in Section 4 evolve as some examples in the target language are added to the training set.

For the NLI task, results are shown in Figure 1. The blue dotted line, dubbed "Supervised", corresponds to training the model in a supervised setting on the target language, using the machine translated training set provided by the XNLI corpus. Sentence Encoder Alignment already obtained scores close to the supervised model in the unsupervised language adaptation setting. By adding 100 instances from the target language, scores increase slightly. However, adding more instances does not affect overall performance. For the remaining models, only when we add $1k$ instances the accuracy starts to increase substantially. As we add more target language instances, accuracy keeps increasing at a consistent rate, reaching the Sentence Encoder Alignment and Supervised baseline when we add $200k$ instances.

For the Sentiment Classification task, results are shown in Figure 2. Adversarial Training remains the best model for this task as we increase learning instances from the target language in the semi-supervised setting. Accuracy scores increase as we add more instances. The Sentence Encoder Alignment is the method that less effectively takes advantage of the added data on the target language. On the other side, the Shared-Private Architecture is the method that makes better use of the added target language instances, surpassing the Sentence Encoder Alignment when we add 800 instances and becoming competitive with Adversarial Training when 1600 instances are added.

In both tasks, the Sentence Encoder Alignment is the method that takes less profit from the added supervision in the target language, while Adversarial Training and Shared-Private Architecture can improve the overall accuracy as more supervision is provided.

6 Conclusions and Future Work

We have studied unsupervised language adaptation approaches on two natural language processing tasks, taking into consideration the assumptions made regarding the availability of unlabeled data in the source and target languages.

Our results indicate that the characteristics of the datasets used in the source language (to train the models) and on the target language (to evaluate the cross-lingual approaches) are an important factor to consider when choosing the architecture to employ. When the source and target datasets present other variations in content besides the language shift, adversarial training approaches outperform those that rely on sentence alignment methods. On the other hand, when the source and target language datasets have the same characteristics, sentence alignment approaches are very effective and obtain scores in the target language that are closer to source language scores.

In future work, we aim to explore recent advances made on multilingual contextualized word embeddings and determine whether they impact the results reported in this work. Hyper-parameter tuning of different loss components is a challenging task that we aim to study in more detail.

Acknowledgments

Gil Rocha is supported by a PhD scholarship (SFRH/BD/140125/2018) from Fundação para a Ciência e a Tecnologia (FCT). This research is supported by project DARGMINTS (POCI/01/0145/FEDER/031460), funded by FCT.

References

Carmen Banea, Rada Mihalcea, Janyce Wiebe, and Samer Hassan. 2008. Multilingual subjectivity analysis using machine translation. In *Proceedings of the Conference on Empirical Methods in Natural Language Processing*, EMNLP '08, pages 127–135, Stroudsburg, PA, USA. Association for Computational Linguistics.

Piotr Bojanowski, Edouard Grave, Armand Joulin, and Tomas Mikolov. 2017. Enriching word vectors with subword information. *Transactions of the Association for Computational Linguistics*, 5:135–146.

Konstantinos Bousmalis, George Trigeorgis, Nathan Silberman, Dilip Krishnan, and Dumitru Erhan. 2016. Domain separation networks. In *Proceedings of the 30th International Conference on Neural Information Processing Systems*, NIPS'16, pages 343–351, USA. Curran Associates Inc.

Samuel R. Bowman, Gabor Angeli, Christopher Potts, and Christopher D. Manning. 2015a. A large annotated corpus for learning natural language inference. In *Proceedings of the 2015 Conference on Empirical Methods in Natural Language Processing*, pages 632–642, Lisbon, Portugal. Association for Computational Linguistics.

Samuel R. Bowman, Christopher Potts, and Christopher D. Manning. 2015b. Recursive neural networks can learn logical semantics. In *Proceedings of the 3rd Workshop on Continuous Vector Space Models and their Compositionality*, pages 12–21, Beijing, China. Association for Computational Linguistics.

Jose Camacho-Collados, Mohammad Taher Pilehvar, Nigel Collier, and Roberto Navigli. 2017. SemEval-2017 task 2: Multilingual and cross-lingual semantic word similarity. In *Proceedings of the 11th International Workshop on Semantic Evaluation (SemEval-2017)*, pages 15–26, Vancouver, Canada. Association for Computational Linguistics.

Julio Javier Castillo. 2011. A wordnet-based semantic approach to textual entailment and cross-lingual textual entailment. *International Journal of Machine Learning and Cybernetics*, 2(3):177–189.

Pi-Chuan Chang, Michel Galley, and Christopher D. Manning. 2008. Optimizing chinese word segmentation for machine translation performance. In *Proceedings of the Third Workshop on Statistical Machine Translation*, StatMT '08, pages 224–232, Stroudsburg, PA, USA. Association for Computational Linguistics.

Qian Chen, Xiaodan Zhu, Zhen-Hua Ling, Si Wei, Hui Jiang, and Diana Inkpen. 2017. Enhanced LSTM for natural language inference. In *Proceedings of the 55th Annual Meeting of the Association for Computational Linguistics (Volume 1: Long Papers)*, pages 1657–1668, Vancouver, Canada. Association for Computational Linguistics.

Xilun Chen, Yu Sun, Ben Athiwaratkun, Claire Cardie, and Kilian Q. Weinberger. 2018. Adversarial deep averaging networks for cross-lingual sentiment classification. *TACL*, 6:557–570.

Alexis Conneau, Ruty Rinott, Guillaume Lample, Adina Williams, Samuel Bowman, Holger Schwenk, and Veselin Stoyanov. 2018. XNLI: Evaluating cross-lingual sentence representations. In *Proceedings of the 2018 Conference on Empirical Methods in Natural Language Processing*, pages 2475–2485, Brussels, Belgium. Association for Computational Linguistics.

Ido Dagan, Dan Roth, Mark Sammons, and Fabio Massimo Zanzotto. 2013. *Recognizing Textual Entailment: Models and Applications*. Synthesis Lectures on Human Language Technologies. Morgan & Claypool Publishers.

Jacob Devlin, Ming-Wei Chang, Kenton Lee, and Kristina Toutanova. 2019. BERT: Pre-training of deep bidirectional transformers for language understanding. In *Proceedings of the 2019 Conference of the North American Chapter of the Association for Computational Linguistics: Human Language Technologies, Volume 1 (Long and Short Papers)*, pages 4171–4186, Minneapolis, Minnesota. Association for Computational Linguistics.

Yaroslav Ganin and Victor Lempitsky. 2015. Unsupervised domain adaptation by backpropagation. In *Proceedings of the 32nd International Conference on Machine Learning*, volume 37 of *Proceedings of Machine Learning Research*, pages 1180–1189, Lille, France. PMLR.

Xavier Glorot, Antoine Bordes, and Yoshua Bengio. 2011. Deep sparse rectifier neural networks. In *Proceedings of the Fourteenth International Conference on Artificial Intelligence and Statistics*, volume 15 of *Proceedings of Machine Learning Research*, pages 315–323, Fort Lauderdale, FL, USA. PMLR.

Stephan Gouws, Yoshua Bengio, and Greg Corrado. 2015. Bilbowa: Fast bilingual distributed representations without word alignments. In *Proceedings of the 32nd International Conference on Machine Learning*, volume 37 of *Proceedings of Machine Learning Research*, pages 748–756, Lille, France. PMLR.

Yulan He, Harith Alani, and Deyu Zhou. 2010. Exploring English lexicon knowledge for Chinese sentiment analysis. In *CIPS-SIGHAN Joint Conference on Chinese Language Processing*.

Sepp Hochreiter and Jürgen Schmidhuber. 1997. Long short-term memory. *Neural Comput.*, 9(8):1735–1780.

Mohit Iyyer, Varun Manjunatha, Jordan Boyd-Graber, and Hal Daumé III. 2015. Deep unordered composition rivals syntactic methods for text classification. In *Proceedings of the 53rd Annual Meeting of the Association for Computational Linguistics and the 7th International Joint Conference on Natural Language Processing (Volume 1: Long Papers)*, pages 1681–1691, Beijing, China. Association for Computational Linguistics.

Armand Joulin, Piotr Bojanowski, Tomas Mikolov, Hervé Jégou, and Edouard Grave. 2018. Loss in translation: Learning bilingual word mapping with a retrieval criterion. In *Proceedings of the 2018 Conference on Empirical Methods in Natural Language Processing*.

Diederik P. Kingma and Jimmy Ba. 2014. Adam: A method for stochastic optimization. *CoRR*, abs/1412.6980.

Philipp Koehn, Hieu Hoang, Alexandra Birch, Chris Callison-Burch, Marcello Federico, Nicola Bertoldi, Brooke Cowan, Wade Shen, Christine Moran, Richard Zens, Chris Dyer, Ondrej Bojar, Alexandra Constantin, and Evan Herbst. 2007. Moses: Open source toolkit for statistical machine translation. In *Proceedings of the 45th Annual Meeting of the Association for Computational Linguistics Companion Volume Proceedings of the Demo and Poster Sessions*, pages 177–180, Prague, Czech Republic. Association for Computational Linguistics.

Guillaume Lample and Alexis Conneau. 2019. Cross-lingual language model pretraining. *CoRR*, abs/1901.07291.

Guillaume Lample, Alexis Conneau, Marc'Aurelio Ranzato, Ludovic Denoyer, and Hervé Jégou. 2018. Word translation without parallel data. In *6th International Conference on Learning Representations, ICLR 2018, Vancouver, BC, Canada, April 30 - May 3, 2018, Conference Track Proceedings*.

Yiou Lin, Hang Lei, Jia Wu, and Xiaoyu Li. 2015. An empirical study on sentiment classification of Chinese review using word embedding. In *Proceedings of the 29th Pacific Asia Conference on Language, Information and Computation: Posters*, pages 258–266, Shanghai, China.

Pengfei Liu, Xipeng Qiu, and Xuanjing Huang. 2017. Adversarial multi-task learning for text classification. In *Proceedings of the 55th Annual Meeting of the Association for Computational Linguistics (Volume 1: Long Papers)*, pages 1–10, Vancouver, Canada. Association for Computational Linguistics.

Christopher Manning, Mihai Surdeanu, John Bauer, Jenny Finkel, Steven Bethard, and David McClosky. 2014. The Stanford CoreNLP natural language processing toolkit. In *Proceedings of 52nd Annual Meeting of the Association for Computational Linguistics: System Demonstrations*, pages 55–60, Baltimore, Maryland. Association for Computational Linguistics.

Ryan McDonald, Slav Petrov, and Keith Hall. 2011. Multi-source transfer of delexicalized dependency parsers. In *Proceedings of the 2011 Conference on Empirical Methods in Natural Language Processing*, pages 62–72, Edinburgh, Scotland, UK. Association for Computational Linguistics.

Yashar Mehdad, Matteo Negri, and Marcello Federico. 2011. Using bilingual parallel corpora for cross-lingual textual entailment. In *Proceedings of the 49th Annual Meeting of the Association for Computational Linguistics: Human Language Technologies*, pages 1336–1345, Portland, Oregon, USA. Association for Computational Linguistics.

Rada Mihalcea, Carmen Banea, and Janyce Wiebe. 2007. Learning multilingual subjective language via cross-lingual projections. In *Proceedings of the 45th Annual Meeting of the Association of Computational Linguistics*, pages 976–983, Prague, Czech Republic. Association for Computational Linguistics.

Saif M. Mohammad, Mohammad Salameh, and Svetlana Kiritchenko. 2016. How translation alters sentiment. *J. Artif. Int. Res.*, 55(1):95–130.

Matthew Peters, Mark Neumann, Mohit Iyyer, Matt Gardner, Christopher Clark, Kenton Lee, and Luke Zettlemoyer. 2018. Deep contextualized word representations. In *Proceedings of the 2018 Conference of the North American Chapter of the Association for Computational Linguistics: Human Language Technologies, Volume 1 (Long Papers)*, pages 2227–2237, New Orleans, Louisiana. Association for Computational Linguistics.

Tim Rocktäschel, Edward Grefenstette, Karl Moritz Hermann, Tomás Kociský, and Phil Blunsom. 2016. Reasoning about entailment with neural attention. In *4th International Conference on Learning Representations, ICLR 2016, San Juan, Puerto Rico, May 2-4, 2016, Conference Track Proceedings*.

Sebastian Ruder. 2017. A survey of cross-lingual embedding models. *CoRR*, abs/1706.04902.

Richard Socher, Alex Perelygin, Jean Wu, Jason Chuang, Christopher D. Manning, Andrew Ng, and Christopher Potts. 2013. Recursive deep models for semantic compositionality over a sentiment treebank. In *Proceedings of the 2013 Conference on Empirical Methods in Natural Language Processing*, pages 1631–1642, Seattle, Washington, USA. Association for Computational Linguistics.

Nitish Srivastava, Geoffrey Hinton, Alex Krizhevsky, Ilya Sutskever, and Ruslan Salakhutdinov. 2014. Dropout: A simple way to prevent neural networks from overfitting. *Journal of Machine Learning Research*, 15:1929–1958.

Ilya Sutskever, Oriol Vinyals, and Quoc V Le. 2014. Sequence to sequence learning with neural networks. In Z. Ghahramani, M. Welling, C. Cortes, N. D. Lawrence, and K. Q. Weinberger, editors, *Advances in Neural Information Processing Systems 27*, pages 3104–3112. Curran Associates, Inc.

Xiaojun Wan. 2008. Using bilingual knowledge and ensemble techniques for unsupervised chinese sentiment analysis. In *Proceedings of the Conference on Empirical Methods in Natural Language Processing*, EMNLP '08, pages 553–561, Stroudsburg, PA, USA. Association for Computational Linguistics.

Adina Williams, Nikita Nangia, and Samuel Bowman. 2018. A broad-coverage challenge corpus for sentence understanding through inference. In *Proceedings of the 2018 Conference of the North American Chapter of the Association for Computational Linguistics: Human Language Technologies, Volume 1 (Long Papers)*, pages 1112–1122, New Orleans, Louisiana. Association for Computational Linguistics.

Ruochen Xu and Yiming Yang. 2017. Cross-lingual distillation for text classification. In *Proceedings of the 55th Annual Meeting of the Association for Computational Linguistics (Volume 1: Long Papers)*, pages 1415–1425, Vancouver, Canada. Association for Computational Linguistics.

David Yarowsky, Grace Ngai, and Richard Wicentowski. 2001. Inducing multilingual text analysis tools via robust projection across aligned corpora. In *Proceedings of the First International Conference on Human Language Technology Research*.

Xiang Zhang, Junbo Zhao, and Yann LeCun. 2015. Character-level convolutional networks for text classification. In *Proceedings of the 28th International Conference on Neural Information Processing Systems - Volume 1*, NIPS'15, pages 649–657, Cambridge, MA, USA. MIT Press.

Xinjie Zhou, Xiaojun Wan, and Jianguo Xiao. 2016. Cross-lingual sentiment classification with bilingual document representation learning. In *Proceedings of the 54th Annual Meeting of the Association for Computational Linguistics (Volume 1: Long Papers)*, pages 1403–1412, Berlin, Germany. Association for Computational Linguistics.

Micha Ziemski, Marcin Junczys-Dowmunt, and Bruno Pouliquen. 2016. The united nations parallel corpus v1.0. In *Proceedings of the Tenth International Conference on Language Resources and Evaluation (LREC 2016)*, Paris, France. European Language Resources Association (ELRA).

A logical-based corpus for cross-lingual evaluation[*]

Felipe Salvatore[1], Marcelo Finger[1†] and R. Hirata Jr[1‡]
[1]Department of Computer Science, Instituto de Matemática e Estatística,
University of São Paulo, Brazil
{felsal, mfinger, hirata}@ime.usp.br

Abstract

At present, different deep learning models are presenting high accuracy on popular inference datasets such as SNLI, MNLI, and SciTail. However, there are different indicators that those datasets can be exploited by using some simple linguistic patterns. This fact poses difficulties to our understanding of the actual capacity of machine learning models to solve the complex task of textual inference. We propose a new set of syntactic tasks focused on contradiction detection that require specific capacities over linguistic logical forms such as: Boolean coordination, quantifiers, definite description, and counting operators. We evaluate two kinds of deep learning models that implicitly exploit language structure: recurrent models and the Transformer network BERT. We show that although BERT is clearly more efficient to generalize over most logical forms, there is space for improvement when dealing with counting operators. Since the syntactic tasks can be implemented in different languages, we show a successful case of cross-lingual transfer learning between English and Portuguese.

1 Introduction

Natural Language Inference (NLI) is a complex problem of Natural Language Understanding which is usually defined as follows: given a pair of textual inputs P and H we need to determine if P entails H, or H contradicts P, or H and P have no logical relationship (they are *neutral*) The Fracas Consortium et al. (1996). P and H, known

as "*premise*" and "*hypothesis*" respectively, can be either simple sentences or full texts.

The task can focus either on the entailment or the contradiction part. The former, which is known as Recognizing Textual Entailment (RTE) Dagan et al. (2013), classifies the pair P, H in "*entailment*" or "*non-entailment*". The latter, which is know as Contradiction Detection (CD), classifies that pair in terms of "*contradiction*" or "*non-contradiction*". Independently of the form that we frame the problem, the concept of inference is the critical issue here.

With this formulation, NLI has been treated as a text classification problem suitable to be solved by a variety of machine learning techniques Bowman et al. (2015a); Williams et al. (2017). Inference itself is also a complex problem. As shown in the following sentence pairs:

1. "*A woman plays with my dog*", "*A person plays with my dog*"

2. "*Jenny and Sally play with my dog*", "*Jenny plays with my dog*"

Both examples are cases of entailment, with different properties. In (1) the entailment is caused by the hypernym relationship between "*person*" and "*woman*". Example (2) deals with interpretation of the coordinating conjunction "*and*" as a Boolean connective. As (1) relies on the meaning of the noun phrases we call it "*lexical inference*". As (2) is invariant under substitution we call it "*structural inference*". The latter is the focus of this work.

In this paper, we propose a new synthetic CD dataset that enables us to:

1. compare the NLI accuracy of different deep learning models.

[*]This study was financed in part by the Coordenação de Aperfeiçoamento de Pessoal de Nível Superior – Brasil (CAPES) – Finance Code 001; and Fapesp 2019/07665-4.

[†]Partly supported by Fapesp project 2014/12236-1 and CNPq grant PQ 303609/2018-4.

[‡]Partly supported by FAPESP projects 2015/01587-0, 2015/24485-9 and 2017/25835-9

Proceedings of the 2nd Workshop on Deep Learning Approaches for Low-Resource NLP (DeepLo), pages 22–30
Hong Kong, China, November 3, 2019. ©2019 Association for Computational Linguistics
https://doi.org/10.18653/v1/P17

2. diagnose the structural (logical and syntactic) competence of each model.

3. verify the cross-lingual performance of each method.

The contributions presented in this paper are: i) the presentation of a structure oriented CD dataset; ii) the comparison of traditional neural recurrent models against the Transformer network BERT; iii) a success case of cross-lingual transfer learning for structural NLI between English and Portuguese.

2 Background and Related Work

The size of NLI datasets has been increasing since the initial proposition of the FraCas test suit composed of 346 examples The Fracas Consortium et al. (1996). Some old datasets like RTE-6 Bentivogli et al. (2009) and SICK Marelli et al. (2014), with 16K and 9.8K examples, respectively, are relatively small if compared with the current ones like SNLI Bowman et al. (2015a) and MNLI Williams et al. (2017), with 570K and 433K examples, respectively. This increase was possible with the use of crowdsource platforms like the Amazon Mechanical Turk Bowman et al. (2015a); Williams et al. (2017). The annotation performed by a formal semanticist, like in RTE 1-3 Giampiccolo et al. (2007), was replaced with the generation of sentence pairs done by average English speakers. This change in dataset construction has been criticised with the argument that it is hard for an average speaker to produce different and creative examples of entailment and contradiction pairs Gururangan et al. (2018). By looking at the hypothesis alone a simple text classifier can achieve an accuracy significantly better than a random classifier in datasets such as SNLI and MNLI. This was explained by a high correlation of occurrences of negative words (*"no"*, *"nobody"*, *"never"*, *"nothing"*) in contradiction instances, and high correlation of generic words (such as *"animal"*, *"instrument"*, *"outdoors"*) with entailment instances. Thus, despite of the large size of the corpora the task was easier to perform than expected Poliak et al. (2018).

The new wave of pre-trained models Howard and Ruder (2018); Devlin et al. (2018); Liu et al. (2019) poses both a challenge and an opportunity for the NLI field. The large-scale datasets are close to being solved (the benchmark for SNLI, MNLI, and SciTail is 91.1%, 85.3%/85.0%, and 94.1%, respectively, as reported in Liu et al. (2019)), giving the impression that NLI will become a trivial problem. The opportunity lies in the fact that, by using pre-trained models, training will no longer need such large datasets. Then we can focus our efforts in creating small, well-thought datasets that reflect the variety of inferential tasks, and so determine the real competence of a model.

Here we present a collection of small datasets designed to measure the competence of detecting contradictions in structural inferences. We have chosen the CD task because it is harder for an average annotator to create examples of contradictions without excessively relying on the same patterns. At the same time, CD has practical importance since it can be used to improve consistency in real case applications, such as chat-bots Welleck et al. (2018).

We choose to focus on structural inference because we have detected that the current datasets are not appropriately addressing this particular feature. In an experiment, we verify the deficiency reported in Gururangan et al. (2018); Glockner et al. (2018). First, we transformed the SNLI and MNLI datasets to a CD task. The transformation is done by converting all instances of entailment and neutral into non-contradiction, and by balancing the classes in both training and test data. Second, we applied a simple Bag-of-Words classifier, destroying any structural information. The accuracy was significantly higher than the random classifier, 63.9% and 61.9% for SNLI and MNLI, respectively. Even the recent dataset focusing on contradiction, Dialog NLI Welleck et al. (2018), presents a similar pattern. The same Bag-of-Words model achieved 76.2% accuracy in this corpus.

Our approach of isolating structural forms by using synthetic data to analyze the logical and syntactical competence of different neural models is similar to Bowman et al. (2015b); Evans et al. (2018); Tran et al. (2018). One main difference between their approach and ours is that we are interested in using a formal language as a tool for performing a cross-lingual analysis.

3 Data Collection

The different datasets that we propose are divided by tasks, such that each task introduces a new linguistic construct. Each task is designed by applying structurally dependent rules to automatically generate the sentence pairs. We first define the pairs in a formal language and then we use it to generate instances in natural language. In this paper, we have decided to work with English and Portuguese.

There are two main reasons to use a formal language as a basis for the dataset. First, this approach allows us to minimize the influence of common knowledge and lexical knowledge, highlighting structural features. Second, we can obtain a structural symmetry between the English and Portuguese corpora.

Hence, our dataset is a tool to measure inference in two dimensions: one defined by the structural forms, which corresponds to different levels in our hierarchical corpus; and other defined by the instantiation of these forms in multiple natural languages.

3.1 Template Language

The *template language* is a formal language used to generate instances of contradictions and non-contradictions in a natural language. This language is composed of two basic entities: people, $Pe = \{x_1, x_2, ..., x_n\}$ and places, $Pl = \{p_1, p_2, ..., p_m\}$. We also define three binary relations: $V(x, y)$, $x > y$, $x \geq y$. It is a simplistic universe with the intended meaning for binary relations such as "*x has visited y*", "*x is taller than y*" and "*x is as tall as y*", respectively.

A *realisation* of the template language r is a function mapping Pe and Pl to nouns such that $r(Pe) \cap r(Pl) = \emptyset$; it also maps the relation symbols and logic operators to corresponding forms in some natural language.

Each task is defined by the introduction of a new structural and logical operator. We define the tasks in a hierarchical fashion: if a logical operator appears on a task n, it can appear in any task k (with $k > n$). The main advantage of our approach compared to other datasets is that we can isolate the occurrences of each operator to have a clear notion in what forces the models to fail (or succeed).

For each task, we provide training and test data with 10K and 1K examples, respectively. All data is balanced; and, as usual, the model's accuracy is evaluated on the test data. To test the model's generalization capability, we have defined two distinct realization functions r_{train} and r_{test} such that $r_{train}(Pe) \cap r_{test}(Pe) = \emptyset$ and $r_{train}(Pl) \cap r_{test}(Pl) = \emptyset$. For example, in the English ver-sion $r_{train}(Pe)$ and $r_{train}(Pl)$ are composed of common English masculine names and names of countries, respectively. Similarly, $r_{test}(Pe)$ and $r_{test}(Pl)$ are composed of feminine names and names of cities from the United States. In the Portuguese version we have done a similar construction, using common masculine and feminine names together with names of countries and names of Brazilian cities.

3.2 Data Generation

A logical rule can be seen as a mapping that transforms a premise P into a conclusion C. To obtain examples of contradiction we start with a premise P and define H as the negation of C. The examples of non-contradiction are different negations that do not necessarily violate P. We repeat this process for each task. What defines the difference from one task to another is the introduction of logical and linguist operators, and subsequently, new rules. We have used more than one template pair to define each task; however, for the sake of brevity, in the description below we will give only a brief overview of each task.

The full dataset in both languages, together with the code to generate it and the detailed list of all templates, can be found online Salvatore (2019).

Task 1: Simple Negation We introduce the negation operator $\neg$, "*not*". The premise P is a collection of facts about some agents visiting different places. Example, $P :=$ $\{V(x_1, p_1), V(x_2, p_2)\}$ ("*Charles has visited Chile, Joe has visited Japan*"). The hypothesis H can be either a negation of one fact that appears in P, $\neg V(x_2, p_2)$ ("*Joe didn't visit Japan*"); or a new fact not related to P, $\neg V(x, p)$ ("*Lana didn't visit France*"). The number of facts that appear in P vary from two to twelve.

Task 2: Boolean Coordination In this task, we add the Boolean conjunction $\wedge$, the coordinating conjunction "*and*". Example, $P := \{V(x1, p) \wedge V(x2, p) \wedge V(x3, p)\}$ ("*Felix, Ronnie, and Tyler have visited Bolivia*"). The new information H can state that one of the mentioned agents did not travel to a mentioned place, $\neg V(x_3, p)$ ("*Tyler didn't visit Bolivia*"). Or it can represent a new fact, $\neg V(x, p)$ ("*Bruce didn't visit Bolivia*").

Task 3: Quantification By adding the quantifiers $\forall$ and $\exists$, "*for every*" and "*some*", respectively, we can construct example of inferences that explicitly exploit the difference between the two basic entities, people and places. Example, P states a general fact about all people, $P := \{\forall x \forall p V(x, p)\}$ (*"Everyone has visited every place"*). H can be the negation of one particular instance of P, $\neg V(x, p)$ (*"Timothy didn't visit El Salvador"*). Or a fact that does not violate P, $\neg V(x, x_1)$ (*"Timothy didn't visit Anthony"*).

Task 4: Definite Description One way to test if a model can capture reference is by using definite description, i.e., by adding the operator ι to perform description and the equality relation $=$. Hence, $x = \iota y Q(y)$ is to be read as *"x is the one that has property Q"*. Here we describe one property of one agent and ask the model to combine the description with a new fact. For example, $P := \{x_1 = \iota y \forall p V(y, p), V(x_1, x_2)\}$ (*"Carlos is the person that has visited every place, Carlos has visited John"*). Two new hypotheses can be introduced: $\neg V(x_1, p)$ (*"Carlos did not visit Germany"*) or $\neg V(x_2, p)$ (*"John did not visit Germany"*). Only the first hypothesis is a contradiction. Although the names *"Carlos"* and *"John"* appear on the premise, we expected the model to relate the property *"being the one that has visited every place"* to *"Carlos"* and not to *"John"*.

Task 5: Comparatives In this task we are interested to know if the model can recognise a basic property of a binary relation: transitivity. The premise is composed of a collection of simple facts $P := \{x_1 > x_2, x_2 > x_3\}$. (*"Francis is taller than Joe, Joe is taller than Ryan"*). Assuming the transitivity of $>$, the hypothesis can be a consequence of P, $x_1 > x_3$ (*"Francis is taller than Ryan"*), or a fact that violates the transitivity property, $x_3 > x_1$ (*"Ryan is taller than Francis"*). The size of the P varies from four to ten. Negation is not employed here.

Task 6: Counting In Task 3 we have added only the basic quantifiers $\forall$ and $\exists$, but there is a broader family of operators called *generalised quantifiers*. In this task we introduce the counting quantifier $\exists_{=n}$ (*"exactly n"*). Example, $P := \{\exists_{=3} p V(x_1, p) \wedge \exists_{=2} x V(x_1, x)\}$ (*"Philip has visited only three places and only two people"*). H can be an information consistent with P, $V(x_1, x_2)$ (*"Philip has visited John"*), or something that contradicts P, $V(x_1, x_2) \wedge V(x_1, x_3) \wedge V(x_1, x_4)$ (*"Philip has visited John, Carla, and Bruce"*). We have added counting quantifiers corresponding to numbers from one to thirty.

Task 7: Mixed In order to guarantee variability, we created a dataset composed of different samples of the previous tasks.

Basic statistics for the English and Portuguese realisations of all tasks can be found in Table 1.

Task	Vocab size	Vocab intersection	Mean input length	Max input length
1 (Eng)	3561	77	230.6	459
2 (Eng)	4117	128	151.4	343
3 (Eng)	3117	70	101.5	329
4 (Eng)	1878	62	100.81	134
5 (Eng)	1311	25	208.8	377
6 (Eng)	3900	150	168.4	468
7 (Eng)	3775	162	160.6	466
1 (Pt)	7762	254	209.4	445
2 (Pt)	9990	393	148.5	388
3 (Pt)	5930	212	102.7	395
4 (Pt)	5540	135	91.8	140
5 (Pt)	5970	114	235.2	462
6 (Pt)	9535	386	87.8	531
7 (Pt)	8880	391	159.9	487

Table 1: Task description. Column 1 presents two realizations of the described tasks - one in English (Eng) and the other in Portuguese (Pt). Column 2 presents the vocabulary size for the task. Column 3 presents the number of words that occurs both in the training and test data. Column 4 presents the average length in words of the input text (the concatenation of P and H). Column 5 presents the maximum length of the input text.

Since we are using a large number of facts in P, the input text is longer than the ones presented in average NLI datasets.

4 Models and Evaluation

To evaluate the accuracy of each CD task we employed three kinds of models:

Baseline The baseline model (Base) is a Random Forest classifier that models the input text, the concatenation of P and H, using the Bag-of-Words representation. Since we have constructed the dataset centered on the notion of structure-based contradictions, we believe that it should perform slightly better than random. At the same time, by using such baseline, we can certify if the proposed tasks are indeed requiring structural knowledge.

Recurrent Models The dominant family of neural models in Natural Language Processing specialised in modelling sequential data is the one composed by the *Recurrent Neural Networks* (RNNs) and its variations, *Long Short-Term Memory* (LSTM), and *Gated Recurrent Unit* (GRU) Goldberg (2015). We consider both the standard and the bidirectional variants of this family of models. As input for these models, we use the concatenation of P and H as a single sentence.

Traditional multilayer recurrent models are not the best choice to improve the benchmark on NLI Glockner et al. (2018). However, in recent works, it has been reported that recurrent models achieve a better performance than Transformer-based models to capture structural patterns for logical inference Evans et al. (2018); Tran et al. (2018). We want to investigate if the same result can be achieved using our tasks as the base of comparison.

Transformer-based Models A recent non-recurrent family of neural models known as *Transformer networks* was introduced in Vaswani et al. (2017). Different from the recurrent models that recursively summarizes all previous input into a single representation, the Transformer network employes a self-attention mechanism to directly attend to all previous inputs (more details of this architecture can be found in Vaswani et al. (2017)). Although, by performing regular training using this architecture alone we do not see surprising results in inference prediction Evans et al. (2018); Tran et al. (2018), when we pre-trained a Transformer network in the language modeling task and fine-tuned afterwards on an inference task we see a significant improvement Devlin et al. (2018).

Among the different Transformer-based models we will focus our analysis on the multilayer bidirectional architecture known as *Bidirectional Encoder Representation from Transformers* (BERT) Devlin et al. (2018). This bidirectional model, pre-trained as a masked language model and as a next sentence predictor, has two versions: $BERT_{BASE}$ and $BERT_{LARGE}$. The difference lies in the size of each architecture, the number of layers and self-attention heads. Since $BERT_{LARGE}$ is unstable on small datasets Devlin et al. (2018) we have used only $BERT_{BASE}$.

The strategy to perform NLI classification using BERT is the same the one presented in Devlin et al. (2018): together with the pair P, H we add new special tokens [CLS] (classification token) and [SEP] (sentence separator). Hence, the textual input is the result of the concatenation:

[CLS] P [SEP] H [SEP]. After we obtain the vector representation of the [CLS] token, we pass it through a classification layer to obtain the prediction class (contradiction / non-contradiction). We fine-tune the model for the CD task in a standard way, the original weights are co-trained with the weights from the new layer.

By comparing BERT with other models we are not only comparing different architectures but different techniques of training. The baseline model uses no additional information. The recurrent models use only a soft version of transfer learning with fine-tuning of pre-trained embeddings (the fine-tuning of one layer only). On the other side, BERT is pre-trained on a large corpus as a language model. It is expected that this pre-training helps the model to capture some general properties of language Howard and Ruder (2018). Since the tasks that we proposed are basic and cover very specific aspects of reasoning, we can use it to evaluate which properties are being learned in the pre-training phase.

The simplicity of the tasks motivated us to use transfer-learning differently: instead of simply using the multilingual version of BERT[1] and fine-tune it on the Portuguese version of the tasks, *we have decided to check the possibility of transferring structural knowledge from high-resource languages (English / Chinese) to Portuguese.*

This can be done because for each pre-trained model there is a tokenizer that transforms the Portuguese input into a collection of tokens that the model can process. Thus, we have decided to use the regular version of BERT trained on an English corpus ($BERT_{eng}$), the already mentioned Multilingual BERT ($BERT_{mult}$), and the version of the BERT model trained on a Chinese corpus ($BERT_{chi}$).

We hypothesize that *most structural patterns learned by the model in English can be transferred to Portuguese.* By the same reasoning, we believe that $BERT_{chi}$ should perform poorly. Not only the tokenizer associated to $BERT_{chi}$ will add noise to the input text, but also Portuguese and Chinese are grammatically different; for example, the latter is overwhelmingly right-branching while the former is more mixed Levy and Manning (2003).

---

[1] Multilingual BERT is a model trained on the concatenation of the entire Wikipedia from 100 languages, Portuguese included. https://github.com/google-research/bert/blob/master/multilingual.md

4.1 Experimental settings

Given the above considerations, four research questions arose:

(i) *How the different models perform on the proposed tasks?*

(ii) *How much each model rely on the occurrence of non-logical words?*

(iii) *Can cross-lingual transfer learning be successfully used for the Portuguese realization of those tasks?*

(iv) *Is the dataset biased? Are the models learning some unexpected text pattern?*

To answer those questions, we evaluated the models performance in four different ways:

(i) Each model was trained on different proportions of the dataset. In this case, $r_{train}(Pe) \cap r_{test}(Pe) = \emptyset$ and $r_{train}(Pl) \cap r_{test}(Pl) = \emptyset$.

(ii) We have trained the models on a version of the dataset where we allow full intersection of the train and test vocabulary, i.e., $r_{train}(Pe) = r_{test}(Pe)$ and $r_{train}(Pl) = r_{test}(Pl)$.

(iii) For the Portuguese corpus, we have fine-tuned the three pre-trained models mentioned previously: $BERT_{eng}$, $BERT_{mult}$, and $BERT_{chi}$.

(iv) We have trained the best model from (i) on the following modified versions of the dataset:

   (a) *Noise label* - each pair P, H is unchanged but we randomly labeled the pair as contradiction or non-contradiction.

   (b) *Premise only* - we keep the labels the same and omit the hypothesis H.

   (c) *Hypothesis only* - the premise P is removed, but the labels remain intact.

4.2 Implementation

All deep learning architectures were implemented using the Pytorch library Paszke et al. (2017). To make use of the pre-trained version of BERT we have based our implementation on the public repository https://github.com/huggingface/pytorch-pretrained-BERT.

The different recurrent architectures were optimized with Adam Kingma and Ba (2014). We have used pre-trained word embedding from Glove Pennington et al. (2014) and Fasttext Joulin et al. (2016), but we also used random initialized embeddings. We random searched across embedding dimensions in $[10, 500]$, hidden layer size of the recurrent model in $[10, 500]$, number of recurrent layer in $[1, 6]$, learning rate in $[0, 1]$, dropout in $[0, 1]$ and batch sizes in $[32, 128]$.

The hyperparameter search for BERT follows the one presented in Devlin et al. (2018) that uses Adam with learning rate warmup and linear decay.

We randomly searched the learning rate in $[2 \cdot 10^{-5}, 5 \cdot 10^{-5}]$, batch sizes in $[16, 32]$ and number of epochs in $[3, 4]$.

All the code for the experiments is public available Salvatore (2019).

4.3 Results

How the different models perform on the proposed tasks?

In most of the tasks, $BERT_{eng}$ presents a clear advantage when compared to all other models. Tasks 3 and 6 are the only ones where the difference in accuracy between $BERT_{eng}$ and the recurrent models is small, as can be seen in Table 2. Even when we look at $BERT_{eng}$'s results on the Portuguese corpus, which are slightly worse when compared to the English one, we still see a similar pattern.

Figure 1 shows that $BERT_{eng}$ is the only model improved by training on more data. All other models remain close to random independently of the amount of training data.

Accuracy improvement over training size indicates the difference in difficulty of each task. On the one hand, Tasks 1, 2 and 4 are practically solved by BERT using only 4K examples of training (99.5%, 99.7%, 97.6% accuracy, respectively). On the other hand, the results for Tasks 3 and 6 remain below average, as seen in Figure 2.

How much each model rely on the occurrence of non-logical words?

With the full intersection of the vocabulary, experiment (ii), we have observed that the average accuracy improvement differs from model to model: Baseline, GRU, $BERT_{eng}$, LSTM and RNN present an average improvement of 17.6%,

Task	Base	RNN	GRU	LSTM	BERT
1 (Eng)	52.1	50.1	50.6	50.4	**99.8**
2 (Eng)	50.7	50.2	50.2	50.8	**100**
3 (Eng)	63.5	50.3	66.1	63.5	**90.5**
4 (Eng)	51.0	51.7	52.7	51.6	**100**
5 (Eng)	50.6	50.1	50.2	50.2	**100**
6 (Eng)	55.5	84.4	82.7	75.1	**87.5**
7 (Eng)	54.1	50.9	53.7	50.0	**94.6**
Avg.	53.9	55.4	58.0	56.2	**96.1**
1 (Pt)	53.9	50.1	50.2	50.0	**99.9**
2 (Pt)	49.8	50.0	50.0	50.0	**99.9**
3 (Pt)	61.7	50.0	70.6	50.1	**78.7**
4 (Pt)	50.9	50.0	50.4	50.0	**100**
5 (Pt)	49.9	50.1	50.8	50.0	**99.8**
6 (Pt)	58.9	66.4	**79.7**	67.2	79.1
7 (Pt)	55.4	51.1	51.6	51.1	**82.7**
Avg.	54.4	52.6	57.6	52.6	**91.4**

Table 2: Results of the experiment (i), accuracy percentage on test data for the English and Portuguese corpora

9.6%, 5.3%, 4.25%, 1.3%, respectively. This may indicate that the recurrent models are relying more on noun phrases than BERT. However, since the difference is not significant, more investigation is required.

Can cross-lingual transfer learning be successfully used for the Portuguese realization of those tasks?

As expected, when we fine-tuned $BERT_{multi}$ to the Portuguese version of the dataset we have observed an overall improvement. Most notably, in Tasks 6 and 7 we have achieved a new accuracy of 87.4% and 92.3% respectively. Surprisingly, $BERT_{chi}$ is able to solve some simple tasks, namely Tasks 1, 2 and 4. But when trained on the mixed version of the dataset, Task 7, this pretrained model had repeatedly present a random performance.

One of the most important features observed by evaluating the different pre-training models is that although $BERT_{eng}$ and $BERT_{mult}$ show a similar result on the Portuguese corpus, $BERT_{eng}$ needs more data to improve its performance, as seen in Figure 3.

Is the dataset biased? Are the models learning some unexpected text pattern?

By taking $BERT_{eng}$ as the best classifier, we repeated the training using all the listed data modification techniques. The results, as shown in Figure 4, indicate that $BERT_{eng}$ is not memorizing random textual patterns, neither excessively relying on information that appears only in the premise P or the hypothesis H. When we applied it on these versions of the data, $BERT_{eng}$ behaves as a random classifier.

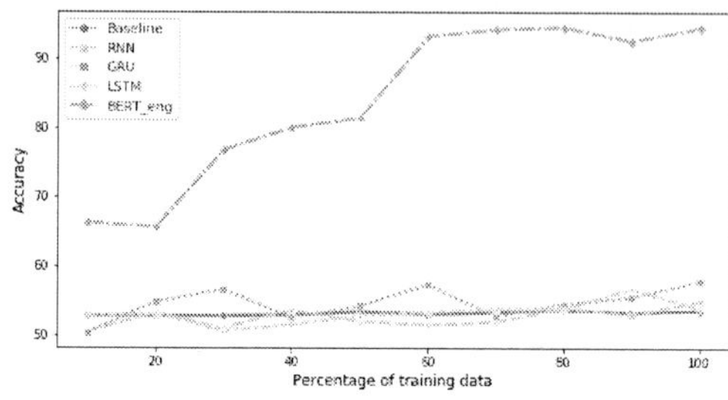

Figure 1: Results of the experiment (i), accuracy for each model on different data proportions (English corpus)

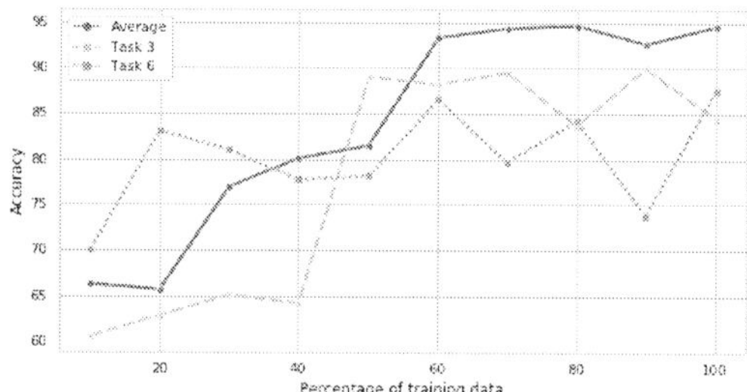

Figure 2: Results of the experiment (i), $BERT_{eng}$'s accuracy on the different different tasks (English corpus)

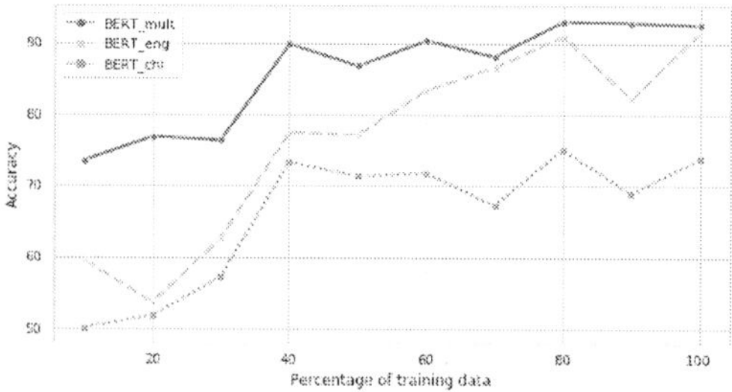

Figure 3: Results of the experiment (iii), different pretrained BERT versions tested on Portuguese corpus

5 Discussion

The results presented above are similar to the ones reported in Goldberg (2019) : *Transformer-based models like BERT can successfully capture syntactic regularities and logical patterns.*

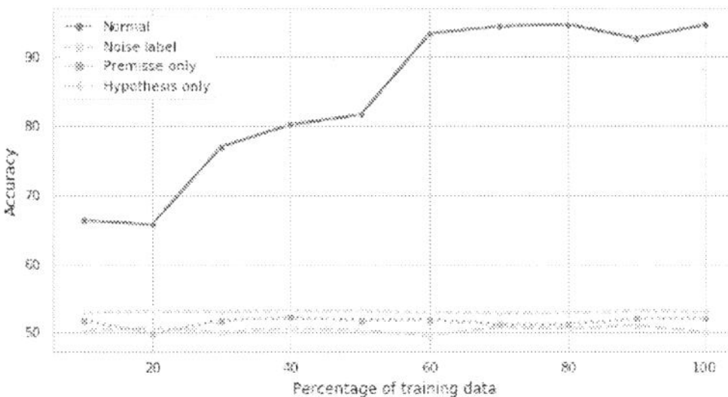

Figure 4: Results of the experiment (iv), BERT$_{eng}$'s accuracy on the different versions of the data (English corpus)

These findings do not contradict the results reported on Evans et al. (2018); Tran et al. (2018), because in both papers, the Transformer models are trained from scratch, while here we have used models that were pre-trained on large datasets with the language model objective.

The results presented both in Table 2 and Figure 3 seem to confirm our initial hypothesis on the effectiveness of transfer learning in a cross-lingual fashion. What has surprised us was the excellent results regarding Tasks 1, 2 and 4 when transferring structural knowledge from Chinese to Portuguese. We offer the following explanation for these results. Take the contradiction pair defined in the template language:

$$P := \{x_1 = \iota y \forall x_2 V(y, x_2), V(x_1, x_3)\}$$
("x_1 is the person that has visited everybody, x_1 has visited x_3")

$$H := \neg V(x_1, x_4) \text{ ("x_1 didn't visit x_4")}$$

If we take one possible Portuguese realization of the pair above and apply the different tokenizers we have the following strings:

1. Original sentence: "*[CLS] gabrielle é a pessoa que <u>visitou</u> todo mundo gabrielle <u>visitou</u> luís [SEP] gabrielle não <u>visitou</u> ianesis [SEP]*".

2. Multilingual tokenizer: "*[CLS] gabrielle a pessoa que visito ##u todo mundo gabrielle visito ##u lu ##s [SEP] gabrielle no visito ##u ian ##esis [SEP]*"

3. English tokenizer: "*[CLS] gabrielle a pe ##sso ##a que visit ##ou tod ##o mundo gabrielle visit ##ou lu ##s [SEP] gabrielle no visit ##ou ian ##esis [SEP]*"

4. Chinese tokenizer: "*[CLS] ga ##b ##rie ##lle a pe ##ss ##oa q ##ue vi ##sit ##ou to ##do mu ##nd ##o ga ##b ##rie ##lle vi ##sit ##ou lu ##s [SEP] ga ##b ##rie ##lle no vi ##sit ##ou ian ##es ##is [SEP]*"

Although the Portuguese words are destroyed by the tokenizers, the model is still able to learn in the fine-tuning phase the *simple* structural pattern between the tokens highlighted above. This may explain why the counting task (Task 4) presents the highest difficulty for BERT. There is some structural grounding for finding contradictions in counting expressions, but to detect contradiction in all cases one must fully grasp the *meaning* of the multiple counting operators.

6   Conclusion

With the possibility of using pre-trained models we can successfully craft small datasets ($\sim$ 10K sentences) to perform fine grained analysis on machine learning models. In this paper, we have presented a new dataset that is able to isolate a few competence issues regarding structural inference. It also allows us to bring to the surface some interesting comparisons between recurrent neural networks and pre-trained Transform-based models. As our results show, *compared to the recurrent models, BERT presents a considerable advantage in learning structural inference. The same result appears even when fine-tuned one version of the model that was not pre-trained on the target language.*

By the stratified nature of our dataset, we can pinpoint BERT's inference difficulties: *there is space for improving the model's counting understanding*. Hence, we can either craft a more realistic NLI dataset centered on the notion of counting or modify BERT's training to achieve better results in the counting task.

The results on cross-lingual transfer learning are stimulating. One possible area for future research is to check if the same results can be attainable using simple structural inferences that occur within complexes sentences. This can be done by carefully selecting sentence pairs in a cross-lingual NLI corpus like Conneau et al. (2018). We plan to explore these paths in the future.

References

Luisa Bentivogli, Peter Clark, Ido Dagan, and Danilo Giampiccolo. 2009. The sixth pascal recognizing textual entailment challenge. In *Text Analysis Conference*.

Samuel R. Bowman, Gabor Angeli, Christopher Potts, and Christopher D. Manning. 2015a. A large annotated corpus for learning natural language inference. In *Empirical Methods in Natural Language Processing, 2015*.

Samuel R. Bowman, Christopher D. Manning, and Christopher Potts. 2015b. Tree-structured composition in neural networks without tree-structured architectures. *CoRR*, abs/1506.04834.

Alexis Conneau, Ruty Rinott, Guillaume Lample, Adina Williams, Samuel R. Bowman, Holger Schwenk, and Veselin Stoyanov. 2018. XNLI: Evaluating cross-lingual sentence representations. Association for Computational Linguistics.

Ido Dagan, Dan Roth, Mark Sammons, and Fabio Massimo Zanzotto. 2013. *Recognizing Textual Entailment: Models and Applications*. Synthesis Lectures on Human Language Technologies. Morgan Claypool Publishers.

Jacob Devlin, Ming-Wei Chang, Kenton Lee, and Kristina Toutanova. 2018. BERT: pre-training of deep bidirectional transformers for language understanding. *CoRR*, abs/1810.04805.

Richard Evans, David Saxton, David Amos, Pushmeet Kohli, and Edward Grefenstette. 2018. Can neural networks understand logical entailment? *CoRR*, abs/1802.08535.

Danilo Giampiccolo, Bernardo Magnini, Ido Dagan, and Bill Dolan. 2007. The third PASCAL recognizing textual entailment challenge. In *Proceedings of the Workshop on Textual Entailment and Paraphrasing, Association for Computational Linguistics, 2007*, pages 1–9.

Max Glockner, Vered Shwartz, and Yoav Goldberg. 2018. Breaking NLI systems with sentences that require simple lexical inferences. *CoRR*, abs/1805.02266.

Yoav Goldberg. 2015. A primer on neural network models for natural language processing. *CoRR*, abs/1510.00726.

Yoav Goldberg. 2019. Assessing bert's syntactic abilities. *CoRR*, abs/1901.05287.

Suchin Gururangan, Swabha Swayamdipta, Omer Levy, Roy Schwartz, Samuel R. Bowman, and Noah A. Smith. 2018. Annotation artifacts in natural language inference data. *CoRR*, abs/1803.02324.

Jeremy Howard and Sebastian Ruder. 2018. Fine-tuned language models for text classification. *CoRR*, abs/1801.06146.

Armand Joulin, Edouard Grave, Piotr Bojanowski, and Tomas Mikolov. 2016. Bag of tricks for efficient text classification. *CoRR*, abs/1607.01759.

Diederik P. Kingma and Jimmy Ba. 2014. Adam: A method for stochastic optimization. *CoRR*, abs/1412.6980.

Roger Levy and Christopher Manning. 2003. Is it harder to parse chinese, or the chinese treebank? In *Association for Computational Linguistics, 2003*.

Xiaodong Liu, Pengcheng He, Weizhu Chen, and Jianfeng Gao. 2019. Multi-task deep neural networks for natural language understanding. *CoRR*, abs/1901.11504.

Marco Marelli, Stefano Menini, Marco Baroni, Luisa Bentivogli, Raffaella Bernardi, and Roberto Zamparelli. 2014. A sick cure for the evaluation of compositional distributional semantic models. In *LREC*.

Adam Paszke, Sam Gross, Soumith Chintala, Gregory Chanan, Edward Yang, Zachary DeVito, Zeming Lin, Alban Desmaison, Luca Antiga, and Adam Lerer. 2017. Automatic differentiation in PyTorch.

Jeffrey Pennington, Richard Socher, and Christopher D. Manning. 2014. Glove: Global vectors for word representation. In *Empirical Methods in Natural Language Processing, 2014*.

Adam Poliak, Jason Naradowsky, Aparajita Haldar, Rachel Rudinger, and Benjamin Van Durme. 2018. Hypothesis only baselines in natural language inference. *CoRR*, abs/1805.01042.

Felipe Salvatore. 2019. Cross-Lingual Contradiction Detection. https://github.com/felipessalvatore/CLCD.

The Fracas Consortium, Robin Cooper, Dick Crouch, Jan Van Eijck, Chris Fox, Josef Van Genabith, Jan Jaspars, Hans Kamp, David Milward, Manfred Pinkal, Massimo Poesio, Steve Pulman, Ted Briscoe, Holger Maier, and Karsten Konrad. 1996. Using the framework.

Ke M. Tran, Arianna Bisazza, and Christof Monz. 2018. The importance of being recurrent for modeling hierarchical structure. *CoRR*, abs/1803.03585.

Ashish Vaswani, Noam Shazeer, Niki Parmar, Jakob Uszkoreit, Llion Jones, Aidan N. Gomez, Lukasz Kaiser, and Illia Polosukhin. 2017. Attention is all you need. *CoRR*, abs/1706.03762.

Sean Welleck, Jason Weston, Arthur Szlam, and Kyunghyun Cho. 2018. Dialogue natural language inference. *CoRR*, abs/1811.00671.

Adina Williams, Nikita Nangia, and Samuel R. Bowman. 2017. A broad-coverage challenge corpus for sentence understanding through inference. *CoRR*, abs/1704.05426.

Bad Form: Comparing Context-Based and Form-Based Few-Shot Learning in Distributional Semantic Models

Jeroen Van Hautte♠♡, Guy Emerson♠ and Marek Rei♠◇♣

♠Dept. of Computer Science & Technology, University of Cambridge, United Kingdom
◇The ALTA Institute, University of Cambridge, United Kingdom
♣Dept. of Computing, Imperial College London, United Kingdom
♡TechWolf, Belgium

`jeroen@vanhautte.be`, `gete2@cam.ac.uk`, `marek.rei@cl.cam.ac.uk`

Abstract

Word embeddings are an essential component in a wide range of natural language processing applications. However, distributional semantic models are known to struggle when only a small number of context sentences are available. Several methods have been proposed to obtain higher-quality vectors for these words, leveraging both this context information and sometimes the word forms themselves through a hybrid approach. We show that the current tasks do not suffice to evaluate models that use word-form information, as such models can easily leverage word forms in the training data that are related to word forms in the test data. We introduce 3 new tasks, allowing for a more balanced comparison between models. Furthermore, we show that hyperparameters that have largely been ignored in previous work can consistently improve the performance of both baseline and advanced models, achieving a new state of the art on 4 out of 6 tasks.

1 Introduction

Word embeddings have impacted almost every aspect of NLP, proving effective in a wide range of use cases. Often used in the form of a pre-trained model, these vectors provide easy to use representations of semantic meaning. However, distributional models are known to struggle with words for which training data is sparse, often resulting in low-quality vector representations (Huang et al., 2012; Adams et al., 2017). The default approach in this case has historically been to ignore these rare words, preferring an incomplete view over an incorrect one (Mikolov et al., 2013). Another option is to use the surface form of a word to obtain a vector, leveraging morphological characteristics (Luong et al., 2013) or subword embeddings (Bojanowski et al., 2017). As neither of these approaches fully resolves the problem, more techniques have been proposed for few-shot learning

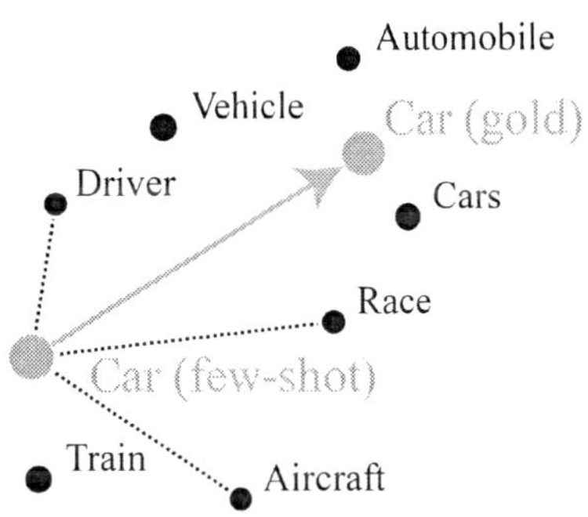

Figure 1: The DN task compares the few-shot vector to the gold vector (arrow), while the Chimera and CRW task compare system and human similarity to a selection of other words (dotted lines).

in distributional models. Each of these aims to correctly position a new word vector inside an existing semantic space. The challenge for few-shot learning is to find a position that accurately reflects the meaning of the word, even if only a small number of usage examples is available.

Making systems better at handling rare words is an obvious practical goal of few-shot learning, as it could substantially improve systems working with technical language or dialects. However, few-shot learning is also interesting from a human language learning perspective: unlike current-day distributional models, humans excel at learning meaning from sparse data through a process called 'fast mapping' (Trueswell et al., 2013; Lake et al., 2017). Lessons learned from psychology might prove effective in machines, and novel few-shot learning techniques might provide insight into fast mapping in humans.

Three evaluation tasks have been proposed to evaluate few-shot learning methods: Definitional Nonce (Herbelot and Baroni, 2017), Chimera (Lazaridou et al., 2017), and Contextual Rare Words (Khodak et al., 2018), which we describe

Proceedings of the 2nd Workshop on Deep Learning Approaches for Low-Resource NLP (DeepLo), pages 31–39
Hong Kong, China, November 3, 2019. ©2019 Association for Computational Linguistics
https://doi.org/10.18653/v1/P17

in Section 2. However, each of these tasks was designed for context-based few-shot learning, without considering hybrid methods, which also have access to word-form information. We show that the existing tasks do not suffice to fully assess the performance of hybrid models, with relatively simple, purely form-based methods dominating two out of three tasks. To provide a better overview and performance comparison, in Section 3 we introduce three new tasks based on these three datasets. In Sections 4–6, we show that, just as hyperparameters are essential to good performance with standard distributional models (Levy et al., 2015), the same is true for few-shot distributional models. With three straightforward modifications, we substantially improve the baseline scores, outperforming several advanced methods from previous work, as well as achieving a new state of the art on 4 out of 6 evaluation tasks.

2   Background & Related Work

2.1   Evaluation Tasks

Three tasks have been used in most previous work to evaluate few-shot learning methods. The goal for each task is to obtain a high-quality vector for a word, given only a small set of sentences in which it appears. An existing semantic space is required,[1] in which a new vector needs to be placed. The embeddings in the existing semantic model are called background embeddings. A simple visualisation of the evaluation strategies is given in Figure 1.

Definitional Nonce   The Definitional Nonce (DN) task (Herbelot and Baroni, 2017) provides a single definitional sentence for each test word. The test words are existing words, which have a high-quality gold vector, due to many occurrences in the training corpus. The aim for a few-shot learning algorithm is to infer a vector close to the gold vector. This is measured by ranking the background vectors by distance from the inferred vector, with the gold vector ideally placed at rank 1. The metrics used for this task are the Mean Reciprocal Rank (MRR) and median rank over the 300 test words. As the DN task uses definitional sentences as opposed to natural word use, we make use of the DN development set to optimise hyperparameters for this dataset separately.

---

[1] In previous work, the model by Herbelot and Baroni (2017) is often used.

Chimera   The Chimera dataset (Lazaridou et al., 2017) consists of a series of novel words that are built as hybrids between two existing words. For each hybrid word, trials with 2, 4 and 6 context sentences are provided, with half of the sentences coming from each of the two source words. Each sentence was manually selected to be informative. Annotators were presented with the context sentences and asked to give similarity scores between the nonsense hybrid word and a range of other words. A few-shot learning algorithm is evaluated based on the rank correlation between the system's cosine similarity scores and the human similarity scores.

Contextual Rare Words   The Contextual Rare Words (CRW) dataset (Khodak et al., 2018; Luong et al., 2013) consists of 255 context sentences selected randomly from Wikipedia for each of 455 existing words. Vectors are inferred for each word using 1, 2, 4, ..., 128 sentences. In similar fashion to the Chimera task, human similarity ratings to a selection of other words are compared to system ratings. For each number of context sentences, the Spearman rank correlation between the human and system similarities is reported. In this paper, we only report scores for up to 64 context sentences. We make use of the CRW development set introduced by Schick and Schütze (2018) to optimise model hyperparameters both for the CRW and Chimera task, as both of these have a similar setup.

2.2   Context-Based Few-Shot Learning

Word2Vec   While the Skip-Gram Word2Vec algorithm (Mikolov et al., 2013) was used to generate the background embeddings provided by Herbelot and Baroni (2017), the method has also been applied as a few-shot learning method. This is done by loading the background embeddings and continuing training on the context sentences for each test word. This approach has been applied to each of the three tasks in previous work, with notably weak performance on the DN and Chimera datasets (Herbelot and Baroni, 2017; Khodak et al., 2018; Schick and Schütze, 2018). However, to our knowledge, thorough hyperparameter optimisation for few-shot learning has not previously been attempted.

Additive Model   In similar fashion to Herbelot and Baroni (2017), we make use of a model that simply adds up all words in the context sentences for the test word. Stopwords[2] are dropped from this sum, as this has been found to consistently improve performance (Khodak et al., 2018).

Nonce2Vec The Nonce2Vec algorithm heavily modifies several aspects of the standard Skip-Gram Word2Vec algorithm. This allows for a higher-risk initial learning approach, followed by a more cautious strategy as more data is presented (Herbelot and Baroni, 2017).

Mem2Vec The Mem2Vec algorithm uses a long-range memory over the whole corpus to find a vector corresponding to a small number of contexts (Sun et al., 2018).

A La Carte The A La Carte model can be seen as an improved additive model: the addition is followed by a linear transformation, which is learned from the co-occurrence matrix of the corpus (Khodak et al., 2018).

2.3 Hybrid Few-Shot Learning

In many words, part of the meaning can be deduced from the word form itself – as such, models that can access and use this information can often perform better at few-shot learning.

FastText FastText (Bojanowski et al., 2017) is an extension of Word2Vec: it is based on the same mechanisms, but adds in the use of character n-gram embeddings, as opposed to only modelling full words. The embedding for a word is calculated as the sum of its word embedding and the contained character n-gram embeddings. These are jointly optimised using the same approach as for Word2Vec. FastText is an interesting choice for few-shot learning due to its ability to generate vectors for out-of-vocabulary words: if a word is not contained in the vocabulary, a vector can be composed using only the character n-gram embeddings.

Form-Context Model In similar fashion to FastText, the Form-Context Model (Schick and Schütze, 2018) combines both form and context information to infer a higher-quality vector. Two variants exist, both estimating the rare word vector $v_{(\mathbf{w},\mathcal{C})}$ using:

$$v_{(\mathbf{w},\mathcal{C})} = \alpha \cdot \hat{v}^{context}_{(\mathbf{w},\mathcal{C})} + (1 - \alpha) \cdot v^{form}_{(\mathbf{w},\mathcal{C})} \qquad (1)$$

where $v^{form}_{(\mathbf{w},\mathcal{C})}$ is the surface form embedding and $\hat{v}^{context}_{(\mathbf{w},\mathcal{C})}$ is the context-based vector. The former is obtained through the subword approach from FastText[3], while the latter vector is obtained through the A La Carte method. The two versions differ in their coefficient α: in the single-parameter variant, α is a learned constant between 0 and 1, while in the gated model, it is a learned function of $v^{form}_{(\mathbf{w},\mathcal{C})}$ and $v^{context}_{(\mathbf{w},\mathcal{C})}$, allowing the model to adapt to different scenarios.

3 Evaluation Setup

Several issues can be observed in the evaluation setup used in previous work. First of all, results on the Chimera task are inconsistent, showing almost no trends between different models. This can largely be attributed to the the size of the test set: only 110 chimera words are used. By using the CRW development set to optimise for both the CRW and Chimera task, we can include the training set as well, resulting in the 'Full Chimera Task' with a total of 330 words.

For the CRW and DN tasks, the issues are not in the consistency of results, but rather in how to interpret the results. Schick and Schütze (2018) observe that, on the CRW task, their form-only model outperforms the full model, which uses both form and context. Whereas in context-based learning, each test word is new by definition, hybrid models typically have access to the vectors of different forms of the same lemma (such as *wanderer* and *wanderers*), meaning data for these words might not be sparse at all once related word forms are considered.

To assess the extent of the available information, we analyse the DN and CRW datasets, looking for words with the same stem[4] as a test word. We ranked these words against the test word's nearest neighbours, with the results shown in Figure 2. For the CRW task, more than 50% of test words have a word with the same stem among their 2 nearest neighbours, with this percentage increasing to more than 75% when we look at the 20 nearest words. This indicates that there is a very high degree of information available to form-based methods that can leverage inflectional morphology. For the Definitional Nonce task, about 28% of test words have a word with the same stem

---

[2]Based on the NLTK stopword list.

[3]These subword embeddings are trained on top of an existing model, unlike those in FastText.

[4]Determined using the NLTK Snowball stemmer.

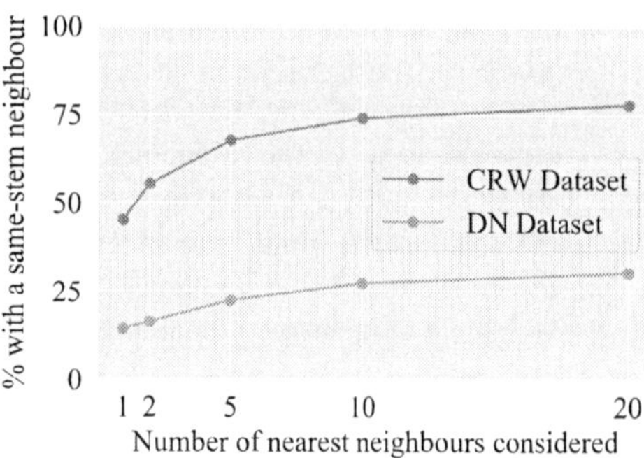

Figure 2: The proportion of words in the CRW and DN test sets that have a neighbour with the same stem, for different numbers of neighbours considered.

among their 20 nearest neighbours.

Based on these insights, we build a simple baseline model that estimates vectors by averaging all vectors for (non-test) words with the same stem. With an MRR of 0.5550 and a median rank of 2 on the DN task, this substantially outperforms the previous best scores of 0.1754 and 49 set by the Form-Context Model (Schick and Schütze, 2018). On the CRW task, the model achieves a score of 0.32, well below the 0.49 score achieved by the form-only model from Schick and Schütze. For both tasks, the top-performing model completely ignores the provided context sentences, implying that both of these tasks focus on new forms of known lemmas, rather than completely novel words.

Both scenarios are important use cases for few-shot distributional semantics, but to get a better view of the second scenario, we introduce the 'Filtered CRW' and 'Filtered DN' tasks, which have the same objectives as their *non-filtered* counterparts, but for which the background embeddings are trained on a restricted corpus, filtering out any words with the same stem as one of the test words. This causes a removal of 2% of the tokens inside the corpus, in similar fashion to how infrequent words[5] are typically dropped before a distributional model is trained. For the CRW dataset, the filtering removes the other word in 83 of the word pairs (for which human similarity scores are available), leaving the filtered version with 479 word pairs.

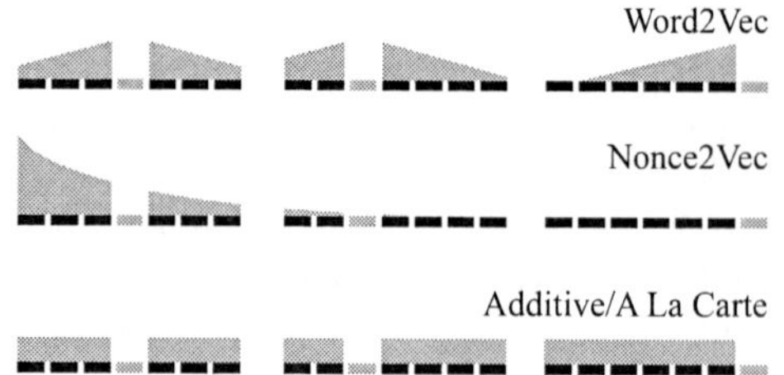

Figure 3: A visual representation of how different methods award importance to words, based on their position relative to the target word (green) and the order in which sentences are processed. The importance of a word can be interpreted as a combination of the selection probability and weight or learning rate used.

4 Novel Methods

We now propose several novel methods, improving both baselines and advanced models through relatively simple modifications.

4.1 Selective Word2Vec & FastText

In previous work the default Word2Vec and Fast-Text implementations are used. This means that not only do the vectors for test words change, but also those for context words. This creates a conflict of interest: to speed up learning of the new vector, a high learning rate might be desirable, but this same learning rate could also distort the background embeddings more heavily, decreasing vector quality. As such, we ensure that only vectors for test words are updated, removing the latter effect.[6]

4.2 Weighted Addition

The additive model, A La Carte model and Form-Context model all make use of a simple, uniformly weighted sum[7] of all words around the test word. However, Word2Vec uses several techniques to focus on those words that are more likely to be meaningful. Below, we describe how these principles are included into each of these models by modifying the weights used in the addition.

4.2.1 Window Weights

The existing models have different strategies to handle the distance at which words co-occur, as shown in Figure 3: while the additive and A La Carte model use each word in a sentence with the

---

[5]Based on a minimum count, for which 50 is used throughout this paper.

[6]We also ensure that test words cannot be used as negative samples, so as to make sure that there is no influence between different samples.

[7]Followed by a transformation for ALC and FCM.

same weight, the exponential parameter decay of Nonce2Vec results in an emphasis on words before the test word. Word2Vec itself uses a sampled window size, meaning the importance of words decreases linearly with distance from the test word (Goldberg and Levy, 2014). We adopt the same approach, as this has been shown to improve performance (Levy et al., 2015). In Word2Vec, given a window size n, a context word m tokens away from the target word has a probability of

$$P_{window}(m) = max\left(\frac{n - m + 1}{n}, 0\right) \quad (2)$$

to be selected as a positive sample. This probability can be seen as the expected weight of the contribution of each word to the final vector, which is how we apply it to the sum in each model.

4.2.2 Negative Sampling & Subsampling

Word2Vec makes use of subsampling, as rare words typically carry more information than overly frequent words (Mikolov et al., 2013; Ramos et al., 2003). For a frequency threshold t (typically 10^{-5}), the probability to keep a word w_i with frequency $f(w_i)$ in the training corpus is given by

$$P_{subsample}(w_i) = 1 - \sqrt{\frac{t}{f(w_i)}} \quad (3)$$

We again use this probability as a weight, multiplying each term with its subsampling probability.

Negative sampling has also been found to improve vector quality in Word2Vec (Goldberg and Levy, 2014). The probability for a word w_j to be selected as a negative sample is given by

$$P_{negative}(w_j) = \frac{f(w_j)^{3/4}}{\sum_{k=0}^{n}\left(f(w_k)^{3/4}\right)} \quad (4)$$

As such, the expected negative sample vector is

$$\hat{v}_{neg} = \sum_{w_i \in V} P_{negative}(w_i) \cdot v_{w_i} \quad (5)$$

where V is the vocabulary and v_{w_i} is the vector for w_i. For a negative sampling rate k, each vector v_{w_i} is now replaced with $v_{w_i} - k \cdot \hat{v}_{neg}$ before being added up, after which the subsample and window probabilities are applied.

4.3 Neural ALC & FCM

The A La Carte model uses a linear transformation, which is efficient, but also severely constrained (Khodak et al., 2018). We propose using a neural network with one hidden layer, allowing for a more flexible transformation. This same neural transformation can then be integrated into a new version of the Form-Context Model as well.

5 Implementation Details

We optimise the hyperparameters on the CRW and DN development sets, using the original evaluation setup. The same settings are used for the novel tasks. All model training described below is done using the Westbury Wikipedia Corpus (Shaoul, 2010), which was used in previous work (Schick and Schütze, 2018; Khodak et al., 2018).

5.1 Background Embeddings

To make the experimental setup less complex, a single background model is used for all new tasks – this can influence scores, but results for different models on the same task can still be compared. Filtering is applied to remove all words with the same stem as a test word, except for the DN words themselves, as these are used as gold vectors during evaluation.

To optimise the background embeddings (for both Word2Vec and FastText), we carry out a grid search for the learning rate (0.025, 0.05 or 0.1), dimension (150, 300 or 450), window size (5 or 10), negative sampling rate (5, 10 or 15) and number of epochs (5, 10 or 100). For FastText, the standard character n-gram length of 3 to 5 characters is used. Evaluating these models on the CRW development set (Schick and Schütze, 2018), we find that for both algorithms, the default configuration[8], while slightly outperformed by a higher-dimensional setup, is not significantly[9] worse than the respective top performer for each algorithm. Therefore, we opt for the default configuration in both cases.

5.2 Previous Work

5.2.1 Context-Based Few-Shot Learning

Word2Vec We conduct the same grid search as for the background embeddings (aside from the dimension, which is fixed to 300). For the CRW

---

[8]Learning rate 0.025, dimension 300, negative sampling 5, window size 5, and 5 epochs.

[9]At the 0.01 level, using a Monte Carlo permutation test.

dataset, we again find the same parameters. For the DN task, a higher number of epochs (100) and window size (10) substantially improve upon the default setup. A possible explanation for the big difference in hyperparameters can be found in the negative sampling mechanism: as only a single context sentence is used in the DN task, a small number of negative samples is used per epoch. This makes the effect of negative sampling on the returned vector more variable, while the gold vector has had sufficient (positive and negative) samples to converge to the expected value. By raising the window size and the number of epochs, the number of negative samples is also increased, allowing for the same to happen even with a single input sentence. On the CRW task, there is no similar tendency, indicating that this 'expected effect of negative sampling' is important for recreating a vector exactly, but less so for the quality of the vector as compared to human judgement.

Nonce2Vec For performance reasons, we implement the Nonce2Vec algorithm ourselves. We use the same parameters reported by Herbelot and Baroni (2017) and confirm that results are comparable to the original.

Mem2Vec As no code was published for Mem2Vec, we have not evaluated the algorithm ourselves. For completeness, we report the results available for the DN and CRW tasks.

A La Carte The code provided with the original paper allows us to easily generate the transformation matrix needed for this model.

5.2.2 Hybrid Few-Shot Learning

FastText For the CRW task, we again find the default settings to be optimal. We only evaluate FastText on the Filtered CRW and Full Chimera tasks, so as to avoid problems with model dependence (DN task) and lexical information leakage.

Form-Context Model We make use of the gated model, training it just like Schick and Schütze (2018). The same character n-gram lengths are used as for FastText.

5.3 Novel Methods

Selective Word2Vec & FastText Based on Gensim's Skip-Gram implementation, we create a selective version of Word2Vec and FastText. All parameters are found to be the same as for the non-selective versions, except for selective Word2Vec

on the DN task, where a higher-risk learning rate of 0.1 is now optimal.

Window Weights To add window weights to the addition-based models, we evaluate both the additive and A La Carte models with a window size of $2, 5, 10, 15$ and 20, finding 10 to be optimal across the board.

Subsampling & Negative Sampling For the subsampling mechanism, the frequency threshold $t = 10^{-5}$ is used, as recommended by Mikolov et al. (2013). For the negative sampling mechanism, rates of $1, 2, 5$ and 10 negative samples per positive sample are considered, with 2 being optimal for both the CRW and DN development set.

Neural ALC & FCM We use a simple architecture with one hidden layer. This hidden layer has 1000 neurons (out of 100, 200, 500, 1000 and 2000) and has a ReLU activation. The output layer has no non-linearity. The network is optimised with the Adam optimiser (Kingma and Ba, 2015) and the mean square error loss function. The model is trained with the same samples as the original A La Carte model. The same window weights are used as before.

6 Results

We now discuss the results for each dataset, with the emphasis on trends in how models adapt to different circumstances. A summary is provided in Section 7.

6.1 Definitional Nonce & Filtered DN

Results for the DN and Filtered DN task are shown in Table 1. The best context-based model on both tasks is the A La Carte model, which significantly[10] outperforms all other context-based models. While the Form-Context model performs significantly better than A La Carte on both tasks, the original DN task is completely dominated by the stem-based model. This shows that using known related word forms is an extremely effective approach for estimating a new embedding. The removal of these related words from the training data heavily impacts the scores for all form-based and hybrid methods, but the Form-Context model still manages to perform strongly on the Filtered DN task, showing that the model is robust to varying amounts of information in both the form and context.

---

[10]Significance testing is applied to the MRR metric.

	Method	Definitional Nonce		Filtered DN		Chimera			Full Chimera		
		MRR	Median	MRR	Median	L2	L4	L6	L2	L4	L6
CONTEXT BASED	Word2Vec	0.0007	5253	0.0110	3546	0.299	0.332	0.404	0.265	0.355	0.363
	Additive	0.0332	870	0.0377	678	0.358	**0.387**	0.420	0.320	0.366	0.388
	Nonce2Vec	0.0415	708	0.0557	583	0.328	0.378	0.401	0.300	0.356	0.369
	A La Carte	**0.0706**	**165**	**0.0697**	**155**	**0.363**	0.384	0.394	0.304	0.355	0.377
	Mem2Vec	0.0542	512	-	-	0.330	0.372	0.390	-	-	-
	Selective Word2Vec	0.0183	1710	0.0255	1570	0.301	0.323	0.410	0.270	0.343	0.365
	Additive + Window	0.0364	937	0.0320	646	0.359	0.370	**0.433**	**0.327**	**0.369**	**0.391**
	Additive + Window/Sub/Neg	0.0523	267	0.0400	418	0.360	0.355	0.422	0.314	0.356	0.388
	A La Carte + Window	0.0426	637	0.0321	591	0.292	0.376	0.390	0.288	0.348	0.372
	A La Carte + Window/Sub/Neg	0.0327	2274	0.0323	510	0.261	0.334	0.375	0.294	0.345	0.365
	Neural A La Carte + Window	0.0472	931	0.0334	1114	0.325	0.374	0.401	0.306	0.367	0.386
FORM + HYBRID	FastText	-	-	-	-	-	-	-	0.129	0.165	0.202
	Form-Context	0.1561	64	**0.0992**	**99**	0.325	**0.367**	0.359	**0.313**	0.339	0.333
	Stem-Based	**0.5550**	**2**	-	-	-	-	-	-	-	-
	Selective FastText	-	-	-	-	-	-	-	0.060	0.087	0.120
	Neural FCM	0.1219	183	0.0735	241	**0.327**	0.361	**0.382**	0.304	**0.351**	**0.360**

Table 1: Results for DN and Chimera tasks. The best result per category (context-based or hybrid) in every column is marked in bold, while setups that were not evaluated have been filled with a dash. Purely form-based methods are not evaluated on the Chimera tasks. The stem-based model is not compatible with the filtered tasks.

Selective Word2Vec and the additive models show that the baseline scores reported by Herbelot and Baroni left much room for improvement, but both normal and selective Word2Vec are still among the worst models evaluated. The effect of weights used in the addition-based models is not consistently positive, which might be explained by the fact that these principles are meant for natural word usage (not definitions, as in the DN dataset).

6.2 Chimera & Full Chimera

The results for the original and Full Chimera tasks are provided in Table 1. On the original task, there are no clear performance trends, presumably caused by the small size of the test set. In that respect, the Full Chimera task is much more useful, allowing for a better comparison between models. The additive model with a window achieves the best score on all trials for the Full Chimera task, as well as one for the original (L6, with strong performance L2 and L4 as well). The most advanced additive model (window, subsampling and negative sampling) and the nonlinear A La Carte model also perform very strongly on the Full Chimera task.

There is a clear divide between the context-based and hybrid models, with the latter being outperformed by almost all of the former. This is caused by the nonsensical word forms used for chimeras: the form information is now misinformation. Looking at the large performance difference between both Form-Context models and the FastText-based models, the advantage of the Form-Context architecture becomes clear: the adaptive weighting between form and context provides much better flexibility. FastText, on the other hand, has a fixed strategy, meaning it cannot disregard the useless form information. The original FastText algorithm outperforms selective FastText, as the subword embeddings are able to overfit on the provided context sentences.

6.3 CRW Tasks

The results for the CRW tasks are provided in Table 2. On the original CRW task, hybrid methods dominate, with the FCM outperforming all other results significantly even with no context sentences. This again shows how much lexical information is available.

On the Filtered CRW task, form-based scores are much lower. However, as shown by the two FastText models and the two Form-Context models, using form information can still provide a clear advantage here by augmenting sparse context-based information. In this situation, the fixed strategy used by FastText allows the selective FastText algorithm to be among the top models on the Filtered CRW task, while the original FastText algorithm suffers from overfitting. The best model overall is the Neural FCM, achieving the top result on all but one trial.

Among the context-based methods, all A La

	Method	Contextual Rare Words								Filtered CRW							
		Number of Context Sentences								Number of Context Sentences							
		0	1	2	4	8	16	32	64	0	1	2	4	8	16	32	64
CONTEXT BASED	Word2Vec	-	0.15	0.19	0.24	0.30	0.35	0.38	0.41	-	0.14	0.18	0.23	0.29	0.33	0.37	0.39
	Additive	-	0.12	0.14	0.16	0.17	0.18	0.19	0.19	-	0.11	0.13	0.15	0.17	0.18	0.18	0.18
	Nonce2Vec	-	0.12	0.15	0.17	0.17	0.16	0.15	0.14	-	0.12	0.15	0.17	0.18	0.17	0.16	0.15
	A La Carte	-	0.19	0.24	0.29	0.34	0.38	0.40	0.40	-	0.20	0.25	0.29	0.34	0.37	0.39	0.40
	Selective Word2Vec	-	0.19	0.23	0.27	0.32	0.36	0.38	0.40	-	0.17	0.22	0.26	0.31	0.34	0.37	0.39
	Additive + Window	-	0.13	0.16	0.18	0.20	0.20	0.21	0.21	-	0.14	0.17	0.20	0.22	0.23	0.24	0.24
	Additive + Window/Sub/Neg	-	0.16	0.20	0.24	0.27	0.29	0.30	0.30	-	0.17	0.21	0.24	0.27	0.29	0.30	0.31
	ALC + Window	-	0.21	0.26	0.32	0.36	0.40	0.41	0.42	-	0.22	0.27	0.32	0.36	**0.39**	0.40	0.41
	ALC + Window/Sub/Neg	-	0.21	0.26	0.31	0.34	0.35	0.36	0.36	-	**0.24**	**0.29**	**0.33**	**0.37**	**0.39**	**0.41**	**0.42**
	Neural ALC + Window	-	**0.22**	**0.27**	**0.33**	**0.37**	**0.41**	**0.43**	**0.44**	-	0.23	0.28	**0.33**	**0.37**	**0.39**	**0.41**	**0.42**
FORM + HYBRID	FastText	-	-	-	-	-	-	-	-	**0.36**	0.31	0.32	0.32	0.32	0.33	0.33	0.34
	Form-Context	**0.49**	0.42	**0.45**	**0.46**	**0.47**	**0.47**	0.47	0.47	**0.36**	0.32	0.35	0.37	**0.39**	0.39	0.39	0.40
	Stem-Based	0.32	-	-	-	-	-	-	-	-	-	-	-	-	-	-	-
	Selective FastText	-	-	-	-	-	-	-	-	**0.36**	**0.36**	**0.36**	0.37	0.37	0.38	0.40	0.42
	Neural FCM	**0.49**	**0.43**	**0.45**	**0.46**	**0.47**	**0.47**	**0.48**	**0.48**	**0.36**	0.33	**0.36**	**0.38**	**0.39**	**0.41**	**0.42**	**0.43**

Table 2: Results on both CRW tasks. The best result per category in every column is marked in bold. The form-based and hybrid categories are shown together, as a hybrid model using 0 context sentences is effectively form-based. The stem-based model is not compatible with the filtered tasks.

Carte models perform strongly, just like the selective Word2Vec algorithm. On the Filtered CRW task, the integration of the principles behind Word2Vec consistently improves performance, both for the additive and A La Carte models, showing that these are particularly effective when working with unfiltered, natural usage examples for new words. In the original CRW task however, these techniques cause a performance drop, most likely caused by the presence of the original words in the model. The Neural ALC model is the best context-based model on both tasks: the extra freedom allowed by the neural network allows this model to adapt better to different situations. Interestingly, performance for Nonce2Vec decreases when more than 16 context sentences are used. This is seems to be caused by the imbalance in the importance of training data (Figure 3).

7 Conclusion

Different situations and goals in few-shot learning have different optimal solutions. The difference between learning from natural language usage and definitions is especially apparent: only the original A La Carte method performs well for both types, while other models that do very well on the latter typically trail on the former. The principles behind Word2Vec work well in other models when using unfiltered, natural usage examples, but are less consistent when the sentences are filtered (Chimera dataset) or of a different type (DN dataset). The available word-form information is a double-edged sword: while real-world scenarios will often allow for the use of such information, a completely novel word form can cause a decrease in performance. With a combination of existing and novel evaluation tasks, we have been able to compare and explain model performance between context-based and hybrid methods in different scenarios.

The success of the newly proposed baseline methods shows that within specific use cases, a simple approach can suffice to achieve very strong performance. More complex methods, such as Nonce2Vec and Mem2Vec, are even outperformed across the board by these new baselines. However, simple methods typically struggle to generalise to multiple sub-tasks. The main benefit of more complex methods is that they are more flexible, at the price of overhead and a risk of overfitting. For both context-based and hybrid few-shot learning, we have achieved a new state of the art on 4 out of the 6 evaluation tasks used, showing that a careful, optimised approach can be the key to success in few-shot learning. Future work could explore other distributional models, such as dependency embeddings (Levy and Goldberg, 2014; Czarnowska et al., 2019), but it is clear from our results that careful optimisation will be required to adapt other models to the few-shot setting.

Acknowledgements

We thank the anonymous reviewers for their valuable feedback. Guy Emerson is supported by a Research Fellowship at Gonville & Caius College, Cambridge.

References

Oliver Adams, Adam Makarucha, Graham Neubig, Steven Bird, and Trevor Cohn. 2017. Cross-lingual word embeddings for low-resource language modeling. In *Proceedings of the 15th Conference of the European Chapter of the Association for Computational Linguistics: Volume 1, Long Papers*, pages 937–947.

Piotr Bojanowski, Edouard Grave, Armand Joulin, and Tomas Mikolov. 2017. Enriching word vectors with subword information. *Transactions of the Association for Computational Linguistics*, 5:135–146.

Paula Czarnowska, Guy Emerson, and Ann Copestake. 2019. Words are vectors, dependencies are matrices: Learning word embeddings from dependency graphs. In *Proceedings of the 13th International Conference on Computational Semantics (IWCS), Long Papers*, pages 91–102.

Yoav Goldberg and Omer Levy. 2014. Word2Vec explained: deriving Mikolov et al.'s negative-sampling word-embedding method. *CoRR*, abs/1402.3722.

Aurélie Herbelot and Marco Baroni. 2017. High-risk learning: acquiring new word vectors from tiny data. In *Proceedings of the 2017 Conference on Empirical Methods in Natural Language Processing*, pages 304–309.

Eric H Huang, Richard Socher, Christopher D Manning, and Andrew Y Ng. 2012. Improving word representations via global context and multiple word prototypes. In *Proceedings of the 50th Annual Meeting of the Association for Computational Linguistics: Long Papers-Volume 1*, pages 873–882. Association for Computational Linguistics.

Mikhail Khodak, Nikunj Saunshi, Yingyu Liang, Tengyu Ma, Brandon Stewart, and Sanjeev Arora. 2018. A la carte embedding: Cheap but effective induction of semantic feature vectors. In *Proceedings of the 56th Annual Meeting of the Association for Computational Linguistics (Volume 1: Long Papers)*, pages 12–22.

Diederik Kingma and Jimmy Ba. 2015. Adam: A method for stochastic optimization. In *Proceedings of the 3rd International Conference on Learning Representations (ICLR)*.

Brenden M Lake, Tomer D Ullman, Joshua B Tenenbaum, and Samuel J Gershman. 2017. Building machines that learn and think like people. *Behavioral and brain sciences*, 40.

Angeliki Lazaridou, Marco Marelli, and Marco Baroni. 2017. Multimodal word meaning induction from minimal exposure to natural text. *Cognitive Science*, 41:677–705.

Omer Levy and Yoav Goldberg. 2014. Dependency-based word embeddings. In *Proceedings of the 52nd Annual Meeting of the Association for Computational Linguistics (Volume 2: Short Papers)*, pages 302–308.

Omer Levy, Yoav Goldberg, and Ido Dagan. 2015. Improving distributional similarity with lessons learned from word embeddings. *Transactions of the Association for Computational Linguistics*, 3:211–225.

Thang Luong, Richard Socher, and Christopher Manning. 2013. Better word representations with recursive neural networks for morphology. In *Proceedings of the Seventeenth Conference on Computational Natural Language Learning*, pages 104–113.

Tomas Mikolov, Kai Chen, Greg Corrado, and Jeffrey Dean. 2013. Efficient estimation of word representations in vector space. *Proceedings of the 1st International Conference on Learning Representations (ICLR), Workshop Track*.

Juan Ramos et al. 2003. Using tf-idf to determine word relevance in document queries. In *Proceedings of the 1st Instructional Conference on Machine Learning*, volume 242, pages 133–142. Piscataway, NJ.

Timo Schick and Hinrich Schütze. 2018. Learning semantic representations for novel words: Leveraging both form and context. *CoRR*, abs/1811.03866.

Cyrus Shaoul. 2010. The Westbury Lab Wikipedia Corpus. Edmonton, AB: University of Alberta.

Jingyuan Sun, Shaonan Wang, and Chengqing Zong. 2018. Memory, show the way: Memory based few shot word representation learning. In *Proceedings of the 2018 Conference on Empirical Methods in Natural Language Processing*, pages 1435–1444.

John C Trueswell, Tamara Nicol Medina, Alon Hafri, and Lila R Gleitman. 2013. Propose but verify: Fast mapping meets cross-situational word learning. *Cognitive psychology*, 66(1):126–156.

Bag-of-Words Transfer:
Non-Contextual Techniques for Multi-Task Learning

Seth Ebner[1]   **Felicity Wang[1,2]***   **Benjamin Van Durme[1]**
[1]Johns Hopkins University
[2]AI Foundation
{seth,vandurme}@cs.jhu.edu, felicity@aifoundation.com

Abstract

Many architectures for multi-task learning (MTL) have been proposed to take advantage of transfer among tasks, often involving complex models and training procedures. In this paper, we ask if the sentence-level representations learned in previous approaches provide significant benefit beyond that provided by simply improving word-based representations. To investigate this question, we consider three techniques that ignore sequence information: a syntactically-oblivious pooling encoder, pre-trained non-contextual word embeddings, and unigram generative regularization. Compared to a state-of-the-art MTL approach to textual inference, the simple techniques we use yield similar performance on a universe of task combinations while reducing training time and model size.[1]

1 Introduction

Multi-task learning (MTL) is usually framed as a discriminative learning problem in which predictors are learned jointly for multiple related tasks, under the premise that jointly optimizing related tasks will yield more robust parameter estimates.

In this work, we consider a collection of two-sequence classification tasks covering sentiment analysis and textual entailment. Previous work has shown that for these kinds of tasks, models incorporating only bag-of-words (BOW) features are competitive with models based on sequence encoders such as recurrent neural networks (RNNs) and convolutional neural networks (CNNs) that build compositional sequence representations (Iyyer et al., 2015; Wieting et al., 2016; Arora et al., 2017). Arora et al. (2017) suggest that BOW models better exploit the semantics of a sequence than RNNs do.

Arora et al. (2017) show that improving context-independent word-level representations may be sufficient for good performance on particular kinds of tasks. Here we ask if those findings extend to the MTL setting, and in particular how well the BOW techniques capture transfer among tasks.

We additionally observe that the standard MTL framing does not make full use of the available labeled data, as it ignores an important type of related task: generative reconstruction of the observations (§2.3). The MTL framework naturally accommodates reconstruction simply as additional tasks.

In this paper, we: (1) consider bag-of-words techniques including pooling encoders, pre-trained word embeddings, and unigram generative regularization, and (2) demonstrate that bag-of-words techniques are competitive with sequence-level techniques in MTL for sentiment analysis and textual inference (§3).

2 Bag-of-Words Techniques

We employ three approaches that use only bag-of-words representations: pooling (aggregation) encoders, pre-trained word embeddings, and unigram generative regularization. These approaches do not model sequence-level interactions. We do not use contextualized encoders such as ELMo (Peters et al., 2018) and BERT (Devlin et al., 2019) because they incorporate sequence-level and positional representations.

2.1 Pooling Encoders

We first consider a variant of the deep averaging network (DAN) encoder (Iyyer et al., 2015). The DAN encoder is a syntactically-oblivious encoder that consists of three steps: average (mean-pool) a sequence's non-contextual word embeddings, pass the average through feed-forward layers, and then perform linear classification on the final layer's

---

*Work done while at Johns Hopkins University.

[1]Our code is available at https://github.com/felicitywang/tfmtl.

Proceedings of the 2nd Workshop on Deep Learning Approaches for Low-Resource NLP (DeepLo), pages 40–46
Hong Kong, China, November 3, 2019. ©2019 Association for Computational Linguistics
https://doi.org/10.18653/v1/P17

representation. We concatenate a max-pooling operation to the mean-pooling used in the first step of the original DAN encoder[2] and use a non-linear transformation in the final layer[3].

Pooling encoders such as DAN and PARAGRAM-PHRASE (which has no parameters) are much faster to train than LSTMs and CNNs, and have been shown to have competitive performance on textual similarity, textual entailment, and sentiment classification tasks (Iyyer et al., 2015; Wieting et al., 2016; Arora et al., 2017).

2.2 Pre-Trained Word Embeddings

A popular way to improve performance over the use of randomly initialized word embeddings is to use pre-trained word embeddings that have been learned from large corpora. The use of pre-trained embeddings is an example of transfer learning, which unlike MTL typically involves a pipeline of tasks rather than a joint training objective. Word embeddings are usually learned by fitting a language model (or other word prediction objective) on an out-of-domain text corpus (Mikolov et al., 2013; Pennington et al., 2014).

Although pre-trained word embeddings are learned in context and can thereby capture distributional syntactic information, good performance using pre-trained word embeddings would be evidence that sequence-aware models may not be necessary for MTL for the tasks we consider here.

Because we restrict our models to use only bag-of-words features, we seek to avoid any syntactic or sequential information that could be derived from our inputs. Any syntactic information present in pre-trained word embeddings comes from the sequences used in pre-training, not from the data in our tasks. By using pre-trained word embeddings, we seek only to determine what benefit is provided by initializing the corresponding parameters with the pre-trained embeddings rather than with random embeddings.

Additionally, contextualized encoders would capture sequential or positional information in our data inputs, so we do not use them. By not using contextualized encoders, each word has only one embedding, which is used regardless of its context.

---

[2]We tried combinations of mean-pooling, max-pooling, and min-pooling, and found mean-pooling + max-pooling performed the best based on held-out dev-set performance.

[3]We tried ELU, ReLU, sigmoid, and tanh, and chose ReLU based on held-out dev-set performance.

2.3 Unigram Generative Regularization

We examine the incorporation of unigram generative regularization (UGR) for all tasks, in which we reconstruct the input sequence using a *conditional* unigram language model $p_\theta(x \mid h)$.[4] Intuitively, generative regularization provides signal that addresses the question, "What do inputs with a particular label tend to look like?" For example, we wish to capture information about inputs that express positive sentiment separately from information about inputs that express negative sentiment.

We explore multi-task UGR in this work because we found that single-task UGR can improve performance (see Table 3). Additionally, multi-task UGR uses no additional data, so we get it "for free." UGR is inherently related to a dataset t's corresponding discriminative task that learns $q_{\phi_t}(y \mid x)$, and it can be viewed as simply another task in the set of auxiliary tasks because it is realized as an auxiliary loss term.

For arbitrary networks $q_{\phi_t}(y \mid x)$ and $p_\theta(x \mid h)$, our loss function, $\mathcal{L}_{\text{GMTL}}$, on a single example is:

$$-[\alpha_t \log q_{\phi_t}(y_i^{(t)} \mid x_i^{(t)}) + \beta_t \log p_\theta(x_i^{(t)} \mid h_i^{(t)})]$$

for input $x_i^{(t)}$ and its label $y_i^{(t)}$ drawn from dataset t. The conditioning vector for the example, $h_i^{(t)}$, may include information about $y_i^{(t)}$. The discriminative and reconstruction task weights are α_t and β_t, respectively.

3 Experiments

As an external baseline, we compare our approach to methods proposed by Augenstein et al. (2018), herein referred to as **ARS**. ARS achieve state-of-the-art performance on topic-based sentiment analysis. We reimplement their baseline model as an additional comparison in our results (Table 3).

The main contributions of ARS are additional architectural components called the label embedding layer (LEL) and the label transfer network (LTN). In the baseline model, an example's two input sequences, x_1 and x_2, are encoded using a two-stage bi-directional RNN and then passed into a task-specific classification layer. In the LEL model, the task-specific classification layers are replaced by a label embedding matrix shared by all tasks. By embedding all the tasks' labels into a shared space, the LEL learns correlations among the tasks' labels.

---

[4]The conditioning vector h is described in §3.2.

The LTN sits on top of the LEL and induces "pseudo-labels" for main task examples based on predicted distributions over labels made by each of the auxiliary tasks. The LTN is added to the main model after a pre-training step.

We note that ARS deliberately avoid pre-trained word embeddings in order to highlight their modeling contributions. We would expect their results to improve if pre-trained embeddings were used.

3.1 Datasets

We use the same two-sequence text classification datasets covering textual entailment and sentiment analysis used by ARS[5]: MultiNLI (Williams et al., 2018), ABSA-L/ABSA-R (Pontiki et al., 2016), Target (Dong et al., 2014), Stance (Mohammad et al., 2016), Topic-2/Topic-5 (Nakov et al., 2016), and FNC-1.[6] All of the inputs have two sequences (x_1, x_2), the second of which (usually a longer text, such as a Tweet or a news document) is read in the context of the first sequence (which is usually shorter, such as the topic/target/aspect of a Tweet, or a news headline). Detailed information about each dataset is shown in Table 1.

For each of our main tasks, we use the best-performing set of auxiliary tasks found by ARS (Table 2). To maintain comparability, we follow the same steps as ARS for preprocessing the data. In particular, MultiNLI was downsampled to the same 10K training examples (2.5%) as ARS, and so we refer to it as MultiNLI$^{2.5\%}$.[7]

3.2 Training Procedure

In all experiments, we seek to optimize performance on the main task, rather than optimize an aggregate metric across main and auxiliary tasks.

We set the discriminative task weights $\alpha_t = \alpha = 1$ for all discriminative tasks, and we fix the reconstruction task weights $\beta_t = \beta$ across all reconstruction tasks for a given set of main and auxiliary tasks. We found performance improves when $\beta \ll \alpha$, which is consistent with the treatment of reconstruction as a regularizing task.[8] In general,

α_t and β_t may be tuned separately for each task.

We use 100-dimensional GloVe 6B[9] word embeddings and initialize the embeddings of words that appear in the GloVe vocabulary with their pre-trained embeddings (Pennington et al., 2014). Other words' embeddings are initialized randomly. All embeddings are fine-tuned during training.

Because we want to see if good performance can be attained without sequence-level information, we reconstruct x_2 using a unigram decoder, which projects the conditioning information h into a distribution over the vocabulary.

The conditioning vector decomposes as $h := [t, y', \pi_1]$, which consists of: (1) a one-hot encoding t of the task index t; this allows the language model to adapt to different tasks (Daumé III, 2007); (2) a task-specific projection $y' = \mathbf{L}_t y$ of the one-hot label vector y, where $\mathbf{L}_t \in \mathbb{R}^{l \times |\mathcal{Y}_t|}$ are trainable task-specific parameters; this projection transforms labels from potentially disparate label spaces $\mathcal{Y}_t$ of different sizes to the same space; and (3) the input encoding π_1, which conveys information about x_1, on which we condition the reading of x_2.[10]

Together, the elements of the conditioning vector h provide for controllable text generation, in which the task, label, and context x_1 together influence the distribution over words of x_2 parametrized by p_θ (Hu et al., 2017).[11]

4 Discussion

Our experimental results are presented in Table 3. For the sake of comparison, we keep with the set of auxiliary tasks used by ARS, which are listed in Table 2. Other combinations of tasks may give better performance for the techniques we examine.

Using just bag-of-words features, our best models outperform the reimplementation of ARS's baseline bi-directional RNN model in 4 of 7 cases and achieve competitive results in the other 3 cases. Our results are also competitive with ARS's best-performing models, which may use the label embedding layer and label transfer network.

The DAN encoder in the single-task learning (STL) setting is competitive with ARS's STL results and with our STL and MTL reimplementa-

---

[5]We do not include results for FNC-1 as a main task because the FNC-1 development set of ARS consists of examples of only a single label type, making model selection (the intent of a dev-set) problematic.

[6]http://www.fakenewschallenge.org/

[7]p.c. with Isabelle Augenstein.

[8]In preliminary experiments, the hyperparameter β was swept from 10^{-5} to 10^5 in powers of 10. Because of poor performance for large β, for subsequent experiments we reduced the range to 10^{-5} to 10^1 in powers of 10.

[9]http://nlp.stanford.edu/data/glove.6B.zip

[10]Single-sequence tasks would not condition on π_1.

[11]Here, the decoder p_θ is coupled with the encoder q_{ϕ_t} both in the representation π_1 and in the word embeddings. In principle, p_θ may be decoupled from q_{ϕ_t} entirely except for the word embeddings.

Dataset	# Labels	# Train	Seq 1	Seq 2	Task
MultiNLI$^{2.5\%}$	3	10,001	Hypothesis	Premise	Natural language inference
ABSA-L	3	2,618	Aspect	Review	Aspect-based sentiment analysis, laptop domain
ABSA-R	3	2,256	Aspect	Review	Aspect-based sentiment analysis, restaurant domain
Target	3	5,623	Target	Text	Target-dependent sentiment analysis
Stance	3	3,209	Target	Tweet	Stance detection
Topic-2	2	5,177	Topic	Tweet	Topic-based sentiment analysis, binary
Topic-5	5	7,236	Topic	Tweet	Topic-based sentiment analysis, fine-grained
FNC-1	4	39,741	Headline	Document	Fake News Detection

Table 1: Size of label set, number of training examples, content of sequences, and task description of each dataset.

Main task	Auxiliary tasks
MultiNLI$^{2.5\%}$	Topic-5
ABSA-L	Topic-5
ABSA-R	Topic-5, ABSA-L, Target
Target	FNC-1, MultiNLI$^{2.5\%}$, Topic-5
Stance	FNC-1, MultiNLI$^{2.5\%}$, Target
Topic-2	FNC-1, MultiNLI$^{2.5\%}$, Target
Topic-5	FNC-1, MultiNLI$^{2.5\%}$, ABSA-L, Target

Table 2: Main tasks and their corresponding auxiliary tasks as used here and by Augenstein et al. (2018).

tions, confirming the findings of previous work discussed in §2.1.

The inclusion of unigram generative regularization (UGR) improves STL DAN performance in 5 of 7 cases (GSTL), motivating its use in the MTL setting. If GSTL performance achieves desired performance, then one saves a search over auxiliary tasks, such as those in (Liu et al., 2016; Augenstein et al., 2018). However, UGR hurts MTL performance in 6 of 7 cases (GMTL). Furthermore, GMTL performance is worse than GSTL performance in all cases, while MTL outperforms GSTL in 5 of 7 cases. These trends suggest that UGR is not needed once the regularization from incorporating auxiliary discriminative tasks takes effect. In other words, the parameter updates resulting from UGR are not as informative as the parameter updates resulting from having additional training examples from similar datasets. However, UGR may still be helpful when auxiliary training sets are not available.

Comparing STL to MTL results, we see that the DAN encoder often facilitates transfer across tasks. The best-performing MTL DAN model outperforms or equals the best-performing STL DAN model in 6 of 7 cases (all but Stance). The use of GloVe embeddings in MTL and GMTL improves performance over the use of randomly initialized embeddings because the task-independent information captured by the pre-trained word embeddings serves as good initialization.

Comparisons in training time, model size, and performance between the reimplemented ARS baseline model and the DAN model are given in Table 4 for MultiNLI$^{2.5\%}$ and Topic-5, the largest dataset and the dataset with the most auxiliary tasks, respectively. The DAN model is 33.4% smaller and 7.7x faster than the ARS model for MultiNLI$^{2.5\%}$ but achieves lower accuracy. DAN (run on a CPU) is 1.2x faster and 14.4% smaller than the ARS model (run on a GPU) for Topic-5 and achieves better performance.[12] As expected based on prior work, the training speed of the DAN encoder is substantially faster than that of the bi-RNN encoder, especially for MultiNLI$^{2.5\%}$.

Although the competitive results of the bag-of-words models are somewhat expected given prior work, we find the magnitude of the gains over the MTL bi-RNN reimplementation surprising, especially on Stance and Topic-2. Overall, our results extend the findings of prior work on simple sentence encoders for sentiment analysis and textual inference to the MTL setting.

5 Related Work

Prior work has shown that bag-of-words pooling encoders compete with sequence encoders on sentiment analysis, textual entailment, and textual similarity for single-task learning (Iyyer et al., 2015; Wieting et al., 2016; Arora et al., 2017). In this work, we explore these tasks in the MTL setting and ask if transfer among the tasks can be captured by bag-of-words features.

Recent work in MTL has explored different parameter sharing schemes in shared neural architectures. Some models incorporate inductive bias by imposing hierarchies over tasks (Søgaard and

---

[12]We would expect the time contrast for Topic-5 to be more pronounced if the DAN and ARS models were run on the same hardware.

	MultiNLI$_\uparrow^{2.5\%}$	ABSA-L$_\uparrow$	ABSA-R$_\uparrow$	Target$_\uparrow$	Stance$_\uparrow$	Topic-2$_\uparrow$	Topic-5$_\downarrow$
Metric	Acc	Acc	Acc	F_1^M	F_1^{FA}	ρ^{PN}	MAE^M
ARS STL (baseline)	49.25	76.74	67.47	64.01	41.1	63.92	0.919
ARS MTL (baseline)	49.39	74.94	82.25	65.73	44.12	80.74	0.859
ARS MTL (best)	49.94*	75.66*†	83.71*†	66.42*	46.26*	80.74	0.803*†
ARS STL (r)	47.71	73.16	72.99	62.44	25.05	63.91	0.903
ARS MTL (r)	49.20	75.03	79.39	63.61	29.30	61.26	0.914
STL DAN (w)	38.82	**74.03**	80.79	63.35	34.31	64.15	0.907
GSTL DAN (w)	41.70	73.53	78.58	63.45	**35.17**	65.09	0.906
MTL DAN (w)	**47.69**	**74.03**	79.86	61.44	31.77	65.42	0.900
MTL DAN + GloVe (w)	43.04	68.91	**81.84**	**63.53**	30.96	**67.85**	**0.856**
GMTL DAN (w)	39.35	69.29	78.23	61.95	25.70	59.88	0.927
GMTL DAN + GloVe (w)	40.41	69.29	80.21	63.01	26.36	61.17	0.958

Table 3: Test results. Acc: accuracy; F_1^M: macro-averaged F_1; F_1^{FA}: macro-averaged F_1 of "favour" and "against" classes; ρ^{PN}: macro-averaged recall, averaged across topics; MAE^M: macro-averaged mean absolute error, averaged across topics. $\uparrow$/$\downarrow$ next to each task name indicates that higher/lower score is better. "STL": single-task setting; "MTL": multi-task setting; "(r)": reimplementation of baseline bi-directional RNN model from ARS (no Label Embedding Layer or Label Transfer Network). *: model uses LEL; †: model uses LTN. Models using only BOW representations are marked with (w). Best results from BOW experiments (bottom section) are **bolded**.

Dataset	Model	Epoch	# Params.	Metric
MNLI$^{2.5\%}$	ARS (r)	268 s	362,608	**49.20**
	DAN	**35 s**	**241,408**	47.69
Topic-5	ARS (r)	93 s (G)	423,918	0.914
	DAN	**75 s**	**362,718**	**0.900**

Table 4: Comparisons of mean training epoch time, number of trainable architecture parameters (i.e., trainable non-word-embedding parameters), and performance of the reimplemented (r) ARS model and the DAN model in the MTL setting for the MultiNLI$^{2.5\%}$ and Topic-5 datasets. (G) denotes the model was run on a GPU, otherwise the model was run on a CPU.

Goldberg, 2016; Hashimoto et al., 2017; Sanh et al., 2019). Ruder et al. (2017) and Liu and Huang (2018) incorporate orthogonality constraints to learn which parameters tasks should share. Previous work in MTL has also lead to non-trivial training procedures. For example, Liu et al. (2017) and Chen and Cardie (2018) use adversarial training, and Ruder and Plank (2018) explore tri-training. The focus of this paper is a collection of BOW tools that form strong baselines upon which architectural or training improvements can be shown.

Ando and Zhang (2005) motivate the inclusion of auxiliary tasks for MTL. They automatically annotate unlabeled data to create a new labeled dataset that is related to the main task. In this work, our auxiliary tasks are pre-existing labeled datasets for which we include discriminative and reconstruction objectives. Criteria and heuristics for the selection of auxiliary tasks are discussed by Alonso

and Plank (2017) and Bingel and Søgaard (2017).

For a given task, it is well-established that the addition of auxiliary word prediction objective terms may help regularize the representations used for prediction (Dai and Le, 2015; Kiros et al., 2015; Rei, 2017). Rei (2017) proposes a semi-supervised MTL framework for sequence tagging that incorporates a secondary language modeling objective. Like that approach, our unigram generative regularization (§2.3) requires no additional data. Our approach differs from Rei (2017) in three ways: we employ a *conditional* language model instead of an unconditional language model, allowing our model to learn in a supervised way from signal derived from the labels; we do not use semi-supervised learning; and we train in a multi-task setting involving both multiple datasets and a compound objective, whereas Rei (2017) optimizes a compound objective on a single dataset for each task (similar to GSTL in Table 3 of this work). To the best of our knowledge, our use of (unigram) generative regularization in the multi-task setting is novel.

6 Conclusion

We showed that bag-of-words techniques such as pooling encoders and non-contextual pre-trained word embeddings can capture transfer among sentiment analysis and textual entailment tasks in multi-task learning. We additionally showed that unigram generative regularization often improved single-task learning performance but not multi-task learning performance, suggesting that generative regularization is not needed once the regularization from incorporating auxiliary discriminative tasks takes effect. The bag-of-words techniques are competitive with a state-of-the-art model, thereby extending the findings of prior work on bag-of-words approaches to sentiment analysis and textual entailment to the multi-task setting.

Acknowledgments

We thank Nicholas Andrews for many helpful discussions throughout the development of this work. We also thank the anonymous reviewers for their feedback. This work was supported in part by IARPA MATERIAL and DARPA AIDA. The views and conclusions contained in this publication are those of the authors and should not be interpreted as representing official policies or endorsements of IARPA, DARPA, or the U.S. Government.

References

Héctor Martínez Alonso and Barbara Plank. 2017. When is multitask learning effective? semantic sequence prediction under varying data conditions. In *15th Conference of the European Chapter of the Association for Computational Linguistics*.

Rie Kubota Ando and Tong Zhang. 2005. A framework for learning predictive structures from multiple tasks and unlabeled data. *J. Mach. Learn. Res.*, 6:1817–1853.

Sanjeev Arora, Yingyu Liang, and Tengyu Ma. 2017. A simple but tough-to-beat baseline for sentence embeddings. *International Conference on Learning Representations*.

Isabelle Augenstein, Sebastian Ruder, and Anders Søgaard. 2018. Multi-task learning of pairwise sequence classification tasks over disparate label spaces. In *Proceedings of the 2018 Conference of the North American Chapter of the Association for Computational Linguistics: Human Language Technologies, Volume 1 (Long Papers)*, volume 1, pages 1896–1906.

Joachim Bingel and Anders Søgaard. 2017. Identifying beneficial task relations for multi-task learning in deep neural networks. In *Proceedings of the 15th Conference of the European Chapter of the Association for Computational Linguistics: Volume 2, Short Papers*, volume 2, pages 164–169.

Xilun Chen and Claire Cardie. 2018. Multinomial adversarial networks for multi-domain text classification. In *Proceedings of the 2018 Conference of the North American Chapter of the Association for Computational Linguistics: Human Language Technologies, Volume 1 (Long Papers)*, volume 1, pages 1226–1240.

Andrew M Dai and Quoc V Le. 2015. Semi-supervised sequence learning. In *Advances in Neural Information Processing Systems*, pages 3079–3087.

Hal Daumé III. 2007. Frustratingly easy domain adaptation. *ACL 2007*, page 256.

Jacob Devlin, Ming-Wei Chang, Kenton Lee, and Kristina Toutanova. 2019. Bert: Pre-training of deep bidirectional transformers for language understanding. In *Proceedings of the 2019 Conference of the North American Chapter of the Association for Computational Linguistics: Human Language Technologies, Volume 1 (Long and Short Papers)*, pages 4171–4186.

Li Dong, Furu Wei, Chuanqi Tan, Duyu Tang, Ming Zhou, and Ke Xu. 2014. Adaptive recursive neural network for target-dependent twitter sentiment classification. In *Proceedings of the 52nd Annual Meeting of the Association for Computational Linguistics (Volume 2: Short Papers)*, volume 2, pages 49–54.

Kazuma Hashimoto, Yoshimasa Tsuruoka, Richard Socher, et al. 2017. A joint many-task model: Growing a neural network for multiple nlp tasks. In *Proceedings of the 2017 Conference on Empirical Methods in Natural Language Processing*, pages 1923–1933.

Zhiting Hu, Zichao Yang, Xiaodan Liang, Ruslan Salakhutdinov, and Eric P Xing. 2017. Toward controlled generation of text. In *International Conference on Machine Learning*, pages 1587–1596.

Mohit Iyyer, Varun Manjunatha, Jordan Boyd-Graber, and Hal Daumé III. 2015. Deep unordered composition rivals syntactic methods for text classification. In *Proceedings of the 53rd Annual Meeting of the Association for Computational Linguistics and the 7th International Joint Conference on Natural Language Processing (Volume 1: Long Papers)*, volume 1, pages 1681–1691.

Ryan Kiros, Yukun Zhu, Ruslan R Salakhutdinov, Richard Zemel, Raquel Urtasun, Antonio Torralba, and Sanja Fidler. 2015. Skip-thought vectors. In *Advances in neural information processing systems*, pages 3294–3302.

Pengfei Liu and Xuanjing Huang. 2018. Meta-learning multi-task communication. *arXiv preprint arXiv:1810.09988*.

Pengfei Liu, Xipeng Qiu, and Xuanjing Huang. 2016. Recurrent neural network for text classification with multi-task learning. In *Proceedings of the Twenty-Fifth International Joint Conference on Artificial Intelligence*, IJCAI'16, pages 2873–2879.

Pengfei Liu, Xipeng Qiu, and Xuanjing Huang. 2017. Adversarial multi-task learning for text classification. In *Proceedings of the 55th Annual Meeting of the Association for Computational Linguistics (Volume 1: Long Papers)*, pages 1–10. Association for Computational Linguistics.

Tomas Mikolov, Ilya Sutskever, Kai Chen, Greg S Corrado, and Jeff Dean. 2013. Distributed representations of words and phrases and their compositionality. In *Advances in neural information processing systems*, pages 3111–3119.

Saif Mohammad, Svetlana Kiritchenko, Parinaz Sobhani, Xiaodan Zhu, and Colin Cherry. 2016. Semeval-2016 task 6: Detecting stance in tweets. In *Proceedings of the 10th International Workshop on Semantic Evaluation (SemEval-2016)*, pages 31–41.

Preslav Nakov, Alan Ritter, Sara Rosenthal, Fabrizio Sebastiani, and Veselin Stoyanov. 2016. Semeval-2016 task 4: Sentiment analysis in twitter. In *Proceedings of the 10th International Workshop on Semantic Evaluation (SemEval-2016)*, pages 1–18.

Jeffrey Pennington, Richard Socher, and Christopher Manning. 2014. Glove: Global vectors for word representation. In *Proceedings of the 2014 conference on empirical methods in natural language processing (EMNLP)*, pages 1532–1543.

Matthew E. Peters, Mark Neumann, Mohit Iyyer, Matt Gardner, Christopher Clark, Kenton Lee, and Luke Zettlemoyer. 2018. Deep contextualized word representations. In *Proc. of NAACL*.

Maria Pontiki, Dimitris Galanis, Haris Papageorgiou, Ion Androutsopoulos, Suresh Manandhar, AL-Smadi Mohammad, Mahmoud Al-Ayyoub, Yanyan Zhao, Bing Qin, Orphée De Clercq, et al. 2016. Semeval-2016 task 5: Aspect based sentiment analysis. In *Proceedings of the 10th international workshop on semantic evaluation (SemEval-2016)*, pages 19–30.

Marek Rei. 2017. Semi-supervised multitask learning for sequence labeling. In *Proceedings of the 55th Annual Meeting of the Association for Computational Linguistics (Volume 1: Long Papers)*, volume 1, pages 2121–2130.

Sebastian Ruder, Joachim Bingel, Isabelle Augenstein, and Anders Søgaard. 2017. Latent multi-task architecture learning. *stat*, 1050:23.

Sebastian Ruder and Barbara Plank. 2018. Strong baselines for neural semi-supervised learning under domain shift. In *Proceedings of the 56th Annual Meeting of the Association for Computational Linguistics (Volume 1: Long Papers)*, pages 1044–1054.

Victor Sanh, Thomas Wolf, and Sebastian Ruder. 2019. A hierarchical multi-task approach for learning embeddings from semantic tasks. In *Proceedings of the AAAI Conference on Artificial Intelligence*, volume 33, pages 6949–6956.

Anders Søgaard and Yoav Goldberg. 2016. Deep multitask learning with low level tasks supervised at lower layers. In *Proceedings of the 54th Annual Meeting of the Association for Computational Linguistics (Volume 2: Short Papers)*, volume 2, pages 231–235.

John Wieting, Mohit Bansal, Kevin Gimpel, and Karen Livescu. 2016. Towards universal paraphrastic sentence embeddings. In *Proceedings of International Conference on Learning Representations*.

Adina Williams, Nikita Nangia, and Samuel Bowman. 2018. A broad-coverage challenge corpus for sentence understanding through inference. In *Proceedings of the 2018 Conference of the North American Chapter of the Association for Computational Linguistics: Human Language Technologies, Volume 1 (Long Papers)*, pages 1112–1122.

BERT is Not an Interlingua and the Bias of Tokenization

Jasdeep Singh[1], Bryan McCann[2], Caiming Xiong[2], Richard Socher[2]
Stanford University[1], Salesforce Research[2]
jasdeep@cs.stanford.edu {bmccann,cxiong,rsocher}@salesforce.com

Abstract

Multilingual transfer learning can benefit both high- and low-resource languages, but the source of these improvements is not well understood. Cananical Correlation Analysis (CCA) of the internal representations of a pretrained, multilingual BERT model reveals that the model partitions representations for each language rather than using a common, shared, interlingual space. This effect is magnified at deeper layers, suggesting that the model does not progressively abstract semantic content while disregarding languages. Hierarchical clustering based on the CCA similarity scores between languages reveals a tree structure that mirrors the phylogenetic trees hand-designed by linguists. The subword tokenization employed by BERT provides a stronger bias towards such structure than character- and word-level tokenizations. We release a subset of the XNLI dataset translated into an additional 14 languages at https://www.github.com/salesforce/xnli_extension to assist further research into multilingual representations.

1 Introduction

Natural language processing (NLP) in multilingual settings often relies on transfer learning between high- and low-resource languages. Word embeddings trained with the Word2Vec (Mikolov et al., 2013b) or GloVe (Pennington et al., 2014) algorithms are trained with large amounts of unsupervised data and transferred to downstream tasks-specific architectures in order to improve performance. Multilingual word embeddings have been trained with varying levels of supervision. Parallel corpora can be leveraged when data is available (Gouws et al., 2015; Luong et al., 2015), monolingual embeddings can be learned separately (Klementiev et al., 2012; Zou et al., 2013; Hermann and Blunsom, 2014) and then aligned

using dictionaries between languages (Mikolov et al., 2013a; Faruqui and Dyer, 2014), and cross-lingual embeddings can be learned jointly through entirely unsupervised methods (Conneau et al., 2017; Artetxe et al., 2018).

Contextualized word embeddings like CoVe, ElMo, and BERT (McCann et al., 2017; Peters et al., 2018; Devlin et al., 2018) improve a wide variety of natural language tasks (Wang et al., 2018; Rajpurkar et al., 2016; Socher et al., 2013; Conneau et al., 2018). A *multilingual* version of BERT trained on over 100 languages achieved state-of-the-art performance across a wide range of languages as well. Performance for low-resource languages has been further improved by additionally leveraging parallel data (Lample and Conneau, 2019) and leveraging machine translation systems for cross-lingual regularization (Singh et al., 2019).

Prior work in zero-shot machine translation has investigated the extent to which multilingual neural machine translation systems trained with a shared subword vocabulary Johnson et al. (2017); Kudugunta et al. (2019) learn a form of interlingua, a common representational space for semantically similar text across languages. We aim to extend this study to language models pretrained with multilingual data in order to investigate the extent to which the resulting contextualized word embeddings represent an interlingua.

Canonical correlation analysis (CCA) is a classical tool from multivariate statistics (Hotelling, 1992) that investigates the relationships between two sets of random variables. Singular value and projection weighted variants of CCA allow for analysis of representations of the same data points from different models in a way that is invariant to affine transformations (Raghu et al., 2017; Morcos et al., 2018), which makes them particularly suitable for analyzing neural networks. They have

Proceedings of the 2nd Workshop on Deep Learning Approaches for Low-Resource NLP (DeepLo), pages 47–55
Hong Kong, China, November 3, 2019. ©2019 Association for Computational Linguistics
https://doi.org/10.18653/v1/P17

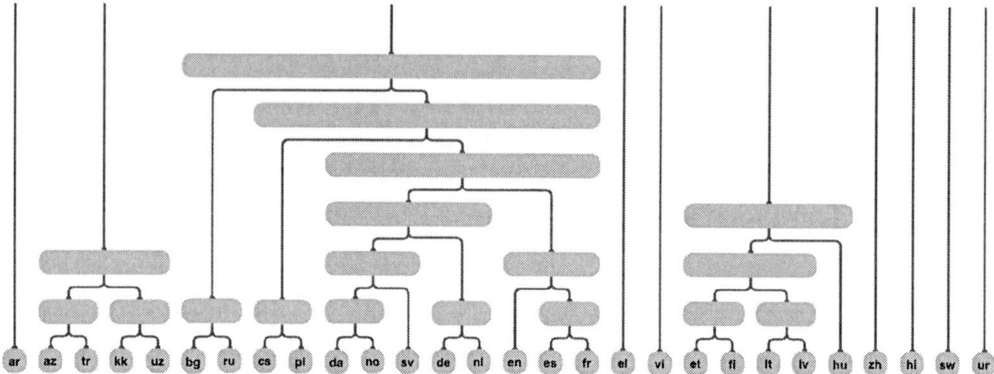

Figure 1: Agglomerative clustering of Languages based on the PWCCA similarity between their represenations, generated from layer 6 of a pretrained multilingual uncased BERT.

been used to explore learning dynamics and representational similarity in computer vision (Morcos et al., 2018) and natural language processing (Saphra and Lopez, 2018; Kudugunta et al., 2019).

We analyze multilingual BERT using projection weighted canonical correlation analysis (PWCCA) between representations from semantically similar text sequences in mulitple languages. We find that the representations from multilingual BERT can be partitioned using PWCCA similarity scores to reflect the linguistic and evolutionary relationships between languages. This suggests that BERT does not represent semantically similar data points nearer to each other in a common space as would be expected of an interlingua. Rather, representations in this space are primarily organized around features that respect the natural differences and similarities between languages. Our analysis shows that the choice of tokenization can heavily influence this space. Subword tokenization, in contrast to word and character level tokenization, provides a strong bias towards discovering these linguistic and evolutionary relationships between languages. As part of our experiments, we translated a subset of the XNLI data set into an additional 14 languages, which we publicly release to assist further research into multilingual representations.

2 Background and Related Work

2.1 Natural Language Inference and XNLI

The Multi-Genre Natural Language Inference (MultiNLI) corpus (Williams et al., 2017) uses data from ten distinct genres of English language for the the task of natural language inference (prediction of whether the relationship between two sentences represents entailment, contradiction, or neither). XNLI (Conneau et al., 2018) is an evaluation set grounded in MultiNLI for cross-lingual understanding (XLU) in 15 different languages that include low-resource languages such as Swahili and Urdu. XNLI serves as the primary testbed for bench marking multilingual understanding. We extend a subset of XNLI to an additional 14 languages for our analysis.

2.2 CCA

Deep network analyses techniques focusing on the weights of a network are unable to distinguish between several invariances such as permutation and scaling. CCA (Hotelling, 1992) and variants that use Singular Value Decomposition (SVD) (Raghu et al., 2017) or projection weighting (Morcos et al., 2018) are apt for analyzing the activations of neural networks because they provide a similarity metric that is invariant to permutations and scaling of neurons. These methods also allow for comparisons between representations for the same data points from different neural networks where there is no naive alignment from neurons of one network to another.

Given a dataset $X = \{x_1, \ldots x_n\}$, let $L_1 \in \mathbb{R}^{m_1 \times n}$ and $L_2 \in \mathbb{R}^{m_2 \times n}$ be two sets of neurons. Often these sets correspond to layers in neural networks. CCA transforms L_1 and L_2 to $a_1^\top L_1$ and $b_1^\top L_2$ respectively where the pair of canonical variables $\{a_1, b_1\}$ is found by maximizing the correlation between the transformed subspaces:

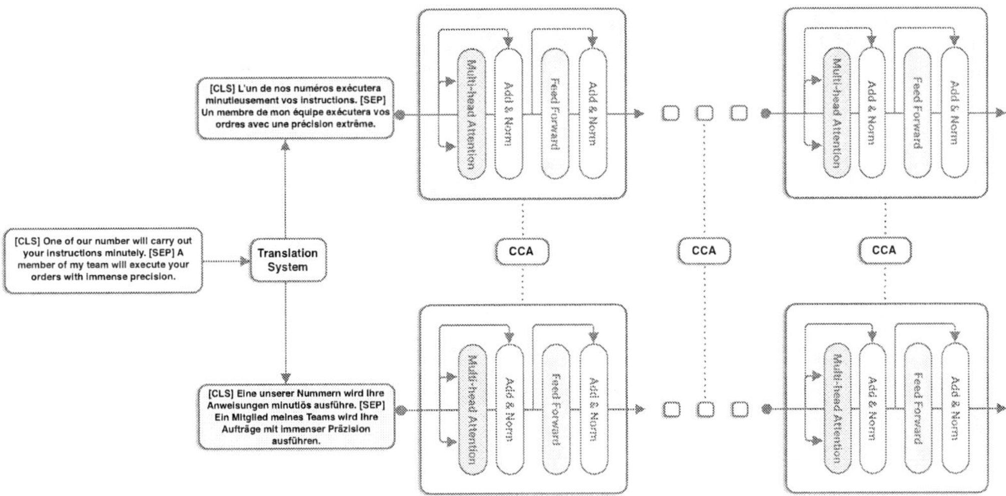

Figure 2: How CCA is used to compare the representations of different languages at different layers in BERT.

$$\rho_1 = \max_{a \in \mathbb{R}^{m_1}, b \in \mathbb{R}^{m_2}} \frac{\langle a^\top L_1, b^\top L_2 \rangle}{\|a^\top L_1\| \cdot \|b^\top L_1\|}$$

Given the set $\{a_1, b_1\}$, we can find another pair $\{a_2, b_2\}$:

$$\rho_2 = \max_{a_2 \in \mathbb{R}^{m_1}, b_2 \in \mathbb{R}^{m_2}} \frac{\langle a_2^\top L_1, b_2^\top L_2 \rangle}{\|a_2^\top L_1\| \cdot \|b_2^\top L_1\|}$$

under the constraints that $\langle a_2, a_1 \rangle = 0$ and $\langle b_2, b_1 \rangle = 0$. This continues until $\{a_{m'}, b_{m'}\}$ and $\rho_{m'}$ have been found such that $m' = \min(m_1, m_2)$.

The average of $\{\rho_1, \dots \rho_{m'}\}$ is often used as an overall similarity measure, as in related work exploring multilingual representations in neural machine translation systems (Kudugunta et al., 2019) and language models (Saphra and Lopez, 2018). Morcos et al. (2018) show that in studying recurrent and convolutional networks, replacing a weighted average leads to a more robust measure of similarity between two sets of activations. For the rest of the paper we use this PWCCA measure to determine the similarity of two sets of activations. The measure lies between [1,0] with 1 being identical and 0 being no similarity between the representations.

CCA is typically employed to compare representations for the same inputs for different models or layers (Raghu et al., 2017; Morcos et al., 2018). We also use CCA to compare representations from the same neural network when fed two translated versions of the same input (Figure 2).

3 Experiments and Discussion

We use the uncased multilingual BERT model (Devlin et al., 2018) and the XNLI data set for most experiments. Multilingual BERT is pretrained on the Wikipedia articles form 102 languages and is 12-layers deep. The XNLI dataset consists of the MultiNLI dataset translated into 15 languages. The uncased multilingual BERT model does not contain tokenization or pretaining for Thai so we focus our analysis on the remaining 14 languages. To provide a more robust study of a broader variety of languages, we supplement the XNLI data set by further translating the first 15 thousand examples using google translate. This allows for analysis of representations for 14 additional languages including Azerbaijani, Czech, Danish, Estonian, Finish, Hungarian, Kazakh, Latvian, Lithuanian, Dutch, Norwegian, Swedish, Ukrainian, and Uzbek.

Following the standard approach to using BERT (Devlin et al., 2018), a [CLS] token is prepended to each example, which consists of a premise, a [SEP] token and a hypothesis. The [CLS] token has been pretrained to extract intersentence relationships between the sentences that follow it. When fine-tuned on XNLI, the final representations for the [CLS] token is used to predict the relationship between sentences as either entailment, contradiction or neutral. This [CLS] token can be thought of as a summary embedding for the input as a whole. We analyze the activations of this [CLS] token for the same XNLI examples across all available languages (Figure 2). These representations have 768 neurons computed over 15 thousand datapoints.

For all fine-tuning experiments we use the hyperparameters and optimization strategies recommended by (Devlin et al., 2018) unless otherwise specified. We use a learning rate warm-up for 10% of training iterations and then linearly decay to zero. The batch size is 32 and the target learning rate after warm-up is $2e - 5$.

3.1 Representations across languages are less similar in the deeper layers of BERT

Figure 3 demonstrates that for all language combinations tested, the summary representation (associated with the [CLS] token) for semantically similar inputs translated into multiple languages is most similar at the shallower layers of BERT, close to the initial embeddings. The representations steadily become more dissimilar in deeper layers until the final layer. The jump in similarity in the final layer can be explained by the common classification layer that contains only three classes. In order to finally choose an output class, the network must project towards one of the three embeddings associated with those classes (Liu et al., 2019).

The trend towards dissimilarity in deeper layers suggests that contextualization in BERT is not a process of semantic abstraction as would be expected of an interlingua. Though semantic features common to the multiple translations of the input might also be extracted, the similarity between representations is dominated by features that differentiate them. BERT appears to preserve and refine features that separate the inputs, which we speculate are more closely related to syntactic and grammatical features of the input.

Representations at the shallower layers, closer to the subword embeddings, exhibit the highest degree of similarity. This provides further evidence for how a subword vocabulary can effectively span a large space of languages.

3.2 Representations diverge with depth after fine-tuning

In the previous set of experiments, BERT had only been pretrained on the unupservised masked language modeling objective. In that setting the

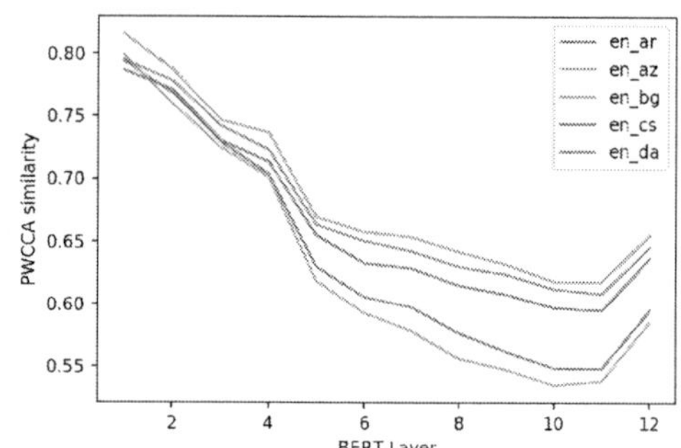

Figure 3: The similarity between representations of different languages decreases deeper into a pretrained uncased multilingual BERT model. Here we show the similarity between English and 5 other languages as a function of model depth

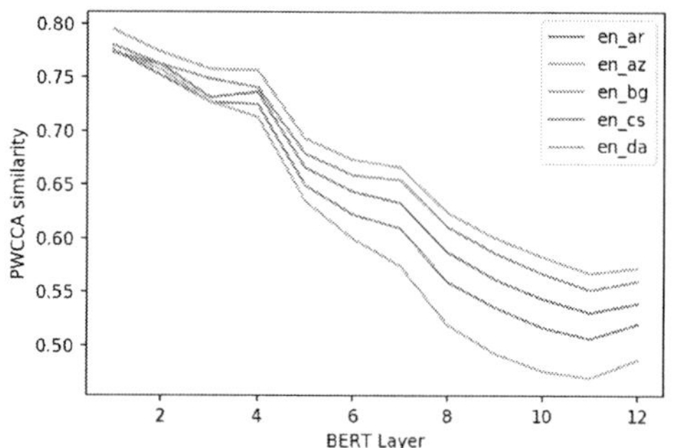

Figure 4: The similarity between representations of different languages decreases deeper into an uncased multilingual BERT model finetuned on XNLI.

[CLS] token was trained to predict whether the second sentence followed the first. This does not align well with the XNLI task in cases in which the hypothesis would not likely follow the premise in the corpora used for pretraining. To alleviate concerns that this might influence the representational similarity, we repeat the above experiments after fine-tuning BERT on several languages. Figure 4 confirms that representations for semantically similar inputs in different languages diverge in PWCCA similarity in deeper layers of BERT.

3.3 Deeper layers change more dramatically during fine-tuning

We also notice that during fine-tuning, the deepest layers of BERT change the most according to PWCCA similarity . In these experiments, we use PWCCA in the more standard setting, in which identical inputs are provided to two different models in order to get two set of neuron activations.

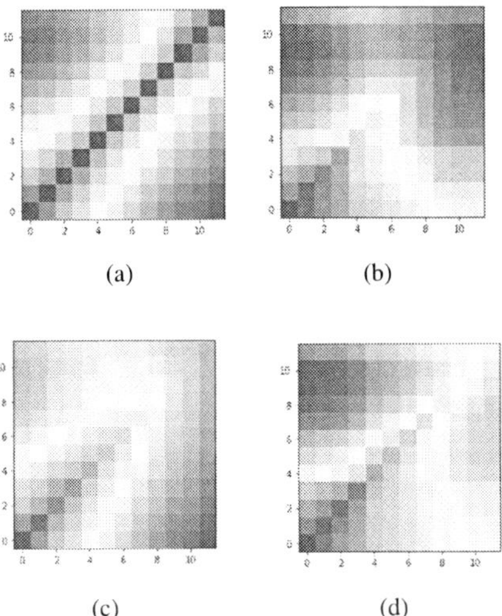

(a)　　　　　　(b)

(c)　　　　　　(d)

Figure 5: CCA experiments showing the finetuning behavior of BERT

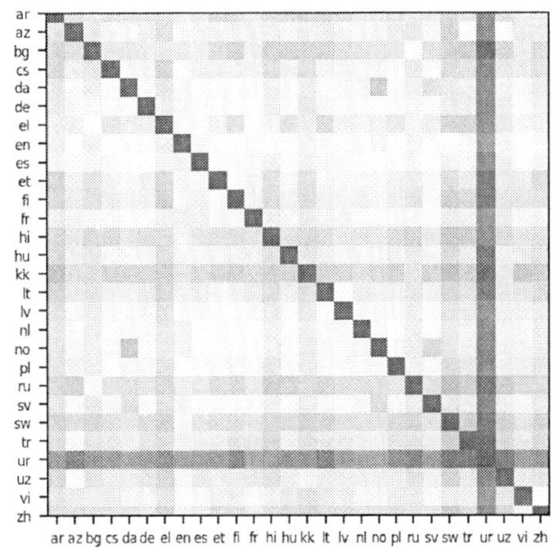

Figure 6: PWCCA generated similarity matrix between languages.

The two different models are different checkpoints of pretrained, multilingual BERT over the course of fine-tuning. Figures 5a - 5d follow a similar structure in which the PWCCA value is computed between all the layers of two models. The matrices are symmetric in expectation, but noise during optimization creates slight asymmetry. Figure 5a shows a baseline case demonstrating that a pretrained, multilingual BERT compared with itself has a PWCCA value of 1 with strong diagonal showing the identity between each layer. The off-diagonal entries show that layer-wise similarity depends on relative depth. This successive and gradual changing of representations is precisely the behavior we expect from networks with residual connections (Raghu et al., 2017).

We compare the pretrained multilingual BERT to a converged BERT fine-tuned on XNLI in Figure 5b and 5c. We use representations for the [CL] token in Figure 5b and the first token in the premise for Figure 5c. Both confirm that the function of early layers remains more similar as the network is fine-tuned. We find this trend to hold for a wide range of tasks including SST and QNLI as well.

Figure 5d shows that deep pretrained networks also converge bottom up during fine-tuning by comparing the representations a quarter of the way through fine-tuning with those of a converged model. Most of the remaining change in the representations between a quarter of the way through training and convergence happens in the later layers. Therefore the changes to middle layers we observe in Figure 5b happen during the first quarter of training.

3.4 Phylogentic Tree of Language Evolution

Figures 3 and 4 show that the representations learned for different languages diverge as we go deeper into the network, as opposed to converging if the network were learning an interlingua or a shared representation space. However, the relative similarities between languages clearly varies for different pairs and changes as a function of depth. To further investigate the internal relationships between representations learned by BERT we create a similarity matrix using PWCCA between all 28 languages for all 12 layers in BERT. For the PWCCA calculations we use the representations of the [CLS] token to generate L_1 and L_2. The resulting similarity matrix for Layer 1 is shown in Figure 6.

To visualize these relationships this matrix can be converted to a phylogentic tree using a cluster algorithm. In Figure 1 we use unweighted pair group method with arithmetic mean (UPGMA), a simple agglomerative (bottom-up) hierarchical clustering method (Sokal, 1958) to generate a phylogentic tree from the representations from Layer 6 of BERT. The generated phylogentic tree closely resembles the language tree constructed by linguists to explain the relationships and evolution of human languages. The details of the linguistic evolutionary phylogentic tree of languages is still debated and a tree model faces some limitations as not all evolutionary relationships are completely hierarchical and it can not easily account for horizontal transmissions. However many of the commonly known relationships between languages are embedded in BERT's representations. We see that BERT's space of its internal representations is finely partitioned into families and subfamiles of languages.

Northern Germanic languages are clustered together and the Western Germanic languages are clustered together before being combined together into the pro-germanic family. Romantic languages are clustered together before the Romantic and Germanic families are combined together. BERT's internal representation of English is in-between that of the Germanic and Romantic sub-families. This captures evolution and structure of English, which is considered a Germanic language but borrows heavily from romantic and latin languages. By varying the layer at which the representations are used to create the phylogentic tree, different structures emerge. Sometimes English is clustered with German before it is combined with the romantic languages, but mostly BERT seems to classify English as a romantic language.

For Layers 6 through 12 the trees generated are almost or exactly like Figure 1. At these layers, Azerbaijani, Turkish, Kazakh, and Uzbek are grouped into the same family although these languages span multiple scripts and have had their official scripts changed multiple times allowing for the possible introduction of confounding differences. Interestingly, at these same layers in Figure 3, languages seem to diverge the most from each other. This seems to suggest that instead of finding a shared latent space for all of the languages, as would be necessary for an interlingua, BERT is actually carefully partitioning its space in a fashion that linguistic and evolutionary relationships are preserved between languages. Trees generated from Layers 1 through 5 seem to make more mistakes than those of later layers. We see that these trees end up failing to group Azerbaijani, Turkish, Kazakh, and Uzbek into the same family, often leaving Kazakh out which is written in Cyrillic script. We can hypothesis that BERT's internal representations are more reliant on the identity of shared subwords earlier in the network as opposed to later in the network. As a matter of fact,

if we use agglomerative clustering to construct a tree from a matrix of subword overlap counts (Figure 7a), we find that it almost exactly matches the tree constructed from BERT's earlier layers.

It seems that BERT's shared multilingual subword vocabulary (Mikolov et al., 2012; Sennrich et al., 2015) provides it with a strong bias towards what linguistic relationships exist between human languages. Instead of then fusing the representations of different languages into one shared representation during training, BERT actually successively refines this partitioned space to better reflect the linguistic relationships between languages at higher layers (Figure 1).

3.5 Tokenization Provides a Strong Bias Towards Knowledge of Linguistic Relationships Between Languages

We tokenize the first 15 thousand examples from XNLI and our translated data using different tokenization methods and compute the token overlap between different languages, generating similarity matrices similar to the one shown in Figure 6. From these matrices we perform agglomerative clustering of languages to generate phylogenetic trees (Figure 7). These trees show how different tokenization schemes can embed different linguistic biases into our models. We investigate subword, word, and character level tokenization. The subword tokenization is done using BERT's learned BPE vocabulary. The word level tokenization is achieved by simply tokenizing at spaces, and the character level tokenization is done using Python's native character level string splitting. Figure 7a is generated from using subwords, and although is not as accurate as the tree generated from BERT's representation at layer 6 (Figure 1), it is still non-trivially close to a linguistically accurate depiction of human language evolution. We see that by using a shared subword vocabulary, multilingual BERT has a very strong bias to discover the linguistic relationships between languages. However, this bias is not as strong if other forms of tokenization are used. Figures 7b and 7c show the trees generated by word level and character level tokenization respectively. We see that word level tokenization splits the Romantic and Germanic languages into completely different trees, and that character level tokenization ends up combining all languages that share the Latin script regardless of their true families. Perhaps the

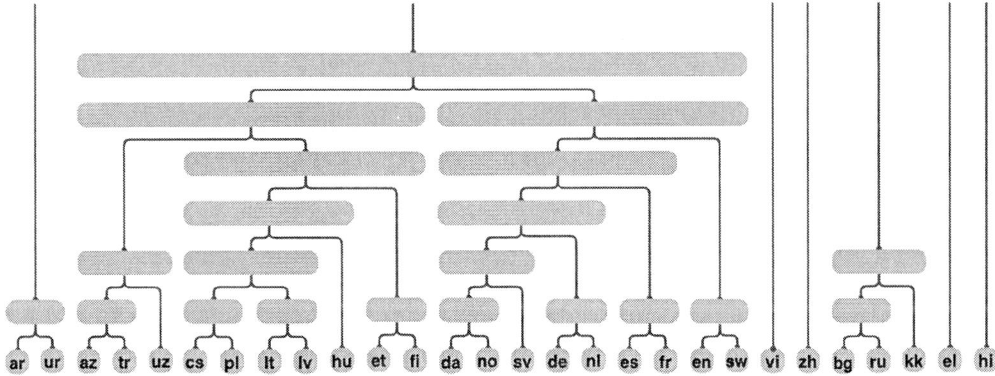

(a) Agglomerative clustering of languages based on subword overlap, generated from using the BERT tokenizer to tokenize the first 15 thousand examples from XNLI and our translated data.

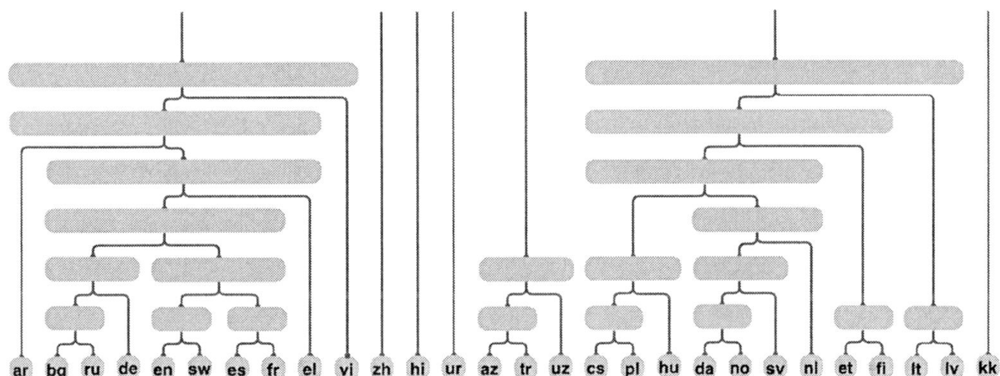

(b) Agglomerative clustering of languages based on word overlap, generated from splitting the first 15 thousand examples from XNLI and our translated data on spaces.

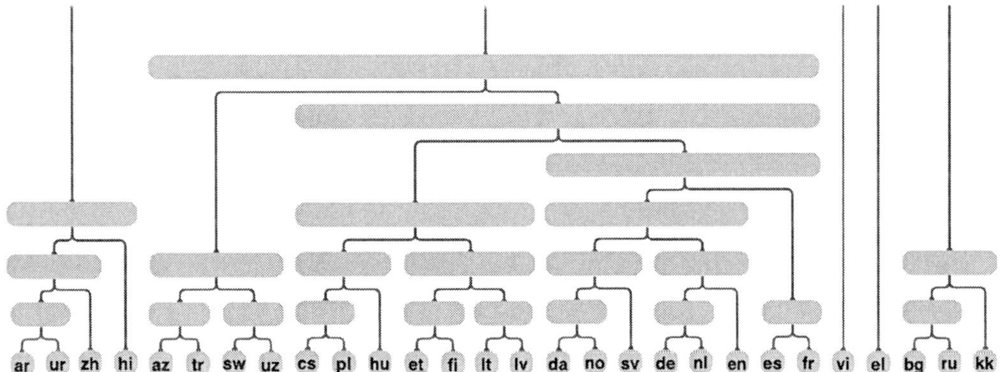

(c) Agglomerative clustering of languages based on character overlap, generated from splitting the first 15 thousand examples from XNLI and our translated.

Figure 7: Different agglomerative clusterings of languages based on subword, word, and character overlap. We see that different tokenization schemes used in NLP embed different linguistic biases into models.

ability of subwords to capture these linguistic relationships between languages has contributed to
their wide success in applications including machine translation and language modeling.

4   Conclusion and Future Directions

While natural language processing systems often
focus on a single language, multilingual transfer
learning has the potential to improve performance,
especially for low-resource languages. Many previous multilingual approaches claim to develop
shared representations of different languages. Recently, multilingual BERT and related models
trained in an unsupervised fashion on monolingual
corpora from over 100 languages achieve state of
the art performance on many tasks involving low
resource languages. Using Cononical Coreelation
Analysis (CCA) on the internal representations of
BERT, we find that it is not embedding different
languages into a shared space. Rather, at deeper
layers, BERT partitions the space to better reflect
the linguistic and evolutionary relationships between languages. We also find that subword tokenization, in contrast to word and character level
tokenization, provides a strong bias to discover
linguistic and evolutionary relationships between
languages.

References

Mikel Artetxe, Gorka Labaka, and Eneko Agirre. 2018.
A robust self-learning method for fully unsupervised
cross-lingual mappings of word embeddings. *arXiv
preprint arXiv:1805.06297.*

Alexis Conneau, Guillaume Lample, Marc'Aurelio
Ranzato, Ludovic Denoyer, and Hervé Jégou. 2017.
Word translation without parallel data. *arXiv
preprint arXiv:1710.04087.*

Alexis Conneau, Guillaume Lample, Ruty Rinott, Adina Williams, Samuel R Bowman, Holger Schwenk,
and Veselin Stoyanov. 2018. Xnli: Evaluating cross-
lingual sentence representations. *arXiv preprint
arXiv:1809.05053.*

Jacob Devlin, Ming-Wei Chang, Kenton Lee, and
Kristina Toutanova. 2018. Bert: Pre-training of deep
bidirectional transformers for language understanding. *arXiv preprint arXiv:1810.04805.*

Manaal Faruqui and Chris Dyer. 2014. Improving vector space word representations using multilingual
correlation. In *Proceedings of the 14th Conference
of the European Chapter of the Association for Computational Linguistics*, pages 462–471.

Stephan Gouws, Yoshua Bengio, and Greg Corrado.
2015. Bilbowa: Fast bilingual distributed representations without word alignments.

Karl Moritz Hermann and Phil Blunsom. 2014. Multilingual models for compositional distributed semantics. *arXiv preprint arXiv:1404.4641.*

Harold Hotelling. 1992. Relations between two sets of
variates. In *Breakthroughs in statistics*, pages 162–
190. Springer.

Melvin Johnson, Mike Schuster, Quoc V Le, Maxim
Krikun, Yonghui Wu, Zhifeng Chen, Nikhil Thorat,
Fernanda Viégas, Martin Wattenberg, Greg Corrado,
et al. 2017. Googles multilingual neural machine
translation system: Enabling zero-shot translation.
*Transactions of the Association for Computational
Linguistics*, 5:339–351.

Alexandre Klementiev, Ivan Titov, and Binod Bhattarai. 2012. Inducing crosslingual distributed representations of words. *Proceedings of COLING 2012*,
pages 1459–1474.

Sneha Reddy Kudugunta, Ankur Bapna, Isaac Caswell,
Naveen Arivazhagan, and Orhan Firat. 2019. Investigating multilingual nmt representations at scale.
arXiv preprint arXiv:1909.02197.

Guillaume Lample and Alexis Conneau. 2019. Cross-
lingual language model pretraining. *arXiv preprint
arXiv:1901.07291.*

Nelson F Liu, Matt Gardner, Yonatan Belinkov,
Matthew Peters, and Noah A Smith. 2019. Linguistic knowledge and transferability of contextual representations. *arXiv preprint arXiv:1903.08855.*

Thang Luong, Hieu Pham, and Christopher D Manning. 2015. Bilingual word representations with
monolingual quality in mind. In *Proceedings of the
1st Workshop on Vector Space Modeling for Natural
Language Processing*, pages 151–159.

Bryan McCann, James Bradbury, Caiming Xiong, and
Richard Socher. 2017. Learned in translation: Contextualized word vectors. In *Advances in Neural Information Processing Systems*, pages 6294–6305.

Tomas Mikolov, Quoc V Le, and Ilya Sutskever. 2013a.
Exploiting similarities among languages for machine translation. *arXiv preprint arXiv:1309.4168.*

Tomas Mikolov, Ilya Sutskever, Kai Chen, Greg S Corrado, and Jeff Dean. 2013b. Distributed representations of words and phrases and their compositionality. In *Advances in neural information processing
systems*, pages 3111–3119.

Tomáš Mikolov, Ilya Sutskever, Anoop Deoras, Hai-
Son Le, Stefan Kombrink, and Jan Cernocky.
2012. Subword language modeling with neural networks. *preprint (http://www. fit. vutbr.
cz/imikolov/rnnlm/char. pdf)*, 8.

Ari Morcos, Maithra Raghu, and Samy Bengio. 2018. Insights on representational similarity in neural networks with canonical correlation. In *Advances in Neural Information Processing Systems*, pages 5727–5736.

Jeffrey Pennington, Richard Socher, and Christopher Manning. 2014. Glove: Global vectors for word representation. In *Proceedings of the 2014 conference on empirical methods in natural language processing (EMNLP)*, pages 1532–1543.

Matthew E Peters, Mark Neumann, Mohit Iyyer, Matt Gardner, Christopher Clark, Kenton Lee, and Luke Zettlemoyer. 2018. Deep contextualized word representations. *arXiv preprint arXiv:1802.05365*.

Maithra Raghu, Justin Gilmer, Jason Yosinski, and Jascha Sohl-Dickstein. 2017. Svcca: Singular vector canonical correlation analysis for deep learning dynamics and interpretability. In *Advances in Neural Information Processing Systems*, pages 6076–6085.

Pranav Rajpurkar, Jian Zhang, Konstantin Lopyrev, and Percy Liang. 2016. Squad: 100,000+ questions for machine comprehension of text. *arXiv preprint arXiv:1606.05250*.

Naomi Saphra and Adam Lopez. 2018. Understanding learning dynamics of language models with svcca. *arXiv preprint arXiv:1811.00225*.

Rico Sennrich, Barry Haddow, and Alexandra Birch. 2015. Neural machine translation of rare words with subword units. *arXiv preprint arXiv:1508.07909*.

Jasdeep Singh, Bryan McCann, Nitish Shirish Keskar, Caiming Xiong, and Richard Socher. 2019. Xlda: Cross-lingual data augmentation for natural language inference and question answering. *arXiv preprint arXiv:1905.11471*.

Richard Socher, Alex Perelygin, Jean Wu, Jason Chuang, Christopher D Manning, Andrew Ng, and Christopher Potts. 2013. Recursive deep models for semantic compositionality over a sentiment treebank. In *Proceedings of the 2013 conference on empirical methods in natural language processing*, pages 1631–1642.

Robert R Sokal. 1958. A statistical method for evaluating systematic relationships. *Univ. Kansas, Sci. Bull.*, 38:1409–1438.

Alex Wang, Amapreet Singh, Julian Michael, Felix Hill, Omer Levy, and Samuel R Bowman. 2018. Glue: A multi-task benchmark and analysis platform for natural language understanding. *arXiv preprint arXiv:1804.07461*.

Adina Williams, Nikita Nangia, and Samuel R Bowman. 2017. A broad-coverage challenge corpus for sentence understanding through inference. *arXiv preprint arXiv:1704.05426*.

Will Y Zou, Richard Socher, Daniel Cer, and Christopher D Manning. 2013. Bilingual word embeddings for phrase-based machine translation. In *Proceedings of the 2013 Conference on Empirical Methods in Natural Language Processing*, pages 1393–1398.

Cross-lingual Joint Entity and Word Embedding to Improve Entity Linking and Parallel Sentence Mining

Xiaoman Pan[*], **Thamme Gowda**[‡], **Heng Ji**[*†], **Jonathan May**[‡], **Scott Miller**[‡]

[*] Department of Computer Science [†] Department of Electrical and Computer Engineering
University of Illinois at Urbana-Champaign
{xiaoman6,hengji}@illinois.edu
[‡] Information Sciences Institute, University of Southern California
{tg,jonmay,smiller}@isi.edu

Abstract

Entities, which refer to distinct objects in the real world, can be viewed as language universals and used as effective signals to generate less ambiguous semantic representations and align multiple languages. We propose a novel method, *CLEW*, to generate cross-lingual data that is a mix of entities and contextual words based on Wikipedia. We replace each anchor link in the source language with its corresponding entity title in the target language if it exists, or in the source language otherwise. A cross-lingual joint entity and word embedding learned from this kind of data not only can disambiguate linkable entities but can also effectively represent unlinkable entities. Because this multilingual common space directly relates the semantics of contextual words in the source language to that of entities in the target language, we leverage it for unsupervised cross-lingual entity linking. Experimental results show that *CLEW* significantly advances the state-of-the-art: up to 3.1% absolute F-score gain for unsupervised cross-lingual entity linking. Moreover, it provides reliable alignment on both the word/entity level and the sentence level, and thus we use it to mine parallel sentences for all $\binom{302}{2}$ language pairs in Wikipedia.[1]

1 Introduction

The sheer amount of natural language data provides a great opportunity to represent named entity mentions by their probability distributions, so that they can be exploited for many Natural Language Processing (NLP) applications. However, named entity mentions are fundamentally different from common words or phrases in three aspects. First, the semantic meaning of a named entity mention (*e.g.,* a person name "*Bill Gates*") is not a simple summation of the meanings of the words it contains ("*Bill*" + "*Gates*"). Second, entity mentions are often highly ambiguous in various local contexts. For example, "*Michael Jordan*" may refer to the basketball player or the computer science professor. Third, representing entity mentions as mere phrases fails when names are rendered quite differently, especially when they appear across multiple languages. For example, "*Ang Lee*" in English is "*Li An*" in Chinese.

Fortunately, entities, the objects which mentions refer to, are unique and equivalent across languages. Many manually constructed entity-centric knowledge base resources such as Wikipedia[2], DBPedia (Auer et al., 2007) and YAGO (Suchanek et al., 2007) are widely available. Even better, they are massively multilingual. For example, up to August 2018, Wikipedia contains 21 million inter-language links[3] between 302 languages. We propose a novel cross-lingual joint entity and word (*CLEW*) embedding learning framework based on multilingual Wikipedia and evaluate its effectiveness on two practical NLP applications: Cross-lingual Entity Linking and Parallel Sentence Mining.

Wikipedia contains rich entity anchor links. As shown in Figure 2, many mentions (*e.g.,* "小米" (*Xiaomi*)) in a source language are linked to the entities in the same language that they refer to (*e.g.,* zh/小米科技 (*Xiaomi Technology*)), and some mentions are further linked to their corresponding English entities (*e.g.,* Chinese mention "苹果" (*Apple*) is linked to entity en/Apple_Inc. in English). We replace each mention (anchor link) in the source language with its corresponding entity title in the target language if it exists, or in

---

[1] We make all software and resources publicly available for research purpose at http://panx27.github.io/wikiann.

[2] https://www.wikipedia.org
[3] https://en.wikipedia.org/wiki/Help:Interlanguage_links

Proceedings of the 2nd Workshop on Deep Learning Approaches for Low-Resource NLP (DeepLo), pages 56–66
Hong Kong, China, November 3, 2019. ©2019 Association for Computational Linguistics
https://doi.org/10.18653/v1/P17

the source language otherwise. After this replacement, each entity mention is treated as a unique disambiguated entity, then we can learn joint entity and word embedding representations for the source language and target language respectively.

Furthermore, we leverage these shared target language entities as pivots to learn a rotation matrix and seamlessly align two embedding spaces into one by linear mapping. In this unified common space, multiple mentions are reliably disambiguated and grounded, which enables us to directly compute the semantic similarity between a mention in a source language and an entity in a target language (*e.g.,* English), and thus we can perform Cross-lingual Entity Linking in an unsupervised way, without using any training data. In addition, considering each pair of Wikipedia articles connected by an inter-language link as comparable documents, we use this multilingual common space to represent sentences and extract many parallel sentence pairs.

The novel contributions of this paper are:

- We develop a novel approach based on rich anchor links in Wikipedia to learn cross-lingual joint entity and word embedding, so that entity mentions across multiple languages are disambiguated and grounded into one unified common space.

- Using this joint entity and word embedding space, entity mentions in any language can be linked to an English knowledge base without any annotation cost. We achieve state-of-the-art performance on unsupervised cross-lingual entity linking.

- We construct a rich resource of parallel sentences for $\binom{302}{2}$ language pairs along with accurate entity alignment and word alignment.

2 Approach

2.1 Training Data Generation

Wikipedia contains rich entity anchor links. For example, in the following sentence from English Wikipedia markup: "[[Apple Inc.|apple]] is a technology company.", where [[Apple Inc.|apple]] is an anchor link that links the anchor text *"apple"* to the entity en/Apple_Inc.[4]

---

[4] In this paper, we use langcode/entity_title to represent entities in Wikipedia in each individual language. For example, en/* refers to an entity in English Wikipedia en.wikipedia.org/wiki/*.

Traditional approaches to derive training data from Wikipedia usually replace each anchor link with its anchor text, for example, "**apple** is a technology company.". These methods have two limitations: (1) **Information loss**: For example, the anchor text *"apple"* itself does not convey information such as the entity is a company; (2) **Ambiguity** (Faruqui et al., 2016): For example, the fruit sense and the company sense of *"apple"* mistakenly share one surface form. Similar to previous work (Wang et al., 2014; Tsai and Roth, 2016; Yamada et al., 2016), we replace each anchor link with its corresponding entity title, and thus treat each entity title as a unique word. For example, "en/Apple_Inc. is a technology company.". Using this kind of data mix of entity titles and contextual words, we can learn joint embedding of entities and words.

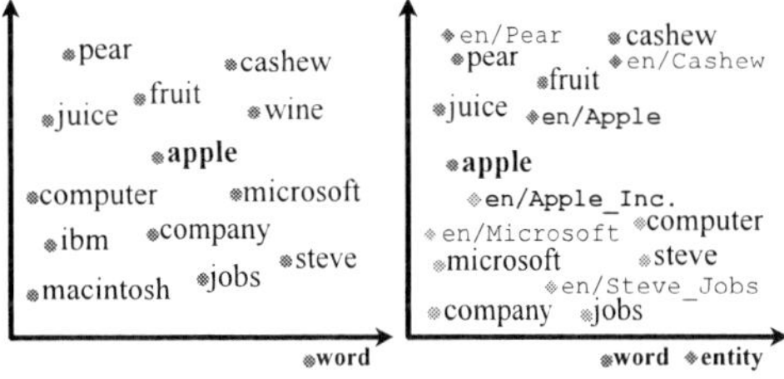

Figure 1: Traditional word embedding (left), and joint entity and word embedding (right).

The results from traditional word embedding and joint entity and word embedding for *"apple"* are visualized through Principal Component Analysis (PCA) in Figure 1. Using the joint embedding we can successfully separate those words referring to fruit and others referring to companies in the vector space. Moreover, the similarity can be computed based on entity-level instead of word-level. For example, en/Apple_Inc and en/Steve_Jobs are close in the vector space because they share many context words and entities.

Moreover, the above approach can be easily extended to the cross-lingual setting by using Wikipedia inter-language links. We replace each anchor link in a source language with its corresponding entity title in a target language if it exists, and otherwise replace each anchor link with its corresponding entity title in the source language. An example is illustrated in Figure 2.

Using this approach, the entities in a target language can be embedded along with words and the entities in a source language, as illustrated in Fig-

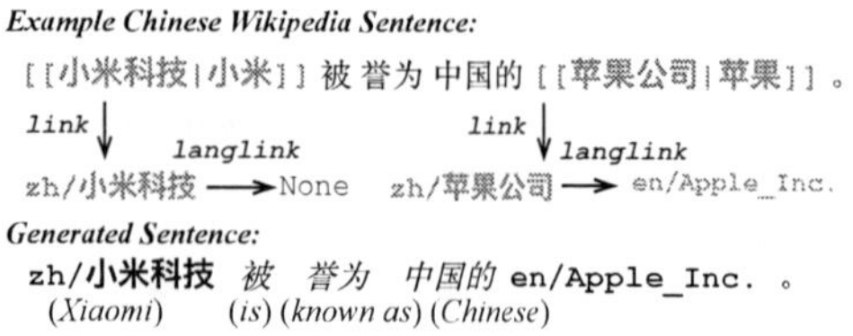

Example Chinese Wikipedia Sentence:

[[小米科技|小米]] 被 誉为 中国的 [[苹果公司|苹果]] 。

Generated Sentence:

zh/小米科技 *被 誉为 中国的* **en/Apple_Inc.** 。
(*Xiaomi*)   (*is*) (*known as*) (*Chinese*)

Figure 2: Using Wikipedia inter-language links to generate sentences which contain words and entities in a source language (*e.g.*, Chinese) and entities in a target language (*e.g.*, English).

Figure 3: Embedding which includes entities in English, and words and entities in Chinese (English words in brackets are human translations of Chinese words).

ure 3.

This joint representation has two advantages: (1) **Disambiguation**: For example, two entities en/Apple_Inc. and en/Apple can be differentiated by their distinct neighbors "电脑" (*computer*) and "水果" (*fruit*) respectively. (2) **Effective representation of unknown entities**: For example, the new entity zh/小米科技 (*Xiaomi Technology*), a Chinese mobile phone manufacturer, may not have an English Wikipedia page yet. But because it's close to neighbors such as en/Microsoft, "手机" (*phone*) and "公司" (*company*), we can infer it's likely to be a technology company.

2.2 Linear Mapping across Languages

Word embedding spaces have similar geometric arrangements across languages (Mikolov et al., 2013b). Given two sets of independently trained word embedding, the source language embedding $\mathcal{Z}^S$ and the target language embedding $\mathcal{Z}^T$, and a set of pre-aligned word pairs, a linear mapping $\mathbf{W}$ is learned to transform $\mathcal{Z}^S$ into a shared space where the distance between the embedding of the source language word and the embedding of its pre-aligned target language word is minimized. For example, given a set of pre-aligned word pairs, we use $\mathbf{X}$ and $\mathbf{Y}$ to denote two aligned matrices which contain the embedding of the pre-aligned words from $\mathcal{Z}^S$ and $\mathcal{Z}^T$ respectively. A linear mapping $\mathbf{W}$ can be learned such that:

$$\underset{\mathbf{W}}{\operatorname{argmin}}||\mathbf{W}\mathbf{X} - \mathbf{Y}||_{\mathrm{F}}$$

Previous work (Xing et al., 2015; Smith et al., 2017) shows that enforcing an orthogonal constraint $\mathbf{W}$ yields better performance. Consequently, the above equation can be transferred to Orthogonal Procrustes problem (Conneau et al., 2017):

$$\underset{\mathbf{W}}{\operatorname{argmin}}||\mathbf{W}\mathbf{X} - \mathbf{Y}||_{\mathrm{F}} = \mathbf{U}\mathbf{V}^{\top}$$

Then $\mathbf{W}$ can be obtained from the singular value decomposition (SVD) of $\mathbf{Y}\mathbf{X}^{\top}$ such that:

$$\mathbf{U}\mathbf{\Sigma}\mathbf{V}^{\top} = \mathrm{SVD}(\mathbf{Y}\mathbf{X}^{\top})$$

In this paper, we propose using entities instead of pre-aligned words as anchors to learn such a linear mapping $\mathbf{W}$. The basic idea is illustrated in Figure 4. We use $\mathcal{E}_T$ and $\mathcal{W}_T$ to denote the sets of entities and words in the target language associated with the target entity and word embedding $\mathcal{Z}^T$:

$$\mathcal{Z}^T = \{\mathbf{z}^t_{e_1}, .., \mathbf{z}^t_{e_{|\mathcal{E}_T|}}, \mathbf{z}^t_{w_1}, .., \mathbf{z}^t_{w_{|\mathcal{W}_T|}}\}$$

Similarly, we use $\mathcal{E}_S$ and $\mathcal{W}_S$ to denote the sets of entities and words in the source language associated with the source entity and word embedding $\mathcal{Z}^S$:

$$\mathcal{Z}^S = \{\mathbf{z}^s_{e_1}, .., \mathbf{z}^s_{e_{|\mathcal{E}_S|}}, \mathbf{z}^s_{w_1}, .., \mathbf{z}^s_{w_{|\mathcal{W}_S|}}\}$$

and use $\mathcal{E}'_T$ to denote the set of entities in the source language which are replaced with the corresponding entities in the target language, where $\mathcal{E}'_T \in \mathcal{E}_T$. Then $\mathcal{Z}^S$ can be represented as

$$\mathcal{Z}^S = \{\mathbf{z}^{t'}_{e_1}, .., \mathbf{z}^{t'}_{e_{|\mathcal{E}'_T|}}, \mathbf{z}^s_{e_1}, .., \mathbf{z}^s_{e_{|\mathcal{E}_S|-|\mathcal{E}'_T|}},$$
$$\mathbf{z}^s_{w_1}, .., \mathbf{z}^s_{w_{|\mathcal{W}_S|}}\}$$

Note that $\mathbf{z}^t_{e_i}$ and $\mathbf{z}^{t'}_{e_i}$ are the embedding of e_i in $\mathcal{Z}^T$ and $\mathcal{Z}^S$ respectively. Therefore, using entities in $\mathcal{E}'_T$ as anchors, we can learn a linear mapping $\mathbf{W}$ that maps $\mathcal{Z}^S$ into the vector space of $\mathcal{Z}^T$, and

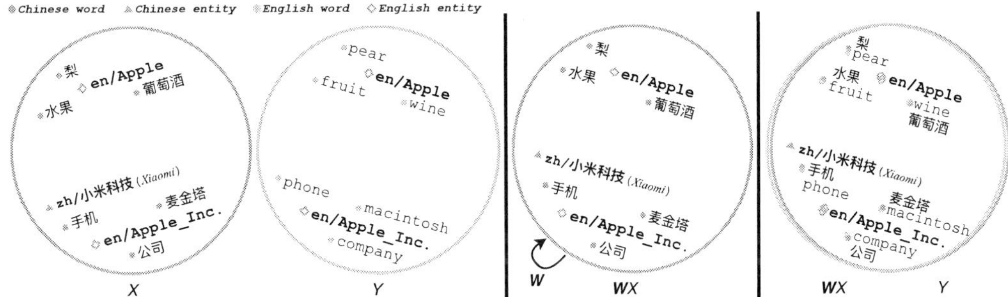

Figure 4: Using the aligned entities as anchors to learn a linear mapping (rotation matrix) which maps a source language embedding space to a target language embedding space.

obtain the cross-lingual joint entity and word embedding $\mathcal{Z}$.

We adopt the refinement procedure proposed by Conneau et al. (2017) to improve the quality of $\mathbf{W}$. A set of new high-quality anchors is generated to refine $\mathbf{W}$ learned from $\mathcal{E}'_T$. High-quality anchors refer to entities that have high frequency (*e.g.,* top 5,000) and entities that are mutual nearest neighbors. We iteratively apply this procedure to optimize $\mathbf{W}$. At each iteration, the new high-quality anchors are exploited to learn a new mapping.

Conneau et al. (2017) also propose a novel comparison metric, Cross-domain Similarity Local Scaling (CSLS), to relieve the hubness phenomenon, where some vectors (*hubs*) are the nearest neighbors of many others. For example, entity en/United_States is a *hub* in the vector space. By employing this metric, the similarity of isolated vectors is increased, while the similarity of vectors in dense areas is decreased. Specifically, given a mapped source embedding $\mathbf{Wx}$ and a target embedding $\mathbf{y}$, the mean cosine similarity of $\mathbf{Wx}$ and $\mathbf{y}$ for their K nearest neighbors in the other language, $r_T(\mathbf{Wx})$ and $r_S(\mathbf{y})$ are computed respectively. The comparison metric is defined as follows:

$$\mathrm{CSLS}(\mathbf{Wx}, \mathbf{y}) = \cos(\mathbf{Wx}, \mathbf{y}) - r_T(\mathbf{Wx})$$
$$- r_S(\mathbf{y})$$

Conneau et al. (2017) show that the performance is essentially the same when $K = 5, 10, 50$. Following this work, we set $K = 10$.

3 Downstream Applications

We apply *CLEW* to enhance two important downstream tasks: Cross-lingual Entity Linking and Parallel Sentence Mining.

3.1 Unsupervised Cross-lingual Entity Linking

Cross-lingual Entity Linking aims to link an entity mention in a source language text to its referent entity in a knowledge base (KB) in a target language (*e.g.,* English Wikipedia). A typical Cross-lingual Entity Linking framework includes three steps: mention translation, entity candidate generation, and mention disambiguation. We use translation dictionaries collected from Wikipedia (Ji et al., 2009) to translate each mention into English. If a mention has multiple translations, we merge the linking results of all translations at the end. We adopt a dictionary-based approach (Medelyan and Legg, 2008) to generate entity candidates for each mention. Then we use *CLEW* to implement the following two widely used mention disambiguation features: Context Similarity and Coherence.

Context Similarity refers to the context similarity between a mention and a candidate entity. Given a mention m, we consider the entire sentence containing m as its local context. Using *CLEW* embedding $\mathcal{Z}$, the vectors of context words are averaged to obtain the context vector representation of m:

$$\mathbf{v}_m = \frac{1}{|\mathcal{W}_m|} \sum_{w \in \mathcal{W}_m} \mathbf{z}_w$$

where $\mathcal{W}_m$ is the set of context words of m, and $\mathbf{z}_w \in \mathcal{Z}$ is the embedding of the context word w. We measure context similarity between m and each of its entity candidates by using the cosine similarity between $\mathbf{v}_m$ and entity embedding $\mathbf{z}_e \in \mathcal{Z}$ such that:

$$\mathcal{F}_{\text{txt}}(e) = \cos(\mathbf{v}_m, \mathbf{z}_e) = \frac{\mathbf{v}_m \cdot \mathbf{z}_e}{\|\mathbf{v}_m\| \|\mathbf{z}_e\|}$$

Feature	Description
$\mathcal{F}_{\text{prior}}(e)$	Entity Prior: $\frac{|A_{e,*}|}{|A_{*,*}|}$, where $A_{e,*}$ is a set of anchor links that link to entity e and $A_{*,*}$ is all anchor links in the KB
$\mathcal{F}_{\text{prob}}(e\|m)$	Mention to Entity Probability: $\frac{|A_{e,m}|}{|A_{*,m}|}$, where $A_{*,m}$ is a set of anchor links with anchor text m and $A_{e,m}$ is a subset that links to entity e.
$\mathcal{F}_{\text{type}}(e\|m,t)$	Entity Type (Ling et al., 2015): $\frac{p(e\|m)}{\sum_{e\mapsto t} p(e\|m)}$, where $e \mapsto t$ indicates that t is one of e's entity types. Conditional probability $p(e\|m)$ can be estimated by $\mathcal{F}_{\text{prob}}(e\|m)$.

Table 1: Mention disambiguation features.

Coherence is driven by the assumption that if multiple mentions appear together within a context window, their referent entities are more likely to be strongly connected to each other in the KB. Previous work (Cucerzan, 2007; Milne and Witten, 2008; Hoffart et al., 2011; Ratinov et al., 2011; Cheng and Roth, 2013; Ceccarelli et al., 2013; Ling et al., 2015) considers the KB as a knowledge graph and models coherence based on the overlapped neighbors of two entities in the knowledge graph. These approaches heavily rely on explicit connections among entities in the knowledge graph and thus cannot capture the coherence between two entities that are implicitly connected. For example, two entities en/Mosquito and en/Cockroach only have very few overlapped neighbors in the knowledge graph, but they usually appear together and have similar contexts in text. Using *CLEW* embedding $\mathcal{Z}$, the coherence score can be estimated by cosine similarity between the embedding of two entities. This coherence metric pays more attention to semantics.

We consider mentions that appear in the same sentence as coherent. Let m be a mention, and $\mathcal{C}_e$ be the set of corresponding entity candidates of m's coherent mentions. The coherence score for each of m's entity candidates is the average:

$$\mathcal{F}_{\text{coh}}(e) = \frac{1}{|\mathcal{C}_e|} \sum_{c_e \in \mathcal{C}_e} \cos(\mathbf{z}_e, \mathbf{z}_{c_e})$$

Finally, we linearly combine these two features with several other common mention disambiguation features as shown in Table 1.

3.2 Parallel Sentence Mining

One major bottleneck of low-resource language machine translation is the lack of parallel sentences. This inspires us to mine parallel sentences from Wikipedia automatically using *CLEW* embedding $\mathcal{Z}$.

Wikipedia contributors tend to translate some content from existing articles in other languages while editing an article. Therefore, if there exists an inter-language link between two Wikipedia articles in different languages, these two articles can be considered comparable and thus they are very likely to contain parallel sentences. We represent a Wikipedia sentence in any of the 302 languages by aggregating the embedding of entities and words it contains. In order to penalize high frequent words and entities, we apply a weighted metric:

$$\text{IDF}(t, \mathcal{S}) = \log \left(\frac{|\mathcal{S}|}{|\{s \in \mathcal{S} : t \in s\}|} \right)$$

where t is a term (entity or word), $\mathcal{S}$ is an article containing $|\mathcal{S}|$ sentences, and $|\{s \in \mathcal{S} : t \in s\}|$ is the total number of sentences containing t. The embedding of a sentence $\mathbf{v}_s$ can be computed as:

$$\mathbf{v}_s = \frac{1}{|\mathcal{T}_s|} \sum_{t \in \mathcal{T}_s} \text{IDF}(t, \mathcal{S}) \cdot \mathbf{z}_t$$

where $\mathcal{T}_s$ is the set of terms of s and $\mathbf{z}_t \in \mathcal{Z}$ is the embedding of t.

Given two comparable Wikipedia articles connected by an inter-language link, we compute the similarity of all possible sentence pairs using the CSLS metric described in Section 2.2 and rank them. If the CSLS score of a sentence pair is greater than a threshold (in this paper, we empirically set the threshold to 0.1 based on a separate small development set), then the sentence pair is considered as parallel. An advantage of our approach is that it provides a similarity score for every term pair, which can be used for improving word alignment and entity alignment.

4 Experiments

4.1 Training Data

We use an April 1, 2018 Wikipedia XML dump to generate data to train the joint entity and word embedding. We only select and analyze those main Wikipedia pages (ns tag is 0) which are not redirected (redirect tag is None) using the approach described in Section 2.1. We use the Skip-gram model in Word2Vec (Mikolov et al., 2013a,c) to learn the unaligned embeddings. The number of dimensions of the embedding is set to 300, and the minimal number of occurrences, the size of the context window, and the learning rate are set to 5, 5, and 0.025 respectively.

4.2 Linear Mapping

A large number of aligned entities can be obtained using the approach described in Section 2.1. For example, there are about 400,000 aligned entities between English and Spanish. However, the mapping algorithm does not perform well if we try to align all anchors, because the embedding of rare entities is updated less often, and thus their contexts are very different across languages. Therefore, we learn the global mapping using only high-quality anchors, and select high-frequency entities only as anchors using the salience metric described in Table 1. We use 5,000 anchors for training and 1,500 anchors for testing for each language pair. Our proposed method is applied to 9 language pairs in our experiments. Table 2 shows the statistics and the performance. We can see that mapping a language to its related language (*e.g.,* Ukrainian to Russian) usually achieves better performance.

Source-Target	$P@1$	$P@5$	$P@10$
es-en	79.1	89.2	92.3
it-en	74.5	86.9	90.5
ru-en	68.4	82.8	86.7
tr-en	59.0	79.9	86.3
uk-en	63.0	79.7	85.9
zh-en	63.1	83.8	89.2
uk-ru	78.1	90.3	92.8
ru-uk	75.8	90.2	93.7

Table 2: Linear entity mapping statistics and performance (Precision (%) at K) (en: English, es: Spanish, it: Italian, ru: Russian, so: Somali, tr: Turkish, uk: Ukrainian, zh: Chinese).

4.3 Cross-lingual Entity Linking

We use the training set and evaluation set (LDC2015E75 and LDC2015E103) in TAC Knowledge Base Population (TAC-KBP) 2015 Tri-lingual Entity Linking Track (Ji et al., 2015) for the cross-lingual entity linking experiments, because these data sets include the most recent and comprehensive gold-standard annotations on this task and we can compare our model with previously reported state-of-the-art approaches on the same benchmark.

We first compare our unsupervised approach to the top TAC2015 unsupervised system reported by Ji et al. (2015). In order to have a fair comparison with the state-of-the-art supervised methods, we also combine the features as described in Section 3.1 in a point-wised learning to rank algorithm based on Gradient Boosted Regression Trees (Friedman, 2000). The learning rate and the maximum depth of the decision trees are set to 0.01 and 4 respectively. The results are shown in Table 3. We can see that our unsupervised and supervised approaches significantly outperform the best TAC15 systems.

Method	ENG	CMN	SPA
Best TAC15 Unsupervised	67.1	78.1	71.5
Our Unsupervised	**70.0**	**81.2**	**73.4**
w/o Context Similarity	66.9	79.0	70.6
w/o Coherence	68.5	78.6	71.4
Best TAC15 Supervised	73.7	83.1	80.4
(Tsai and Roth, 2016)	-	83.6	80.9
(Sil et al., 2017)	-	84.4	82.3
Our Supervised	**74.8**	84.2	82.1
w/o Context Similarity	72.2	80.4	79.5
w/o Coherence	73.3	82.1	77.8

Table 3: F1 (%) of the evaluation set in TAC KBP 2015 Tri-lingual Entity Linking Track (Ji et al., 2015) (ENG: English, CMN: Chinese, SPA: Spanish).

We further observe that Context Similarity and Coherence features derived from $\mathcal{Z}$ play significant roles. Without such features, the performance drops significantly, as shown in Table 3. For example, in the following sentence: "欧盟委员会副主席雷丁就此表示... (European Commission vice president ***Redding*** said that...)", without Context Similarity feature, mention "雷丁(***Redding***)" is likely to be linked to the football club en/Reading_F.C. or the city en/Redding,_California. Using contextual words such as "委员会(*commission*)" and "主

席(*president*)", we can successfully link this mention to the target entity en/Viviane_Reding.

4.4 Parallel Sentence Mining

The proposed parallel sentence mining approach can be applied to any two languages in Wikipedia. Therefore, we have mined parallel sentences from a total number of $\binom{302}{2}$ language pairs and made this data set publicly available for research purpose. Table 4 shows some examples of mined parallel sentences from Wikipedia, with word and entity alignment highlighted.

Language Pairs	Prefect	Partial	Word	Entity
Chinese-English	81%	10%	92.3%	95.5%
Spanish-English	75%	13%	89.7%	91.1%
Russian-Ukrainian	70%	16%	82.4%	90.3%

Table 5: Quality of the mined parallel sentences (Perfect and Partial stand for the percentage of perfect and partial respectively; Word and Entity stand for the Accuracy of word and entity alignments respectively).

Amharic - English
* ዓርብ የሳምንቱ ስድስተኛ ቀን ሲሆን ሐሙስ በኋላ ቅዳሜ በፊት ይገኛል ።
* Friday is the day after Thursday and the day before Saturday .
Yoruba - English
* Glasgow ni ilu totobijulo ni orile-ede Skotlandi ati eyi totobijulo keta ni Britani .
* Glasgow is the largest city in Scotland , and third largest in the United Kingdom .
Uyghur - English
جۇمە ، پەيشەنبە بىلەن شەنبە نىڭ ئوتتۇرىسىدىكى ، ھەپتىنىڭ بەشىنچى كۈنىدۇر *
* Friday is the day after Thursday and the day before Saturday .
Vietnamese - English
* Bardolph là một làng thuộc quận McDonough , tiểu bang Illinois , HoaKỳ .
* Bardolph is a village in McDonough County , Illinois , United States .
Russian - Ukrainian
* Статья 2 - я Конституции СССР 1977 года провозглашала : « Вся власть в СССР принадлежит народу .
* Стаття 2 - га Конституції СРСР 1977 року проголошувала : " Вся влада в СРСР належить народові .
(*Article 2 of the Constitution of the USSR in 1977 proclaimed: "All power in the USSR belongs to the people."*)
Classical Chinese - Modern Chinese
* 至二战之时，南斯拉夫屡败，终为德意志、义大利所分。
* 在二次世界大战期间，南斯拉夫多次战败，分别被德国、意大利占领。
(*During the World War II, Yugoslavia was defeated several times and was occupied by Germany and Italy.*)

Table 4: Examples of mined parallel sentences from Wikipedia. A portion of alignments are highlighted using the same colors.

We randomly select 100 mined parallel sentence pairs for each of 3 language pairs, and ask linguistic experts to judge the quality of these sentence pairs (perfect, partial, or not parallel). The results are shown in Table 5. We can see that the quality of mined parallel sentence is promising and the quality of word and entity alignment is decent.

Furthermore, we evaluate the quality of mined parallel sentences extrinsically using a neural machine translation (NMT) model. We use the Transformer model (Vaswani et al., 2017) implemented by Tensor2Tensor[5]. Our Transformer model has 6 encoder and decoder layers, 8 attention heads, 512-dimension hidden states, 2048-dimension feed-forward layers, dropout of 0.1 and label smoothing of 0.1. The model is trained up to 128,000 optimizer steps.

Using the NMT model as a black box, we perform two experiments using the following training and tuning settings:

- *Baseline:* 44,000 training and 1,000 tuning sentences randomly sampled from the WMT17 News Commentary v12 Russian-English Corpus (Bojar et al., 2016).

- *Our approach:* Adding 44,000 training and 1,000 tuning sentences mined from Wikipedia using *CLEW*.

Using 1,000 randomly selected sentences from WMT 17 corpus for testing, the baseline achieves 19.0% BLEU score while our approach achieves 20.8% BLEU score.

5 Related Work

Cross-lingual Word Embedding Learning. Mikolov et al. (2013b) first notice that word embedding spaces have similar geometric arrangements across languages. They use this property to learn a linear mapping between two spaces. After that, several methods attempt to improve the mapping (Faruqui and Dyer, 2014; Xing et al., 2015; Lazaridou et al., 2015; Ammar et al., 2016; Artetxe et al., 2017; Smith et al., 2017). The measures used to compute similarity between a foreign word and an English word often include distributed monolingual representations on character-level (Costa-jussà and Fonollosa, 2016; Luong and Manning, 2016), subword-level (Anwarus Salam et al., 2012; Rei et al.,

---

[5]`https://github.com/tensorflow/tensor2tensor`

2016; Sennrich et al., 2016; Yang et al., 2017), and bi-lingual word embedding (Madhyastha and España-Bonet, 2017). Recent attempts have shown that it is possible to derive cross-lingual word embedding from unaligned corpora in an unsupervised fashion (Zhang et al., 2017; Conneau et al., 2017; Artetxe et al., 2018).

Another strategy for cross-lingual word embedding learning is to combine monolingual and cross-lingual training objectives (Zou et al., 2013; Klementiev et al., 2012; Luong et al., 2015; Ammar et al., 2016; Vulić et al., 2017). Compared to our direct mapping approach, these methods generally require large size of parallel data.

Our work is largely inspired from (Conneau et al., 2017). However, our work focuses on better representing entities, which are fundamentally different from common words or phrases in many aspects as described in Section 1. Previous multilingual word embedding efforts including (Conneau et al., 2017) do not explicitly handle entity representations. Moreover, we perform comprehensive extrinsic evaluations based on down-stream NLP applications including cross-lingual entity linking and machine translation, while previous work on cross-lingual embedding only focused on intrinsic evaluations.

Cross-lingual Joint Entity and Word Embedding Learning. Previous work on cross-lingual joint entity and word embedding methods largely neglect unlinkable entities (Tsai and Roth, 2016) and heavily rely on parallel or comparable sentences (Cao et al., 2018). Tsai and Roth (2016) apply a similar approach to generate code-switched data from Wikipedia, but their framework does not keep entities in the source language. Using all aligned entities as a dictionary, they adopt canonical correlation analysis to project two embedding spaces into one. In contrast, we only choose salient entities as anchors to learn a linear mapping. Cao et al. (2018) generate comparable data via distant supervision over multilingual knowledge bases, and use an entity regularizer and a sentence regularizer to align cross-lingual words and entities. Further, they design knowledge attention and cross-lingual attention to refine the alignment. Essentially, they train cross-lingual embedding jointly, while we align two embedding spaces that trained independently. Moreover, compared to their approach that relies on comparable data, aligned entities are easier to acquire.

Parallel Sentence Mining. Automatic mining parallel sentences from comparable documents is an important and useful task to improve Statistical Machine Translation. Early efforts mainly exploited bilingual word dictionaries for bootstrapping (Fung and Cheung, 2004). Recent approaches are mainly based on bilingual word embeddings (Marie and Fujita, 2017) and sentence embeddings (Schwenk, 2018) to detect sentence pairs or continuous parallel segments (Hangya and Fraser, 2019). To the best of our knowledge, this is the first work to incorporate joint entity and word embedding into parallel sentence mining. As a result the sentence pairs we include reliable alignment between entity mentions which are often out-of-vocabulary and ambiguous and thus receive poor alignment quality from previous methods.

6 Conclusions and Future Work

We developed a simple yet effective framework to learn cross-lingual joint entity and word embedding based on rich anchor links in Wikipedia. The learned embedding strongly enhances two downstream applications: cross-lingual entity linking and parallel sentence mining. The results demonstrate that our proposed method advances the state-of-the-art for unsupervised cross-lingual entity linking task. We have also constructed a valuable repository of parallel sentences for all language pairs in Wikipedia to share with the community. In the future, we will extend the framework to capture better representation of other types of knowledge elements such as relations and events.

Acknowledgments

This research is based upon work supported in part by U.S. DARPA LORELEI Program HR0011-15-C-0115, the Office of the Director of National Intelligence (ODNI), Intelligence Advanced Research Projects Activity (IARPA), via contract FA8650-17-C-9116, and ARL NS-CTA No. W911NF-09-2-0053. The views and conclusions contained herein are those of the authors and should not be interpreted as necessarily representing the official policies, either expressed or implied, of DARPA, ODNI, IARPA, or the U.S. Government. The U.S. Government is authorized to reproduce and distribute reprints for governmental purposes notwithstanding any copyright annotation therein.

References

Waleed Ammar, George Mulcaire, Yulia Tsvetkov, Guillaume Lample, Chris Dyer, and Noah A. Smith. 2016. Massively multilingual word embeddings. *CoRR*, abs/1602.01925.

Khan Md. Anwarus Salam, Setsuo Yamada, and Tetsuro Nishino. 2012. Sublexical translations for low-resource language. In *Proceedings of the Workshop on Machine Translation and Parsing in Indian Languages*, pages 39–52, Mumbai, India. The COLING 2012 Organizing Committee.

Mikel Artetxe, Gorka Labaka, and Eneko Agirre. 2017. Learning bilingual word embeddings with (almost) no bilingual data. In *Proceedings of the 55th Annual Meeting of the Association for Computational Linguistics (Volume 1: Long Papers)*, pages 451–462. Association for Computational Linguistics.

Mikel Artetxe, Gorka Labaka, and Eneko Agirre. 2018. A robust self-learning method for fully unsupervised cross-lingual mappings of word embeddings. In *Proceedings of the 56th Annual Meeting of the Association for Computational Linguistics (Volume 1: Long Papers)*, pages 789–798. Association for Computational Linguistics.

Sören Auer, Christian Bizer, Georgi Kobilarov, Jens Lehmann, Richard Cyganiak, and Zachary Ives. 2007. Dbpedia: A nucleus for a web of open data. In *The Semantic Web*, pages 722–735, Berlin, Heidelberg. Springer Berlin Heidelberg.

Ondrej Bojar, Rajen Chatterjee, Christian Federmann, Yvette Graham, Barry Haddow, Matthias Huck, Antonio Jimeno Yepes, Philipp Koehn, Varvara Logacheva, Christof Monz, et al. 2016. Findings of the 2016 conference on machine translation. In *Proceedings of the First Conference on Machine Translation: Volume 2, Shared Task Papers*, pages 131–198. Association for Computational Linguistics.

Yixin Cao, Lei Hou, Juanzi Li, Zhiyuan Liu, Chengjiang Li, Xu Chen, and Tiansi Dong. 2018. Joint representation learning of cross-lingual words and entities via attentive distant supervision. In *Proceedings of the 2018 Conference on Empirical Methods in Natural Language Processing*, pages 227–237. Association for Computational Linguistics.

Diego Ceccarelli, Claudio Lucchese, Salvatore Orlando, Raffaele Perego, and Salvatore Trani. 2013. Learning relatedness measures for entity linking. In *Proceedings of the 22Nd ACM International Conference on Information & Knowledge Management*, CIKM '13, pages 139–148, New York, NY, USA. ACM.

Xiao Cheng and Dan Roth. 2013. Relational inference for wikification. In *Proceedings of the 2013 Conference on Empirical Methods in Natural Language Processing*, pages 1787–1796, Seattle, Washington, USA. Association for Computational Linguistics.

Alexis Conneau, Guillaume Lample, Marc'Aurelio Ranzato, Ludovic Denoyer, and Hervé Jégou. 2017. Word translation without parallel data. *arXiv preprint arXiv:1710.04087*.

Marta R. Costa-jussà and José A. R. Fonollosa. 2016. Character-based neural machine translation. In *Proceedings of the 54th Annual Meeting of the Association for Computational Linguistics (Volume 2: Short Papers)*, pages 357–361, Berlin, Germany. Association for Computational Linguistics.

Silviu Cucerzan. 2007. Large-scale named entity disambiguation based on Wikipedia data. In *Proceedings of the 2007 Joint Conference on Empirical Methods in Natural Language Processing and Computational Natural Language Learning (EMNLP-CoNLL)*, pages 708–716, Prague, Czech Republic. Association for Computational Linguistics.

Manaal Faruqui and Chris Dyer. 2014. Improving vector space word representations using multilingual correlation. In *Proceedings of the 14th Conference of the European Chapter of the Association for Computational Linguistics*, pages 462–471. Association for Computational Linguistics.

Manaal Faruqui, Yulia Tsvetkov, Pushpendre Rastogi, and Chris Dyer. 2016. Problems with evaluation of word embeddings using word similarity tasks. In *Proceedings of the 1st Workshop on Evaluating Vector-Space Representations for NLP*, pages 30–35, Berlin, Germany. Association for Computational Linguistics.

Jerome H. Friedman. 2000. Greedy function approximation: A gradient boosting machine. *Annals of Statistics*, 29:1189–1232.

Pascale Fung and Percy Cheung. 2004. Mining very-non-parallel corpora: Parallel sentence and lexicon extraction via bootstrapping and e. In *Proceedings of the 2004 Conference on Empirical Methods in Natural Language Processing*, pages 57–63, Barcelona, Spain. Association for Computational Linguistics.

Viktor Hangya and Alexander Fraser. 2019. Unsupervised parallel sentence extraction with parallel segment detection helps machine translation. In *Proceedings of the 57th Annual Meeting of the Association for Computational Linguistics*, pages 1224–1234, Florence, Italy. Association for Computational Linguistics.

Johannes Hoffart, Mohamed Amir Yosef, Ilaria Bordino, Hagen Fürstenau, Manfred Pinkal, Marc Spaniol, Bilyana Taneva, Stefan Thater, and Gerhard Weikum. 2011. Robust disambiguation of named entities in text. In *Proceedings of the 2011 Conference on Empirical Methods in Natural Language Processing*, pages 782–792. Association for Computational Linguistics.

Heng Ji, Ralph Grishman, Dayne Freitag, Matthias Blume, John Wang, Shahram Khadivi, Richard Zens, and Hermann Ney. 2009. Name extraction and translation for distillation. *Handbook of Natural Language Processing and Machine Translation: DARPA Global Autonomous Language Exploitation.*

Heng Ji, Joel Nothman, Ben Hachey, and Radu Florian. 2015. Overview of tac-kbp2015 tri-lingual entity discovery and linking. In *Proc. Text Analysis Conference (TAC2015).*

Alexandre Klementiev, Ivan Titov, and Binod Bhattarai. 2012. Inducing crosslingual distributed representations of words. In *Proceedings of COLING 2012*, pages 1459–1474. The COLING 2012 Organizing Committee.

Angeliki Lazaridou, Georgiana Dinu, and Marco Baroni. 2015. Hubness and pollution: Delving into cross-space mapping for zero-shot learning. In *Proceedings of the 53rd Annual Meeting of the Association for Computational Linguistics and the 7th International Joint Conference on Natural Language Processing (Volume 1: Long Papers)*, pages 270–280. Association for Computational Linguistics.

Xiao Ling, Sameer Singh, and Daniel S. Weld. 2015. Design challenges for entity linking. *Transactions of the Association for Computational Linguistics*, 3:315–328.

Minh-Thang Luong and Christopher Manning. 2016. Achieving open vocabulary neural machine translation with hybrid word-character models. In *Proceedings of ACL2016.*

Thang Luong, Hieu Pham, and Christopher D. Manning. 2015. Bilingual word representations with monolingual quality in mind. In *Proceedings of the 1st Workshop on Vector Space Modeling for Natural Language Processing*, pages 151–159. Association for Computational Linguistics.

Pranava Swaroop Madhyastha and Cristina España-Bonet. 2017. Learning bilingual projections of embeddings for vocabulary expansion in machine translation. In *Proceedings of the 2nd Workshop on Representation Learning for NLP*, pages 139–145, Vancouver, Canada. Association for Computational Linguistics.

Benjamin Marie and Atsushi Fujita. 2017. Efficient extraction of pseudo-parallel sentences from raw monolingual data using word embeddings. In *Proceedings of the 55th Annual Meeting of the Association for Computational Linguistics (Volume 2: Short Papers)*, pages 392–398, Vancouver, Canada. Association for Computational Linguistics.

O. Medelyan and C. Legg. 2008. Integrating cyc and wikipedia: Folksonomy meets rigorously defined common-sense. In *Proc. AAAI 2008 Workshop on Wikipedia and Artificial Intelligence.*

Tomas Mikolov, Kai Chen, Greg Corrado, and Jeffrey Dean. 2013a. Efficient estimation of word representations in vector space. *CoRR.*

Tomas Mikolov, Quoc V. Le, and Ilya Sutskever. 2013b. Exploiting similarities among languages for machine translation. *CoRR.*

Tomas Mikolov, Ilya Sutskever, Kai Chen, Greg S Corrado, and Jeff Dean. 2013c. Distributed representations of words and phrases and their compositionality. In *Advances in Neural Information Processing Systems 26.*

D. Milne and I.H. Witten. 2008. Learning to link with wikipedia. In *Proc. ACM international conference on Information and knowledge management (CIKM 2008).*

Lev Ratinov, Dan Roth, Doug Downey, and Mike Anderson. 2011. Local and global algorithms for disambiguation to Wikipedia. In *Proceedings of the 49th Annual Meeting of the Association for Computational Linguistics: Human Language Technologies*, pages 1375–1384, Portland, Oregon, USA. Association for Computational Linguistics.

Marek Rei, Gamal Crichton, and Sampo Pyysalo. 2016. Attending to characters in neural sequence labeling models. In *Proceedings of COLING 2016, the 26th International Conference on Computational Linguistics: Technical Papers*, pages 309–318, Osaka, Japan. The COLING 2016 Organizing Committee.

Holger Schwenk. 2018. Filtering and mining parallel data in a joint multilingual space. In *Proceedings of the 56th Annual Meeting of the Association for Computational Linguistics.*

Rico Sennrich, Barry Haddow, and Alexandra Birch. 2016. Neural machine translation of rare words with subword units. In *Proceedings of ACL2016.*

Avirup Sil, Gourab Kundu, Radu Florian, and Wael Hamza. 2017. Neural cross-lingual entity linking. *CoRR*, abs/1712.01813.

Samuel L. Smith, David H. P. Turban, Steven Hamblin, and Nils Y. Hammerla. 2017. Offline bilingual word vectors, orthogonal transformations and the inverted softmax. *CoRR*, abs/1702.03859.

Fabian M. Suchanek, Gjergji Kasneci, and Gerhard Weikum. 2007. Yago: a core of semantic knowledge. In *Proceedings of the 16th international conference on World Wide Web*, pages 697–706.

Chen-Tse Tsai and Dan Roth. 2016. Cross-lingual wikification using multilingual embeddings. In *Proceedings of the 2016 Conference of the North American Chapter of the Association for Computational Linguistics: Human Language Technologies*, pages 589–598, San Diego, California. Association for Computational Linguistics.

Ashish Vaswani, Noam Shazeer, Niki Parmar, Jakob Uszkoreit, Llion Jones, Aidan N Gomez, Łukasz Kaiser, and Illia Polosukhin. 2017. Attention is all you need. In *Advances in Neural Information Processing Systems*, pages 5998–6008.

Ivan Vulić, Nikola Mrkšić, and Anna Korhonen. 2017. Cross-lingual induction and transfer of verb classes based on word vector space specialisation. In *Proceedings of the 2017 Conference on Empirical Methods in Natural Language Processing*, pages 2546–2558. Association for Computational Linguistics.

Zhen Wang, Jianwen Zhang, Jianlin Feng, and Zheng Chen. 2014. Knowledge graph and text jointly embedding. In *Proceedings of the 2014 Conference on Empirical Methods in Natural Language Processing (EMNLP)*, pages 1591–1601. Association for Computational Linguistics.

Chao Xing, Dong Wang, Chao Liu, and Yiye Lin. 2015. Normalized word embedding and orthogonal transform for bilingual word translation. In *Proceedings of the 2015 Conference of the North American Chapter of the Association for Computational Linguistics: Human Language Technologies*, pages 1006–1011. Association for Computational Linguistics.

Ikuya Yamada, Hiroyuki Shindo, Hideaki Takeda, and Yoshiyasu Takefuji. 2016. Joint learning of the embedding of words and entities for named entity disambiguation. In *Proceedings of The 20th SIGNLL Conference on Computational Natural Language Learning*, pages 250–259, Berlin, Germany. Association for Computational Linguistics.

Baosong Yang, Derek F. Wong, Tong Xiao, Lidia S. Chao, and Jingbo Zhu. 2017. Towards bidirectional hierarchical representations for attention-based neural machine translation. In *Proceedings of the 2017 Conference on Empirical Methods in Natural Language Processing*, pages 1432–1441, Copenhagen, Denmark. Association for Computational Linguistics.

Meng Zhang, Yang Liu, Huanbo Luan, and Maosong Sun. 2017. Adversarial training for unsupervised bilingual lexicon induction. In *Proceedings of the 55th Annual Meeting of the Association for Computational Linguistics (Volume 1: Long Papers)*, pages 1959–1970. Association for Computational Linguistics.

Will Y. Zou, Richard Socher, Daniel Cer, and Christopher D. Manning. 2013. Bilingual word embeddings for phrase-based machine translation. In *Proceedings of the 2013 Conference on Empirical Methods in Natural Language Processing*, pages 1393–1398. Association for Computational Linguistics.

Deep Bidirectional Transformers for Relation Extraction without Supervision

Yannis Papanikolaou, Ian Roberts, Andrea Pierleoni
Healx, Cambridge, UK
{yannis.papanikolaou, ian.roberts, andrea.pierleoni}@healx.io

Abstract

We present a novel framework to deal with relation extraction tasks in cases where there is complete lack of supervision, either in the form of gold annotations, or relations from a knowledge base. Our approach leverages syntactic parsing and pre-trained word embeddings to extract few but precise relations, which are then used to annotate a larger corpus, in a manner identical to distant supervision. The resulting data set is employed to fine tune a pre-trained BERT model in order to perform relation extraction. Empirical evaluation on four data sets from the biomedical domain shows that our method significantly outperforms two simple baselines for unsupervised relation extraction and, even if not using any supervision at all, achieves slightly worse results than the state-of-the-art in three out of four data sets. Importantly, we show that it is possible to successfully fine tune a large pre-trained language model with noisy data, as opposed to previous works that rely on gold data for fine tuning.

1 Introduction

The last years have seen a number of important advances in the field of Relation Extraction (RE), mainly based on deep learning models (Zeng et al., 2014, 2015; Lin et al., 2016; Zeng et al., 2016; Wu et al., 2017; Verga et al., 2018). These advances have led to significant improvements in benchmark tasks for RE. The above cases assume the existence of some form of supervision either manually annotated or distantly supervised data (Mintz et al., 2009), where relations from a knowledge base are used in order to automatically annotate data, which then can be used as a noisy training set. For most real-world cases manually labeled data is either limited or completely missing, so typically one resorts to distant supervision to tackle a RE task.

Verb	Relation	Similarity
apply use	treat	0.40
investigate administer	treat	0.51
have manage	treat	0.60
evaluate improve	treat	0.41
be eradicate	treat	0.55
develop cause	cause	0.81
induce exacerbate	cause	0.58
know contribute	cause	0.41
result lead	cause	0.57
relate induce	cause	0.47

Table 1: Examples of verb mappings for compound-disease relation. Each verb (can be n-gram as well) is mapped to its closest class (*cause*, *treat*) with pre-trained word embeddings.

There exist cases though, where even the distant supervision approach cannot be followed due to the lack of a knowledge base. This is often the case in domains like the Web or the biomedical literature, where entities of interest might be related with other entities and no available supervision signal exists.

In this work, we propose an approach to deal with such a scenario, from a purely unsupervised approach, that is without providing any manual annotation or any supervision whatsoever. Our goal is to provide a framework that enables a pre-trained language model to be *self-fine tuned*[1] on a set of predefined relation types, in situations without any existing training data and without the possibility or budget for human supervision.

Our method proceeds as follows:

- The data are first parsed syntactically, extracting relations of the form subject-verb-object. The resulting verbs are embedded in a

---

[1] We employ the term *self-fine tuned* to denote that the model creates its own data set, without any supervision.

Proceedings of the 2nd Workshop on Deep Learning Approaches for Low-Resource NLP (DeepLo), pages 67–75
Hong Kong, China, November 3, 2019. ©2019 Association for Computational Linguistics
https://doi.org/10.18653/v1/P17

vector space along with the relation types that we are interested to learn and each is mapped to their most similar relation type. Table 1 shows an example of this mapping process. This process is entirely automatic, we only provide the set of relation types that we are interested in and a threshold below which a verb is mapped to a *Null* class.

- Subsequently, we use these extracted relations identically to a distant supervision signal to annotate automatically all co-occurrences of entities on a large corpus.

- The resulting data set is used to fine tune a Deep Bidirectional Transformer (BERT) model (Devlin et al., 2018).

Importantly, the first step ensures that the resulting relations will have high precision (although at the expense of low recall), since they largely exclude the possibility of the two entities co-occurring randomly in the sentence, through the subject-verb-object association. In other words, we end up with a small, but high quality set of relations, which can then be used in a way identical to distant supervision.

The main contribution of this work is the introduction of a novel framework to deal with RE tasks without any supervision, either manually annotated data or known relations. Our approach is empirically evaluated on four data sets. A secondary implication of our work involves how we employ a pre-trained language model such as BERT: unlike previous approaches that employ a small gold data set, we show that it is possible to instead use a large noisy data set to successfully fine tune such a model.

The rest of the paper is organized as follows: we describe the related work in Section 2, subsequently describing our method in Section 3 and presenting the empirical evaluation results in Section 4.

2   Related work

Dealing with relation extraction in the absence of training data is not a novel task: for more than a decade, researchers have employed successfully techniques to tackle the lack of supervision, mainly by resorting to distant supervision (Mintz et al., 2009; Riedel et al., 2010). This approach assumes the existence of a knowledge base, which contains already known relations between specific entities. These relations are then used to automatically annotate texts containing these entity pairs. Although this approach leads to noisy labelling, it is cheap and has the ability to leverage a vast amount of training data. A great body of work has built upon this approach aiming to alleviate the noise in annotations, using formulations such as multi-label multi-instance learning (Surdeanu et al., 2012; Zeng et al., 2015), employing generative models to reduce wrong labelling (Takamatsu et al., 2012), developing different loss functions for relation extraction (dos Santos et al., 2015; Wang et al., 2016) or using side information to constraint predicted relations (Vashishth et al., 2018).

More recently, a number of other interesting approaches have been presented aiming to deal with the lack of training data, with direct application to RE: data programming (Ratner et al., 2016) provides a framework that allows domain experts to write labelling functions which are then denoised through a generative model. Levy et al. (2017) have formulated the relation extraction task as a reading comprehension problem by associating one or more natural language questions with each relation. This approach enables generalization to unseen relations in a zero-shot setting.

Our work is different from the aforementioned approaches, in that it does not rely on the existence of any form of supervision. We build a model that is driven by the data, discovering a small set of precise relations, using them to annotate a larger corpus and being self-fine tuned to extract new relationships.

To train the RE classifier, we employ BERT, a recently proposed deep language model that achieved state-of-the-art results across a variety of tasks. BERT, similarly to the works of Radford et al. (2018a) and Radford et al. (2018b), builds upon the idea of pre-training a deep language model on massive amounts of data and then applies it (by fine tuning) to solve a diverse set of tasks. The building block of BERT is the Tranformer model (Vaswani et al., 2017), a neural network cell that uses a multi-head, self-attention mechanism.

The first step of our approach is highly reminiscent of approaches from the open Information Extraction (openIE) literature (Banko et al., 2007). Indeed, similar to openIE approaches, we also use syntactic parsing to extract relations. Neverthe-less, unlike openIE we are interested in a) specific types of entities which we assume that have been previously extracted with Named Entity Recognition (NER) and b) in specific, predefined types of relations between entities. We use syntactic parsing only as a means to extract a few precise relations and then follow an approach similar to distant supervision to train a neural relation extraction classifier. It should be noted though, that as a potential extension of this work we could employ more sophisticated techniques instead of syntactic parsing, similar to the latest openIE works (Yahya et al., 2014)

3   Method and Implementation Details

We present here the details of our method. First, we describe how we create our training set which results from a purely unsupervised procedure during which the only human intervention is to define the relation types of interest, e.g., 'treat' or 'associate'. Subsequently, we describe BERT, the model that we use in our approach.

3.1   Training Set Creation

Our method assumes that the corpus is split in sentences[2], which are then passed through a NER model and a syntactic parser. We use the spaCy library[3] for the above steps.

Given a pair of two entities A and B, we find their shortest dependency path and if one or more verbs V are in that path we assume that A is related to B with V. The next step involves mapping the verbs to a set of predefined relation types, as shown in Table 1. To do so, we embed both relation types and verbs to a continuous, lower-dimensional space with a pre-trained skip gram model (Mikolov et al., 2013), and map each verb to its closest relation type, if the cosine similarity of the two vectors is greater than a threshold (in initial small scale experiments using a validation set, we have found that a $threshold = 0.4$ works well). Otherwise, the verb is not considered to represent a relation. In our experiments we used the pre-trained BioASQ word vectors[4], since our re-

lation extraction tasks come from the biomedical domain.

It is important to note that in the above procedure the only human involvement is defining the set of relation types that we are interested in. In that sense, this approach is neither domain or scale dependent: any set of relations can be used (coming from any domain) and likewise we can consider any number of relation types.

The above procedure results in a small but relatively precise set of relations which can then be used in a way similar to distant supervision, to annotate all of our corpus. Nevertheless, there are a number of caveats to be taken into consideration:

- As expected, there will be errors in the relations that come from the syntactic parsing and verbs mapping procedure.

- Our distant supervision-like approach comes also with inherent noise: we end up with a training set that has a lot of false negative and also a few false positive errors.

- The resulting training set will be largely imbalanced, since the way that we extract relations sacrifices recall for precision.

To deal with the above noise, we employ BERT as a relation extraction classifier. Furthermore, we use a balanced bagging approach to deal with class imbalance. Both approaches are described in detail in the following section.

3.2   Deep Bidirectional Transformers

BERT is a deep learning network that focus in learning general language representations which can then be used in downstream tasks. Much like the work of Radford et al. (2018a) and Radford et al. (2018b), the general idea is to leverage the expressive power of a deep Transformer architecture that is pre-trained on a massive corpus on a language modelling task. Indeed, BERT comes in two flavors of 12 and 24 layers and 110M and 340M parameters respectively and is pre-trained on a concatenation of the English Wikipedia and the Book Corpus (Zhu et al., 2015). The resulting language model can then be fine tuned across a variety of different NLP tasks.

The main novelty of BERT is its ability to pre-train bidirectional representations by using a masked language model as a training objective. The idea behind the masked language model is to

---

[2]We can easily extend to cross-sentence relations, since the Transformer models which are the basis of BERT do not suffer from the problems encountered in LSTMs or CNNs for longer sequences, thanks to their self-attention mechanism.

[3]https://spacy.io/

[4]http://bioasq.lip6.fr/tools/
BioASQword2vec/

randomly mask some of the word tokens from the input, the objective being to predict what that word actually is, based on its context. The model is simultaneously trained on a second objective in order to model sentence relationships, that is, given two sentences $sent_a$ and $sent_b$ predict if $sent_b$ is the next sentence after $sent_a$.

BERT has achieved state-of-the-art across eleven NLP tasks using the same pre-trained model and only with some simple fine tuning. This makes it particularly attractive for our use case, where we need a strong language model that will be able to learn from noisy patterns.

In order to further deal with the challenges mentioned in the previous section, in our experiments we fine tuned BERT for up to 5 epochs, since in early experiments we noticed that the model started overfitting to noise and validation loss started increasing after that point.

3.3 Balanced Bagging

In order to deal with class imbalance we employed balanced bagging (Tao et al., 2006), an ensembling technique where each component model is trained on a sub-sample of the data, such that the negative examples are roughly equal to the positive ones. To train each model of the ensemble, we sub-sample only the negative class so as to end up with a balanced set of positives and negatives.

This sub-sampling of the negative class is important not only in order to alleviate the data imbalance, but also because the negative class will contain more noise than the positive by definition of our approach. In other words, since we consider as positives only a small set of relations coming from syntax parsing and verb mapping, it is more likely that a negative is in reality a positive sample rather than the opposite.

4 Experiments

In this section we first describe the data sets used in experiments and the experimental setup and then present the results of our experiments.

4.1 Data Sets and Setup

We evaluate our method on four data sets coming from the biomedical domain, expressing disease-drug and disease-gene relations. Three of them are well known benchmark data sets for relation extraction: The Biocreative chemical-disease relations (CDR) data set (Li et al., 2016), the Genetic Association Database (GAD) data set (Bravo et al., 2015) and the EU-ADR data set (Van Mulligen et al., 2012). Additionally, we present a proprietary manually curated data set, Healx CD, expressing therapeutic drug-disease relations. We consider only sentence-level relations, so we split CDR instances into sentences (the rest of the data sets are already at sentence-level). Statistics for the data sets are provided in Table 2. We should note that for our approach we map each verb to the respective relation class that is depicted in Table 2 in parentheses.

As stated, we are mainly interested to understand how our proposed method performs under complete lack of training signal, so we compare it with two simple baselines for unsupervised relation extraction. The first, assumes that a sentence co-occurrence of two entities signals a positive relation, while the second is equivalent to the first two steps of our method, syntactic parsing followed by verb mapping to the relation types of interest. In other words, if two entities are connected in the shortest dependency path through a verb that is mapped to a class, they are considered to be related with that class.

Additionally, we would like to understand how our method performs against supervised methods, so for the first three data sets we compare it with a BERT model trained on the respective gold data, reporting also the current state-of-the-art, while for the Healx CD data set since there are no manual annotations, we compare our method against a distant supervision approach, retrieving ground truth relations from our internal knowledge base.

Across all experiments and for all methods we use the same BERT model, BioBERT (Lee et al., 2019), which is a BERT model initialized with the model from Devlin et al. (2018) and then pre-trained on PubMed, and thus more relevant to our tasks. That model is fine tuned on relation extraction classification using the code provided by the BioBERT authors, either on the gold or the distantly supervised or our approach's training set. We fine tune for up to 5 epochs with a learning rate of 0.00005 and a batch size of 128, keeping the model that achieves the best loss on the respective validation set.

Finally, for the distant supervision as well as for our method, we use the previously mentioned balanced bagging approach, fine tuning an ensemble of ten models for each relation.

Data set	Relation (class)	# Train (pos)	# Dev (pos)	# Test (pos)
Annotated				
CDR	Drug-Disease (*cause*)	3,596(1,453)	3,875(1,548)	3,805(1,482)
GAD	Disease-Gene (*cause*)	5,330(1,834)	-	-
EUADR	Disease-Gene (*cause*)	355(243)	-	-
Healx CD	Drug-Disease (*treat*)	564(325)	-	-
Dist.Sup.				
250k	Drug-Disease (*treat*)	250k(35k)	-	-
full	Drug-Disease (*treat*)	8m(1.1m)	-	-
Our approach				
250k	Drug-Disease (*treat*, *cause*)	250k(70k 10k)	-	-
full	Drug-Disease (*treat*, *cause*)	8m(2.2m 325k)	-	-
250k	Disease-Gene (*cause*)	250k(62k)	-	-
full	Disease-Gene (*cause*)	9.1m(2.2m)	-	-

Table 2: Data sets used in our experiments. 'Our approach' stands for the procedure described in Section 3.1. The Drug-Disease relation for our approach yields two positive classes, *treat* and *cause*, therefore we report accordingly positives from each class in parentheses.

4.2 Results

Table 3 shows the results for the four data sets, reporting the average over five runs. For the GAD and EU-ADR data sets, we use the train and test splits provided by Lee et al. (2019). Also, for CDR, since the state-of-the-art results (Verga et al., 2018) are given at the abstract level, we re-run their proposed algorithm on our transformed sentence-level CDR data set, reporting results for a single model, without additional data (Verga et al. (2018) reports also results when adding weakly labeled data).

Let us first focus on the two unsupervised baselines. The first, dubbed 'co-occurrences', achieves a perfect recall since it considers all entity pairs co-occurrences as expressing a relation, but is clearly sub-optimal with regards to precision. The opposite behaviour is observed for the second baseline (syntactic parsing with verb mapping) since that one focuses in extracting high-precision relations, sacrificing recall: only entity pairs with a verb in between that is mapped to a relation are considered positives. Notably, this baseline achieves the highest precision in two out of four data sets, even compared to the supervised methods.

Our method proves significantly better compared to the other two unsupervised baselines, outperforming them by a large margin in all cases apart for EUADR. In that case our method is slightly worse than the co-occurrences baseline, since EUADR contains a big percentage of positives. Specifically, it is interesting to observe the improvement over the second baseline, which acts as a training signal for our method. Thanks to the predictive power and the robustness of BERT, our method manages to learn useful patterns from a noisy data set and actually improve substantially upon its training signal.

An additional advantage of our method compared to the two other unsupervised baselines and similar approaches in general, is that it outputs a probability. Unlike the other methods, this probability allows us to tune our method for better precision or recall, depending on the application.

We then focus on comparing our proposed approach against the same BERT model fine tuned on supervised data, either manually annotated for the first three data sets, or distantly annotated for the fourth. For the first three data sets, we also report the current state-of-the-art results. Interestingly, even if our method is completely unsupervised, it is competitive with the state-of-the-art of fully supervised methods in three out of four cases, being inferior to them from 3.7 to 14.1 F1 points. On average, our method is worse by 7.5 F1 points against the best supervised model (either BERT or current state-of-the-art).

These results are particularly important, if we take into account that they come from a procedure that is fully unsupervised and which entails substantial noise from its sub-steps: the syntactic parsing may come with errors and mapping the verbs to relevant relation types is a process

Data set		Method	Precision	Recall	F1
CDR					
	Unsupervised	Co-occurrences	30.9	100.0	47.2
		syntactic parsing+verb mapping	84.0	8.5	15.4
		Our method on BERT (250k)	49.4	76.3	60.4
		Our method on BERT (full)	50.1	81.3	**62.2**
	Supervised	SOTA (Verga et al., 2018)	64.2	68.5	66.3
		Gold Data on BERT	61.1	80.3	**70.4**
GAD					
	Unsupervised	Co-occurrences	34.4	100.0	51.2
		syntactic parsing+verb mapping	71.9	9.9	17.4
		Our method on BERT (250k)	53.1	82.8	64.6
		Our method on BERT (full)	56.9	90.1	**69.8**
	Supervised	SOTA (Bhasuran and Natarajan, 2018)	79.2	89.2	**83.9**
		Gold Data on BERT	76.4	87.7	81.7
EUADR					
	Unsupervised	Co-occurrences	68.5	100.0	**81.3**
		syntactic parsing+verb mapping	70.1	6.9	12.1
		Our method on BERT (250k)	71.7	79.4	75.5
		Our method on BERT (full)	75.5	87.9	81.2
	Supervised	SOTA (Bhasuran and Natarajan, 2018)	76.4	98.0	**85.3**
		Gold Data on BERT	78.0	93.9	85.2
Healx CD					
	Unsupervised	Co-occurrences	57.6	100.0	73.0
		syntactic parsing+verb mapping	91.0	17.9	29.9
		Our method on BERT (250k)	73.4	85.1	79.0
		Our method on BERT (full)	74.4	90.0	**81.4**
	Supervised	Distant Supervision on BERT (250k)	83.3	83.1	83.4
		Distant Supervision on BERT (full)	87.1	83.2	**85.1**

Table 3: Results on relation classification. State-of-the-art results were obtained from the corresponding papers. We averaged over five runs and report the evaluation metrics for a 0.5 probability threshold.

largely subject to the quality of the embeddings. Even worse, the relations obtained from the previous steps are used to automatically annotate all co-occurrences in a distant supervision-like fashion, which leads to even more noise.

What we show empirically here is that despite all that noise coming from the above unsupervised procedure, we manage to successfully fine tune a deep learning model so as to achieve comparable performance to a fully supervised model. BERT is the main factor driving this robustness to noise and it can be mainly attributed to the fact that it consists of a very deep language model (112M parameters) and that it is pre-trained generatively on a massive corpus (3.3B words). The significance of these results is further amplified if we consider how scarce are labeled data for tasks such as relation extraction.

4.3 Qualitative Analysis

Although we showed empirically that our proposed approach is consistently capable to achieve results comparable to the SOTA, we would like to further focus on what are the weak points of the syntax parsing method and of our approach compared to a fully supervised approach.

To this end we inspected manually examples of predictions of the three aforementioned methods on the CDR data set, focusing on failures of our method and the syntactic parsing method which acts as training signal of our approach. Table 4 shows some characteristic cases:

- In the first sentence, the syntactic parsing+verb mapping baseline (SP+VM) fails since the verb (*developed*) is not associated with cause. Conversely our method, BERT

Sentence	class	BERT+gold	BERT+SP+VM	SP+VM
A patient with renal disease developed coombs-positive DISEASE while receiving COMPOUND therapy.	cause	0.98	0.69	Null (developed)
Five cases of DISEASE during treatment of loiasis with COMPOUND.	cause	0.97	0.95	Null
COMPOUND induced bradycardia in a patient with DISEASE.	Null	0.04	0.99	cause (induced)
Neuroleptic drugs such as haloperidol, which block COMPOUND receptors, also cause DISEASE in rodents.	Null	0.92	0.99	treat (block)
The results provide new insight into the potential role of ectopic hilar granule cells in the COMPOUND model of DISEASE.	cause	0.89	0.05	Null (provide)

Table 4: Examples of predictions from the three methods on the CDR data set. $SP+VM$ stands for the syntactic parsing+verb mapping baseline, while $BERT+SP+VM$ stands for our method. $BERT+gold$ is a BERT model trained on the gold CDR training set. For $SP+VM$ we also provide the phrase verb in parentheses.

with SP+VM manages to model correctly the sentence and extract the relation.

- SP+VM fails in the second example for the same reason, although the sentence is relatively simple.

- The third sentence represents also an interesting case, with SP+VM being "tricked" by the verb *induced*. Our method also fails here, failing to attend correctly to the DISEASE masked entity.

- The fourth example represents a similar case, both BERT-based models are being tricked by the language. The SP+VM baseline is erroneously associating the verb *block* to the relation *treat* instead of cause.

- The fifth sentence resembles the first two: SP+VM fails to extract the relation for the same reason (verb in between). Our method fails too in that case, perhaps due to the relatively uncommon way that the causal relation is expressed (*COMPOUND model of DISEASE*.

While further inspecting the results, we also noticed a steady tendency of SP+VM to be able to capture relations in simpler (from a syntax perspective) and shorter sentences, while failing in the opposite case.

Overall, we observe, as expected, that the SP+VM method is largely dependent on the simplicity of the expressed relation. Our method is clearly dependent on the quality of the syntax parsing, but manages up to a point to overcome low quality training data. To conclude, we can safely assume that our method would further benefit by replacing the SP+VM method with a more sophisticated unsupervised approach as the training signal, a future direction that we intend to take.

5 Conclusions

This work has introduced a novel framework to deal with relation extraction tasks in settings where there is complete lack of supervision. Our method employs syntactic parsing and word embeddings to extract a small set of precise relations which are then used to annotate a larger corpus, in the same way as distant supervision. With that data, we fine tune a pre-trained BERT model to perform relation extraction.

We have empirically evaluated our method against two unsupervised baselines, a BERT model trained with gold or distantly supervised data and the current state-of-the-art. The results showed that our approach is significantly better than the unsupervised baselines, ranking slightly worse than the state-of-the-art in three out of four cases.

Apart from presenting a novel perspective on how to train a relation extraction model in the absence of supervision, our work also shows empirically that it is possible to successfully fine tune a deep pre-trained language model with substantially noisy data.

We are interested in extending this paradigm to other areas of natural language processing tasks or adjusting our framework for more complex relation extraction tasks, as well as using more sophisticated unsupervised methods as training signal.

Acknowledgments

We would like to thank Saatviga Sudhahar, for her insightful comments that greatly helped in improving this paper.

References

Michele Banko, Michael J Cafarella, Stephen Soderland, Matthew Broadhead, and Oren Etzioni. 2007. Open information extraction from the web. In *IJCAI*, pages 2670–2676.

Balu Bhasuran and Jeyakumar Natarajan. 2018. Automatic extraction of gene-disease associations from literature using joint ensemble learning. *PloS one*, 13(7):e0200699.

Àlex Bravo, Janet Piñero, Núria Queralt-Rosinach, Michael Rautschka, and Laura I Furlong. 2015. Extraction of relations between genes and diseases from text and large-scale data analysis: implications for translational research. *BMC bioinformatics*, 16(1):55.

Jacob Devlin, Ming-Wei Chang, Kenton Lee, and Kristina Toutanova. 2018. Bert: Pre-training of deep bidirectional transformers for language understanding. *arXiv preprint arXiv:1810.04805*.

Jinhyuk Lee, Wonjin Yoon, Sungdong Kim, Donghyeon Kim, Sunkyu Kim, Chan Ho So, and Jaewoo Kang. 2019. Biobert: pre-trained biomedical language representation model for biomedical text mining. *arXiv preprint arXiv:1901.08746*.

Omer Levy, Minjoon Seo, Eunsol Choi, and Luke Zettlemoyer. 2017. Zero-shot relation extraction via reading comprehension. *arXiv preprint arXiv:1706.04115*.

Jiao Li, Yueping Sun, Robin J Johnson, Daniela Sciaky, Chih-Hsuan Wei, Robert Leaman, Allan Peter Davis, Carolyn J Mattingly, Thomas C Wiegers, and Zhiyong Lu. 2016. Biocreative v cdr task corpus: a resource for chemical disease relation extraction. *Database*, 2016.

Yankai Lin, Shiqi Shen, Zhiyuan Liu, Huanbo Luan, and Maosong Sun. 2016. Neural relation extraction with selective attention over instances. In *Proceedings of the 54th Annual Meeting of the Association for Computational Linguistics (Volume 1: Long Papers)*, volume 1, pages 2124–2133.

Tomas Mikolov, Ilya Sutskever, Kai Chen, Greg S Corrado, and Jeff Dean. 2013. Distributed representations of words and phrases and their compositionality. In *Advances in neural information processing systems*, pages 3111–3119.

Mike Mintz, Steven Bills, Rion Snow, and Dan Jurafsky. 2009. Distant supervision for relation extraction without labeled data. In *Proceedings of the Joint Conference of the 47th Annual Meeting of the ACL and the 4th International Joint Conference on Natural Language Processing of the AFNLP: Volume 2-Volume 2*, pages 1003–1011. Association for Computational Linguistics.

Alec Radford, Karthik Narasimhan, Tim Salimans, and Ilya Sutskever. 2018a. Improving language understanding by generative pre-training. Technical report, Technical report, OpenAi.

Alec Radford, Jeffrey Wu, Rewon Child, David Luan, Dario Amodei, and Ilya Sutskever. 2018b. Language models are unsupervised multitask learners. Technical report, Technical report, OpenAi.

Alexander J Ratner, Christopher M De Sa, Sen Wu, Daniel Selsam, and Christopher Ré. 2016. Data programming: Creating large training sets, quickly. In *Advances in neural information processing systems*, pages 3567–3575.

Sebastian Riedel, Limin Yao, and Andrew McCallum. 2010. Modeling relations and their mentions without labeled text. In *Joint European Conference on Machine Learning and Knowledge Discovery in Databases*, pages 148–163. Springer.

Cicero dos Santos, Bing Xiang, and Bowen Zhou. 2015. Classifying relations by ranking with convolutional neural networks. In *Proceedings of the 53rd Annual Meeting of the Association for Computational Linguistics and the 7th International Joint Conference on Natural Language Processing (Volume 1: Long Papers)*, volume 1, pages 626–634.

Mihai Surdeanu, Julie Tibshirani, Ramesh Nallapati, and Christopher D Manning. 2012. Multi-instance multi-label learning for relation extraction. In *Proceedings of the 2012 joint conference on empirical methods in natural language processing and computational natural language learning*, pages 455–465. Association for Computational Linguistics.

Shingo Takamatsu, Issei Sato, and Hiroshi Nakagawa. 2012. Reducing wrong labels in distant supervision for relation extraction. In *Proceedings of the 50th Annual Meeting of the Association for Computational Linguistics: Long Papers-Volume 1*, pages 721–729. Association for Computational Linguistics.

Dacheng Tao, Xiaoou Tang, Xuelong Li, and Xindong Wu. 2006. Asymmetric bagging and random subspace for support vector machines-based relevance feedback in image retrieval. *IEEE Transactions on Pattern Analysis & Machine Intelligence*, (7):1088–1099.

Erik M Van Mulligen, Annie Fourrier-Reglat, David Gurwitz, Mariam Molokhia, Ainhoa Nieto, Gianluca Trifiro, Jan A Kors, and Laura I Furlong. 2012. The eu-adr corpus: annotated drugs, diseases, targets, and their relationships. *Journal of biomedical informatics*, 45(5):879–884.

Shikhar Vashishth, Rishabh Joshi, Sai Suman Prayaga, Chiranjib Bhattacharyya, and Partha Talukdar. 2018. Reside: Improving distantly-supervised neural relation extraction using side information. In *Proceedings of the 2018 Conference on Empirical Methods in Natural Language Processing*, pages 1257–1266.

Ashish Vaswani, Noam Shazeer, Niki Parmar, Jakob Uszkoreit, Llion Jones, Aidan N Gomez, Łukasz Kaiser, and Illia Polosukhin. 2017. Attention is all you need. In *Advances in neural information processing systems*, pages 5998–6008.

Patrick Verga, Emma Strubell, and Andrew McCallum. 2018. Simultaneously self-attending to all mentions for full-abstract biological relation extraction. In *Proceedings of the 2018 Conference of the North American Chapter of the Association for Computational Linguistics: Human Language Technologies, Volume 1 (Long Papers)*, volume 1, pages 872–884.

Linlin Wang, Zhu Cao, Gerard de Melo, and Zhiyuan Liu. 2016. Relation classification via multi-level attention cnns. In *Proceedings of the 54th Annual Meeting of the Association for Computational Linguistics (Volume 1: Long Papers)*, volume 1, pages 1298–1307.

Yi Wu, David Bamman, and Stuart Russell. 2017. Adversarial training for relation extraction. In *Proceedings of the 2017 Conference on Empirical Methods in Natural Language Processing*, pages 1778–1783.

Mohamed Yahya, Steven Whang, Rahul Gupta, and Alon Halevy. 2014. Renoun: Fact extraction for nominal attributes. In *Proceedings of the 2014 Conference on Empirical Methods in Natural Language Processing (EMNLP)*, pages 325–335.

Daojian Zeng, Kang Liu, Yubo Chen, and Jun Zhao. 2015. Distant supervision for relation extraction via piecewise convolutional neural networks. In *Proceedings of the 2015 Conference on Empirical Methods in Natural Language Processing*, pages 1753–1762.

Daojian Zeng, Kang Liu, Siwei Lai, Guangyou Zhou, Jun Zhao, et al. 2014. Relation classification via convolutional deep neural network.

Wenyuan Zeng, Yankai Lin, Zhiyuan Liu, and Maosong Sun. 2016. Incorporating relation paths in neural relation extraction. *arXiv preprint arXiv:1609.07479*.

Yukun Zhu, Ryan Kiros, Rich Zemel, Ruslan Salakhutdinov, Raquel Urtasun, Antonio Torralba, and Sanja Fidler. 2015. Aligning books and movies: Towards story-like visual explanations by watching movies and reading books. In *Proceedings of the IEEE international conference on computer vision*, pages 19–27.

Domain Adaptation with BERT-based Domain Classification and Data Selection

Xiaofei Ma, Peng Xu, Zhiguo Wang, Ramesh Nallapati, Bing Xiang
AWS AI Labs
{xiaofeim, pengx, zhiguow, rnallapa, bxiang}@amazon.com

Abstract

The performance of deep neural models can deteriorate substantially when there is a domain shift between training and test data. For example, the pre-trained BERT model can be easily fine-tuned with just one additional output layer to create a state-of-the-art model for a wide range of tasks. However, the fine-tuned BERT model suffers considerably at zero-shot when applied to a different domain. In this paper, we present a novel two-step domain adaptation framework based on curriculum learning and domain-discriminative data selection. The domain adaptation is conducted in a mostly unsupervised manner using a small target domain validation set for hyper-parameter tuning. We tested the framework on four large public datasets with different domain similarities and task types. Our framework outperforms a popular discrepancy-based domain adaptation method on most transfer tasks while consuming only a fraction of the training budget.

1 Introduction

Modern deep NLP models with millions of parameters are powerful learners in that they can easily adapt to a new learning task and dataset when enough supervision is given. However, they are also very fragile when deployed in the wild since the data distribution and sometimes even the task type can be very different between the training and inference time. Domain adaptation (Csurka, 2017), a prominent approach to mitigate this problem, aims to leverage labeled data in one or more related source domains to learn a classifier for unseen or unlabeled data in a target domain.

Fine-tuning deep neural networks (Chu et al., 2016) is a popular supervised approach for domain adaptation in which a base network is trained with the source data, and then the first n layers of the base network are fixed while the target domain labeled data is used to fine-tune the last few layers of the network. However, this approach requires a significant amount of labeled data from the target domain to be successful.

While classical methods such as instance reweighting and feature transformation (Pan and Yang, 2010) are among the most popular and effective early solutions of domain adaptation for classical machine learning algorithms, deep learning architectures specifically designed for domain adaptation is more promising for deep domain adaptation. The major idea in unsupervised domain adaptation is to learn a domain invariant representation (Wang and Deng, 2018) leveraging both labeled data from the source domains and unlabeled data from the target domain. Various methods and architectures have been proposed which often fall into discrepancy-based or adversarial-based domain adaptation categories. In discrepancy-based methods, domain discrepancy based on maximum mean discrepancy (MMD) (Smola et al., 2006) or Wasserstein Distance (Shen et al., 2017) defined between corresponding activation layers of the two streams of the Siamese architecture is often used as a regularization term to enforce the learning of domain non-discriminative representations. In adversarial-based approaches, which can be either generative or non-generative, the aim is to encourage domain confusion through an adversarial objective. In the generative approach, a Generative Adversarial Network (GAN) is used to generate synthetic target data to pair with synthetic source data to share label information (Liu and Tuzel, 2016). Inspired by GAN, in the non-generative approach, a domain confusion loss produced by the domain discriminator helps to learn the domain-invariant representations. For example, Ganin et al. implemented a domain-adversarial net-

Proceedings of the 2nd Workshop on Deep Learning Approaches for Low-Resource NLP (DeepLo), pages 76–83
Hong Kong, China, November 3, 2019. ©2019 Association for Computational Linguistics
https://doi.org/10.18653/v1/P17

work in which unsupervised domain adaptation is achieved by adding a domain classifier. The domain classifier is trained via a gradient reversal layer that multiplies the gradient by a certain negative constant during the backpropagation. As the training progresses, the approach promotes the emergence of a representation that is discriminative for the main learning task and indiscriminate with respect to the shift between the domains. However, such type of models are usually hard to train since the optimization problem involves a minimization with respect to some parameters, as well as a maximization with respect to the others.

Very early approaches in NLP utilized instance re-weighting (Jiang and Zhai, 2007) and target data co-training (Chen et al., 2011) to achieve domain adaptation. Recently, Denoising Autoencoders (Glorot et al., 2011), domain discrepancy regularization and domain adversarial training (Shah et al., 2019; Shen et al., 2017) have been employed to learn a domain invariant representation for neural network models. Many domain adaptation studies have focused on tasks such as sentiment analysis (Glorot et al., 2011; Shen et al., 2017) , Part-Of-Speech (POS) tagging (Ruder et al., 2017a) and paraphrase detection (Shah et al., 2019), and tested on neural network models such as multilayer perceptron (MLP) and Long Short-term Memory (LSTM). In terms of multiple source domain adaptation, while some of the methods of single-source adaptation can be directly extended to the multiple sources case, models that specially designed for multiple sources domain adaptation such as the mixture of experts and knowledge adaptation (teacher-student network) (Ruder et al., 2017b) are more effective.

BERT model (Devlin et al., 2018) is one of the latest models that leverage heavily on language model pre-training. It has achieved state-of-the-art performance in many natural language understanding tasks ranging from sequence classification and sequence-pair classification to question answering. Although pre-trained BERT can be easily fine-tuned with just one additional output layer on a supervised dataset, sometimes the zero-shot transfer of the fine-tuned model from a source domain is necessary due to the very limited labeled data in the target domain. The performance of the fine-tuned BERT can deteriorate substantially if there is a domain shift between the fine-tuning and the test data (see section 4.3). Due

to the complex attention mechanisms and large parameter size, it is hard to train BERT for domain adaptation using the domain-adversarial approach. Our initial experiments demonstrated the unsteadiness of this approach when applied to BERT. Unsupervised language model (LM) fine-tuning method (Howard and Ruder, 2018) consisting of general-domain LM pre-training and target task LM fine-tuning is effective using a AWD-LSTM language model on many text classification tasks such as sentimental analysis, question classification and topic classification. However, due to the unique objective of BERT language model pre-training (masked LM and next sentence prediction) which requires multi-sentences natural language paragraphs, unsupervised fine-tuning of BERT LM does not apply to many sentence-pair classification datasets.

In this work, we propose a novel domain adaptation framework, in which the idea of domain-adversarial training is effectively executed in two separate steps. In the first step, a BERT-based domain classifier is trained on data from different domains with domain labels. In the second step, a small subset of source domain data is selected based on the domain classifier for fine-tuning BERT. The order of presentation of the selected source domain data to the model learner (training curriculum) also plays an important role and is determined by the point-wise domain probability. We demonstrate the effectiveness of our framework by comparing it against an MMD-based domain adaptation method and a naive zero-shot baseline. Our method achieved the best performance on most transfer tasks while only consuming a portion of the training budget.

2 Related Work

Our method is inspired by the work on curriculum learning and recent work on data selection for transfer learning.

Curriculum Learning: Curriculum Learning (Bengio et al., 2009) deals with the question of how to use prior knowledge about the difficulty of the training examples, to boost the rate of learning and the performance of the final model. The ranking or weighting of the training examples is used to guide the order of presentation of examples to the learner. The idea is to build a curriculum of progressively harder samples in order to significantly accelerate a neural network's training. While curriculum learning can leverage label information (loss of the model, training progress) (Weinshall and Amir, 2018) to guide data selection, this work assumes no or few labeled data in the new domain.

Data Selection: Not all the data points from the source domain are equally important for target domain transfer. Irrelevant source data points only add noise and overfit the training model. Recent work from Ruder and Plank, applied Bayesian optimization to learn a scoring function to rank the source data points. Data selection method was also used by Tsvetkov et al. to learn the curriculum for task-specific word representation learning, and by Axelrod et al.; Duh et al. for machine translation using a neural language model.

3 Approach

In this section, we propose a domain adaptation framework based on domain-discriminative data selection. Specifically, instead of training a deep neural network model in a domain-adversarial way, we effectively execute the idea in two separate steps. In the first step, we train a domain classifier with the same model architecture on the data from different domains with domain labels. In the second step, we select a subset of source domain data based on the domain probability from the domain classifier, and train the original model on the selected source data. We further design the training curriculum by presenting first the data points that are most similar to the target domain as ranked by the domain probability. Compared with the integrated training of domain classifier and task classifier based on batch-wise input of source and target data, the advantage of our two-step approach is that all the source data can be ranked at the same time and only the source data that are most similar to the target domain are selected for training the task classifier. We apply this framework to the domain adaptation of the fine-tuned BERT model.

BERT Domain Classifier BERT representations are very discriminative of texts from different domains due to the extensive language model pre-training. A t-SNE plot of BERT embeddings is presented at Figure 3, on which the data points from different domains are grouped into well-separated regions. In order to effectively select source data that is most similar to the target domain distribution, we train a BERT-based domain classifier on mixed data points with domain labels.

The probability score from the domain classifier quantifies the domain similarity.

Learning Curriculum As demonstrated in many curriculum learning papers, the order of training data presented to the learning algorithm plays an important role in convergence rate and final model performance. The idea is to build a curriculum of progressively harder samples so that a neural network can learn from easy samples first and gradually adjust its parameters. As part of the proposed domain adaptation framework, we propose a learning curriculum based on the domain probability from the domain classifier. In the context of domain adaptation, an "easy" source sample is a sample very similar to the target domain data, while a "hard" sample is a sample very different from the target domain data.

Domain Regularization Method We compare our framework with a popular domain adaptation method: MMD-based domain regularization. Specifically, we enforce domain regularization by minimizing the maximum mean discrepancy (MMD) in the BERT latent space between the source and target domains. Formally, the squared MMD between the probability distributions P and Q in the reproducing kernel Hilbert space $\mathcal{H}_k$ (RKHS) with kernel k is defined as:

$$d_k^2(P, Q) := \|\mathbf{E}_P[x] - \mathbf{E}_Q[x]\|_{\mathcal{H}_k}^2$$

With that, we have the following domain regularized training objective for the BERT model:

$$\min_\theta \frac{1}{S} \Sigma_{(x_i, y_i) \in S} \mathscr{L}(x_i, y_i; \theta) + \lambda \cdot d_k^2(D_s, D_t; \theta)$$

where S is the collection of labeled source domain data, and λ is the regularization parameter. We choose rational quadratic kernel of the form:

$$k(x, x') = \sigma^2 (1 + \frac{(x - x')^2}{2al^2})^{-\alpha}$$

as the characteristic kernel in the experiment. The lengthscale l determines the length of the "wiggles" in the function. The parameter α determines the relative weighting of large-scale and small-scale variations.

4 Experiment

In this section, we conduct both qualitative and quantitative studies of the proposed method, and compare its performance against the MMD-based domain regularization method and naive zero-shot transfer from the source domain. In the experiments, in order to determine the optimal number of data points selected from the source domain, we set aside a small target domain dataset for validation. Starting from only a hundred examples, we double the training data size every time we observe a significant change in transfer performance evaluated on the validation set.

4.1 Datasets

We tested our framework on four large public datasets across three task categories: natural language inference (SNLI and MNLI), answer sentence selection (QNLI) and paraphrase detection (Quora). Large datasets usually have a much smaller variance in evaluation metrics compared with smaller datasets. We used the pre-processed datasets from GLUE natural language understanding benchmark (Wang et al., 2018). A summary of the dataset statistics and the details of the experiment setup are presented in Table 1.

Task Category	Dataset	Train Size	Dev Size
Natural Language Inference	SNLI	510,711	9,831
Natural Language Inference	MNLI	392,702	9,815
Answer Sentence Selection	QNLI	108,436	5,732
Paraphrase Detection	Quora	363,847	40,430

Table 1: Summary of the datasets

SNLI The Stanford Natural Language Inference (SNLI) Corpus (Bowman et al., 2015) is a collection of 570k human-written English sentence pairs supporting the task of natural language inference. Given a premise sentence and a hypothesis sentence, the task is to predict whether the premise entails the hypothesis (entailment), contradicts the hypothesis (contradiction), or neither (neutral). In order to make the label set the same across all the datasets, we convert the original three-label classification task into a binary classification task with "entailment" as the positive label, and "contradiction" and "neutral" as negative.

MNLI The Multi-Genre Natural Language Inference (MNLI) corpus (Williams et al., 2017) is a crowd-sourced collection of 433k sentence pairs annotated with textual entailment information. The corpus is modeled on the SNLI corpus but differs in that it covers a range of genres including transcribed speech, fiction, and government reports, and supports a distinctive cross-genre generalization evaluation. We used the training data from GLUE but evaluate only on the matched (in-domain) section. Similar as in SNLI, we convert the three-label classification task into a binary classification task.

QNLI The Question-answering Natural Language Inference (QNLI) is a dataset converted from the Stanford Question Answering Dataset (SQuAD) (Rajpurkar et al., 2016). Although its name contains "natural language inference", the text domain and task type of QNLI are fundamentally different from those of SNLI and MNLI. The original SQuAD dataset consists of question-paragraph pairs, where one of the sentences in the paragraph (drawn from Wikipedia) contains the answer to the corresponding question (written by an annotator). GLUE converts the task into sentence pair classification by forming a pair between each question and each sentence in the corresponding context and filtering out pairs with low lexical overlap between the question and the context sentence. The task is to determine whether the context sentence contains the correct answer to the question.

QQP The Quora Question Pairs (QQP) dataset is a collection of question pairs from the community question-answering website Quora (Wang et al., 2017). The task is to determine whether a pair of questions are semantically equivalent. One source of negative examples are pairs of "related questions" which, although pertaining to similar topics, are not truly semantically equivalent. Due to community nature, the ground-truth labels contain some amount of noise.

4.2 Experiment Setup

BERT Domain Classifier The setup for training the BERT domain classifier is shown in Figure 1. Basically, the setup is similar to that for fine-tuning BERT on sequence-pair classification task (since we test our method on sequence-pair classification tasks). We take the hidden state of the [CLS] token of the input sequence pair, and feed it into a two-layer feedforward neural network with hidden units of 100 and 10 in each layer and ReLU as the activation function. The label for each data point is the domain that the data point belongs to.

MMD-based Domain Regularization The goal of domain regularization is to train the BERT model on the source domain but learn domain-invariant latent representations. The computation pipeline of training BERT model using MMD-based domain regularization is presented in Fig-

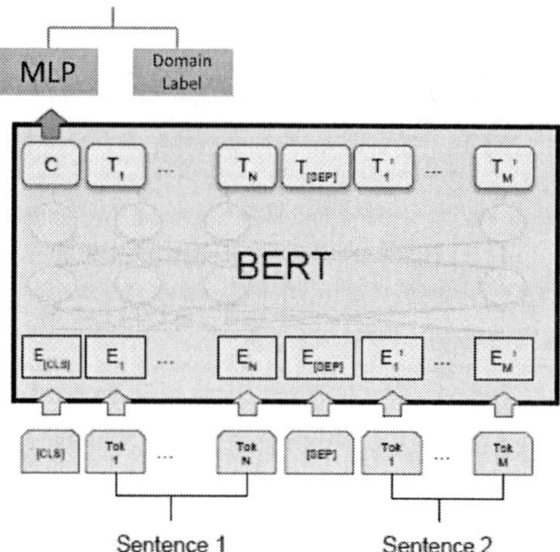

Figure 1: Setup for training a BERT domain classifier. Picture adapted from (Devlin et al., 2018)

ure 2. Basically, we feed both labeled source domain data and unlabelled target domain data to the model, a classification loss is calculated based on source labels and model prediction, and an MMD domain loss is calculated from the BERT representations of source domain data and target domain data. We combine the two losses as the training objective. It is straightforward to optimize this objective using stochastic gradient methods.

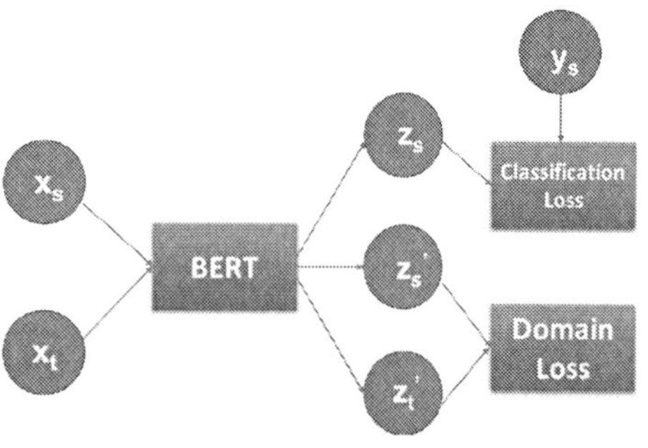

Figure 2: Setup for BERT domain adaptation with MMD-based domain regularization.

Experiment Details The experiments were conducted in three phases. In the first phase, a BERT-based domain classifier is trained to distinguish samples from a pair of datasets. In the second phase, all source domain training samples are ranked based on the output from the BERT domain classifier, and a subset of data points is selected from the source domain training set. The selected subset of source data and their ground truth labels are then used to fine-tune a BERT model in the

final phase.

We train one binary domain classifier for each pair of source-target datasets. For each dataset, $5,000$ data points were randomly selected to make up the training set, and another $1,000$ data points were sampled as the test set. We train the BERT domain classifier for a fixed step of 100, using a small learning rate of $2e - 6$ and batch size of 64. Due to the domain discriminative nature of pre-trained BERT representations, the BERT domain classifier can easily achieve an accuracy $> 99\%$ domain classification performance on the holdout test dataset.

The trained domain classifier is then used to predict the target domain probability for each data point from the source domain. Source data points with the highest target domain probability are selected for fine-tuning BERT for domain adaptation. For each target domain, we set aside a small validation set (1 percent of the target training set) for tuning the hyper-parameters such as batch size. We incrementally increase the size of the selected source data. For each batch size and number of selected source data combination, we fine-tuned the BERT model for 10 epochs, and record the best performance for each configuration.

4.3 Results

BERT Representations The fact that pre-trained BERT can be easily fine-tuned with just one additional output layer to create state-of-the-art models for a wide range of tasks suggests that BERT representations are potential universal text embeddings. In order to visualize BERT representations, we randomly select $5,000$ training samples from each dataset and extract the BERT embeddings of them. Figure 3 presents the t-SNE plot of the BERT representations. As we can see from the figure, data points from different datasets are grouped into well-separated regions. This shows that BERT is extremely effective at mapping text from different domains to different locations within its representation space.

Transfer Performance The transfer performance of different methods is presented in Table 2. As the first baseline, we evaluate the performance of naive zero-shot transfer of fine-tuned BERT models. The results are presented in the column "NZS". Each fine-tuned BERT model is trained to convergence using all the source domain data, and zero-shot transferred to the target do-

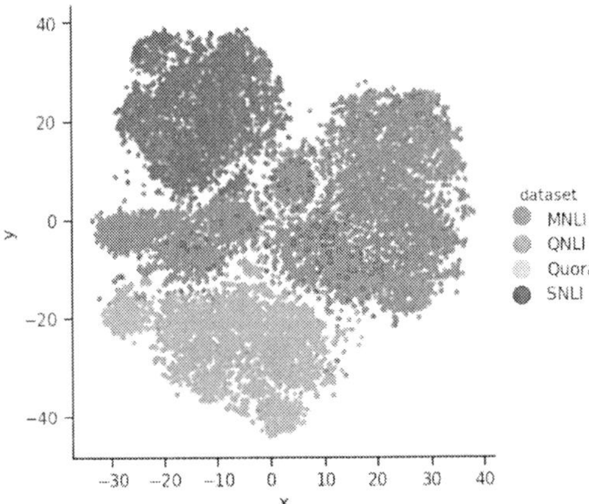

Figure 3: t-SNE plot of [CLS] token activations from the second-to-last encoder of BERT for four datasets in this paper. Second-to-last layer is used since the last layer embeddings may be biased to the target of BERT pre-training tasks.

Source	Target	IFT	NZS	MMD	DDS	% Data
MNLI	QNLI	85.3	49.8	58.0	**58.5**	0.1 %
MNLI	Quora	89.3	73.7	71.5	**73.9**	26.1 %
MNLI	SNLI	92.9	87.4	87.6	**88.3**	26.1 %
QNLI	MNLI	88.3	63.7	66.0	**67.2**	0.4 %
QNLI	Quora	89.3	61.8	66.1	**67.6**	1.5 %
QNLI	SNLI	92.9	56.1	65.3	**66.6**	0.4 %
Quora	MNLI	88.3	71.0	70.6	**83.6**	3.5 %
Quora	QNLI	85.3	50.8	58.8	**59.1**	1.8 %
Quora	SNLI	92.9	69.1	**72.4**	71.6	1.8 %
SNLI	MNLI	88.3	77.0	**82.2**	80.2	5.0 %
SNLI	QNLI	85.3	49.0	54.9	**56.7**	0.1 %
SNLI	Quora	89.3	67.0	70.8	**70.9**	1.3 %

Table 2: Transfer performance (accuracy) of different domain adaptation methods. "IFT": in-domain fine-tuning. "NZS": naive zero-shot. "MMD": MMD-based domain regularization. "DDS": discriminative data selection. "% Data": percentage of source domain data selected in DDS method.

main. While in-domain fine-tuned BERT models usually achieve state-of-the-art performance, their zero-shot performance on the target domain can be significantly degraded. For transfers between dissimilar domains such as SNLI to QNLI, naive zero-shot can lead to more than 40% loss in accuracy compared with in-domain supervised training. By learning a domain invariant representation, the MMD-based domain adaptation method (column "MMD") significantly outperforms the naive zero-shot baseline in almost all the transfer tasks. However, our discriminative data selection method (column "DDS") achieves the best transfer performance in 10 out of the 12 pairwise transfer tasks while training on only a small fraction of source domain data (column "% Data"). The relative improvement is as large as 18% over the naive zero-shot and 3.3% over the MMD-based domain regularization. Even though we doubled the training data size every time we observe an increase in transfer performance, the cumulative training time is still much smaller than fine-tuning on the whole source dataset. Compared with the batch-wise iterative adaptation or regularization techniques, our method ranks all the source domain data at the same time, and the learner is trained on the most target-domain-similar data first. This difference is critical since early stage updates usually play an important role in the final model performance.

The Effect of Learning Curriculum In order to evaluate the effectiveness of our learning cur-riculum, we designed experiments to compare the learning curves of five learning curricula. The five learning curricula are described as the following: "Most Similar": is the curriculum adopted in this paper, in which all the source training samples are ranked based on the target domain probability. A subset of source data is selected and presented to the model learner according to the curriculum that the samples with the highest target domain probability are trained first. "Most Dissimilar": the curriculum ranks the source data reversely according to the target domain probability, selects and trains the most dissimilar samples first. In "Random Sample" curriculum, a subset of source samples are randomly selected and fed into the training model. In "Random Order within Selected" case, the subset is selected first based on target domain probability. However, the order of presentation during training is random. In "Reverse Order within Selected" scenario, the subset is selected based on target domain proba-bility, and the order of presentation during train-ing is based on the reverse order of target domain probability. As we can see from the figure, both the data selection strategy and learning curriculum have a clear effect on the transfer performance. "Most Similar" curriculum enjoys the highest con-vergence rate when trained on a small amount of source data, while "Most Dissimilar" curriculum has the lowest convergence rate. The transfer per-formance of all the learning curricula benefits ini-tially from adding more training data and eventu-ally saturates. Overall, "Most Similar" curriculum converges to the best performance among other curricula. The observation demonstrates the effectiveness of using target domain probability as a measure of learning "hardness".

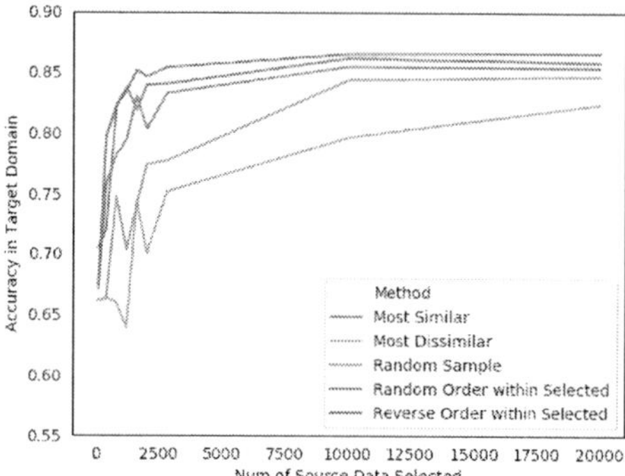

Figure 4: Transfer performance from MNLI to SNLI for five learning curricula. "Most Similar" curriculum achieves the best convergence rate and transfer performance.

5 Conclusion

In conclusion, we propose a novel domain adaptation framework for fine-tuned BERT models through a two-step domain-discriminative data selection and curriculum learning. Our approach significantly outperforms the baseline models on four large datasets, which demonstrates the effectiveness of both the data selection strategy and curriculum design. The method can be readily extended to multi-source domain adaptation, or applied to few-shot learning scenarios in which the selected source domain data can be used to augment the limited target domain training data.

References

Amittai Axelrod, Xiaodong He, and Jianfeng Gao. 2011. Domain Adaptation Via Pseudo In-Domain Data Selection. *EMNLP (Empirical Methods in Natural Language Processing)*, pages 355–362.

Yoshua Bengio, Jérôme Louradour, Ronan Collobert, and Jason Weston. 2009. Curriculum learning. *Proceedings of the 26th annual international conference on machine learning*, pages 41–48.

Samuel R. Bowman, Gabor Angeli, Christopher Potts, and Christopher D. Manning. 2015. A large annotated corpus for learning natural language inference.

Minmin Chen, Kilian Q Weinberger, and John Blitzer. 2011. Co-training for domain adaptation. *Advances in neural information processing systems*, pages 2456–2464.

Brian Chu, Vashisht Madhavan, Oscar Beijbom, Judy Hoffman, and Trevor Darrell. 2016. Best Practices for Fine-Tuning Visual Classifiers to New Domains. *ECCV Workshops*, pages 435–442.

Gabriela Csurka. 2017. A comprehensive survey on domain adaptation for visual applications. In *Advances in Computer Vision and Pattern Recognition*, 9783319583464, pages 1–35.

Jacob Devlin, Ming-Wei Chang, Kenton Lee, and Kristina Toutanova. 2018. BERT: Pre-training of Deep Bidirectional Transformers for Language Understanding.

Kevin Duh, Graham Neubig, Katsuhito Sudoh, and Hajime Tsukada. 2013. Adaptation Data Selection using Neural Language Models: Experiments in Machine Translation. In *ACL-2013: 51st Annual Meeting of the Association for Computational Linguistics*, 1, pages 678–683.

Yaroslav Ganin, Evgeniya Ustinova, Hana Ajakan, Pascal Germain, Hugo Larochelle, François Laviolette, Mario Marchand, and Victor Lempitsky. 2015. Domain-Adversarial Training of Neural Networks. 17:1–35.

Xavier Glorot, Antoine Bordes, and Yoshua Bengio. 2011. Domain Adaptation for Large-Scale Sentiment Classification: A Deep Learning Approach. *Proceedings of the 28th International Conference on Machine Learning*, (1):513–520.

Jeremy Howard and Sebastian Ruder. 2018. Universal Language Model Fine-tuning for Text Classification.

Jing Jiang and Chengxiang Zhai. 2007. Instance Weighting for Domain Adaptation in NLP. *Proceedings of the 45th Annual Meeting of the Association of Computational Linguistics*, (October):264–271.

Ming-yu Liu and Oncel Tuzel. 2016. Coupled Generative Adversarial Networks. (Nips).

Sinno Jialin Pan and Qiang Yang. 2010. A survey on transfer learning. *IEEE Transactions on Knowledge and Data Engineering*, 22(10):1345–1359.

Pranav Rajpurkar, Jian Zhang, Konstantin Lopyrev, and Percy Liang. 2016. SQuAD: 100,000+ Questions for Machine Comprehension of Text. (ii).

Sebastian Ruder, Joachim Bingel, Isabelle Augenstein, and Anders Søgaard. 2017a. Learning what to share between loosely related tasks.

Sebastian Ruder, Parsa Ghaffari, and John G. Breslin. 2017b. Knowledge Adaptation: Teaching to Adapt.

Sebastian Ruder and Barbara Plank. 2017. Learning to select data for transfer learning with Bayesian Optimization.

Darsh Shah, Tao Lei, Alessandro Moschitti, Salvatore Romeo, and Preslav Nakov. 2019. Adversarial Domain Adaptation for Duplicate Question Detection. pages 1056–1063.

Jian Shen, Yanru Qu, Weinan Zhang, and Yong Yu. 2017. Wasserstein Distance Guided Representation Learning for Domain Adaptation.

A. J. Smola, H.-P. Kriegel, M. J. Rasch, B. Scholkopf, K. M. Borgwardt, and A. Gretton. 2006. Integrating structured biological data by Kernel Maximum Mean Discrepancy. *Bioinformatics*, 22(14):e49–e57.

Yulia Tsvetkov, Manaal Faruqui, Wang Ling, Brian MacWhinney, and Chris Dyer. 2016. Learning the Curriculum with Bayesian Optimization for Task-Specific Word Representation Learning. pages 130–139.

Alex Wang, Amapreet Singh, Julian Michael, Felix Hill, Omer Levy, and Samuel R Bowman. 2018. GLUE: A Multi-Task Benchmark and Analysis Platform for Natural Language Understanding.

Mei Wang and Weihong Deng. 2018. Deep visual domain adaptation: A survey. *Neurocomputing*, 312:135–153.

Zhiguo Wang, Wael Hamza, and Radu Florian. 2017. Bilateral multi-perspective matching for natural language sentences. *IJCAI International Joint Conference on Artificial Intelligence*, pages 4144–4150.

Daphna Weinshall and Dan Amir. 2018. Theory of Curriculum Learning, with Convex Loss Functions. pages 1–18.

Adina Williams, Nikita Nangia, and Samuel R. Bowman. 2017. A Broad-Coverage Challenge Corpus for Sentence Understanding through Inference. pages 1112–1122.

Empirical Evaluation of Active Learning Techniques for Neural MT

Xiangkai Zeng[1*]   **Sarthak Garg**[2]   **Rajen Chatterjee**[2]   **Udhyakumar Nallasamy**[2]   **Matthias Paulik**[2]

[1]Carnegie Mellon University

[2]Apple Inc.

xiangkaiz@cs.cmu.edu,{sarthak_garg, rajen_c, udhay, mpaulik}@apple.com

Abstract

Active learning (AL) for machine translation (MT) has been well-studied for the phrase-based MT paradigm. Several AL algorithms for data sampling have been proposed over the years. However, given the rapid advancement in neural methods, these algorithms have not been thoroughly investigated in the context of neural MT (NMT). In this work, we address this missing aspect by conducting a systematic comparison of different AL methods in a simulated AL framework. Our experimental setup to compare different AL methods uses: i) State-of-the-art NMT architecture to achieve realistic results; and ii) the same dataset (WMT'13 English-Spanish) to have fair comparison across different methods. We then demonstrate how recent advancements in unsupervised pre-training and paraphrastic embedding can be used to improve existing AL methods. Finally, we propose a neural extension for an AL sampling method used in the context of phrase-based MT - Round Trip Translation Likelihood (RTTL). RTTL uses a bidirectional translation model to estimate the loss of information during translation and outperforms previous methods.

1 Introduction

Active learning (AL) is an iterative supervised learning procedure where the learner is able to query an oracle for labeling new data points. Since the learner chooses the data points for annotation, the amount of labeling needed to learn a concept can be much lower than annotating the whole unlabeled dataset (Balcan et al., 2009). This approach is useful in low-resource scenarios where unlabeled data is abundant but manual labeling is expensive. AL has been successfully applied to many areas of NLP like classification, sequence labeling, spoken language understanding (Cohn

et al., 1994; Guo and Greiner, 2007; Dagan and Engelson, 1995; Settles and Craven, 2008; Tur et al., 2005) as well as machine translation (MT) (Ambati, 2011; Haffari et al., 2009; Eck, 2008; Peris and Casacuberta, 2018; Zhang et al., 2018). In MT, most of the AL methods have been investigated under the phrase-based paradigm. Although neural MT has dominated the field (Barrault et al., 2019), there has only been limited effort to investigate and compare existing AL algorithms in this newer paradigm. The few recently published papers in this direction (Peris and Casacuberta, 2018; Zhang et al., 2018) use LSTM-based MT systems, whereas, the latest state-of-the-art systems are based on the Transformer architecture (Vaswani et al., 2017). Moreover, these papers either investigate different algorithms of the same class or compare only a handful of methods from different classes. Thus a global picture showing the effect of different AL methods on the same dataset for the state-of-the-art (SotA) MT system has been missing.

In this work, we fill this missing gap by performing a comprehensive evaluation of different AL algorithms on a publicly available dataset (WMT'13) using the SotA NMT architecture. To make our analysis thorough, we take into account different evaluation metrics to avoid any bias arising because of similarity between the evaluation metric and some components of the AL algorithm. Finally, we propose two extensions of existing AL algorithms. One leverages recent advances in paraphrastic embeddings (Wieting and Gimpel, 2018) and other is based on round-trip translation - a neural variant of the approach proposed in phrase-based MT (Haffari et al., 2009). Both of these approaches outperform existing methods with the latter showing the best results.

---

* Work done during internship at Apple Inc.

Proceedings of the 2nd Workshop on Deep Learning Approaches for Low-Resource NLP (DeepLo), pages 84–93

Hong Kong, China, November 3, 2019. ©2019 Association for Computational Linguistics

https://doi.org/10.18653/v1/P17

2 Active Learning Framework

We simulate AL in a batch setup because it is more practical to send batches of data for manual translation rather than a single sentence at disjoint intervals of time. Algorithm 1 summarizes the procedure. It expects: i) a labeled parallel corpus ($\mathcal{L}$), which is used to train the NMT system ($\mathcal{M}$); ii) an unlabeled monolingual corpus ($\mathcal{U}$), which is used to sample new data points for manual translation; iii) a scoring function (ψ), which is used to estimate the importance of data points in ($\mathcal{U}$); and iv) batch size (B), which indicates the number of data points to sample in each iteration.[1] In practice, the AL algorithm will iterate until we exhaust the budget for annotation (step 2). However, in our simulation we already have reference translations for all the unlabeled data points (see Footnote 1), therefore, we iterate until we exhaust all the data points in $\mathcal{U}$. In each iteration, we first train an NMT system from scratch using $\mathcal{L}$ (step 3). We then score all the sentences in $\mathcal{U}$ with ψ that takes in to account $\mathcal{L}$, $\mathcal{U}$, and $\mathcal{M}$ (step 4-6). The ψ function is a key component in all AL algorithms, which is discussed in detail along with its variants in the next section. We then select the highest scoring B sentences for manual translation (step 7-8). These sentences are removed from $\mathcal{U}$ (step 9), and added to $\mathcal{L}$ along with their reference translations (step 10). The algorithm then proceeds to step 2 for the next round.

Algorithm 1 Batch Active Learning for NMT

1: **Given:** Parallel data $\mathcal{L}$, Monolingual source language data $\mathcal{U}$, Sampling strategy $\psi(\cdot)$, Sampling batch size B.
2: **while** Budget $\neq$ EMPTY **do**
3:     $\mathcal{M} = TrainNMTsystem(\mathcal{L})$;
4:     **for** $x \in \mathcal{U}$ **do**
5:        $f(x) = \psi(x, \mathcal{U}, \mathcal{L}, \mathcal{M})$;
6:     **end for**
7:     $X_B = TopScoringSamples(f(x), B)$;
8:     $Y_B = HumanTranslation(X_B)$;
9:     $\mathcal{U} = \mathcal{U} - X_B$;
10:     $\mathcal{L} = \mathcal{L} \cup \{X_B, Y_B\}$;
11: **end while**
12: **return** $\mathcal{L}$

---

[1] In our simulation, $\mathcal{U}$ is basically the source side of a parallel corpus $\mathcal{L}'$ ($\mathcal{L}' \neq \mathcal{L}$), and to label new data points from $\mathcal{U}$ we simply extract the corresponding references from $\mathcal{L}'$ rather than asking a human annotator.

3 Methodology

In this section we outline the AL methods - i.e. the scoring functions (ψ), which have been proposed to work best for NMT, SMT and various sequence labeling tasks (Peris and Casacuberta, 2018; Zhang et al., 2018; Ambati, 2011; Haffari et al., 2009; Settles and Craven, 2008). These approaches can be broadly categorized into two classes: model-driven and data-driven.

Model-driven approaches sample instances based on the model, the labeled dataset and the unlabeled dataset, i.e. $\psi(x, \dots) = \psi(x, \mathcal{M}, \mathcal{U}, \mathcal{L})$. These methods receive direct signal from the model, which can potentially help in sampling more sentences from regions of the input space, where the model is weak. We first describe several model-driven approaches from the above works, all of which sample instances where the model $\mathcal{M}$ is least certain about the prediction. We then propose Round Trip Translation Likelihood, a neural extension of an existing method, which outperforms other model-driven methods substantially.

Data-driven approaches on the other hand only rely on $\mathcal{U}$ and $\mathcal{L}$ to sample sentences, i.e. $\psi(x, \dots) = \psi(x, \mathcal{U}, \mathcal{L})$. Since these methods are model independent, model training in step 3 of Algorithm 1 can be ignored, making these methods computationally faster. We summarize various existing data-driven approaches from MT literature and demonstrate how these approaches can benefit considerably from sentence embeddings specifically trained for capturing semantic similarity.

3.1 Model-Driven

In this class of methods, we explore uncertainty sampling (Lewis and Catlett, 1994) strategies that have been widely used in MT. In this strategy an unlabeled example x is scored with some measure of uncertainty in the probability distribution over the label classes assigned by the model $p_{\mathcal{M}}(y|x)$. In the case of classification tasks, using the entropy $H(p_{\mathcal{M}}(y|x))$ is the most obvious choice, but in the case of structure prediction tasks, the space of all possible labels is usually exponential, making entropy calculation intractable. Settles and Craven (2008) found two heuristics: Least Confidence and N-best Sequence Entropy, which seemed to be the most effective estimators of model uncertainty across for two sequence labeling tasks. In addition to these, we also investigate Coverage Sampling (Peris and Casacuberta, 2018) proposed for interactive NMT, and our version of Round Trip Translation Likelihood inspired from the work in phrase-based MT (Haffari et al., 2009).

3.1.1 Least Confidence (LC)

This method estimates the model uncertainty of a source sentence x by averaging token-level log probability of the corresponding decoded translation $\hat{y}$. In our formulation, we further add length normalization to avoid any bias towards the length of the translations.

$$\psi_{\text{LC}}(x, \mathcal{M}) = -\frac{1}{L} \log p_{\mathcal{M}}(\hat{y}|x), \qquad (1)$$

where L denotes the length of $\hat{y}$.

3.1.2 N-best Sequence Entropy (NSE)

Another tractable approximator of model uncertainty is computing the entropy of the n-best hypothesis. Corresponding to a source sentence x, let $\mathcal{N} = \{\hat{y}_1, \hat{y}_2 \ldots \hat{y}_n\}$ denote the set of n-best translations. The normalized probability $\hat{P}$ of each hypothesis can be computed as:

$$\forall \hat{y} \in \mathcal{N}, \quad \hat{P}(\hat{y}) = \frac{p_{\mathcal{M}}(\hat{y}|x)}{\sum_{\hat{y} \in \mathcal{N}} p_{\mathcal{M}}(\hat{y}|x)}. \qquad (2)$$

Each source sentence is scored with the entropy of the probability distribution $\hat{P}$:

$$\psi_{\text{NSE}}(x, \mathcal{M}) = -\sum_{\hat{y} \in \mathcal{N}} \hat{P}(\hat{y}) \log \hat{P}(\hat{y}). \qquad (3)$$

3.1.3 Coverage Sampling (CS)

Under-translation is a well known problem in NMT (Tu et al., 2016), wherein not all source tokens are translated during decoding. The attention mechanism in LSTM based encoder-decoder architecture (Bahdanau et al., 2015) can model word alignment between translation and source to some degree. The extent of coverage of the attention weights over the source sentence can be an indicator of the quality of the translation. Peris and Casacuberta (2018) proposed Coverage Sampling (CS), which uses this coverage to estimate uncertainty. Formally:

$$\psi_{\text{CS}}(x, \mathcal{M}) = -\frac{\sum_{j=1}^{|x|} \log(\min(\sum_{i=1}^{|\hat{y}|} \alpha_{i,j}, 1))}{|x|}$$
$$(4)$$

where x and $\hat{y}$ are the source sentence and the decoded translation respectively, $|\cdot|$ denotes the number of tokens and $\alpha_{i,j}$ denotes the attention probability on the jth word of x while predicting the ith word of the $\hat{y}$.

3.1.4 Round Trip Translation Likelihood (RTTL)

Ott et al. (2018) showed that even a well trained NMT model does not necessarily assign higher probabilities to better translations. This behavior can be detrimental for methods like **LC** in which sentences with highly probable translations are not selected for human translations. In this scenario we assume that a low quality translation will lose some source-side information and it will become difficult to reconstruct the original source from this translation. To this end, we train models $\mathcal{M}$ and $\mathcal{M}_{rev}$ to translate from source language to target language and the reverse direction respectively. $\mathcal{M}_{rev}$ is identical to $\mathcal{M}$ except that it is trained on data obtained by flipping source and target sentences in $\mathcal{L}$. Formally, for any source sentence x of length L, we first translate it to a target sentence $\hat{y}$ using $\mathcal{M}$. Then we translate $\hat{y}$ back using $\mathcal{M}_{rev}$, but instead of decoding, we compute the probability of the original source sentence x and use it as a measure of uncertainty.

$$\hat{y} \approx \operatorname*{argmax}_{y} p_{\mathcal{M}}(y|x). \quad \text{(beam search)} \qquad (5)$$

$$\psi_{\text{RTTL}}(x, \mathcal{M}, \mathcal{M}_{rev}) = -\frac{1}{L} \log p_{\mathcal{M}_{rev}}(x|\hat{y}). \qquad (6)$$

RTTL is inspired by one of the methods proposed by Haffari et al. (2009), but differs from it in terms of modeling uncertainty. In their formulation, x is first translated to $\hat{y}$ like us but instead of scoring the likelihood of x given $\hat{y}$, under $\mathcal{M}_{rev}$, they use $\mathcal{M}_{rev}$ to translate $\hat{y}$ to a new source sentence $\hat{x}$ and measure uncertainty using sentence-level BLEU between x and $\hat{x}$. They showed that their approach did not perform better than a random baseline, however, in our experiments, RTTL outperforms the random baseline as well as all other model-driven methods. We suspect that this might be due to model log probability being a much finer grained metric than sentence-level BLEU.

3.2 Data-Driven

The data-driven approaches usually score sentences based on optimizing either one or a tradeoff between the following two metrics:

- Density: This metric scores sentences based on how similar they are with respect to the entire data in $\mathcal{U}$. In other words, sentences with higher likelihood under the data distribution of $\mathcal{U}$ are scored higher. This strategy assumes that the test set has the same distribution as $\mathcal{U}$, which makes achieving good translations on the *dense regions* of $\mathcal{U}$ more important.

- Diversity: This metric compliments the above and encourages sampling sentences which are less similar to the data in $\mathcal{L}$. This eventually leads to $\mathcal{L}$ containing a *diverse* set of sentences, leading to better generalization performance of model $\mathcal{M}$.

A key component in the above two metrics is how the similarity between two sentences is measured. We select the two common practices in literature are using n-gram overlap and cosine similarity between sentence embeddings. In the sections below, we describe the formulation of various data-driven methods based on how sentence similarity is measured.

3.2.1 N-gram Overlap

Ambati (2011) and Eck (2008) investigated density and diversity metrics using n-gram overlap for phrase-based MT and concluded that the best approach is to combine both of them together in the scoring function. Therefore, we select Density Weighted Diversity method from the former and Static Sentence Sorting from the latter in our study. Both methods use the following notations:

- $\mathcal{I}$: denotes the indicator function,

- n-gram(x): denotes the multiset of n-grams in a sentence (or a set of sentence) x,

- $\#(a|\mathcal{X})$: denotes the frequency of an n-gram a in n-gram($\mathcal{X}$).

Density Weighted Diversity (DWDS) combines the density and diversity metrics using a harmonic mean. Equation 7 and 8 respectively define the density (α) and diversity (β) metrics, which are combined together in Equation 9 to obtain the DWDS scoring function.

$$\alpha(x, \mathcal{U}, \mathcal{L}) = \frac{\sum\limits_{s \in \text{n-gram(x)}} \#(s|\mathcal{U}) e^{-\lambda \#(s|\mathcal{L})}}{|\text{n-gram}(x)||\text{n-gram}(\mathcal{U})|} \quad (7)$$

Here, λ is used as a decay parameter to give discount the n-grams which have already been seen in the bilingual data.

$$\beta(x, \mathcal{U}, \mathcal{L}) = \frac{\sum\limits_{x \in \text{n-gram}(x)} \mathcal{I}(s \notin \text{n-gram}(\mathcal{L}))}{|\text{n-gram}(x)|} \quad (8)$$

$$\psi_{\text{DWDS}}(x, \mathcal{U}, \mathcal{L}) = \frac{\alpha(x, \mathcal{U}, \mathcal{L})\beta(x, \mathcal{U}, \mathcal{L})}{k\alpha(x, \mathcal{U}, \mathcal{L}) + \beta(x, \mathcal{U}, \mathcal{L})} \quad (9)$$

Here, k controls the relative weighting of α and β.

Static Sentence Sorting (SSS) is a much simpler formulation which samples sentences from dense regions of $\mathcal{U}$, containing n-grams which are absent in $\mathcal{L}$.

$$\psi_{\text{SSS}}(x, \mathcal{U}, \mathcal{L}) = \frac{\sum\limits_{s \in \text{n-gram}(x)} \mathcal{I}(s \notin \mathcal{L}) \#(s|\mathcal{U})}{|x|} \quad (10)$$

3.2.2 Cosine Similarity

Zhang et al. (2018) proposed **S-Score (SS)** to use cosine similarity between sentence embeddings rather than n-gram overlap as a measure of sentence similarity. S-Score mainly relies on the diversity metric for selection. It samples sentences from $\mathcal{U}$ which are furthest from their nearest neighbors in $\mathcal{L}$. Essentially sentences which are semantically different from all the sentences in $\mathcal{L}$ would be selected. Let $\mathbf{e}(x)$ denote the embedding vector of the sentence x and $cos(\cdot, \cdot)$ denote the cosine similarity, then S-Score is defined as:

$$\psi_{SS}(x, \mathcal{L}) = \min_{y \in \mathcal{L}} cos(\mathbf{e}(x), \mathbf{e}(y)) \quad (11)$$

Zhang et al. (2018) used learnt sentence embeddings starting from `fasttext` (Bojanowski et al., 2017) and fine-tuned using Paragraph Vector (Le and Mikolov, 2014).

To better understand how recent advances in unsupervised pre-training can benefit active learning, we perform an ablation study of the S-Score method with varying the source of embeddings. We experiment with the following three increasingly expressive sentence representations:

Bag of words (SS-BoW): This is the simplest method in which the sentence embeddings are computed by taking the average of all the word embeddings. The word embeddings are obtained from the `fasttext` tool.

Contextual embedding (SS-CE): In this method, we leverage unsupervised pre-training techniques like BERT which have significantly advanced the SotA in NLP (Devlin et al., 2019). Specifically, we train the Transformer Encoder using the Masked Language Modeling (MLM) objective proposed in BERT (Devlin et al., 2019). We then compute the sentence embedding by averaging outputs from the trained encoder corresponding to all the sentence tokens.

Paraphrastic embedding (SS-PE): The sentence embedding methods listed above and those used by Zhang et al. (2018) are all trained with the objective of predicting tokens based on their context. While this allows the embeddings to be somewhat correlated with the semantics, explicitly fine-tuning the embeddings on semantic similarity can be helpful for our use case. Therefore, we fine-tune the contextual embedding model discussed above on the paraphrase task as proposed in Wieting and Gimpel (2018).

Wieting and Gimpel (2018) created a dataset[2] containing pairs of English paraphrases by back-translating the Czech side of an English-Czech corpus. We fine-tune the embeddings of the paraphrase pairs to be close to each other using a contrastive loss. We specifically choose this task because it does not utilize any supervised human annotated corpus for semantic similarity while achieving competitive performance on SemEval semantic textual similarity (STS) benchmarks.

We show that using contextual sentence embeddings does not give any noticeable gains over simply using bag of words embeddings, however fine-tuning the embeddings on semantic similarity tasks improves the performance of S-Score substantially, enabling it to outperform other data-driven approaches.

4 Experiments

4.1 Dataset

Our setup is based on the WMT'13 English-Spanish news translation task. We use the Europarl and News Commentary Corpus consisting of $\sim$ 2M sentence pairs. We randomly sample 10% of the whole bilingual data to create the base parallel dataset $\mathcal{L}$ ($\sim$ 200K) which is used to train

an initial NMT model. We then randomly sample 50% from the remaining data to the unlabeled dataset $\mathcal{U}$ ($\sim$ 1M) used for simulating the AL experiments. Note that we do the random sampling just once and fix $\mathcal{L}$ and $\mathcal{U}$ for all the experiments for fair comparison. Since we experiment in a simulated AL framework, the target sentences in $\mathcal{U}$ are hidden while scoring source sentences with different AL strategies. Once the AL algorithm samples a batch B containing 100k source sentences from $\mathcal{U}$, the sampled sentences along with their corresponding "hidden" translations are added to $\mathcal{L}$. We use `newstest-2012` as the validation set and `newstest-2013` as the test set, each consisting of about 3000 sentence pairs. For training the contextual embeddings, we use the English News Crawl corpus from years 2007-17, consisting of $\sim$ 200M sentences. For preprocessing, we apply the Moses tokenizer (Koehn et al., 2007) without aggressive hyphen splitting and with punctuation normalization. We learn a joint source and target Byte-Pair-Encoding (BPE, Sennrich et al. (2016)) on the whole bilingual data with 32k merge operations.

4.2 Training and Model Hyperparameters

For the NMT models in all the experiments, we use the `base` Transformer configuration with 6 encoder and decoder layers, 8 attention heads, embedding size of 512, shared input and output embeddings, `relu` activation function and sinusoidal positional embeddings. We train with a batch size of 2000 tokens on 8 Volta GPUs using half-precision for 30 epochs. Furthermore we use Adam optimizer (Kingma and Ba, 2015) with a learning rate of $0.001, \beta_1 = 0.9, \beta_2 = 0.98$, learning rate warmup over the first 4000 steps and inverse square root learning rate scheduling. We also apply dropout and label smoothing of 0.1 each. We average the weights of 5 checkpoints with the best validation loss and run inference with a beam size of 5.

While training the Transformer Encoder using the Masked Language Modeling (MLM) objective, we switch to the `big` configuration with an embedding size of 1024 and 16 attention heads. The masking probabilities are the same as described in Devlin et al. (2019), however instead of pair of sentences, we use text streams spanning across multiple sentences (truncated at 256 tokens) (Lample and Conneau, 2019). This model is trained using 64 Volta GPUs, each processing a batch of 128 segments. We use a learning rate of 0.0003, with other hyperparameters similar to the NMT model. The above model is fine-tuned on the task of Paraphrastic Sentence Embeddings. Specifically we use a margin of 0.4, learning rate 0.0005, batch size 3500 tokens and megabatches consisting of 32 batches. We train for 5 epochs using 8 Volta GPUs. Lastly for DWDS, we set $k = 1, \lambda = 1$. For both the n-gram based methods, we consider up to tri-grams. In case of NSE, we restrict the n-best list to be of size 5. Our baseline is a system that randomly selects sentences from the unlabeled data.

5 Results and Discussion

In this section, we compare the performance of different AL algorithms of each class: model-driven and data-driven. For a comprehensive comparison, we evaluate the best approaches of both classes on:

- **Various MT evaluation metrics**. N-gram overlap based metrics like BLEU (Papineni et al., 2002) might be biased towards AL methods based on n-gram similarity (DWDS, SSS). For a fair comparison, we evaluate the AL approaches on BLEU, TER (Snover et al., 2006), which is based on edit distance, and BEER (Stanojević and Sima'an, 2015), which uses a linear model trained on human evaluations dataset.

- **Out-of-domain evaluation sets**. Since AL algorithms are sensitive to the labeled ($\mathcal{L}$) and unlabeled data ($\mathcal{U}$) distributions, it is possible that some AL algorithms perform worse, when evaluated on out-of-domain test sets. To compare the robustness of different AL approaches, we evaluate them on a test set sourced from biological domain, which is very different from the training data distribution (parliament speech and news).

- **Evaluation sets without any translationese source sentences**. Translationese refers to the distinctive style of sentences which are translated by human translators. These sentences tend to be a simplistic, standardized, explicit and lack complicated constructs like idioms etc. These properties might make it easy to reconstruct source sentences from

the translationese domain, hence discouraging them to be sampled by RTTL. Presence of translationese source sentences in the test sets might unfairly penalize RTTL.

5.1 Model-Driven Approaches

Figure 1 and Table 1 compares the results of model-driven approaches and random sampling baseline. We observe that CS performs worse than the random baseline. This is in contrast to the results reported in Peris and Casacuberta (2018) where it is amongst the best performing methods. The performance of CS is dependent upon the assumption that attention probabilities are good at modeling word alignments. While this assumption is valid in the case Peris and Casacuberta (2018), which uses attentional sequence-sequence models with LSTMs/GRUs, it breaks down in the presence of multi-layered, multi-headed attention mechanism of the Transformer architecture. Upon closer inspection, we found that this method sampled very long sentences with rare words and many BPE splits, resulting in sub-optimal performance. LC has slightly better performance than NSE, while RTTL outperforms all the other methods consistently by a non-trivial margin. This demonstrates that our proposed extension is an effective approximation of model uncertainty.

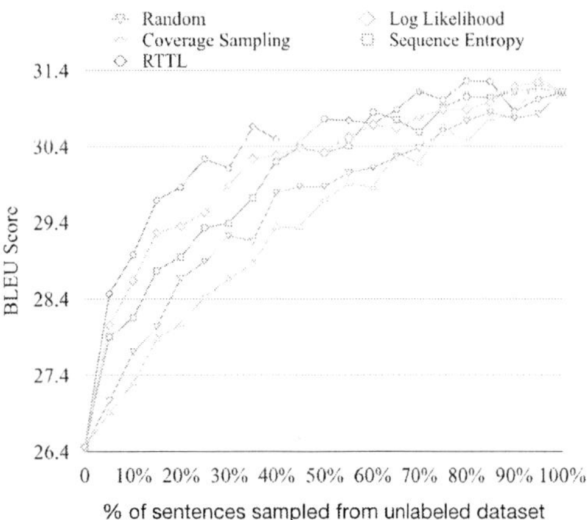

Figure 1: Results of model-driven approaches.

5.2 Data-Driven Approaches

Figure 2 shows the results of n-gram based data-driven approaches. As illustrated in Figure 2, these computationally inexpensive methods can consistently outperform the random baseline by a

Table 1: Results for Model-Driven and Data-Driven approaches. We report the average BLEU scores across 20 active learning iterations. Best methods within each category are boldened.

Random	Model-Driven				Data-Driven (N-Gram)		Data-Driven (Embedding)		
	LC	CS	NSE	RTTL	DWDS	SSS	SS-BoW	SS-CE	SS-PE
29.54	30.06	29.35	29.93	**30.29**	30.22	30.21	29.84	30	**30.17**

large margin. In spite of modeling density and diversity in very different ways, both the methods achieve similar performance.

Figure 3 shows the results of embedding based data-driven approaches (SS) corresponding to different sources of embeddings. It is noteworthy that using bag-of-words (SS-BoW) and contextual embeddings (SS-CE) results in roughly the same performance, barely beating the random baseline. However, fine-tuning the contextual embeddings on the paraphrase task (SS-PE), brings about a large performance gain, emphasizing the effectiveness of fine-tuning on semantic similarity tasks for AL.

The above trends are inline with the results reported in Table 1 as well.

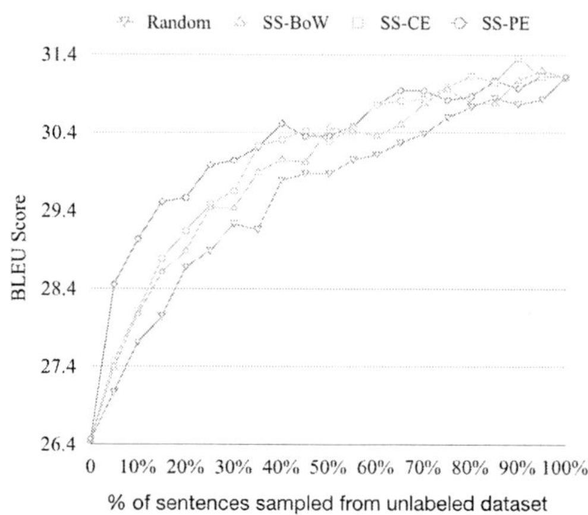

Figure 3: Results of the SS method with various sources of embeddings.

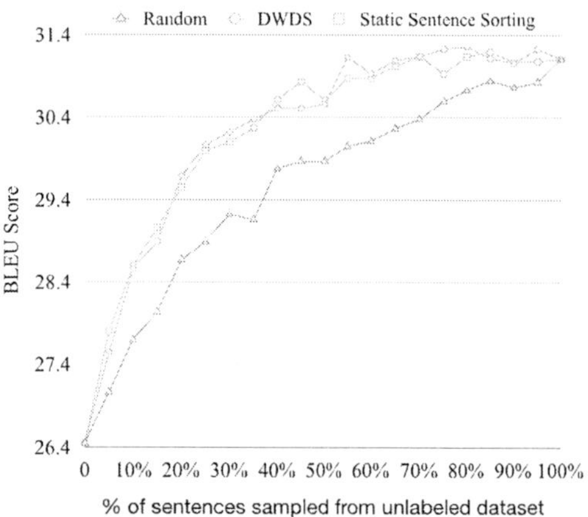

Figure 2: Results of data-driven approaches based on n-gram similarity.

5.3 Performance on Different Evaluation Metrics

Figure 4 compares the top three AL methods (RTTL, DWDS, SS-PE) using BLEU. All three methods are quite competitive, with RTTL and SS-PE performing slightly better than DWDS in the beginning. Figures 4 and 5 show consistent performance trends using all the three metrics. It is worth noting from figure 4, that all the methods

are able to achieve the same BLEU (as with using the whole bitext) with using only 70% of the bitext. This outlines that AL can be quite effective for NMT.

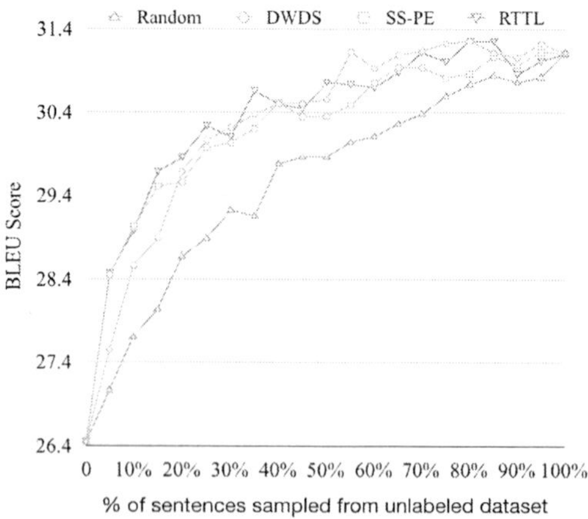

Figure 4: Results of best performing approaches with BLEU.

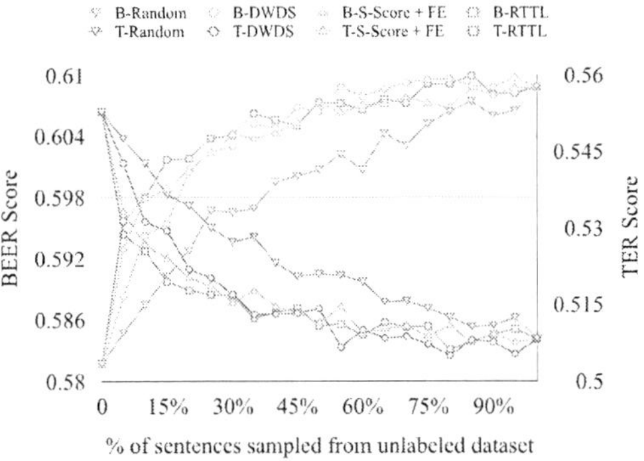

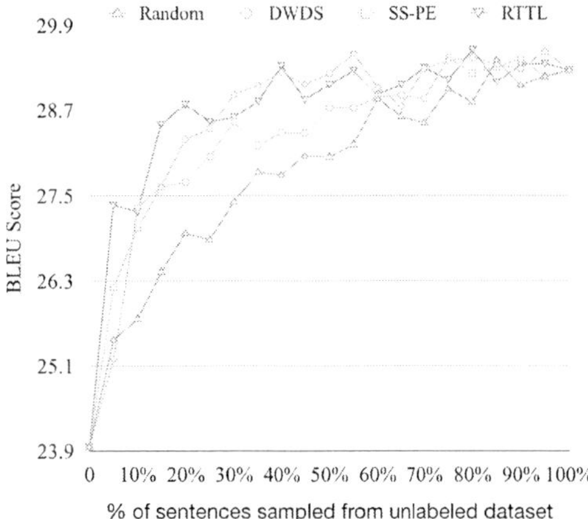

Figure 6: Results of the best performing approaches on Biomedical Translation test set

Figure 5: Results of best performing approaches with BEER (B-X) and TER (T-X) evaluation metrics.

5.4 Evaluation on Test Sets Without Translationese

Zhang and Toral (2019) brought to light the effect of having translationese in the source side of the evaluation sets used in WMT over the years. The situation is even worse for `newstest2013` which contains translations of sentences from 5 different languages, in the source side. We create a new test set, by collecting $\sim$ 2000 sentences from `newstest2009-13` except `newstest2012` (since we use `newstest2012` as validation set) which are originally from English. The BLEU scores of all the methods are much higher on this test set corrected for translationese ($\sim$38 BLEU), as compared to `newstest2013` ($\sim$31 BLEU), however the relative performance trends remain the same.

5.5 Evaluation on Out-of-Domain Test Sets

Figure 6 shows the results on out-of-domain test set from the WMT16 Shared Task on Biomedical Translation. It can be observed from figure 6 that, while RTTL and DWDS are quite robust to the test domain, and strongly outperform the random baseline, there is some degradation in the performance of SS-PE.

6 Related Work

Early work on AL for MT includes Ambati (2011); Eck (2008); Haffari et al. (2009) among others. These papers investigated the AL approaches for phrase-based MT systems. Given that the current SotA MT systems are neural-based, in this work, we investigate the effectiveness of their proposed methods in the neural paradigm. Couple of works

that did investigate the AL methods for NMT are Peris and Casacuberta (2018) and Zhang et al. (2018). Both of these used RNN/LSTM based NMT architecture, whereas, we use the latest SotA Transformer in our investigation. Peris and Casacuberta (2018) used an interactive NMT setup and mostly focused on model-driven approaches disregarding data-driven methods. Zhang et al. (2018) did compare methods from both the classes but considered only a handful of methods. Our work is closer to Zhang et al. (2018), but we cover much a wider spectrum of methods in AL. We also go one step further and show that the cosine similarity based methods proposed in Zhang et al. (2018) are more effective when the embeddings are optimized for the paraphrase task. As far as we know, most of the prior work concluded that data-driven methods outperform model-driven methods, however, our model-driven RTTL formulation obtains slight gain over the best data-driven method.

7 Conclusion

In this work, we performed an empirical evaluation of different AL methods for the state-of-the-art neural MT architecture, a missing aspect in prior work. We explored two classes of approaches: data-driven and model-driven, and observed that all the methods outperform a random baseline, except coverage sampling which relies on the attention mechanism. Coverage sampling was shown to be amongst the best approaches in prior work that used LSTM-based NMT model. Given Transformer's more complex attention architecture (multi-headed and multi-layered), it appears that the attention scores are not reliable enough to be used with the AL methods.

From our ablation study on using different sources of embeddings, we discovered that optimizing the embeddings towards a semantic similarity task can give significant performance improvements in data-driven AL methods. Also, for the first time, we observed that a model-driven approach can outperform data-driven methods. The improvement was more evident in the out-of-domain evaluation results. This was possible with our proposed neural extension - RTTL, which computes the likelihood score of re-constructing the original source from its translation using a reverse translation model. Overall, we observed that the performance trends of different AL methods were consistent with all the three evaluation metrics (BLEU, BEER, and TER) and on different evaluation sets (in-domain and out-of-domain).

Acknowledgments

We would like to thank Tom Gunter, Andrew Finch, Russ Webb and the anonymous reviewers for their helpful comments. Many thanks to the Siri Machine Translation Team for helpful discussions and support.

References

Vamshi Ambati. 2011. *Active learning and crowdsourcing for machine translation in low resource scenarios*. Ph.D. thesis, Carnegie Mellon University.

Dzmitry Bahdanau, Kyunghyun Cho, and Yoshua Bengio. 2015. Neural machine translation by jointly learning to align and translate. In *International Conference on Learning Representations*, San Diego, CA, USA.

Maria-Florina Balcan, Alina Beygelzimer, and John Langford. 2009. Agnostic active learning. *Journal of Computer and System Sciences*, 75(1):78–89.

Loïc Barrault, Ondrej Bojar, Marta R. Costa-jussà, Christian Federmann, Mark Fishel, Yvette Graham, Barry Haddow, Matthias Huck, Philipp Koehn, Shervin Malmasi, Christof Monz, Mathias Müller, Santanu Pal, Matt Post, and Marcos Zampieri. 2019. Findings of the 2019 conference on machine translation (wmt19). In *Proceedings of the Fourth Conference on Machine Translation*, pages 128–188. Association for Computational Linguistics.

Piotr Bojanowski, Edouard Grave, Armand Joulin, and Tomas Mikolov. 2017. Enriching word vectors with subword information. *Transactions of the Association for Computational Linguistics*, 5:135–146.

David Cohn, Les Atlas, and Richard Ladner. 1994. Improving generalization with active learning. *Machine Learning - Special issue on structured connectionist systems*, 15(2):201–221.

Ido Dagan and Sean P Engelson. 1995. Committee-based sampling for training probabilistic classifiers. In *Machine Learning Proceedings 1995*, pages 150–157. Elsevier, Tahoe City, California, USA.

Jacob Devlin, Ming-Wei Chang, Kenton Lee, and Kristina Toutanova. 2019. Bert: Pre-training of deep bidirectional transformers for language understanding. In *Proceedings of the 2019 Conference of the North American Chapter of the Association for Computational Linguistics: Human Language Technologies, Volume 1 (Long and Short Papers)*, pages 4171–4186, Minneapolis, Minnesota.

Matthias Eck. 2008. *Developing deployable spoken language translation systems given limited resources*. Ph.D. thesis, Verlag nicht ermittelbar.

Yuhong Guo and Russell Greiner. 2007. Optimistic active-learning using mutual information. In *Proceedings of the 20th International Joint Conference on Artificial Intelligence*, volume 7, pages 823–829, Hyderabad, India.

Gholamreza Haffari, Maxim Roy, and Anoop Sarkar. 2009. Active learning for statistical phrase-based machine translation. In *Proceedings of Human Language Technologies: The 2009 Annual Conference of the North American Chapter of the Association for Computational Linguistics*, pages 415–423, Boulder, Colorado, USA. Association for Computational Linguistics.

Diederik P Kingma and Jimmy Ba. 2015. Adam: A method for stochastic optimization. In *International Conference on Learning Representations*, San Deigo, CA, USA.

Philipp Koehn, Hieu Hoang, Alexandra Birch, Chris Callison-Burch, Marcello Federico, Nicola Bertoldi, Brooke Cowan, Wade Shen, Christine Moran, Richard Zens, Chris Dyer, Ondrej Bojar, Alexandra Constantin, and Evan Herbst. 2007. Moses: Open source toolkit for statistical machine translation. pages 177–180, Prague, Czech Republic.

Guillaume Lample and Alexis Conneau. 2019. Cross-lingual language model pretraining. *arXiv preprint arXiv:1901.07291*.

Quoc Le and Tomas Mikolov. 2014. Distributed representations of sentences and documents. In *International Conference on Machine Learning*, pages 1188–1196, Beijing, China.

David D Lewis and Jason Catlett. 1994. Heterogenous uncertainty sampling for supervised learning.

In *Machine Learning Proceedings 1994: Proceedings of the Eighth International Conference*, pages 148–156, New Brunswick, NJ, USA. Morgan Kaufmann Publishers Inc.

Myle Ott, Michael Auli, David Grangier, et al. 2018. Analyzing uncertainty in neural machine translation. In *International Conference on Machine Learning*, pages 3953–3962, Stockholm, Sweden.

Kishore Papineni, Salim Roukos, Todd Ward, and Wei-Jing Zhu. 2002. BLEU: A method for automatic evaluation of machine translation. pages 311–318, Philadelphia, PA, USA.

Álvaro Peris and Francisco Casacuberta. 2018. Active learning for interactive neural machine translation of data streams. In *Proceedings of the 22nd Conference on Computational Natural Language Learning*, pages 151–160, Brussels, Belgium.

Rico Sennrich, Barry Haddow, and Alexandra Birch. 2016. Neural machine translation of rare words with subword units. pages 1715–1725, Berlin, Germany.

Burr Settles and Mark Craven. 2008. An analysis of active learning strategies for sequence labeling tasks. In *Proceedings of the 2008 Conference on Empirical Methods in Natural Language Processing*, pages 1070–1079, Waikiki, Honolulu, Hawaii.

Matthew Snover, Bonnie Dorr, Richard Schwartz, Linnea Micciulla, and John Makhoul. 2006. A study of translation edit rate with targeted human annotation. In *Proceedings of Association for Machine Translation in the Americas*, pages 223–231, Cambridge, Massachusetts.

Miloš Stanojević and Khalil Sima'an. 2015. Beer 1.1: Illc uva submission to metrics and tuning task. In *Proceedings of the Tenth Workshop on Statistical Machine Translation*, pages 396–401, Lisbon, Portugal.

Zhaopeng Tu, Zhengdong Lu, Yang Liu, Xiaohua Liu, and Hang Li. 2016. Modeling coverage for neural machine translation. In *Proceedings of the 54th Annual Meeting of the Association for Computational Linguistics (Volume 1: Long Papers)*, volume 1, pages 76–85.

Gokhan Tur, Dilek Hakkani-Tür, and Robert E Schapire. 2005. Combining active and semi-supervised learning for spoken language understanding. *Speech Communication*, 45(2):171–186.

Ashish Vaswani, Noam Shazeer, Niki Parmar, Jakob Uszkoreit, Llion Jones, Aidan N. Gomez, Lukasz Kaiser, and Illia Polosukhin. 2017. Attention is all you need. pages 1–11, Long Beach, CA, USA.

John Wieting and Kevin Gimpel. 2018. Paranmt-50m: Pushing the limits of paraphrastic sentence embeddings with millions of machine translations. In *Proceedings of the 56th Annual Meeting of the Association for Computational Linguistics (Volume 1: Long Papers)*, pages 451–462, Melbourne, Australia.

Mike Zhang and Antonio Toral. 2019. The effect of translationese in machine translation test sets. *arXiv preprint arXiv:1906.08069*.

Pei Zhang, Xueying Xu, and Deyi Xiong. 2018. Active learning for neural machine translation. In *2018 International Conference on Asian Language Processing (IALP)*, pages 153–158, Bandung, Indonesia. IEEE.

Fast Domain Adaptation of Semantic Parsers via Paraphrase Attention

Avik Ray, Yilin Shen and **Hongxia Jin**
Samsung Research America, Mountain View, California, USA
{avik.r, yilin.shen, hongxia.jin}@samsung.com

Abstract

Semantic parsers are used to convert user's natural language commands to executable logical form in intelligent personal agents. Labeled datasets required to train such parsers are expensive to collect, and are never comprehensive. As a result, for effective post-deployment domain adaptation and personalization, semantic parsers are continuously retrained to learn new user vocabulary and paraphrase variety. However, state-of-the art attention based neural parsers are slow to retrain which inhibits real time domain adaptation. Secondly, these parsers do not leverage numerous paraphrases already present in the training dataset. Designing parsers which can simultaneously maintain high accuracy and fast retraining time is challenging. In this paper, we present novel paraphrase attention based sequence-to-sequence/tree parsers which support fast near real time retraining. In addition, our parsers often boost accuracy by jointly modeling the semantic dependencies of paraphrases. We evaluate our model on benchmark datasets to demonstrate upto 9X speedup in retraining time compared to existing parsers, as well as achieving state-of-the-art accuracy.

1 Introduction

Semantic parsers are used in modern intelligent personal agents (e.g. Alexa, Bixby, Jibo) to allow users carry out a wide variety of tasks using natural language commands/queries. Specifically, these parsers convert the input query to an executable logical form representation. However, labeled datasets required to train state-of-the-art neural semantic parsers are difficult to collect due to their annotation complexity. Secondly, users from different locale tend to use different vocabulary, and paraphrases making it nearly impossible to collect a comprehensive dataset covering all possible variety of queries. As a result,

once deployed, the semantic parsers require frequent retraining for adaptation to the locale and user specific vocabulary (Thomason et al., 2015; Azaria et al., 2016; Ray et al., 2018). Such domain adaptation and personalization is a key feature in current commercial personal agents (Kim et al., 2018).

Recently, neural semantic parsers based on attention based sequence-to-sequence/tree models were proposed (Jia and Liang, 2016; Dong and Lapata, 2016). These are attractive for commercial personal agents, since unlike previous approaches these can be trained end-to-end without requiring hand crafted domain specific grammar/lexicon, thereby improving scalability. However, these parsers are particularly prone to error when queries contain out-of-vocabulary (OOV) words (Ray et al., 2018). They are also slow to retrain since the attention layer, which is critical for boosting accuracy (Dong and Lapata, 2016), also constraints the encoder and decoder to be retrained simultaneously. As an example, in benchmark ATIS dataset with 4,485 training queries, a sequence-to-sequence semantic parser requires over 1 hour retraining time using a single GPU.

In this paper, we present novel sequence-to-sequence/tree parsers with two key advantages over previous parsers. First, our parser is trained to use either attention from input query or attention from its paraphrase (referred as paraphrase attention) when available. For learning new vocabulary from paraphrased queries (Azaria et al., 2016; Ray et al., 2018), this naturally enables our parsers to be retrained much faster, since in our parser only the encoder requires retraining. Secondly, by jointly modeling the semantic dependencies between paraphrases, our parser often achieves better accuracy over previous models. Our main contributions are summarized below.

- We propose novel sequence-to-sequence and

Proceedings of the 2nd Workshop on Deep Learning Approaches for Low-Resource NLP (DeepLo), pages 94–103
Hong Kong, China, November 3, 2019. ©2019 Association for Computational Linguistics
https://doi.org/10.18653/v1/P17

tree parsers with paraphrase attention which can be retrained much faster than previous models, enabling real time domain adaptation of intelligent agents.

- Our models explicitly leverage paraphrases in the training dataset resulting in better semantic understanding. On benchmark datasets our models achieve similar or better parsing accuracy over previous models.

- On OOV datasets, our models can learn new personalized words/phrases upto 9X faster than previous attention based parsers after re-training.

1.1 Related work

In this section we highlight the most related prior literature. In the last few decades a wide variety of semantic parsers have been proposed using both rule based and supervised approaches (Zelle and Mooney, 1996; Wong and Mooney, 2007; Zettle-moyer and Collins, 2005, 2007; Kwiatkowski et al., 2010, 2011; Artzi and Zettlemoyer, 2013). More recently, end-to-end neural network models are being explored due to their superior performance and ease of training (Jia and Liang, 2016; Dong and Lapata, 2016; Iyer et al., 2017; Dong and Lapata, 2018). The use of paraphrases to boost performance of semantic parsers have been studied (Berant and Liang, 2014; Ray et al., 2018).

Domain adaptation of semantic parsers have been explored in both pre–deployment (Herzig and Berant, 2017; Fan et al., 2017) and post–deployment (Thomason et al., 2015; Azaria et al., 2016; Iyer et al., 2017; Ray et al., 2018) settings, and using both CCG based and neural network parsers. In (Ray et al., 2018), the authors propose new models to effectively learn user specific OOV words by retraining neural semantic parsers.

Neural semantic parsers are mainly based on attention based sequence-to-sequence networks. Although sequence-to-sequence networks were first proposed to solve the problem of machine translation (Sutskever et al., 2014; Bahdanau et al., 2015), it has been applied successfully in a wide range of NLP tasks (Cho et al., 2014; Vinyals et al., 2015b; Prakash et al., 2016). While adding extra context information from the input in the form of attention network greatly improves the performance of these models (Bahdanau et al., 2015; Vinyals et al., 2015a; Dong and Lapata, 2016), they also slow down their retraining time by constraining both the encoder and decoder networks to be retrained simultaneously.

Our work lie in the intersection of these areas. We propose new sequence-to-sequence/tree parsers using paraphrase attention, which facilitates faster domain adaptation, while maintaining competitive parsing accuracy as current models.

This paper is organized as follows. Section 2 formally defines our problem and discuss related background. We describe our new paraphrase attention based parsers in Section 3. In Section 4 we present our numerical evaluation results. Finally, we conclude in Section 5.

2 Problem and Background

In this section, we concretely define our problem and discuss related notations. A semantic parser $\mathcal{P}$ converts an user provided query $\mathbf{q} = (w_1, \ldots, w_n)$ to its corresponding logical form representation $\mathbf{l}(\mathbf{q}) = (l_1, \ldots, l_m)$, where w_i-s represents words from vocabulary $\mathcal{V}$, and l_j-s correspond to logical expression tokens. The parser $\mathcal{P}$ is trained over a labeled training set T. After deployment, users often use their own personal or locale specific vocabulary in queries, some of which are absent in the training vocabulary $\mathcal{V}$. Let $\mathbf{p}^*$ be a query with OOV words which parser $\mathcal{P}$ cannot parse. We follow the post–deployment domain adaptation settings similar to (Azaria et al., 2016; Ray et al., 2018), where using user feedback/dialog, a paraphrased query $\mathbf{q}^*$ of $\mathbf{p}^*$ is obtained which is parsable. The main task of domain adaptation is to retrain $\mathcal{P}$ using both the given paraphrased sample $(\mathbf{p}^*, \mathbf{q}^*, \mathbf{l}(\mathbf{q}^*))$, and the training set T to obtain an improved personalized parser $\mathcal{P}'$.

2.1 Sequence-to-sequence/tree parsers

In (Dong and Lapata, 2016; Jia and Liang, 2016), the authors demonstrate that attention based sequence-to-sequence/tree models can be utilized to solve the semantic parsing task. A basic attention based sequence-to-sequence/tree parser consists of an encoder, a decoder, and an attention layer. The encoder, and the decoder again consists of recurrent neural networks (e.g. LSTM). The model is trained by maximizing the simplified likelihood function:

$$P(l_1, .., l_m | w_1, .., w_n) = \amalg_{t=1}^{m} P(l_t | l_1, .., l_{t-1}, \mathbf{c})$$

$$(1)$$

where **c** is the context vector (or final encoder hidden state).

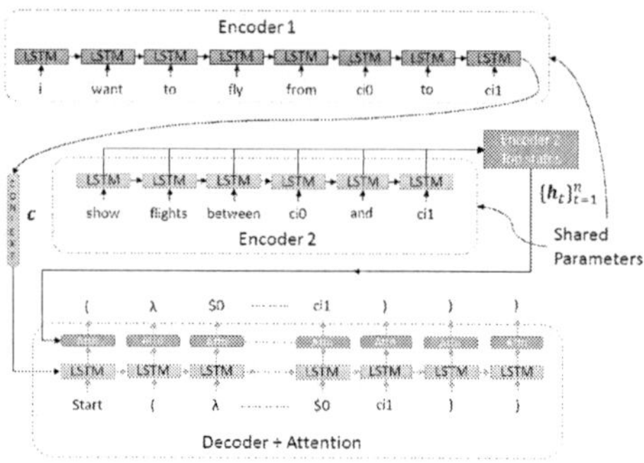

Figure 1: Figure showing our new sequence-to-sequence parser with paraphrase attention. During training, encoder 1 encodes a query (*"i want to fly from $ci0$ to $ci1$"*), and encoder 2 encodes its paraphrase (*"show flights between $ci0$ and $ci1$"*). For decoding, the context state is provided by encoder 1 and attention is computed from encoder 2 top states. Both encoders share same LSTM parameters. During inference, a single encoder is used to compute both context and attention states.

3 Our Model

In this section we describe our new sequence-to-sequence/tree parser using paraphrase attention. The motivation behind our parser is as follows. Existing attention based sequence-to-sequence/tree parsers are slow to retrain since both the encoder and decoder needs to be retrained simultaneously to achieve satisfactory accuracy, hindering real time domain adaptation. While it may be possible to freeze the decoder parameters, and finetune only the encoder, however this is still slow since the error gradients need to be propagated all the way back to the encoder. Freezing the encoder parameters and finetuning just the decoder results in poor performance (shown in evaluation Section 4) since the model fails to learn the proper encoder representation corresponding to new OOV words.

Recall that, to teach a query $\mathbf{p}^*$ with OOV words to an intelligent agent, user provides a paraphrased query $\mathbf{q}^*$ with known words which the parser $\mathcal{P}$ understands. Since $\mathbf{p}^*$ and $\mathbf{q}^*$ have the same meaning (hence the same logical form), their context representation c should be the same. We make two key observations. First, to learn new query $\mathbf{p}^*$ we can finetune just the encoder

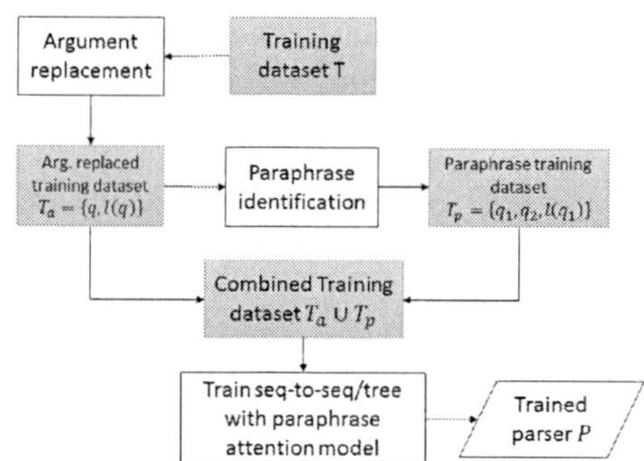

Figure 2: Illustration of data pre-processing and training process of our sequence-to-sequence/tree with paraphrase attention parser.

by treating the context vector **c** (computed from paraphrased query $\mathbf{q}^*$) as ground-truth. However, the top encoder states corresponding to query $\mathbf{p}^*$, which are required for attention computation, are still unknown. We make a second observation that, if during training the model is taught to use attention either from a query, or its paraphrase, we can simply use attention from $\mathbf{q}^*$ to decode $\mathbf{p}^*$. Therefore, we do not require knowledge of top encoder states of $\mathbf{p}^*$, instead we just need to know those of $\mathbf{q}^*$. This can be obtained since $\mathcal{P}$ can correctly parse $\mathbf{q}^*$. Before describing our model details, we discuss another essential data processing step which identifies paraphrased sentences for model training.

3.1 Data preprocessing

We now describe two key preprocessing steps required to train our paraphrase attention model. Figure 2 provides an overview of these data processing steps.

Argument replacement: In (Dong and Lapata, 2016; Ray et al., 2018), the authors use an important preprocessing step called argument replacement. This step replaces certain words/phrases in the user query (e.g. entities or numbers), which correspond to logical form arguments, using special argument tokens before training. This greatly improves parsing accuracy by reducing the input variability (Dong and Lapata, 2016). Figure 1 shows an example of argument replaced query *"i want to fly from $ci0$ to $ci1$"* for the original query *"i want to fly from atlanta to philadelphia"* in ATIS dataset, where $ci0, ci1$ are special argument tokens. As a first preprocessing step, we perform this argument replacement to convert original training set T to an argument replaced training set

T_a.

Paraphrase identification: In order to train a sequence-to-sequence parser which can use attention either from a query or its paraphrase, first we need to identify sentential paraphrases in the training dataset. Intuitively, if two paraphrased queries have the same meaning, they must share the same logical form. However, in the original training set T there are not many paraphrases, since often logical forms differ only by a constant. Instead, if we consider the argument replaced training set T_a, where such constants have been replaced by argument tokens, many identical logical forms exist. In our second paraphrase identification step, using the queries in T_a whose paraphrase exist, we construct a new **paraphrase training set** $T_p = \{\mathbf{q}_1^i, \mathbf{q}_2^i, \mathrm{l}(\mathbf{q}_1^i)\}_{i=1}^p$ of a given size p, where $\mathbf{q}_1^i, \mathbf{q}_2^i$ are paraphrases. An example of such paraphrase pair is shown in Figure 1.

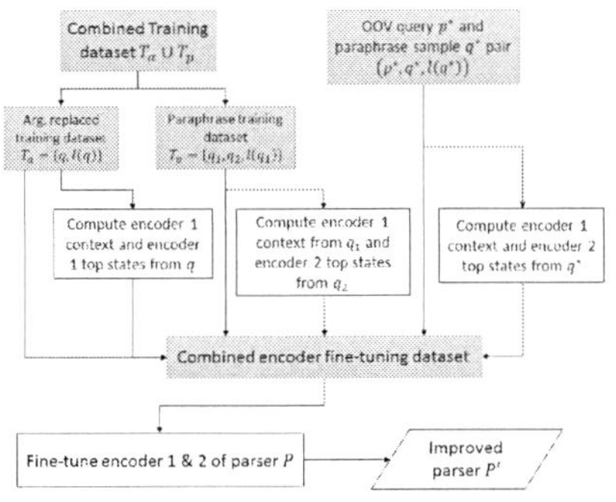

Figure 3: Illustration of fast encoder fine-tuning process in our sequence-to-sequence/tree parser $\mathcal{P}$.

3.2 Sequence-to-sequence/tree with paraphrase attention

Now we describe our sequence-to-sequence with paraphrase attention model. Our model consists of two encoders (with shared parameters), one decoder, and one attention layer as shown in Figure 1. Sequence encoders 1 and 2 encode a query and its paraphrase respectively. During, decoding the decoder context is initialized from encoder 1 final hidden state, however the attention states are computed using the top hidden states of encoder 2. This enables our model to jointly capture the semantic dependence between the paraphrase pair.

Training: A key feature of our model is that the attention network is able to generate attention signals from both the query, or its paraphrase.

To ensure this, we train our model on a combined dataset $T_a \bigcup T_p$ using a multi-task objective. For a sample without a paraphrase $(\mathbf{q}, \mathrm{l}(\mathbf{q})) \in T_a$, we perform forward/backward propagation identical to sequence-to-sequence with attention parsers using a single encoder (either 1 or 2 since they share parameters). For a sample with paraphrase $(\mathbf{q}_1, \mathbf{q}_2, \mathrm{l}(\mathbf{q}_1)) \in T_p$, we perform forward/backward propagation using both encoders, and use the attention from encoder 2. We use the overall negative log-likelihood function as our training objective.

$$\mathcal{L} = -\log P(\mathrm{l}(\mathbf{q}_1)|\mathbf{q}_1, \mathbf{q}_2)$$

Figure 2 provides an overview of the data processing steps and training procedure of our new parser.

Inference: During model inference/testing we only have one user provided query $\mathbf{q}$ and no paraphrase. However, thanks to the shared encoder parameters, both encoder context and top states can be computed from this query $\mathbf{q}$. Therefore, during inference the model essentially acts as a normal sequence-to-sequence/tree parser.

Fast domain adaptation: For domain adaptation, user provides a OOV query $\mathbf{p}^*$ and its paraphrase $\mathbf{q}^*$. In end-to-end neural network models it is straight-forward to fine-tuning the parser $\mathcal{P}$ after adding this new sample $(\mathbf{p}^*, \mathbf{q}^*, \mathrm{l}(\mathbf{q}^*))$ to the training set. As mentioned before, in previous sequence-to-sequence parsers such fine-tuning is slow since it involves updating the entire model parameters. In our model, a faster alternative is to fine-tune just the encoder. We can perform this by using a MSE objective as follows.

$$\mathcal{L} = \sum_{t=1}^{|\mathbf{q}|} \|\bar{\mathbf{h}}_t - \hat{\mathbf{h}}_t\|^2 + \|\bar{\mathbf{c}} - \hat{\mathbf{c}}\|^2$$

where $\{\hat{\mathbf{h}}_t\}_{t=1}^{|\mathbf{q}|}, \hat{\mathbf{c}}$ are the predicted top encoder states, and context vector respectively; while $\{\bar{\mathbf{h}}_t\}_{t=1}^{|\mathbf{q}|}, \bar{\mathbf{c}}$ are their ground-truths. For all training samples of $\mathcal{P}$, the ground-truths can be computed by a single forward pass using $\mathcal{P}$. Unfortunately, in sequence-to-sequence with attention parser, the ground-truth top encoder states $\{\bar{\mathbf{h}}_t\}_{t=1}^{|\mathbf{p}^*|}$, for the new OOV query $\mathbf{p}^*$, are unknown. This cannot be computed even from the paraphrase $\mathbf{q}^*$ since they may have different lengths (example in Figure 1). In our paraphrase attention model, we can naturally fine-tune the encoder, since the attention is computed from a paraphrase $\mathbf{q}^*$. Specifically,

1. The ground-truth encoder 1 context $\bar{\mathbf{c}}$ is computed by encoding $\mathbf{q}^*$ using encoder 2, since query $\mathbf{p}^*$ should have the same meaning representation as $\mathbf{q}^*$.

2. The ground-truth encoder 2 states $\{\bar{\mathbf{h}}_t\}_{t=1}^{|\mathbf{q}^*|}$ are also computed by encoding $\mathbf{q}^*$ using encoder 2. Since only encoder 2 provides the attention signal, the different length of query $\mathbf{p}^*$ is irrelevant.

Figure 3 illustrates the encoder fine-tuning process for our parser. Note that, so far we have mainly described our sequence-to-sequence with paraphrase attention parser. However we can easily construct a similar sequence-to-tree with paraphrase attention parser by simply replacing the sequence decoder with the tree decoder in (Dong and Lapata, 2016).

Discussion: Note that, by fine-tuning using a MSE objective may result in a new context vector $\hat{\mathbf{c}}$ which is perturbed from the original semantic feature space that represented training queries. Thankfully, we observe in our experiments that the intermediate neural network layers are robust to small perturbations from the context feature space, and may not result in any significant changes in final classification output (or accuracy). Such robustness of intermediate layers have also been observed in works on neural network model compression (Denton et al., 2014; Aghasi et al., 2017; Kasiviswanathan et al., 2018).

To the best of our knowledge, this is the first work to use attention from paraphrase to improve parsing accuracy, and retraining time. Observe that, we harness accurate paraphrases from the training dataset itself as opposed to noisy auto-generated paraphrases from external resource like PPDB (Ganitkevitch et al., 2013; Dong et al., 2017), or a domain specific KB (Berant and Liang, 2014) used in recent literature. Moreover, in low resource languages such external paraphrase resource are generally unavailable. In (Ray et al., 2018) the authors train a paraphrase generator by first training an auto-encoder, and subsequently fine-tuning it with user provided paraphrases. In contrast, our model is trained using paraphrases identified within the training data even without any user input. Our model can also be trained end-to-end, unlike the hybrid parser model of (Ray et al., 2018).

4 Experiments

In this section we present our evaluation results. We have the following objectives. First we show that our new parsers using paraphrase attention can achieve a competitive or better parsing accuracy over previous models on benchmark datasets. Next, we present the main result that our new models can be retrained significantly faster to learn new OOV words/phrases than previous models.

4.1 Datasets

In order to test the performance of our model we consider three benchmark semantic parsing datasets:

1. *airline queries* dataset (ATIS) with 5,410 queries (4,480 training, 480 validation, 450 test)
2. *geographical queries* dataset (GEO) with 880 queries
3. *job queries* dataset (JOB) with 640 queries

For ATIS dataset we use the standard train-test split for our evaluation. However, for GEO and JOB datasets, owing to their small size, the parsing accuracy can vary significantly depending on the chosen split. Hence, in these smaller datasets we perform a 10 fold validation similar to (Wong and Mooney, 2007; Lu et al., 2008; Ray et al., 2018).

To test domain adaptation, we use OOV datasets used in (Ray et al., 2018) referred as PARA-ATIS and PARA-GEO datasets respectively (examples in Table 1). These datasets were constructed from benchmark datasets by substituting words w in the benchmark queries by synonymous OOV words and phrases $s \in Syn(w)$, to generate candidate paraphrases. For a given train–test split, the dataset is in the form of tuple pairs (word w, synonym s, $T_{trn}(w, s)$, $T_{tst}(w, s)$), where $T_{trn}(w, s)/T_{tst}(w, s)$ denotes the subset of queries from original train/test set where w has been replaced by s. The PARA-GEO dataset contains 180 word–synonym pairs and 5,783 OOV queries; while the PARA-ATIS dataset contains 161 word–synonym pairs and 13,501 OOV queries. Note that, the crowdsourced benchmark datasets contain typical queries that most users may ask. However, in order to test domain adaptation we need to consider atypical queries which are rare overall, but important for a particular user or locale. Hence, these OOV datasets containing atypical queries are suitable for this evaluation task.

Benchmark	Original benchmark query q^*	OOV substituted query p^*	Logical form $l(q^*)$	OOV dataset
ATIS	list all flights departing from $ap0$	list all flights taking off from $ap0$	(λ \$0 (and (flight \$0) (from \$0 $ap0$)))	PARA-ATIS
ATIS	i need a flight from $ci0$ to $ci1$	i require a flight from $ci0$ to $ci1$	(λ \$0 (and (flight \$0) (from \$0 $ci0$) (to \$0 $ci1$)))	PARA-ATIS
GEO	how many big cities are in $s0$	how many large cities are in $s0$	(count (λ \$0 (and (major \$0) (city \$0) (loc \$0 $s0$))))	PARA-GEO
GEO	which state has the highest elevation	which state has the highest natural elevation	(argmax (λ \$0 (state \$0)) (λ \$1 (elevation \$1)))	PARA-GEO

Table 1: Table showing examples from OOV datasets PARA-GEO and PARA-ATIS which were constructed from the benchmark GEO and ATIS datasets (Ray et al., 2018). Underlined words in the original benchmark queries are replaced with synonymous out-of-vocabulary words and phrases.

Model	10 fold accuracy %
COCKTAIL (Tang and Mooney, 2001)	79.40
argument transfer (Ray et al., 2018)	88.59
seq-to-seq + attention (our baseline)	93.75
seq-to-tree + attention (our baseline)	**95.31**
seq-to-seq + paraphrase attention (our model)	**95.31**
seq-to-tree + paraphrase attention (our model)	**95.31**

Table 2: Comparison of best 10 fold accuracy of all models on benchmark JOB dataset. In our paraphrase attention models we use $p = 50$ paraphrase pairs.

4.2 Methodology

First we train our parsers $\mathcal{P}$ on the combined dataset $T_a \cup T_p$, where T_a correspond to the argument replaced benchmark dataset, and T_p contain p^1 randomly sampled paraphrase pairs from the dataset T_a. We compare the parsing accuracy (computed as exact logical form match) on the test set with baseline attention based sequence-to-sequence and tree models by (Dong and Lapata, 2016). Next, to evaluate retraining performance, we follow the same experimental setup as (Ray et al., 2018). We fine-tune the parser $\mathcal{P}$ adding at most 5 samples (i.e. user provides 5 paraphrase pairs) from OOV training set $T_{trn}(w, s)$ to training set of $\mathcal{P}$, and test accuracy on the corresponding OOV test set $T_{tst}(w, s)$ (referred as the **retrained accuracy**). Within an appropriate retraining period, let t_b be the minimum time required by the baseline model to achieve best retrained accuracy, and t_p be the minimum time required by our paraphrase attention model to achieve the same retrained accuracy. We compute the retraining speedup t_b/t_p achieved by our parser over baseline. An alternative evaluation methodology involves crowdsourcing sentence level paraphrase datasets (from benchmark dataset) and split it into train–test sets containing different sentential paraphrases. However, such evaluation is less interpretable, since it is not clear exactly which words/phrases are leaned by the model. We defer this for our future work.

<hr>

[1]The number of paraphrase pairs p is treated as an additional hyperparameter.

Model	10 fold accuracy %
λ-WASP (Wong and Mooney, 2007)	86.60
generative model + EM (Lu et al., 2008)	81.80
paraphrase + arg. transfer (Ray et al., 2018)	88.30
seq-to-seq + attention (our baseline)	89.77
seq-to-tree + attention (our baseline)	90.91
seq-to-seq + paraphrase attention (our model)	90.91
seq-to-tree + paraphrase attention (our model)	**92.05**

Table 3: Comparison of best 10 fold accuracy of all models on benchmark GEO dataset. In our paraphrase attention models we use $p = 150$ paraphrase pairs.

4.3 Parameters

We implemented our models using Torch 7. All baseline model hyper-parameters were tuned on validation data. To test the performance gain, our models use the same hyper-parameters as the baseline model. To compare retraining time, all models were trained/retrained on a server with NVIDIA Tesla K80 GPU. At the encoder, we initialize all embedding vectors (including OOV words) with GLOVE embeddings (Pennington et al., 2014). RMSProp was used as the optimization algorithm. We restrict the embedding dimension, and hidden state dimension $d \in \{100, 200, 300\}$. The learning rate was chosen in the range $[0.0125, 0.005]$, and dropout rates among $\{0.5, 0.4, 0.3, 0.2\}$. For paraphrase attention models we choose the number of paraphrase pairs $p \in \{50, 100, 150, 200, 250\}$. For the baseline model, we use the code made available by the authors of (Dong and Lapata, 2016).

Model	test accuracy %
online CCG (Zettlemoyer and Collins, 2007)	84.60
seq-to-seq + attn + copy (Jia and Liang, 2016)	83.30
seq-to-seq + attn (Dong and Lapata, 2016)	84.20
seq-to-tree + attn (Dong and Lapata, 2016)	84.60
seq-to-seq + attn + arg. transfer (Ray et al., 2018)	85.27
coarse2fine (Dong and Lapata, 2018)	**87.70**
seq-to-seq + attention (our baseline)	85.71
seq-to-tree + attention (our baseline)	82.59
seq-to-seq + paraphrase attention (our model)	86.16
seq-to-tree + paraphrase attention (our model)	82.37

Table 4: Comparison of best test accuracy of all models on benchmark ATIS dataset. In our paraphrase attention models we use $p = 200$ paraphrase pairs.

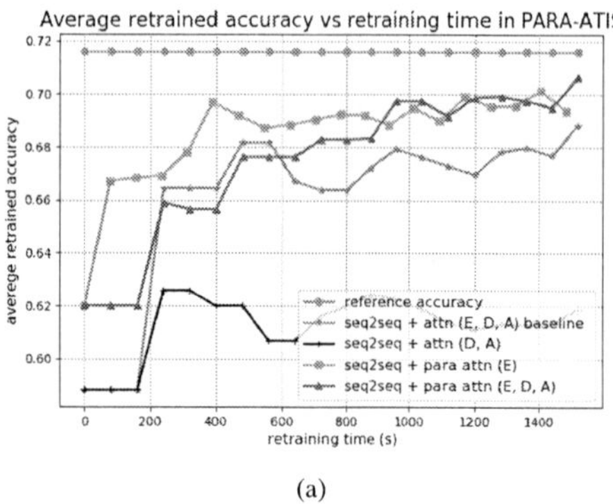

Average retrained accuracy vs retraining time in PARA-ATIS

(a)

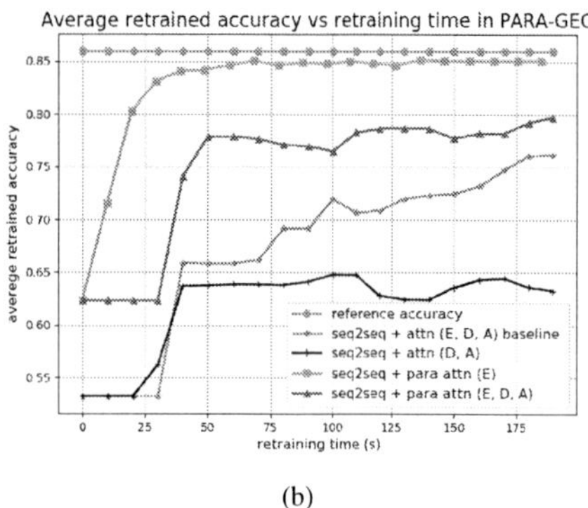

Average retrained accuracy vs retraining time in PARA-GEO

(b)

Figure 4: Comparison of the average retrained accuracy of all sequence-to-sequence based models with retraining time in (a) PARA-ATIS (b) PARA-GEO datasets. We show in brackets the part of the model being fine-tuned; where **Encoder=E, Decoder=D, Attention=A**. Our paraphrase attention model with encoder fine-tuning **seq2seq + para attn (E)**, reaches the retrained accuracy of baseline seq-to-seq + attention model 4X faster in PARA-ATIS, and 9X faster in PARA-GEO dataset.

4.4 Results

First, we compare the accuracy of our models to baseline sequence-to-sequence/tree with attention parsers (Dong and Lapata, 2016). Table 2 compares the best 10 fold accuracy achieved by all models in JOB dataset, while Table 3 compares the same in GEO dataset. For our paraphrase attention models we randomly choose $p = 50$ paraphrase pairs in JOB dataset, and $p = 150$ paraphrase pairs in GEO dataset. We observe our paraphrase attention parsers to outperform most baseline models achieving state-of-the-art 10 fold accuracy. In Table 4 we report the best test accuracy achieved in ATIS dataset. In this dataset we use $p = 200$ paraphrase pairs for our paraphrase attention models. Our sequence-to-sequence + paraphrase attention model achieves a highly competitive accuracy of

86.16% on the benchmark test set outperforming all baselines except (Dong and Lapata, 2018). We remind that, our models do not use any external data compared to baselines since the paraphrases are harnessed from the training data itself.

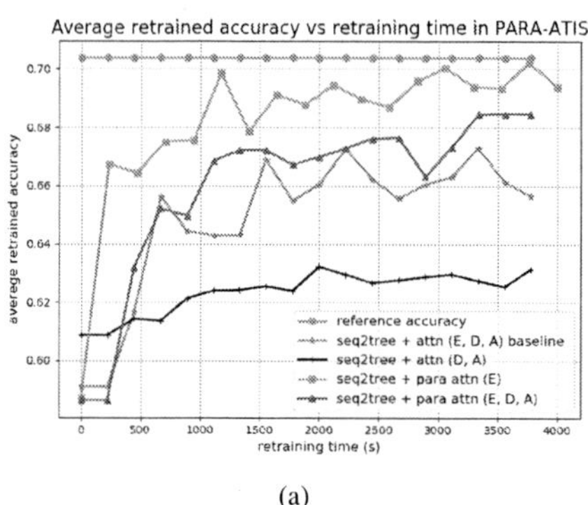

Average retrained accuracy vs retraining time in PARA-ATIS

(a)

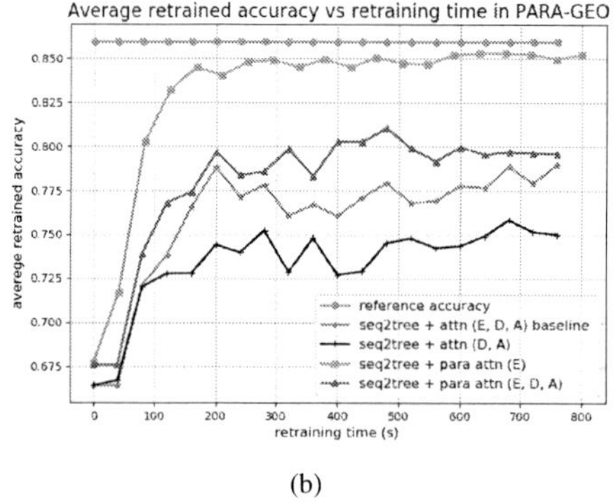

Average retrained accuracy vs retraining time in PARA-GEO

(b)

Figure 5: Comparison of the average retrained accuracy of all sequence-to-tree based models with retraining time in (a) PARA-ATIS (b) PARA-GEO datasets. We show in brackets the part of the model being fine-tuned; where **Encoder=E, Decoder=D, Attention=A**. Our paraphrase attention model with encoder fine-tuning **seq2tree + para attn (E)**, reaches the retrained accuracy of baseline seq-to-tree + attn model 3X faster in PARA-ATIS, and 5X faster in PARA-GEO dataset.

Next, we present our main domain adaptation results by comparing the retraining performance of all models using the OOV datasets. In Figure 4, we plot the average retrained accuracy versus retraining time for PARA-ATIS and PARA-GEO datasets using sequence-to-sequence based models. The average retrained accuracy is computed on the OOV test set $T_{tst}(w, s)$, and further averaged over all word–synonym pairs in this dataset. We observe that, our sequence-to-sequence + paraphrase attention model with fast encoder fine-tuning (referred as *seq2seq+para attn (E))*, achieves the maximum retrained accuracy of baseline sequence-to-sequence + attention model (denoted as *seq2seq+attn (E,D,A)*) **4X faster** in PARA-ATIS, and **9X faster** in PARA-GEO dataset. The **reference accuracy** denotes the accuracy of the original parser $\mathcal{P}$, on the subset of test queries from which the OOV test set $T_{tst}(w, s)$ was obtained, and acts as a soft upper bound on retrained accuracy. Ideally, the fine-tuned parser $\mathcal{P}'$ should achieve retrained accuracy comparable to this target reference. In PARA-GEO dataset, our model achieves accuracy close to the reference. As discussed in Section 3, the baseline parser can also be fine-tuned faster by freezing encoder parameters, and retraining only the decoder + attention layers. This however achieves a poor retrained accuracy as shown in Figure 4 (denoted as *seq2seq+attn (D,A)*) since proper encoder representations corresponding to OOV words are not learned. In Figure 5 we compare the retraining performance of all sequence-to-tree based models. We again observe that sequence-to-tree with paraphrase attention model achieves maximum retrained accuracy of baseline model **3X faster** in PARA-ATIS, and **5X faster** in PARA-GEO dataset.

Finally, in Figure 6 we plot the average retraining time with epochs, for all sequence-to-sequence models. As expected, our paraphrase attention model with fast encoder fine-tuning (seq2seq + para attn (E)) is the fastest, and it shows a runtime speedup of 3X-4X over baseline models in both OOV datasets. When we fine-tune the entire paraphrase attention model, this too takes similar runtime as the baseline (with full model fine-tuning). When the baseline model is fine-tuned with frozen encoder parameters, it is relatively faster since the gradients need not be back-propagated to the encoder. However, as shown earlier in Figure 4, this model achieves very poor retrained accuracy. Note that, it is possible to fine-tune the baseline model with frozen decoder + attention layers, updating only encoder parameters. However, this is not expected to be significantly faster than full model fine-tuning, since it still needs to compute all decoder and attention gradients in order to back-propagate the gradients to the encoder.

5   Conclusion

Post-deployment domain adaptation of intelligent agent to better understand user and locale specific vocabulary require frequent retraining of

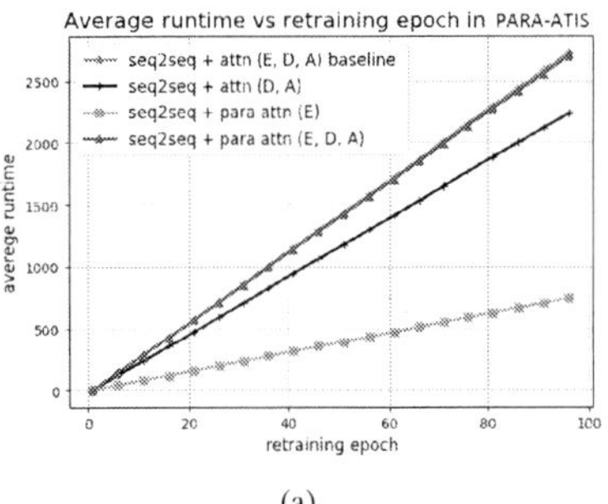

(a)

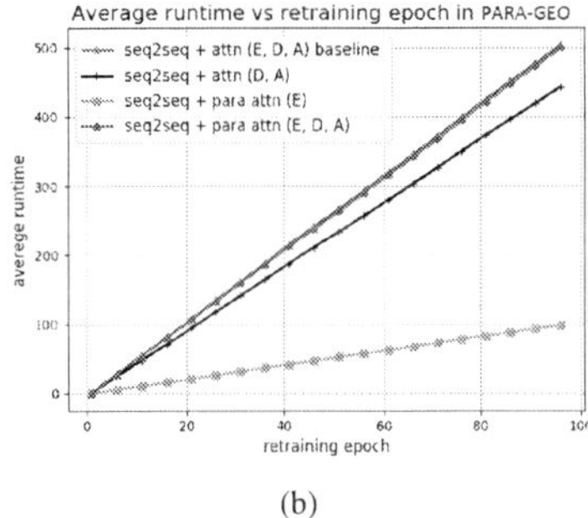

(b)

Figure 6: Figure showing the average runtime of all sequence-to-sequence models with retraining epochs in (a) PARA-ATIS (b) PARA-GEO datasets. We show in brackets the part of the model being fine-tuned; where **Encoder=E, Decoder=D, Attention=A**. Our paraphrase attention model, with fast encoder fine-tuning, achieves a 3X-4X runtime speedup over baseline seq-to-seq + attention model in both dataset.

its semantic parser. In this paper, we propose novel paraphrase attention based sequence-to-sequence/tree models for semantic parsing, which enables near real-time domain adaptation. Our parsers can be retrained quickly by fine-tuning just the encoder network; which was not possible in previous attention based parsers. On OOV datasets our parsers are shown to achieve target retrained accuracy over 3-9X faster than baseline parsers. Moreover, by jointly learning the semantic relationship between paraphrases within the model, our parsers can achieve better or comparable parsing accuracy to previous models on benchmark datasets. Our models can also be easily adapted to transformer based sequence networks, which outperform recurrent networks for many NLP tasks (Vaswani et al., 2017; Devlin et al., 2019), as shown recently.

References

Alireza Aghasi, Afshin Abdi, Nam Nguyen, and Justin Romberg. 2017. Net-trim: Convex pruning of deep neural networks with performance guarantee. In *Proc. of NIPS, 2017*, pages 3180–3189.

Yoav Artzi and Luke Zettlemoyer. 2013. Weakly supervised learning of semantic parsers for mapping instructions to actions. *TACL*, 1:49–62.

Amos Azaria, Jayant Krishnamurthy, and Tom M Mitchell. 2016. Instructable intelligent personal agent. In *Proc. of the 30th AAAI*, pages 2681–2689.

Dzmitry Bahdanau, Kyunghyun Cho, and Yoshua Bengio. 2015. Neural machine translation by jointly learning to align and translate. In *Proceedings of the ICLR, San Diego, California*.

Jonathan Berant and Percy Liang. 2014. Semantic parsing via paraphrasing. In *Proc. of ACL (1)*, pages 1415–1425.

Kyunghyun Cho, Bart van Merrienboer, Çaglar Gülçehre, Dzmitry Bahdanau, Fethi Bougares, Holger Schwenk, and Yoshua Bengio. 2014. Learning phrase representations using RNN encoder-decoder for statistical machine translation. In *Proc. of the 2014 EMNLP*, pages 1724–1734.

Emily L. Denton, Wojciech Zaremba, Joan Bruna, Yann LeCun, and Rob Fergus. 2014. Exploiting linear structure within convolutional networks for efficient evaluation. In *Annual Conference on Neural Information Processing Systems NIPS, 2014*, pages 1269–1277.

Jacob Devlin, Ming-Wei Chang, Kenton Lee, and Kristina Toutanova. 2019. BERT: pre-training of deep bidirectional transformers for language understanding. In *Proceedings of the 2019 Conference of the North American Chapter of the Association for Computational Linguistics: Human Language Technologies, NAACL-HLT 2019, Minneapolis, MN, USA, June 2-7, 2019, Volume 1 (Long and Short Papers)*, pages 4171–4186.

Li Dong and Mirella Lapata. 2016. Language to logical form with neural attention. In *Proc. of the 54th ACL 2016*.

Li Dong and Mirella Lapata. 2018. Coarse-to-fine decoding for neural semantic parsing. In *Proc. of ACL 2018, Volume 1: Long Papers*, pages 731–742.

Li Dong, Jonathan Mallinson, Siva Reddy, and Mirella Lapata. 2017. Learning to paraphrase for question answering. In *Proc. of EMNLP 2017*, pages 875–886.

Xing Fan, Emilio Monti, Lambert Mathias, and Markus Dreyer. 2017. Transfer learning for neural semantic parsing. In *Proceedings of the 2nd Workshop on Representation Learning for NLP, Rep4NLP@ACL 2017, Vancouver, Canada, August 3, 2017*, pages 48–56.

Juri Ganitkevitch, Benjamin Van Durme, and Chris Callison-Burch. 2013. PPDB: the paraphrase database. In *Human Language Technologies: Conference of the North American Chapter of the Association of Computational Linguistics, Proceedings, June 9-14, 2013, Westin Peachtree Plaza Hotel, Atlanta, Georgia, USA*, pages 758–764.

Jonathan Herzig and Jonathan Berant. 2017. Neural semantic parsing over multiple knowledge-bases. In *Proceedings of the 55th Annual Meeting of the Association for Computational Linguistics, ACL 2017, Vancouver, Canada, July 30 - August 4, Volume 2: Short Papers*, pages 623–628.

Srinivasan Iyer, Ioannis Konstas, Alvin Cheung, Jayant Krishnamurthy, and Luke Zettlemoyer. 2017. Learning a neural semantic parser from user feedback. In *Proc. of the ACL 2017, Volume 1: Long Papers*, pages 963–973.

Robin Jia and Percy Liang. 2016. Data recombination for neural semantic parsing. In *Proc. of the 54th ACL*.

Shiva Prasad Kasiviswanathan, Nina Narodytska, and Hongxia Jin. 2018. Network approximation using tensor sketching. In *Proc. of the 27th IJCAI 2018*, pages 2319–2325.

Young-Bum Kim, Dongchan Kim, Anjishnu Kumar, and Ruhi Sarikaya. 2018. Efficient large-scale neural domain classification with personalized attention. In *Proc. of the ACL 2018, Volume 1: Long Papers*, pages 2214–2224.

Tom Kwiatkowski, Luke Zettlemoyer, Sharon Goldwater, and Mark Steedman. 2010. Inducing probabilistic ccg grammars from logical form with higher-order unification. In *Proc. of the 2010 EMNLP*, pages 1223–1233. ACL.

Tom Kwiatkowski, Luke Zettlemoyer, Sharon Goldwater, and Mark Steedman. 2011. Lexical generalization in ccg grammar induction for semantic parsing. In *Proc. of EMNLP, 2011*, pages 1512–1523. ACL.

Wei Lu, Hwee Tou Ng, Wee Sun Lee, and Luke S. Zettlemoyer. 2008. A generative model for parsing natural language to meaning representations. In *Proc. of EMNLP 2008*, pages 783–792.

Jeffrey Pennington, Richard Socher, and Christopher D. Manning. 2014. Glove: Global vectors for word representation. In *Proc. of EMNLP 2014*, pages 1532–1543.

Aaditya Prakash, Sadid A. Hasan, Kathy Lee, Vivek V. Datla, Ashequl Qadir, Joey Liu, and Oladimeji Farri. 2016. Neural paraphrase generation with stacked residual LSTM networks. In *Proc. of COLING 2016*, pages 2923–2934.

Avik Ray, Yilin Shen, and Hongxia Jin. 2018. Learning out-of-vocabulary words in intelligent personal agents. In *Proc. of the 27th International Joint Conference on Artificial Intelligence, IJCAI 2018*, pages 4309–4315.

Ilya Sutskever, Oriol Vinyals, and Quoc V Le. 2014. Sequence to sequence learning with neural networks. In *Proc. of NIPS*, pages 3104–3112.

Lappoon R. Tang and Raymond J. Mooney. 2001. Using multiple clause constructors in inductive logic programming for semantic parsing. In *Proc. of EMCL 2001*, pages 466–477.

Jesse Thomason, Shiqi Zhang, Raymond J. Mooney, and Peter Stone. 2015. Learning to interpret natural language commands through human-robot dialog. In *Proc. of IJCAI 2015,*, pages 1923–1929.

Ashish Vaswani, Noam Shazeer, Niki Parmar, Jakob Uszkoreit, Llion Jones, Aidan N. Gomez, Lukasz Kaiser, and Illia Polosukhin. 2017. Attention is all you need. In *Advances in Neural Information Processing Systems 30: Annual Conference on Neural Information Processing Systems 2017, 4-9 December 2017, Long Beach, CA, USA*, pages 6000–6010.

Oriol Vinyals, Meire Fortunato, and Navdeep Jaitly. 2015a. Pointer networks. In *Proc. of NIPS*, pages 2692–2700.

Oriol Vinyals, Lukasz Kaiser, Terry Koo, Slav Petrov, Ilya Sutskever, and Geoffrey E. Hinton. 2015b. Grammar as a foreign language. In *Proc. of NIPS*, pages 2773–2781.

Yuk Wah Wong and Raymond J Mooney. 2007. Learning synchronous grammars for semantic parsing with lambda calculus. In *ACL*, volume 45, page 960.

John M Zelle and Raymond J Mooney. 1996. Learning to parse database queries using inductive logic programming. In *Proceedings of the national conference on artificial intelligence*, pages 1050–1055.

Luke S Zettlemoyer and Michael Collins. 2005. Learning to map sentences to logical form: Structured classification with probabilistic categorial grammars. In *Proc. of the 21st UAI*, pages 658–666.

Luke S Zettlemoyer and Michael Collins. 2007. Online learning of relaxed ccg grammars for parsing to logical form. In *EMNLP-CoNLL*, pages 678–687.

Few-Shot and Zero-Shot Learning for Historical Text Normalization

Marcel Bollmann[♣] and **Natalia Korchagina**[◇] and **Anders Søgaard**[♣]

[♣]Department of Computer Science, University of Copenhagen
[◇]Institute of Computational Linguistics, University of Zurich
marcel@di.ku.dk, korchagina@ifi.uzh.ch, soegaard@di.ku.dk

Abstract

Historical text normalization often relies on small training datasets. Recent work has shown that multi-task learning can lead to significant improvements by exploiting synergies with related datasets, but there has been no systematic study of different multi-task learning architectures. This paper evaluates 63 multi-task learning configurations for sequence-to-sequence-based historical text normalization across ten datasets from eight languages, using autoencoding, grapheme-to-phoneme mapping, and lemmatization as auxiliary tasks. We observe consistent, significant improvements across languages when training data for the target task is limited, but minimal or no improvements when training data is abundant. We also show that zero-shot learning outperforms the simple, but relatively strong, identity baseline.

1 Introduction

Historical text normalization is the task of mapping variant spellings in historical documents—e.g., digitized medieval manuscripts—to a common form, typically their modern equivalent. The aim is to make these documents amenable to search by today's scholars, processable by NLP tools, and accessible to lay people. Many historical documents were written in the absence of standard spelling conventions, and annotated datasets are rare and small, making automatic normalization a challenging task (cf. Piotrowski, 2012; Bollmann, 2018).

In this paper, we experiment with datasets in eight different languages: English, German, Hungarian, Icelandic, Portuguese, Slovene, Spanish, and Swedish. We use a standard neural sequence-to-sequence model, which has been shown to be competitive for this task (e.g., Korchagina, 2017; Bollmann, 2018; Tang et al., 2018). Our main focus is on analyzing the usefulness of multi-task

learning strategies (a) to leverage whatever supervision is available for the language in question (*few-shot learning*), or (b) to do away with the need for supervision in the target language altogether (*zero-shot learning*).

Bollmann et al. (2017) previously showed that multi-task learning with grapheme-to-phoneme conversion as an auxiliary task improves a sequence-to-sequence model for historical text normalization of German texts; Bollmann et al. (2018) showed that multi-task learning is particularly helpful in low-resource scenarios. We consider three auxiliary tasks in our experiments—grapheme-to-phoneme mapping, autoencoding, and lemmatization—and focus on extremely low-resource settings.

Our paper makes several contributions:

(a) We evaluate 63 multi-task learning configurations across ten datasets in eight languages, and with three different auxiliary tasks.

(b) We show that in few-shot learning scenarios (ca. 1,000 tokens), multi-task learning leads to robust, significant gains over a state-of-the-art, single-task baseline.[1]

(c) We are, to the best of our knowledge, the first to consider *zero-shot historical text normalization*, and we show significant improvements over the simple, but relatively strong, identity baseline.

While our focus is on the specific task of historical text normalization, we believe that our results can be of interest to anyone looking to apply multi-task learning in low-resource scenarios.

---

[1]We note that 1,000 tokens is more instances than is typically considered in few-shot learning; e.g., Kimura et al. (2018) use up to 200 instances. We argue that for structured prediction it is reasonable to assume more data, yet we also consider scenarios down to as little as 100 instances.

Proceedings of the 2nd Workshop on Deep Learning Approaches for Low-Resource NLP (DeepLo), pages 104–114
Hong Kong, China, November 3, 2019. ©2019 Association for Computational Linguistics
https://doi.org/10.18653/v1/P17

Dataset/Language		Tokens (Dev)
DE$_A$	German (Anselm)	45,996
DE$_R$	German (RIDGES)	9,712
EN	English	16,334
ES	Spanish	11,650
HU	Hungarian	16,707
IS	Icelandic	6,109
PT	Portuguese	26,749
SL$_B$	Slovene (Bohorič)	5,841
SL$_G$	Slovene (Gaj)	20,878
SV	Swedish	2,245

Table 1: Historical datasets used in our experiments and the size of their development sets. (Size of the training sets is fixed in all our experiments.)

Datasets We consider ten datasets spanning eight languages, taken from Bollmann (2019).[2] Table 1 gives an overview of the languages and the size of the development set, which we use for evaluation.

2 Model architecture

We use a standard attentional encoder–decoder architecture (Bahdanau et al., 2014) with words as input sequences and characters as input symbols.[3] Following the majority of previous work on this topic (cf. Sec. 5), we limit ourselves to word-by-word normalization, ignoring problems of contextual ambiguity. Our model consists of the following parts (which we will also refer to using the bolded letters):

- **S**ource embedding layer: transforms input characters into dense vectors.

- **E**ncoder: a single bidirectional LSTM that encodes the embedded input sequence.

- **A**ttention layer: calculates attention from the encoded inputs and the current decoder state using a multi-layer perceptron (as in Bahdanau et al., 2014).

- **T**arget embedding layer: transforms output characters into dense vectors.

- **D**ecoder: a single LSTM that decodes the encoded sequence one character at a time, using

the attention vector and the embedded previous output characters as input.

- **P**rediction layer: a final feed-forward layer that linearly transforms the decoder output and performs a softmax to predict a distribution over all possible output characters.

Hyperparameters We tuned our hyperparameters on the English development section. We use randomly initialized embeddings of dimensionality 60, hidden layers of dimensionality 300, a dropout of 0.2 and a batch size of 30. We train the model for an unspecified number of epochs, instead relying on early stopping on a held-out validation set. Since we experiment with varying amounts of training data, we choose to derive this held-out data from the given training set, using only 90% of the tokens as actual training data and the remaining 10% to determine early stopping.

3 Multi-task learning

Multi-task learning (MTL) is a technique to improve generalization by training a model jointly on a set of related tasks. We follow the common approach of hard parameter sharing suggested by Caruana (1993), in which certain parts of a model architecture are shared across all tasks, while others are kept distinct for each one. Such approaches have been applied successfully to a variety of problems, e.g., machine translation (Dong et al., 2015), sequence labelling (Yang et al., 2016; Peng and Dredze, 2017), or discourse parsing (Braud et al., 2016).

Auxiliary tasks We experiment with the following auxiliary tasks:

- **Autoencoding.** We use data extracted from Wikipedia[4] and train our model to recreate the input words. In the normalization task, large parts of the input words often stay the same, so autoencoding might help to reinforce this behavior in the model.

- **Grapheme-to-phoneme mapping (g2p).** This task uses the data by Deri and Knight

---

[2]The datasets are available from: `https://github.com/coastalcph/histnorm`

[3]Our implementation uses the XNMT toolkit (Neubig et al., 2018, `https://github.com/neulab/xnmt`).

[4]Whenever possible, we used the dumps provided by the Polyglot project: `https://sites.google.com/site/rmyeid/projects/polyglot` Since an Icelandic text dump was not available from Polyglot, we generated one ourselves using the Cirrus Extractor: `https://github.com/attardi/wikiextractor` All dumps were cleaned from punctuation marks.

(2016) to map words (i.e., sequences of graphemes) to sequences of phonemes. Bollmann et al. (2017) previously showed that this task can improve historical normalization, possibly because changes in spelling are often motivated by phonological processes, an assumption also made by other normalization systems (Porta et al., 2013; Etxeberria et al., 2016).

- **Lemmatization.** We use the UniMorph dataset (Kirov et al., 2018)[5] to learn mappings from inflected word forms to their lemmas. This task is similar to normalization in that it maps a set of different word forms to a single target form, which typically bears a high resemblance to the input words.

Since we train separate models for each historical dataset, we always use auxiliary data from the same language as the dataset.

Training details When training an MTL model, we make sure that each training update is based on a balanced combination of main and auxiliary task inputs; i.e., for each batch of 30 tokens of the historical normalization task, the model will see 10 tokens from each auxiliary task. Epochs are still counted based on the normalization task only. This way, we try to make up for the imbalanced quantity of different auxiliary datasets.

3.1 Experiment 1: What to share?

In previous work on multi-task learning, there is no clear consensus on which parts of a model to share and which to keep separate. Bollmann et al. (2017) share all parts of the model except for the final prediction layer, while other multi-task sequence-to-sequence models keep task-specific encoders and decoders (cf. also Sec. 5). In principle, though, the decision to share parameters between tasks can be made for each of the encoder–decoder components individually, allowing for many more possible MTL configurations.

Setup We explore the effect of different sharing configurations. The architecture described in Sec. 2 leaves us with $2^6 = 64$ possible model configurations. When all parameters are shared, this is identical to training a single model to perform all tasks at once; when none are shared, this is identical to a single-task model trained on historical

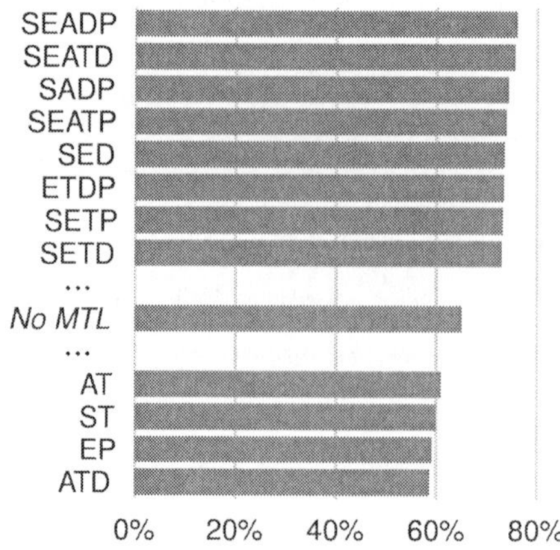

Figure 1: Normalization accuracy on the English-1k dataset, trained jointly with all three auxiliary tasks; letters indicate which model components (cf. Sec. 2) are shared between tasks.

normalization only. We identify an MTL configuration using letters (cf. the bold letters from Sec. 2) to indicate which parts of the model are shared; e.g., an "SE" model would share the source embeddings and the encoder, an "SEATD" model would share everything except the final prediction layer, and so on.

In Experiment 1, we only use the first 1,000 tokens of the English historical dataset for training. We combine this with all three auxiliary tasks (using their full datasets) and train one MTL model for each of the 64 different sharing configurations.

Results Figure 1 shows an excerpt of the results, evaluated on the dev set of the English dataset. The best MTL model achieves a normalization accuracy of 75.9%, while the worst model gets 58.6%. In total, 49 configurations outperform the single-task model, showing the general effectiveness of the MTL approach. Sharing more is generally better; nine out of the top ten configurations share at least four components. Figure 2 visualizes the accuracy distribution by the number of shared components in the MTL model, supporting this conclusion.

3.2 Experiment 2: Which auxiliary tasks?

In the previous experiment, we trained the models using all three auxiliary tasks at the same time. However, not all of these tasks might be equally helpful for learning the normalization task. While Bollmann et al. (2017) show the effectiveness of

---

[5]https://unimorph.github.io/

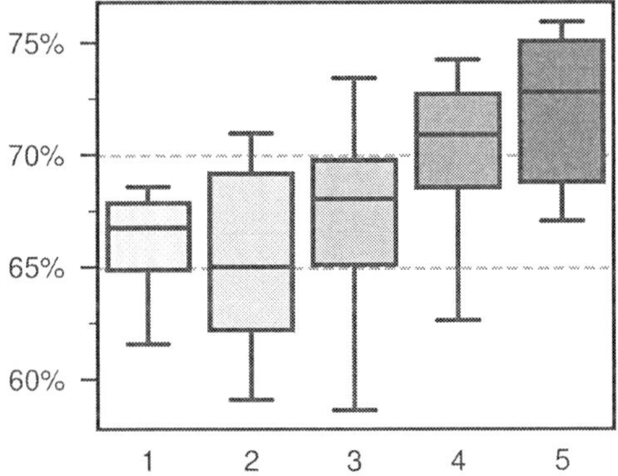

Figure 2: Quartiles of the normalization accuracies (on English-1k) by the number of shared components in the MTL model; bottom dashed line indicates no shared components (= single-task), top dashed line indicates all (= 6) shared components.

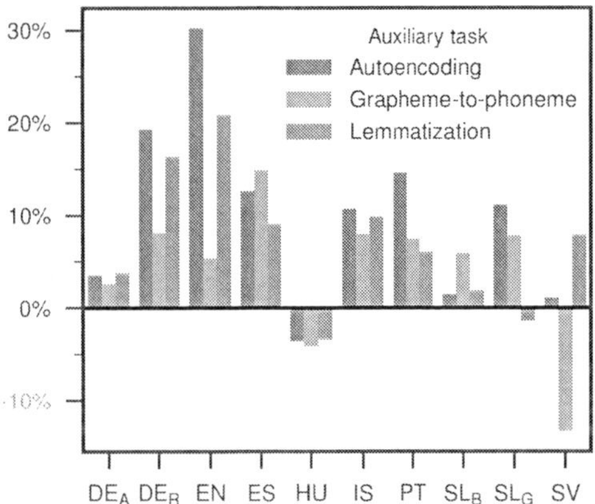

Figure 3: Error reduction for the SEADP configuration by auxiliary task, using 1,000 tokens from the historical datasets for training.

the grapheme-to-phoneme task, they only evaluate on German, and autoencoding and lemmatization have so far not been evaluated at all for improving historical text normalization.

Setup We want to investigate the improvements from each auxiliary task in isolation compared to (a) the single-task baseline and (b) the previous approach of training with all three auxiliary tasks simultaneously. For this, we select the best MTL configuration from Sec. 3.1, which is to share everything except the target embeddings ("SEADP"), and train one single-task model and four MTL models per dataset: one for each of the three auxiliary tasks, and one that uses all three tasks at the same time.

As before, we only use the first 1,000 tokens of each historical dataset. This also makes the results more comparable across datasets, as the size of the training set for the main task can affect the usefulness of multi-task learning.[6]

Results Figure 3 shows the error reduction of the MTL models compared to the single-task setup. For most datasets, MTL improves the results; the main exception is Hungarian, where all three auxiliary tasks lead to a loss in accuracy. The results show that not all auxiliary tasks

are equally beneficial. Autoencoding provides the largest error reduction in most cases, while lemmatization is often slightly worse, but provides the best result for German (Anselm) and Swedish. The grapheme-to-phoneme task, on the other hand, performs worst on average, yielding much less benefits on German (Ridges) and English, and even *increases* the error on Swedish.

Table 2a shows the accuracy scores for all datasets and models. The full MTL model—training jointly on all tasks—only achieves the best performance on four of the datasets. Since the dev sets used for this evaluation vary strongly in size, we also calculate the *micro-average* of the accuracy scores, i.e., the accuracy obtained over the concatenation of all datasets. Here, we can see that using only autoencoding as an auxiliary task actually produces the highest average accuracy.

3.3 Experiment 3: How much training data?

All previous experiments have used 1,000 tokens from each historical dataset for training. Bollmann et al. (2018) show that the benefits of multi-task learning depend on training data quantity, so it is unclear whether the findings generalize to smaller or larger datasets.

Setup We analyze the benefit of MTL depending on the amount of training data that is used for the main task. We do this by training MTL models (using all three auxiliary tasks, as in Sec. 3.1) with varying amounts of historical training data, ranging from 100 tokens to 50,000 tokens. Different

---

[6]The same is true, of course, for the size of the auxiliary datasets. We try to balance out this factor by balancing the training updates as described in Sec. 3 "Training details", but we also note that we do not observe a correlation between auxiliary dataset size and its effectiveness for MTL in Fig. 3.

Dataset	Single	Multi-task				Dataset	Best in (a)	from Bollmann (2019)		
		Autoenc	Lemma	g2p	ALL 3			Norma	SMT	NMT
DE_A	54.84	56.41	**56.55**	55.99	56.52	DE_A	56.55	**61.27**	58.60	52.74
DE_R	56.72	**65.05**	63.79	60.25	64.49	DE_R	65.05	73.62	**75.04**	60.61
EN	66.95	**76.94**	73.84	68.72	72.01	EN	76.94	**84.53**	83.81	66.93
ES	74.68	77.87	76.97	78.45	**79.09**	ES	79.09	**86.21**	85.89	76.32
HU	**42.44**	40.39	40.49	40.07	38.64	HU	42.44	**55.75**	53.00	40.52
IS	63.40	67.31	67.02	66.31	**68.51**	IS	68.51	70.86	**72.30**	62.80
PT	72.23	**76.28**	73.89	74.27	75.55	PT	76.28	**82.94**	82.00	71.43
SL_B	74.06	74.44	74.54	**75.59**	74.39	SL_B	75.59	78.97	**82.90**	73.83
SL_G	86.34	87.86	86.15	87.40	**89.45**	SL_G	89.45	84.36	**90.00**	86.31
SV	69.98	70.29	72.34	65.97	**73.05**	SV	73.05	74.54	**78.51**	66.43
Micro-Avg	64.46	**67.46**	66.47	65.79	67.04	Micro-Avg	68.13	**73.30**	73.07	63.80

(a) Single-task vs. multi-task models (b) Comparison to previous work

Table 2: Normalization accuracy on dev sets after training on 1,000 tokens. Best results highlighted in bold.

sharing configurations might conceivably give different benefits based on the training set size. We therefore evaluate each of the top three MTL configurations from Sec. 3.1, as well as the single-task model, across different data sizes.

Results Figure 4 shows learning curves for all of our historical datasets. The quantity of improvements from MTL differs between datasets, but there is a clear tendency for MTL to become less beneficial as the size of the normalization training set increases. In some cases, using MTL with larger training set sizes even results in *lower* accuracy compared to training a single-task model to do normalization only. This suggests that multi-task learning—at least with the auxiliary tasks we have chosen here—is mostly useful when the training data for the main task is sparse.

Since the accuracy scores of the different models are often within close range of each other, Figure 5 visualizes the three MTL configurations in terms of error reduction compared to the single-task model, averaged over all ten datasets. This again highlights the decreasing gains from MTL with increasing amounts of training data.

3.4 Comparison to previous work

Bollmann (2019) compares normalization models when trained with different amounts of data, including a setting with 1,000 tokens for training, allowing us to directly compare our results with those reported there.[7] These results are shown in Table 2b. Comparing our single-task system with

---

[7]Bollmann (2019) only shows graphical plots for these results, but the exact figures were released at: `https://github.com/coastalcph/histnorm/blob/master/appendix_tab6.pdf`

their NMT model (which is very similar to ours), we see that the scores are overall comparable, suggesting that our implementation is sound. At the same time, our best scores with MTL are still far below those produced by SMT or the rule-based "Norma" tool. This, unfortunately, is a negative result for the neural approach in this low-resource scenario, and the diminishing gains from MTL that were shown in Sec. 3.3 suggest that our presented approach will not be sufficient for elevating the neural model above its non-neural alternatives for this particular task.

3.5 Experiment 4: Zero-shot learning

Most previous work on historical text normalization has focused on a supervised scenario where some labeled data is available for the target domain, i.e., the particular historical language you are interested in. Since spelling variation is highly idiosyncratic in the absence of normative spelling guidelines, models are not expected to generalize beyond specific language stages, or sometimes even manuscript collections. This means that many historical text normalization projects require resources to annotate new data. This paper is the first to experiment with a zero-shot learning scenario that leverages existing data from other languages, but assumes *no* labeled data for the target language.

Setup For the zero-shot experiments, we use the same model as for the single-task baseline; in other words, all layers are shared between all tasks and languages. Instead, to allow the model to discern between languages and tasks, we prepend two extra symbols to all model inputs: a *lan-*

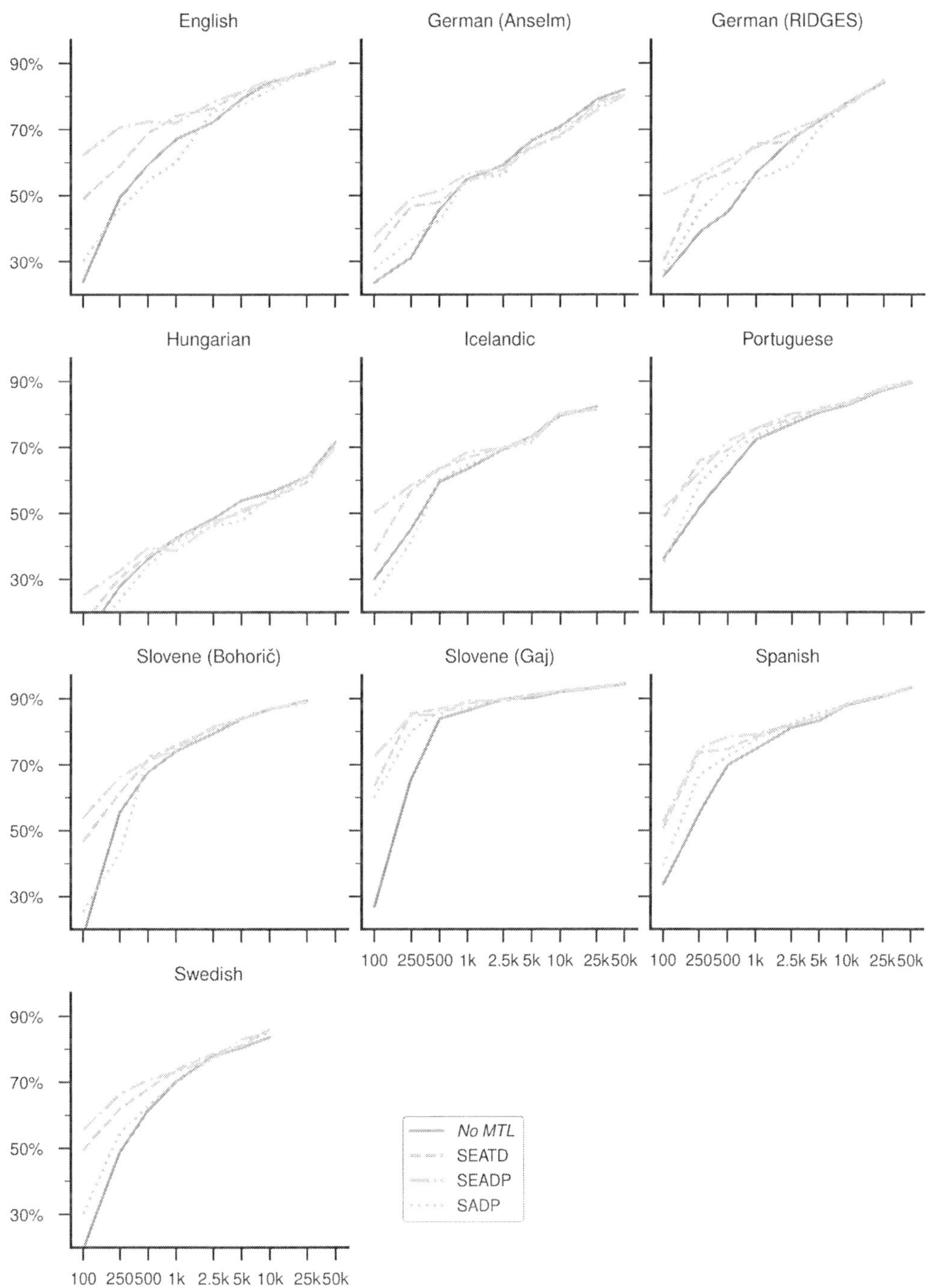

Figure 4: Learning curves for all datasets, showing the normalization accuracy of a single-task and three multi-task learning models in relation to the training set size; note that the x-axis is log-scaled.

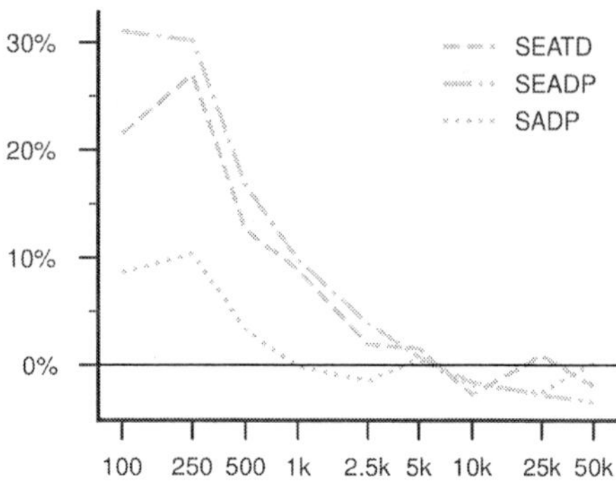

Figure 5: Error reduction for three MTL configurations by training set size, (micro-)averaged over all datasets.

Dataset	Identity	Zero-shot
DE_A	30.16	**40.94**
DE_R	43.57	**55.92**
EN	**75.47**	56.31
ES	**72.29**	64.39
HU	17.81	**20.58**
IS	**47.77**	42.95
PT	65.18	**67.64**
SL_B	39.84	**50.21**
SL_G	**85.58**	84.99
SV	**59.24**	50.65
Micro-Avg	50.17	**52.96**

Table 3: Normalization accuracy on dev sets for zero-shot experiments. Best results highlighted in bold.

4 Analysis

The experiment in Sec. 3.2 has shown that not all auxiliary tasks are equally useful; furthermore, autoencoding is, on average, the most useful auxiliary task of the three, closely followed by lemmatization. This gives rise to the hypothesis that MTL mostly helps the model learn the identity mappings between characters.

To analyze this, we feed the historical data into the *auxiliary models;* i.e., we treat them *as if* they were a historical text normalization model. We then correlate their normalization accuracy with the error reduction over the baseline of the MTL model using this auxiliary task. Figure 6a shows a strong correlation for the autoencoding task, suggesting that the synergy between autoencoding and historical text normalization is higher *when the two tasks are very related.* Figure 6b shows the same correlation for lemmatization.

We can also compare the error reduction from MTL to the identity baseline (cf. Tab. 3). Figure 7 shows the correlation of these scores for the full MTL model trained with all three auxiliary tasks.[8] The strong correlation suggests that the regularization effect introduced by MTL is particularly helpful with tasks where there is a strong similarity between input and output; or, in other words, that *multi-task learning prevents the model from over-generalizing* based on the training data.

The previous correlation scores only consider the performance of models trained on 1,000 tokens of historical data. Sec. 3.3 showed that the benefit of MTL diminishes when the size of the historical training sets gets larger. Figure 8 presents learning

guage identifier and a *task identifier.* For each language, we then train a single model on all tasks— normalization, lemmatization, autoencoding, and grapheme-to-phoneme transduction—and all languages, *except* for the normalization task of the target language. This way, the model can observe data from the normalization task (albeit in other languages) and from the target language (albeit from auxiliary tasks only), but does not see any normalization data from the target language. In those cases where there are two datasets from the same language, we leave out *both* of them from the training step. The model is similar to previous work on zero-shot neural machine translation (Johnson et al., 2016).

As before, we include only 1,000 tokens from each historical dataset for training. In each training update, we use an equal number of samples from each dataset/task combination, and define an epoch to consist of 1,000 samples from each of these combinations. Since we do not want to feed the model any normalization data from the target language during training, we cannot use early stopping, but instead train for a fixed number of 10 epochs.

Results   Table 3 shows the accuracy of zero-shot normalization compared to the naive *identity baseline,* i.e., the accuracy obtained by simply leaving the input word forms unchanged. The zero-shot approach improves over this baseline for half of the datasets, sometimes by up to 12 percentage points (DE_R). Micro-averaging the results shows an overall advantage for zero-shot learning.

---

[8]The correlation is similar when using longest common subsequence or Levenshtein distance instead of accuracy.

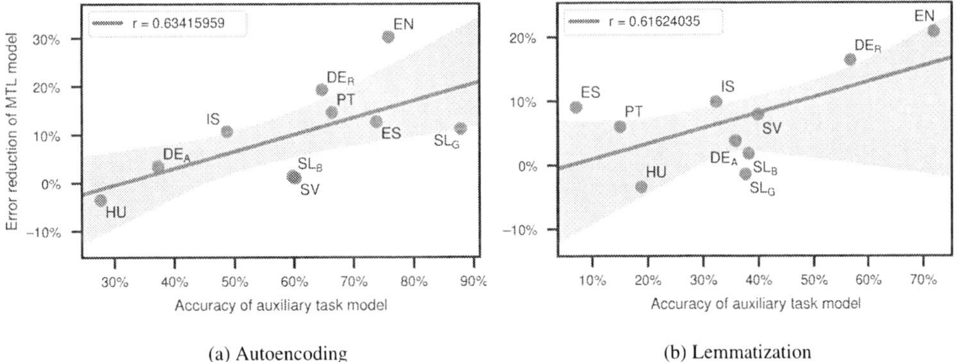

(a) Autoencoding   (b) Lemmatization

Figure 6: Correlations (with 95% confidence intervals) between the performance of an auxiliary task model applied to normalization data and the error reduction when using this task in a multi-task learning setup.

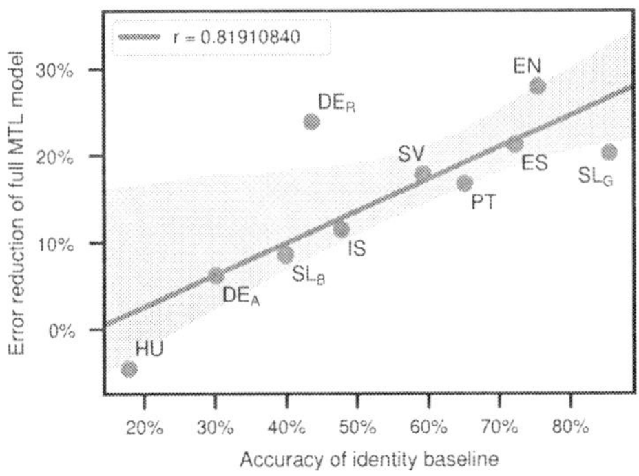

Figure 7: Correlation (with 95% confidence interval) between the identity baseline and the error reduction of the full MTL model with all three auxiliary tasks.

curves that have been micro-averaged over all ten datasets, but evaluated on different subsets of the data: (a) tokens that have been seen during training ("knowns") or not ("unknowns"); and (b) tokens that stay identical in the reference normalization or not. On average, the performance of the MTL models is comparable to that of the single-task model for known tokens and non-identity normalizations. In other words, most of the gain from MTL comes from helping the model learn the identity mappings, which becomes less relevant the more historical training data is available.

5   Related work

On previous approaches to historical text normalization, Bollmann (2019, Sec. 2) gives an extensive overview. Common approaches include rule-based algorithms—with either manually crafted or automatically learned rules—or distance metrics to compare historical spellings to modern lexicon forms (Baron and Rayson, 2008; Bollmann, 2012; Pettersson et al., 2013a). Finite-state transducers are sometimes used to model this, but also to explicitly encode phonological transformations which often underlie the spelling variation (Porta et al., 2013; Etxeberria et al., 2016).

Character-based statistical machine translation (CSMT) has been successfully applied to normalization on many languages (Pettersson et al., 2013b; Scherrer and Erjavec, 2016; Domingo and Casacuberta, 2018); neural encoder–decoder models with character-level input can be seen as the neural equivalent to the statistical MT approach (Bollmann et al., 2017; Tang et al., 2018) and have been shown to be competitive with it (Robertson and Goldwater, 2018; Hämäläinen et al., 2018), although Bollmann (2019) suggests that they are still inferior to CSMT in low-resource scenarios.

All these methods rely on individual word forms as their input; there is almost no work on incorporating sentence-level context for this task (but cf. Jurish, 2010).

MTL architectures   In Sec. 3.1, we explored *what to share* between tasks in our multi-task architecture. A common approach is to share only the first layers (e.g., Yang et al., 2016; Peng and Dredze, 2017). Multi-task encoder–decoder models will often keep the whole encoder and decoder task- or language-specific (Dong et al., 2015; Luong et al., 2015). Firat et al. (2016) explore the effect of sharing the attentional component across

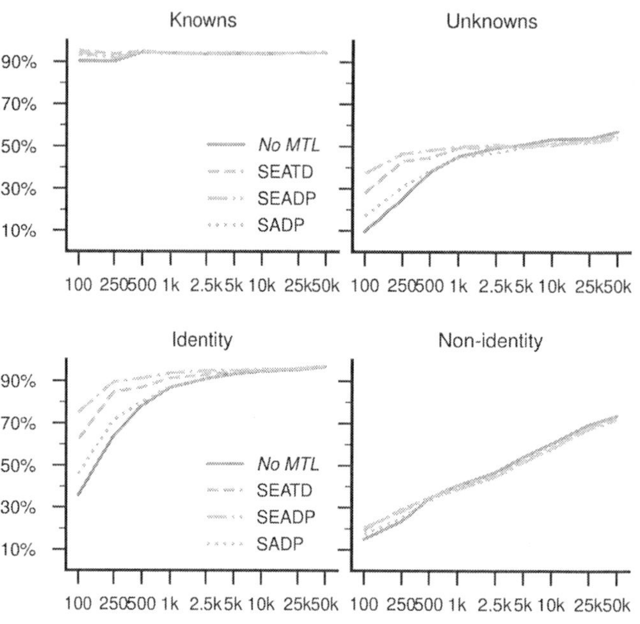

Figure 8: Learning curves, micro-averaged over all datasets, for different subsets of the data.

all languages, while Anastasopoulos and Chiang (2018) compare both parallel and cascading model configurations.

A different MTL approach is to share *all* parts of a model, but prepend a task-specific symbol to the input string to enable it to learn task-specific features (cf. Sec. 3.5). Milde et al. (2017) use this approach for grapheme-to-phoneme conversion; Kann et al. (2017) apply it to morphological paradigm completion.

Auxiliary tasks for MTL For *which auxiliary task(s) to use* (Sec 3.2), few systematic studies exist. Most approaches use tasks that are deemed to be related to the main task—e.g., combining machine translation with syntactic parsing (Kiperwasser and Ballesteros, 2018)—and justify their choice by the effectiveness of the resulting model. Bingel and Søgaard (2017) analyze beneficial task relations for MTL in more detail, but only consider sequence labelling tasks. For zero-shot learning (Sec. 3.5), we use an architecture very similar to Johnson et al. (2016), also used for grapheme-to-phoneme mapping in Peters et al. (2017).

6 Conclusion

We performed an extensive evaluation of a neural encoder–decoder model on historical text normalization, using little or even no training data for the target language, and using multi-task learning (MTL) strategies to improve accuracy. We found that sharing more components between main and auxiliary tasks is usually better, and autoencoding generally provides the most benefit for our task. Analysis showed that this is mainly because MTL helps the model learn that most characters should stay the same, and that its beneficial effect vanishes as the size of the training set increases. While our models did not beat the non-neural models of Bollmann (2019), we believe our work still provides interesting insights into the impact of MTL for low-resource scenarios.

Acknowledgments

We would like to thank the anonymous reviewers of this as well as previous iterations of this paper for several helpful comments.

This research has received funding from the European Research Council under the ERC Starting Grant LOWLANDS No. 313695. Marcel Bollmann was partly funded from the European Union's Horizon 2020 research and innovation programme under the Marie Skodowska-Curie grant agreement No. 845995.

References

Antonios Anastasopoulos and David Chiang. 2018. Tied multitask learning for neural speech translation. In *Proceedings of the 2018 Conference of the North American Chapter of the Association for Computational Linguistics: Human Language Technologies, Volume 1 (Long Papers)*, pages 82–91, New Orleans, Louisiana. Association for Computational Linguistics.

Dzmitry Bahdanau, Kyunghyun Cho, and Yoshua Bengio. 2014. Neural machine translation by jointly learning to align and translate. *CoRR*, abs/1409.0473.

Alistair Baron and Paul Rayson. 2008. VARD 2: A tool for dealing with spelling variation in historical corpora. In *Proceedings of the Postgraduate Conference in Corpus Linguistics*.

Joachim Bingel and Anders Søgaard. 2017. Identifying beneficial task relations for multi-task learning in deep neural networks. In *Proceedings of the 15th Conference of the European Chapter of the Association for Computational Linguistics: Volume 2, Short Papers*, pages 164–169, Valencia, Spain. Association for Computational Linguistics.

Marcel Bollmann. 2012. (Semi-)automatic normalization of historical texts using distance measures and the Norma tool. In *Proceedings of the Second Workshop on Annotation of Corpora for Research in the Humanities (ACRH-2)*, Lisbon, Portugal.

Marcel Bollmann. 2018. Normalization of historical texts with neural network models. *Bochumer Linguistische Arbeitsberichte*, 22.

Marcel Bollmann. 2019. A large-scale comparison of historical text normalization systems. In *Proceedings of the 2019 Conference of the North American Chapter of the Association for Computational Linguistics: Human Language Technologies, Volume 1 (Long and Short Papers)*, pages 3885–3898. Association for Computational Linguistics.

Marcel Bollmann, Joachim Bingel, and Anders Søgaard. 2017. Learning attention for historical text normalization by learning to pronounce. In *Proceedings of the 55th Annual Meeting of the Association for Computational Linguistics (Volume 1: Long Papers)*, pages 332–344, Vancouver, Canada. Association for Computational Linguistics.

Marcel Bollmann, Anders Søgaard, and Joachim Bingel. 2018. Multi-task learning for historical text normalization: Size matters. In *Proceedings of the Workshop on Deep Learning Approaches for Low-Resource NLP*, pages 19–24. Association for Computational Linguistics.

Chloé Braud, Barbara Plank, and Anders Søgaard. 2016. Multi-view and multi-task training of RST discourse parsers. In *Proceedings of COLING 2016, the 26th International Conference on Computational Linguistics: Technical Papers*, pages 1903–1913, Osaka, Japan. The COLING 2016 Organizing Committee.

Rich Caruana. 1993. Multitask learning: A knowledge-based source of inductive bias. In *Proceedings of the 10th International Conference on Machine Learning (ICML)*, pages 41–48.

Aliya Deri and Kevin Knight. 2016. Grapheme-to-phoneme models for (almost) any language. In *Proceedings of the 54th Annual Meeting of the Association for Computational Linguistics (Volume 1: Long Papers)*, pages 399–408, Berlin, Germany. Association for Computational Linguistics.

Miguel Domingo and Francisco Casacuberta. 2018. Spelling normalization of historical documents by using a machine translation approach. In *Proceedings of the 21st Annual Conference of the European Association for Machine Translation*, pages 129–137.

Daxiang Dong, Hua Wu, Wei He, Dianhai Yu, and Haifeng Wang. 2015. Multi-task learning for multiple language translation. In *Proceedings of the 53rd Annual Meeting of the Association for Computational Linguistics and the 7th International Joint Conference on Natural Language Processing (Volume 1: Long Papers)*, pages 1723–1732, Beijing, China. Association for Computational Linguistics.

Izaskun Etxeberria, Iñaki Alegria, Larraitz Uria, and Mans Hulden. 2016. Evaluating the noisy channel model for the normalization of historical texts: Basque, Spanish and Slovene. In *Proceedings of the Tenth International Conference on Language Resources and Evaluation (LREC 2016)*, pages 1064–1069, Portorož, Slovenia. European Language Resources Association (ELRA).

Orhan Firat, Kyunghyun Cho, and Yoshua Bengio. 2016. Multi-way, multilingual neural machine translation with a shared attention mechanism. *CoRR*, abs/1601.01073.

Mika Hämäläinen, Tanja Säily, Jack Rueter, Jörg Tiedemann, and Eetu Mäkelä. 2018. Normalizing early english letters to present-day english spelling. In *Proceedings of the Second Joint SIGHUM Workshop on Computational Linguistics for Cultural Heritage, Social Sciences, Humanities and Literature*, pages 87–96. Association for Computational Linguistics.

Melvin Johnson, Mike Schuster, Quoc V. Le, Maxim Krikun, Yonghui Wu, Zhifeng Chen, Nikhil Thorat, Fernanda B. Viégas, Martin Wattenberg, Greg Corrado, Macduff Hughes, and Jeffrey Dean. 2016. Google's multilingual neural machine translation system: Enabling zero-shot translation. *CoRR*, abs/1611.04558.

Bryan Jurish. 2010. More than words: using token context to improve canonicalization of historical German. *Journal for Language Technology and Computational Linguistics*, 25(1):23–39.

Katharina Kann, Ryan Cotterell, and Hinrich Schütze. 2017. One-shot neural cross-lingual transfer for paradigm completion. In *Proceedings of the 55th Annual Meeting of the Association for Computational Linguistics (Volume 1: Long Papers)*, pages 1993–2003, Vancouver, Canada. Association for Computational Linguistics.

Akisato Kimura, Zoubin Ghahramani, Koh Takeuchi, Tomoharu Iwata, and Naonori Ueda. 2018. Few-shot learning of neural networks from scratch by pseudo example optimization. *arXiv e-prints*, abs/1802.03039.

Eliyahu Kiperwasser and Miguel Ballesteros. 2018. Scheduled multi-task learning: From syntax to translation. *Transactions of the Association for Computational Linguistics*, 6:225–240.

Christo Kirov, Ryan Cotterell, John Sylak-Glassman, Graldine Walther, Ekaterina Vylomova, Patrick Xia, Manaal Faruqui, Arya D. McCarthy, Sandra Kbler, David Yarowsky, Jason Eisner, and Mans Hulden. 2018. UniMorph 2.0: Universal morphology. In *Proceedings of the Eleventh International Conference on Language Resources and Evaluation (LREC 2018)*, pages 1868–1873. European Language Resources Association (ELRA).

Natalia Korchagina. 2017. Normalizing medieval German texts: from rules to deep learning. In *Proceedings of the NoDaLiDa 2017 Workshop on Processing Historical Language*, pages 12–17, Gothenburg. Linköping University Electronic Press.

Minh-Thang Luong, Quoc V. Le, Ilya Sutskever, Oriol Vinyals, and Lukasz Kaiser. 2015. Multi-task sequence to sequence learning. *CoRR*, abs/1511.06114.

Benjamin Milde, Christoph Schmidt, and Joachim Khler. 2017. Multitask sequence-to-sequence models for grapheme-to-phoneme conversion. In *Proceedings of Interspeech 2017*, pages 2536–2540.

Graham Neubig, Matthias Sperber, Xinyi Wang, Matthieu Felix, Austin Matthews, Sarguna Padmanabhan, Ye Qi, Devendra Singh Sachan, Philip Arthur, Pierre Godard, John Hewitt, Rachid Riad, and Liming Wang. 2018. XNMT: The extensible neural machine translation toolkit. In *Conference of the Association for Machine Translation in the Americas (AMTA) Open Source Software Showcase*, Boston.

Nanyun Peng and Mark Dredze. 2017. Multi-task domain adaptation for sequence tagging. In *Proceedings of the 2nd Workshop on Representation Learning for NLP*, pages 91–100, Vancouver, Canada. Association for Computational Linguistics.

Ben Peters, Jon Dehdari, and Josef van Genabith. 2017. Massively multilingual neural grapheme-to-phoneme conversion. In *Proceedings of the First Workshop on Building Linguistically Generalizable NLP Systems*, pages 19–26, Copenhagen, Denmark. Association for Computational Linguistics.

Eva Pettersson, Beáta Megyesi, and Joakim Nivre. 2013a. Normalisation of historical text using context-sensitive weighted Levenshtein distance and compound splitting. In *Proceedings of the 19th Nordic Conference of Computational Linguistics (NODALIDA 2013)*, pages 163–179, Oslo, Norway. Linköping University Electronic Press.

Eva Pettersson, Beáta Megyesi, and Jörg Tiedemann. 2013b. An SMT approach to automatic annotation of historical text. In *Proceedings of the Workshop on Computational Historical Linguistics at NODAL-IDA 2013*, NEALT Proceedings Series 18, pages 54–69. Linköping University Electronic Press.

Michael Piotrowski. 2012. *Natural Language Processing for Historical Texts*. Number 17 in Synthesis Lectures on Human Language Technologies. Morgan & Claypool.

Jordi Porta, José-Luis Sancho, and Javier Gómez. 2013. Edit transducers for spelling variation in Old Spanish. In *Proceedings of the Workshop on Computational Historical Linguistics at NODAL-IDA 2013*, NEALT Proceedings Series 18, pages 70–79. Linköping University Electronic Press.

Alexander Robertson and Sharon Goldwater. 2018. Evaluating historical text normalization systems: How well do they generalize? In *Proceedings of the 2018 Conference of the North American Chapter of the Association for Computational Linguistics: Human Language Technologies, Volume 2 (Short Papers)*, pages 720–725. Association for Computational Linguistics.

Yves Scherrer and Tomaž Erjavec. 2016. Modernising historical Slovene words. *Natural Language Engineering*, 22(6):881–905.

Gongbo Tang, Fabienne Cap, Eva Pettersson, and Joakim Nivre. 2018. An evaluation of neural machine translation models on historical spelling normalization. In *Proceedings of the 27th International Conference on Computational Linguistics*, pages 1320–1331, Santa Fe, New Mexico, USA. Association for Computational Linguistics.

Zhilin Yang, Ruslan Salakhutdinov, and William W. Cohen. 2016. Multi-task cross-lingual sequence tagging from scratch. *CoRR*, abs/1603.06270.

From Monolingual to Multilingual FAQ Assistant using Multilingual Co-training

Mayur Patidar, Surabhi Kumari, Manasi Patwardhan, Shirish Karande
Puneet Agarwal, Lovekesh Vig, Gautam Shroff
TCS Research, New Delhi, India
{patidar.mayur, surabhi.kumari6, manasi.patwardhan,
shirish.karande, puneet.a, lovekesh.vig,
gautam.shroff}@tcs.com

Abstract

Recent research on cross-lingual transfer show state-of-the-art results on benchmark datasets using pre-trained language representation models (PLRM) like BERT. These results are achieved with the traditional training approaches, such as Zero-shot with no data, Translate-train or Translate-test with machine translated data. In this work, we propose an approach of "Multilingual Co-training" (MCT) where we augment the expert annotated dataset in the source language (English) with the corresponding machine translations in the target languages (e.g. Arabic, Spanish) and fine-tune the PLRM jointly. We observe that the proposed approach provides consistent gains in the performance of BERT for multiple benchmark datasets (e.g. 1.0% gain on MLDocs, and 1.2% gain on XNLI over translate-train with BERT), while requiring a single model for multiple languages. We further consider a FAQ dataset where the available English test dataset is translated by experts into Arabic and Spanish. On such a dataset, we observe an average gain of 4.9% over all other cross-lingual transfer protocols with BERT. We further observe that domain-specific joint pre-training of the PLRM using HR policy documents in English along with the machine translations in the target languages, followed by the joint finetuning, provides a further improvement of 2.8% in average accuracy.

1 Introduction

Achievement of scale, agility, and quality in support functions of large enterprises is a key demand. Conversational systems are increasingly being deployed to this effect. Such systems try to classify users' utterances into one of the FAQ (Khurana et al., 2017), usually referred to as intent, and then show an answer that is mapped to the chosen intent. In specific geographies such as Europe,

Latin America, and India such FAQ based conversational systems may be required to work in more than one language. Similar requirements are also presented to us by many international consumer oriented businesses such as airlines, shipping companies, and banks.

The straight-forward approach is to build a different classification model for every language, which is hard to maintain because of manual effort involved in preparing the training data in every language, and training time for every model. We therefore look into cross-lingual transfer learning approaches such as a) *Translate-Train* (Schuster et al., 2019): here we translate the training data from English[1] into all the other languages and train a different model for every language; b) *Translate-Test* (Artetxe and Schwenk, 2018): here we maintain single model (usually for English), and use machine translation at the inference time before using the classification model; c) *Zero-shot* (Artetxe and Schwenk, 2018): here we employ multi-lingual pre-trained language representation model (PLRM) such as LASER (Artetxe and Schwenk, 2018), and train the model in high resource language (English) only and use the target language at the inference time only; d) *Joint training* (Upadhyay et al., 2018a,b): here the same model is trained on all the languages on which it is expected to be used. All these approaches are also shown in Figure 1. Either the accuracy of above mentioned models is low (Zero-Shot, or Translate-Test) or they are too hard to maintain in production system (Translate-Train, or Joint training). We therefore require an approach that performs better than all these approaches and is easier to maintain.

In this paper, we propose a new method for cross-lingual transfer learning, i.e., Multi-Lingual

---

[1]Most often English is the most common language in all deployments of FAQ systems

Proceedings of the 2nd Workshop on Deep Learning Approaches for Low-Resource NLP (DeepLo), pages 115–123
Hong Kong, China, November 3, 2019. ©2019 Association for Computational Linguistics
https://doi.org/10.18653/v1/P17

Co-Training (MCT). Here, we jointly train single model on all the languages (upto 15 languages), using different multi-lingual PLRMs. When the training data is not available for certain language, we use translate-train paradigm and use machine translations as the training data. To the best of our knowledge, such an approach has not been used by prior works in the related area. We demonstrate the efficacy of our approach on a real world dataset taken from "Watt" (Khurana et al., 2017) project. Finally, we also demonstrate the robustness on publicly available datasets such as XNLI (Conneau et al., 2018) and MLDoc (Schwenk and Li, 2018). For MLDoc dataset, MCT provides 1.0% gain for the 8 languages, whereas for the XNLI dataset it provides 1.2% gain for 15 languages.

The rest of the paper is organized as follows: We describe our problem in Section 2 and the proposed approach in Section 3. We present the results of the proposed and other baseline approaches in Section 4. We later describe related work in Section 5 and conclude in Section 6.

2 Problem Description

A labeled dataset (D) for the deployed FAQ assistant in the source language (i.e., English) was created by HR domain experts using policy documents. It consists of a set of intents i.e. $D = \{I_1, I_2, ..., I_n\}$ where, each I_j comprises of a set of semantically similar queries $Q_j = \{q_{j1}, q_{j2}, ..., q_{jm}\}$ and a common corresponding answer ans_j i.e. $I_j = <Q_j, ans_j>$. Our objective here is to find a relevant intent I corresponding to a user's query q and then retrieve and show the answer associated with that intent. This can be modeled as a multiclass sentence classification where $I = \underset{I_j \epsilon D}{\operatorname{argmax}} P(I_j/q)$.

In the context of a multilingual FAQ assistant, we assume that there exists complete overlap between the intents of source and target languages (T_i, $i = 1, 2, ..., k$) with no availability of human labeled data in any target language. The objective in the case of multilingual FAQ assistant is similar to the monolingual case except that user is free to ask a query in any language. In a multilingual FAQ system, along with intent identification, a language detection module is also required to respond to a user's query in an appropriate language.

3 Proposed Approach

In the context of a multilingual FAQ assistant, we assume that there exists complete overlap between the intents of source and target languages (T_i, $i = 1, 2, ..., k$) with no availability of human-labeled data in any target language. To create a labeled dataset D_{T_i} for a target language T_i, each set of semantically similar queries Q_j in the source language are translated to the target language to obtain Q_{jT_i}, using machine translation (MT)[2] and ans_{jT_i} is created by the respective HR domain experts.

To obtain a single multilingual labeled dataset D' comprising of data from the source as well as all the target languages, we combine D with all the datasets D_{T_i} created for all T_i. Each intent $I_j = < Q'_j, ans'_j >$ in the final labeled dataset (D') is comprised of queries $Q'_j = \{Q_j \cup Q_{jT_i} \cup ... \cup Q_{jT_k}\}$ and answers $ans'_j = \{ans_j \cup ans_{jT_i} \cup ... \cup ans_{jT_k}\}$ from the source and target languages.

We propose an approach referred to as Multilingual Co-training (MCT), where we use multilingual labeled dataset D' to train a multiclass classifier for intent identification. In this work, we propose three variants of MCT, which differ in terms of how we train a classifier given multilingual labeled dataset D', which we discuss in next subsections.

In all variants of MCT, we need a translation system only to create the dataset D'. Unlike translate-test, we do not require to translate each user query to source language during the inference. Also, we need to maintain only a single multilingual FAQ assistant for all languages. However, in case of translate-train, in general, we need to create multiple FAQ assistants, one for each language. We use D' to train a multilingual FAQ system, which may not be the best but perform better than solely relying on representations from PLRM (zero-shot) for cross-lingual transfer.

3.1 MCT using Multilingual Sentence Representation (MCT-MSR)

MCT-MSR is the simplest variant of MCT, where we obtain vector representation for all the queries present in dataset D' from the PLRM. Corresponding to each user query q_t, we obtain vector representation $\boldsymbol{q_t} \in R^d$ where d is the dimension

---

[2] we use google translation api for machine translation.

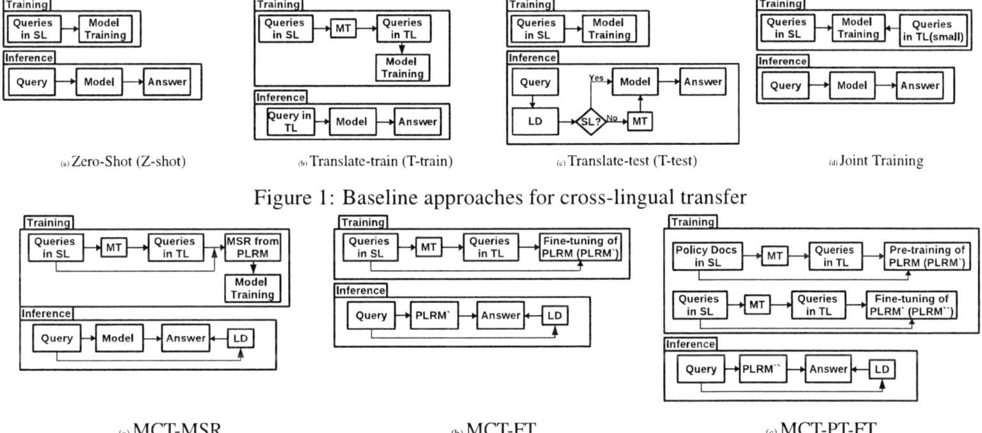

Figure 1: Baseline approaches for cross-lingual transfer

Figure 2: Proposed approaches for MCT

of query representation. We use these query representations to train a multiclass classifier by minimizing the categorical cross entropy loss as shown in Equation 3, where $I_i \in I$, N is the total number of queries in D', n is the number of intents in D' and y is 1 only for the target intent and zero otherwise. We build the classifier using a two layered feed forward network as described in Equations 1 and 2 where W_1, W_2 represent the weights and b_1, b_2 represent the biases of the two layers. We also use dropout (Srivastava et al., 2014) for regularization and *tanh* as the nonlinear activation function.

Finally, as shown in Figure 2a, we use trained classifier with language detection module i.e., Multilingual FAQ assistant to answer user's query in source or target language.

$$o_t = dropout(tanh(W_1 * q_t + b_1)) \quad (1)$$

$$p(I \mid q_t) = \text{softmax}(W_2 * o_t + b_2) \quad (2)$$

$$\mathcal{L}_{CE} = -\frac{1}{N} \sum_{t=1}^{N} \sum_{i=1}^{n} y \cdot log(p(I_i \mid q_t)) \quad (3)$$

3.2 MCT using Fine Tuning (MCT-FT)

In the recent work (Devlin et al., 2019; Lample and Conneau, 2019; Wu and Dredze, 2019), it is shown that fine-tuning of all or a few layers of PLRM on end task performs better than task-specific models. Unlike in MCT-MSR, in MCT-FT we use D' to fine-tune all the parameters of PLRM along with the weights W_3 and biases b_3 of a task-specific linear layer as shown in Equation 4 which is similar to (Devlin et al., 2019). In Equation 4, q_t refers to vector representation of user's query i.e., q_t ob-

tained from PLRM.

$$p(I \mid q_t) = \text{softmax}(W_3 * q_t + b_3) \quad (4)$$

Finally, as shown in Figure 2b, we use PLRM, obtained after fine-tuning with language detection module i.e., Multilingual FAQ assistant to answer user's query in source or target language.

3.3 MCT via pre-training followed by fine-tuning (MCT-PT-FT)

In (Devlin et al., 2019), it is shown that additional pre-training of PLRMs on domain-specific text corpus improve the performance on the end task. In this work, addition to D', we also use policy documents to create our multilingual FAQ assistant. A policy document is a semi-structured document which contains information (e.g., purpose, applicability, approval workflow, etc.) about leave type in the form of tables, plain text, etc. In this work, we only use plain text from policy documents. Due to unavailability of policy documents in the target languages, we use MT to translate them to target languages.

In MCT-PT-FT, we perform domain-specific pre-training of existing PLRM using policy documents on tasks specific to PLRM. For example, we pre-train BERT (Devlin et al., 2019) using MLM and NSP tasks. Similar to MCT-FT, we fine-tune the PLRM obtained after pre-training on policy documents.

Finally, as shown in Figure 2c, we use a PLRM, obtained after domain-specific pre-training and fine-tuning with language detection (LD) module forming the Multilingual FAQ assistant to answer user's query in source or target language.

Table 1: We compare the existing baselines with **MCT-MSR** using **LASER**, **BERT** and **XLM** as PLRMs **without fine-tuning** on "Leave Dataset". Bold with * denotes the best and underline denotes the second best average classification accuracy on test set.

Language Code	LASER (Artetxe and Schwenk, 2018)				XLM (MLM+TLM) (Lample and Conneau, 2019)				BERT (Devlin et al., 2019)			
	Z-shot	T-train	T-test	MCT-MSR (Ours)	Z-shot	T-train	T-test	MCT-MSR (Ours)	Z-shot	T-train	T-test	MCT-MSR (Ours)
en	85.5	85.5	85.5	82.4	47.1	47.1	47.1	44.2	59.5	59.5	59.5	53.9
ar	45.6	52.4	48.7	58.1	4.7	13.1	23.1	17.4	3.9	18.5	22.8	19.1
es	63.6	73.3	63.9	72.3	17.5	29.9	28.0	29.8	6.6	35.1	28.7	31.5
Average	64.9	70.4	66.0	**70.9***	23.1	30.0	**32.7***	30.5	23.3	**37.7***	37.0	34.8

Table 2: We compare the existing baselines with **MCT-FT** using **Watt**, **BERT** and **XLM** as PLRMs **with fine-tuning** on "Leave Dataset". Bold with * denotes the best and underline denotes the second best average classification accuracy on test set.

Language Code	Watt (BiLSTM + SQRT-KLD) (Khurana et al., 2017)				XLM (MLM+TLM) (Lample and Conneau, 2019)				BERT (Devlin et al., 2019)			
	Z-shot	T-train	T-test	MCT-FT (Ours)	Z-shot	T-train	T-test	MCT-FT (Ours)	Z-shot	T-train	T-test	MCT-FT (Ours)
en	83.5	83.5	83.5	79.4	82.3	82.3	82.3	85.6	90.0	90.0	90.0	89.8
ar	-	18.1	24.1	31.5	15.0	39.6	41.5	52.4	9.4	44.9	44.4	56.5
es	-	56.3	34.0	63.9	28.0	62.7	50.1	72.2	26.5	78.5	58.5	81.8
Average	-	52.6	47.2	**58.3***	41.8	61.5	58.0	**69.9***	42.0	71.1	64.3	**76.0***

Table 3: Dataset description. SPL refers to Samples Per Language

Property ↓ / Dataset →	Leave	MLDoc	XNLI
Train-SPL	2801	1000	392,702
Validation-SPL	934	1000	2490
Test-SPL	832	4000	5010
No. of classes	199	4	3
No. of languages	3	8	15

4 Experiments and Results

In this section, we describe the various datasets and also give details of the different hyper-parameters of the models used in our experiments. We later present all the results and note some key observations from them.

4.1 Dataset Description

We evaluate proposed approaches on three datasets as shown in Table 3.

Leave dataset (Khurana et al., 2017) is created by HR domain experts in English and for our purpose, we translate training and validation set in target languages (Arabic and Spanish) using MT, while test set is translated by respective target language experts.

MLDoc[3] (Schwenk and Li, 2018) is a four class, multilingual document classification dataset containing news stories in eight languages, where stories in target languages are written by respective target language experts. Similar to (Wu and Dredze, 2019), we take first two sentences from each document in our experiments and use NLTK[4] for sentence tokenization.

The Cross-lingual Natural Language Inference (XNLI) (Conneau et al., 2018) dataset is an extension of Multi-Genre Natural Language Inference (MultiNLI)[5] corpus, where objective is to classify a pair of sentences (premise and hypothesis) in one of the three classes. Validation and test set are translated by domain experts and the training set by a machine translation system in 14 target languages.

4.2 Training Details

For training Watt, the final hyper-parameters are selected from the sets as mentioned in (Khurana et al., 2017). The datasets mentioned in the Table 3 are not pre-processed in any form during our experiments. All the final hyper-parameters are selected based on the performance on a validation set. We use Adam (Kingma and Ba, 2014) for optimization and dropout for regularization (Srivastava et al., 2014). The batch size is selected from the set {16, 32}.

We use multilingual variants of PLRMs, viz. BERT[6], XLM(MLM+TLM)[7] (Lample and Conneau, 2019) and LASER[8] (Artetxe and Schwenk, 2018) in our experiments.

MCT-MSR The number of hidden units and layers are selected from the sets {512, 1024,

---

[3] https://trec.nist.gov/data/reuters/reuters.html

[4] https://www.nltk.org/

[5] https://www.nyu.edu/projects/bowman/multinli/

[6] https://storage.googleapis.com/bert_models/2018_11_23/multi_cased_L-12_H-768_A-12.zip

[7] https://dl.fbaipublicfiles.com/XLM/mlm_tlm_xnli15_1024.pth

[8] https://github.com/facebookresearch/LASER

Table 4: We compare the results of **Fine-tuning** vs **Pre-training followed by Fine-tuning** of various models on "Leave Dataset". For MCT we use BERT as a PLRM. Bold with * denotes the best and underline denotes the second best average classification accuracy on test set.

Language Code		Fine-tuning					Pre-training followed by Fine-tuning			
||	|| Z-shot	T-train	T-test	MCT-FT (Ours) ||	Z-shot	T-train	T-test	MCT-PT-FT (Ours) ||
|| en	|| 90.0	90.0	90.0	89.8 ||	90.3	90.3	90.3	90.5 ||
|| ar	|| 9.4	44.9	44.4	56.5 ||	10.9	44.9	44.8	59.4 ||
|| es	|| 26.5	78.5	58.5	81.8 ||	30.8	79.2	60.0	86.4 ||
|| Average	|| 42.0	<u>71.1</u>	64.3	**76.0*** ||	44.0	<u>71.5</u>	65.0	**78.8*** ||

Table 5: We compare the results of different approaches to bilingual co-training (BCT) on "Leave Dataset". We use LASER (Artetxe and Schwenk, 2018), BERT (Devlin et al., 2019) and XLM (MLM+TLM) (Lample and Conneau, 2019) as PLRMs. Bold with * denotes the best and underline denotes the second best average classification accuracy on test set for each approach. Bold with ** denotes the overall best. The first three rows showcase results of the billingual models created on en-ar pair and later 3 rows on en-es pair.

Language Code		BCT-MSR				BCT-FT			BCT-PT-FT	
||	|| LASER	XLM (MLM+TLM)	BERT ||	Watt	XLM (MLM+TLM)	BERT ||	BERT ||
|| en	|| 81.9	39.5	53.3 ||	75.0	82.4	89.5 ||	90.0 ||
|| ar	|| 55.1	16.3	18.1 ||	20.7	48.3	59.8 ||	63.5 ||
|| Average	|| **68.5***	27.9	<u>35.7</u> ||	47.8	<u>65.3</u>	**74.6*** ||	**76.7**** ||
|| en	|| 84.7	48.3	56.6 ||	78.1	85.1	90.5 ||	90.6 ||
|| es	|| 73.9	34.7	36.0 ||	61.6	72.5	82.7 ||	84.0 ||
|| Average	|| **79.3***	41.5	<u>46.3</u> ||	69.8	<u>78.8</u>	**86.6*** ||	**87.3**** ||

2048} and {1, 2} respectively with *tanh* as the non-linearity. The learning rate and dropout are selected from the sets {$1e - 2$, $1e - 3$} and {0.1, 0.2, 0.3} respectively.

MCT-FT For fine tuning of PLRMs based on the end task, we use dropout of 0.1 and the learning rate is selected from the set {2e-5, 3e-5, 5e-5}. For MLDoc dataset, we also use L2 weight decay of 0.01 in addition to dropout for regularization. For XNLI (Conneau et al., 2018) and MLDoc (Schwenk and Li, 2018) datasets, the number of epochs for fine-tuning are selected from the set {3,4}. However for Leave dataset due to high number of classes and small data size, we have used early stopping.

MCT-PT-FT To utilize domain-specific corpus i.e., policy documents, we have run additional steps of pre-training starting from the existing Multilingual BERT model. We have used a masking probability of 0.15, learning rate of $2e-5$, 50% noise for data creation for NSP, batch size of 32 and a maximum of 20 masked LM predictions per sequence. The number of epochs for pre-training of BERT are selected from the set {5, 10, 15}.

4.3 Results And Discussion

In this work, we compare proposed approaches with existing baselines. For fair comparison, we compare proposed approaches with existing baselines under different scenarios, i.e. use of PLRMs with/without finetuning and/or pre-training. In all our experiments we assume that the accuracy of the language detection (LD) module is 100%. This is not an unreasonable assumption, as IP address, employee number, scripts and vocabulary can all be used together for language detection.

MCT-MSR vs Baselines In first scenario (without fine-tuning of PLRMs), we obtain multilingual sentence representations (MSRs) for each sentence in a given dataset and train a classifier as described in subsection 3.1. According to Table 1, on Leave dataset, for LASER, MCT-MSR perform slightly better than other baseline approaches. However, in case of BERT and XLM, baseline approaches perform better than MCT-MSR. Overall, LASER-based approaches perform better than BERT and XLM since, pre-training objective of LASER, "machine translation using single encoder for 93 languages", seems to explicitly force alignment of sentence representations in

Table 6: We compare **MCT-FT** with the existing baselines on "MLDoc" (Schwenk and Li, 2018) Dataset. We use BERT (Devlin et al., 2019; Wu and Dredze, 2019) as a PLRM for **MCT-FT**. Bold with * denotes the best classification accuracy on test set for each language and also for the average across all languages.

Language Code	Z-shot			T-train		MCT-FT(Ours)
	MLDoc	LASER	BERT	MLDoc	BERT	BERT
en	92.2	89.9	94.2	92.2	94.2	**94.3***
de	81.2	84.8	80.2	93.7	93.3	**96.6***
zh	74.7	71.9	76.9	87.3	89.3	**91.7***
es	72.5	77.3	72.6	94.5	95.7	**96.0***
fr	72.4	78.0	72.6	92.1	93.4	**94.2***
it	69.4	69.4	68.9	85.6	**88.0***	87.7
ja	67.6	60.3	56.5	85.4	88.4	**89.6***
ru	60.8	67.8	73.7	85.7	87.5	**87.7***
Average	73.9	74.9	74.5	89.5	91.2	**92.2***

Table 7: We compare **MCT-FT (Ours)** with the existing baselines on "XNLI Dataset" (Conneau et al., 2018) Dataset. We use BERT and XLM (MLM+TLM) as PLRMs for **MCT-FT (Ours)**. Bold with * denotes the best classification accuracy on test set for each language and also for the average across all languages.

Language Code	XLM (MLM+TLM) (Lample and Conneau, 2019)				BERT (Devlin et al., 2019; Wu and Dredze, 2019)		
	Z-shot	T-train	T-test	MCT-FT (Ours)	Z-shot	T-train	MCT-FT (Ours)
en	**85.0***	**85.0***	**85.0***	83.5	**82.1***	**82.1***	80.6
fr	78.7	**80.2***	79.0	79.3	73.8	76.9	**77.4***
es	78.9	**80.8***	79.5	80.2	74.3	**78.5***	78.2
de	77.8	**80.3***	78.1	78.7	71.1	74.8	**76.3***
el	76.6	**78.1***	77.8	78.0	66.4	72.1	**74.3***
bg	77.4	**79.3***	77.6	77.8	68.9	**75.4***	75.1
ru	75.3	**78.1***	75.5	75.6	69.0	**74.3***	73.6
tr	72.5	**74.7***	73.7	72.8	61.1	70.6	**71.2***
ar	73.1	**76.5***	73.7	75.0	64.9	**70.8***	70.5
vi	76.1	76.6	70.8	**77.1***	69.5	67.8	**75.3***
th	73.2	75.5	70.4	**76.4***	55.8	63.2	**65.7***
zh	76.5	**78.6***	73.6	78.5	69.3	**76.2***	75.9
hi	69.6	**72.3***	69.0	71.9	60.0	65.3	**67.2***
sw	68.4	**70.9***	64.7	70.4	50.4	65.3	**66.3***
ur	67.3	63.2	**65.1***	63.8	58.0	60.6	**64.53***
Average	75.1	**76.7***	74.2	75.9	66.3	71.6	**72.8***

multiple languages.

MCT-FT vs Baselines In second scenario (fine-tuning of PLRMs), we fine-tune PLRMs as described in subsection 3.2. However, Watt is not based on PLRMs and for comparison we train it from scratch as described in (Khurana et al., 2017). As LASER (Artetxe and Schwenk, 2018) is typically used to obtain MSRs, we have not considered it for comparison here. According to Table 2, for Leave dataset, proposed approach MCT-FT performs significantly better than baseline approaches in all cases and for BERT we gain 4.9% in terms of average classification accuracy compared to translate-train. For MLDoc dataset we achieve better accuracy in seven out of eight languages with 1.0% average improvement over existing baselines as shown in Table 6. According to Table 7, for XLM, baseline translate-train performs better than the proposed approach by 0.8%. However, in case of BERT we achieve better accuracy in nine out of fifteen languages with an improvement of 1.2% in terms of average classification accuracy compared to translate-train.

MCT-PT-FT vs Baselines In third scenario (pre-training followed by fine-tuning of PLRMs), we pre-train PLRM using domain-specific unlabeled text corpus (policy documents) and fine-tune it on labeled dataset as discussed in subsection 3.3. Since BERT outperformed XLM during fine-tuning we use BERT as a PLRM for all baselines and as well as the proposed approach MCT-PT-FT. According to Table 4, MCT-PT-FT outperforms translate-train by a margin of 7.3% and gains an improvement of 2.8% over MCT-FT. MCT-PT-FT was tested on Leave dataset only as for other datasets their domain-specific unlabeled text corpora were unavailable.

Bilingual Co-training (BCT) For completeness, we also report results on bilingual co-training which is type of MCT, where unlike bilingual joint-training we use machine translated data for target language. According to Table 5, BERT based MCT-PT-FT performs better for both language pairs i.e., en-es and en-ar as compared to MCT-MSR and MCT-FT.

Does noisy translation affect MCT ?

It is interesting to note, from Table 4, the gains obtained by MCT-PT-FT over Translate-train on Spanish (*es*) (86.4% over 79.2%) and Arabic (*ar*) (59.4% over 44.9%). Apart from these gains in performance, the poorer performance on *ar* compared to *es* can be attributed to the noise induced by MT when translating the domain-specific words from English to target languages. To verify this, we translate the test set of English into *es* and *ar* (one set for each) using MT. We then evaluate the performance of MT in terms of BLEU (Papineni et al., 2002) score by considering the manually labeled test sets of *es* and *ar* as the reference translations. These are found to be 40.0 for *ar* and 63.0 for *es*, further validating our observation regarding the noisy MT system. In future, one can consider approaches which compensate for the translator noise. For example, during MCT one could use different weights for each language in the cost function.

5   Related Work

In this section, we provide an outline of existing FAQ assistants, followed by an overview of the recent work on multilingual language modelling and cross-lingual transfer methods.

5.1   FAQ Assistants

Recent years have seen significant advances in conversational systems, with various models considering context, affect, goal, external knowledge etc. However, all these systems can be categorized into two types i.e. those which seek to generate responses or those which use a retrieval based approach. (Zhou et al., 2018; Pei and Li, 2018) are examples where the ability to generate responses is learnt from patterns in dialogues found in the training set. On the contrary, there exist several industrial scenarios where the domain is sufficiently restricted, or there exist legal ramifications associated with the responses, and hence pre-defined answers are preferred. Therefore, research on retrieval based conversational models continues to be active, for example see (Das et al., 2016; Lai et al., 2015). Our work builds upon the retrieval-based model for a domain-specific leave dataset used in (Khurana et al., 2017), where a Bi-LSTM based architecture was employed.

Multilingual and cross-lingual conversational models for virtual assistants are an emerging field of research. Some research work has been done to capture different languages in one conversational system. In (Gupta et al., 2018), machine translation and information retrieval approaches were used for multilingual question answering in English and Hindi languages. In (Schuster et al., 2019), the authors use different cross-lingual embeddings eg. XLU (Schuster et al., 2019), ELMo (Peters et al., 2018), CoVe (McCann et al., 2017), etc. for cross-lingual learning in English, Spanish and Thai. In this paper, we propose an approach to extend an FAQ system to other languages such as Arabic and Spanish.

5.2   Multilingual Sentence Representation

There are approaches which have specifically been developed for capturing cross-lingual sentence representations. An encoder was used to align a parallel set of sentences to learn joint space embeddings in (Hermann and Blunsom, 2014; Conneau et al., 2018), an encoder pre-trained on the translation task with multiple source languages was utilized in (Artetxe and Schwenk, 2018; Eriguchi et al., 2018; Yu et al., 2018; Schwenk et al., 2017), Transformer based approaches such as BERT further extended to the multilingual setting (Wu and Dredze, 2019) and XLM (Lample and Conneau, 2019) having a cross-lingual objective for language modeling can be used to obtain multilingual sentence representations for cross-lingual transfer. The cross-lingual sentence representation obtained from these models can be further utilized for multilingual downstream tasks, e.g. (Schwenk and Li, 2018; Conneau et al., 2018). In our work, as we are trying to extend our FAQ assistant to the multilingual setting, we use the

BERT, XLM models (Devlin et al., 2019; Lample and Conneau, 2019; Artetxe and Schwenk, 2018) as base models and further fine-tune them with domain-specific and task-specific data.

5.3 Cross-Lingual Transfer

For low resource languages, due to insufficient (or no) data availability, it is difficult to get good task-specific accuracies. In case of complete unavailability of low resource language data, various approaches are defined in the literature: (i) zero-shot approaches, which train task-specific models on high resource languages and then use these models directly for low resource languages (Artetxe and Schwenk, 2018). (ii) Using predefined word or sentence embeddings (Schwenk and Li, 2018). (iii) Making use of translated high resource language data for training a low resource language model (Schuster et al., 2019). For cases where a small amount of low resource language data is available, there are approaches which make use of joint training using high resource language data augmented with a small amount of target (low resource) language data, which leads to better task-specific accuracy for target languages than zero shot (Upadhyay et al., 2018a,b). These approaches are applicable for the bi-lingual as well as multilingual settings. There are studies which help determine the applicability of using a particular high resource source language for a (set-of) low resource target language(s) (Lin et al., 2019). Our work is inspired by the joint-training approach of cross-lingual transfer, however, we assume unavailability of target language data and use machine translations for the same.

6 Conclusions and Future Work

There are a few baseline observations that need to be highlighted before commenting upon the key conclusions about the proposed "Multi-lingual Co-training". With regards to our Multilingual FAQ bot, when compared with Watt (Khurana et al., 2017), it seems that the use of PLRMs can improve the performance even for English. Therefore, it was reasonable to base the study in this work on the three recently proposed PLRMs, viz. LASER, BERT and XLM. With regards to cross-lingual transfer, if one were to use the PLRMs purely as feature extractors, then LASER provide the best baselines. Meanwhile, if one were to allow fine-tuning, then BERT provides the best

baselines. In both cases the best baseline is provided by Translate-Train. The proposed variants MCT-MSR of LASER and MCT-FT of BERT are able to beat the corresponding baselines. In fact, one can observe that while Watt and XLM do not provide the best baselines for fine-tuning, even for these models, multilingual co-training does help. Finally, we explored the use of pre-training in the multilingual setting. While human translations have been used by LASER, the use of machine translations as a self-supervised language modeling task has not been explored in the past. Translation noise can potentially lead to a lot of error propagation. However, we observed that use of translations for pre-training provides the best baseline with BERT, and a joint multilingual pre-training is able to beat this baseline.

As a part of the future work, we would like to explore distinct strategies for a further boost in the performance. We comment upon a few possibilities. (1) The essence of MCT lies in the use of target language translations. Translator noise can have a big impact on the performance, and training bias in favor of a particular language. We believe that there are several approaches that can be attempted to overcome such a challenge. One could identify a set of languages that can mutually benefit from and share a quality MT. Thus, instead of training a single model for all languages, one could train a model for each set. One can also bias the cost function by using language-specific weights; these weights could potentially be used to model translator noise. One could also use a training schedule (along with adapting the learning rate) instead of weights to bias the training in favor of a language or language set. (2) Finally, we admit, for the purposes of illustration, we have made a rather strict assumption of zero human-translated data. It remains of interest to explore the impact of a small volume of human translated data on the performance of MCT, further whether an MCT can be used to sample queries which if translated by a human can help to maximally boost performance, in an active learning framework.

References

Mikel Artetxe and Holger Schwenk. 2018. Massively multilingual sentence embeddings for zero-shot cross-lingual transfer and beyond. *CoRR*.

Alexis Conneau, Ruty Rinott, et al. 2018. XNLI: Evaluating cross-lingual sentence representations. In

Proceedings of the 2018 Conference on Empirical Methods in Natural Language Processing.

Arpita Das, Harish Yenala, et al. 2016. Together we stand: Siamese networks for similar question retrieval. In *Proceedings of the 54th Annual Meeting of the Association for Computational Linguistics.*

Jacob Devlin et al. 2019. BERT: pre-training of deep bidirectional transformers for language understanding. In *Proceedings of the 2019 Conference of the North American Chapter of the Association for Computational Linguistics: Human Language Technologies.*

Akiko Eriguchi, Melvin Johnson, et al. 2018. Zero-shot cross-lingual classification using multilingual neural machine translation. *CoRR.*

Deepak Gupta, Surabhi Kumari, et al. 2018. MMQA: A Multi-domain Multi-lingual Question-Answering Framework for English and Hindi. In *Proceedings of the Eleventh International Conference on Language Resources and Evaluation (LREC 2018).*

Karl Moritz Hermann and Phil Blunsom. 2014. Multilingual models for compositional distributed semantics. In *Proceedings of the 52nd Annual Meeting of the Association for Computational Linguistics.*

Prerna Khurana, Puneet Agarwal, et al. 2017. Hybrid bilstm-siamese network for faq assistance. In *Proceedings of the 2017 ACM on Conference on Information and Knowledge Management (CIKM 2017).*

Diederik P. Kingma and Jimmy Ba. 2014. Adam: A method for stochastic optimization. *CoRR.*

Siwei Lai, Liheng Xu, et al. 2015. Recurrent convolutional neural networks for text classification. In *Proceedings of the Twenty-Ninth AAAI Conference on Artificial Intelligence.*

Guillaume Lample and Alexis Conneau. 2019. Cross-lingual language model pretraining. *CoRR.*

Yu-Hsiang Lin, Chian-Yu Chen, et al. 2019. Choosing transfer languages for cross-lingual learning. In *The 57th Annual Meeting of the Association for Computational Linguistics (ACL).*

Bryan McCann, James Bradbury, et al. 2017. Learned in translation: Contextualized word vectors. In *Advances in Neural Information Processing Systems.*

Kishore Papineni, Salim Roukos, Todd Ward, and Wei-Jing Zhu. 2002. Bleu: A method for automatic evaluation of machine translation. In *Proceedings of the 40th Annual Meeting on Association for Computational Linguistics.*

Jiaxin Pei and Chenliang Li. 2018. S2SPMN: A simple and effective framework for response generation with relevant information. In *Proceedings of the 2018 Conference on Empirical Methods in Natural Language Processing.*

Matthew Peters, Mark Neumann, et al. 2018. Deep contextualized word representations. In *Proceedings of the 2018 Conference of the North American Chapter of the Association for Computational Linguistics: Human Language Technologies, Volume 1 (Long Papers).*

Sebastian Schuster, Sonal Gupta, et al. 2019. Cross-lingual transfer learning for multilingual task oriented dialog. In *Proceedings of the 2019 Conference of the North American Chapter of the Association for Computational Linguistics: Human Language Technologies.*

Holger Schwenk and Xian Li. 2018. A corpus for multilingual document classification in eight languages. In *Proceedings of the Eleventh International Conference on Language Resources and Evaluation (LREC-2018).*

Holger Schwenk, Ke Tran, et al. 2017. Learning joint multilingual sentence representations with neural machine translation. *CoRR.*

Nitish Srivastava, Geoffrey E Hinton, et al. 2014. Dropout: a simple way to prevent neural networks from overfitting. *Journal of Machine Learning Research.*

Shyam Upadhyay, Manaal Faruqui, et al. 2018a. (almost) zero-shot cross-lingual spoken language understanding. In *Proceedings of the IEEE ICASSP.*

Shyam Upadhyay, Nitish Gupta, et al. 2018b. Joint multilingual supervision for cross-lingual entity linking. In *Proceedings of the 2018 Conference on Empirical Methods in Natural Language Processing.*

Shijie Wu and Mark Dredze. 2019. Beto, bentz, becas: The surprising cross-lingual effectiveness of bert. *CoRR.*

Katherine Yu, Haoran Li, et al. 2018. Multilingual seq2seq training with similarity loss for cross-lingual document classification. In *The 56th Annual Meeting of the Association for Computational Linguistics.*

Xiangyang Zhou, Lu Li, et al. 2018. Multi-turn response selection for chatbots with deep attention matching network. In *Proceedings of the 56th Annual Meeting of the Association for Computational Linguistics.*

Generation-Distillation for Efficient Natural Language Understanding in Low-Data Settings

Luke Melas-Kyriazi
lmelaskyriazi@college.harvard.edu

George Han
hanz@college.harvard.edu

Celine Liang
cliang@college.harvard.edu

Abstract

Over the past year, the emergence of transfer learning with large-scale language models (LM) has led to dramatic performance improvements across a broad range of natural language understanding tasks. However, the size and memory footprint of these large LMs makes them difficult to deploy in many scenarios (e.g. on mobile phones). Recent research points to knowledge distillation as a potential solution, showing that when training data for a given task is abundant, it is possible to distill a large (teacher) LM into a small task-specific (student) network with minimal loss of performance. However, when such data is scarce, there remains a significant performance gap between large pretrained LMs and smaller task-specific models, even when training via distillation. In this paper, we bridge this gap with a novel training approach, called *generation-distillation*, that leverages large finetuned LMs in two ways: (1) to generate new (unlabeled) training examples, and (2) to distill their knowledge into a small network using these examples. Across three low-resource text classification datsets, we achieve comparable performance to BERT while using $300\times$ fewer parameters, and we outperform prior approaches to distillation for text classification while using $3\times$ fewer parameters.

1 Introduction

Over the past year, rapid progress in unsupervised language representation learning has led to the development of increasingly powerful and generalizable language models (Radford et al., 2019; Devlin et al., 2018). Widely considered to be NLP's "ImageNet moment" (Ruder, 2018), this progress has led to dramatic improvements in a wide range of natural language understanding (NLU) tasks, including text classification, sentiment analysis, and question answering (Wang et al., 2018; Rajpurkar et al., 2016). The now-common approach for employing these systems using transfer learning is to (1) pretrain a large language model (LM), (2) replace the top layer of the LM with a task-specific layer, and (3) finetune the entire model on a (usually relatively small) labeled dataset. Following this pattern, Peters et al. (2018), Howard and Ruder (2018), Radford et al. (2019), and Devlin et al. (2018) broadly outperform standard task-specific NLU models (i.e. CNNs/LSTMs), which are initialized from scratch (or only from word embeddings) and trained on the available labeled data.

Notably, transfer learning with LMs vastly outperforms training task-specific from scratch in low data regimes. For example, GPT-2 is capable of generating coherent text in a particular style (i.e. poetry, Java code, questions and answers) when conditioned on only a handful of sentences of that style (Radford et al., 2019). Similarly, on discriminative tasks such as question answering, BERT reaches accuracies comparable to previous task-specific models with orders of magnitude less labeled data (Devlin et al., 2018).

At the same time however, these large language models are extremely unwieldy. The largest versions of GPT-2 and BERT have over 1.5B and 340M parameters, respectively; it is challenging to use either of these models on a modern GPU (with 12GB of VRAM) and nearly impossible to deploy them on mobile or embedded devices. Thus, there is a strong need for efficient task-specific models that can leverage the knowledge from large pretrained models, while remaining highly compressed.

In this project, we attempt to bridge this gap for the task of low-resource text classification. We propose a new approach, called *generation-distillation*, to improve the training of small, task-specific text classification models by utilizing

Proceedings of the 2nd Workshop on Deep Learning Approaches for Low-Resource NLP (DeepLo), pages 124–131
Hong Kong, China, November 3, 2019. ©2019 Association for Computational Linguistics
https://doi.org/10.18653/v1/P17

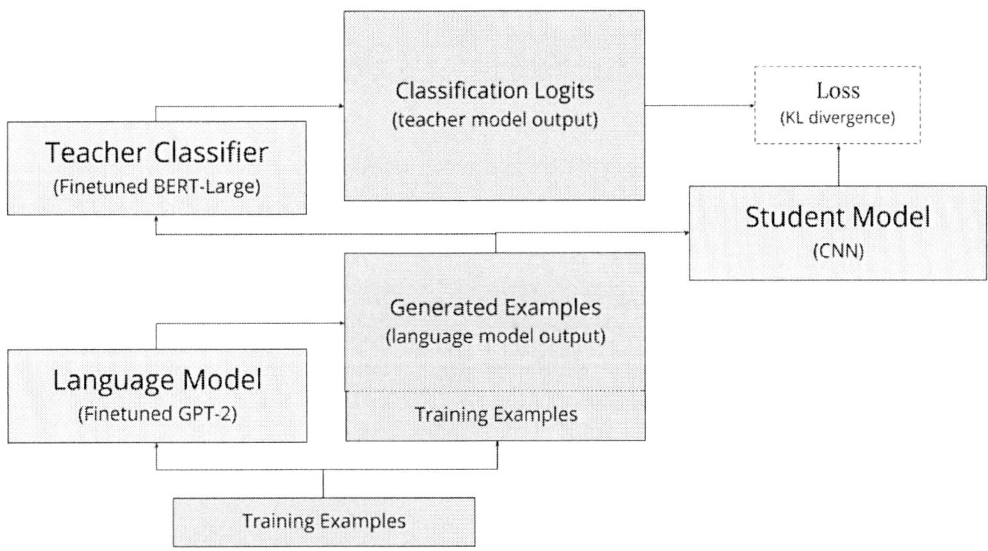

Figure 1: Our proposed generation-distillation training procedure. First, we use a large language model to augment our set of training examples, and second we train our student via distillation with a large language model-based classifier. In the diagram above, green blocks indicate models and purple blocks indicate text data.

multiple large pretrained language models. First, we use a large LM (GPT-2) to generate text in the style of our training examples, augmenting our data with unlabeled synthetic examples. Second, we use the synthetic examples to distill a second large LM (BERT), which has already been fine-tuned for classification, into a small task-specific model (CNN).

In our experiments, we show that this procedure delivers significant gains over a standard distillation approach in low-data regimes. Specifically, on low-data versions of three widely-adopted text classification datasets (AG News, DBPedia, Yahoo Answers), we obtain 98% of BERT's performance with $300\times$ fewer parameters. Moreover, compared to prior work on distilling BERT (Chia et al., 2018) on these datasets, we outperform past approaches while using $3\times$ fewer parameters.

2 Related Work

Designed to produce contextual word embeddings, large language models (LMs) build upon the now-classic idea of using pretrained word embeddings to initialize the first layer of deep natural language processing models (Collobert et al., 2011). Early proponents of contextual word vectors, including CoVe, ULMFit, and ELMo (McCann et al., 2017;

Howard and Ruder, 2018; Peters et al., 2018), extracted word representations from the activations of LSTMs, which were pretrained for either machine translation (CoVe) or for language modeling (ULMFit, ELMo).

Recent work has adopted the transformer architecture for large-scale language representation. BERT (Devlin et al., 2018) trains a transformer using masked language modeling and next sentence prediction objectives, giving state-of-the-art performance across NLU tasks. GPT/GPT-2 (Radford et al., 2019) trains a unidirectional objective, showing the ability to generate impressively coherent text.

Due to the unwieldy size of these models, a line of recent research has investigated how to best compress these models (Tang et al., 2019). In the most popular of these approaches, knowledge distillation (Hinton et al., 2015), the outputs of a larger "teacher" model are used to train a smaller "student" model. These outputs may contain more information than is available in the true label, helping bring the performance of the student closer to that of the teacher. On the task of text classification, (Tang et al., 2019) and (Chia et al., 2018) both recently showed that it is possible to compress transformer-based LMs into

Model	Params (1000s)	AG News	DBPedia	Yahoo Answers
Baseline - TFIDF + SVM (Ramos et al., 2003)	18.1	81.9	94.1	54.5
Baseline - FastText (Joulin et al., 2016)	N/A	75.2	91.0	44.9
BERT-Large	340,000	*89.9*	**97.1**	**67.0**
Chia et al. (2018) - BlendCNN*	3617	87.6	94.6	58.3
Chia et al. (2018) - BlendCNN + *Dist**	3617	**89.9**	96.0	63.4
Ours (Kim-style)	1124	85.7	94.3	62.4
Ours (Res-style)	1091	86.2	94.7	60.9
Ours + *Dist* (Kim-style)	1124	86.9	95.0	62.9
Ours + *Dist* (Res-style)	1091	87.3	95.4	62.2
Ours + *Gen-Dist* (Kim-style)	1124	*89.9*	*96.3*	64.2
Ours + *Gen-Dist* (Res-style)	1091	89.8	96.0	*65.0*

Table 1: *(Results)* A comparison of model size and accuracy on 3 text classification datasets. Bold font indicates best accuracy and italics+underline indicates second-best accuracy. Generation-distillation broadly improves small model performance over distillation, which in turn broadly improves performance over training from scratch. * results from other papers.

CNNs/LSTMs with fewer parameters, at the cost of a small (but nontrivial) drop in accuracy.

Our project builds on prior work in multiple ways. When performing generation-distillation, we employ a finetuned GPT-2 (Radford et al., 2019) as our generator and a finetuned BERT (Devlin et al., 2018) as our teacher classifier. Additionally, the distillation component of our generation-distillation approach is similar to the method used in (Chia et al., 2018), but with a different loss function (KL divergence in place of mean absolute error).

3 Methodology

As shown in Figure 1, our *generation-distillation* approach is divided into three steps: finetuning, generation and distillation.

3.1 Finetuning

The first step in our approach involves finetuning two different large LMs on our small task-specific dataset. First, we finetune a generative model (in our case, GPT-2) using only the text of the dataset. This model is used to generate new synthetic examples in the *generation* step. Second, we finetune a large LM-based classifier (in our case, BERT with an added classification head) using both the text and the labels of the dataset. This model is used as the teacher in the *distillation* step.

3.2 Generation

In the generation step, we used a large generative LM, finetuned in the first step, to augment our training dataset with synthetic examples. Specifically, we use GPT-2 to generate new sentences in the style of our training dataset and add these to our training dataset. We do not have labels for these generated sentences, but labels are not necessary because we train with distillation; our goal in generating synthetic examples is not to improve the large LM-based classifier, but rather to improve our ability to distill a large LM-based classifier into a small task-specific classifier.

3.3 Distillation

We combine both the real training examples and our synthetic examples into one large training set for distillation. We distill a large LM-based teacher classifier, finetuned in the first step, into our smaller student model via standard distillation as in Hinton et al. (2015). For our loss function, like Hinton et al. (2015), we use the KL divergence between the teacher logits and the student logits; this differs from Chia et al. (2018), who use the mean absolute error between the logits.

4 Experiments

4.1 Data

We perform text classification on three widely-used datasets: *AG News*, *DBPedia*, and *Yahoo Answers* (Gulli; Auer et al., 2007; Labrou and Finin, 1999). For purposes of comparison, we select our training set using the same procedure as Chia et al. (2018), such that the training set contains 100 examples from each class. For the generation-distillation experiments, we use GPT-2 to generate 13600 synthetic training examples on AG News and 25000 synthetic training examples on DBPedia and Yahoo Answers. Combining these with the $400, 1400$, and 1000 original (labeled) examples yields a total of $14000, 26400$, and 26000 examples on AG News, DBPedia, and Yahoo Answers, respectively.

4.2 Finetuning Details and Examples

We finetune GPT-2 345M using Neil Shepperd's fork of GPT-2: `https://github.com/nshepperd/gpt-2/blob/finetuning/train.py`

Finetuning is performed for a single epoch with a learning rate of $2e - 5$ with the Adam optimizer. We use batch size 1 and gradient checkpointing in order to train on a single GPU with 12GB of VRAM. We choose to train for only 1 epoch after examining samples produced by models with different amounts of finetuning; due to the small size of the dataset relative to the number of parameters in GPT-2, finetuning for more than 1 epoch results in significant dataset memorization.

For sampling, we perform standard sampling (i.e. sampling from the full output distribution, not top-p or top-k sampling) with temperature parameter $T = 1$. Although we do not use top-k or top-p sampling, we believe it would be interesting to compare the downstream effect of different types of sampling in the future.

In Supplementary Table 3, we show examples of synthetic training texts generated by sampling from the finetuned GPT-2 model, for both DBPedia and Yahoo Answers.

In Supplementary Table 4, we show two synthetic training texts along with their nearest neighbors in the training set. Nearest neighbors were calculated by ranking all examples from the training dataset (1400 examples) according to cosine similarity of TF-IDF vectors. As can be seen in the example in the right column, the GPT-2 language model has memorized some of the entities in the training dataset (i.e. the exact words "Ain Dara Syria"), but provides a novel description of the entity. This novel description is factually incorrect, but it may still be helpful in training a text classification model in a low-resource setting, because the words the model generates (i.e. "Syria", "Turkey", "Karzahayel") are broadly related to the original topic/label. For example, they may help the model learn the concept of the class "village", which is the label of Nearest Neighbor 1.

4.3 Student Models & Optimization

We experiment with two main CNN architectures. The first is a standard CNN architecture from Kim (2014). The second is a new CNN based on ResNet (He et al., 2016). This "Res-style" model has 3 hidden layers, each with hidden size 100, and dropout probability $p = 0.5$. We use multiple models to demonstrate that our performance improvements over previous approaches are not attributable to architectural changes, and to show that our approach generalizes across architectures.

We train the CNNs using Adam (Kingma and Ba, 2014; Loshchilov and Hutter, 2017) with learning rate 10^{-3}. Additionally, the CNNs both use 100-dimensional pretrained subword embeddings (Heinzerling and Strube, 2018), which are finetuned during training.

4.4 Results

We report the performance of our trained models in Table 1.

When trained with standard distillation, our KimCNN and ResCNN models perform as would be expected given the strong results in Chia et al. (2018). Our models perform slightly worse than the 8-layer BlendCNN from Chia et al. (2018) on AG News and DBPedia, while performing slightly better on Yahoo Answers. Standard distillation improves their performance, but there remains a significant gap between the CNNs and the BERT-Large based classifier. Training with the proposed generation-distillation approach significantly reduces the gap between the CNNs and BERT-Large; across all datasets, the model trained with generation-distillation matches or exceeds both the model the model trained with standard distillation and the BlendCNN.

4.5 Ablation

In Figure 2, we show how the accuracy of the final distilled model varies with the number of syn-

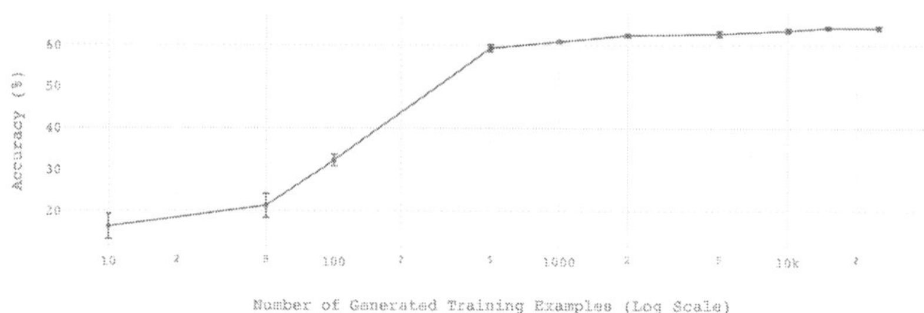

Figure 2: Above, we show how the accuracy of the final distilled model varies with the number of synthetic training examples generated by GPT-2. Error bars show the standard deviation of accuracies on five separate runs. The same GPT-2 model (trained on 100 examples per class, or a total of 1000 examples) was used to generate all synthetic texts.

Hard Labeling vs. Distillation on Generated Examples (Yahoo Answers)

	Hard Labeling with BERT	Distillation with BERT
Accuracy	62.9 ±0.22	64.2 ±0.13

Table 2: Above, we show a comparison of hard labeling and distillation for labeling the synthetic examples produced by our generator network. We report the the mean and standard error of the student (Kim) model accuracy across 5 random restarts on the Yahoo Answers dataset. Generation and distillation significantly outperforms generation and hard labeling.

thetic training examples generated by GPT-2. The distilled model is trained entirely on synthetic examples, without ever seeing the original data. The model shows strong performance (60% accuracy) with as few as 500 generated training examples, or 50 per class. Moreover, model performance continues to increase with more generated training examples, up to $25,000$.

In Table 2, we compare two different methods of labeling the synthetic examples produced by our generator network (GPT-2): hard labeling and distillation. Hard labeling refers to taking the maximum-probability class according to our finetuned BERT model as the label for each generated example and using a standard cross entropy loss function. Distillation refers to using the probability distribution outputted by BERT as the label for each generated examtple and using a KL divergence loss function. Put differently, in the former we use BERT to generate labels, whereas in the latter we use BERT to generate perform distillation. We find that generation and distillation outperforms generation and hard labeling by a significant margin, consistent with previous work on knowledge distillation (Hinton et al., 2015).

5 Conclusion

In this work, we present a new approach to compressing natural language understanding models in low-data regimes. Our approach leverages large finetuned language models in two ways: (1) to generate new (unlabeled) training examples, and (2) to distill their knowledge into a small network using these examples. Across three low-resource text classification datsets, we achieve comparable performance to BERT while using $300\times$ fewer parameters, and we outperform prior approaches to distillation for text classification while using $3\times$ fewer parameters. Although we focus on text classification in this paper, our proposed method may be extended to a host of other natural language understanding tasks in low-data settings, such as question answering or extractive summarization.

References

Sören Auer, Christian Bizer, Georgi Kobilarov, Jens Lehmann, Richard Cyganiak, and Zachary Ives. 2007. Dbpedia: A nucleus for a web of open data. In *The semantic web*, pages 722–735. Springer.

Yew Ken Chia, Sam Witteveen, and Martin Andrews.

2018. Transformer to cnn: Label-scarce distillation for efficient text classification.

Ronan Collobert, Jason Weston, Léon Bottou, Michael Karlen, Koray Kavukcuoglu, and Pavel P. Kuksa. 2011. Natural language processing (almost) from scratch. *CoRR*, abs/1103.0398.

Jacob Devlin, Ming-Wei Chang, Kenton Lee, and Kristina Toutanova. 2018. Bert: Pre-training of deep bidirectional transformers for language understanding. *arXiv preprint arXiv:1810.04805*.

Antonio Gulli. [link].

Kaiming He, Xiangyu Zhang, Shaoqing Ren, and Jian Sun. 2016. Deep residual learning for image recognition. In *Proceedings of the IEEE conference on computer vision and pattern recognition*, pages 770–778.

Benjamin Heinzerling and Michael Strube. 2018. BPEmb: Tokenization-free Pre-trained Subword Embeddings in 275 Languages. In *Proceedings of the Eleventh International Conference on Language Resources and Evaluation (LREC 2018)*, Miyazaki, Japan. European Language Resources Association (ELRA).

Geoffrey Hinton, Oriol Vinyals, and Jeff Dean. 2015. Distilling the knowledge in a neural network. *arXiv preprint arXiv:1503.02531*.

Jeremy Howard and Sebastian Ruder. 2018. Universal language model fine-tuning for text classification. *ACL 2018*.

Armand Joulin, Edouard Grave, Piotr Bojanowski, Matthijs Douze, Hérve Jégou, and Tomas Mikolov. 2016. Fasttext.zip: Compressing text classification models. *arXiv preprint arXiv:1612.03651*.

Yoon Kim. 2014. Convolutional neural networks for sentence classification. *arXiv preprint arXiv:1408.5882*.

Diederik P Kingma and Jimmy Ba. 2014. Adam: A method for stochastic optimization. *arXiv preprint arXiv:1412.6980*.

Yannis Labrou and Tim Finin. 1999. Yahoo! as an ontology: using yahoo! categories to describe documents. In *Proceedings of the eighth international conference on Information and knowledge management*, pages 180–187. ACM.

Ilya Loshchilov and Frank Hutter. 2017. Fixing weight decay regularization in adam. *arXiv preprint arXiv:1711.05101*.

Bryan McCann, James Bradbury, Caiming Xiong, and Richard Socher. 2017. Learned in translation: Contextualized word vectors. In *Advances in Neural Information Processing Systems*, pages 6294–6305.

Matthew E Peters, Mark Neumann, Mohit Iyyer, Matt Gardner, Christopher Clark, Kenton Lee, and Luke Zettlemoyer. 2018. Deep contextualized word representations. *NAACL 2018*.

Alec Radford, Jeffrey Wu, Rewon Child, David Luan, Dario Amodei, and Ilya Sutskever. 2019. Language models are unsupervised multitask learners. *OpenAI Blog*, 1:8.

Pranav Rajpurkar, Jian Zhang, Konstantin Lopyrev, and Percy Liang. 2016. Squad: 100, 000+ questions for machine comprehension of text. *CoRR*, abs/1606.05250.

Juan Ramos et al. 2003. Using tf-idf to determine word relevance in document queries.

Sebastian Ruder. 2018. Nlp's imagenet moment has arrived.

Raphael Tang, Yao Lu, Linqing Liu, Lili Mou, Olga Vechtomova, and Jimmy Lin. 2019. Distilling task-specific knowledge from bert into simple neural networks. *arXiv preprint arXiv:1903.12136*.

Alex Wang, Amapreet Singh, Julian Michael, Felix Hill, Omer Levy, and Samuel R Bowman. 2018. Glue: A multi-task benchmark and analysis platform for natural language understanding. *arXiv preprint arXiv:1804.07461*.

Examples of Generated Training Texts

DBPedia
Landmine: Landmine[1] (also known as LNG mine) is a landmine created by the Chernobyl nuclear powerplant. It is a slurry subterranean mine typically laid in shallow pools of water. The mines are connected by run-off points and can be faced off against one another.
Naukembe Consolidated School: Naukembe is a boarder boarding and lodging school based in the township of Naushere East Sussex England. The school is a member of the N30 co-education network. The school holds around 750 students from grade six to eleven.
Peter Moldegrd: Peter Moldegrd (born 6 July 1940) is a Swedish film director known for his 1972 Melancholia. He later worked in Zurich and Hong Kong.
Ain Dara Syria: Ain Dara (Arabic: Andin Qasim Qasim; also Romanized as Andin Qs Qasim and Madd Drqt) is a small village in Doubs Governorate southwestern Syria close to the Turkey-Syria border. Nearby localities include Afrin to the north Karzahayel to the east and Siloamfara to the northwest. Ain Dara is settled by around 30 families.
Yahoo Answers
Why is America the most geographically illiterate first world country?
Where I can get program that erases voice from music track?: Where I can get program that erases voice from music track? nowhere
does anyone know the name of the song that's used in the ADIDAS commercial Jos +10? (That's adidas, by the way)?: This commercial was recently in a recent adidas commercial, and they apparently used the credits for the commercial, so I saw it and thought it was pretty cool.
What would be a good way to express how you feel about another person?: say something nice, thoughtful, creative, professional... whatever . just let it go and move on, someone else will take care of the rest

Table 3: Examples of captions generated by GPT-2 for the DBPedia and Yahoo Answers datasets. The GPT-2 model that generated these texts was trained on 100 examples per class, or a total of 1000 examples for Yahoo Answers and 1400 for DBPedia. These examples were picked randomly from all generated sentences.

Generated Training Examples and their Nearest Neighbors in the Real Training Data
(DBPedia)

Generated Example	Naukembe Consolidated School: Naukembe is a boarder boarding and lodging school based in the township of Naushere East Sussex England. The school is a member of the N30 co-education network. The school holds around 750 students from grade six to eleven.	Ain Dara Syria: Ain Dara (Arabic: Andin Qasim Qasim; also Romanized as Andin Qs Qasim and Madd Drqt) is a small village in Doubs Governorate southwestern Syria close to the Turkey-Syria border. Nearby localities include Afrin to the north Karzahayel to the east and Siloamfara to the northwest. Ain Dara is settled by around 30 families.
Nearest Neighbor 1	East High School (Erie Pennsylvania): East High School part of the Erie City School District is a public high school located in Erie Pennsylvania United States. The school colors are scarlet and gray. The school mascot is a Native American Warrior. People associated with East High may be referred to as East High School Warriors East High Warriors or Warriors.	Ain Dara Syria: Ain Dara (Arabic: Ł \u200e also spelled Ayn Darah) is a small village in northern Syria administratively part of the Afrin District of the Aleppo Governorate located northwest of Aleppo. Nearby localities include Afrin to the north Karzahayel to the east and Bassouta to the south. According to the Syria Central Bureau of Statistics (CBS) Ain Dara had a population of 248 in the 2004 census.The modern-day settlement of Ain Dara is situated just east of the ancient Ain Dara temple.
Nearest Neighbor 2	Calvert School: Calvert School is a lower and middle co-educational private school with a day school operation in Baltimore Maryland and an associated homeschooling division that administers a curriculum shipped to families around the United States and the world. Developed in 1906 the home school curriculum grew by being advertised in the National Geographic magazine as a kindergarten program for those wishing to offer a better education to their children.	Carabus hemprichi:,Carabus hemprichi is a species of black-coloured ground beetle in the Carabinae subfamily that can be found in Israel Lebanon Syria and Turkey
Nearest Neighbor 3	South Elgin High School: South Elgin High School (SEHS) opened 2004 is a four-year high school located in South Elgin Illinois a northwest suburb of Chicago Illinois in the United States. It is part of Elgin Area School District U46 which also includes Elgin High School Larkin High School Bartlett High School and Streamwood High School. The class of 2008 was the first to graduate at the high school. The class of 2009 was the first four year graduating class from the high school.	Retowy:,Retowy [rtv] (German: Rettauen) is a village in the administrative district of Gmina Spopol within Bartoszyce County Warmian-Masurian Voivodeship in northern Poland close to the border with the Kaliningrad Oblast of Russia. It lies approximately 10 kilometres (6 mi) north-west of Spopol 14 km (9 mi) north-east of Bartoszyce and 68 km (42 mi) north-east of the regional capital Olsztyn.Before 1945 the area was part of Germany (East Prussia).

Table 4: Above, we show two example sentences from DPedia along with their nearest neighbors from the training dataset (DBPedia). Nearest neighbors were calculated by selecting the three examples from the training dataset (1400 examples) with the greatest TF-IDF vector cosine distance to the generated example.

Unlearn Dataset Bias in Natural Language Inference by Fitting the Residual

He He[1,2] and **Sheng Zha**[1] and **Haohan Wang**[3]

[1]Amazon Web Services, [2]New York University, [3]Carnegie Mellon University

`{hehea,zhasheng}@amazon.com, haohanw@cs.cmu.edu`

Abstract

Statistical natural language inference (NLI) models are susceptible to learning *dataset bias*: superficial cues that happen to associate with the label on a particular dataset, but are not useful in general, e.g., negation words indicate contradiction. As exposed by several recent challenge datasets, these models perform poorly when such association is absent, e.g., predicting that *"I love dogs."* contradicts *"I don't love cats."*. Our goal is to design learning algorithms that guard against *known* dataset bias. We formalize the concept of dataset bias under the framework of distribution shift and present a simple debiasing algorithm based on residual fitting, which we call DRiFt. We first learn a biased model that only uses features that are known to relate to dataset bias. Then, we train a debiased model that fits to the residual of the biased model, focusing on examples that cannot be predicted well by biased features only. We use DRiFt to train three high-performing NLI models on two benchmark datasets, SNLI and MNLI. Our debiased models achieve significant gains over baseline models on two challenge test sets, while maintaining reasonable performance on the original test sets.

1 Introduction

Machine learning models have surpassed human-performance on multiple language understanding benchmarks. However, transferring the success to real-world applications has been much slower due to the brittleness of these systems. For example, McCoy et al. (2019) show that models blindly predict the entailment relation for two sentences with high word overlap even if they have very different meanings, e.g., *"The man hit a dog"* and *"The dog hit a man"*. Jia and Liang (2017) show that reading comprehension models are easily distracted by irrelevant sentences containing key phrases from the

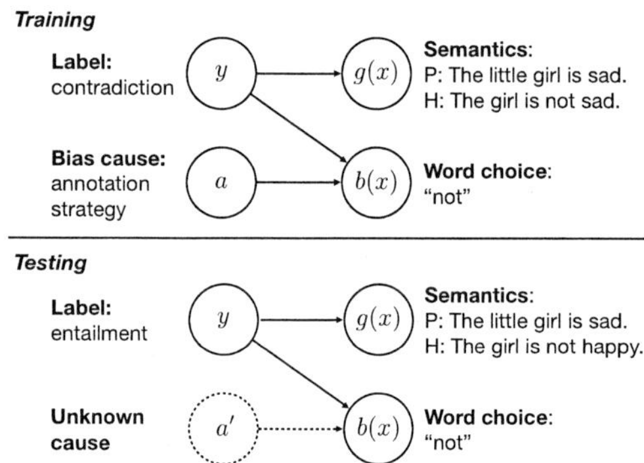

Figure 1: An example of dataset bias in NLI. On the training data, the biased feature (*"not"*) is affected by crowd workers' strategy of negating the premise to create a contradicting pair. However, at test time the word choice is affected by *unknown* sources, thus *"not"* may not be associated with the label "contradiction". A model relying on the negation word to predict "contradiction" would fail on the shown test example.

question. Similar failures have also been observed on paraphrase identification (Zhang et al., 2019c) and story cloze test (Schwartz et al., 2017).

A common problem behind these failures is distribution shift. Our training data is often not a representative sample of real-world data due to their different data-generating processes, thus models are susceptible to learning simple cues (e.g., lexical overlap) that work well on the majority of training examples but fail on more challenging test examples. Consider generating a contradicting pair of sentences for natural language inference (NLI) in Figure 1. Crowd workers tend to mechanically negate the premise sentence to save time, introducing an association between negation words (e.g., *"not"*) and the contradiction label. However, at test time, such association may not exist as data is now generated by end users. Thus, a model that heavily relies on the biased feature *"not"* would

Proceedings of the 2nd Workshop on Deep Learning Approaches for Low-Resource NLP (DeepLo), pages 132–142
Hong Kong, China, November 3, 2019. ©2019 Association for Computational Linguistics
https://doi.org/10.18653/v1/P17

fail. In this paper, we formalize *dataset bias* (Torralba and Efros, 2011) under the label shift assumption: the conditional distribution of the label given biased features changes at test time. Our goal is to design learning algorithms that are robust to dataset bias with a focus on NLI, i.e. predicting whether the *premise* sentence entails the *hypothesis* sentence.

Typical debiasing approaches aim to remove biased features (e.g., gender and image texture) in the learned representation (Wang et al., 2019b,a). However, biased features in textual data often conflate useful semantic information and superficial cues, thus completely removing them might significantly hurt prediction performance. Even when we are confident that the bias is irrelevant to prediction (e.g., gender), Gonen and Goldberg (2019) show that existing bias removal methods are insufficient.

Instead of debiasing the data representation, our method (along with the concurrent work of Clark et al. (2019)) accounts for label shift given biased features by focusing on "hard" examples that cannot be predicted well using only biased features. We train a model in two steps. First, we train a *biased model* using insufficient features such as overlapping words between the premise and the hypothesis. Next, we train a *debiased model* by fitting to the residuals of the biased model. This step "unlearns" the bias by taking additional negative gradient updates on examples with low loss under the biased model (Section 3.2).[1] At test time, only the debiased model is used for prediction. We call this learning algorithm DRiFt (**D**ebias by **R**esidual **F**itting).

We use DRiFt to train three high-performing NLI models on two benchmark datasets, SNLI (Bowman et al., 2015) and MNLI (Williams et al., 2017). Compared to baseline models trained by maximum likelihood estimation, our debiased models improve performance on several challenge datasets with only slight degradation on the original test sets.

2 Problem Statement

Dataset bias. Let $x \in \mathcal{X}$ be the input and $y \in \mathcal{Y}$ be the label we want to predict. Given training examples (x, y) drawn from a distribution P, we

---

[1] Note that dataset bias is flagged by good performance despite insufficient input, e.g., a high-accuracy hypothesis-only classifier (Gururangan et al., 2018).

define *dataset bias* as (partial) representation of x that exhibits label shift (Lipton et al., 2018; Scholkopf et al., 2012) on the test distribution Q. Formally, assume that x can be represented by two components $b(x)$ and $g(x)$ conditionally independent given y. We have

$$p(x, y) = p(b(x), g(x), y) \qquad (1)$$
$$= p(g(x) \mid y)p(y \mid b(x))p(b(x)). \qquad (2)$$

Let $g(x)$ be the true effect of y such that their relationship does not change normally, i.e. $p(g(x) \mid y) = q(g(x) \mid y)$. Let $b(x)$ be *biased features* that happen to be predictive of y on P. For example, in Figure 1, $g(x)$ represents semantics of the premis and hypothesis sentences, whereas $b(x)$ represents specific word choices affected by varying sources. In the training data, the word "*not*" has a strong association with "contradiction" due to crowd workers' writing strategies. Consequently, a model learned on the training data distribution P would degrade when such association no longer exists. Formally, both training and testing examples may exhibit biased features: $p(b(x)) = q(b(x))$, but dependence between these features and the label can change: $p(y \mid b(x)) \neq q(y \mid b(x))$.

In a typical supervised learning setting with dataset bias, we do not observe examples from Q thus $b(x)$ is unknown. Without additional information, achieving good performance on Q is impossible. Fortunately, oftentimes we do have domain-specific knowledge on what $b(x)$ might be, e.g., the word overlapping heuristic in NLI. Therefore, our goal is to correct the model trained on P to perform well on Q given *known* dataset bias.

Bias in NLI data. Dataset bias in SNLI (Bowman et al., 2015) and MNLI (Williams et al., 2017) are largely due to the crowdsourcing process. Both are created by asking crowd workers to write three sentences (hypotheses) that are entailed by, neutral with, or contradict a given sentence drawn from a corpus (the premise). Gururangan et al. (2018); Poliak et al. (2018) show that certain words in the hypothesis have high pointwise mutual information with class labels regardless of the premise, which could be artifacts of specific annotation strategies. For example, one can create a neutral sentence by adding a cause ("*because*") to the premise and create a contradicting sentence by negating ("*no*", "*never*") the premise. As a result, the majority of training examples can be solved without much reasoning about sentence meanings. Subsequently, McCoy et al. (2019) report that models rely on high word overlap to predict entailment; Glockner et al. (2018); Naik et al. (2018) demonstrate that models struggle at even lexical-level inference involving antonyms, hypernyms, etc.

A natural question to ask then is whether there exist better data collection procedures that guard against these biases. We argue that this is not easy because in practice, we almost always have different data-generating processes during training (generated from selected corpora and annotators) and test (generated by end users). Then, can we remove biased features from training examples? This is also infeasible because sometimes they contain the necessary information for prediction, e.g., removing words may destroy the sentence meaning. It is not the features that are biased but their relation with the label. Next, we describe our approach to mitigating this biased relation.

3 Approach

3.1 Overview

The key idea of our approach is to first detect biased examples given prior knowledge on potential dataset bias, then focus on learning from unbiased, hard examples. We describe the two steps in details below.

Detect biased examples. How do we know if an example exhibits biased features? Although we cannot directly measure label shift without accessing the test data, we know that NLI models are unlikely to work well given insufficient features. When it does work well given only partial semantics of the input, the good performance is likely due to dataset bias. For example, Gururangan et al. (2018) exposes annotation artifacts by showing that hypothesis-only models have unexpected high accuracy. Similarly, we train a *biased classifier* using insufficient features $I(x)$, e.g., the hypothesis sentence. We assume that examples predicted well by the biased classifier exhibit dataset bias, i.e. $p(y \mid I(x))$ is high but $q(y \mid I(x))$ is low.

Importantly, while $I(x)$ approximates $b(x)$ given our prior knowledge, it does not necessarily capture all dataset bias, which depends on the unknown test distribution. In addition, $I(x)$ may include useful information. For example, although bag-of-words (BOW) features are insufficient to represent precise sentence meaning, it encodes a distribution of possible meanings. Thus good performance of a BOW classifier is not fully due to fitting dataset bias. In practice, as we will see in the experiments (Section 4.5), good choices of $I(x)$ capture biased features precisely, resulting in significant performance drop of the biased classifier on Q.

Learn residuals of the biased classifier. Our intuition is that the debiased classifier should capture information beyond those contained in the biased classifier. If the biased classifier already has a small loss on an example, then there is not much to learn beyond the biased features; otherwise, the debiased classifier should correct predictions of the biased classifier.

We implement the idea through a residual fitting procedure (DRiFt). Let $f_s \colon \mathcal{X} \to \mathbb{R}$ and $f_d \colon \mathcal{X} \to \mathbb{R}$ be the biased and the debiased classifiers, and let L be the loss function. First, we learn f_s with insufficient features $I(x)$ as the input:

$$\theta^* = \arg\min_{\theta} \mathbb{E}_P \left[L(f_s(I(x); \theta), y) \right]. \quad (3)$$

Let $f^*(x)$ be the optimal predictor that minimizes the empirical risk on P. We define

$$f^*(x) \stackrel{\text{def}}{=} f_s(I(x); \theta^*) + f_d(x; \phi^*). \quad (4)$$

Thus f_d fits the residual of f_s with respect to the target f^*. To estimate parameters ϕ of f_d, we fix parameters of f_s and minimize the loss:

$$\min_{\phi} \mathbb{E}_P \left[L(f_s(I(x); \theta^*) + f_d(x; \phi), y) \right]. \quad (5)$$

At test time, we only use the debiased classifier f_d.

Consider the typical empirical risk minimization approach that estimates ϕ by minimizing $\mathbb{E}_P \left[L(f_d(x; \phi), y) \right]$. It is susceptible to relying on biased features when they predict well on the majority examples. In contrast, DRiFt first learns f_s which is intended to fit potential bias in the data. It then learns f_d that compensates f_s without fitting to the bias already captured by it.

Next, we analyze the behavior of DRiFt using the cross-entropy loss function, which is typically used for classification problems.

3.2 Analysis with the Cross-Entropy Loss

In this section, we show that DRiFt adjusts the gradient on each example depending on how well it is predicted by the pretrained biased classifier.

Given the cross-entropy loss, our goal is to maximize the expected conditional log-likelihood of the data, $\mathbb{E}_P[\log p(y \mid x)]$. A classifier outputs a vector of scores for each of the K classes, $f(x) = (f^1(x), \ldots, f^K(x)) \in \mathbb{R}^K$, which are then mapped to a probability distribution $p(y \mid x)$ by the softmax function. Given classifiers f_s and f_d, we have three choices of parametrization of the conditional probability $p(y \mid x)$:

$$p_s(y \mid I(x)) \propto \exp\left(f_s^y(I(x); \theta)\right) \quad (6)$$

$$p_d(y \mid x) \propto \exp\left(f_d^y(x; \phi)\right) \quad (7)$$

$$p_a(y \mid x) \propto \exp\left(f_s^y(I(x); \theta) + f_d^y(x; \phi)\right)$$
$$\propto p_s(y \mid I(x)) p_d(y \mid x). \quad (8)$$

To learn the classifier f_d, standard maximum likelihood estimation (MLE) uses $p_d(y \mid x)$, whereas DRiFt uses $p_a(y \mid x)$ given pretrained f_s with fixed parameters.

Let us first compare the two learning objectives. Denote $p_s(y \mid I(x); \theta^*)$ by $p_s^*(y \mid I(x))$. DRiFt maximizes

$$J_{\mathrm{D}}(\phi) = \sum_{(x,y) \sim \mathcal{D}} \log p_a(y \mid x; \theta^*, \phi) \quad (9)$$

$$= C + \sum_{(x,y) \sim \mathcal{D}} [\log p_d(y \mid x; \phi) -$$

$$\log \sum_{k=1}^{K} p_s^*(k \mid I(x)) p_d(k \mid x; \phi)], \quad (10)$$

where $\mathcal{D}$ denotes the training set and $C = \sum_{(x,y) \sim \mathcal{D}} \log p_s^*(k \mid I(x))$ is a constant. Compare (10) with the MLE objective:

$$J_{\mathrm{MLE}}(\phi) = \sum_{(x,y) \sim \mathcal{D}} \log p_d(y \mid x; \phi) . \quad (11)$$

We see that $J_{\mathrm{D}}(\phi)$ has an additional regularizer for each example x:

$$R(x) \stackrel{\text{def}}{=} -\log \sum_{k=1}^{K} p_s^*(k \mid I(x)) p_d(k \mid x) . \quad (12)$$

Geometrically, it encourages output from the debiased classifier, p_d, to have minimal projection on p_s predicted by the biased classifier.

Next, let's look at the effect of this regularizer through its gradient. Let $Z(x)$ be the normalizer $\sum_k p_s^*(k \mid I(x)) p_d(k \mid x)$. Then, we have

$$\nabla_\phi R(x) = -\frac{\sum_k p_s^*(k \mid I(x)) \nabla_\phi p_d(k \mid x)}{\sum_k p_s^*(k \mid I(x)) p_d(k \mid x)}$$

$$= -\sum_k p_a(k \mid x) \nabla_\phi \log p_d(k \mid x),$$

which is derived by writing $\nabla_\phi p_d$ as $p_d \nabla_\phi \log p_d$. Taking a negative step in the direction of $\nabla_\phi \log p_d(k \mid x)$ corresponds to down-weighting the probability $p_d(k \mid x)$. Intuitively, the model tries to reweight the output distribution by the gradient weights $p_a(k \mid x)$. Note that

$$p_a(k \mid x) \propto p_s^*(k \mid I(x)) p_d(k \mid x) . \quad (13)$$

For an example (x, y), large values of $p_s^*(y \mid I(x))$ indicate that $I(x)$ is likely to contain biased features. If $p_d(y \mid x)$ is also large, the model is probably picking up the bias since p_d has access to complete information in x including the biased features, in which case a relatively large negative step is taken to correct it. In the extreme case where the biased classifier makes perfect prediction, we have $p_s^*(y \mid I(x)) \to 1$ thus $\nabla_\phi R(x) \to -\nabla_\phi \log p_d(y \mid x)$, canceling the MLE gradient $\nabla_\phi \log p_d(y \mid x)$. As a result, the gradient on this example is zero, and there is nothing to be learned. At the other end where $I(x)$ does not provide any useful information, the biased classifier outputs a uniform distribution $p_s^*(y \mid I(x)) = 1/K$, thus $p_a(y \mid x) = p_d(y \mid x)$ and the gradient on this example is reduced to the MLE gradient.

4 Experiments

We first evaluate our method using synthetic bias to show its effectiveness under different amount of dataset bias. We then test on two challenge datasets using different biased classifiers. We show that DRiFt consistently outperforms MLE on the challenge datasets given different NLI models, especially when the insufficient features capture dataset bias exploited by the challenge data.

4.1 Training Data

We evaluate DRiFt on two benchmarking NLI datasets: SNLI (Bowman et al., 2015) and MNLI (Williams et al., 2017). Each pair of premise and hypothesis sentences has a label from one of "entailment", "contradiction", or "neutral". Sentences from SNLI are derived from image captions, whereas MNLI covers a broader range of styles and topics. Statistics of the two datasets are shown in Table 1. All MNLI results are on the matched development set.[2]

[2] MNLI has two development sets, one from the same source as the training data (matched) and one from different sources (mismatched). We trained two sets of models using their corresponding development sets for model selection and obtained similar results. Thus we focus on the "matched" results.

Dataset	Train	Dev	Test
SNLI	549,367	9842	9842
MNLI	392,702	9815	-

Table 1: Statistics of training datasets. The test sets of MNLI are hosted through Kaggle competitions.

4.2 Models and Training Details

DRiFt is a general learning algorithm that works with any biased/debiased models. Below we describe the three key components of our approaches: the learning algorithm, the biased model with its insufficient features, and the debiased model.

Learning algorithms. We compare DRiFt with MLE, as well as a simpler variant of DRiFt: instead of the residual fitting, we remove the examples predicted correctly by the biased classifier and train on the rest. We call this baseline RM, which is also conceived by Gururangan et al. (2018). MLE only trains the debiased model. Both DRiFt and RM rely on an additional biased model that captures potential dataset bias.

Biased models. We consider three insufficient representations that exploit various NLI dataset biases reported in prior work.

HYPO is a finetuned BERT classifier that uses only the hypothesis sentence.

CBOW is a continuous bag-of-words classifier. Similar to Mou et al. (2016), we represent both the premise and the hypothesis as the respective sums of their word embeddings. We then concatenate the premise and the hypothesis embeddings, their difference, and their element-wise product. The final representation is passed through a one-layer fully connected network with ReLU activation.

HAND is a classifier using handcrafted features based on error analysis in Naik et al. (2018). Specifically, we include tokens in the hypothesis that are also in the premise, tokens unique to the hypothesis, Jaccard similarity between the two sentences, whether negation words ("*not*" and "*n't*") are included, and length difference computed by $\frac{|L_p - L_h|}{L_p + L_h}$ where L_p and L_h are numbers of tokens in the premise and the hypothesis. We represent the overlapping and the non-overlapping tokens as the respective sums of their word embeddings. The embeddings are then concatenated with the dense features and passed through a one-layer fully connected network with ReLU activation.

Debiased models. We choose three high-performing models of different capability.

DA is the Decomposable Attention model introduced by Parikh et al. (2016), which relies on the interaction between words in the premise and the hypothesis. It does not use any word order information. We used the variant without intra-sentence attention.[3]

ESIM is the Enhanced Sequential Inference Model (Chen et al., 2017). It first encodes the premise and the hypothesis by a bidirectional LSTM, aligns the contextual word embeddings similar to Parikh et al. (2016), and uses another "inference" bidirectional LSTM to aggregate information. Thus it has access to the non-local context.

BERT is the Bidirectional Encoder Representations from Transformers (Devlin et al., 2019) that recently improved performance on MNLI significantly. It uses contextual embeddings pretrained from large corpora.

Hyperparameters. For non-BERT models, word embeddings are initialized with the `840B.300d` pretrained GloVe (Pennington et al., 2014) word vectors and finetuned during training. For DA and ESIM, hyperparameters of the model architecture are the same as those reported in the original papers. We finetune all BERT models from the pretrained `BERT-base-uncased` model.[4] We train all models using the Adam (Kingma and Ba, 2014) optimizer with $\beta_1 = 0.9$, $\beta_2 = 0.999$, L2 weight decay of 0.01, learning rate warmup for the first 10% of updates and linear decay afterwards. We use a dropout rate of 0.1 for all models except ESIM, which has a dropout rate of 0.5. BERT and non-BERT models are trained with a learning rate of 2e-5 and 1e-4, respectively. For MLE, we train BERT for 4 epochs and the rest for 30 epochs. When training the debiased model in DRiFt, we find that the models converge slowly thus we train BERT for 8 epochs and the rest for 80 epochs.

---

[3] We removed the projection layers of the word embeddings as it speeds up training without hurting performance in our experiments.

[4] `http://gluon-nlp.mxnet.io/model_zoo/bert/index.html`

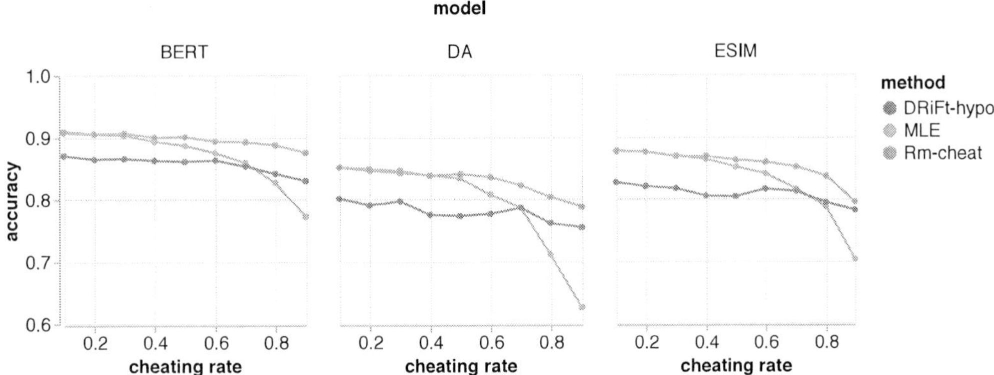

Figure 2: Accuracy on SNLI test set augmented with cheating features, which leak the groundtruth labels on training data but not on test data. Models trained by MLE degrade significantly when a majority of examples are cheatable, whereas debiased models trained by DRiFt maintain similar accuracies across different cheating rates.

4.3 In-Distribution Performance

We first evaluate the models' in-distribution performance where they are trained and evaluated on splits from the same dataset. Results of the biased models are reported in Table 2. All exceeds the majority-class baseline by a large margin, indicating that a majority of examples can be solved by superficial cues.

Results of the debiased models are reported in Table 3. Baseline results from our implementations are comparable to prior reported performance (row "MLE"). Debiased models trained by DRiFt show some degradation on in-distribution data, especially for the less powerful DA and ESIM models. The accuracy drop is expected due to two reasons. First, DRiFt assumes distribution shift thus does not optimize performance on the training distribution P. Second, the effective training data size is reduced by negative gradients on potentially biased examples; this effect is exaggerated by RM, which shows significant in-distribution degradation. Similar trade-off between in-distribution accuracy and robustness on out-of-distribution data has also been observed in adversarial training (Zhang et al., 2019b; Tsipras et al., 2019).

Dataset	majority	HYPO	CBOW	HAND
SNLI	34.2	61.8	81.2	76.7
MNLI	35.4	52.5	66.1	65.4

Table 2: Accuracy of biased classifiers on SNLI test set and MNLI development set. All exceeds the majority-class baseline by a large margin, signaling dataset bias.

	SNLI			MNLI		
	BERT	DA	ESIM	BERT	DA	ESIM
MLE	90.8	85.3	88.0	84.5	72.2	78.1
DRiFt-HYPO	89.8	83.9	86.3	84.3	68.6	75.0
DRiFt-CBOW	84.7	62.6	62.3	82.1	56.3	68.8
DRiFt-HAND	86.5	75.0	79.2	81.7	58.8	68.9
RM-HYPO	71.2	67.0	70.3	65.5	57.5	63.0
RM-CBOW	35.8	27.1	22.2	54.9	26.8	27.1
RM-HAND	46.3	37.2	38.1	51.7	34.6	37.4

Table 3: Accuracy of models trained by MLE, DRiFt, and RM with different biased models. Training and test examples are from the same dataset. Intensity of the red highlights corresponds to *absolute* drop in accuracy with respect to the MLE baseline. RM significantly hurts in-distribution performance. DRiFt maintains reasonable performance.

4.4 Synthetic Bias

In this section, we evaluate our model under controlled, synthetic dataset bias on SNLI. Recall our definition of dataset bias: the conditional distribution of the label y given biased features are different on training and test sets. Therefore, we inject bias into each example by adding a *cheating feature* that encodes its label. On training and development examples, the cheating feature encodes the ground truth label with probability p_{cheat} (the cheating rate), and a random label otherwise. On test examples, the cheating feature always encodes a random label. Thus a model relying on the cheating feature would perform poorly on the test set.

Specifically, we prepend the hypothesis with a string "{label} *and*" where label $\in$ {entailment, contradiction, neutral}. To simulate the fact that we often cannot pinpoint biased features until the model fails on some test examples, we choose HYPO as our biased classifier. That is to say, we have a rough idea that the bias might be in the hypothesis but do not know what it is exactly.

We train all three base models (DA, ESIM, and BERT) using MLE and DRiFt, respectively. Our results are shown in Figure 2. All MLE models are reasonably robust to a mild amount of bias. However, when a majority ($p_{\text{cheat}} > 0.6$) of training examples contains the bias, their accuracy decreases significantly: about 20% drop at $p_{\text{cheat}} = 0.9$ compared to the baseline accuracy when no cheating features are injected. BERT is slightly more robust than DA and ESIM, possibly due to the regularization effect of pretrained embeddings. In contrast, our debiased models (DRiFt-HYPO) maintain similar accuracies with increasing cheating rates and have a maximum accuracy drop of about 5%.

Two questions remain, though: (1) Why does the accuracy of debiased models still drop a bit at high cheating rates? (2) Why is the baseline accuracy of DRiFt lower than MLE? We answer these questions by analyzing the upper bound performance of our method below.

Best-case scenario. In the ideal case, we know precisely what the bias is. Consider a biased classifier that only uses the cheating feature as its input. It predicts biased examples perfectly, i.e. $p_s(y \mid b(x)) = 1$ and $p_s(k \mid b(x)) = 0 \ \forall k \neq y$, and predicts the rest unbiased examples uniformly at random. Based on our discussion at the end of Section 3.2, the biased examples have zero gradients and unbiased examples have the same gradients as in MLE. In this case, our method is equivalent to removing biased examples and training a classifier on the rest, i.e. RM-cheat. In Figure 2, we see that it completely dominates MLE. The accuracy of RM-cheat still drops when p_{cheat} is large, because there are fewer "good" examples to learn from, not due to fitting the bias. Similarly, DRiFt-HYPO has lower overall accuracy compared to RM-cheat, because HYPO captures additional (unbiased) features that cannot be fully learned by the debiased model.

Worst-case scenario. In the extreme case when $p_{\text{cheat}} = 1$, all models' predictions on the test set are random guesses. For MLE, the biased features are no longer differentiable from the gener-

alizable ones, thus there is no reason not to use them. For DRiFt, since the biased model achieves perfect prediction on all training examples, the debiased model receives zero gradient. Therefore, when strong bias presents on all examples, we need more information to correct the bias, e.g., collecting additional data or augmenting examples.

method	lexical		subseq		const	
	E	$\neg E$	E	$\neg E$	E	$\neg E$
HYPO	52.6	44.4	54.5	44.3	45.6	16.7
CBOW	63.2	16.0	66.2	33.7	63.2	38.5
HAND	66.7	0.0	66.7	0.0	66.7	0.0
model: BERT						
MLE	67.2	7.8	66.7	0.4	68.1	11.9
DRiFt-HYPO	84.7	79.8	69.0	23.7	72.7	40.8
DRiFt-CBOW	80.8	75.2	68.5	29.5	71.5	40.3
DRiFt-HAND	77.4	70.9	71.2	41.2	75.8	61.0
RM-HYPO	67.2	46.0	65.2	36.6	75.5	72.2
RM-CBOW	5.4	66.4	8.5	64.2	34.8	65.3
RM-HAND	10.0	66.0	4.7	66.3	9.1	67.3
model: DA						
MLE	66.6	0.5	66.6	0.3	66.5	0.4
DRiFt-HYPO	66.3	1.7	66.9	5.5	66.3	8.4
DRiFt-CBOW	65.3	7.2	66.1	9.6	65.1	9.1
DRiFt-HAND	60.5	27.1	61.4	44.9	55.9	48.3
RM-HYPO	65.1	9.6	66.2	15.0	66.2	18.8
RM-CBOW	0.4	66.6	1.3	66.7	0.8	66.5
RM-HAND	10.3	65.8	8.9	65.7	13.9	64.7
model: ESIM						
MLE	65.8	3.2	67.2	4.6	65.5	2.8
DRiFt-HYPO	64.3	10.5	68.3	16.3	68.1	29.3
DRiFt-CBOW	63.2	14.4	66.8	20.1	64.9	22.7
DRiFt-HAND	61.2	19.6	63.7	39.4	64.8	48.3
RM-HYPO	63.3	12.8	64.1	24.8	71.3	46.0
RM-CBOW	4.5	65.7	6.0	65.2	16.9	63.8
RM-HAND	25.8	60.8	18.3	67.3	13.1	65.9

Table 4: F1 scores of the entailment (E) and non-entailment ($\neg E$) classes on HANS. All models are trained on MNLI and results are shown on three subsets targeting at different biases: lexical overlap (lexical), subsequence overlap (subseq), and constituent overlap (const). Intensity of the Blue and red highlights corresponds to *absolute* increase and decrease of scores with respect to MLE. DRiFt significantly improves results on challenging $\neg E$ examples without hurting performance on E, whereas RM improves scores on $\neg E$ at the cost of performance on E.

4.5 Word Overlap Bias

We evaluate our method on word overlap bias in NLI. McCoy et al. (2019) show that models trained on MNLI largely rely on word overlap between the premise and the hypothesis to make entailment predictions. They created a challenge dataset (HANS) where premises may not entail high word-overlapping hypotheses. Specifically, a model biased by word overlap would fail on three types of non-entailment examples: (1) Lexical overlap, e.g., *"The doctor visited the lawyer."* $\nRightarrow$ *"The lawyer visited the doctor.".* (2) Subsequence, e.g., *"The senator near the lawyer danced."* $\nRightarrow$ *"The lawyer danced.".* (3) Constituent, e.g., *"The lawyers resigned, or the artist slept."* $\nRightarrow$ *"The artist slept.".*

We evaluate both biased and debiased models on the three subsets of HANS and show F1 scores for each class in Table 4. As expected, models trained by MLE almost always predict entailment (E), and thus performs poorly for the non-entailment class ($\neg E$). DRiFt improves performance on $\neg E$ in all cases with little degradation on E. In contrast, RM improves performance on $\neg E$ at the cost of significant degradation on E.

Among all biased models, HAND produces the best debiasing results because it is designed to fit the word overlap bias, and indeed has zero recall on $\neg E$ when tested on HANS. On the contrary, the improvement from HYPO is lower because it does not capture any word overlap bias. Correspondingly, its performance drop on HANS is minimal compared to its in-distribution performance. Among all debiased models, BERT has the best overall performance. We hypothesize that pre-training on large data improves model robustness in addition to the debiasing effect from DRiFt.

4.6 Stress Tests

In addition to the word overlap bias exploited by HANS, there are other known biases such as negation words and sentence lengths. Naik et al. (2018) conduct a detailed error anlaysis on MNLI and create six stress test sets (STRESS) targeting at each type of error. We focus on the word overlap and negation stress test sets, which expose dataset bias as opposed to model weakness according to Liu et al. (2019). A model biased by word overlap rate and negation words are expected to have low accuracy on the entailment class on challenge data. The complete results are shown in Appendix A.

In Table 5, we show the F1 scores of each class for all models on STRESS.[5] Compared to results

method	Negation			Overlap		
	E	C	N	E	C	N
HYPO	41.2	52.4	50.5	44.2	52.8	51.7
CBOW	20.1	48.2	53.9	49.7	52.9	55.6
HAND	37.5	45.0	57.3	56.7	50.1	57.8
model: BERT						
MLE	2.4	81.1	56.5	19.2	83.3	59.4
DRiFt-HYPO	7.3	80.7	55.6	27.5	81.1	59.1
DRiFt-CBOW	17.9	81.7	55.5	18.3	80.0	56.6
DRiFt-HAND	4.3	80.6	55.5	15.0	81.9	57.4
model: DA						
MLE	17.4	47.3	55.3	46.7	60.5	57.8
DRiFt-HYPO	11.8	47.0	51.8	41.6	59.4	55.6
DRiFt-CBOW	28.4	21.4	39.5	35.2	41.7	43.8
DRiFt-HAND	24.7	42.0	46.4	42.2	56.0	49.9
model: ESIM						
MLE	12.0	72.7	54.6	27.6	76.4	57.5
DRiFt-HYPO	22.8	67.7	54.0	37.5	73.2	56.7
DRiFt-CBOW	32.7	62.3	46.9	30.4	65.6	49.8
DRiFt-HAND	15.8	64.6	51.8	39.2	70.7	53.9

Table 5: F1 scores of each class on STRESS. Intensity of the Blue and red highlights corresponds to *absolute* increase and decrease of scores with respect to MLE. DRiFt improves results on E (that exhibits label shift) with some degradation on other classes for DA and ESIM.

on HANS, STRESS sees lower overall improvement from debiasing. One reason is that STRESS decreases word overlap *rate* and injects negation words by appending distractor phrases, i.e. *"true is true"* and *"false is not true".* While this introduces label shift on biased features, it also introduces covariate shift on the input. For example, although HAND contains features designed to use word overlap rate (Jaccard similarity) and negation words, its does not have big performance drop on the challenge data compared to its in-distribution performance, showing that that distractor phrases may affect the model in other ways.

While all debiased models show improvement on E, both DA and ESIM suffer from degradation on the other two classes, especially when trained by DRiFt-CBOW. We posit two reasons. First, while CBOW is insufficient to represent complete sentence meaning, it does encode a distribution of possible meanings. Thus models debiased by DRiFt-CBOW might discard useful information. Second, model capacity limits what is learned beyond a BOW representation. DA shows the most

---

[5] Since results of RM are similar to those in Table 4, we put them in Appendix A.

degradation since it only uses local word interaction, thus is essentially a BOW model. In contrast, BERT has little degradation on in-distribution examples regardless of the biased classifier.

5 Related Work and Discussion

Adversarial data collection. Aside from NLI, dataset bias has been exposed on benchmarks for other NLP tasks as well, e.g., paraphrase identification (Zhang et al., 2019c,a), story close test (Schwartz et al., 2017), reading comprehension (Kaushik and Lipton, 2018), coreference resolution (Zhao et al., 2018a), and visual question answering (Agrawal et al., 2016). Most bias is resulted from artifacts in the data selection procedure and shortcuts taken by crowd workers. To systematically minimize bias during data collection, adversarial filtering methods (Sakaguchi et al., 2019; Zellers et al., 2019) have been proposed to discard examples predicted well by a simple classifier. This is similar to the RM baseline, except that we apply "filtering" at training time. In general, our debiasing methods are complementary to adversarial data collection methods.

Debiased representation. Our work is closely related to the line of work on removing bias in data representations. Bolukbasi et al. (2016); Zhao et al. (2018b) learn gender-neutral word embeddings by forcing certain dimensions to be free of gender information. Similarly, Wang et al. (2019a) construct a biased classifier and project its representation out of the model's representation. For NLI, Belinkov et al. (2019) use adversarial learning to remove hypothesis-related bias in the sentence representations. However, for some NLP applications it may not be easy to separate biased features from useful semantic representations, thus we correct the conditional distribution of the class label given these biased features instead of removing them from the input. Concurrently, Clark et al. (2019) take the same approach and further show its effectiveness on additional tasks including reading comparehension and visual question answering.

Distribution shift. Covariate shift (Shimodaira, 2000; Ben-David et al., 2006) and label shift (Lipton et al., 2018; Zhang et al., 2013) are two well-studied settings under distribution shift, which makes different assumptions on how $p(x, y)$ changes. However, most works in these settings assume access to unlabeled data from the target distribution. Our objective is more related to distributionally robust optimization (Duchi and Namkoong, 2018; Hu et al., 2018), which does not assume access to target data and optimizes the worst-case performance under *unknown*, bounded distribution shift. In contrast, we leverage prior knowledge on potential dataset bias.

Data augmentation. An effective way to tackle the challenge datasets is to train or finetune on similar examples (McCoy et al., 2019; Liu et al., 2019; Jia and Liang, 2017), which explicitly correct the training data distribution. However, constructing challenge examples often rely on handcrafted rules that target a specific type of bias, e.g., swapping male and female entities (Zhao et al., 2018a, 2019), synonym/antonym substitution (Glockner et al., 2018), and syntactic rules (McCoy et al., 2019; Ribeiro et al., 2018), and may require human verification (Zhang et al., 2019c; Jia and Liang, 2017). Data augmentation provides a way to encode our prior knowledge on the task, e.g., swapping genders does not affect coreference resolution result, and syntactic transformations may affect sentence meanings. Therefore, a related direction is to develop generic augmentation techniques with linguistic priors (Andreas, 2019; Karpukhin et al., 2019).

6 Conclusion

Across all different dataset biases, the fundamental problem is that the majority training examples are not representative of the real-world data distribution (including the challenge data), thus minimizing the average training loss no longer accurately describes our objective. In this paper, we tackle the problem by adapting the learning objective to focus on examples that cannot be easily solved by biased features. We show that our debiasing method improves model performance on challenge data given *known* dataset bias. However, current improvements largely rely on task-specific prior knowledge, thus an important next step is to develop more general methods that tackle different types of biases.

Acknowledgments

Yanchao Ni worked on an earlier version of this project while he was at New York University. We thank the GluonNLP community for their support on reproducing prior results.

References

A. Agrawal, D. Batra, and D. Parikh. 2016. Analyzing the behavior of visual question answering models. In *Empirical Methods in Natural Language Processing (EMNLP)*.

J. Andreas. 2019. Good-enough compositional data augmentation. *arXiv*.

Y. Belinkov, A. Poliak, S. M. Shieber, B. V. Durme, and A. M. Rush. 2019. Don't take the premise for granted: Mitigating artifacts in natural language inference. In *Association for Computational Linguistics (ACL)*.

S. Ben-David, J. Blitzer, K. Crammer, and F. Pereira. 2006. Analysis of representations for domain adaptation. In *Advances in Neural Information Processing Systems (NeurIPS)*, pages 137–144.

T. Bolukbasi, K. Chang, J. Y. Zou, V. Saligrama, and A. T. Kalai. 2016. Man is to computer programmer as woman is to homemaker? debiasing word embeddings. In *Advances in Neural Information Processing Systems (NeurIPS)*, pages 4349–4357.

S. Bowman, G. Angeli, C. Potts, and C. D. Manning. 2015. A large annotated corpus for learning natural language inference. In *Empirical Methods in Natural Language Processing (EMNLP)*.

Q. Chen, X. Zhu, Z. Ling, S. Wei, H. Jiang, and D. Inkpen. 2017. Enhanced LSTM for natural language inference. In *Association for Computational Linguistics (ACL)*.

C. Clark, M. Yatskar, and L. Zettlemoyer. 2019. Don't take the easy way out: Ensemble based methods for avoiding known dataset biases. In *Empirical Methods in Natural Language Processing (EMNLP)*.

J. Devlin, M. Chang, K. Lee, and K. Toutanova. 2019. Bert: Pre-training of deep bidirectional transformers for language understanding. In *North American Association for Computational Linguistics (NAACL)*.

J. Duchi and H. Namkoong. 2018. Learning models with uniform performance via distributionally robust optimization. *arXiv preprint arXiv:1810.08750*.

M. Glockner, V. Shwartz, and Y. Goldberg. 2018. Breaking NLI systems with sentences that require simple lexical inferences. In *Association for Computational Linguistics (ACL)*.

H. Gonen and Y. Goldberg. 2019. Lipstick on a pig: Debiasing methods cover up systematic gender biases in word embeddings but do not remove them. *arXiv preprint arXiv:1903.03862*.

S. Gururangan, S. Swayamdipta, O. Levy, R. Schwartz, S. R. Bowman, and N. A. Smith. 2018. Annotation artifacts in natural language inference data. In *North American Association for Computational Linguistics (NAACL)*.

W. Hu, G. Niu, I. Sato, and M. Sugiyama. 2018. Does distributionally robust supervised learning give robust classifiers? In *International Conference on Machine Learning (ICML)*.

R. Jia and P. Liang. 2017. Adversarial examples for evaluating reading comprehension systems. In *Empirical Methods in Natural Language Processing (EMNLP)*.

V. Karpukhin, O. Levy, J. Eisenstein, and M. Ghazvininejad. 2019. Training on synthetic noise improves robustness to natural noise in machine translation. *arXiv*.

D. Kaushik and Z. C. Lipton. 2018. How much reading does reading comprehension require? a critical investigation of popular benchmarks. In *Empirical Methods in Natural Language Processing (EMNLP)*.

D. Kingma and J. Ba. 2014. Adam: A method for stochastic optimization. *arXiv preprint arXiv:1412.6980*.

Z. C. Lipton, Y. Wang, and A. J. Smola. 2018. Detecting and correcting for label shift with black box predictors. In *International Conference on Machine Learning (ICML)*.

N. F. Liu, R. Schwartz, and N. A. Smith. 2019. Inoculation by fine-tuning: A method for analyzing challenge datasets. In *North American Association for Computational Linguistics (NAACL)*.

R. T. McCoy, E. Pavlick, and T. Linzen. 2019. Right for the wrong reasons: Diagnosing syntactic heuristics in natural language inference. *arXiv preprint arXiv:1902.01007*.

L. Mou, R. Men, G. Li, Y. Xu, L. Zhang, R. Yan, and Z. Jin. 2016. Natural language inference by tree-based convolution and heuristic matching. In *Association for Computational Linguistics (ACL)*.

A. Naik, A. Ravichander, N. Sadeh, C. Rose, and G. Neubig. 2018. Stress test evaluation for natural language inference. In *International Conference on Computational Linguistics (COLING)*.

A. Parikh, O. Täckström, D. Das, and J. Uszkoreit. 2016. A decomposable attention model for natural language inference. In *Empirical Methods in Natural Language Processing (EMNLP)*.

J. Pennington, R. Socher, and C. D. Manning. 2014. GloVe: Global vectors for word representation. In *Empirical Methods in Natural Language Processing (EMNLP)*, pages 1532–1543.

A. Poliak, J. Naradowsky, A. Haldar, R. Rudinger, and B. V. Durme. 2018. Hypothesis only baselines in natural language inference. *arXiv preprint arXiv:1805.01042*.

M. T. Ribeiro, S. Singh, and C. Guestrin. 2018. Semantically equivalent adversarial rules for debugging NLP models. In *Association for Computational Linguistics (ACL)*.

K. Sakaguchi, R. L. Bras, C. Bhagavatula, and Y. Choi. 2019. WINOGRANDE: An adversarial winograd schema challenge at scale. *arXiv preprint arXiv:1907.10641*.

B. Scholkopf, D. Janzing, J. Peters, E. Sgouritsa, K. Zhang, and J. Mooij. 2012. On causal and anticausal learning. In *International Conference on Machine Learning (ICML)*.

R. Schwartz, M. Sap, Y. Konstas, L. Zilles, Y. Choi, and N. A. Smith. 2017. The effect of different writing tasks on linguistic style: A case study of the ROC story cloze task. In *Computational Natural Language Learning (CoNLL)*.

H. Shimodaira. 2000. Improving predictive inference under covariate shift by weighting the log-likelihood function. *Journal of Statistical Planning and Inference*, 90:227–244.

A. Torralba and A. Efros. 2011. Unbiased look at dataset bias. In *Computer Vision and Pattern Recognition (CVPR)*.

D. Tsipras, S. Santurkar, L. Engstrom, A. Turner, and A. Madry. 2019. Robustness may be at odds with accuracy. In *International Conference on Learning Representations (ICLR)*.

H. Wang, Z. He, Z. C. Lipton, and E. P. Xing. 2019a. Learning robust representations by projecting superficial statistics out. In *International Conference on Learning Representations (ICLR)*.

T. Wang, J. Zhao, M. Yatskar, K. Chang, and V. Ordonez. 2019b. Balanced datasets are not enough: Estimating and mitigating gender bias in deep image representations. In *International Conference on Computer Vision (ICCV)*.

A. Williams, N. Nangia, and S. R. Bowman. 2017. A broad-coverage challenge corpus for sentence understanding through inference. *arXiv preprint arXiv:1704.05426*.

R. Zellers, A. Holtzman, Y. Bisk, A. Farhadi, and Y. Choi. 2019. HellaSwag: Can a machine really finish your sentence? In *Association for Computational Linguistics (ACL)*.

G. Zhang, B. Bai, J. Liang, K. Bai, S. Chang, M. Yu, C. Zhu, and T. Zhao. 2019a. Selection bias explorations and debias methods for natural language sentence matching datasets. In *Association for Computational Linguistics (ACL)*.

H. Zhang, Y. Yu, J. Jiao, E. P. Xing, L. E. Ghaoui, and M. I. Jordan. 2019b. Theoretically principled tradeoff between robustness and accuracy. *arXiv preprint arXiv:1901.08573*.

K. Zhang, B. Schlkopf, K. Muandet, and Z. Wang. 2013. Domain adaptation under target and conditional shift. In *International Conference on Machine Learning (ICML)*.

Y. Zhang, J. Baldridge, and L. He. 2019c. PAWS: Paraphrase adversaries from word scrambling. In *North American Association for Computational Linguistics (NAACL)*.

J. Zhao, T. Wang, M. Yatskar, R. Cotterell, V. Ordonez, and K. Chang. 2019. Gender bias in contextualized word embeddings. In *North American Association for Computational Linguistics (NAACL)*.

J. Zhao, T. Wang, M. Yatskar, V. Ordonez, and K. Chang. 2018a. Gender bias in coreference resolution:evaluation and debiasing methods. In *North American Association for Computational Linguistics (NAACL)*.

J. Zhao, Y. Zhou, Z. Li, W. Wang, and K. Chang. 2018b. Learning gender-neutral word embeddings. In *Empirical Methods in Natural Language Processing (EMNLP)*.

Metric Learning for Dynamic Text Classification

Jeremy Wohlwend   Ethan R. Elenberg   Samuel Altschul   Shawn Henry   Tao Lei

ASAPP, Inc.

{jeremy,eelenberg,saltschul,shawn,tao}@asapp.com

Abstract

Traditional text classifiers are limited to predicting over a fixed set of labels. However, in many real-world applications the label set is frequently changing. For example, in intent classification, new intents may be added over time while others are removed.

We propose to address the problem of dynamic text classification by replacing the traditional, fixed-size output layer with a learned, semantically meaningful metric space. Here the distances between textual inputs are optimized to perform nearest-neighbor classification across overlapping label sets. Changing the label set does not involve removing parameters, but rather simply adding or removing support points in the metric space. Then the learned metric can be fine-tuned with only a few additional training examples.

We demonstrate that this simple strategy is robust to changes in the label space. Furthermore, our results show that learning a non-Euclidean metric can improve performance in the low data regime, suggesting that further work on metric spaces may benefit low-resource research.

1 Introduction

Text classification often assumes a static set of labels. While this assumption holds for tasks such as sentiment analysis and part-of-speech tagging (Pang and Lee, 2005; Kim, 2014; Brants, 2000; Collins, 2002; Toutanova et al., 2003), it is rarely true for real-world applications. Consider the example of news categorization in Figure 1 (a). A domain expert may decide that the *Sports* class should be separated into two distinct *Soccer* and *Baseball* sub-classes, and conversely merge the two *Cars* and *Motorcycles* classes into a single *Auto* category. Another example is user intent classification in task-oriented dialog systems. In

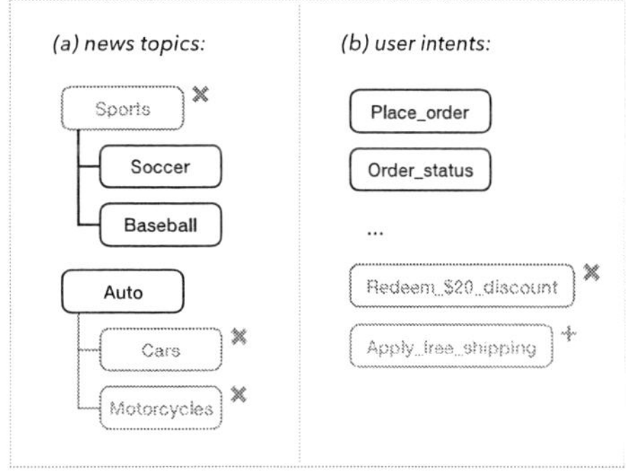

Figure 1: Examples of dynamic classification. In the hierarchical setting (left), new labels are created by splitting and merging old labels. In the flat setting (right), arbitrary labels can be added or removed.

Figure 1 (b) for example, an intent to redeem a reward can be removed when the option is no longer available, while a new intent to apply free shipping can be added to the system. In all of these applications, the classifier must remain applicable for *dynamic classification*, a task where the label set is rapidly evolving.

Several factors make the dynamic classification problem difficult. First, traditional classifiers are not suited to changes in the label space. These classifiers produce a fixed sized output which aligns each of the dimensions to an existing label. Thus, adding or removing any label requires changing the model architecture. Second, while it is possible to retain some model parameters, such as in hierarchical classification models, these architectures must still learn separate weights for every new class or sub-class (Cai and Hofmann, 2004; Kowsari et al., 2017). This is problematic because the new class labels often come with very few training examples, providing insufficient information for learning accurate model weights. Furthermore, these models do not leverage infor-

Proceedings of the 2nd Workshop on Deep Learning Approaches for Low-Resource NLP (DeepLo), pages 143–152
Hong Kong, China, November 3, 2019. ©2019 Association for Computational Linguistics
https://doi.org/10.18653/v1/P17

mation across similar labels, which weakens their ability to adapt to new target labels (Kowsari et al., 2017; Tsochantaridis et al., 2005; Cai and Hofmann, 2004).

We propose to address these issues by learning an embedding function which maps input text into a semantically meaningful metric space. The parameterized metric space, once trained on an initial set of labeled data, can be used to perform classification in a nearest-neighbor fashion (by comparing the distance from the input text to reference texts with known label). As a result, the classifier becomes agnostic to changes in the label set. One remaining design challenge, however, is to learn a representation that best leverages the relationship between old and new labels. In particular, the label split example in Figure 1 (b) shows that new labels are often formed by partitioning an old label. This suggests that the classifier may benefit from a metric space that can better represent the structural relationships between labels. Given the hierarchical relationship between the old and new labels, we choose a space of negative curvature (hyperbolic), which has been shown to better embed tree-like structure (Nickel and Kiela, 2017; Sala et al., 2018; Gu et al., 2019).

Our two main contributions are outlined below:

1. We design an experimental framework for *dynamic text classification*, and propose a classification strategy based on prototypical networks, a simple but powerful metric learning technique (Snell et al., 2017).

2. We construct a novel prototypical network adapted to hyperbolic geometry. This requires deriving useful prototypes to represent a set of points on the negatively curved Riemannian manifold. We state sufficient theoretical conditions for the resulting optimization problem to converge. To the best of our knowledge, this is the first application of hyperbolic geometry to text classification beyond the word level.

We perform a thorough experimental analysis by considering the model improvements across several aspects – low-resource fine-tuning, impact of pretraining, and ability to learn new classes. We find that the metric learning approach adapts more gracefully to changes in the label distribution, and outperforms traditional, fixed size classifiers in every aspect of the analysis. Further-more, our proposed hyperbolic prototypical network outperforms its Euclidean counterpart in the low-resource setting, when fewer than 10 examples per class are available.

2 Related Work

Prototypical Networks and Manifold Learning: This paper builds on the prototypical network architecture (Snell et al., 2017), which was originally proposed in the context of few-shot learning. In both their work and ours, the goal is to embed training data in a space such that the distance to *prototype* centroids of points with the same label define good decision boundaries for labeling test data with a nearest neighbor classifier. Building on earlier work in metric learning (Vinyals et al., 2016; Ravi and Larochelle, 2017), the authors show that learned prototype points also help the network classify inputs into test classes for which minimal data exists. This architecture has found success in computer vision applications such as image and video classification (Weinberger and Saul, 2009; Ustinova and Lempitsky, 2016; Luo et al., 2017). Very recently, prototypical network architectures have shown promising results on relational classification tasks (Han et al., 2018; Gao et al., 2019). To the best of our knowledge, our work is the first application of prototypical network architectures to text classification using non-Euclidean geometry.[1]

Concurrent with the writing of this paper, (Khrulkov et al., 2019) applied several hyperbolic neural networks to few-shot image classification tasks. However, their prototypical network uses the Einstein midpoint rather than the Karcher mean we use in Section 3.3. In (Chen et al., 2019) the authors embed the labels and data separately, then predict hierarchical class membership using an interaction model. Our model directly links embedding distances to model predictions, and thus learns an embedded space that is more amenable to low-resource, dynamic classification tasks.

Hyperbolic geometry has been deeply explored in classical works of differential geometry (Thurston, 2002; Cannon et al., 1997; Berger,

---

[1]Snell et al. (2017) discuss their formulation in the context of Euclidean distance, cosine distance (spherical manifold), and general Bregman divergences; however, classical Bregman divergence does not easily generalize to hyperbolic space (Section 3.3).

2003). More recently, hyperbolic space has been studied in the context of developing neural networks with hyperbolic parameters (Ganea et al., 2018b). In particular, recent work has successfully applied hyperbolic geometry to graph embeddings (Sarkar, 2011; Nickel and Kiela, 2017, 2018; Sala et al., 2018; Ganea et al., 2018a; Gu et al., 2019). In all of these prior works, the model's parameters correspond to node vectors in hyperbolic space that require Riemannian optimization. In our case, only the model's outputs live in hyperbolic space—not its parameters, which avoids propagating gradients in hyperbolic space and facilitates optimization. This is explained in more detail in Section 3.3.

Hierarchical or Few-shot Text Classification: Many classical models for multi-class classification incorporate a hierarchical label structure (Tsochantaridis et al., 2005; Cai and Hofmann, 2004; Yen et al., 2016; Naik et al., 2013; Sinha et al., 2018). Most models proceed in a top-down manner: a separate classifier (logistic regression, SVM, etc.) is trained to predict the correct child label at each node in the label hierarchy. For instance, HDLTex (Kowsari et al., 2017) addresses large hierarchical label sets explicitly by training a stacked, hierarchical neural network architecture. Such approaches do not scale well to deep and large label hierarchies, while our method can adapt to more flexible settings, such as adding or removing labels, without adding extra parameters.

Our work also relates to text classification in a low-resource setting. While a wide range of methods improve accuracy by leveraging external data such as multi-task training (Miyato et al., 2016; Chen et al., 2018; Yu et al., 2018; Guo et al., 2018), semi-supervised pretraining (Dai and Le, 2015), and unsupervised pretraining (Peters et al., 2018; Devlin et al., 2018), our method makes use of the structure of the data via metric learning. As a result, our method can be easily combined with any of these methods to further improve model performance.

3 Model Framework

This section provides the details of each component of our framework, starting with a more detailed formulation of *dynamic classification*. We then provide some background on prototypical networks, before introducing our hyperbolic variant and its theoretical guarantees.

3.1 Dynamic Classification

Mathematically, we formulate *dynamic classification* as the following problem: given access to an old, labeled training corpus $(x_i, y_i) \in \mathcal{X}_{old} \times \mathcal{Y}_{old}$, we are interested in training a classifier $h : \mathcal{X}_{new} \mapsto \mathcal{Y}_{new}$ with a few examples $(x_j, y_j) \in \mathcal{X}_{new} \times \mathcal{Y}_{new}$. Unlike few-shot learning, the old and new datasets need not be disjoint ($\mathcal{X}_{old} \cap \mathcal{X}_{new} \neq \emptyset$, $\mathcal{Y}_{old} \cap \mathcal{Y}_{new} \neq \emptyset$).

We consider two different cases: 1) new labels arrive as a consequence of new input data $\mathcal{X}_{new} \setminus \mathcal{X}_{old}$, and 2) during label splitting/merging, some new examples may be constructed by relabeling old examples from $y_i \in \mathcal{Y}_{old}$ to $y_j \in \mathcal{Y}_{new} \setminus \mathcal{Y}_{old}$. This latter case is of particular interest as the classifier may be able to leverage its knowledge of old labels in learning to classify new ones.

There are many natural approaches to this problem. First, a fixed model trained on $\mathcal{X}_{old} \times \mathcal{Y}_{old}$ may be applied directly to classify examples in $\mathcal{X}_{new} \times \mathcal{Y}_{new}$, which we refer to as an *un-tuned* model. Alternately, a pretrained model may also be fine-tuned on $\mathcal{X}_{new} \times \mathcal{Y}_{new}$. Finally, it is also possible to train from scratch on $\mathcal{X}_{new} \times \mathcal{Y}_{new}$, disregarding the model weights trained on the old data distribution. We compare strategies in Sections 4–5.

3.2 Episodic Training

The standard prototypical network is trained using episodic training, as described in (Snell et al., 2017). We view our model as an embedding function which takes textual inputs and outputs points in the metric space. Let $d(x, y)$ denote the distance between two points x and y in our metric space, and let f denote our embedding function. At each iteration, we form a new episode by sampling a set of target labels, as well as support and query points for each of the sampled labels. Let N_C, N_S, and N_Q, be the number of classes tested, the number of support points used, and the number of query points used in each episode, respectively.

For each episode, we first sample N_C classes, $C = \{c_i | i = 1, \ldots, N_C\}$, uniformly across all training labels. We then build a set of support points $S_i = \{s_{i,j} | j = 1, \ldots, N_S\}$ for each of the selected classes by sampling N_S training examples from each selected class. For each support set, we compute a prototype vector p_i^*. For the standard Euclidean prototypical network, we use the mean of the embedded support set:

$$p_i^* = \frac{1}{N_S} \sum_{j=1}^{N_S} f(s_{i,j}) \ .\tag{1}$$

To compute the loss for an episode, we further sample N_Q query points $Q = \{x_{i,j} | j = 1, \ldots, N_Q\}$ which do not appear in the support set of the episode, for each selected class c_i. We then encode each query sequence and apply a softmax function over the negative distances from the query points to the episode's class prototypes. This yields a probability distribution over classes, and we take the negative log probability of the true class, averaged over the query points, to get the loss for the episode.

$$\frac{-1}{N_C N_Q} \sum_{i=1}^{N_C} \sum_{j=1}^{N_Q} \log \left[\frac{\exp(-d(f(x_{i,j}), p_i^*))}{\sum_k \exp(-d(f(x_{i,j}), p_k^*))} \right],$$

where k in the denominator ranges from 1 to N_C. The steps of a single episode are summarized in Algorithm 1.

Once episodic training is finished, the prototype vectors for a class can be computed as the mean of the embeddings of any number of items in the class. In our experiments, we use the whole training set to compute the final class prototypes, but under lower resources, fewer support points could also be used.

3.3 Hyperbolic Prototypical Networks

In this section we discuss the hyperbolic prototypical network which can better model structural relationships between labels. We first review the hyperboloid model of hyperbolic space and its distance formula. Then we describe the main technical challenge of computing good prototypes in hyperbolic space. Proofs of our uniqueness and convergence will be provided in an extended version. We also describe a second, *distinct* method for computing prototypes which is used to initialize our main method during experiments (a detailed discussion of this point will be provided in an extended version).

Hyperbolic space can be interpreted as a continuous analogue of a tree (Cannon et al., 1997; Krioukov et al., 2010). While trees on n vertices can be embedded in Euclidean space with $\log(n)$ dimensions, hyperbolic space needs only

---

Algorithm 1 Prototypical Training Episode

Input: D – set of (x, y) pairs
D_i – all pairs with $y = i$
N_C – number of classes sampled each episode
N_S – number of support points
N_Q – number of query points

1: **procedure** EPISODE(D, N_C,N_S, N_Q)
2:      $C \leftarrow$ SAMPLE(D, N_C)
3:      **for** $i \in C$ **do**
4:          $S_i \leftarrow$ SAMPLE(D_i, N_S)
5:          $Q_i \leftarrow$ SAMPLE($D_i \setminus S_i, N_Q$)
6:          $c_i \leftarrow$ PROTOTYPE(S_i)
7:      $P \leftarrow$ CONCAT($c_0; c_1; ...; c_{N_C}$)
8:      Loss $\leftarrow 0$
9:      **for** each Q_i **do**
10:         $d_i \leftarrow$ PAIRWISEDIST(Q_i, P)
11:         Loss $\leftarrow$ Loss $- \frac{1}{N_C N_Q} \log \left[\frac{e^{-d_i}}{\sum_j e^{-d_j}} \right]$

---

2 dimensions. Additionally, the circumference of a hyperbolic disk grows exponentially with its radius. Therefore, hyperbolic models have room to place many prototypes equidistant from a common parent while maintaining separability from other classes. We argue that this property helps text classification with latent hierarchical structures (e.g. dynamic label splitting).

The reader is referred to Section 2.6 of (Thurston, 2002) for a detailed introduction to hyperbolic geometry, and to (Cannon et al., 1997) for a more gentle introduction. In this section we have adopted the sign convention of (Sala et al., 2018).

Hyperbolic space in d dimensions is the unique, simply connected, d-dimensional, Riemannian manifold with constant curvature -1. The hyperboloid (or Lorentz) model realizes d-dimensional hyperbolic space as an isometric embedding inside $\mathbb{R}^{d+1}$ endowed with a signature $(1, d)$ bilinear form. Specifically, let the coordinates of any $a \in \mathbb{R}^{d+1}$ be $a = (a_0, a_1, ..., a_d)$. Then we can define a bilinear form on $\mathbb{R}^{d+1}$ by

$$B(x, y) = x_0 y_0 - \sum_{j=1}^{d} x_j y_j \ ,\tag{2}$$

which allows us to define the hyperboloid to be the set $\{x \in \mathbb{R}^{d+1} | B(x,x) = 1 \text{ and } x_0 > 0\}$. We induce a Riemannian metric on the hyperboloid by restricting $B(\cdot, \cdot)$ to the hyperboloid's tangent space. The resulting Riemannian manifold is hyperbolic space $\mathbb{H}^d$. For $x, y \in \mathbb{H}^d$ the hyperbolic distance is given by

$$d_{\mathbb{H}}(x, y) = \operatorname{arccosh}(B(x, y)). \qquad (3)$$

There are several equivalent ways of defining hyperbolic space. We choose to work primarily in the hyperboloid model over other models (*e.g.* Poincaré disk model) for improved numerical stability. We use the d-dimensional output vector h of our network and project it on the hyperboloid embedded in $d + 1$ dimensions:

$$h_0 = \sqrt{\sum_{i=1}^{d} h_i^2 + 1} \ , \qquad \bar{h} = [h_0; h] \ . \qquad (4)$$

A key algorithmic difference between the Euclidean and the hyperbolic model is the computation of prototype vectors. There are multiple definitions that generalize the notion of a mean to general Riemannian manifolds. One sensible mean $p_X^\star$ of a set X is given by the point which minimizes the sum of squared distances to each point in X.

$$
\begin{aligned}
p_X^\star &= \arg\min_{p \in \mathbb{H}^d} \phi_X(p) \\
&= \arg\min_{p \in \mathbb{H}^d} \sum_{x \in X} d_{\mathbb{H}^d}(p, x)^2 \ .
\end{aligned}
\qquad (5)
$$

A proof for the following proposition will be provided in an extended version. We note that concurrent with the writing of this paper, a generalized version of our result appeared in (Gu et al., 2019) as Lemma 2.

Proposition 1. *Every finite collection of points X in $\mathbb{H}^d$ has a unique mean $p_X^\star$. Furthermore, solving the optimization problem (5) with Riemannian gradient descent will converge to $p_X^\star$.*

In an effort to derive a closed form for $p_X^\star$ (rather than solve a Riemannian optimization problem), we conjecture that the following expression is a good approximation. It is computed by averaging the vectors in X and scaling them by the constant which projects this average back to the hyperboloid:

$$\hat{p} = \frac{1}{|X|} \sum_{x \in X} x, \quad \tilde{p} = \frac{\hat{p}}{\sqrt{B(\hat{p}, \hat{p})}}. \qquad (6)$$

$p_X^\star \neq \tilde{p}$ can be shown to differ through a simple counterexample, although in practice we find little difference between their values during experiments. The proof will be provided in an extended version.

3.4 Implementation and Stability

Our final hyperbolic prototypical model combines both definitions with the following heuristic: initialize problem (5) with $\tilde{p}$ and then run several iterations of Riemannian gradient descent. We find that it is possible to backpropagate through a few steps of the gradient descent procedure described above during prototypical model training. However, we also find that the model can be trained successfully when detaching the gradients with respect to the support points. This suggests that prototypical models can be trained in metric spaces where the mean or its gradient cannot be computed efficiently. Further experimental details are provided in the next section.

Our prototypical network loss function uses both squared Euclidean distance and squared hyperbolic distance for similar reasons. Namely, the distance between two close points is much less numerically stable than the squared distance. In the Euclidean case, the derivative of $\sqrt{s}$ is undefined at zero. In the hyperbolic case, the derivative of $\operatorname{arccosh}(s)$ at 1 is undefined, and $B(x, x) = 1$ for points on the hyperboloid. If we instead use the *squared* hyperbolic distance, L'Hôpital's rule implies that the derivative of $\operatorname{arccosh}(b)^2$ as $b \to 1+$ is 2, allowing gradients to backpropagate through the squared hyperbolic distance without issue.

4 Experiments

We evaluate the performance of our framework on several text classification benchmarks, two of which exhibit a hierarchical label set. We only use the label hierarchy to simulate the label splitting discussed in Figure 1 (a). The models are not trained with explicit knowledge of the hierarchy, as we assume that the full hierarchy is not known *a priori* in the dynamic classification setting. A description of the datasets is provided below:

- 20 Newsgroups (NEWS): This dataset is composed of nearly 20,000 documents, distributed across 20 news categories. We use the provided label hierarchy to form the depth 3 tree used throughout our experiments. We use 9,044 documents for training, 2,668 for validation, and 7,531 for testing.

- Web of Science (WOS): This dataset was used in two previous works on hierarchical text classification (Kowsari et al., 2017; Sinha et al., 2018). It contains 134 topics, split across 7 parent categories. It contains 46,985 documents collected from the Web of Science citation index. We use 25,182 documents for training, 6,295 for validation, and 15,503 for testing.

- Twitter Airline Sentiment (SENT): This dataset consists of public tweets from customers to American-based airlines labeled with one of 10 reasons for negative sentiment (*e.g.* Late Flight, Lost Luggage).[2] We preprocess the data by keeping only the negative tweets with confidence over 60%. This dataset is non-hierarchical and composed of nearly 7500 documents. We use 5,975 documents for training, 742 for validation, and 754 for testing.

Dynamic Setup: We construct training data for the task of dynamic classification as follows. First, we split our training data in half. The first half is used for pretraining and the second for fine-tuning. To simulate a change in the label space, we randomly remove $p > 0$ fraction of labels in the pretraining data. This procedure yields two label sets, with $\mathcal{Y}_{old}$ (pretraining) $\subset \mathcal{Y}_{new}$ (fine-tuning). In our experiments, we further vary the amount of data available in the fine-tuning set. For the flat dataset, the labels to be removed are sampled uniformly. In the hierarchical case, we create $\mathcal{Y}_{old}$ by randomly collapsing leaf labels into their parent classes, as shown previously in Figure 1.

Hyperparameters and Implementation Details: We apply the same encoder architecture throughout all experiments. We use a 4 layer recurrent neural network, with SRU cells (Lei et al., 2018) and a hidden size of 128. We use pretrained GloVe embeddings (Pennington et al., 2014), which are fixed during training. A sequence level embedding is computed by passing a sequence of word embeddings through the recurrent encoder, and taking the embedding for the last token to represent the sequence. We use the ADAM optimizer with default learning of 0.001, and train for 100 epochs for the baseline models and 10,000 episodes for the prototypical models, with early stopping. In our experiments, we use $N_S = 4$, $N_Q = 64$. We use the full label set every episode for all datasets except WOS, for which we use $N_C = 50$. We use a dropout rate of 0.5 on NEWS and SENT, and 0.3 for the larger WOS dataset. We tuned the learning rate and dropout for each model on a held-out validation set.

For the hyperbolic prototypical network, we follow the initialization and update procedure outlined at the end of Section 3.3 with 5 iterations of Riemannian gradient descent during training and 100 iterations during evaluation. We utilize negative squared distance in the softmax computation in order to improve numerical stability. The means are computed via (5) during both training and model inference. However, this computation is treated as a constant during backpropagation as described in Section 3.3.

Baseline: Our baseline model consists of the same recurrent encoder and an extra linear output layer which computes the final probabilities over the target classes. In order to fine-tune this multilayer perceptron (MLP) model on a new label ontology, we reuse the encoder, and learn a new output layer. This differs from the prototypical models for which the architecture is kept unchanged.

Evaluation: We evaluate the performance of our models using accuracy with respect to the new label set $\mathcal{Y}_{new}$. We also highlight accuracy on only the classes introduced during label addition/splitting, *i.e.* $\mathcal{Y}_{new} \setminus \mathcal{Y}_{old}$. All results are averaged over 5 random label splits with $p = 0.3$.

Results: Table 1 shows the accuracy of the fine tuned models for all three methods. The SENT dataset shows performance in the case where completely new labels are added during fine tuning. In the NEWS and WOS datasets new labels originate from the splits of old labels.

In all cases, the prototypical models outperform the baseline MLP model significantly, especially when the data in the new label distribution is in the low-resource regime (+5–15% accuracy). We also see an increase in performance in the high data regime of up to 5%.

Table 1 further shows that the hyperbolic model outperforms its Euclidean counterpart in the low

---

[2]`https://www.kaggle.com/crowdflower/twitter-airline-sentiment`

Dataset	Model	$n_{fine} = 5$	$n_{fine} = 10$	$n_{fine} = 20$	$n_{fine} = 100$
SENT	MLP	37.3 ± 2.9	43.8 ± 3.5	45.7 ± 3.8	57.4 ± 3.5
	EUC	39.6 ± 6.4	45.5 ± 1.8	47.7 ± 4.7	$\mathbf{62.7 \pm 2.1}$
	HYP	$\mathbf{42.2 \pm 3.5}$	$\mathbf{47.1 \pm 4.8}$	$\mathbf{53.0 \pm 2.3}$	$\mathbf{62.7 \pm 2.2}$
NEWS	MLP	49.2 ± 1.0	55.9 ± 2.5	68.5 ± 1.1	76.3 ± 0.5
	EUC	56.5 ± 0.4	65.6 ± 1.0	$\mathbf{74.2 \pm 0.6}$	$\mathbf{79.8 \pm 0.2}$
	HYP	$\mathbf{64.8 \pm 2.8}$	$\mathbf{69.7 \pm 1.0}$	72.9 ± 0.5	78.8 ± 0.4
WOS	MLP	36.6 ± 1.1	46.8 ± 1.2	62.8 ± 0.6	68.9 ± 0.5
	EUC	49.4 ± 1.0	59.2 ± 0.4	$\mathbf{70.4 \pm 0.4}$	73.3 ± 0.2
	HYP	$\mathbf{54.5 \pm 1.4}$	$\mathbf{60.7 \pm 0.9}$	70.2 ± 0.7	$\mathbf{73.5 \pm 0.5}$

Table 1: Test accuracy for each dataset and method. Columns indicate the number of examples per label n_{fine} used in the fine tuning stage. In all cases, the prototypical models outperform the baseline. The hyperbolic model performs best in the low data regime, but both metrics perform comparably when data is abundant.

data regime on the NEWS and WOS datasets. This is consistent with our hypothesis (and previous work) that hyperbolic geometry is well suited for hierarchical data. Interestingly, the hyperbolic model also performs better on the non-hierarchical SENT dataset when given few examples, which implies that certain metric spaces may be generally stronger in the low-resource setting. In the high data regime, however, both prototypical models perform comparably.

5 Analysis

In this section, we examine several aspects of our experimental setup more closely, and use the SENT and NEWS datasets for this analysis.

Benefits of Pretraining We wish to isolate the effect of pretraining on an older label set by measuring the performance of our models on the new label distribution with and without pretraining. Figure 2 shows accuracy without pretraining as solid bars, with the gains due to pretraining shown as translucent bars above them. In the low-data regime without pretraining, all models often perform similarly. Nevertheless, our models do improve substantially over the baseline once pretraining is introduced.

With only a few new examples, our models better leverage knowledge gained from old pretraining data. On the NEWS dataset in particular, with only 5 fine-tune examples per class, the relative reduction in classification error for metric learning models exceeds 53% (Euclidean) and 62% (hyperbolic), while the baseline only reduces relative error by about 45%. This shows that the prototypical network, and particularly the hyperbolic

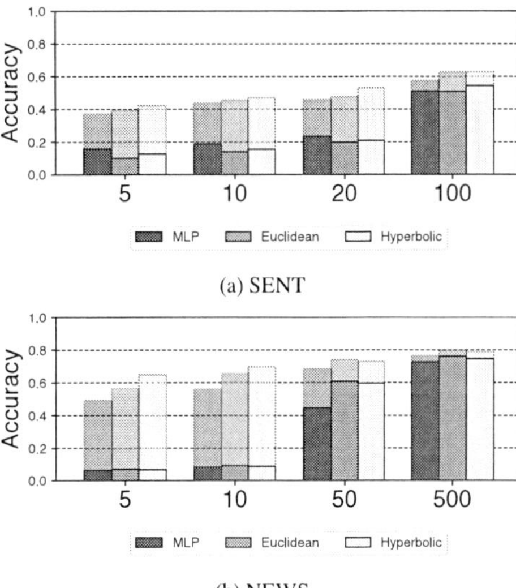

(a) SENT

(b) NEWS

Figure 2: Accuracy gains from pretraining as a function of the number of examples per class available in the new label distribution. While the models are comparable in the pretraining stage (solid bards), the prototypical models make better use of pretraining, showing higher gain during fine-tuning in both the low and high data data regimes (translucent bars).

model can adapt more quickly to dynamic label shifts. Furthermore, the prototypical models conserve their advantage over the baseline in the high data regime, though the margins become smaller.

Benefits of Fine-tuning An important advantage of the prototypical model is its ability to predict classes that were unseen during training with as few as a single support point for the new class. A natural question is whether fine-tuning on these new class labels immediately improves per-

Model	5	10	20	100
MLP (un-tuned)	38.2	46.7	42.4	46.3
EUC	39.6	45.5	47.7	**62.7**
EUC (un-tuned)	43.4	51.2	47.6	55.8
HYP	42.2	47.1	53.0	**62.7**
HYP (un-tuned)	**45.7**	**52.4**	**53.3**	53.1

(a) SENT

Model	5	10	50	500
MLP (un-tuned)	29.5	34.6	40.3	42.7
EUC	56.5	65.6	**74.2**	**79.8**
EUC (un-tuned)	53.2	56.5	59.6	60.8
HYP	**64.8**	**69.7**	72.9	78.8
HYP (un-tuned)	60.1	62.9	65.4	66.7

(b) NEWS

Table 2: Test accuracy for each dataset and method. Columns indicate the number of examples per label used for fine-tuning and/or creating prototype vectors.

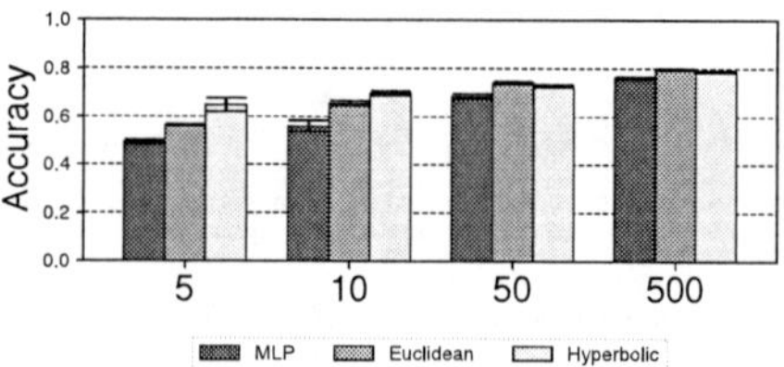

(a) Accuracy with respect to the full label set

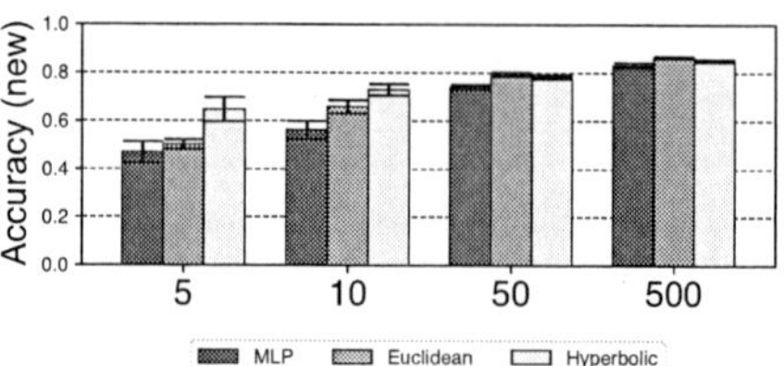

(b) Accuracy with respect to new classes only

Figure 3: Accuracy on the NEWS Dataset against number of fine tune examples: (a) all classes and (b) newly introduced classes only. The mean is taken over 5 random label splits, and error bars are given at ± 1 standard deviation. The gap between the hyperbolic models and the others is even larger on the new classes.

formance, or whether fine-tuning should only be done once a significant amount of data has been obtained from the new distribution. We study this question by comparing the performance of tuned and un-tuned models on the new label distribution.

Table 2 compares the accuracy of two types of pretrained prototypical models provided with a variable number of new examples. The fine-tuned model uses this data for both additional training and for constructing new prototypes. The *un-tuned* model constructs prototypes using the pretrained model's representations without additional training. We also construct an un-tuned MLP baseline by fitting a nearest neighbor classifier (KNN) on the encodings of the penultimate layer of the network. We experimented with fitting the KNN on the output predictions but found that using the penultimate layer was more effective.

We find that the models generally benefit from fine-tuning once a significant amount of data for the new classes is provided (> 20). In the low data regime, however, the results are less consistent, and suggests that the performance may be very dataset dependant. We note however that all metric learning models significantly outperform the MLP-KNN baseline in both the low and high data regimes. This shows that regardless of fine-tuning, our approach is more robust on previously unseen classes.

Learning New Classes An important factor in the dynamic classification setup is the ability for the model to not only keep performing well on the old classes, but also to smoothly adapt to new ones. We highlight the performance of the models on the newly introduced labels in Figure 3, where we see that the improvement in accuracy is dominated by the performance on the new classes.

6 Conclusions

We propose a framework for dynamic text classification in which the label space is considered flexible and subject to frequent changes. We apply a metric learning method, namely prototypical network, and demonstrate its robustness for this task in a variety of data regimes. Motivated by the idea that new labels often originate from label splits, we extend prototypical networks to hyperbolic geometry, derive expressions for hyperbolic prototypes, and demonstrate the effectiveness of our model in the low-resource setting. Our experimental findings suggest that metric learning improves dynamic text classification models, and offer insights on how to combine low-resource training data from overlapping label sets. In the future we hope to explore other applications of metric learning to low-resource research, possibly in combination with explicit models for label entailment (tree learning, fuzzy sets), and/or Wasserstein distance.

References

Marcel Berger. 2003. *A Panoramic View of Riemannian Geometry*. Springer-Verlag Berlin Heidelberg, Heidelberg, Germany.

Thorsten Brants. 2000. Tnt: a statistical part-of-speech tagger. In *Proceedings of the sixth conference on Applied natural language processing*, pages 224–231. Association for Computational Linguistics.

Lijuan Cai and Thomas Hofmann. 2004. Hierarchical document categorization with support vector machines. In *CKIM*, pages 78–87.

James Cannon, William Floyd, Richard Kenyon, and Walter Parry. 1997. Hyperbolic geometry. http://library.msri.org/books/Book31/files/cannon.pdf.

Boli Chen, Xin Huang, Lin Xiao, Zixin Cai, and Liping Jing. 2019. Hyperbolic interaction model for hierarchical multi-label classification. https://arxiv.org/pdf/1905.10802.pdf.

Xilun Chen, Yu Sun, Ben Athiwaratkun, Claire Cardie, and Kilian Weinberger. 2018. Adversarial deep averaging networks for cross-lingual sentiment classification. *Transactions of the Association for Computational Linguistics*, 6.

Michael Collins. 2002. Discriminative training methods for hidden markov models: Theory and experiments with perceptron algorithms. In *EMNLP*, pages 1–8. Association for Computational Linguistics.

Andrew M Dai and Quoc V Le. 2015. Semi-supervised sequence learning. In *NeurIPS*, pages 3079–3087.

Jacob Devlin, Ming-Wei Chang, Kenton Lee, and Kristina Toutanova. 2018. Bert: Pre-training of deep bidirectional transformers for language understanding. In *NAACL*.

Octavian-Eugen Ganea, Gary Bécigneul, and Thomas Hofmann. 2018a. Hyperbolic entailment cones for learning hierarchical embeddings. In *ICML*.

Octavian-Eugen Ganea, Gary Bécigneul, and Thomas Hofmann. 2018b. Hyperbolic neural networks. In *NeurIPS*.

Tianyu Gao, Xu Han, Zhiyuan Liu, and Maosong Sun. 2019. Hybrid attention-based prototypical networks for noisy few-shot relation classification. In *AAAI*.

Albert Gu, Frederic Sala, Beliz Gunel, and Christopher Ré. 2019. Learning mixed-curvature representations in products of model spaces. In *ICLR*.

Jiang Guo, Darsh Shah, and Regina Barzilay. 2018. Multi-source domain adaptation with mixture of experts. In *EMNLP*. Association for Computational Linguistics.

Xu Han, Hao Zhu, Pengfei Yu, Ziyun Wang, Yuan Yao, Zhiyuan Liu, and Maosong Sun. 2018. Fewrel: A large-scale supervised few-shot relation classification dataset with state-of-the-art evaluation. In *EMNLP*.

Valentin Khrulkov, Leyla Mirvakhabova, Evgeniya Ustinova, Ivan Oseledets, and Victor Lempitsky. 2019. Hyperbolic image embeddings. https://arxiv.org/pdf/1904.02239.pdf.

Yoon Kim. 2014. Convolutional neural networks for sentence classification. In *EMNLP*, page 17461751.

Kamran Kowsari, Donald E. Brown, Mojtaba Heidarysafa, Kiana Jafari Meimandi, Matthew S. Gerber, and Laura E. Barnes. 2017. HDLTex: hierarchical deep learning for text classification. In *IEEE ICMLA*, pages 364–371.

Dmitri Krioukov, Fragkiskos Papadopoulos, Maksim Kitsak, Amin Vahdat, and Marián Boguñá. 2010. Hyperbolic geometry of complex networks. *Phys. Rev. E*, 82.

Tao Lei, Yu Zhang, Sida I. Wang, Hui Dai, and Yoav Artzi. 2018. Simple recurrent units for highly parallelizable recurrence. In *EMNLP*.

Zelun Luo, Yuliang Zou, Judy Hoffman, and Li Fei-Fei. 2017. Label efficient learning of transferable representations across domains and tasks. In *NeurIPS*.

Takeru Miyato, Andrew M Dai, and Ian Goodfellow. 2016. Adversarial training methods for semi-supervised text classification. *arXiv preprint arXiv:1605.07725*.

Azad Naik, Anveshi Charuvaka, and Huzefa Rangwala. 2013. Classifying documents within multiple hierarchical datasets using multi-task learning. In *IEEE International Conference on Tools with Artificial Intelligence*.

Maximilian Nickel and Douwe Kiela. 2018. Learning continuous hierarchies in the lorentz model of hyperbolic geometry. In *ICML*, pages 3776–3785.

Maximillian Nickel and Douwe Kiela. 2017. Poincaré embeddings for learning hierarchical representations. In *NeurIPS*, pages 6338–6347.

Bo Pang and Lillian Lee. 2005. Seeing stars: Exploiting class relationships for sentiment categorization with respect to rating scales. In *Proceedings of the annual meeting on assocation for computational lingustics*, pages 115–224.

Jeffrey Pennington, Richard Socher, and Christopher D. Manning. 2014. Glove: Global vectors for word representation. In *EMNLP*, pages 1532–1543.

Matthew E. Peters, Mark Neumann, Mohit Iyyer, Matt Gardner, Christopher Clark, Kenton Lee, and Luke Zettlemoyer. 2018. Deep contextualized word representations. In *NAACL*.

Sachin Ravi and Hugo Larochelle. 2017. Optimization as a model for few-shot learning. In *ICLR*.

Frederic Sala, Chris De Sa, Albert Gu, and Christopher Ré. 2018. Representation tradeoffs for hyperbolic embeddings. In *ICML*, pages 4460–4469.

R. Sarkar. 2011. Low distortion Delaunay embedding of trees in hyperbolic plane. In *Proc. of the International Symposium on Graph Drawing (GD 2011)*, pages 355–366.

Koustuv Sinha, Yue Dong, Jackie Chi Kit Cheung, and Derek Ruths. 2018. A hierarchical neural attention-based text classifier. In *EMNLP*, pages 817–823.

Jake Snell, Kevin Swersky, and Richard Zemel. 2017. Prototypical networks for few-shot learning. In *NeurIPS*, pages 4077–4087.

William Thurston. 2002. The geometry and topology of three-manifolds: Chapter 2, elliptic and hyperbolic geometry. `http://library.msri.org/books/gt3m/PDF/2.pdf`.

Kristina Toutanova, Dan Klein, Christopher D Manning, and Yoram Singer. 2003. Feature-rich part-of-speech tagging with a cyclic dependency network. In *NAACL*, pages 173–180. Association for Computational Linguistics.

Ioannis Tsochantaridis, Thorsten Joachims, Thomas Hofmann, and Yasemin Altun. 2005. Large margin methods for structured and interdependent output variables. *JMLR*, 6:1453–1484.

Evgeniya Ustinova and Victor Lempitsky. 2016. Learning deep embeddings with histogram loss. In *NeurIPS*, pages 4170–4178.

Oriol Vinyals, Charles Blundell, Timothy Lillicrap, Koray Kavukcuoglu, and Daan Wierstra. 2016. Matching networks for one shot learning. In *NeurIPS*, pages 3630–3638.

Kilian Weinberger and Lawrence Saul. 2009. Distance metric learning for large margin nearest neighbor classification. *Journal of Machine Learning Research*, 10:207–244.

Ian En-Hsu Yen, Xiangru Huang, Pradeep Ravikumar, Kai Zhong, and Inderjit Dhillon. 2016. Pd-sparse: A primal and dual sparse approach to extreme multiclass and multilabel classification. In *ICML*, pages 3069–3077.

Mo Yu, Xiaoxiao Guo, Jinfeng Yi, Shiyu Chang, Saloni Potdar, Yu Cheng, Gerald Tesauro, Haoyu Wang, and Bowen Zhou. 2018. Diverse few-shot text classification with multiple metrics. In *NAACL*.

Hongyi Zhang and Suvrit Sra. 2016. First-order methods for geodesically convex optimization. In *COLT*, volume 49, pages 1617–1638.

Evaluating Lottery Tickets Under Distributional Shifts

Shrey Desai[*,1], **Hongyuan Zhan**[2], and **Ahmed Aly**[2]

[1]The University of Texas at Austin
[2]Facebook Assistant
shreydesai@utexas.edu
{hyzhan, ahhegazy}@fb.com

Abstract

The Lottery Ticket Hypothesis (Frankle and Carbin, 2019) suggests large, over-parameterized neural networks consist of small, sparse subnetworks that can be trained in isolation to reach a similar (or better) test accuracy. However, the initialization and generalizability of the obtained sparse subnetworks have been recently called into question. Our work focuses on evaluating the initialization of sparse subnetworks under distributional shifts. Specifically, we investigate the extent to which a sparse subnetwork obtained in a source domain can be re-trained in isolation in a dissimilar, target domain. In addition, we examine the effects of different initialization strategies at transfer-time. Our experiments show that sparse subnetworks obtained through lottery ticket training do not simply overfit to particular domains, but rather reflect an inductive bias of deep neural networks that can be exploited in multiple domains.

1 Introduction

Recent research has suggested deep neural networks are dramatically over-parameterized. In natural language processing alone, most state-of-the-art neural networks have computational and memory complexities that scale with the size of the vocabulary. Practitioners have developed numerous methods to reduce the complexity of these models—either before, during, or after training—while retaining existing performance. Some of these methods include quantization (Gong et al., 2014; Hubara et al., 2017), and different flavors of pruning (Zhu and Gupta, 2017; Liu et al., 2018b; Frankle and Carbin, 2019; Gale et al., 2019).

In particular, the Lottery Ticket Hypothesis (Frankle and Carbin, 2019) proposes that small, sparse subnetworks are embedded within large,

over-parametrized neural networks. When trained in isolation, these subnetworks can achieve commensurate performance using the same initialization as the original model. The lottery ticket training procedure is formalized as an iterative three-stage approach: (1) train an over-parametrized model with initial parameters θ_0; (2) prune the trained model by applying a mask $m \in \{0, 1\}^{|\theta|}$ identified by a sparsification algorithm; (3) reinitialize the sparse subnetwork by resetting its non-zero weights to the initial values ($m \odot \theta_0$) and retrain it. These three stages are repeated for multiple rounds. If the final subnetwork achieves similar (or better) test performance in comparison to the original network, a winning *lottery ticket* has been identified.

Evidence of the existence of winning tickets has been empirically shown on a range of tasks, including computer vision, reinforcement learning, and natural language processing (Frankle and Carbin, 2019; Yu et al., 2019). However, the merits of lottery ticket training has recently been called into question. In particular, (1) whether keeping the same initialization (e.g., θ_0) is crucial for acquiring tickets (Liu et al., 2018b); and (2) if tickets can generalize across multiple datasets (Morcos et al., 2019).

Our paper investigates the efficacy of lottery tickets when the data distribution changes. We define multiple data domains such that their input distributions are varied. Then, we consider whether subnetworks obtained in a source domain $\mathcal{D}_s$ can be used to specify and train subnetworks in a target domain $\mathcal{D}_t$ where $s \neq t$. Inspired by Liu et al. (2018b), we also experiment with different initialization methods at transfer-time, probing at the importance of initial (source domain) values in disparate target domains. We find that subnetworks obtained through lottery ticket training do not completely overfit to particular input dis-

---

[*]Work done during an internship at Facebook.

Proceedings of the 2nd Workshop on Deep Learning Approaches for Low-Resource NLP (DeepLo), pages 153–162
Hong Kong, China, November 3, 2019. ©2019 Association for Computational Linguistics
https://doi.org/10.18653/v1/P17

tributions, showing some generalization potential when distributional shifts occur. In addition, we discover a *phase transition* point, at which subnetworks reset to their initial values show better and more stable generalization performance when transferred to an arbitrary target domain.

In summary, our contributions are (1) continuing the line of work on the Lottery Ticket Hypothesis (Frankle and Carbin, 2019), showing that tickets exist in noisy textual domains; (2) performing comprehensive experiments pointing towards the transferability of lottery tickets under distributional shifts in natural language processing; and (3) publicly releasing our code and datasets to promote further discussion on these topics[1].

2   Related Work

There is a large body of work on transfer learning for neural networks (Deng et al., 2013; Yosinski et al., 2014; Liu et al., 2017; Zoph et al., 2018; Kornblith et al., 2019). Most of these works focus on improving the transferred representation across tasks and datasets. The representation from a source dataset is fine-tuned or learned collaborately on a target dataset. In contrast, we focus on understanding whether the *architecture* can be transferred and retrained, and whether transferring the initialization is required. Our work is also related to Neural Architecture Search (NAS) (Zoph et al., 2018; Liu et al., 2018a; Elsken et al., 2018). The goal of NAS is to identify well-performing neural networks automatically. Network pruning can be viewed as a form of NAS, where the search space is the sparse topologies within the original over-parameterized network (Liu et al., 2018b; Gale et al., 2019; Frankle and Carbin, 2019).

Iterative magnitude pruning (Frankle and Carbin, 2019; Frankle et al., 2019) is a recently proposed method for finding small, sparse subnetworks from large, over-parameterized neural networks that can be trained in isolation to reach a similar (or better) test accuracy. To obtain these re-trainable sparse subnetworks, Frankle and Carbin (2019) uses an iterative pipeline that involves training a model, removing "redundant" network connections identified by a sparsification algorithm, re-training the subnetwork with the remaining connections. In particular, the experiments in Frankle and Carbin (2019) show it is critical to re-initialize the subnetworks using the

---
[1] https://github.com/facebookresearch/pytext

same initial values after each round of the iterative pipeline.

However, the importance of re-using the original initialization is questioned in Liu et al. (2018b), where the authors show that competitive performance of the sparse subnetworks can be achieved with random initialization as well. Morcos et al. (2019) investigate the transferability of lottery tickets across multiple optimizers and datasets for supervised image classification, showing that tickets can indeed generalize (Morcos et al., 2019). Beyond the differences between our domain, task, and datasets, our work carries an important distinction. In Morcos et al. (2019), the authors refer to the *transfer of initialization* as both the *transfer of the sparse topologies* and the *transfer of the initial values* of the subnetworks. Therefore, it is unclear whether the *sparse topology* alone can be transferred across datasets or the topology combined with the initial values must be exploited jointly to achieve transferability. In our work, we decouple this question by investigating the influence of different initialization strategies on the sparse architecture during the process of finding the winning tickets and after the transfer to other domains.

3   Task and Datasets

Distributional Shifts   Let $(x_i^s, y_i^s) \in \mathcal{X} \times \mathcal{Y}$ denote a pair of training samples from domain $\mathcal{D}_s$. Let $f(x; \theta)$ be a function (e.g., deep neural network) that maps an input from $\mathcal{X}$ to the label space $\mathcal{Y}$, parameterized by θ. In this work, the sparsity of θ is induced by the lottery ticket training process (Frankle and Carbin, 2019). To model distributional shifts, we characterize each domain $\mathcal{D}_i$ as a dataset from the Amazon Reviews corpus (McAuley and Leskovec, 2013). The differences in unigram frequencies, semantic content, and random noise mimic the type of distributional shifts that occur in machine learning.

Subword Vocabulary   We ensure each domain $\mathcal{D}$ shares an identical support on $\mathcal{X}$ by encoding the inputs using a vocabulary common across all datasets. Word-level vocabularies may introduce problems during domain transfer as certain words potentially only appear within a particular domain. On the other end of the spectrum, character-level vocabularies ameliorate this issue but may not contain enough expressive power to model the data. We elect to use a subword vo-

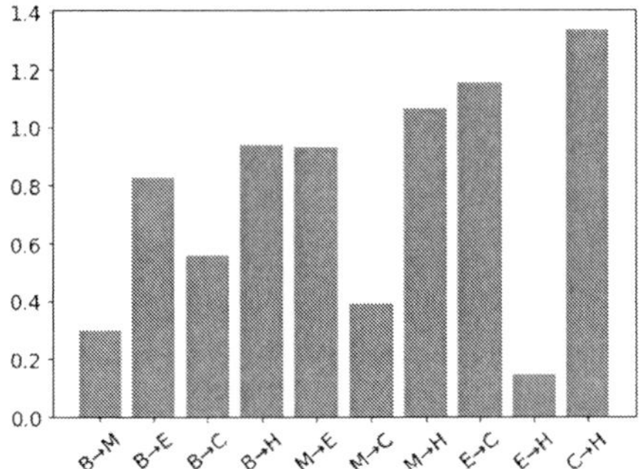

Figure 1: Jenson-Shannon Divergence scores on subword unigram distributions for each domain pair $(\mathcal{D}_i, \mathcal{D}_{i'})$. Domains include Books (B), Electronics (E), Movies (M), CDs (C), and Home (H). Values are scaled by $1e^5$ for presentation.

cabulary, balancing the out-of-vocabulary and effectiveness problems introduced by the word- and character-level vocabularies, respectively. Technical details for creating the shared subword vocabulary are presented in §4.1.

Divergence Scores Given an identical support for all data distributions, we now quantify the distributional shifts between our domains using Jenson-Shannon Divergence (JSD). JSD is a symmetric measure of similarity between two (continuous) probability distributions p and q with a proxy, averaged distribution $m = \frac{1}{2}(p + q)$:

$$\mathrm{JSD}(p||q) = \frac{1}{2}\mathrm{KL}(p||m) + \frac{1}{2}\mathrm{KL}(q||m) \quad (1)$$

where $\mathrm{KL}(p||q)$ in Eq. 1 denotes the Kullback-Leibler divergence, defined as:

$$\mathrm{KL}(p||q) = \int_{-\infty}^{\infty} p(x)\log\frac{p(x)}{q(x)}dx \quad (2)$$

Figure 1 displays the divergence scores between our datasets. On average, there is high disagreement with respect to the prevalence and usage of subwords in each domain, with Electronics→Home the most similar and CDs→Home the most dissimilar.

Sentiment Analysis Finally, we introduce our base task for experimentation. Our models are evaluated on a binary sentiment analysis task constructed from five categories in the Amazon Reviews corpus: books (B), electronics (E), movies (M), CDs (C), and home (H). The dataset originally provides fine-grained sentiment labels (1

through 5) so we group 1, 2 as negative and 4, 5 as positive. Following Peng et al. (2018), reviews with neutral ratings (3) are discarded. We sample 20K train, 10K validation, and 10K test samples from each category, ensuring there is an equal distribution of positive and negative reviews.

4   Methods

In this section, we discuss our technical methods. First, we describe the subword vocabulary creation process (§4.1). Second, we cover the underlying model used in the sentiment analysis task (§4.2). Third, we detail the lottery ticket training and transferring methods (§4.3).

4.1   Vocabulary

We use the SentencePiece[2] library to create a joint subword vocabulary for our datasets (Kudo and Richardson, 2018). The subword model is trained on the concatenation of all five training datasets (100K sentences) using the byte-pair encoding algorithm (Sennrich et al., 2016). We set the vocabulary size to 8K. The final character coverage is 0.9995, ensuring minimal out-of-vocabulary problems during domain transfer.

4.2   Model

We use convolutional networks (CNN) as the underlying model given their strong performance on numerous text classification tasks (Kim, 2014; Mou et al., 2016; Gehring et al., 2017). Let V and n represent the vocabulary of the corpus and maximum sequence length, respectively. Sentences are encoded as an integer sequence $t_1, \cdots, t_n$ where $t_i \in V$. The embedding layer replaces each token t_i with a vector $\mathbf{t}_i \in \mathbb{R}^d$ that serves as the corresponding d-dimensional embedding. The vectors $\mathbf{t}_1, \cdots, \mathbf{t}_n$ are concatenated row-wise to form a token embedding matrix $\mathbf{T} \in \mathbb{R}^{n \times d}$.

Our model ingests the embedding matrix $\mathbf{T}$, then performs a series of convolutions to extract salient features from the input. We define a convolutional filter $\mathbf{W} \in \mathbb{R}^{h \times d}$ where h represents the *height* of the filter. The filter is not strided, padded, or dilated, Let $\mathbf{T}[i : j] \in \mathbb{R}^{h \times d}$ represent a sub-matrix of $\mathbf{T}$ extracted from rows i through j, inclusive. The feature map $\mathbf{c} \in \mathbb{R}^{n-h+1}$ is induced by applying the filter to each possible window of h words, i.e.,

$$c_i = f\left(\langle \mathbf{T}[i : i + h], \mathbf{W}\rangle_{\mathrm{fro}} + b\right) \quad (3)$$

---

[2]https://github.com/google/sentencepiece

for $1 \leq i \leq n - h + 1$, where $b \in \mathbb{R}$ is a bias term, f is a non-linear function, and the Frobenius inner product is denoted by $\langle \mathbf{A}, \mathbf{B} \rangle_{\text{fro}} = \sum_{i=1}^{h} \sum_{j=1}^{d} \mathbf{A}_{ij} \mathbf{B}_{ij}$. 1-max pooling (Collobert et al., 2011) is applied on $\mathbf{c}$, defined as $\hat{c} = \max\{\mathbf{c}\}$. This is performed to propagate the maximum signal throughout the network and reduce the dimensionality of the input.

The process described above creates *one* feature from *one* convolution with window h followed by a pooling operation. To extract multiple features, the model uses several convolutions with varying h to obtain features from different sized n-grams in the sequence. The convolutional (and pooled) outputs are concatenated along the channel dimension, then fed into a one-layer MLP to obtain a distribution over the c classes.

4.3 Lottery Tickets

4.3.1 Initialization

The embedding matrix is initialized from a unit Gaussian, $\mathbf{T} \sim \mathcal{N}(0, 1)$. The convolutional and MLP layers use He initialization (He et al., 2015), whose bound is defined as

$$b = \sqrt{\frac{6}{(1 + a^2) \times \text{fan\_in}}} \quad (4)$$

where a and fan_in are parameters calculated for each weight. The resulting weights have values uniformly sampled from $\mathcal{U}(-b, b)$.

4.3.2 Training

We use iterative pruning with alternating cycles of training and pruning to obtain the tickets (Han et al., 2015; Frankle and Carbin, 2019). For clarity, we define a *round* as training a network for a fixed number of epochs. We begin with a seed round r_0 where the model does not undergo any pruning, then begin to procure tickets in a series of lottery ticket training rounds.

In each successive round $r_{i>0}$, a fraction p of the weights that survived round r_{i-1} are pruned (according to a sparsification algorithm, discussed below) to obtain a smaller, sparser subnetwork; this is denoted by $f(x; m_i \odot \theta_i)$ where m_i and θ_i represent the sparse mask and weights at round r_i. The weights θ_i of this subnetwork are set according to an *initialization strategy* and the subnetwork is re-trained to convergence. We refer to the *sparsity* as the fraction of weights in the network that are exactly zero. In each round, we prune $p\%$ of

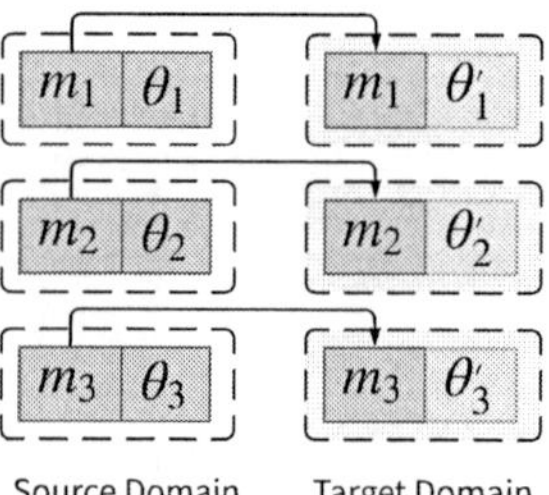

Figure 2: Visualization of the subnetwork transfer process. Purple denotes elements from the source domain, while blue denotes elements from the target domain. Tickets are composed of two elements: (1) the sparsified mask (m_i) and (2) the initial parameter values (θ_i). During transfer, we create subnetworks in the source domain with the mask borrowed from the source domain, but with potentially different parameters. We use θ_i' to denote that these parameters are set according to some *initialization strategy*, which we discuss further in our experiments (§5).

the weights in the model. Therefore, the resulting ticket has sparsity $1 - (1 - p\%)^{r_{total}}$, where r_{total} is the total number of lottery ticket training rounds.

Next, we discuss the sparsification algorithm used to prune weights in each round r_i. Let $\mathbf{p}_i$ denote the vectorized collection of trainable parameters in layer $i \geq 0$, with the embedding layer as layer 0. After re-training the (sub-)networks in each round, we apply the ℓ_0 projection on the parameters in each layer, i.e.

$$\underset{\mathbf{p}}{\arg\min} ||\mathbf{p} - \mathbf{p}_i||_2^2 \quad (5)$$

subject to $\text{card}(\mathbf{p}) \leq k_i$, where $\text{card}(\mathbf{p})$ denotes the number of non-zeros in $\mathbf{p}$. The optimization problem in Eq. 5 can be solved analytically by sorting the elements of $\mathbf{p}_i$ with respect to their absolute values and picking the top k_i elements with the largest magnitude (Jain et al., 2017; Zhu and Gupta, 2017). We use the sparsity hyperparameter p introduced above to decide k_i for each layer. Let $\text{len}(\mathbf{p}_i)$ denote the total number of trainable parameters in layer i. We set $k_i = p\% \times \text{len}(\mathbf{p}_i)$ for each layer. In accordance with our training procedure, once a weight is pruned, it is no longer a trainable parameter; hence, $\text{len}(\mathbf{p}_i)$ is strictly decreasing after each round.

4.3.3 Transferring

The lottery ticket training procedure outlined in §4.3.2 yields a batch of subnetworks $f(x^s; m_1 \odot$

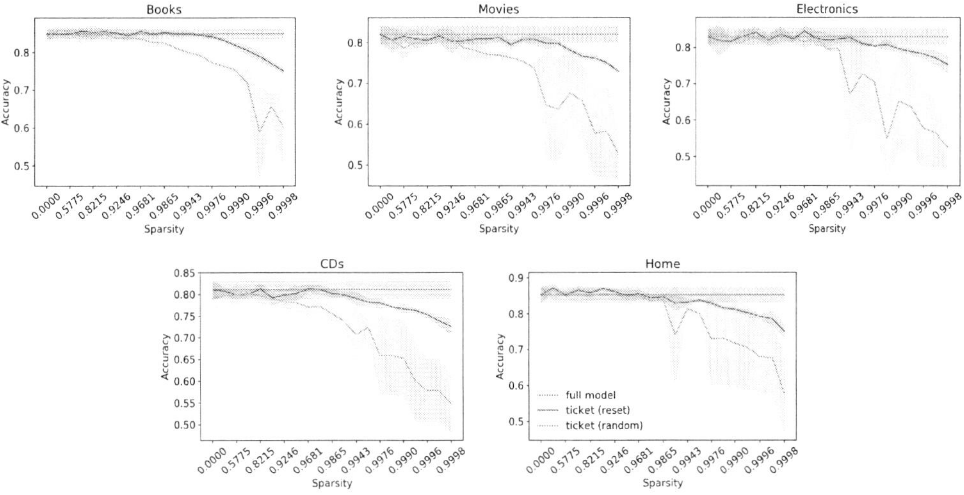

Figure 3: Results obtaining lottery tickets on the Books, Movies, Electronics, CDs, and Home categories of the Amazon Reviews dataset (McAuley and Leskovec, 2013). Experiments are repeated five times, where the solid lines represent the mean and shaded regions represent the standard deviation. Note that the x-axis ticks are *not* uniformly spaced.

$\theta), \cdots, f(x^s; m_n \odot \theta)$ where x^s represents the inputs from a *source* domain $\mathcal{D}_s$ and m_i represents the sparse mask used to prune weights at round r_i. During transfer, we construct a new batch of subnetworks $f(x^t; m_1 \odot \theta'), \cdots, f(x^t; m_n \odot \theta')$ to be evaluated on inputs from a (non-identical) *target* domain $\mathcal{D}_t$ with masks derived from the *source* domain. The change in parameter notation $(\theta \rightarrow \theta')$ implies that the subnetworks evaluated in a disparate domain can potentially use a different *transfer* initialization strategy. We clarify this process in Figure 2. In contrast, Morcos et al. (2019) transfers the entire ticket (sparse masks and initial values) to the target domain. Finally, using the new batch of subnetworks, we evaluate each subnetwork $f(x^t; m_i \odot \theta')$ in the target domain for r_{total} rounds. Unlike the canonical ticket training rounds, we do not (additionally) sparsify the subnetworks during transfer. All in all, our transfer task is designed to answer the following question: can the *sparse masks* found in a source domain using lottery ticket training (§4.3) be transferred to a target domain with *different initialization strategies* to match the performance of a ticket obtained in same target domain?

5 Experiments

5.1 Settings

Our CNN uses three filters ($h \in [3, 4, 5]$), each with 127 channels, and ReLU activation (Nair and Hinton, 2010). We fix the maximum sequence length to 500 subwords. The embeddings are 417-dimensional and trained alongside the model. We opt not to use pre-trained embeddings to ensure the generalizability of our results. Additionally, we regularize the embeddings with dropout (Srivastava et al., 2014), $p = 0.285$. The MLP contains one hidden layer with a dimension of 117. Hyperparameters were discovered using Bayesian hyperparameter optimization (Snoek et al., 2012) on the Books validation set. The models are trained with a batch size of 32 for a maximum of 15 epochs. Early stopping is used to save iterative model versions that perform well on a development set. We use the Adam optimizer (Kingma and Ba, 2014) with a learning rate of $1e^{-3}$ and ℓ_2 regularization with a weight of $1e^{-5}$.

5.2 Obtaining Tickets

First, we use the lottery ticket training procedure outlined in §4.3.2 to obtain tickets for our five datasets with $p = 35\%$ and $r_{total} = 20$. We compare the test performance of the subnetworks using the following baselines:

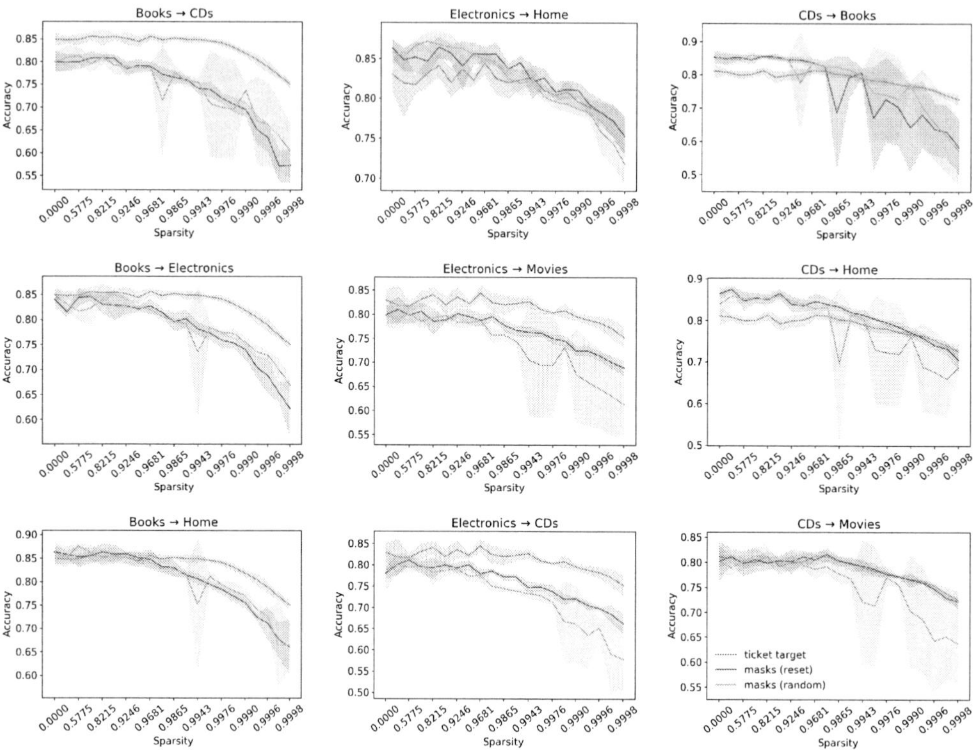

Figure 4: Results transferring lottery tickets on nine transfer tasks constructed from the five categories of the Amazon Reviews dataset (McAuley and Leskovec, 2013). Experiments are repeated five times, where the solid lines represent the mean and shaded regions represent the standard deviation. Note that the x-axis ticks are *not* uniformly spaced.

- FULL-MODEL: This baseline evaluates the performance of the original network *without* any pruning. In other words, we train a model for a seed round r_0, then record its performance.

- TICKET-RESET: The values of the subnetwork are reset to their *original values* before training. This initialization strategy was used in the earliest formation of the Lottery Ticket Hypothesis (Frankle and Carbin, 2019).

- TICKET-RANDOM: The values of the subnetwork are reset to *random values* drawn from the initialization distribution(s) of the original network. We sample weights from the distributions outlined in §4.3.1 to initialize the subnetworks.

The results are shown in Figure 3. For all datasets, TICKET-RESET shows the best performance, notably outperforming FULL-MODEL

in early stages of sparsification (0-90%) for the Books, Electronics, and Home datasets. This demonstrates that deep neural networks—especially those for sentiment analysis—are highly over-parameterized, and the sparsity induced by lottery ticket training can help to increase performance. This observation is consistent with Louizos et al. (2018), which also showed sparse networks fashion a regularization effect that results in better generalization performance. In addition, we observe that TICKET-RESET and TICKET-RANDOM have similar test performance until about 96% sparsity. This casts some doubt around whether the initial values truly matter for sparse models as the randomly sampled values seem to fit sparse masks well.

However, a *phase transition* occurs in the high sparsity regime, where the differences between TICKET-RESET and TICKET-RANDOM are significantly enlarged. The performance of TICKET-

RANDOM becomes highly unstable and drops off much faster than TICKET-RESET after 96% sparsity. In contrast, TICKET-RESET remains relatively stable—even with sparsity levels over 99.9%—pointing towards the enigmatic importance of original values in extreme levels of sparsity.

5.3 Transferring Tickets

Next, we use the lottery ticket transferring procedure outlined in §4.3 to transfer (obtained) subnetworks from a *source* domain to a non-identical *target* domain. Identical to the previous experiment, we use $r_{total} = 20$. We compare the test performance of the *transferred* subnetworks using the following baselines:

- TICKET-TARGET: This baseline is comprised of the subnetworks obtained in the target domain using lottery ticket training. We borrow the values for this baseline (without modification) from the TICKET-RESET subnetworks shown in Figure 3, albeit from the domain of interest.

- MASKS-RESET: Under this initialization strategy, the masks obtained in the source domain is used on the target domain and the subnetwork is trained from the *same* initial values as in the source domain.

- MASKS-RANDOM: Under this initialization strategy, *only* the masks are used from the subnetwork obtained in the source domain. The parameters are randomly initialized from the distributions outlined in §4.3.1 before training on the target domain.

The results are shown in Figure 4. Both MASKS-RESET and MASKS-RANDOM show signs of generalization in the early stages of sparsification. Most notably, subnetworks obtained in the CDs domain are extremely robust; both the MASKS-RESET and MASKS-RANDOM results show stronger performance than TICKET-TARGET, even in sparsity levels over 99%. This is relatively surprising as the FULL-MODEL in §5.2 achieved the worst performance in the CDs domain. Further inspection of representations learned in this domain will be required to understand its strong ticket performance, which may or may not be a coincidence.

We see a 3-5% dropoff in performance (up to 90% sparsity) from tickets identified from the Books and Electronics tasks after transferring. These results together imply that tickets are not completely immune to distributional shifts, although the degradation in test accuracy is not substantial until reaching high sparsity. Nevertheless, we notice the accuracies of MASKS-RESET and MASKS-RANDOM stay relatively stable from 0-90% sparsity; they only begin to steadily decline after this point.

Finally, we compare the performance of MASKS-RESET and MASKS-RANDOM. In the Books tasks, MASKS-RANDOM performs better overall in comparison to MASKS-RESET. Its performance is slightly worse in the Electronics and CDs tasks, although it is relatively comparable to MASKS-RESET up to 96%. Similar to the results in §5.2, we notice a *phase transition* point where the initial values (e.g., MASKS-RESET) play a much bigger role in maintaining stability and performance in the deeper stages of sparsification.

6 Discussion

In this section, we briefly recap our findings, highlighting key points observed through our ticket procuring and transfer experiments. For each section, we also touch on areas for future work.

Evidence of transferability of winning tickets in natural language processing. Our experiments show that "winning tickets" can indeed be identified in a sentiment task formulated from noisy, user-generated datasets. Moreover, the "winning tickets", up to extreme level of sparsity (e.g., 90%), can be transferred across domains without much loss in accuracy. The fact that tickets can be obtained in noisy environments shows its prominence across multiple data sources. However, our work only considers a binary sentiment analysis task. Future work can explore other tasks such as multi-class text classification, language modeling, and machine translation.

Randomly initialized tickets are strong baselines. Consistent with the observations in Liu et al. (2018b), initializing tickets to their *original values* before training is not necessarily required for strong performance. In our experiments, we show that in high sparsity conditions (up to 90%), there is no noticeable difference between the performance of the *originally* and *randomly* initialized subnetworks. Although the sparse masks build on top of each other from round r_i to r_{i+1}, randomly initialized subnetworks are still able to settle in a local minima with comparable performance to that of the originally initialized subnetworks. However, our work fixes the optimizer and learning rate across experiments. It may be possible that randomly initialized subnetworks using varying optimization reach better minima.

A *phase transition* point largely influences ticket performance. As alluded to above, there is almost no difference in performance when considering originally and randomly initialized subnetworks. However, our experiments point towards a crucial turning point—the *phase transition*—in which the initialization begins to matter. In particular, especially in extreme levels of sparsity (e.g., 99.99%) originally initialized networks exhibit less variance than randomly initialized tickets in test accuracy. However, the specific sparsity at which the phase transition happens is dataset-dependent. Understanding why this occurs and its relation with other models, datasets, and optimization algorithms can further unveil and explain the phenomena behind lottery tickets.

7 Applications in Federated Learning

Federated learning is a scenario where a centralized model is trained over decentralized data, distributed across millions (if not billions) of clients (e.g., electronic devices) (Konen et al., 2016; Bonawitz et al., 2019). Crucially, the clients are not allowed to exchange *data* with the central server or each other. Instead, each client can fine-tune a model for a couple of iterations on their own data, then send their (encrypted) parameters or gradients to a server for aggregation. This "collaborative learning" setup effectively maintains a level of user privacy by ensuring the data always stays on-device. However, this poses several challenges for optimization; as the centralized server does not have access to the data distribution of each client, any neural architecture selection has to be done on either (a) a *different* data source the server has access to or (b) on each individual client. Since (b) is generally quite expensive, the server usually maintains some seed data, as alluded to in (a).

With the transferability of lottery tickets, the server can procure lottery tickets on server-accessible data, then retrain the tickets on client data under the federated learning framework. While there may be a large performance drop when transferring *extremely* sparse networks, our results show that clients can still re-train *moderately* sparse networks with commensurate performance. We believe that this "sparsify and transfer" procedure has two immediate benefits: (1) past work—including the original incarnation of the lottery ticket hypothesis—has shown that sparse networks can be, under certain conditions, easier to optimize (Frankle and Carbin, 2019; Morcos et al., 2019; Gale et al., 2019); and (2) sparser subnetworks have significantly less capacity than their large, over-parameterized counterparts, which can alleviate client-server communication costs (e.g., model uploading and downloading) (Konen et al., 2016; Sattler et al., 2019).

8 Conclusion

The Lottery Ticket Hypothesis (Frankle and Carbin, 2019) posits that large, over-parameterized networks contain small, sparse subnetworks that can be re-trained in isolation with commensurate test performance. In this paper, we examine whether these tickets are robust against distributional shifts. In particular, we set up domain transfer tasks with the Amazon Reviews dataset (McAuley and Leskovec, 2013) to obtain tickets in a *source* domain and transfer them in a disparate *target* domain. Moreover, we experiment with the *transfer* initialization of the networks, determining if resetting to initial values (obtained in the source domain) are required for strong performance in the target domain. Our experiments show that tickets (under several initialization strategies) can be transferred across different text domains without much loss up to a very high level of sparsity.

In addition, there is a lot of debate on whether initial value resetting is critical to achieve commensurate test performance. While Frankle and Carbin (2019); Frankle et al. (2019) present evidence supporting the importance of resetting, Gale et al. (2019); Liu et al. (2018b) show that sparse retrainable subnetworks can be found independent of resetting. Our experiments show that this is *not* a yes or no question. Specifically, we show there is a *phase transition* related to sparsity. Resetting is not critical before extreme levels of sparsity (i.e., below 99%), but the effect of resetting is magnified in high sparsity regimes. Finally, we demonstrate the practical applications of our results in federated learning.

Acknowledgments

Thanks to Veselin Stoyanov and our anonymous reviewers for their helpful comments.

References

Keith Bonawitz, Hubert Eichner, Wolfgang Grieskamp, Dzmitry Huba, Alex Ingerman, Vladimir Ivanov, Chloe Kiddon, Jakub Konecny, Stefano Mazzocchi, H Brendan McMahan, et al. 2019. Towards federated learning at scale: System design. *arXiv preprint arXiv:1902.01046*.

Ronan Collobert, Jason Weston, Léon Bottou, Michael Karlen, Koray Kavukcuoglu, and Pavel Kuksa. 2011. Natural language processing (almost) from scratch. *Journal of machine learning research*, 12(Aug):2493–2537.

Jun Deng, Zixing Zhang, Erik Marchi, and Björn Schuller. 2013. Sparse autoencoder-based feature transfer learning for speech emotion recognition. In *2013 Humaine Association Conference on Affective Computing and Intelligent Interaction*, pages 511–516. IEEE.

Thomas Elsken, Jan Hendrik Metzen, and Frank Hutter. 2018. Neural architecture search: A survey. *arXiv preprint arXiv:1808.05377*.

Jonathan Frankle and Michael Carbin. 2019. The lottery ticket hypothesis: Finding sparse, trainable neural networks. In *International Conference on Learning Representations*.

Jonathan Frankle, Gintare Karolina Dziugaite, Daniel M Roy, and Michael Carbin. 2019. Stabilizing the lottery ticket hypothesis. *arXiv preprint arXiv:1903.01611v2*.

Trevor Gale, Erich Elsen, and Sara Hooker. 2019. The state of sparsity in deep neural networks. *arXiv preprint arXiv:1902.09574*.

Jonas Gehring, Michael Auli, David Grangier, Denis Yarats, and Yann N Dauphin. 2017. Convolutional sequence to sequence learning. In *Proceedings of the 34th International Conference on Machine Learning-Volume 70*, pages 1243–1252. JMLR. org.

Yunchao Gong, Liu Liu, Ming Yang, and Lubomir Bourdev. 2014. Compressing deep convolutional networks using vector quantization. *arXiv preprint arXiv:1412.6115*.

Song Han, Jeff Pool, John Tran, and William Dally. 2015. Learning both weights and connections for efficient neural network. In *Advances in neural information processing systems*, pages 1135–1143.

Kaiming He, Xiangyu Zhang, Shaoqing Ren, and Jian Sun. 2015. Delving deep into rectifiers: Surpassing human-level performance on imagenet classification. In *Proceedings of the IEEE international conference on computer vision*, pages 1026–1034.

Itay Hubara, Matthieu Courbariaux, Daniel Soudry, Ran El-Yaniv, and Yoshua Bengio. 2017. Quantized neural networks: Training neural networks with low precision weights and activations. *The Journal of Machine Learning Research*, 18(1):6869–6898.

Prateek Jain, Purushottam Kar, et al. 2017. Nonconvex optimization for machine learning. *Foundations and Trends® in Machine Learning*, 10(3-4):142–336.

Yoon Kim. 2014. Convolutional neural networks for sentence classification. In *Proceedings of the 2014 Conference on Empirical Methods in Natural Language Processing (EMNLP)*, pages 1746–1751.

Diederik P Kingma and Jimmy Ba. 2014. Adam: A method for stochastic optimization. *arXiv preprint arXiv:1412.6980*.

Jakub Konen, H. Brendan McMahan, Felix X. Yu, Peter Richtarik, Ananda Theertha Suresh, and Dave Bacon. 2016. Federated learning: Strategies for improving communication efficiency. In *NIPS Workshop on Private Multi-Party Machine Learning*.

Simon Kornblith, Jonathon Shlens, and Quoc V Le. 2019. Do better imagenet models transfer better? In *Proceedings of the IEEE Conference on Computer Vision and Pattern Recognition*, pages 2661–2671.

Taku Kudo and John Richardson. 2018. Sentencepiece: A simple and language independent subword tokenizer and detokenizer for neural text processing. *arXiv preprint arXiv:1808.06226*.

Hanxiao Liu, Karen Simonyan, and Yiming Yang. 2018a. Darts: Differentiable architecture search. *arXiv preprint arXiv:1806.09055*.

Jiaming Liu, Yali Wang, and Yu Qiao. 2017. Sparse deep transfer learning for convolutional neural network. In *Thirty-First AAAI Conference on Artificial Intelligence*.

Zhuang Liu, Mingjie Sun, Tinghui Zhou, Gao Huang, and Trevor Darrell. 2018b. Rethinking the value of network pruning. *arXiv preprint arXiv:1810.05270*.

Christos Louizos, Max Welling, and Diederik P. Kingma. 2018. Learning sparse neural networks through l_0 regularization. In *International Conference on Learning Representations*.

Julian McAuley and Jure Leskovec. 2013. Hidden factors and hidden topics: understanding rating dimensions with review text. In *Proceedings of the 7th ACM conference on Recommender systems*, pages 165–172. ACM.

Ari S Morcos, Haonan Yu, Michela Paganini, and Yuandong Tian. 2019. One ticket to win them all: generalizing lottery ticket initializations across datasets and optimizers. *arXiv preprint arXiv:1906.02773*.

Lili Mou, Zhao Meng, Rui Yan, Ge Li, Yan Xu, Lu Zhang, and Zhi Jin. 2016. How transferable are neural networks in nlp applications? In *Proceedings of the 2016 Conference on Empirical Methods in Natural Language Processing*, pages 479–489.

Vinod Nair and Geoffrey E Hinton. 2010. Rectified linear units improve restricted boltzmann machines. In *Proceedings of the 27th international conference on machine learning (ICML-10)*, pages 807–814.

Minlong Peng, Qi Zhang, Yu-gang Jiang, and Xuanjing Huang. 2018. Cross-domain sentiment classification with target domain specific information. In *56th Annual Meeting of the Association for Computational Linguistics (Long Papers)*.

Felix Sattler, Simon Wiedemann, Klaus-Robert Müller, and Wojciech Samek. 2019. Robust and communication-efficient federated learning from non-iid data. *arXiv preprint arXiv:1903.02891*.

Rico Sennrich, Barry Haddow, and Alexandra Birch. 2016. Neural machine translation of rare words with subword units. In *Proceedings of the 54th Annual Meeting of the Association for Computational Linguistics (Volume 1: Long Papers)*, pages 1715–1725.

Jasper Snoek, Hugo Larochelle, and Ryan P Adams. 2012. Practical bayesian optimization of machine learning algorithms. In *Advances in neural information processing systems*, pages 2951–2959.

Nitish Srivastava, Geoffrey Hinton, Alex Krizhevsky, Ilya Sutskever, and Ruslan Salakhutdinov. 2014. Dropout: a simple way to prevent neural networks from overfitting. *The journal of machine learning research*, 15(1):1929–1958.

Jason Yosinski, Jeff Clune, Yoshua Bengio, and Hod Lipson. 2014. How transferable are features in deep neural networks? In *Advances in neural information processing systems*, pages 3320–3328.

Haonan Yu, Sergey Edunov, Yuandong Tian, and Ari S. Morcos. 2019. Playing the lottery with rewards and multiple languages: lottery tickets in RL and NLP. *CoRR*, abs/1906.02768.

Michael Zhu and Suyog Gupta. 2017. To prune, or not to prune: exploring the efficacy of pruning for model compression. *arXiv preprint arXiv:1710.01878*.

Barret Zoph, Vijay Vasudevan, Jonathon Shlens, and Quoc V Le. 2018. Learning transferable architectures for scalable image recognition. In *Proceedings of the IEEE conference on computer vision and pattern recognition*, pages 8697–8710.

Cross-lingual Parsing with Polyglot Training and Multi-treebank Learning: A Faroese Case Study

James Barry and **Joachim Wagner** and **Jennifer Foster**
ADAPT Centre
School of Computing, Dublin City University, Ireland
`firstname.lastname@adaptcentre.ie`

Abstract

Cross-lingual dependency parsing involves transferring syntactic knowledge from one language to another. It is a crucial component for inducing dependency parsers in low-resource scenarios where no training data for a language exists. Using Faroese as the target language, we compare two approaches using annotation projection: first, projecting from multiple *monolingual* source models; second, projecting from a single *polyglot* model which is trained on the combination of all source languages. Furthermore, we reproduce multi-source projection (Tyers et al., 2018), in which dependency trees of multiple sources are combined. Finally, we apply multi-treebank modelling to the projected treebanks, in addition to or alternatively to polyglot modelling on the source side. We find that polyglot training on the source languages produces an overall trend of better results on the target language but the single best result for the target language is obtained by projecting from monolingual source parsing models and then training multi-treebank POS tagging and parsing models on the target side.

1 Introduction

Cross-lingual transfer methods, i.e. methods that transfer knowledge from one or more source languages to a target language, have led to substantial improvements for low-resource dependency parsing (Rosa and Mareček, 2018; Agić et al., 2016; Guo et al., 2015; Lynn et al., 2014; McDonald et al., 2011; Hwa et al., 2005) and part-of-speech (POS) tagging (Plank and Agić, 2018). In low-resource scenarios, there may be not enough data for data-driven models to learn how to parse. In cases where no annotated data is available, knowledge is often transferred from annotated data in other languages and when there is only a small amount of annotated data, additional knowl-

edge can be induced from external corpora such as by learning distributed word representations (Mikolov et al., 2013; Al-Rfou' et al., 2013) and more recent contextualized variants (Peters et al., 2018; Devlin et al., 2019).

This work focuses on dependency parsing for low-resource languages by means of annotation projection (Yarowsky et al., 2001) and synthetic treebank creation (Tiedemann and Agić, 2016). We build on recent work by Tyers et al. (2018) who show that in the absence of annotated training data for the target language, a lexicalized treebank can be created by translating a target language corpus into a number of related source languages and parsing the translations using models trained on the source language treebanks.[1] These annotations are then projected to the target language using separate word alignments for each source language, combined into a single graph for each sentence and decoded (Sagae and Lavie, 2006), resulting in a treebank for the target language, Faroese in the case of Tyers et al.'s and our experiments.

Inspired by recent literature involving multilingual learning (Mulcaire et al., 2019; Smith et al., 2018; Vilares et al., 2016), we investigate whether additional improvements can be made by:

1. using a single polyglot[2] parsing model which is trained on the combination of all source languages to create synthetic source treebanks (which are subsequently projected to the target language)

---

[1] In this paper, *source language* and *target language* always refer to the projection, not the direction of translation.

[2] We adopt the same terminology used in Mulcaire et al. (2019), who use the term *cross-lingual transfer* to describe methods involving the use of one or more source languages to process a target language. They reserve the term *polyglot learning* for training a single model on multiple languages and where parameters are shared between languages. For the polyglot learning technique applied to multiple treebanks of a single language, we use the term *multi-treebank learning*.

Proceedings of the 2nd Workshop on Deep Learning Approaches for Low-Resource NLP (DeepLo), pages 163–174
Hong Kong, China, November 3, 2019. ©2019 Association for Computational Linguistics
https://doi.org/10.18653/v1/P17

2. training a multi-treebank model on the individually projected treebanks and the treebank produced with multi-source projections.

The former differs from the approach of Tyers et al. (2018), who use multiple discrete, monolingual models to parse the translated sentences, whereas in this work we use a single model trained on multiple source treebanks. The latter differs from training on the target treebank produced by multi-source projection in that the information of the individual projections is still available and training data is not reduced to cases where all source languages provide a projection.

In other words, we aim to investigate whether the current state-of-the-art approach for Faroese, which relies on cross-lingual transfer, can be improved upon by adopting an approach based on source-side polyglot learning and/or target-side multi-treebank learning. We hypothesize that a polyglot model can exploit similarities in morphology and syntax across the included source languages, which will result in a better model to provide annotations for projection. On the target side, we expect that combining different sources of information will result in a more robust target model.

We evaluated our various models on the Faroese test set and experienced considerable gains for three of the four source languages (Danish, Norwegian Bokmål and Swedish) by adopting a polyglot model. However, for Norwegian Nynorsk, a stronger monolingual model was able to outperform the polyglot approach. When we extended multi-treebank learning to the target side, we experienced additional gains for all cases. Our best result of 71.5 – an absolute improvement of 7.2 points over the result reported by Tyers et al. (2018) – was achieved with multi-treebank target learning over the monolingual projections.

2   Background

Tyers et al. (2018) describe a method for creating synthetic treebanks for Faroese based on previous work which uses machine translation and word alignments to transfer trees from source language(s) to the target language. Sentences from Faroese are translated into the four source languages Danish, Swedish, Norwegian Nynorsk and Norwegian Bokmål. The translated sentences are then tokenized, POS tagged and parsed using the relevant source language model trained on the source language treebank. The resulting trees are projected back to the Faroese sentences using word alignments. The four trees for each sentence are combined into a graph with edge scores one to four (the number of trees that support them), from which a single tree per sentence is produced using the Chu-Liu-Edmonds algorithm (Chu and Liu, 1965; Edmonds, 1967). The resulting trees make up a synthetic treebank for Faroese which is then used to train a Faroese parsing model. The parser output is evaluated using the gold-standard Faroese test treebank developed by Tyers et al. (2018). The approach is compared to a delexicalized baseline, which it outperforms by a large margin. It is also shown that, for Faroese, a combination of the four source languages (multi-source projection) is superior to individual language projection.

The idea of annotation projection using word-alignments originates from (Yarowsky et al., 2001) who used word alignments to transfer information such as POS tags from source to target languages. This method was later used in dependency parsing by Hwa et al. (2005), who project dependencies to a target language and use a set of heuristics to form dependency trees in the target language. A parser is then trained on the projected treebank and evaluated against gold-standard treebanks. Zeman and Resnik (2008) introduced the idea of delexicalized dependency parsing whereby a parser is trained using only POS information and is then applied to a target language.

McDonald et al. (2011) perform delexicalized dependency parsing using direct transfer and show that this approach outperforms unsupervised approaches for grammar induction. Importantly, this approach can be extended to the multi-source case by training on multiple source languages and predicting a target language. In an additional experiment, they combine annotation projection and multi-source transfer.

Tiedemann and Agić (2016) present a thorough comparison of pre-neural cross-lingual parsing. Various forms of projected annotation methods are compared to delexicalized baselines, and the use of machine translation instead of parallel corpora to produce synthetic treebanks in the target language is explored. In contrast to Tyers et al. (2018), they translate a target sentence and project the source parse tree back to the target during test time instead of using this approach to obtain training data for the target language.

Agić et al. (2016) leverage massively multilingual parallel corpora such as translations of the Bible and web-scraped data from the Watchtower Online Library website[3] for low-resource POS tagging and dependency parsing using annotation projection. They project weight matrices (as opposed to decoded dependency arcs) from multiple source languages and average the matrices weighted by word alignment confidences. They then decode the weight matrices into dependency trees on the target side, which are then used to train a parser. This approach utilizes dense information from multiple source languages, which helps reduce noise from source side predictions but to the best of our knowledge, the source-side parsing models learn information between source languages independently and the cross-lingual interaction only occurs when projecting the edge scores into multi-source weight matrices.

The idea of projecting dense information in the form of a weighted graph has been further extended by Schlichtkrull and Søgaard (2017) who bypass the need to train the target parser on decoded trees and develop a parser which can be trained directly on weighted graphs.

Plank and Agić (2018) use annotation projection for POS tagging. They find that choosing high quality training instances results in superior accuracy than randomly sampling a larger training set. To this end, they rank the target sentences by the percentage of words covered by word alignments across all source languages and choose the top k covered sentences for training.

Meechan-Maddon and Nivre (2019) carry out an evaluation on cross-lingual parsing for three low-resource languages which are supported by related languages. They include three experiments: first, training a *monolingual* model on a small number of sentences in the target language; second, training a *cross-lingual* model on related source languages which is then applied to the target data and lastly, training a *multilingual* model which includes target data as well as data from the related support languages. They found that training a monolingual model on the target data was always superior to training a cross-lingual model. Interestingly, they found that the best results were achieved by training a model on the various support languages as well as the target data, i.e. their multilingual model. While we do not combine the synthetic target treebanks with the source treebanks in our experiments, the results of Meechan-Maddon and Nivre (2019) motivate us to carry out this experiment in the future.

3 Method

We outline the process used for creating a synthetic treebank for cross-lingual dependency parsing. We use the following resources: raw Faroese sentences taken from Wikipedia, a machine translation system to translate these sentences into all source languages (Danish, Swedish, Norwegian Nynorsk and Norwegian Bokmål), a word-aligner to provide word alignments between the words in the target and source sentences, treebanks for the four source languages on which to train parsing models, POS tagging and parsing tools, and, lastly a target language test set. We use the same raw corpus, alignments and tokenized and segmented versions of the source translations[4] as Tyers et al. (2018) who release all of their data.[5] In this way, the experimental pipeline is the same as theirs but we predict POS tags and dependency annotations using our own models.

Target Language Corpus We use the target corpus built by Tyers et al. (2018) which comprises 28,862 sentences which were extracted from Faroese Wikipedia dumps[6] using the WikiExtractor script[7] and further pre-processed to remove any non-Faroese texts and other forms of unsuitable sentences.

Machine Translation As noted by Tyers et al. (2018), popular repositories for developing machine translation systems such as OPUS (Tiedemann, 2016) contain an inadequate amount of sentences to train a data-driven machine translation system for Faroese. For instance, there are fewer than 7,000 sentence pairs between Faroese and Danish, Faroese and English, Faroese and Norwegian and Faroese and Swedish. Consequently, to create parallel source sentences, Tyers et al. (2018) use a rule-based machine translation system available in Apertium[8] to translate from Faroese to

---

[3] https://wol.jw.org/

[4] The original authors tokenize and segment the source translations with UDPipe.

[5] https://github.com/ftyers/cross-lingual-parsing

[6] https://dumps.wikimedia.org/

[7] https://github.com/attardi/wikiextractor

[8] https://github.com/apertium

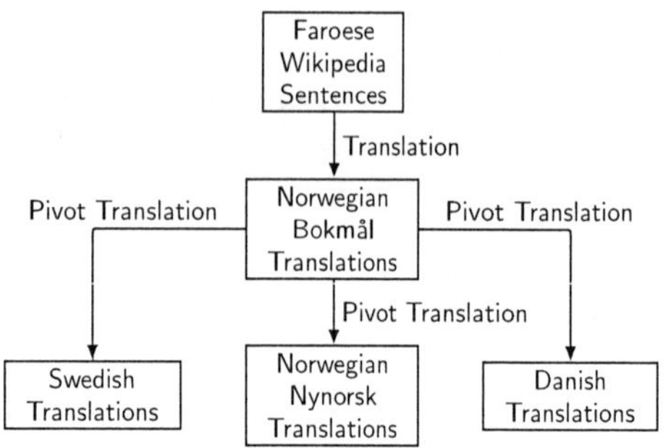

Figure 1: Overview of the machine translation process. The Faroese sentences are first translated into Norwegian Bokmål and then from Norwegian Bokmål into the other source languages (pivot translation).

Norwegian Bokmål. There also exists translation systems from Norwegian Bokmål to Norwegian Nynorsk, Swedish and Danish in Apertium. As a result, the authors use *pivot translation* from Norwegian Bokmål into the other source languages. The process is illustrated in Fig. 1. For a more thorough description of the machine translation process and for resource creation in general, see the work of Tyers et al. (2018).

Word Alignments We use word alignments between the Faroese text and the source translations generated by Tyers et al. (2018) using fast_align (Dyer et al., 2013), a word alignment tool based on IBM Model 2.[9]

Source Treebanks We use the Universal Dependencies v2.2 treebanks (Nivre et al., 2018) to train our source parsing models. This is the version used for the 2018 CoNLL shared task on Parsing Universal Dependencies (Zeman et al., 2018).

Source Tagging and Parsing Models In order for our parsers to work well with predicted POS tags, we follow the same steps as used in the 2018 CoNLL shared task for creating training and development treebanks with automatically predicted POS tags (henceforth referred to as silver POS). Since we are required to parse translated text which only has lexical features available, we

disregard lemmas, language-specific POS (XPOS) and morphological features and only use the word form and universal POS (UPOS) tag as input features to our parsers. We develop our POS tagging and parsing models using the AllenNLP library (Gardner et al., 2018).

We use jackknife resampling to predict the UPOS tags for the training treebanks. We split the training treebank into ten parts, train models on nine parts and predict UPOS for the excluded part. The process is repeated until all ten parts are predicted and they are then combined to recreate the treebank with silver POS tags. Only token features are used to predict the UPOS tag.[10] Finally, we train a model per source language on the full training data to check performance on the respective development set and to POS tag the source language translations before parsing.

We train two variants of parsing models. The first is a monolingual biaffine dependency parser (Dozat and Manning, 2017) trained on the individual source treebanks. The second is a polyglot model trained on all source treebanks using the multilingual parser of Schuster et al. (2019), which is the same graph-based biaffine dependency parser, extended to enable parsing with multiple treebanks. We additionally include a treebank embedding (Ammar et al., 2016; Stymne et al., 2018) to the input of the polyglot parser to help the parser differentiate between the source languages. We optimize the model for average development set LAS across the included languages. The process is illustrated in Fig. 2.

To ensure that our parser is realistic, we add a pre-trained monolingual word embedding to each monolingual parser, giving a considerable improvement in accuracy on the development sets of the source languages. We use the precomputed Word2Vec embeddings[11] released as part of the 2017 CoNLL shared task on UD parsing (Zeman et al., 2017) which were trained on CommonCrawl and Wikipedia.

In order to use pre-trained word embeddings for the polyglot setting, we need to consider that a polyglot model uses a shared vocabulary across all input languages. In our experiments, we simply

---

[9]Note that previous related work (Agić et al., 2016) report better results using IBM Model 1 with a more diverse language setup. They claim that IBM Model 2 introduces a bias towards more closely related languages. As we are working with related languages and translations and alignments are largely word-for-word, we expect that this will have less of an impact on our experiments although IBM Model 1 should also be tried in future work.

[10]We observe slightly lower POS tagging scores on fully annotated test sets than UDPipe, which uses gold lemmas, XPOS and morphological features to predict the UPOS label and therefore cannot be applied to the translated text without also building predictors for these features.

[11]`https://lindat.mff.cuni.cz/repository/xmlui/handle/11234/1-1989`

use the union of the word embeddings and average the word vector for words that occur in more than one language. Future work should explore cross-lingual word embeddings with limited amount of parallel data or use aligned contextual embeddings as in (Schuster et al., 2019).

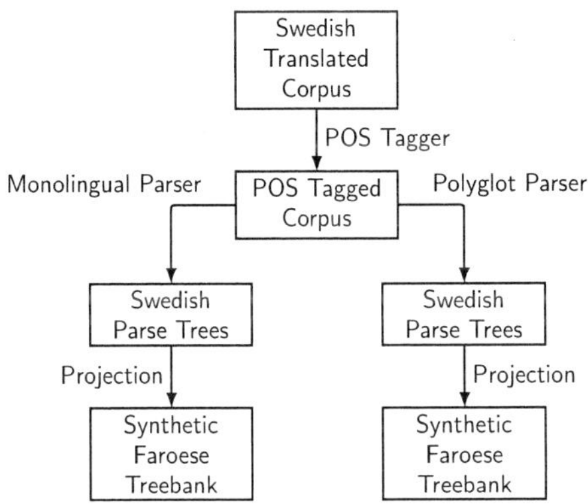

Figure 2: Overview of the *monolingual* and *polyglot* parse experiments using Swedish translations as an example. This process is repeated for all source languages.

Synthetic Source Treebanks   Source translations are tokenized with UDPipe (Straka and Straková, 2017) by Tyers et al. (2018). For each source language, the POS model trained on the full training data (see previous section) is used to tag the tokenized translations. Once the text is tagged, we predict dependency arcs and labels with the parsing models of the previous section, and use annotation projection (described below) to provide syntactic annotations for the target sentences.

Annotation Projection   Once the synthetic source treebanks are compiled, i. e. the translations are parsed, the annotations are then projected from the source translations to the target language using the word alignments and Tyers et al.'s projection tool, resulting in a Faroese treebank. In some cases, not all tokens are aligned and Tyers et al. (2018) work around this by falling back to a 1:1 mapping between the target index and the source index. There are also cases where there is a mismatch in length between the source and target sentences and some dependency structures cannot be projected to the target language. Tyers et al.'s projection setup removes unsuitable projected trees containing e. g. more than one root token, a token that is its own head or a token with a head outside the range of the sentence.

Multi-source Projection   For multi-source projection, the four source-language dependency trees for a Faroese sentence are projected into a single graph, scoring edges according to the number of trees that contain them (Sagae and Lavie, 2006; Nivre et al., 2007). The dependency structure is first built by voting over the directed edges. Afterward, dependency labels and POS tags are decided using the same voting procedure. The process is illustrated in Fig. 3.

Target Tagging and Parsing Models   At this stage we have Faroese treebanks to train our POS tagging and parsing models. The Faroese treebanks come in two variants: the result of projection from source trees produced by either 1) a monolingual, or 2) the polyglot model. For each case, we train our POS tagging and parsing models directly on these synthetic treebanks and do not make use of word embeddings as we do not have them for Faroese.

Multi-treebank Target Parsing   Since we have several synthetic Faroese treebanks, we have the option of training on a single treebank or using a multi-treebank approach where we train on all target treebanks in the same way as we did for inducing the polyglot source model. The process is illustrated in Fig. 4. When training a multi-treebank target model, for each target treebank, we add a treebank embedding denoting the source model used to project annotations to the target treebank. At predict time, we must include one of these treebank embeddings as input to the model. As we do not have real Faroese data in our target training treebanks, we must choose the treebank embedding of one of the synthetic target treebanks. Stymne et al. (2018) introduce the term "proxy treebank" to refer to cases where the test treebank is not in the training set and a treebank embedding from the training set must be used instead.

4   Experiments

In this section, we describe our experiments, which include a replication of the main findings of Tyers et al. (2018), using AllenNLP (Gardner et al., 2018) for POS tagging and parsing instead of UDPipe (Straka and Straková, 2017).[12]

---

[12] All of the code and scripts to reproduce the experiments can be found at `https://github.com/Jbar-ry/`

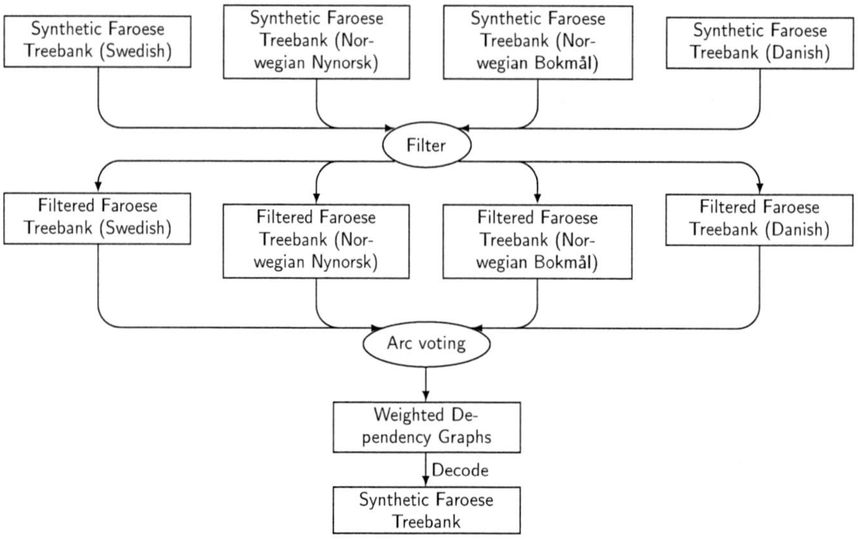

Figure 3: Multi-source projection. The source language is listed in brackets.

4.1 Details

The hyper-parameters of our POS tagging and parsing models are given in Table 1. For POS tagging, we adopt a standard architecture with a word and character-level Bi-LSTM (Plank et al., 2016; Graves and Schmidhuber, 2005) to learn context-sensitive representations of our words. These representations are passed to a multilayer perceptron (MLP) classifier followed by a softmax function to choose a tag with the highest probability. For both the POS tagging and parsing models, we use a word embedding dimension of size 100 and a character embedding dimension of size 64. POS tag embeddings of dimension 50 are included in the parser. We train our Faroese models for fifty epochs. We do not split the synthetic Faroese treebanks into training/development portions though we suspect doing so will help the models to not overfit on the training data. For all experiments we report labelled attachment scores produced by the official CoNLL 2018 evaluation script.[13]

4.2 Results

The development results of our monolingual and polyglot models on the source language treebanks are shown in Table 2. The results for the polyglot model are better for three out of four source languages, whereas for no_nynorsk, the monolingual model marginally outperforms the polyglot one. These results suggest that the polyglot model will contribute better syntactic annotations for Faroese treebanks.

The statistics of the filtered Faroese treebanks obtained via projection with our source parsing models are given in Table 3. The treebank sizes are fairly similar regardless of whether source annotations are provided by a monolingual or a polyglot model which is expected because the word alignments are the major factor in determining whether a projection is successful. There is a proportionally lower number of sentences for multi-source projection. This is because this method only uses the intersection of sentences which are present across all synthetic treebanks after filtering. The treebank originating from Norwegian Bokmål has the highest number of valid sentences, suggesting that it could be a good candidate for projection to Faroese. It also has the highest source language parsing accuracy (Table 2).

The results of training on our various synthetic Faroese treebanks and predicting the Faroese test set are shown in the first result column of Table 4 (SINGLE). In terms of monolingual vs. polyglot, we find that projecting from a polyglot model helps with four out of the five possible treebanks (with three of them being statistically

```
multilingual-parsing
```
[13]`https://github.com/ufal/conll2018/blob/master/evaluation_script/conll18_ud_eval.py`

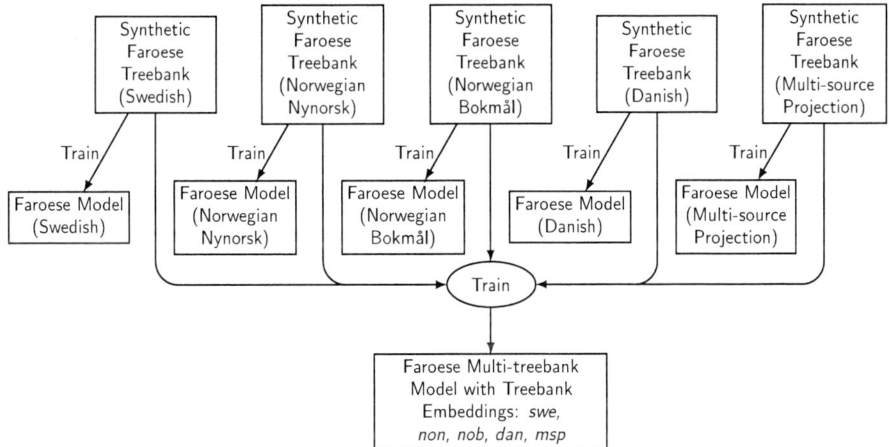

Figure 4: Single versus multi-treebank training. The source language is listed in brackets.

POS Tagger Architecture	
Parameter	**Value**
Char-BiLSTM layers	2
BiLSTM layers	2
BiLSTM size	400
Dropout LSTMs	0.33
Dropout MLP	0.33
Dropout embeddings	0.33
Nonlinear act. (MLP)	ELU
Parser Architecture	
Parameter	**Value**
Char-BiLSTM layers	2
BiLSTM layers	3
BiLSTM size	400
Arc MLP size	500
Label MLP size	100
Dropout LSTMs	0.33
Dropout MLP	0.33
Dropout embeddings	0.33
Nonlinear act. (MLP)	ELU
Embeddings	
Parameter	**Size**
Word embedding (both)	100
Char embedding (both)	64
POS embedding (parser)	50
Treebank embedding (both)	12
Training	
Parameter	**Value**
Optimizer	Adam
Learning rate	0.001
Adam epsilon	1e-08
beta1 (both)	0.9
beta2 (parser)	0.9
beta2 (tagger)	0.999

Table 1: Chosen hyperparameters for our POS tagging and parsing models. *both* means the feature is common to both the POS tagger and parser.

TREEBANK	MONOLINGUAL	POLYGLOT
da_ddt	81.10	**82.75**
sv_talbanken	80.61	**83.85**
no_nynorsk	**88.54**	88.29
no_bokmaal	89.29	**90.29**
average	84.88	**86.30**

Table 2: Source model LAS scores on the development treebanks using silver POS tags.

SOURCE	MONOLINGUAL	POLYGLOT
Danish	13,950	13,944
Swedish	10,894	10,874
Norwegian Nynorsk	13,177	13,194
Norwegian Bokmål	17,345	17,378
Multi-source	6,716	6,833

Table 3: The number of valid sentences in the Faroese synthetic treebank for each source language after annotation projection and sentence filtering.

formed by the monolingual model using Norwegian Nynorsk for projection though the difference is not statistically significant. On the source side, the monolingual Norwegian Nynorsk model also performed slightly better than the polyglot model (Table 2). This observation supports the intuition that the quality of the projected annotations can be improved by contributing better source annotations, i. e. improving the source model(s) is one way to improve performance of the target model. This is supported by the fact that the source lan-

significant).[14] The polyglot model was outper-

---

[14]Statistical significance is tested with udapi-python

LAS differences are reported as significant if $p < 0.05$.

Source Language	Source Model	Target Model	
		Single	Multi
Danish	Monolingual	61.24	63.40
	Polyglot	65.29[†]	**65.53[†]**
Swedish	Monolingual	65.93	66.15
	Polyglot	68.60[†]	**69.69[†]**
Norwegian Nynorsk	Monolingual	70.27	**71.51**
	Polyglot	69.80	71.13
Norwegian Bokmål	Monolingual	67.46	67.94
	Polyglot	70.51[†]	**70.58[†]**
Multi-source	Monolingual	68.00	69.80
	Polyglot	68.55	**70.07**
Average	Monolingual	66.58	67.76
	Polyglot	68.55	**69.40**

Table 4: LAS on the target Faroese test treebank. *Single* refers to using a single synthetic Faroese treebank to train a Faroese model, *Multi* uses both a multi-treebank POS tagger and a multi-treebank parser with all synthetic Faroese treebanks. The multi-treebank model is tested with each of the five training treebanks (four projected from individual source languages and one using multi-source projection) as proxy treebank. Statistically significant differences between the monolingual and polyglot setting are indicated by † for each result pair, excluding averages.

Source Language	Monolingual	Polyglot
Danish	61.13	**64.43**
Swedish	63.19	**67.46**
Norwegian Nynorsk	68.72	**69.28**
Norwegian Bokmål	66.13	**68.77**
Multi-source	68.00	**68.55**
Average	65.43	**67.70**

Table 5: LAS scores between target models trained on the subset of sentences eligible for multi-source projection (with annotations from the stated source).

guage with the highest LAS (Norwegian Bokmål) is also the best choice for projection (in this single target model setting).

The multi-source approach was not that effective in our case and some individual better sources were able to surpass this combination approach. One could argue that this may be due to the lower amount of training data when using the multi-source treebank. We test this hypothesis by only including those sentences which contributed to multi-source projection in the single-source synthetic treebanks. The results are given in Table 5. Comparing the results in Tables 4 and 5, we see that LAS scores tend to be slightly lower than on the version which included all target sen-

Work	Result
Rosa and Mareček (2018)	49.4
Tyers et al. (2018)	64.4
Our implementation of Tyers et al. (2018)	68.0
Our Best Model	**71.5**

Table 6: Comparison to previous work. LAS on Faroese test set. Note that the first results uses predicted segmentation and tokenization whereas the rest used gold.

tences, indicating that we did lose some information by filtering out a large number of sentences. However, Norwegian Nynorsk still outperforms the multi-source model for the monolingual setting and both Norwegian models perform better than the multi-source model in the polyglot setting, suggesting that size alone does not explain the under-performance of the multi-source model. It is also worth noting that polyglot training is superior to all monolingual models which hints that for no_nynorsk (the previously better performing model), the monolingual model was not able to achieve its full potential with the reduced data while the polyglot model was able to provide richer annotations.

Another reason why the multi-source model does not work as well in our experiments as it does in those of Tyers et al. (2018) might be that we use pre-trained embeddings whereas Tyers et al. (2018) do not. In this way, our monolingual models are stronger and likely do not benefit as much from voting.

The second result column (MULTI) of Table 4 shows the effect of training a multi-treebank POS tagger and parser on the Faroese treebanks created by each of the four source languages as well as the treebank which is produced by multi-source projection. This experiment is orthogonal to the experiment using a polyglot model on the source side and so we also test a combination of polyglot source side parsing and multi-treebank target side parsing. We see improvements over the single treebank setting for all cases.[15]

---

[15]The multi-treebank tagger closely resembles the dependency parser, where we add a treebank embedding and optimize for average accuracy across the included treebanks. To the best of our knowledge, this is the first reported use of a multi-treebank POS tagger using a treebank embedding (Stymne et al., 2018). We also tested the effect of training only the dependency parser using multiple treebanks

Table 6 places our systems in the context of previous results on the same Faroese test set. The highest scoring system in the 2018 CoNLL shared task was that of Rosa and Mareček (2018) who achieved a LAS score of 49.4 on the Faroese test set. Note that they use predicted tokenization and segmentation whereas our experiments and Tyers et al.'s use gold tokenization and segmentation, which provides a small artificial boost. Tyers et al. (2018) report an LAS of 64.43 with a monolingual multi-source approach. Our implementation which uses a different parser (AllenNLP versus UDPipe) and pre-trained word embeddings achieves an LAS of 68. Our highest score of 71.51 is achieved through the combination of projecting from strong monolingual source models and then training multi-treebank POS tagging and parsing models on the outputs.

5   Conclusion

We have presented parsing results on Faroese, a low-resource language, using annotation projection from multiple monolingual sources versus a single polyglot model. We also extended the idea of multi-treebank learning to the target treebanks.

The results of our experiments show that the use of a polyglot source model helps in four out of five cases using single treebank target models. The two source languages that have lowest LAS when using monolingual parsers, namely Danish and Swedish, see significant improvements when switching to a polyglot model. Our best performing single target model is trained on Faroese trees projected from Norwegian Bokmål trees produced by a polyglot model. However, the strongest language with monolingual modelling, Norwegian Nynorsk, does not benefit from switching to a polyglot model. When we filtered the target treebank to the subset of sentences selected by multi-source projection, the polyglot model is superior to all five monolingual models, even outperforming the Norwegian Nynorsk model. One explanation of the improvements seen with polyglot modelling is that it introduces a new interaction point for cross-lingual features via the feature extractor of the polyglot parser. With monolingual source models, cross-lingual features only interact indirectly in the graph-decoding stage of multi-source projection.

We also applied the multi-treebank approach to the target-side POS tagger and parser and see improvements for all settings. The overall best result is with the setting that uses monolingual source models to create the source trees that are projected to Faroese and combined in a multi-treebank model. The proxy treebank for the multi-treebank model is the treebank that also gave best results with single treebank target models, projected from Norwegian Nynorsk.

We presented a simple solution to deal with using multiple pre-trained embeddings in a model with a shared vocabulary. It was a rather naïve solution and we want to explore the use of available cross-lingual word embedding tools. Additionally, the use of contextual embeddings such as ELMo (Peters et al., 2018) or multilingual BERT (Devlin et al., 2019) would likely provide better representations, with the effect of contributing better annotations for the target language. Indeed, recent work has already shown promising work in this area (Schuster et al., 2019; Kondratyuk, 2019).

In the multi-source projection experiments, our criteria for filtering is based on whether the sentence was present across all target treebanks and more sophisticated approaches could be used to select better training instances as in Plank and Agić (2018).

More generally, we would like to investigate how our findings might change when the number of source languages or treebanks is changed and how the observations carry over to other languages than Faroese. It would also be interesting to use multiple sources of arc weights in a dense graph as in (Agić et al., 2016) but with models induced from training on multiple source languages together. To work with language pairs with more deviating word orders and/or translations that are not word-for-word, the choice of word alignment algorithm and the projection algorithm may have to be revised.

Acknowledgments

This research is supported by Science Foundation Ireland through the ADAPT Centre for Digital Content Technology, which is funded under the SFI Research Centres Programme (Grant 13/RC/2106) and is co-funded under the European Regional Development Fund. We thank Tyers et al. (2018) for releasing their data and the anonymous reviewers for their helpful feedback.

---

but found that it always helps to also perform multi-treebank training for the POS tagger.

References

Željko Agić, Anders Johannsen, Barbara Plank, Héctor Martínez Alonso, Natalie Schluter, and Anders Søgaard. 2016. Multilingual projection for parsing truly low-resource languages. *Transactions of the Association for Computational Linguistics*, 4:301–312.

Rami Al-Rfou', Bryan Perozzi, and Steven Skiena. 2013. Polyglot: Distributed word representations for multilingual NLP. In *Proceedings of the Seventeenth Conference on Computational Natural Language Learning*, pages 183–192, Sofia, Bulgaria. Association for Computational Linguistics.

Waleed Ammar, George Mulcaire, Miguel Ballesteros, Chris Dyer, and Noah A. Smith. 2016. Many languages, one parser. *Transactions of the Association for Computational Linguistics*, 4:431–444.

Yoeng-Jin Chu and Tseng-Hong Liu. 1965. On the shortest arborescence of a directed graph. *Scientia Sinica*, 14:1396–1400.

Jacob Devlin, Ming-Wei Chang, Kenton Lee, and Kristina Toutanova. 2019. BERT: Pre-training of deep bidirectional transformers for language understanding. In *Proceedings of the 2019 Conference of the North American Chapter of the Association for Computational Linguistics: Human Language Technologies, Volume 1 (Long and Short Papers)*, pages 4171–4186, Minneapolis, Minnesota. Association for Computational Linguistics.

Timothy Dozat and Christopher D. Manning. 2017. Deep biaffine attention for neural dependency parsing. In *Proceedings of the 5th International Conference on Learning Representations (ICLR 2017)*.

Chris Dyer, Victor Chahuneau, and Noah A. Smith. 2013. A simple, fast, and effective reparameterization of IBM model 2. In *Proceedings of the 2013 Conference of the North American Chapter of the Association for Computational Linguistics: Human Language Technologies*, pages 644–648, Atlanta, Georgia. Association for Computational Linguistics.

Jack Edmonds. 1967. Optimum branchings. *Journal of Research of the national Bureau of Standards B*, 71(4):233–240.

Matt Gardner, Joel Grus, Mark Neumann, Oyvind Tafjord, Pradeep Dasigi, Nelson F. Liu, Matthew Peters, Michael Schmitz, and Luke Zettlemoyer. 2018. AllenNLP: A deep semantic natural language processing platform. In *Proceedings of Workshop for NLP Open Source Software (NLP-OSS)*, pages 1–6, Melbourne, Australia. Association for Computational Linguistics.

Alex Graves and Jürgen Schmidhuber. 2005. Framewise phoneme classification with bidirectional lstm and other neural network architectures. *Neural networks*, 18(5-6):602–610.

Jiang Guo, Wanxiang Che, David Yarowsky, Haifeng Wang, and Ting Liu. 2015. Cross-lingual dependency parsing based on distributed representations. In *Proceedings of the 53rd Annual Meeting of the Association for Computational Linguistics and the 7th International Joint Conference on Natural Language Processing (Volume 1: Long Papers)*, pages 1234–1244, Beijing, China. Association for Computational Linguistics.

Rebecca Hwa, Philip Resnik, Amy Weinberg, Clara Cabezas, and Okan Kolak. 2005. Bootstrapping parsers via syntactic projection across parallel texts. *Natural language engineering*, 11(3):311–325.

Daniel Kondratyuk. 2019. 75 languages, 1 model: Parsing universal dependencies universally. *CoRR*, abs/1904.02099.

Teresa Lynn, Jennifer Foster, Mark Dras, and Lamia Tounsi. 2014. Cross-lingual transfer parsing for low-resourced languages: An Irish case study. In *Proceedings of the First Celtic Language Technology Workshop*, pages 41–49, Dublin, Ireland. Association for Computational Linguistics and Dublin City University.

Ryan McDonald, Slav Petrov, and Keith Hall. 2011. Multi-source transfer of delexicalized dependency parsers. In *Proceedings of the 2011 Conference on Empirical Methods in Natural Language Processing*, pages 62–72, Edinburgh, Scotland, UK. Association for Computational Linguistics.

Ailsa Meechan-Maddon and Joakim Nivre. 2019. How to parse low-resource languages: Cross-lingual parsing, target language annotation, or both? In *Proceedings of DepLing*.

Tomas Mikolov, Ilya Sutskever, Kai Chen, Greg S Corrado, and Jeff Dean. 2013. Distributed representations of words and phrases and their compositionality. In *Advances in neural information processing systems*, pages 3111–3119.

Phoebe Mulcaire, Jungo Kasai, and Noah A. Smith. 2019. Polyglot contextual representations improve crosslingual transfer. In *Proceedings of the 2019 Conference of the North American Chapter of the Association for Computational Linguistics: Human Language Technologies, Volume 1 (Long and Short Papers)*, pages 3912–3918, Minneapolis, Minnesota. Association for Computational Linguistics.

Joakim Nivre, Mitchell Abrams, Željko Agić, Lars Ahrenberg, Lene Antonsen, Maria Jesus Aranzabe, Gashaw Arutie, Masayuki Asahara, Luma Ateyah, Mohammed Attia, Aitziber Atutxa, Liesbeth Augustinus, Elena Badmaeva, Miguel Ballesteros, Esha Banerjee, Sebastian Bank, Verginica Barbu Mititelu, John Bauer, Sandra Bellato, Kepa Bengoetxea, Riyaz Ahmad Bhat, Erica Biagetti, Eckhard Bick, Rogier Blokland, Victoria Bobicev, Carl Börstell, Cristina Bosco, Gosse Bouma, Sam Bowman, Adriane Boyd, Aljoscha Burchardt, Marie

Candito, Bernard Caron, Gauthier Caron, Gülşen Cebiroğlu Eryiğit, Giuseppe G. A. Celano, Savas Cetin, Fabricio Chalub, Jinho Choi, Yongseok Cho, Jayeol Chun, Silvie Cinková, Aurélie Collomb, Çağrı Çöltekin, Miriam Connor, Marine Courtin, Elizabeth Davidson, Marie-Catherine de Marneffe, Valeria de Paiva, Arantza Diaz de Ilarraza, Carly Dickerson, Peter Dirix, Kaja Dobrovoljc, Timothy Dozat, Kira Droganova, Puneet Dwivedi, Marhaba Eli, Ali Elkahky, Binyam Ephrem, Tomaž Erjavec, Aline Etienne, Richárd Farkas, Hector Fernandez Alcalde, Jennifer Foster, Cláudia Freitas, Katarína Gajdošová, Daniel Galbraith, Marcos Garcia, Moa Gärdenfors, Kim Gerdes, Filip Ginter, Iakes Goenaga, Koldo Gojenola, Memduh Gökırmak, Yoav Goldberg, Xavier Gómez Guinovart, Berta Gonzáles Saavedra, Matias Grioni, Normunds Grūzītis, Bruno Guillaume, Céline Guillot-Barbance, Nizar Habash, Jan Hajič, Jan Hajič jr., Linh Hà Mỹ, Na-Rae Han, Kim Harris, Dag Haug, Barbora Hladká, Jaroslava Hlaváčová, Florinel Hociung, Petter Hohle, Jena Hwang, Radu Ion, Elena Irimia, Tomáš Jelínek, Anders Johannsen, Fredrik Jørgensen, Hüner Kaşıkara, Sylvain Kahane, Hiroshi Kanayama, Jenna Kanerva, Tolga Kayadelen, Václava Kettnerová, Jesse Kirchner, Natalia Kotsyba, Simon Krek, Sookyoung Kwak, Veronika Laippala, Lorenzo Lambertino, Tatiana Lando, Septina Dian Larasati, Alexei Lavrentiev, John Lee, Phng Lê H`ông, Alessandro Lenci, Saran Lertpradit, Herman Leung, Cheuk Ying Li, Josie Li, Keying Li, KyungTae Lim, Nikola Ljubešić, Olga Loginova, Olga Lyashevskaya, Teresa Lynn, Vivien Macketanz, Aibek Makazhanov, Michael Mandl, Christopher Manning, Ruli Manurung, Cătălina Mărănduc, David Mareček, Katrin Marheinecke, Héctor Martínez Alonso, André Martins, Jan Mašek, Yuji Matsumoto, Ryan McDonald, Gustavo Mendonça, Niko Miekka, Anna Missilä, Cătălin Mititelu, Yusuke Miyao, Simonetta Montemagni, Amir More, Laura Moreno Romero, Shinsuke Mori, Bjartur Mortensen, Bohdan Moskalevskyi, Kadri Muischnek, Yugo Murawaki, Kaili Müürisep, Pinkey Nainwani, Juan Ignacio Navarro Horñiacek, Anna Nedoluzhko, Gunta Nešpore-Bērzkalne, Lng Nguy˜ên Thị, Huy`ên Nguy˜ên Thị Minh, Vitaly Nikolaev, Rattima Nitisaroj, Hanna Nurmi, Stina Ojala, Adédayo Olúòkun, Mai Omura, Petya Osenova, Robert Östling, Lilja Øvrelid, Niko Partanen, Elena Pascual, Marco Passarotti, Agnieszka Patejuk, Siyao Peng, Cenel-Augusto Perez, Guy Perrier, Slav Petrov, Jussi Piitulainen, Emily Pitler, Barbara Plank, Thierry Poibeau, Martin Popel, Lauma Pretkalniņa, Sophie Prévost, Prokopis Prokopidis, Adam Przepiórkowski, Tiina Puolakainen, Sampo Pyysalo, Andriela Rääbis, Alexandre Rademaker, Loganathan Ramasamy, Taraka Rama, Carlos Ramisch, Vinit Ravishankar, Livy Real, Siva Reddy, Georg Rehm, Michael Rießler, Larissa Rinaldi, Laura Rituma, Luisa Rocha, Mykhailo Romanenko, Rudolf Rosa, Davide Rovati, Valentin Roca, Olga Rudina, Shoval Sadde, Shadi Saleh, Tanja Samardžić, Stephanie Samson, Manuela Sanguinetti, Baiba Saulīte, Yanin Sawanakunanon, Nathan Schneider, Sebastian Schuster, Djamé Seddah, Wolfgang Seeker, Mojgan Seraji, Mo Shen, Atsuko Shimada, Muh Shohibussirri, Dmitry Sichinava, Natalia Silveira, Maria Simi, Radu Simionescu, Katalin Simkó, Mária Šimková, Kiril Simov, Aaron Smith, Isabela Soares-Bastos, Antonio Stella, Milan Straka, Jana Strnadová, Alane Suhr, Umut Sulubacak, Zsolt Szántó, Dima Taji, Yuta Takahashi, Takaaki Tanaka, Isabelle Tellier, Trond Trosterud, Anna Trukhina, Reut Tsarfaty, Francis Tyers, Sumire Uematsu, Zdeňka Urešová, Larraitz Uria, Hans Uszkoreit, Sowmya Vajjala, Daniel van Niekerk, Gertjan van Noord, Viktor Varga, Veronika Vincze, Lars Wallin, Jonathan North Washington, Seyi Williams, Mats Wirén, Tsegay Woldemariam, Tak-sum Wong, Chunxiao Yan, Marat M. Yavrumyan, Zhuoran Yu, Zdeněk Žabokrtský, Amir Zeldes, Daniel Zeman, Manying Zhang, and Hanzhi Zhu. 2018. Universal dependencies 2.2. LINDAT/CLARIN digital library at the Institute of Formal and Applied Linguistics (ÚFAL), Faculty of Mathematics and Physics, Charles University.

Joakim Nivre, Johan Hall, Sandra Kübler, Ryan McDonald, Jens Nilsson, Sebastian Riedel, and Deniz Yuret. 2007. The CoNLL 2007 shared task on dependency parsing. In *Proceedings of the CoNLL Shared Task Session of EMNLP-CoNLL 2007*, pages 915–932, Prague, Czech Republic. Association for Computational Linguistics.

Matthew Peters, Mark Neumann, Mohit Iyyer, Matt Gardner, Christopher Clark, Kenton Lee, and Luke Zettlemoyer. 2018. Deep contextualized word representations. In *Proceedings of the 2018 Conference of the North American Chapter of the Association for Computational Linguistics: Human Language Technologies, Volume 1 (Long Papers)*, pages 2227–2237, New Orleans, Louisiana. Association for Computational Linguistics.

Barbara Plank and Željko Agić. 2018. Distant supervision from disparate sources for low-resource part-of-speech tagging. In *Proceedings of the 2018 Conference on Empirical Methods in Natural Language Processing*, pages 614–620, Brussels, Belgium. Association for Computational Linguistics.

Barbara Plank, Anders Søgaard, and Yoav Goldberg. 2016. Multilingual part-of-speech tagging with bidirectional long short-term memory models and auxiliary loss. In *Proceedings of the 54th Annual Meeting of the Association for Computational Linguistics (Volume 2: Short Papers)*, pages 412–418, Berlin, Germany. Association for Computational Linguistics.

Rudolf Rosa and David Mareček. 2018. CUNI x-ling: Parsing under-resourced languages in CoNLL 2018 UD shared task. In *Proceedings of the CoNLL 2018 Shared Task: Multilingual Parsing from Raw Text to Universal Dependencies*, pages 187–196, Brussels, Belgium. Association for Computational Linguistics.

Kenji Sagae and Alon Lavie. 2006. Parser combination by reparsing. In *Proceedings of the Human Language Technology Conference of the NAACL, Companion Volume: Short Papers*, pages 129–132, New York City, USA. Association for Computational Linguistics.

Michael Schlichtkrull and Anders Søgaard. 2017. Cross-lingual dependency parsing with late decoding for truly low-resource languages. In *Proceedings of the 15th Conference of the European Chapter of the Association for Computational Linguistics: Volume 1, Long Papers*, pages 220–229, Valencia, Spain. Association for Computational Linguistics.

Tal Schuster, Ori Ram, Regina Barzilay, and Amir Globerson. 2019. Cross-lingual alignment of contextual word embeddings, with applications to zero-shot dependency parsing. In *Proceedings of the 2019 Conference of the North American Chapter of the Association for Computational Linguistics: Human Language Technologies, Volume 1 (Long and Short Papers)*, pages 1599–1613, Minneapolis, Minnesota. Association for Computational Linguistics.

Aaron Smith, Bernd Bohnet, Miryam de Lhoneux, Joakim Nivre, Yan Shao, and Sara Stymne. 2018. 82 treebanks, 34 models: Universal dependency parsing with multi-treebank models. In *Proceedings of the CoNLL 2018 Shared Task: Multilingual Parsing from Raw Text to Universal Dependencies*, pages 113–123, Brussels, Belgium. Association for Computational Linguistics.

Milan Straka and Jana Straková. 2017. Tokenizing, POS tagging, lemmatizing and parsing UD 2.0 with UDPipe. In *Proceedings of the CoNLL 2017 Shared Task: Multilingual Parsing from Raw Text to Universal Dependencies*, pages 88–99, Vancouver, Canada. Association for Computational Linguistics.

Sara Stymne, Miryam de Lhoneux, Aaron Smith, and Joakim Nivre. 2018. Parser training with heterogeneous treebanks. In *Proceedings of the 56th Annual Meeting of the Association for Computational Linguistics (Volume 2: Short Papers)*, pages 619–625. Association for Computational Linguistics.

Jörg Tiedemann. 2016. Opus–parallel corpora for everyone. *Baltic Journal of Modern Computing*, page 384.

Jrg Tiedemann and Željko Agić. 2016. Synthetic treebanking for cross-lingual dependency parsing. *Journal of Artificial Intelligence Research*, 5.

Francis Tyers, Mariya Sheyanova, Aleksandra Martynova, Pavel Stepachev, and Konstantin Vinogorodskiy. 2018. Multi-source synthetic treebank creation for improved cross-lingual dependency parsing. In *Proceedings of the Second Workshop on Universal Dependencies (UDW 2018)*, pages 144–150, Brussels, Belgium. Association for Computational Linguistics.

David Vilares, Carlos Gómez-Rodríguez, and Miguel A. Alonso. 2016. One model, two languages: training bilingual parsers with harmonized treebanks. In *Proceedings of the 54th Annual Meeting of the Association for Computational Linguistics (Volume 2: Short Papers)*, pages 425–431, Berlin, Germany. Association for Computational Linguistics.

David Yarowsky, Grace Ngai, and Richard Wicentowski. 2001. Inducing multilingual text analysis tools via robust projection across aligned corpora. In *Proceedings of the first international conference on Human language technology research*, pages 1–8. Association for Computational Linguistics.

Daniel Zeman, Jan Hajič, Martin Popel, Martin Potthast, Milan Straka, Filip Ginter, Joakim Nivre, and Slav Petrov. 2018. CoNLL 2018 shared task: Multilingual parsing from raw text to universal dependencies. In *Proceedings of the CoNLL 2018 Shared Task: Multilingual Parsing from Raw Text to Universal Dependencies*, pages 1–21, Brussels, Belgium. Association for Computational Linguistics.

Daniel Zeman, Martin Popel, Milan Straka, Jan Hajic, Joakim Nivre, Filip Ginter, Juhani Luotolahti, Sampo Pyysalo, Slav Petrov, Martin Potthast, Francis Tyers, Elena Badmaeva, Memduh Gokirmak, Anna Nedoluzhko, Silvie Cinkova, Jan Hajic jr., Jaroslava Hlavacova, Václava Kettnerová, Zdenka Uresova, Jenna Kanerva, Stina Ojala, Anna Missilä, Christopher D. Manning, Sebastian Schuster, Siva Reddy, Dima Taji, Nizar Habash, Herman Leung, Marie-Catherine de Marneffe, Manuela Sanguinetti, Maria Simi, Hiroshi Kanayama, Valeria de-Paiva, Kira Droganova, Héctor Martínez Alonso, Çağr Çöltekin, Umut Sulubacak, Hans Uszkoreit, Vivien Macketanz, Aljoscha Burchardt, Kim Harris, Katrin Marheinecke, Georg Rehm, Tolga Kayadelen, Mohammed Attia, Ali Elkahky, Zhuoran Yu, Emily Pitler, Saran Lertpradit, Michael Mandl, Jesse Kirchner, Hector Fernandez Alcalde, Jana Strnadová, Esha Banerjee, Ruli Manurung, Antonio Stella, Atsuko Shimada, Sookyoung Kwak, Gustavo Mendonca, Tatiana Lando, Rattima Nitisaroj, and Josie Li. 2017. Conll 2017 shared task: Multilingual parsing from raw text to universal dependencies. In *Proceedings of the CoNLL 2017 Shared Task: Multilingual Parsing from Raw Text to Universal Dependencies*, pages 1–19, Vancouver, Canada. Association for Computational Linguistics.

Daniel Zeman and Philip Resnik. 2008. Cross-language parser adaptation between related languages. In *Proceedings of the IJCNLP-08 Workshop on NLP for Less Privileged Languages*.

Inject Rubrics into Short Answer Grading System

Tianqi Wang[1,3]   **Naoya Inoue**[1,3]   **Hiroki Ouchi**[3]   **Tomoya Mizumoto**[2,3]   **Kentaro Inui**[1,3]

[1] Tohoku University   [2] Future Corporation   [3] RIKEN Center for Advanced Intelligence Project
{outenki, naoya-i, inui}@ecei.tohoku.ac.jp
hiroki.ouchi@riken.jp
t.mizumoto.yb@future.co.jp

Abstract

Short Answer Grading (SAG) is a task of scoring students' answers in examinations. Most existing SAG systems predict scores based only on the answers, including the model (Riordan et al., 2017) used as baseline in this paper, which gives the-state-of-the-art performance. But they ignore important evaluation criteria such as rubrics, which play a crucial role for evaluating answers in real-world situations. In this paper, we present a method to inject information from rubrics into SAG systems. We implement our approach on top of word-level attention mechanism to introduce the rubric information, in order to locate information in each answer that are highly related to the score. Our experimental results demonstrate that injecting rubric information effectively contributes to the performance improvement and that our proposed model outperforms the state-of-the-art SAG model on the widely used ASAP-SAS dataset under low-resource settings.

1 Introduction

Short Answer Grading (SAG) is the task of automatically evaluating the correctness of students' answers to a given prompt in an examination (Mohler et al., 2011). It would be beneficial particularly in an educational context where teachers' availability is limited (Mohler and Mihalcea, 2009). Motivated by this background, SAG has been studied mainly with machine learning-based approaches, where the task is considered as inducing a regression model from a given set of manually scored sample answers (i.e., training instances). As observed in a variety of other NLP tasks, recently proposed neural models have been yielding strong results (Riordan et al., 2017).

In general, a prompt is provided along with a scoring rubric. Figure 1 shows a typical example. Students are required to answer the steps involved

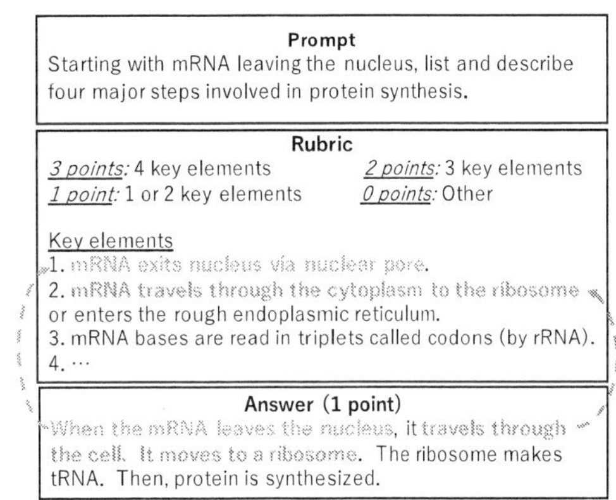

Figure 1: Example prompt and rubric from the ASAP-SAS dataset.

in protein synthesis. Each answer is scored based on a rubric, which contains several scoring criteria called *key elements*. Each of them stipulates different aspects of the conditions for an answer to gain a score. Based on the number of the key elements mentioned in an answer, its final score is determined. In Figure 1, the answer mentions two key elements, so it gains 1 point. Thus, rubrics and key elements play an essential role in SAG. Few previous studies, however, use information from rubrics for SAG.

In this paper, we present a method to incorporate rubric information into neural SAG models. Our idea is to enable neural models to capture alignments between an answer and each key element. Specifically, we use a word-level attention mechanism to compute alignments and generate an attentional feature vector for each pair of an answer and a key element.

The contributions of this study is summarized as follows:

- This is the first study that explores how to incorporate rubric information into neural SAG

Proceedings of the 2nd Workshop on Deep Learning Approaches for Low-Resource NLP (DeepLo), pages 175–182
Hong Kong, China, November 3, 2019. ©2019 Association for Computational Linguistics
https://doi.org/10.18653/v1/P17

models.

- We propose a general framework to extend existing neural SAG models with a component for exploiting rubric information.
- Our empirical evaluation shows that our proposed model achieves a significant performance improvement particularly in low-resource settings.

2   Related Work

A lot of existing SAG studies have a main interest in exploring better representations of answers and similarity measures between student answers and reference answers. A wide variety of methods have been explored so far, ranging from Latent Semantic Analysis (LSA) (Mohler et al., 2011), edit distance-based similarity, and knowledge-based similarity using WordNet (Pedersen et al., 2004) (Magooda et al., 2016) to word embedding-based similarity (Sultan et al., 2016). Recently, Riordan et al. (2017) report that neural network-based feature representation learning (Taghipour and Ng, 2016) is effective for SAG.

In contrast to the popularity of learning answer representations, the use of rubric information for SAG has been gained little attention so far. In Sakaguchi et al. (2015), the authors compute similarities, such as BLEU (Papineni et al., 2002), between an answer and each key element in a rubric, and use them as features in a support vector regression (SVR) model. Ramachandran et al. (2015). Ramachandran et al. (2015) generates text patterns from top answers and rubrics, and reports the automatically generated pattern performances better than manually generated regex pattern. Nevertheless, it still remains an open issue (i) whether a rubric is effective or not even in the context of a neural representation learning paradigm (Riordan et al., 2017), and (ii) what kinds of neural architectures should be employed for the efficient use of rubrics.

Another issue in SAG is on low-resource settings. Heilman and Madnani (2015) investigate the importance of the training data size on non-neural SAG models with discrete features. Horbach and Palmer (2016) show that active learning is effective for increasing useful training instances. This is orthogonal to our approach: combining active learning with our rubric-aware SAG model is an interesting future direction.

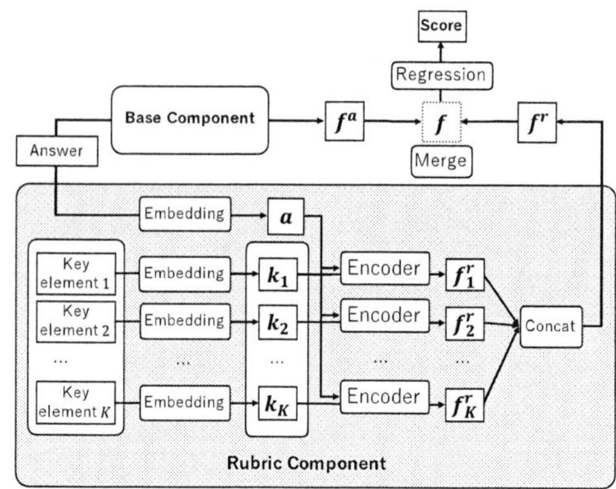

Figure 2: The proposed rubric-aware SAG architecture, consisting of base component and rubric component.

3   Proposed model

3.1   Overall architecture

Figure 2 illustrates our proposed model, which consists of (i) *base component* and (ii) *rubric component*.

We assume the base component encodes an answer into a feature vector f^a. We also assume that a given rubric stipulates a set of key elements in natural language. We build a *rubric component* to encode rubric information, based on the relevance between the answer a and each key element $k \in \{k_1, k_2, \cdots, k_K\}$ provided in the rubric.

The rubric component first encodes each key element that consists of m words, $k = (w_1, w_2, \cdots, w_m)$, into its feature vector k and the answer a into a. Then, it computes the relevance between the given answer a and each key element $k \in \{k_1, k_2, \cdots, k_K\}$ using a word-level attention mechanism, and generates attentional feature vectors $f_1^r, \cdots, f_K^r$, which represent the aggregated information of each key element. A rubric feature f^r is generated based on the obtained K attentional feature vectors. Finally, f^a and f^r are merged into one vector f, which is used for scoring:

$$\text{score}(a) = \beta \, \text{sigmoid}(w \cdot f + b), \quad (1)$$

where w is a parameter vector, β is a prompt-specific scaling constant, and b is a bias term.

Note that the model does not require explicit annotation of key elements on the training answer samples because the model implicitly estimates which key elements are included in each student answer in the course of training. It is also

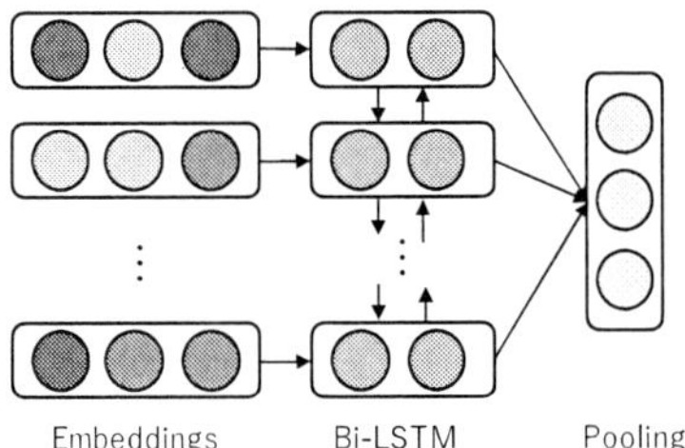

Figure 3: The base component.

important to note that our framework is encoder-agnostic; namely, any answer encoder that produces a fixed-length feature vector can be used as the base component.

3.2 Base component

As the base component, we employ the neural SAG model proposed by Riordan et al. (2017), which is the state-of-the-art SAG system among published methods. As shown in Figure 3, this model consists of three layers, namely (i) the embedding layer, (ii) the BiLSTM (bidirectional Long Short-Term Memory (Schuster and Paliwal, 1997)) layer and (iii) the pooling layer.

Given an answer $a = (w_1, w_2, ..., w_n)$, the embedding layer outputs a vector $e_i^a \in \mathbb{R}^d$ for each word w_i. Taking a sequence of these vectors $(e_1^a, e_2^a, \cdots, e_n^a)$ as input, the BiLSTM layer then produces a contextualized vector $f_i^a = [\overrightarrow{h_i}; \overleftarrow{h_i}]$ for each word, where $\overrightarrow{h_i} \in \mathbb{R}^h$, $\overleftarrow{h_i} \in \mathbb{R}^h$ are the hidden states of the forward and backward LSTM, respectively. Finally, the pooling layer averages these contextualized vectors to obtain a feature vector for the answer as follows:

$$f^a = \frac{1}{n} \sum_{i=1}^{n} f_i^a \qquad (2)$$

3.3 Rubric component

Inspired by Chen et al. (2016), we compute word-level attention between each key element and an given answer as illustrated in Figure 4. The rubric component captures how relevant a key element is to the given answer in this way.

Given word embedding sequences of an answer $(e_1^a, e_2^a, \cdots, e_n^a)$ and a key element $(e_1^k, e_2^k, \cdots, e_m^k)$, the rubric component first calculates the word-level attention between e_i^k and e_j^a:

- Calculate the inner-products between word

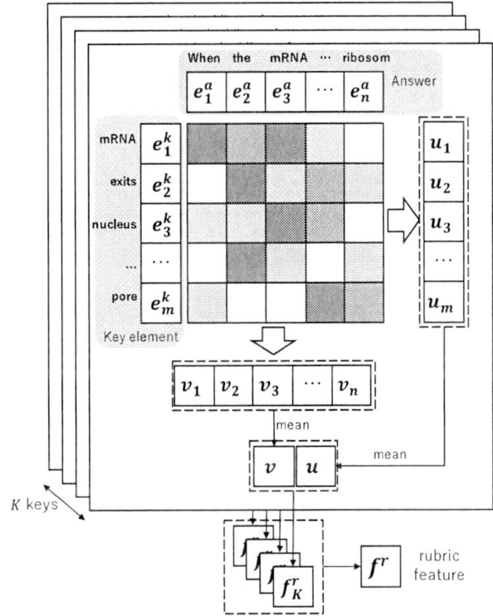

Figure 4: Calculation of rubric feature based on word-level attention. Words of answers lay on x-axes, and words of the key elements lay on y-axes.

embeddings from the answer and key element: $z_{i,j} = e_i^k \cdot e_j^a$

- Calculate softmax of $z_{i,j}$ over the rows and columns respectively:

$$\alpha_i^k = \mathrm{softmax}(z_{i,1}, z_{i,2}, \cdots, z_{i,n}) \qquad (3)$$
$$\alpha_j^a = \mathrm{softmax}(z_{1,j}, z_{2,j}, \cdots, z_{m,j}) \qquad (4)$$

Note that $\alpha_i^k \in \mathbb{R}^n$ stands for the attention from the i-th word of a key element to each word in the answer a. Similarly, $\alpha_j^a \in \mathbb{R}^m$ stands for the attention from the j-th word of answer to each word in the key element k.

Next, attentional vectors of key-to-answer (v) and answer-to-key (u) are calculated by the sum of word embeddings weighted by α^a and α^k as follows:

$$u = \frac{1}{m} \sum_{i=1}^{m} \sum_{j=1}^{n} \alpha_{i,j}^k e_j^a \qquad (5)$$

$$v = \frac{1}{n} \sum_{j=1}^{n} \sum_{i=1}^{m} \alpha_{j,i}^a e_i^k \qquad (6)$$

Intuitively, vectors u and v are the aggregation of answer tokens that are highly relevant to a key element, and tokens in the key elements that are highly relevant to the answer. We then concatenate u, v to obtain a feature vector for the key element.

Finally, we generate feature vectors $\boldsymbol{f}_1^r, \cdots, \boldsymbol{f}_K^r$ for all key elements in this manner, and then generate rubric feature $\boldsymbol{f}^r$ based on them.

3.4 Merge features

We introduce two methodologies to merge $\boldsymbol{f}^a$ and $\boldsymbol{f}^r$ into one single feature $\boldsymbol{f}$.

Concatenation We concatenate $\boldsymbol{f}^a$ and $\boldsymbol{f}^r$:

$$\boldsymbol{f}^r = [\boldsymbol{f}_1^r; \boldsymbol{f}_2^r; ...; \boldsymbol{f}_K^r] \tag{7}$$

$$\boldsymbol{f} = [\boldsymbol{f}^a; \boldsymbol{f}^r], \boldsymbol{f} \in \mathbb{R}^{2h+2dK} \tag{8}$$

In this case, we expect the regression layer learns weights for the two feature space at the same time.

Weighted Sum Besides, we introduce a trainable parameter λ, which represents the influence of the rubric component. We then generate a rubric-aware answer feature as follows:

$$\boldsymbol{f}^r = \frac{1}{K} \sum_{i=1}^{K} \boldsymbol{f}_i^r \tag{9}$$

$$\boldsymbol{f} = \lambda \boldsymbol{f}^a + (1 - \lambda)(\boldsymbol{f}^r M), \boldsymbol{f} \in \mathbb{R}^{2h} \tag{10}$$

where $M \in \mathbb{R}^{2d \times 2h}$ is a transformation matrix to learn, projecting $\boldsymbol{f}^r$ to the space of $\boldsymbol{f}^a$. To reduce parameters to learn, we compute $\boldsymbol{f}^r$ by average instead of concatenation. λ is initialized with 0.5 in our experiments.

Finally, the answer a is scored as follows: $\text{score}(a) = \beta \text{sigmoid}(\boldsymbol{w} \cdot \boldsymbol{f} + b)$, where $\boldsymbol{w} \in \mathbb{R}^{2h+2dK}$ (or $\boldsymbol{w} \in \mathbb{R}^{2h}$ for 'weighted sum' strategy) is a model parameter, β is a prompt-specific scaling constant, and b is a bias term.

4 Experiments

4.1 Settings

We apply the proposed model on a widely-used, rubric-rich ASAP-SAS dataset[2], which includes 10 prompts, with 2,226 answers for each prompt on average, including around 1,704 training data and 522 test data. In this paper, we choose the prompts 1, 2, 5, 6 and 10, where key elements are explicitly provided in their rubric, and we randomly take 20% of answers from the training data as the development data. On average, we have 1,308 answers as training data, 327 answers as development data and 545 answers as test data.

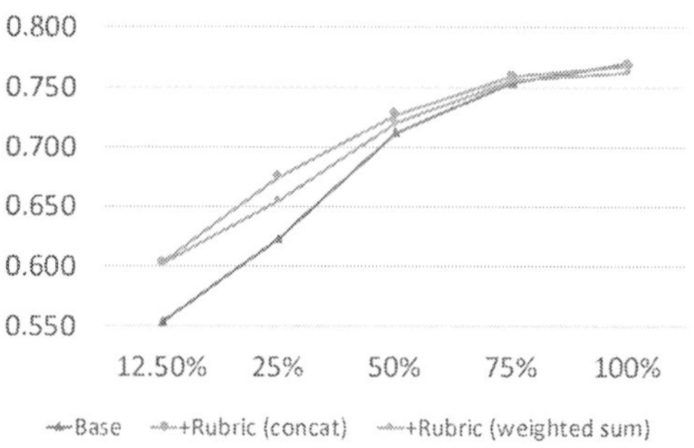

Figure 5: Mean performance across different size of training data. The performance is shown in average QWK over all prompts.

For both the base and rubric components, we use 300-dimensional GloVe embeddings pretrained on Wikipedia and Gigaword5 (Pennington et al., 2014) to initialize the word embedding layer ($d = 300$), and update them during the training phase.

For the bi-LSTM layer of base component, we set $h = 256$, set the dropout probability for linear transformation as 0.5, and set the dropout probability for recurrent state as 0.1, following the setting of (Riordan et al., 2017).

Mean Squared Error (MSE) is used as the loss function, and optimized by RMSprop optimizer with a learning rate of 0.001. The batch size is set to 32.

The model is trained on each prompt. We first train the base component, then fix the base component and train the whole model, and run the training phase for 50 epochs to choose the best model on the development data. For each prompt, we repeat the experiments 5 times with different random seeds from 0 to 4 for initialization, and evaluate the model with Quadratic Weighted Kappa (QWK) independently, then we take average QWK over all the random seeds as the final performance of the model on the corresponding prompt.

To evaluate the robustness of our model in low-resource settings, we train our model on various sizes of the training data (12.5%, 25%, 50%, 75% and 100%).

4.2 Results

The experimental results under different sizes of training data are shown in Figure 5. The performance of the base component ('Base') with 100% training data was 0.770, which is comparable to

Table 1: Performance across different sizes of training data. * indicates a statistically significant improvement by Wilcoxon's signed-rank test ($p < 0.05$).[1] 'B' indicates baseline, and '+R' indicates our model (base component + rubric component)

(a) Merge base feature and rubric feature by concatenation.

Prompt		1	2	5	6	10	mean
12.5%	B	**.588**	.331	.617	.611	**.618**	.553
	+R	.579*	**.408***	**.723***	**.721***	.582*	**.603**
		-.009	+.077.	+.107.	+.110	-.036	+.050
25%	B	**.656**	.473	.641	.627	**.719**	.623
	+R	.652*	**.544***	**.719***	**.743***	.712*	**.674**
		-.004	+.072	+.078	+.116	-.007	+.051
50%	B	**.748**	.637	.748	.718	**.705**	.711
	+R	.745*	**.641**	**.790***	**.756***	.700*	**.726**
		-.003	+.004	+.042	+.038	-.005	+.015
75%	B	.776	**.700**	.798	**.748**	.744	.753
	+R	**.780***	.696	**.803***	.759*	**.755***	**.759**
		+.004	-.004	+.005	-.011	+.011	+.006
100%	B	**.792**	.713	**.804**	.788	**.753**	**.770**
	+R	.784	**.714***	.797*	**.793***	.751	.768
		-.008	+.001	-.008	+.005	-.002	-.002

(b) Merge base feature and rubric feature by weighted sum.

Prompt		1	2	5	6	10	mean
12.5%	B	.588	.331	.617	.611	**.618**	.553
	+R	**.599***	**.424***	**.689***	**.679***	.617	**.602**
		+.012	+.093	+.073	+.068	-.001	+.049
25%	B	.656	.473	.641	.627	**.719**	.623
	+R	**.661***	**.529***	**.687***	**.697***	.698	**.654**
		+.005	+.056	+.046	+.070	-.020	+.031
50%	B	.748	.637	.748	.718	**.705**	.711
	+R	**.747***	**.643**	**.784***	**.723***	.702*	**.720**
		+.000	+.006	+.036	+.006	-.004	+.009
75%	B	.776	.700	**.798**	.748	.744	.753
	+R	**.783***	.704	.787*	**.750***	**.784***	**.762**
		+.007	+.004	-.010	+.002	+.040	+.009
100%	B	.792	.713	**.804**	.788	**.753**	**.770**
	+R	.789	.695*	.786*	**.790***	.748	.762
		-.003	-.018	-.018	+.002	-.005	-.008

the best performance of QWK 0.773 on the corresponding 5 prompts reported in (Riordan et al., 2017). This indicates that we successfully replicated their best performing model.

Also, by adding the rubric component ('+Rubric'), the performance was improved especially when less training data is available. This suggests that the rubric component compensates the lack of training data. This is consistent with (Sakaguchi et al., 2015), a non-neural counter-part of our study.

Performance on each prompt is shown in Table 1. The results indicate that the benefit we obtain from rubric component varies with prompts. For instance, we achieve more improvements on prompt 2, 5 and 6 compared to the others. One of the reasons is that the rubrics vary on prompts. For instance in prompt 5 and 6, all key elements with which an answer can get points are listed, while in prompt 10 only four example answers are provided.

4.3 Analysis

Contribution of components Figure 5 demonstrates that when trained with full training data, our rubric-aware model ('+Rubric') achieved a comparable performance to the base component. To reveal reasons for this, we conduct two analyses.

First, for '+Rubric (concat)', we investigate the distribution of the learned weights of regression layer corresponding to the base and rubric components following the idea from Meftah et al. (2019). The distribution is shown in Figure 6. When the model was trained on 100% training data, the weights for the rubric component were closer to 0, while the weights for the base component were more dispersed (Figure 6b), compared to the distribution for 12.5% training data (Figure 6a).

Second, for '+Rubric (weighted sum)', we plot the values of trained λ in Figure 7, representing the weights of base component. Generally, the values of λ grow with data size, which is consistent with Figure 6. This means that as training data increases, the rubric component makes less contribution to the performance, thus little improvement was obtained from the rubric component. Addressing this issue is an interesting direction of our future research.

Word-level attention To get further insights on the rubric component, we analyzed 1-point answers in the test set. We show two typical examples of 1-point answers in Table 2, where each answer is graded (a) correctly and (b) incorrectly by the system trained with 12.5% training data. Both the two answers are graded incorrectly as 0-points

Table 2: Instance 1-point answers.

ID	Answer	Score	Base	+Rubric
13278	the mRNA gets transcribed, it leaves the nucleus by the ribosomes, then it travels on the Endocplasmic reticulum, and goes to the lysomes and gets translated to proteins.	1	0	1
13174	mRNA leaves the nulceus, travels to the endoplasmic reticulum, then to cell membrane and exits the cell	1	0	0

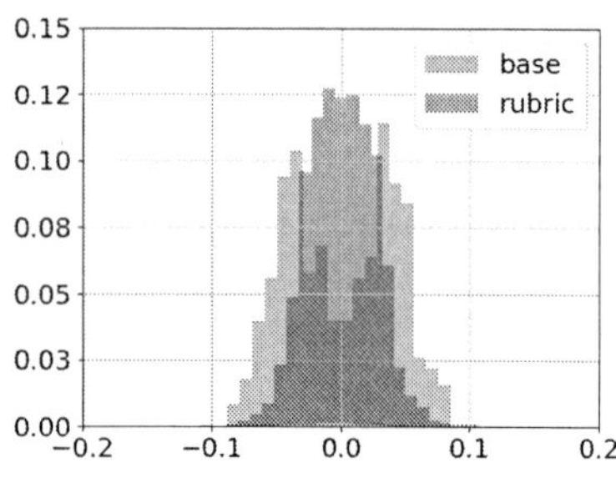

(a) Training data size: 12.5%

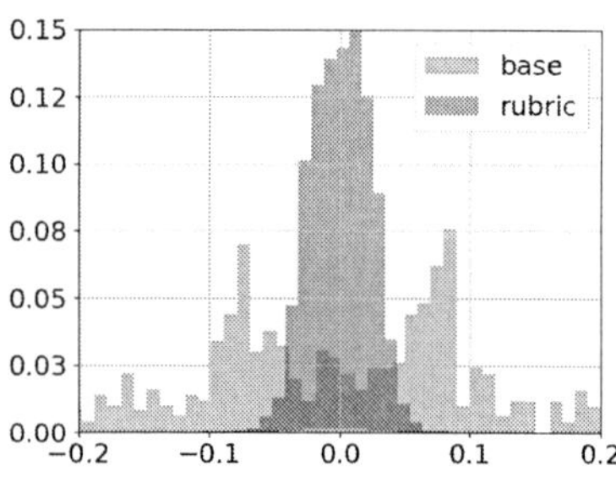

(b) Training data size: 100%

Figure 6: Value distribution of learned weights of regression layer corresponding to base and rubric component for prompt 5.

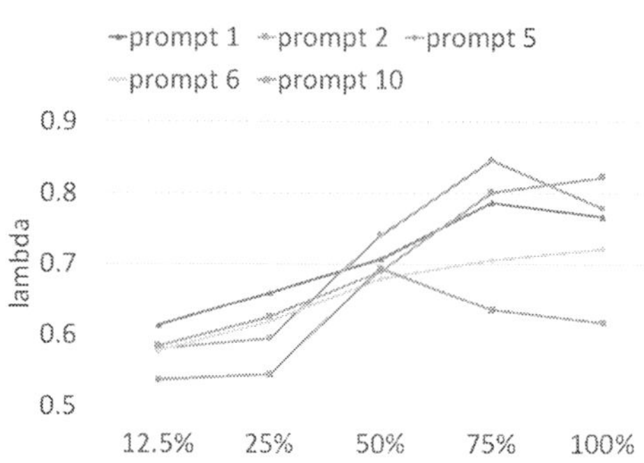

Figure 7: Values of λ trained by various of data size.

by the baseline.

The corresponding prompt and its rubric are shown in Figure 1. Both the answers only contain the first key element provided in rubric. The first answer is graded as 1-point correctly while the second is graded as 0-points.

The word-level attention shown in Figure 8 indicates how the proposed model identified the relevancy of the answer towards the key element. Figure 8a shows that the model successfully found words and phrases most related to the key element, helping the model improve the performance. On the other hand, Figure 8b shows that the model incorrectly aligned words in the answer and key element. Specifically, the model aligned *exists* in the answer with *exists* in the key element. However, these two verbs should *not* be aligned because their objects are different from each other (i.e. *the cell* in the answer, but *nucleus* in the key element). Because the attention is calculated on word-level, the model tends to simply find similar words that appear in the key element, ignoring the context around the words.

5 Conclusion

Rubrics play a crucial role for SAG but have attracted little attention in the SAG community. In this paper, we present an approach for incorporating rubrics into neural SAG models. We replicated a state-of-the-art neural SAG model as the base component, and injected rubrics (key elements) through the rubric component as an extension. In the low-resource setting where the base component had difficulty learning key elements directly from answers, our experimental results showed that the rubric component significantly improved the performance of SAG. When all training data was used, the rubric component did not have a negative effect on the overall performance.

Overall, the proposed model still has much room for improvement. For example, the approach to calculate the alignment between answers and key elements could be improved by taking context into account, instead of using word-level at-

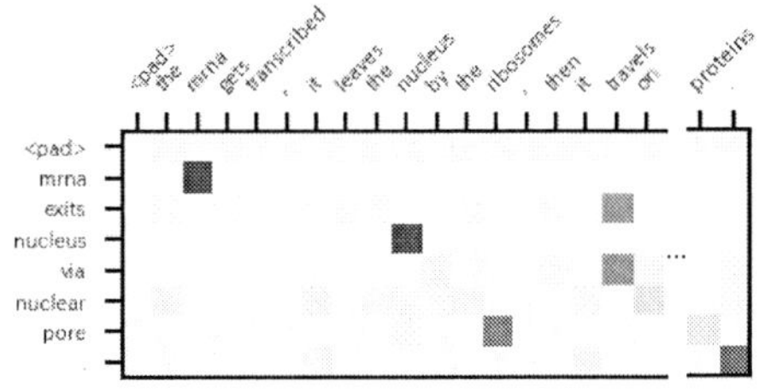

(a) Attention for answer 13278

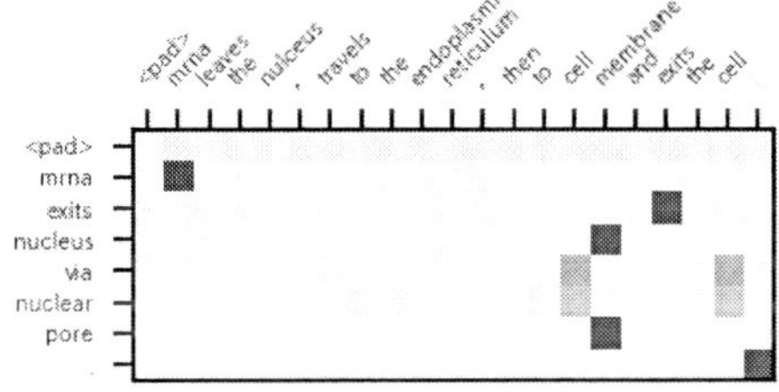

(b) Attention for answer 13174

Figure 8: Word-level attention. Words of answers lay on x-axes, and words of the key element lay on y-axes.

tention. Moreover, other types of rubrics could be explored in the SAG task, especially for prompts where key elements are not provided explicitly. We also expect to obtain a further improvement when full training data is available, by increasing the weights of rubric component feature, as discussed in Figure 6. Beyond SAG, we would like to explore approaches for generating feedback based on the computed attention to key elements.

References

Qian Chen, Xiaodan Zhu, Zhenhua Ling, Si Wei, Hui Jiang, and Diana Inkpen. 2016. Enhanced lstm for natural language inference. *arXiv preprint arXiv:1609.06038*.

Michael Heilman and Nitin Madnani. 2015. The impact of training data on automated short answer scoring performance. In *Proceedings of the Tenth Workshop on Innovative Use of NLP for Building Educational Applications*, pages 81–85.

Andrea Horbach and Alexis Palmer. 2016. Investigating active learning for short-answer scoring. In *Proceedings of the 11th Workshop on Innovative Use of NLP for Building Educational Applications*, pages 301–311.

Ahmed Ezzat Magooda, Mohamed A Zahran, Mohsen Rashwan, Hazem M Raafat, and Magda B Fayek. 2016. Vector based techniques for short answer grading. In *FLAIRS Conference*, pages 238–243.

Sara Meftah, Youssef Tamaazousti, Nasredine Semmar, Hassane Essafi, and Fatiha Sadat. 2019. Joint learning of pre-trained and random units for domain adaptation in part-of-speech tagging. *arXiv preprint arXiv:1904.03595*.

Michael Mohler, Razvan Bunescu, and Rada Mihalcea. 2011. Learning to grade short answer questions using semantic similarity measures and dependency graph alignments. In *Proceedings of the ACL*, pages 752–762. Association for Computational Linguistics.

Michael Mohler and Rada Mihalcea. 2009. Text-to-text semantic similarity for automatic short answer grading. In *Proceedings of the EACL*, pages 567–575. Association for Computational Linguistics.

Kishore Papineni, Salim Roukos, Todd Ward, and Wei-Jing Zhu. 2002. Bleu: a method for automatic evaluation of machine translation. In *Proceedings of the 40th annual meeting on association for computational linguistics*, pages 311–318. Association for Computational Linguistics.

Ted Pedersen, Siddharth Patwardhan, and Jason Michelizzi. 2004. Wordnet:: Similarity: measuring the relatedness of concepts. In *Demonstration papers at HLT-NAACL 2004*, pages 38–41. Association for Computational Linguistics.

Jeffrey Pennington, Richard Socher, and Christopher Manning. 2014. Glove: Global vectors for word representation. In *Proceedings of the 2014 conference on empirical methods in natural language processing (EMNLP)*, pages 1532–1543.

Lakshmi Ramachandran, Jian Cheng, and Peter Foltz. 2015. Identifying patterns for short answer scoring using graph-based lexico-semantic text matching. In *Proceedings of the Tenth Workshop on Innovative Use of NLP for Building Educational Applications*, pages 97–106.

Brian Riordan, Andrea Horbach, Aoife Cahill, Torsten Zesch, and Chong Min Lee. 2017. Investigating neural architectures for short answer scoring. In *Proceedings of the 12th Workshop on Innovative Use of NLP for Building Educational Applications*, pages 159–168.

Keisuke Sakaguchi, Michael Heilman, and Nitin Madnani. 2015. Effective Feature Integration for Automated Short Answer Scoring. In *Proceedings of NAACL*, pages 1049–1054.

Mike Schuster and Kuldip K Paliwal. 1997. Bidirectional recurrent neural networks. *IEEE Transactions on Signal Processing*, 45(11):2673–2681.

Md Arafat Sultan, Cristobal Salazar, and Tamara Sumner. 2016. Fast and easy short answer grading with high accuracy. In *Proceedings of the 2016 Conference of the North American Chapter of the Association for Computational Linguistics: Human Language Technologies*, pages 1070–1075.

Kaveh Taghipour and Hwee Tou Ng. 2016. A neural approach to automated essay scoring. In *Proceedings of the 2016 Conference on Empirical Methods in Natural Language Processing*, pages 1882–1891.

Instance-based Inductive Deep Transfer Learning by Cross-Dataset Querying with Locality Sensitive Hashing

Somnath Basu Roy Chowdhury
IIT Kharagpur
brcsomnath@gmail.com

K M Annervaz
Indian Institute of Science
annervaz@iisc.ac.in

Ambedkar Dukkipati
Indian Institute of Science
ambedkar@iisc.ac.in

Abstract

Supervised learning models are typically trained on a single dataset and the performance of these models rely heavily on the size of the dataset i.e., the amount of data available with ground truth. Learning algorithms try to generalize solely based on the data that it is presented with during the training. In this work, we propose an inductive transfer learning method that can augment learning models by infusing similar instances from different learning tasks in Natural Language Processing (NLP) domain. We propose to use instance representations from a source dataset, *without inheriting anything* else from the source learning model. Representations of the instances of *source* and *target* datasets are learned, retrieval of relevant source instances is performed using soft-attention mechanism and *locality sensitive hashing* and then augmented into the model during training on the target dataset. Therefore, while learning from a training data, we also simultaneously exploit and infuse relevant local *instance-level information* from an external data. Using this approach we have shown significant improvements over the baseline for three major news classification datasets. Experimental evaluations also show that the proposed approach reduces dependency on labeled data by a significant margin for comparable performance. With our proposed cross dataset learning procedure we show that one can achieve competitive/better performance than learning from a single dataset.

1   Introduction

A fundamental issue with performance of supervised learning techniques (like classification) is the requirement of enormous amount of labeled data, which in some scenarios maybe expensive or impossible to acquire. Every supervised task requires a dedicated labeled dataset and training

state-of-the-art deep learning model requires extensive computational power. In this paper, we propose a deep transfer learning method that can enhance the performance of learning models by incorporating information from a secondary dataset belonging to a similar domain.

We present our approach in an *inductive transfer learning* (Pan and Yang, 2010) framework, with a labeled *source* ($\mathcal{D}_S$ domain and task $\mathcal{T}_S$) and *target* ($\mathcal{D}_T$ domain and task $\mathcal{T}_T$) dataset, the aim is to boost the performance of target predictive function $f_T(\cdot)$ using available knowledge in $\mathcal{D}_S$ and $\mathcal{T}_S$, given $\mathcal{T}_S \neq \mathcal{T}_T$. Knowledge transfer in our approach takes place in four ways (a) instance-transfer (b) feature-representation-transfer (c) parameter-transfer and (d) relational-knowledge-transfer. Parameter and relational knowledge transfer are studied exhaustively in inductive transfer literature. Our work is based on a simple inductive bias (also used in (Snell et al., 2017)), that there exists an embedding space where instances belonging to the same class cluster around a central point. We utilize the instance-level information in the source dataset, and also make the newly learnt target instance representation similar to the retrieved source instances. This allows the learning algorithm to improve generalization across the source and target datasets. We use *instance-based learning* that actively looks for similar instances in the source dataset given a target instance. The intuition behind retrieving similar instances comes from instance-based learning perspective, where simplification of the class distribution takes place within the locality of a test instance. As a result, modeling of similar instances become easier (Aggarwal, 2014). Similar instances have the maximum amount of information necessary to classify an unseen instance, as exploited by techniques like k-nearest neighbours.

We derived inspiration to propose this method

Proceedings of the 2nd Workshop on Deep Learning Approaches for Low-Resource NLP (DeepLo), pages 183–191
Hong Kong, China, November 3, 2019. ©2019 Association for Computational Linguistics
https://doi.org/10.18653/v1/P17

from the working of the human brain, where *memory consolidation* (McGaugh, 2000) occurs, in which new memory representations are consolidated slowly over time for efficient retrieval in future. According to (McGaugh, 2000), newly learnt memory representation remain in a fragile state and are affected as further learning takes place. In our approach, we make use of encodings of instances precipitated while training for the source task using an independent model. This model being independently used for an source task and can be adapted as required, is in alignment with memory consolidation in human brain.

One of the attractive features of the proposed method is that the search mechanism allows us to use more than one source dataset during training the joint model to achieve inductive transfer learning. Our approach differs from the standard instance-based learning in two major aspects. First, the instances retrieved are not necessarily from the same dataset, but can be from various secondary datasets. Secondly, our model simultaneously makes use of local instance level information as well as the macro-statistical view point of the dataset, where typical instance-based learning like k-nearest neighbour search make use of only the local instance level information.

2 Background

Locality Sensitive Hashing (LSH): Locality Sensitive Hashing (Gao et al., 2014; Gionis et al., 1999) is an algorithm which performs approximate nearest neighbor similarity search for high-dimensional data in sub-linear time. LSH is a data independent hashing technique as the hash functions are selected at random, which makes LSH perfectly suited for our purpose. Latent vectors encountered during training cannot be accessed, which is required for constructing data-driven hash functions.

The locality sensitive hash family, $\mathcal{H}$ has to satisfy certain constraints mentioned in (Indyk and Motwani, 1998) for nearest neighbor retrieval. The LSH Index maps each point p into a bucket in a hash table with a label $g(p) = (h_1(p), h_2(p), \ldots, h_k(p))$, where $h_1, h_2, \ldots, h_k$ are chosen independently with replacement from $\mathcal{H}$. We generate l different hash functions of length k given by $G_j(p) = (h_{1j}(p), h_{2j}(p), \cdots, h_{kj}(p))$ where $j \in 1, 2, \ldots, l$ denotes the index of the hash table. Given a collection of data points

$\mathcal{C}$, we hash them into l hash tables by concatenating randomly sampled k hash functions from $\mathcal{H}$ for each hash table. While returning the nearest neighbors of a query Q, it is mapped into a bucket in each of the l hash tables. The union of all points in the buckets $G_j(Q), j = 1, 2, \ldots, l$ is returned. Therefore, all points in the collection $\mathcal{C}$ is not scanned and the query is executed in sublinear time. The storage overhead for LSH is subquadratic in n, the number of points in the collection $\mathcal{C}$.

LSH Forests (Bawa et al., 2005) are an improvement over LSH Index which relaxes the constraints on hash family $\mathcal{H}$ with better practical performance guarantees. LSH Forests utilizes l prefix trees (LSH trees) instead of having hash tables, each constructed from independently drawn hash functions from $\mathcal{H}$. The hash function of each prefix tree is of variable length (k) with an upper bound k_m. The length of the hash label of a point is increased whenever a collision occurs to form leaf nodes from the parent node in the LSH tree. For m nearest neighbour query of a point p, the l prefix trees are traversed in a top-down manner to find the leaf node with highest similarity with point p. From the leaf node, we traverse in a bottom-up fashion to collect M points from the forest, where $M = cl$, c being a small constant. It has been shown in (Bawa et al., 2005), that for practical cases the LSH Forests execute each query in constant time with storage cost linear in n, the number of points in the collection $\mathcal{C}$.

Instance-based transfer learning: Instance-based transfer learning has been extensively studied in literature (Zadrozny, 2004) (Gretton et al., 2009) (Huang et al., 2007) (Sugiyama et al., 2008) (Dai et al., 2007). These methods primarily focus on the problem of distribution mismatch between data from two different sources. They also assume that the training instances are sampled from a homogenous distribution and have the same target label space. In our approach, we are not assuming any constraints on the distribution of data or label space, our only assumption is that the datasets should have certain feature overlap in some embedding space. The feature overlap may not necessarily be substantial, as we also enforce the instance representations to be similar using a penalty function. The penalty function performs structural transformation of the feature space, which is usually an attribute of feature-

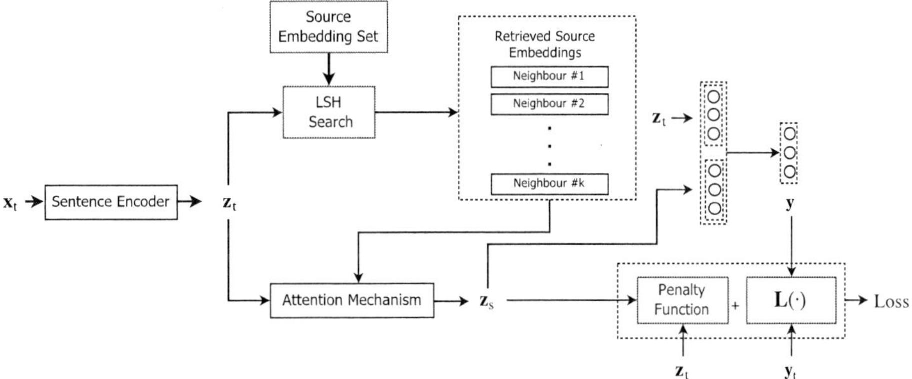

Figure 1: Proposed Model Architecture

based transfer learning methods (Pan et al., 2011).

3 Proposed Model

Given the data x with the ground truth y, supervised learning models aim to find the parameters Θ that maximizes the log-likelihood as

$$\Theta = \underset{\Theta}{\operatorname{argmax}} \log P(y|\mathrm{x}, \Theta). \qquad (1)$$

To augment the learning by infusing similar source instances latent representations, a latent vector from source dataset z_s is retrieved using the data sample x_t (target dataset instance). Thus, our modified objective function can be expressed as

$$\underset{\Theta}{\max} P(y|\mathrm{x}_t, \mathrm{z}_s, \Theta). \qquad (2)$$

To enforce latent representations of the instances to be similar, for better generalization across the tasks, we add a suitable penalty to the objective. The modified objective then becomes,

$$\Theta = \underset{\Theta}{\operatorname{argmax}} \log P(y|\mathrm{x}_t, \mathrm{x}_s, \Theta) - \lambda \mathcal{L}(\mathrm{z}_s, \mathrm{z}_t) \quad (3)$$

where $\mathcal{L}$ is the penalty function and λ (scale-factor) is a hyperparameter.

The subsequent sections focus on the methods to retrieve instance latent vector z_s using the data sample x_t. It is important to note that, we do not assume any structural form for P. Hence the proposed method is applicable to augment any supervised learning setting with any form for P. In the experiments we have used softmax using the bi-LSTM (Greff et al., 2015) encodings of the input as the form for P. Any state of the art text encoding scheme (Le and Mikolov, 2014) can be used

here instead. The schematic representation of the model is shown in Figure 1. In the following section, we discuss the in-detail working of individual modules in Figure 1 and formulation of the penalty function $\mathcal{L}$.

Sentence Encoder: The purpose of this module is to create a vector in some latent space, encoding the semantic context of a sentence from the input sequence of words. The context vector c is obtained from an input sentence which is a sequence of word vectors $\mathbf{x} = (x_1, x_2, \ldots, x_T)$, using a bi-LSTM (Sentence Encoder shown in Figure 1) as

$$h_t = f(x_t, h_{t-1}), \qquad (4)$$

where $h_t \in \mathbb{R}^n$ is the hidden state of the bi-LSTM at time t and n is the embedding size. We combine the states at multiple time steps using a linear function g. We have,

$$o = g(\{h_1, \ldots, h_T\}), \ c = \operatorname{ReLU}(o^T W), \quad (5)$$

where $W \in \mathbb{R}^{n \times m}$ and m is a hyper parameter representing the dimension of the context vector. g in our experiments is set as

$$g(\{h_1, h_2, \ldots, h_T\}) = \frac{1}{T} \sum_{t=1}^{T} h_t. \qquad (6)$$

The bi-LSTM module is responsible for generating the context vector c is pre-trained on the target classification task. A separate bi-LSTM module (sentence encoder for the source dataset) is trained on the source classification task. In our experiments we used similar modules for creating the instance embeddings of the source and target dataset, this is not constrained by the method and different modules can be used here.

Instance Retrieval: Using the obtained context vector c_t (c in Equation 5) corresponding to a target instance as a query, k-nearest neighbours are searched from the source dataset $(z_1^s, z_2^s, \ldots, z_k^s)$ using Locality Sensitive Hashing (LSH). The search mechanism using LSH takes constant time in practical scenario (Bawa et al., 2005) and therefore does not affect the training duration by large margins. Although LSH returns approximate nearest neighbours it doesn't introduce any extra loss (compared to exact nearest neighbour retrieval) in our model, as our objective is to retrieve similar instances in order to determine the class label. Even if the ranking of the instances retrieved are not accurate, retrieving multiple instances (k) reduces the chance of missing out very similar instances. The retrieved source dataset instance embeddings receive attention α_i^z, using soft-attention mechanism based on inner product similarity given as,

$$\alpha_i^z = \frac{\exp(c_t^T z_i^s)}{\sum\limits_{j=1}^{k} \exp(c_t^T z_j^s)}, \quad (7)$$

where $c_t \in \mathbb{R}^m$ and $z_i^s, z_j^s \in \mathbb{R}^m$.

The fused instance embedding vector z_s formed after soft attention mechanism is given by,

$$z_s = \sum\limits_{i=1}^{k} \alpha_i^z z_i^s, \quad (8)$$

where $z_s \in \mathbb{R}^m$. The retrieved instance is concatenated with the context vector c (in Equation 5) as

$$s = [c_t, z_s] \text{ and } y = \text{softmax}(s^T W^{(1)}), \quad (9)$$

where $W^{(1)} \in \mathbb{R}^{2m \times u}$, y is the output of the final target classification task. This model is then trained jointly with the initial parameters from the pre-trained classification module. The pre-training of the classification module is necessary because if we start from a randomly initialized context vector c_t, the LSH Forest retrieves arbitrary vectors and the model as a whole fails to converge. As the error only propagates through the attention values and penalty function it is impossible to simultaneously rectify the query and search results of the hashing mechanism.

It is important to note that the proposed model adds only a limited number of parameters over the baseline model. The extra trainable weight matrix in the model is $W^{(1)} \in \mathbb{R}^{2m \times u}$, adding only $2m \times$

u, where m is the size of the context vector c and u is the number of classes.

Penalty Function: In instance-based learning, a test instance is assigned the label of the majority of its nearest-neighbour instances. This follows from the fact that similar instances belong to the same class distribution. Following the retrieval of latent vector embeddings from the source dataset, the target latent embedding is constrained to be similar to the retrieved source instances. In order to enforce this, we introduce an additional penalty along with the loss function (shown in Figure 1). The modified objective function is given as

$$\min_\theta L(\mathbf{y}, y_t) + \lambda ||z_s - z_t||_F^2 , \quad (10)$$

where $|| \bullet ||_F$ stands for Frobenius norm of a matrix, $\mathbf{y}$ and z_s are the outputs of the model and retrieved latent embedding respectively, y_t is the label, λ is the scale factor and z_t is the latent vector embedding of the target instance. $L(\cdot)$ in the above equation denotes the loss function used to train the model (depicted as $\mathbf{L}(\cdot)$ in Figure 1) and θ denotes the model parameters. The additional penalty term enables the latent vectors to be similar across multiple datasets, which aids performance in the subsequent stages.

4 Experiments & Results

The experiments are designed in a manner to compare the performance of the baseline model with that of external dataset augmented model. A simple *bi-LSTM (target-only)* model is trained without consideration for source-domain instances (no source-instance retrieval branch included into the network), which acts as the baseline. The embeddings of the source instances are also trained using bi-LSTM classifier. The only constraint on the embeddings is that their shape should be same across multiple domain for LSH search to take place. Our experiments shows performance enhancement across several datasets by incorporating relevant instance information from a source dataset in varying setups. Our experiments also illustrate that our proposed model continues to perform better even when the size of training set is reduced, thereby reducing the dependence on labeled data. We also demonstrate the efficacy of our model through latent vector visualizations.

Datasets & Setup: For our experiments, we have chosen three popular publicly-available news classification datasets (a) 20 Newsgroups

METHOD	TARGET SOURCE	NEWS20 BBC		BBC NEWS20		BBC SPORTS BBC	
		Acc	F1	Acc	F1	Acc	F1
Bi-LSTM (*target only*)		65.17	0.6328	91.33	0.9122	84.22	0.8395
Instance-Infused Bi-LSTM		76.44	0.7586	95.35	0.9531	88.78	0.8855
Instance-Infused Bi-LSTM (*with penalty*)		**78.29**	**0.7773**	**96.09**	**0.9619**	**91.56**	**0.9100**

Table 1: Classification accuracies and F1-Scores for news arcticle classifications for different source and target domains. The first row corresponds to the baseline performance trained on the target dataset. The next two rows shows the performance of instance-infusion method with and without the penalty function.

Dataset	Train Size	Test Size	#Classes
News20	18000	2000	20
BBC	2000	225	5
BBC Sports	660	77	5

Table 2: Dataset Specifications

(News20)[1] (Lichman, 2013) (b) BBC[2] (Greene and Cunningham, 2006), (c) BBC Sports[2] (Greene and Cunningham, 2006). The datasets are chosen in such a way that all of them share common domain knowledge and have small number of training examples so that the improvement observed using instance-infusion is significant. The statistics of the three real-world datasets are mentioned in Table 2.

The mentioned datasets do not have a dedicated test set, so the evaluations were performed using *k-fold cross validation* scheme. All performance scores that are reported in this paper are the mean performance over all the folds.

Parameter	News20	BBC	BBC-Sports
Batch size	256	32	16
Learning rate	0.01	0.01	0.01
Word vector dim	300	300	300
Latent dim (m)	50	50	50
#Neighbours (k)	5	5	5
Scale factor (λ)	10^{-4}	10^{-4}	10^{-4}
# Epochs	30	20	20

Table 3: Hyper-parameters which were used in experiments for News20, BBC & BBC-Sports

The word embeddings were randomly initialized and trained along with the model. The learning rate is regulated over the training epochs, it is decreased to 0.3 times its previous value every 10 epochs. The relevant hyper-parameters are listed in Table 3.

Results: Table 1 shows the details results of our approach for all the datasets. The source and target are chosen in such a manner so that the source dataset is able to provide relevant information. In Table 1, we have shown improvements by a high margin for all datasets. For 20Newsgroups the improvement over baseline model is 12%, BBC and BBC Sports datasets show an improvement of 5%. As the proposed approach is independent of the source encoding procedure, the source instance embeddings are kept constant during training, source instances from multiple datasets can be incorporated. In the subsequent sections, we describe various setups to prove the efficacy of our model.

Instance Infusion from Same Dataset: We study the results of using the target dataset as the source for instance retrieval. This setting is same as the conventional instance-based learning setup. However, our approach not only uses the instance based information, but also leverage the macro statistics of the target dataset. The intuition behind this experimental setup is that instances from the same dataset is also useful in modeling other instances especially when a class imbalance exists in the target dataset. In this experimental setup, the *nearest neighbour retrieved is ignored* as it would be same as the instance sample being modeled during training. The performance of this setup is shown in Table 4.

Dataset Reduction with Single Source: We will discuss a set of experiments performed to support our hypothesis that the proposed model is capable of reducing the dependency on labeled instances. In these set of experiments, we show that the cross-dataset augmented models perform sig-

[1] http://qwone.com/ jason/20Newsgroups/
[2] http://mlg.ucd.ie/datasets/bbc.html

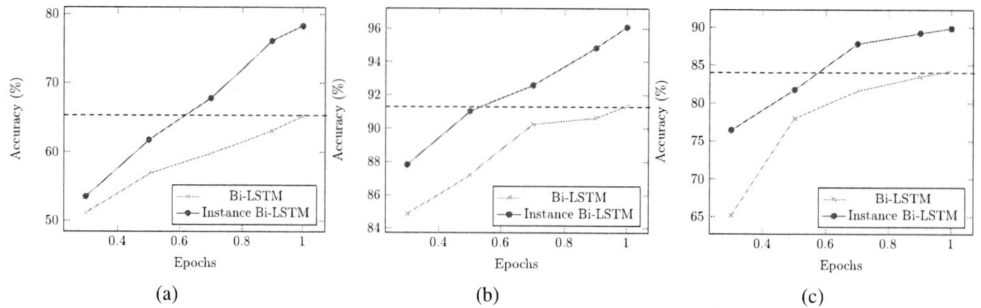

(a)   (b)   (c)

Figure 2: Accuracy Plot over dataset fractions for baseline and proposed model for (a) News20 (b) BBC (c) BBC Sports datasets. The proposed approach (in blue) beats the baseline (in red) performance by a significant margin across varying dataset fractions for all datasets.

Dataset	Acc	F1	Source
News20	77.51	0.7707	News20
BBC	96.17	0.9606	BBC
BBC Sports	90.63	0.8931	BBC Sports

Table 4: Test Accuracy for proposed model using instances from the same target dataset

nificantly better than baseline models when varying fractions of the training data is used. Figure 2 shows the variation of *instance-infused bi-LSTM* and *bi-LSTM (target-only)* performance for 20Newsgroups, BBC and BBC Sports datasets. In these set of experiments 20Newsgroups had BBC, BBC had 20Newsgroup and BBC Sports had BBC as source dataset. As shown in the plot, 0.3, 0.5, 0.7, 0.9 and 1.0 fraction of the dataset are used for performance analysis. The dashed line in the plots indicates the baseline model performance with 100% dataset support. It is observed that the performance of instance-infused bi-LSTM with 70% dataset, is better than the baseline model trained on the entire dataset. This observation shows that our proposed approach is successful in reducing the dependency on the training examples by at least 30% across all datasets.

Dataset Reduction with Multiple Source:. We design an experimental setup in which only 0.5 fraction of the target dataset is utilized and study the influence of multiple source dataset infusion. Table 6 compares the results, when single source and multiple source datasets are used for 50% dataset fraction. The results improves as and when more source datasets are used in the infusion process. This can be effectively leveraged for improving the performance of very lean datasets, by

heavily deploying large datasets as source. For the single source setup, the same source datasets are used as mentioned in results section. In multiple source experiment setup, for a given target dataset the other two datasets are used as source.

Comparative Study: Table 5 gives the experimental results for our proposed approach, baselines and other conventional learning techniques on the 20 Newsgroups, BBC and BBC Sports datasets. Literature involving these datasets mostly focus on non-deep learning based approaches, we compare our results with some popular conventional learning techniques. The experiments involving conventional learning were performed using *scikit-learn* (Pedregosa et al., 2011) library in Python[3]. For the k-NN-ngram experiments, the number of nearest neighbours k was set to 5. In Table 5, the models studied are Multinomial Naive Bayes, k-nearest neighbour classifier, Support Vector Machine (SVM) (Bishop, 2006) and Random Forests Classifier. The input vectors were initialized using n-grams, bi-gram or term frequency-inverse document frequency (tf-idf). For the mentioned datasets, conventional models outperform our baseline Bi-LSTM model, however upon *instance infusion* the deep learning based model is able to achieve competitive performance across all datasets. Moreover by instance infusion the simple bi-LSTM model approaches the classical models in performance on News20 and BBC Sports dataset, whereas on BBC Dataset the proposed instance infused bi-LSTM model beats all the mentioned models. The improvement by instance infusion is 13% for News20, 5% for BBC and 8% for BBC Sports datasets. The

---

[3]https://www.python.org/

MODEL		NEWS20		BBC		BBC SPORTS	
		Accuracy	**F1-Score**	**Accuracy**	**F1-Score**	**Accuracy**	**F1-Score**
k-NN-ngrams		35.25	0.3566	74.61	0.7376	94.59	0.9487
Multinomial NB-bigram		**79.21**	**0.7841**	95.96	0.9575	95.95	0.9560
SVM-bigram		75.04	0.7474	94.83	0.9456	93.92	0.9393
SVM-ngrams		78.60	0.7789	95.06	0.9484	95.95	0.9594
Random Forests-bigram		69.01	0.6906	87.19	0.8652	85.81	0.8604
Random Forests-ngrams		78.36	0.7697	94.83	0.9478	94.59	0.9487
Random Forests- tf-idf		78.6	0.7709	95.51	0.9547	**96.62**	**0.9660**
Bi-LSTM		65.17	0.6328	91.33	0.9122	84.22	0.8395
Instance-Infused Bi-LSTM		78.29	0.7773	**96.09**	**0.9619**	91.56	0.9100

Table 5: Comparison of results using other learning schemes on News20, BBC and BBC Sports datasets. Our approach achieves competitive performance compared to other methods across all datasets.

Dataset	Single Source		Multiple Source	
	Acc	F1	Acc	F1
News20	61.72	0.6133	67.32	0.6650
BBC	91.01	0.9108	91.41	0.9120
BBC Sports	81.72	0.7990	82.81	0.8027

Table 6: Test Accuracy using instances from multiple source datasets with 50% target dataset

important point to note here is that although for News20 dataset we are not able to beat the state of the art(by less than 1%), by instance infusion we are able to improve the performance of the deep learning model by a significant margin of 13%.

Visualization: We show visualizations of latent space embeddings formed using *bi-LSTM (target only)* and with *instance infusion*. In Figure 3, the latent vector embeddings of BBC Sports dataset with News20 support is shown for 0.3 in (a) & (b), 0.5 in (c) & (d) and 0.7 in (e) & (f), fraction of the target training dataset (BBC Sports). Figure 3 (f) is the embeddings representation with 70% data for which best performance (among the 6 visualizations) is observed.

It is evident from the figure that even with 30% and 50% of the data *instance infusion* tries to make the embedding distribution similar to Figure 3 (f) as seen in Figure 3 (b) and (d), when the *bi-LSTM (target-only)* instances representations in Figure 3 (a) and (c) are quite different. This illustrates that

by instance infusion the latent space evolves faster to the better performing shape compared to the scenario where no instance infusion is done.

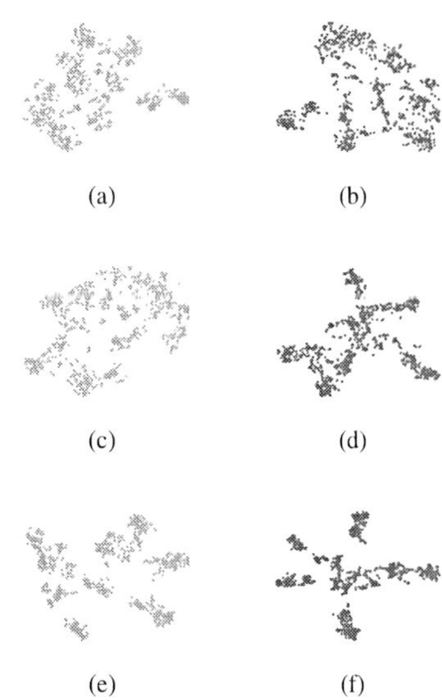

Figure 3: t-SNE visualization of LSTM latent space vectors (in red) and instance-infused embeddings (in blue) of BBC Sports with News20 as source dataset for varying dataset fractions. (a) & (b) show embeddings for 30% data fraction, (c) & (d) for 50% data, and (e) & (f) for 70% data. This figures shows the efficacy of our approach in shaping embedding space which leads to enhanced performance.

5 Related Work

The motivation behind our model comes from memory networks (Graves et al., 2014) that have an augmented long-term memory component and our model follows the general workflow in (Weston et al., 2014; Sukhbaatar et al., 2015). In our work we have incorporated instance level information using content-based attention from support dataset memory. Attention based approaches are widely used in text analysis (Bahdanau et al., 2014; Lin et al., 2017) . This approach has gained popularity in works with limited sample space. (Vinyals et al., 2016) uses a similar approach for one-shot learning however they form inference based on only support instance labels. (Snell et al., 2017) extends the idea to few shot learning in a discriminative manner by measuring distance from a class representative from a support set. (Triantafillou et al., 2017) introduced a scoring function to rank instances in a batch and optimize mean Average Precision (mAP) for few-shot learning. (Edwards and Storkey, 2016) used a generative approach for selecting representative samples for inference.

In our work, like memory network we maintain a fixed long term memory from source dataset but do not perform any modifications to it during training. We sample instances from the memory using content-based similarity but our model does not access labels like few-shot learning techniques. We present our work as a generalized approach for transfer learning across datasets sharing a common domain.

6 Conclusion & Future Work

In this work, we posit that while learning from a training data, infusion of instance level local information from an external data will improve the performance of learning algorithm, which we show through extensive experimentation on our proposed model. Although instance based learning is extensively studied in AI literature, this has rarely been used in a deep learning setup for transfer learning. An aspect of work which can be pursued to improve our setup is to incorporate a sophisticated search paradigm for instance retrieval in order to reduce latency. In this work, we have shown that our method is able to reduce the dependency on labeled data, which can also be extended to analyse performance in an unsupervised setup. Improved feature modification techniques can be augmented along with the search module in order to enhance the query formulation. We also assumed that the datasets share a common domain, in future work means to tackle domain discrepancy needs to be formulated to incorporate instances from a range of datasets.

References

Charu C Aggarwal. 2014. Instance-based learning: A survey.

Dzmitry Bahdanau, Kyunghyun Cho, and Yoshua Bengio. 2014. Neural machine translation by jointly learning to align and translate. *arXiv preprint arXiv:1409.0473*.

Mayank Bawa, Tyson Condie, and Prasanna Ganesan. 2005. Lsh forest: self-tuning indexes for similarity search. In *Proceedings of the 14th international conference on World Wide Web*, pages 651–660. ACM.

Christopher M Bishop. 2006. *Pattern recognition and machine learning*. springer.

Wenyuan Dai, Qiang Yang, Gui-Rong Xue, and Yong Yu. 2007. Boosting for transfer learning. In *Proceedings of the 24th international conference on Machine learning*, pages 193–200. ACM.

Harrison Edwards and Amos Storkey. 2016. Towards a neural statistician. *arXiv preprint arXiv:1606.02185*.

Jinyang Gao, Hosagrahar Visvesvaraya Jagadish, Wei Lu, and Beng Chin Ooi. 2014. Dsh: data sensitive hashing for high-dimensional k-nnsearch. In *Proceedings of the 2014 ACM SIGMOD international conference on Management of data*, pages 1127–1138. ACM.

Aristides Gionis, Piotr Indyk, Rajeev Motwani, et al. 1999. Similarity search in high dimensions via hashing. In *VLDB*, volume 99, pages 518–529.

Alex Graves, Greg Wayne, and Ivo Danihelka. 2014. Neural turing machines. *arXiv preprint arXiv:1410.5401*.

Derek Greene and Pádraig Cunningham. 2006. Practical solutions to the problem of diagonal dominance in kernel document clustering. In *Proceedings of the 23rd International Conference on Machine learning (ICML'06)*, pages 377–384. ACM Press.

Klaus Greff, Rupesh Kumar Srivastava, Jan Koutník, Bas R Steunebrink, and Jürgen Schmidhuber. 2015. Lstm: A search space odyssey. *arXiv preprint arXiv:1503.04069*.

Arthur Gretton, Alexander J Smola, Jiayuan Huang, Marcel Schmittfull, Karsten M Borgwardt, and Bernhard Schölkopf. 2009. Covariate shift by kernel mean matching.

Jiayuan Huang, Arthur Gretton, Karsten M Borgwardt, Bernhard Schölkopf, and Alex J Smola. 2007. Correcting sample selection bias by unlabeled data. In *Advances in neural information processing systems*, pages 601–608.

Piotr Indyk and Rajeev Motwani. 1998. Approximate nearest neighbors: towards removing the curse of dimensionality. In *Proceedings of the thirtieth annual ACM symposium on Theory of computing*, pages 604–613. ACM.

Quoc Le and Tomas Mikolov. 2014. Distributed representations of sentences and documents. In *International Conference on Machine Learning*, pages 1188–1196.

M. Lichman. 2013. UCI machine learning repository.

Zhouhan Lin, Minwei Feng, Cicero Nogueira dos Santos, Mo Yu, Bing Xiang, Bowen Zhou, and Yoshua Bengio. 2017. A structured self-attentive sentence embedding. *arXiv preprint arXiv:1703.03130*.

James L McGaugh. 2000. Memory–a century of consolidation. *Science*, 287(5451):248–251.

Sinno Jialin Pan, Ivor W Tsang, James T Kwok, and Qiang Yang. 2011. Domain adaptation via transfer component analysis. *IEEE Transactions on Neural Networks*, 22(2):199–210.

Sinno Jialin Pan and Qiang Yang. 2010. A survey on transfer learning. *IEEE Transactions on knowledge and data engineering*, 22(10):1345–1359.

F. Pedregosa, G. Varoquaux, A. Gramfort, V. Michel, B. Thirion, O. Grisel, M. Blondel, P. Prettenhofer, R. Weiss, V. Dubourg, J. Vanderplas, A. Passos, D. Cournapeau, M. Brucher, M. Perrot, and E. Duchesnay. 2011. Scikit-learn: Machine learning in Python. *Journal of Machine Learning Research*, 12:2825–2830.

Jake Snell, Kevin Swersky, and Richard Zemel. 2017. Prototypical networks for few-shot learning. In *Advances in Neural Information Processing Systems*, pages 4080–4090.

Masashi Sugiyama, Shinichi Nakajima, Hisashi Kashima, Paul V Buenau, and Motoaki Kawanabe. 2008. Direct importance estimation with model selection and its application to covariate shift adaptation. In *Advances in neural information processing systems*, pages 1433–1440.

Sainbayar Sukhbaatar, Jason Weston, Rob Fergus, et al. 2015. End-to-end memory networks. In *Advances in neural information processing systems*, pages 2440–2448.

Eleni Triantafillou, Richard Zemel, and Raquel Urtasun. 2017. Few-shot learning through an information retrieval lens. In *Advances in Neural Information Processing Systems*, pages 2252–2262.

Oriol Vinyals, Charles Blundell, Tim Lillicrap, Daan Wierstra, et al. 2016. Matching networks for one shot learning. In *Advances in Neural Information Processing Systems*, pages 3630–3638.

Jason Weston, Sumit Chopra, and Antoine Bordes. 2014. Memory networks. *CoRR*, abs/1410.3916.

Bianca Zadrozny Zadrozny. 2004. Learning and evaluating classifiers under sample selection bias. In *In International Conference on Machine Learning ICML04*, pages 903–910.

Multimodal, Multilingual Grapheme-to-Phoneme Conversion for Low-Resource Languages

James Route, Steven Hillis, Isak C. Etinger,* Han Zhang,* Alan Black
Language Technologies Institute
Carnegie Mellon University
Pittsburgh, PA, USA
{jroute, shillis, ice, awb}@cs.cmu.edu, hanz3@andrew.cmu.edu

Abstract

Grapheme-to-phoneme conversion (g2p) is the task of predicting the pronunciation of words from their orthographic representation. Historically, g2p systems were transition- or rule-based, making generalization beyond a monolingual (high resource) domain impractical. Recently, neural architectures have enabled multilingual systems to generalize widely; however, all systems to date have been trained only on spelling-pronunciation pairs. We hypothesize that the sequences of IPA characters used to represent pronunciation do not capture its full nuance, especially when cleaned to facilitate machine learning. We leverage audio data as an auxiliary modality in a multi-task training process to learn a more optimal intermediate representation of source graphemes; this is the first multimodal model proposed for *multilingual* g2p. Our approach is highly effective: on our in-domain test set, our multimodal model reduces phoneme error rate to 2.46%, a more than 65% decrease compared to our implementation of a unimodal spelling-pronunciation model—which itself achieves state-of-the-art results on the Wiktionary test set. The advantages of the multimodal model generalize to wholly unseen languages, reducing phoneme error rate on our out-of-domain test set to 6.39% from the unimodal 8.21%, a more than 20% relative decrease. Furthermore, our training and test sets are composed primarily of low-resource languages, demonstrating that our multimodal approach remains useful when training data are constrained.

1 Introduction

Graphemic and phonemic representations of words are often no more than loosely related within languages and can be in direct contradiction between them. These inconsistencies introduce errors into any application of speech technol-

ogy which has to convert between these two representations: namely text-to-speech and speech-recognition systems.

Very early grapheme to phoneme systems were monolingual and often restricted to English due to dataset availability (Weide, 1998; Kingsbury et al., 1997; Sejnowski, 1987). These early systems were designed to address the problem of intra-language discrepancies through rule based transition systems. These systems required painstaking tailoring to individual languages, and their performance was largely limited to that language's domain. Recent work has extended finite state automata constructed in this way for high resource languages to very similar low resource languages by applying distance metrics and linguistic expertise (Deri and Knight, 2016), but this approach is limited in application and performance.

Relieving some of the burden of technical expertise, statistical methods surpassed rule-based ones, with emphasis on joint sequence modeling (Chen, 2003; Bisani and Ney, 2008; Jiampojamarn et al., 2007). These methods improved performance, but they mandate explicit training alignments. This can be avoided by using neural attentional models, as in Toshniwal and Livescu (2016). Their work makes clear the parallel between this sequence prediction task and more traditional machine translation; this parallel inspires the model proposed in Peters et al. (2017), which, motivated by similarities in vocabularies, spellings, writing systems, and phonemic inventories between low and high resource languages, applies multilingual MT techniques to train a massively multilingual g2p system.

This application is effective, but it—like all work on this task before it—neglects perhaps the most rich source of information on pronunciation available: speech data. All existing grapheme to phoneme systems have been trained on spelling-

---

* Equal contribution

Proceedings of the 2nd Workshop on Deep Learning Approaches for Low-Resource NLP (DeepLo), pages 192–201
Hong Kong, China, November 3, 2019. ©2019 Association for Computational Linguistics
https://doi.org/10.18653/v1/P17

pronunciation data alone, neglecting the audio modality largely due to constraints imposed by available datasets. Suspecting that the preprocessed IPA sequences used to represent pronunciation encode it insufficiently, we propose to learn more optimal grapheme representations and thus make more accurate phoneme predictions by novelly leveraging an auxiliary audio modality as part of a multi-task training process.

2 Datasets

We discuss two datasets in this paper. We focus on the newer Wilderness dataset (Black, 2019), which is multilingual and contains paired text and speech data. We compare results of our multimodal model with all baselines on the Wilderness data. We also include the Wiktionary dataset (Deri and Knight, 2016), which consists of textual data only, because it has been commonly used in prior works on multilingual g2p systems. Wiktionary and Wilderness have incompatible IPA character sets which prevent us from training a model on Wilderness and testing with Wiktionary. We report baseline results only on Wiktionary to offer an approximate means of comparison between the two datasets.

2.1 Wiktionary

The Wiktionary dataset, introduced in Deri and Knight (2016), consists of single word spelling-pronunciation pairs scraped from the open-source multilingual dictionary maintained by Wikimedia. Entries are extracted from high resource language sites, which have instances for multiple languages. This heavily biases the distribution, with English, French, and German accounting for 51% of all pairs. Filtering for length, each Wiktionary pronunciation is mapped to Phoible phonemes after accounting for a phoneme distance metric original to this work. Following Peters et al. (2017), we use the cleaned pronunciations and randomly sample 10% of the corpus' training split to use for validation.

	Train	Test
Languages	311	507
Words	631,828	25,894
Scripts	42	45

Table 1: Corpus statics for Wiktionary dataset

2.2 Wilderness

We use the CMU Wilderness dataset[1], introduced in Black (2019), which contains of audio, aligned text, and word pronunciations for over 700 languages. The source material consists of versions of the New Testament, which speakers read in their own language. Pronunciations are generated from the audio by an HMM aligner and are transcribed in X-SAMPA (Wells, 1995), an extension of the Speech Assessment Methods Phonetic Alphabet (SAMPA). X-SAMPA was used to encode symbols of the International Phonetic Alphabet (IPA) into 7-bit ASCII before the advent of Unicode. We convert the X-SAMPA representations into true IPA characters.

We represent the audio data from the CMU Wilderness dataset as 39-dimensional MFCC (Mel Frequency Cepstral Coefficients) features (Sahidullah and Saha, 2012; Zheng et al., 2001; Ganchev et al., 2005; Ittichaichareon et al., 2012), a spectral-based parameter commonly used to vectorize audio data which represents the short-term power spectrum of an audio stream. The first 13 dimensions are the Mel frequency cepstral coefficients of the first 13 coefficients of the Fourier transform of the audio stream. The next 13 dimensions are the time-derivatives of those coefficients, and the last 13 are the double time-derivatives. The first 13 dimensions were calculated with the Librosa python package (McFee et al., 2015) method `librosa.feature.mfcc`. Other dimensions were calculated with the `librosa.feature.delta` method.

Directly comparing those dimensions has no physical meaning, so we normalize those features as

$$f_{i,u} \rightarrow \frac{f_{i,u} - \min_{u' \in U}(f_{i,u'})}{\max_{u' \in U}(f_{i,u'}) - \min_{u' \in U}(f_{i,u'})} \cdot 0.95^i$$

where U are the utterances and $i \in \{1..39\}$. We used a sliding window of 25ms with 10ms stride. MFCCs are not the only way to vectorize audio data, and they are not necessarily the best, but they are a sufficient representation to facilitate our experiments.

The Wilderness dataset ranks the quality of alignment for a language on the basis of the reconstruction score over a held out test set for a

[1] `https://github.com/festvox/datasets-CMU_Wilderness`

grapheme-based speech synthesizer trained on the remaining language data. Reconstruction score is measured in Mel Cepstral Distortion (MCD) (Toda et al., 2007), a scaled Euclidean distortion metric for comparing synthesized utterances to true ones. Lower is better. For this dataset, when MCD scores are less than 7, the synthesized outputs are usually intelligible, and when they are less than 6, the outputs are easily understood. We chose languages with MCD scores less than 6 for our experiments; see Table 2 for more on these languages.

Resources constrain our experiments to a total of 20 languages out of the available 700. Ten of those languages are used for training, development, and in-domain (ID) experiments; the remaining ten are used for out-of-domain (OoD) experiments. Fifteen different language families are represented. For training and validation, 1000 and 100 utterances are used for each ID language respectively. Note that all languages trained on are themselves low resource—a major departure from previous work. For more details on each of the languages, as well as expansions of the abbreviations, see Table 9 at the end of the paper.

In-Domain		Out-of-Domain	
Language	**MCD**	**Language**	**MCD**
SHIRBD	4.96	MYYWBT	5.80
COKWBT	5.37	SABWBT	5.80
LTNNVV	5.82	LONBSM	5.83
XMMLAI	5.20	NHYTBL	5.92
TS1BSM	5.24	ALJOMF	5.93
GAGIBT	5.26	BFABSS	5.20
KNETBL	5.68	HUBWBT	5.98
TPPTBL	5.72	TWBOMF	5.98
HAUCLV	5.74	ENXBSP	5.99
ESSWYI	5.79	POHPOC	5.29

Table 2: MCD scores for Wilderness languages[2]

	Verses	**Words**	**Length (min)**
Train	10,000	139,796	1060
Dev	1,000	13,937	106
ID Test	1,000	13,815	104
OoD Test	1,000	15,418	107

Table 3: Statistics for Wilderness-based corpus

3 Baseline

Multilingual neural machine translation techniques have recently been applied to the g2p problem (Peters et al., 2017) to accommodate the lack of data for low-resource languages. With many low-resource languages sharing similar writing systems with high-resource languages, orthographic representations of words in any language are mapped to the corresponding phonemic representations in a multisource sequence-to-sequence model. We reproduce their architecture as our performance baseline using OpenNMT (Klein et al., 2017) on the Wiktionary and Wilderness datasets. Briefly, the source graphemes (augmented with language tags) and target phonemes are first processed as character-based embedding sequences. The model uses an encoder-decoder structure and the global attention layer proposed by Luong et al. (2015). We selected this model because it achieved state-of-the-art results on Wiktionary and represents a strong baseline for sequence-to-sequence model performance on g2p.

Two common evaluation metrics for g2p models are Phoneme Error Rate (PER) and Word Error Rate (WER). Phoneme Error Rate represents the Levenshtein distance over the target and predicted phonemes, normalized by the target sequence length. Word Error Rate represents the percentage of predicted phoneme words which do not exactly match their target phoneme words. For our experiments, we extend the concept of Word Error Rate to a metric that we term Sequence Error Rate (SER), which measures the percentage of incorrectly predicted phoneme sequences. This alteration is necessary because Wilderness utterances consist of multiple words, and the phoneme sequences are not segmented by word. WER

Examples	**SER**	**PER**
Example #1: 'An example'		
Predicted: [ə n ɪ g z æ m p ə l]		
Gold: [ə n ɪ g z æ m p ə l]	0.00	0.00
Example #2: 'And a second'		
Predicted: [æ n d ə s ə k ə n]		
Gold: [æ n d ə s ɛ k ə n d]	100.00	20.00
Total Scores	**50.00**	**10.00**

Table 4: Examples for SER and PER calculations

and SER are functionally identical for Wiktionary, which comprises single-word grapheme-phoneme pairs.

We note that other multilingual g2p systems exist, such as Deri and Knight (2016) and Epitran (Mortensen et al., 2018), although we do not include these systems in the results. The Peters et al. (2017) model previously outperformed the Deri and Knight (2016) system on Wiktionary by a significant margin, and Epitran is a rule-based system that does not support the vast majority of the low-resource languages we use.

4   Multimodal Approach

Multimodal models have been frequently explored for feature mining (e.g., text, image, audio). Multimodal learning commonly focuses on three areas: fusion of information, cross-modality learning, and shared representation mining (Ngiam et al., 2011). A deep multimodal learning method for automatic speech recognition was designed (Mroueh et al., 2015) to fuse both audio and visual modalities. In this case, the latent audio and video features were concatenated and used jointly for the prediction of speech. Recent work on multimodal sentiment analysis (Pham et al. (2018b) and Pham et al. (2018a)) demonstrated that an auxiliary task of translating from a source to one or more target modalities results in a joint representation that captures interactions between the modalities. We base our model on this approach and apply it to a sequence prediction task on multilingual data.

We develop a recurrent sequence-to-sequence model with attention that learns a robust joint representation for graphemes and speech data across multiple languages, which is then used to predict a phoneme sequence given only graphemes[3]. We hypothesize that the inclusion of the speech modality will enable the model to learn a better multilingual representation than text alone, and that a multimodal representation will generalize to unseen languages better than a text-only model. A key feature of our model is that speech data are only required for training; during inference the model only uses grapheme inputs.

Our model is an LSTM sequence-to-sequence model with a single encoder and two decoders (Figure 1). One decoder predicts MFCC coef-

---

[3]Model code is available at `https://github.com/jamesrt95/Multimodal-Multilingual-G2P`

ficients from graphemes (auxiliary task) and the other predicts IPA character sequences (primary task). Each task corresponds to a separate loss function.

During training, three sequences are available to the model: grapheme characters X_t, speech MFCCs S_t, and phoneme characters Y_t. The encoder is a biLSTM, with the output based on the previous hidden state and the current grapheme character in the input sequence:

$$h_{e,t} = LSTM(h_{e,t-1}, X_t) \qquad (1)$$

The decoders use the same basic architecture with minor differences. The MFCC decoder consists of an LSTM whose input is a concatenation of the previous MFCC output $\hat{S}_{t-1}$ and previous attention context $a_{s,t-1}$. The LSTM hidden state is fed to an MLP to produce the attention query $q_{s,t}$. The sequence of encoder hidden states is passed through two separate MLPs to obtain attention keys and values K and V. A dot-product global attention mechanism from Vaswani et al. (2017) follows. The resulting attention context $a_{s,t}$ is then projected by MLP down to a 39-dimension MFCC vector $\hat{S}_t$.

$$h_{s,t} = LSTM(h_{s,t-1}, [\hat{S}_{t-1}; a_{s,t-1}]) \qquad (2)$$
$$q_{s,t} = MLP(h_{s,t}) \qquad (3)$$
$$K, V = MLP(h_e), MLP(h_e) \qquad (4)$$
$$a_{s,t} = \sum softmax(q_{s,t}K^T)V \qquad (5)$$
$$\hat{S}_t = MLP(a_{s,t}) \qquad (6)$$

The phoneme decoder follows the same design except that its output $\hat{Y}_t$ is a distribution over the IPA character vocabulary. No parameters are shared between the decoders.

$$h_{y,t} = LSTM(h_{y,t-1}, [\hat{Y}_{t-1}; a_{y,t-1}]) \qquad (7)$$
$$q_{y,t} = MLP(h_{y,t}) \qquad (8)$$
$$K, V = MLP(h_e), MLP(h_e) \qquad (9)$$
$$a_{y,t} = \sum softmax(q_{y,t}K^T)V \qquad (10)$$
$$\hat{Y}_t = softmax(MLP(a_{y,t})) \qquad (11)$$

Model parameters are learned during training by empirical risk minimization over input graphemes and paired MFCC vectors and phoneme characters $\{X_t, S_t, Y_t\}$, across all languages in the training set. A separate loss is

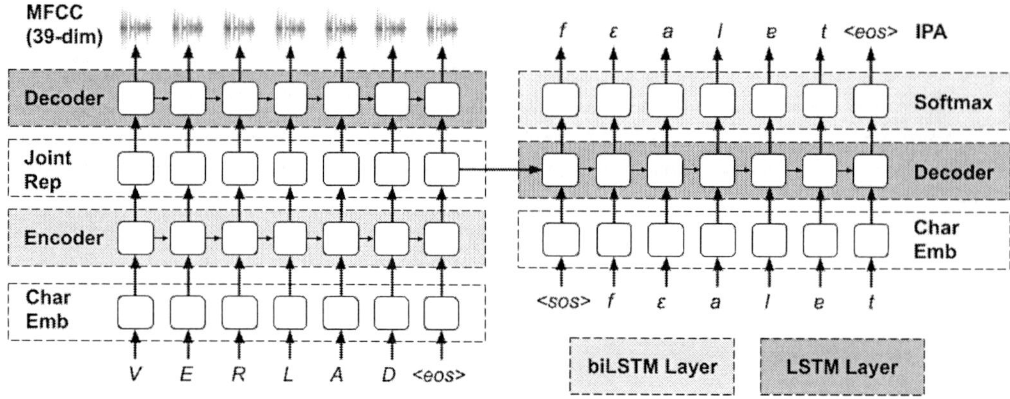

Figure 1: Diagram of Multimodal g2p Model

calculated from the output of each decoder. We use mean-squared error as loss function ℓ_S for the MFCC output and cross-entropy as loss function ℓ_Y for the IPA output. The entire network is trained end-to-end using a weighted sum of the two losses where λ is a hyperparameter.

$$\mathcal{L}_S = \mathbb{E}[\ell_S(\hat{S}, S)] \tag{12}$$

$$\mathcal{L}_Y = \mathbb{E}[\ell_Y(\hat{Y}, Y)] \tag{13}$$

$$\mathcal{L} = \mathcal{L}_Y + \lambda \mathcal{L}_S \tag{14}$$

The encoder learns a joint embedding that models interactions between the grapheme and speech modalities. This is accomplished via gradient descent, as parameter updates for the encoder and MFCC decoder are dependent on the grapheme and speech sequences. The model is then able to infer speech data when given only grapheme inputs. At test time, the model is given only grapheme inputs and the MFCC output is ignored. We then perform beam search over the IPA decoder output to generate the final predicted sequence.

5   Experiments

First, we implemented the Peters et al. (2017) baseline model separately on the Wiktionary and Wilderness datasets. We then trained two variants of our sequence-to-sequence model on the in-domain Wilderness data to compare the effects of the multimodal representation. The first variant was multimodal (referred to as the *Multimodal Model*). The parameters for this model are given in Table 5. The second variant was unimodal (referred to as the *Unimodal Model*) and treated as

an additional baseline. During training for this model, the loss term for the MFCC decoder was ignored, so learned parameters were based solely on the grapheme inputs and phoneme outputs. The unimodal model also used the parameters given in the table, except the MSE loss weight was zero.

We selected layer size parameters for the both models that were similar to Peters et al. (2017) so that differences in performance could be more clearly attributed to the multimodal training process. We set teacher forcing to 90% so that the model's inferences were not completely dependent on seeing correct labels at each time step. For the multimodal model, we weighted the MSE loss from MFCC prediction at 0.1 because it was an auxiliary objective, and the model's learning process tended to be more stable when weighted lower than the primary cross-entropy objective. We used results from the dev set to choose this value. We also averaged the MFCC values over 10 consecutive frames; this helped the model to learn more quickly and allowed for larger batch sizes.

The models were each trained on all languages in the training set (i.e., each model was trained to be multilingual). The training set was shuffled so that there was no systematic ordering of languages during training. The models were then evaluated separately on the in-domain and out-of-domain test sets.

6   Results

The results on the Wilderness datasets are presented in Table 7. We are only able to provide a direct comparison between the performance of the baseline model and of our models on the Wilder-

Enc. type	biLSTM
Dec. type	LSTM
Enc. & dec. layers	1
Attention type	Dot
Hidden layer size	128
Source emb. size	64
Target emb. size	64
Batch size	16
Optimizer	Adam
Learning rate	1e-3
Teacher forcing rate	0.9
MSE loss weight (λ)	0.1
Training epochs	14
Beam size	10

Table 5: Multimodal Model Parameters

ness data: the Wiktionary dataset uses a different and incompatible IPA character vocabulary, which prevents us from training a model on Wilderness and testing on Wiktionary. We report baseline results on Wiktionary to offer an approximate means of comparison between Wiktionary (an established dataset) and Wilderness, which is newly created.

Model	SER	PER
Peters et al. Baseline Model	43.23	37.85
Our Impl. of Peters et al.	**37.87**	**26.00**

Table 6: Comparison of Models on Wiktionary Dataset

For the Wilderness data, we report results on two test sets (In-Domain and Out-of-Domain) to illustrate generalization to unseen languages. The ID test set consists of 100 unseen utterances from each of the same 10 languages used in training, whereas the OoD test set consists of 100 utterances each from 10 languages that were not used in training.

7 Discussion

Although we were pleasantly surprised to see the performance of our implementation of the baseline system from Peters et al. (2017) increase so drastically from the results they report on the Wiktionary dataset, we take little credit for this result; it can perhaps be attributed to improvements made to the OpenNMT platform over the past two years, but we replicated their experiments as faithfully as

Model	SER	PER
In-Domain Test Results		
Baseline Model	46.90	25.06
Unimodal Model	31.20	7.05
Multimodal Model	**9.50**	**2.46**
Out-of-Domain Test Results		
Baseline Model	84.20	43.16
Unimodal Model	49.30	8.21
Multimodal Model	**38.10**	**6.39**

Table 7: Comparison of Models on Wilderness Dataset

we were able.

On the other hand, we are happy to take credit for the relative performances of our models on the Wilderness dataset. We attribute much of the improvement to a more expressive attention mechanism and to improved hyperparameter tuning, as our underlying model used similar layer sizes to the baseline.

Our hypothesis about the value of including audio data during training is heartily confirmed by the performance of our multimodal model: the multimodal model performs better for both metrics not only on in-domain languages but also on very different, wholly unseen languages. Our multimodal approach to the task of grapheme to phoneme conversion improves both performance and generalization.

We note the multimodal model's SER is much worse on out-of-domain languages than in-domain ones, albeit still surpassing the unimodal model's

	In-Domain			Out-of-Domain	
Lang	**PER**	**SER**	**Lang**	**PER**	**SER**
SHI	5.24	14.00	MYY	14.10	100.00
COK	3.07	14.00	SAB	6.59	50.00
LTN	1.92	8.00	LON	1.51	14.00
XMM	1.91	8.00	NHY	18.60	22.00
TS1	1.62	6.00	ALJ	2.60	4.00
GAG	2.71	7.00	BFA	7.41	90.00
KNE	1.29	3.00	HUB	1.60	5.00
TPP	5.03	20.00	TWB	2.86	7.00
HAU	0.56	7.00	ENX	17.00	71.00
ESS	0.23	8.00	POH	3.36	18.00

Table 8: Multimodal Model Error Rates by Language

In-Domain			Out-of-Domain		
Code	**Name**	**Family**	**Code**	**Name**	**Family**
SHIRBD	Shilha	Afro-Asiatic	MYYWBT	Macuna	Tucanoan
COKWBT	Cora, Santa Teresa	Uto-Aztecan	SABWBT	Buglere	Chibchan
LTNNVV	Latin	Indo-European	LONBSM	Elhomwe	Niger-Congo
XMMLAI	Manadonese Malay	Austronesian/Indo-Euro.	NHYTBL	Nahuatl	Uto-Aztecan
TS1BSM	Tsonga	Niger-Congo	ALJOMF	Alangan	Austronesian
GAGIBT	Gagauz	Turkic	BFABSS	Bari	Nilo-Saharan
KNETBL	Kankanaey	Austronesian	HUBWBT	Huambisa	Jivaroan
TPPTBL	Tepehua	Totonacan	TWBOMF	Tawbuid	Austronesian
HAUCLV	Hausa	Afro-Asiatic	ENXBSP	Enxet	Mascoyan
ESSWYI	Yupik	Eskimo-Aleut	POHPOC	Pokomchi	Mayan

Table 9: More Information on Wilderness languages

(Table 8). The out-of-domain languages contain characters that are out of vocabulary (OOV) from the training set, and in most cases OOV characters comprise 15-20% of the input sequence. One mistake in the output results in the entire sequence being scored incorrect for SER, so even small PER increases can lead to large swings in SER. In particular, the large increase in SER is primarily due to four languages in the Out-of-Domain test set. In the case of Macuna (MYY, 100 SER), the IPA character ʉ appears in nearly every utterance but never occurs in the training set, so the model is unable to predict it. Bari (BFA, 90.0 SER) is similar, where ŋ is highly common but never appears in the training set. Enxet (ENX, 71.0 SER) and Buglere (SAB, 50.0 SER) both frequently contain ɲ, which occurs only once in the training set.

We also note that our reimplementation of the Peters et al. (2017) baseline produces a lower Sequence Error Rate on the single-word utterances in the Wiktionary dataset than on the multi-word utterances in the Wilderness sets. Longer sequence pairs result in more opportunities for a model to make a mistake. This effect is acute for the sequence-level error, but even for PER, an incorrect output at one timestep may lead to cascading mistakes at future timesteps. The comparable PER scores on the Wiktionary and In-Domain Wilderness set suggest that the datasets are comparable in difficulty. Although we are unable to directly measure the multimodal model's performance on Wiktionary, its substantial improvements on a comparable task convince us of its efficacy.

8 Future Work

With recent advancements in language embeddings, we identify significant potential for improving the generalization of the model to unseen languages. Including language tags was shown to be beneficial in previous work, and we predict that exchanging the three-character tag for a high-dimensional embedding to capture taxonomic relationships between languages would only magnify the effect. Similarly, we have demonstrated the advantages of incorporating audio data during training, but MFCCs are not necessarily the most effective method of vectorizing that audio data. It would be interesting to investigate the effects of using other techniques, such as those in Haque et al. (2019) and Chung and Glass (2018), for generating high-dimensional representations of audio data.

We trained our model on approximately 0.1% of the data included in the Wilderness dataset, leaving tremendous opportunity for further learning. The incorporation of more training data is likely to improve results on its own, but it may also facilitate the use of a Transformer encoder-decoder model (Vaswani et al., 2017), which we know to require larger datasets than the LSTM variants.

We are very interested in experimenting with graphemes encoded in non-Roman scripts. This capacity is one of the most compelling facets of the Peters et al. (2017) model, but we were unable to explore it with our multimodal model: the New Testament text is almost always Romanized in the Wilderness data. We were furthermore unable to effectively evaluate our multimodal model on the

Wiktionary data after training on the Wilderness, as the IPA character space over the Wilderness dataset is much smaller than that of the Wiktionary dataset. In the future, we would like to reconcile these differences, both in order to evaluate our multimodal model on the Wiktionary test set and to explore its performance over widely varying scripts.

Acknowledgments

We thank Bhiksha Raj for helpful comments on our development of the multimodal model. We also appreciate the suggestions and comments from the anonymous reviewers.

References

Maximilian Bisani and Hermann Ney. 2008. Joint-sequence models for grapheme-to-phoneme conversion. *Speech communication*, 50(5):434–451.

Alan W. Black. 2019. Cmu wilderness multilingual speech dataset. *ICASSP*.

Stanley F Chen. 2003. Conditional and joint models for grapheme-to-phoneme conversion. In *Eighth European Conference on Speech Communication and Technology*.

Yu-An Chung and James Glass. 2018. Speech2vec: A sequence-to-sequence framework for learning word embeddings from speech. *arXiv preprint arXiv:1803.08976*.

Aliya Deri and Kevin Knight. 2016. Grapheme-to-phoneme models for (almost) any language. In *ACL*.

Todor Ganchev, Nikos Fakotakis, and George Kokkinakis. 2005. Comparative evaluation of various mfcc implementations on the speaker verification task. In *Proceedings of the SPECOM*, volume 1, pages 191–194.

Albert Haque, Michelle Guo, Prateek Verma, and Li Fei-Fei. 2019. Audio-linguistic embeddings for spoken sentences. *arXiv preprint arXiv:1902.07817*.

Chadawan Ittichaichareon, Siwat Suksri, and Thaweesak Yingthawornsuk. 2012. Speech recognition using mfcc. In *International Conference on Computer Graphics, Simulation and Modeling (ICGSM'2012) July*, pages 28–29.

Sittichai Jiampojamarn, Grzegorz Kondrak, and Tarek Sherif. 2007. Applying many-to-many alignments and hidden markov models to letter-to-phoneme conversion. In *Human Language Technologies 2007: The Conference of the North American Chapter of the Association for Computational Linguistics; Proceedings of the Main Conference*, pages 372–379.

Paul Kingsbury, Stephanie Strassel, Cynthia McLemore, and Robert MacIntyre. 1997. Callhome american english lexicon (pronlex). *Linguistic Data Consortium, Philadelphia*.

Guillaume Klein, Yoon Kim, Yuntian Deng, Jean Senellart, and Alexander M. Rush. 2017. OpenNMT: Open-source toolkit for neural machine translation. In *Proc. ACL*.

Minh-Thang Luong, Hieu Pham, and Christopher D. Manning. 2015. Effective approaches to attention-based neural machine translation. *CoRR*, abs/1508.04025.

Brian McFee, Colin Raffel, Dawen Liang, Daniel P.W. Ellis, Matt McVicar, Eric Battenberg, and Oriol Nieto. 2015. librosa: Audio and Music Signal Analysis in Python. In *Proceedings of the 14th Python in Science Conference*, pages 18 – 24.

David R. Mortensen, Siddharth Dalmia, and Patrick Littell. 2018. Epitran: Precision G2P for many languages. In *Proceedings of the Eleventh International Conference on Language Resources and Evaluation (LREC 2018)*, Paris, France. European Language Resources Association (ELRA).

Y. Mroueh, E. Marcheret, and V. Goel. 2015. Deep multimodal learning for audio-visual speech recognition. In *2015 IEEE International Conference on Acoustics, Speech and Signal Processing (ICASSP)*, pages 2130–2134.

Jiquan Ngiam, Aditya Khosla, Mingyu Kim, Juhan Nam, Honglak Lee, and Andrew Y. Ng. 2011. Multimodal deep learning. In *Proceedings of the 28th International Conference on International Conference on Machine Learning*, ICML'11, pages 689–696, USA. Omnipress.

Ben Peters, Jon Dehdari, and Josef van Genabith. 2017. Massively multilingual neural grapheme-to-phoneme conversion. *CoRR*, abs/1708.01464.

Hai Pham, Paul Pu Liang, Thomas Manzini, Louis-Philippe Morency, and Barnabas Poczos. 2018a. Found in translation: Learning robust joint representations by cyclic translations between modalities. *arXiv preprint arXiv:1812.07809*.

Hai Pham, Thomas Manzini, Paul Pu Liang, and Barnabas Poczos. 2018b. Seq2seq2sentiment: Multimodal sequence to sequence models for sentiment analysis. *arXiv preprint arXiv:1807.03915*.

Md Sahidullah and Goutam Saha. 2012. Design, analysis and experimental evaluation of block based transformation in mfcc computation for speaker recognition. *Speech Communication*, 54(4):543–565.

Terry Sejnowski. 1987. Net talk: A parallel network that learns to read aloud. *Complex Systems*, 1:145–168.

Tomoki. Toda, Alan. Black, and Keiichi. Tokuda. 2007. Voice converstion based on maximum-likelihood estimation of speech parameter trajectory. *IEEE Transaction of Audio, Speech and Language Processing*, 15(8):2222–2236.

Shubham Toshniwal and Karen Livescu. 2016. Jointly learning to align and convert graphemes to phonemes with neural attention models. In *2016 IEEE Spoken Language Technology Workshop (SLT)*, pages 76–82. IEEE.

Ashish Vaswani, Noam Shazeer, Niki Parmar, Jakob Uszkoreit, Llion Jones, Aidan N Gomez, Łukasz Kaiser, and Illia Polosukhin. 2017. Attention is all you need. In *Advances in neural information processing systems*, pages 5998–6008.

Robert L Weide. 1998. The cmu pronouncing dictionary. *URL: http://www. speech. cs. cmu. edu/cgibin/cmudict*.

John C Wells. 1995. Computer-coding the ipa: a proposed extension of sampa. *Revised draft*, 4(28):1995.

Fang Zheng, Guoliang Zhang, and Zhanjiang Song. 2001. Comparison of different implementations of mfcc. *Journal of Computer science and Technology*, 16(6):582–589.

Natural Language Generation for Effective Knowledge Distillation

Raphael Tang, Yao Lu, and **Jimmy Lin**
David R. Cheriton School of Computer Science
University of Waterloo

Abstract

Knowledge distillation can effectively transfer knowledge from BERT, a deep language representation model, to traditional, shallow word embedding-based neural networks, helping them approach or exceed the quality of other heavyweight language representation models. As shown in previous work, critical to this distillation procedure is the construction of an unlabeled transfer dataset, which enables effective knowledge transfer. To create transfer set examples, we propose to sample from pretrained language models fine-tuned on task-specific text. Unlike previous techniques, this directly captures the purpose of the transfer set. We hypothesize that this principled, general approach outperforms rule-based techniques. On four datasets in sentiment classification, sentence similarity, and linguistic acceptability, we show that our approach improves upon previous methods. We outperform OpenAI GPT, a deep pretrained transformer, on three of the datasets, while using a single-layer bidirectional LSTM that runs at least ten times faster.

1 Introduction

That bigger neural networks plus more data equals higher quality is a tried-and-true formula. In the natural language processing (NLP) literature, the recent darling of this mantra is the deep, pretrained language representation model. After pretraining hundreds of millions of parameters on vast amounts of text, models such as BERT (Bidirectional Encoder Representations from Transformers; Devlin et al., 2018) achieve remarkable state of the art in question answering, sentiment analysis, and sentence similarity tasks, to list a few.

Does this progress mean, then, that classic, shallow word embedding-based neural networks are noncompetitive? Not quite. Recently, Tang et al. (2019) demonstrate that knowledge distillation (Ba and Caruana, 2014; Hinton et al., 2015) can transfer knowledge from BERT to small, traditional neural networks, helping them approach or exceed the quality of much larger pretrained long short-term memory (LSTM; Hochreiter and Schmidhuber, 1997) language models, such as ELMo (Embeddings from Language Models; Peters et al., 2018).

As shown in Tang et al. (2019), crucial to knowledge distillation is constructing a transfer dataset of unlabeled examples. In this paper, we explore how to construct such an effective transfer set. Previous approaches comprise manual data curation, a meticulous method where the end user manually selects a corpus similar enough to the present task, and rule-based techniques, where a transfer set is fabricated from the training set using a set of data augmentation rules. However, these rules only indirectly model the purpose of the transfer set, which is to provide more input drawn from the task-specific data distribution. Hence, we instead propose to construct the transfer set by generating text with pretrained language models fine-tuned on task-specific text. We validate our approach on four small- to mid-sized datasets in sentiment classification, sentence similarity, and linguistic acceptability.

We claim two contributions: first, we elucidate a novel approach for constructing the transfer set in knowledge distillation. Second, we are the first to outperform OpenAI GPT (Radford et al., 2018) in sentiment classification and sentence similarity with a single-layer bidirectional LSTM (Bi-LSTM) that runs more than ten times faster, *without* pretraining or domain-specific data curation. We make our datasets and codebase public in a GitHub repository.[1]

---

[1] https://github.com/castorini/d-bert

Proceedings of the 2nd Workshop on Deep Learning Approaches for Low-Resource NLP (DeepLo), pages 202–208
Hong Kong, China, November 3, 2019. ©2019 Association for Computational Linguistics
https://doi.org/10.18653/v1/P17

2   Background and Related Work

Ba and Caruana (2014) propose knowledge distillation, a method for improving the quality of a smaller *student* model by encouraging it to match the outputs of a larger, higher-quality *teacher* network. Concretely, suppose $h_S(\cdot)$ and $h_T(\cdot)$ respectively denote the untrained student and trained teacher models, and we are given a training set of inputs $\mathcal{S} = \{x_1, \ldots, x_N\}$. On classification tasks, the model outputs are log probabilities; on regression tasks, the outputs are as-is. Then, the distillation objective $\mathcal{L}_{\text{KD}}$ is

$$\mathcal{L}_{\text{KD}} = \frac{1}{N} \sum_{i=1}^{N} \|h_S(x_i) - h_T(x_i)\|_2^2 \qquad (1)$$

Hinton et al. (2015) alternatively use Kullback–Leibler divergence for classification, along with additional hyperparameters. For simplicity and generality, we stick with the original mean-squared error (MSE) formulation. We minimize $\mathcal{L}_{\text{KD}}$ end-to-end with backpropagation, updating the student's parameters and fixing the teacher's. $\mathcal{L}_{\text{KD}}$ can optionally be combined with the original, supervised cross-entropy or MSE loss; following Tang et al. (2019) and Shi et al. (2019), we optimize only $\mathcal{L}_{\text{KD}}$ for training the student.

Using only the given training set for $\mathcal{S}$, however, is often insufficient. Thus, Ba and Caruana (2014) augment $\mathcal{S}$ with a *transfer* set comprising unlabeled input, providing the student with more examples to distill from the teacher. Techniques for constructing this transfer set consist of either manual data curation or unprincipled data synthesis rules. Ba and Caruana (2014) choose images from the 80 million tiny images dataset, which is a superset of their dataset. In the NLP domain, Tang et al. (2019) propose text perturbation rules for creating a transfer set from the training set, achieving results comparable to ELMo using a BiLSTM with 100 times fewer parameters.

We wish to avoid these previous approaches. Manual data curation requires the researcher to select an unlabeled set similar enough to the target dataset, a difficult-to-impossible task for many datasets in, for example, linguistic acceptability and sentence similarity. Rule-based techniques, while general, unfortunately deviate from the *true* purpose of modeling the input distribution; hence, we hypothesize that they are less effective than a principled approach, which we detail below.

3   Our Approach

In knowledge distillation, the student perceives the oracular teacher to be the true $p(Y|X)$, where X and Y respectively denote the input sentence and label. This is reasonable, since the student treats the teacher output y as ground truth, given some sentence x comprising words $\{w_1, \ldots, w_n\}$. The purpose of the transfer set is, then, to provide additional input sentences for querying the teacher. To construct such a set, we propose the following: first, we parameterize $p(X)$ directly as a language model $p(w_1, \ldots, w_n) = \Pi_{i=1}^{n} p(w_i|w_1, \ldots, w_{i-1})$ trained on the given sentences $\{x_1, \ldots, x_N\}$. Then, to generate unlabeled examples, we sample from the language model, i.e., the ith word of a sentence is drawn from $p(w_i|w_1, \ldots, w_{i-1})$. We stop upon generating the special end-of-sentence token [EOS], which we append to each sentence while fine-tuning the language model (LM).

Unlike previous methods, our approach directly parameterizes $p(X)$ to provide unlabeled examples. We hypothesize that this approach outperforms ad hoc rule-based methods, which only indirectly model the input distribution $p(X)$.

Sentence-pair modeling. To language model sentence pairs, we follow Devlin et al. (2018) and join both sentences with a special separator token [SEP] between, treating the resulting sequence as a single contiguous sentence.

3.1   Model Architecture

For simplicity and efficient inference, our student models use the same single-layer BiLSTM models from Tang et al. (2019)—see Figures 1 and 2.

First, we map an input sequence of words to their corresponding word2vec embeddings, trained on Google News. Next, for single-sentence tasks, these embeddings are fed into a single-layer BiLSTM encoder to yield concatenated forward and backward states $\mathbf{h} = [\mathbf{h}_f; \mathbf{h}_b]$. For sentence-pair tasks, we encode each sentence separately using a BiLSTM to yield $\mathbf{h}_1$ and $\mathbf{h}_2$. To produce a single vector $\mathbf{h}$, following Wang et al. (2018), we compute $\mathbf{h} = [\mathbf{h}_1; \mathbf{h}_2; \delta(\mathbf{h}_1, \mathbf{h}_2); \mathbf{h}_1 \cdot \mathbf{h}_2]$, where $\cdot$ denotes elementwise multiplication and δ denotes elementwise absolute difference. Finally, for both single- and paired-sentence tasks, $\mathbf{h}$ is passed through a multilayer perceptron (MLP) with one hidden layer that uses a rectified linear unit (ReLU) activation. For classification, the fi-

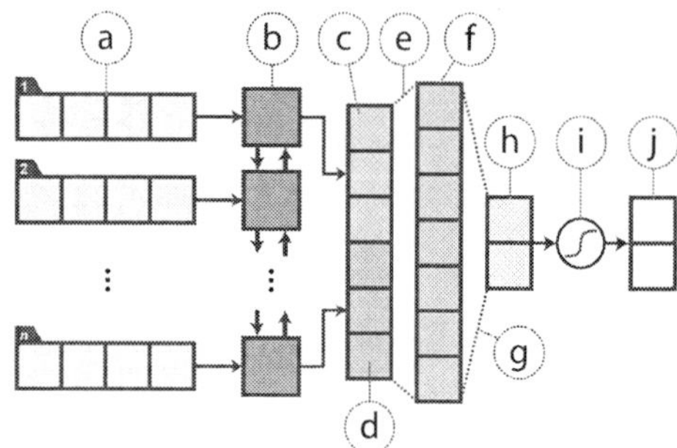

Figure 1: Illustration of the single-sentence BiLSTM, copied from Tang et al. (2019). The labels are as follows: (a) word embeddings (b) BiLSTM layer (c) final forward hidden state (d) final backward hidden state (e) nonlinear layer (f) the final representation (g) fully-connected layer (h) logits or similarity score (i) softmax activation for classification tasks; identity for regression (j) final probabilities or score.

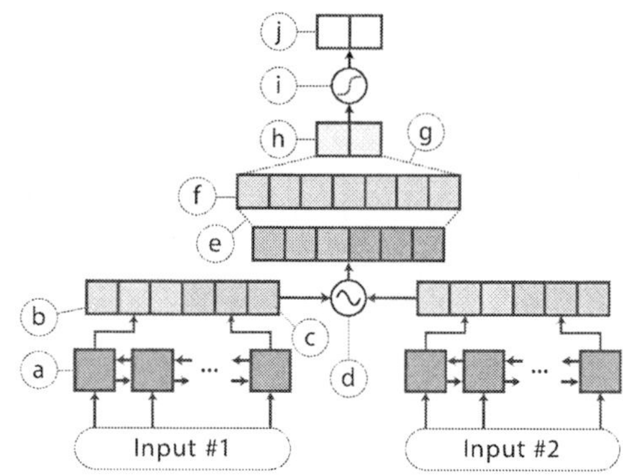

Figure 2: Illustration of the sentence-pair BiLSTM, copied from Tang et al. (2019). The labels are as follows: (a) BiLSTM layer (b) final forward hidden state (c) final backward hidden state (d) comparison unit, as detailed in the text (e) nonlinear layer (f) the final representation (g) fully-connected layer (h) logits or similarity score (i) softmax activation for classification tasks; identity for regression (j) final probabilities or score.

nal output is interpreted as the logits of each class; for real-valued sentence similarity, the final output is a single score.

Our teacher model is the large variant of BERT, a deep pretrained language representation model that achieves close to state of the art (SOTA) on our tasks. Extremely recent, improved pretrained models like XLNet (Yang et al., 2019) and RoBERTa (Liu et al., 2019) likely offer greater benefits to the student model, but BERT is widely used and sufficient for the point of this paper. We follow the same experimental procedure in Devlin et al. (2018) and fine-tune BERT end-to-end for each task, varying only the final classifier layer for the desired number of classes.

Language modeling. For creating the transfer set, we apply two public, state-of-the-art language models: the word-level Transformer-XL (TXL; Dai et al., 2019) pretrained on WikiText-103 (Merity et al., 2017), which is derived from Wikipedia, and the subword-level GPT-2 (345M version; Radford et al., 2019) pretrained on Web-Text, which represents a large web corpus that *excludes* Wikipedia. Other models exist, but we choose these two since they represent the state of the art. We name the GPT-2 and TXL-constructed transfer sets TS_{GPT-2} and TS_{TXL}, respectively.

4 Experimental Setup

We validate our approach on four datasets in sentiment classification, linguistic acceptability, sen-

tence similarity, and paraphrasing: Stanford Sentiment Treebank-2 (SST-2; Socher et al., 2013), the Corpus of Linguistic Acceptability (CoLA; Warstadt et al., 2018), Semantic Textual Similarity Benchmark (STS-B; Cer et al., 2017), and Microsoft Research Paraphrase Corpus (MRPC; Dolan and Brockett, 2005). SST-2 is a binary polarity dataset of single-sentence movie reviews. CoLA is a single-sentence grammaticality task, with expertly annotated binary judgements. STS-B comprises sentence pairs labeled with real-valued similarity between 1 and 5. Lastly, MRPC has sentence pairs with binary labels denoting semantic equivalence. We pick these four tasks from the General Language Understanding Evaluation (GLUE; Wang et al., 2018) benchmark, and submit results to their public evaluation server.[2]

4.1 Baselines

As a sanity check, we attempt knowledge distillation *without* a transfer set, as well as training our BiLSTM from scratch on the original labels. We compare to the best official GLUE test results reported for single- and multi-task ELMo models, OpenAI GPT, single- and multi-task single-layer BiLSTMs, and the SOTA before GPT. ELMo and GPT are pretrained language representation models with around a hundred million parameters. We name our distilled model $BiLSTM_{KD}$.

---

[2] http://gluebenchmark.com

Transfer set construction baselines. For our rule-based baseline, we use the masking and part of speech (POS)-guided word swapping rules as originally suggested by Tang et al. (2019), which consist of the following: iterating through a dataset's sentences, we replace 10% of the words with the masking token [MASK]. We swap another mutually exclusive 10% of the words with others of the same POS tag from the vocabulary, randomly sampling by unigram probability. For sentence-pair tasks, we apply the rules to the first sentence only, then the second only, and, finally, both. Discarding any duplicates, we repeat this entire process until meeting the target number of transfer set sentences. Tang et al. (2019) also suggest to sample n-grams; however, we omit this rule, since our preliminary experiments find that it hurts accuracy. We call this method TS_{MP}.

For our unlabeled dataset baseline, we choose the document-level IMDb movie reviews dataset (Diao et al., 2014) as our transfer set for SST-2. To match the single-sentence SST-2, we break paragraphs into individual linguistic sentences and, hence, multiple transfer set examples. To confirm that this is domain sensitive, we also apply it to the out-of-domain CoLA task in linguistic acceptability. We are unable to find a suitable unlabeled set for our other tasks—by construction, most sentence-pair datasets require manual balancing to prevent an overabundance of a single class, e.g., dissimilar examples in sentence similarity. We call this method TS_{IMDb}.

4.2 Training and Hyperparameters

We fine-tune our pretrained language models using largely the same procedure from Devlin et al. (2018). For fair comparison, we use 800K sentences for *all* transfer sets, including TS_{IMDb}. For our BiLSTM student models, we follow Tang et al. (2019) and use ADADELTA (Zeiler, 2012) with its default LR of 1.0 and $\rho = 0.95$. We train our models for 30 epochs, choosing the best performing on the standard development set. As is standard, for classification tasks, we minimize the negative log-likelihood; for regression, the mean-squared error. Depending on the loss on the development set, we choose either 150 or 300 LSTM units, and 200 or 400 hidden MLP units. This results in a model size between 1–3 million parameters. We use the 300-dimensional word2vec vectors trained on Google News, initial-izing out-of-vocabulary (OOV) vectors from UNI-FORM$[-0.25, 0.25]$, following Kim (2014), along with multichannel embeddings.

To fine-tune our pretrained language models, we use Adam (Kingma and Ba, 2014) with a learning rate (LR) linear warmup proportion of 0.1, linearly decaying the LR afterwards. We choose a batch size of eight and one fine-tuning epoch, which is sufficient for convergence. We tune the LR from $\{1, 5\} \times 10^{-5}$ based on word-level perplexity on the development set.

5 Results and Discussion

We present our results in Table 1. As an initial sanity check, we confirm that our BiLSTM (row 11) is acceptably similar to the previous best reported BiLSTM (row 5). We also verify that a transfer set is necessary—see rows 10 and 11, where using only the training dataset for distillation is insufficient. We further confirm that TS_{IMDb} works poorly for the out-of-domain CoLA dataset (row 8). Note that the absolute best result on SST-2 before BERT is 93.2, from Radford et al. (2017), but that approach demands copious amounts of domain-specific data from the practitioner.

5.1 Quality and Efficiency

Of the transfer set construction approaches, our principled generation methods consistently achieve the highest results (see Table 1, rows 6 and 7), followed by the rule-based TS_{MP} and the manually curated TS_{IMDb} (rows 8 and 9). TS_{GPT-2} is especially effective for CoLA, yielding a respective 12.5- and 30-point increase in Matthew's Correlation Coefficient (MCC) over TS_{MP} and training from scratch.

Interestingly, on SST-2, the synthetic GPT-2 samples outperform handwritten movie reviews from IMDb. Unlike the rule-based TS_{MP}, our LM-driven approaches outperform ELMo on all four tasks. TS_{GPT-2}, our best method, reaches GPT parity on all but CoLA, establishing domain-agnostic, pre-BERT SOTA on SST-2 and STS-B.

Our models use between one and three million parameters, which is at least 30 and 40 times smaller than ELMo and GPT, respectively. This represents an improvement over the previous SOTA—see the official GLUE leaderboard and Devlin et al. (2018) for specifics.

It should be emphasized that using fewer model parameters does *not* necessarily reduce the total

#	Model	SST-2 Acc.	CoLA MCC	STS-B r/ρ	MRPC F_1/Acc.
1	BERT$_{large}$ (Devlin et al., 2018)	94.9	60.5	86.5/87.6	89.3/85.4
2	OpenAI GPT (Radford et al., 2018)	91.3	**45.4**	82.0/80.0	82.3/75.7
3	Pre-OpenAI SOTA (Devlin et al., 2018)	90.2†	35.0	81.0/–	**86.0/80.4**
4	ELMo BiLSTM (Wang et al., 2018)	90.4	36.0	74.2/72.3	84.9/78.0
5	BiLSTM scratch (GLUE leaderboard)	85.9	15.7	70.3/67.8	81.8/74.3
6	BiLSTM$_{KD}$+TS$_{GPT-2}$	**92.7**	40.0	**82.1/80.7**	85.5/80.2
7	BiLSTM$_{KD}$+TS$_{TXL}$	91.9	36.5	82.0/80.4	85.1/79.3
8	BiLSTM$_{KD}$+TS$_{IMDb}$	92.0	18.8	–	–
9	BiLSTM$_{KD}$+TS$_{MP}$	90.7	27.5	81.1/79.3	82.4/76.1
10	BiLSTM$_{KD}$ (no TS)	88.4	0.0	68.2/65.8	78.0/69.7
11	BiLSTM scratch (ours)	87.6	9.5	66.9/64.3	80.9/69.4

Table 1: GLUE test results for our models, along with previous comparison points. Bolded are the best scores from rows 2–11. †For fair comparison, this result is copied from Looks et al. (2017), which represents the best *domain-agnostic* approach; the rest in row 3 is from Devlin et al. (2018) and the GLUE website.

#	Dataset	SST-2 U3$_\%$	SST-2 p/n	CoLA U3$_\%$	CoLA p/n	STS-B U3$_\%$	MRPC U3$_\%$	MRPC p/n
1	TS$_{GPT-2}$	77%	1.14	88%	2.71	83%	82%	0.41
2	TS$_{TXL}$	76%	1.29	87%	1.51	80%	82%	0.25
3	TS$_{IMDb}$	65%	1.65	65%	8.35	–	–	–
4	TS$_{MP}$	44%	1.23	69%	1.10	62%	60%	1.38
5	Training	20%	1.26	64%	2.38	66%	64%	2.07

Table 2: Diversity and generation statistics.

Model	SST-2 OOV	ppl	bpc	CoLA OOV	ppl	bpc	STS-B OOV	ppl	bpc	MRPC OOV	ppl	bpc
GPT-2	0%	67	1.3	0%	60	1.1	0%	35	1.2	0%	19	1.3
TXL	2.9%	77	1.8	0.1%	32	1.2	1.4%	32	1.9	1.0%	17	2.5

Table 3: Language modeling statistics.

disk usage. All traditional, word embedding-based models require storing the word vectors, which obviously precludes many on-device applications. Instead, the main benefit is that these shallow BiLSTMs perform inference an order of magnitude faster than GPT, which is mostly important for server-based, in-production NLP systems.

5.2 Language Generation Analysis

To characterize the transfer sets, we present diversity statistics in Table 2. U3$_\%$ denotes the average percentage of unique trigrams (Fedus et al., 2018) across sequential dataset chunks of size M, where M matches the original dataset size for fairness. Specifically, it represents the following:

$$\frac{1}{K} \sum_{i=1}^{K} \frac{\text{\# unique trigrams in } x_{((i-1)M+1):iM}}{\text{\# total trigrams in } x_{((i-1)M+1):iM}} \quad (2)$$

where $K = \lfloor N/M \rfloor$ and $\{x_1, \ldots, x_N\}$ the dataset. We find that TS$_{GPT-2}$ and TS$_{TXL}$ (rows 1 and 2) contain more unique trigrams than TS$_{MP}$, the original training set, and, surprisingly, handwritten movie reviews from IMDb (see rows 3–5).

To examine whether the class distribution of the transfer sets matches the original, we compute p/n, the positive-to-negative label ratio. Based on the statistics, we conclude that p/n varies wildly among the methods and datasets, with our LM-generated transfer sets differing substantially on MRPC, e.g., TS$_{GPT-2}$'s 0.41 versus the original's 2.07. This suggests that similar examples are more difficult to generate than dissimilar ones.

Finally, to characterize the LMs, we report GPT-2's and TXL's word-level perplexity (PPL) and bits per character (BPC) on the development sets, as well as the percentage of OOV tokens on the dataset—see Table 3, where lower scores are better. GPT-2 has practically no OOV for English, due to its byte-pair encoding scheme. In spite of using half as many parameters, GPT-2 is better at character-level language modeling than TXL is on all datasets, and its word-level PPL is similar, except on CoLA. As a rough analysis, BPC is a stronger predictor of improved quality than PPL is. Across the datasets, distillation quality strictly increases with decreasing BPC, unlike PPL, suggesting that character-level modeling is more important for constructing an effective transfer set.

Set	Example
TS$_{\text{GPT-2}}$	cansfield 's further oeuvre encompasses it somehow , and the surreal feels natural . [EOS]
TS$_{\text{TXL}}$	ethereal and plot of irony and irony and , most importantly , subtle suspense and spirit game - of - humor . [EOS]
TS$_{\text{MP}}$	what should have been a cutting hollywood satire is [MASK] about as fresh as last week 's issue of variety . [EOS]
TS$_{\text{IMDb}}$	but it the end, the film is a big steaming pile of...y'know. [EOS]
Training	the cinematography to the outstanding soundtrack and unconventional narrative [EOS]

Table 4: Generation examples on SST-2.

Generation examples. We present a random example from each transfer set in Table 4 for SST-2. The generated samples ostensibly consist of movie reviews and contain acceptable linguistic structure, despite only one epoch of fine-tuning. Due to space limitations, we show only SST-2; however, the other transfer sets are public for examination in our GitHub repository.

6   Conclusions and Future Work

We propose using text generation for constructing the transfer set in knowledge distillation. We validate our hypothesis that generating text using pretrained LMs outperforms manual data curation and rule-based techniques: the former in generality, and the latter efficacy. Across multiple datasets, we achieve OpenAI GPT-level quality using a single-layer BiLSTM.

The presented techniques can be readily extended to sequence-to-sequence-level knowledge distillation for applications in neural machine translation and logical form induction. Another line of future work involves applying the techniques to knowledge distillation for traditional, in-production NLP systems.

Acknowledgments

This research was supported by the Natural Sciences and Engineering Research Council (NSERC) of Canada. This research was enabled in part by resources provided by Compute Ontario and Compute Canada.

References

Jimmy Ba and Rich Caruana. 2014. Do deep nets really need to be deep? In *Advances in Neural Information Processing Systems*.

Daniel Cer, Mona Diab, Eneko Agirre, Inigo Lopez-Gazpio, and Lucia Specia. 2017. SemEval-2017 task 1: Semantic textual similarity multilingual and crosslingual focused evaluation. In *Proceedings of the 11th International Workshop on Semantic Evaluation (SemEval-2017)*.

Zihang Dai, Zhilin Yang, Yiming Yang, William W. Cohen, Jaime Carbonell, Quoc V. Le, and Ruslan Salakhutdinov. 2019. Transformer-XL: Attentive language models beyond a fixed-length context. *arXiv:1901.02860*.

Jacob Devlin, Ming-Wei Chang, Kenton Lee, and Kristina Toutanova. 2018. BERT: Pre-training of deep bidirectional transformers for language understanding. *arXiv:1810.04805*.

Qiming Diao, Minghui Qiu, Chao-Yuan Wu, Alexander J. Smola, Jing Jiang, and Chong Wang. 2014. Jointly modeling aspects, ratings and sentiments for movie recommendation (JMARS). In *Proceedings of the 20th ACM SIGKDD International Conference on Knowledge Discovery and Data Mining*.

William B. Dolan and Chris Brockett. 2005. Automatically constructing a corpus of sentential paraphrases. In *Proceedings of the Third International Workshop on Paraphrasing (IWP2005)*.

William Fedus, Ian Goodfellow, and Andrew M. Dai. 2018. MaskGAN: Better text generation via filling in the _______. In *International Conference on Learning Representations*.

Geoffrey Hinton, Oriol Vinyals, and Jeff Dean. 2015. Distilling the knowledge in a neural network. *arXiv:1503.02531*.

Sepp Hochreiter and Jürgen Schmidhuber. 1997. Long short-term memory. *Neural Computation*.

Yoon Kim. 2014. Convolutional neural networks for sentence classification. In *Proceedings of the 2014 Conference on Empirical Methods in Natural Language Processing*.

Diederik P. Kingma and Jimmy Ba. 2014. Adam: A method for stochastic optimization. In *International Conference on Learning Representations*.

Yinhan Liu, Myle Ott, Naman Goyal, Jingfei Du, Mandar Joshi, Danqi Chen, Omer Levy, Mike Lewis, Luke Zettlemoyer, and Veselin Stoyanov. 2019. RoBERTa: A robustly optimized BERT pretraining approach. *arXiv:1907.11692*.

Moshe Looks, Marcello Herreshoff, DeLesley Hutchins, and Peter Norvig. 2017. Deep learning with dynamic computation graphs. In *International Conference on Learning Representations*.

Stephen Merity, Caiming Xiong, James Bradbury, and Richard Socher. 2017. Pointer sentinel mixture models. In *International Conference on Learning Representations*.

Matthew Peters, Mark Neumann, Mohit Iyyer, Matt Gardner, Christopher Clark, Kenton Lee, and Luke Zettlemoyer. 2018. Deep contextualized word representations. In *Proceedings of the 2018 Conference of the North American Chapter of the Association for Computational Linguistics: Human Language Technologies, Volume 1 (Long Papers)*.

Alec Radford, Rafal Jozefowicz, and Ilya Sutskever. 2017. Learning to generate reviews and discovering sentiment. *arXiv:1704.01444*.

Alec Radford, Karthik Narasimhan, Tim Salimans, and Ilya Sutskever. 2018. Improving language understanding by generative pre-training.

Alec Radford, Jeffrey Wu, Rewon Child, David Luan, Dario Amodei, and Ilya Sutskever. 2019. Language models are unsupervised multitask learners. *OpenAI Blog*.

Yangyang Shi, Mei-Yuh Hwang, Xin Lei, and Haoyu Sheng. 2019. Knowledge distillation for recurrent neural network language modeling with trust regularization. In *2019 IEEE International Conference on Acoustics, Speech and Signal Processing (ICASSP)*.

Richard Socher, Alex Perelygin, Jean Wu, Jason Chuang, Christopher D. Manning, Andrew Ng, and Christopher Potts. 2013. Recursive deep models for semantic compositionality over a sentiment treebank. In *Proceedings of the 2013 Conference on Empirical Methods in Natural Language Processing*.

Raphael Tang, Yao Lu, Linqing Liu, Lili Mou, Olga Vechtomova, and Jimmy Lin. 2019. Distilling task-specific knowledge from BERT into simple neural networks. *arXiv:1903.12136*.

Alex Wang, Amapreet Singh, Julian Michael, Felix Hill, Omer Levy, and Samuel R. Bowman. 2018. GLUE: A multi-task benchmark and analysis platform for natural language understanding. *arXiv:1804.07461*.

Alex Warstadt, Amanpreet Singh, and Samuel R. Bowman. 2018. Neural network acceptability judgments. *arXiv:1805.12471*.

Zhilin Yang, Zihang Dai, Yiming Yang, Jaime G. Carbonell, Ruslan Salakhutdinov, and Quoc V. Le. 2019. XLNet: Generalized autoregressive pretraining for language understanding. *arXiv:1906.08237*.

Matthew D. Zeiler. 2012. ADADELTA: an adaptive learning rate method. *arXiv:1212.5701*.

Neural Unsupervised Parsing Beyond English

Katharina Kann, Anhad Mohananey, Kyunghyun Cho and **Samuel R. Bowman**
New York University, USA
{kann, anhad, kyunghyun.cho, bowman}@nyu.edu

Abstract

Recently, neural network models which automatically infer syntactic structure from raw text have started to achieve promising results. However, earlier work on unsupervised parsing shows large performance differences between non-neural models trained on corpora in different languages, even for comparable amounts of data. With that in mind, we train instances of the PRPN architecture (Shen et al., 2018a)—one of these unsupervised neural network parsers—for Arabic, Chinese, English, and German. We find that (i) the model strongly outperforms trivial baselines and, thus, acquires at least some parsing ability for all languages; (ii) good hyperparameter values seem to be universal; (iii) how the model benefits from larger training set sizes depends on the corpus, with the model achieving the largest performance gains when increasing the number of sentences from 2,500 to 12,500 for English. In addition, we show that, by sharing parameters between the related languages German and English, we can improve the model's unsupervised parsing F1 score by up to 4% in the low-resource setting.

1 Introduction

Unsupervised parsing, the task of inducing hierarchical syntactic structure from a large amount of unlabeled text, has been widely studied in natural language processing (NLP) (Carroll and Charniak, 1992; Pereira and Schabes, 1992; Klein and Manning, 2002, 2004). Work on this task bears on open research questions involving human language learning and grammar design by demonstrating what can be learned without substantial prior knowledge. Further, it can also be practically relevant for low-resource languages or language styles.

Recently, multiple types of neural network models have been added to the line of research on

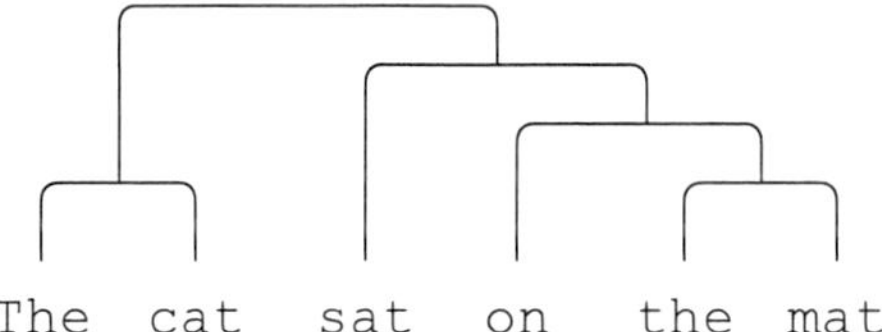

Figure 1: The constituency parse tree of the sentence *The cat sat on the mat*. In this work, we experiment with models that discover such syntactic structures in an unsupervised manner.

unsupervised parsing. Latent tree learning models learn to parse via optimization of a downstream task objective (Yogatama et al., 2017; Maillard et al., 2017; Choi et al., 2018). In contrast, generative unsupervised parsing models learn to model syntactic structure while being trained to language model (Shen et al., 2018a,c). While the latter model family has been able to generate parse trees which show a high accordance with expert annotations, its members, with the prominent Parsing Reading Predict-Network (PRPN) being no exception, have mostly been evaluated on English.[1] Thus, it is not obvious whether and when obtained results would hold true for other languages, especially if they are unrelated to English or dispose of significantly smaller training corpora. Some non-neural models for grammar induction—i.e., models which perform unsupervised parsing—show language-dependent performance variation (Snyder et al., 2009), which motivates our investigation of recent neural models.

In this work, we first aim to answer the following research questions, focusing on the parsing-reading-predict network (PRPN; Shen et al., 2018a) and experimenting with Arabic, Chinese,

---

[1] Some work, e.g. Kim et al. (2019a), present PRPN results on Chinese, but without further analysis of language-dependent differences.

Proceedings of the 2nd Workshop on Deep Learning Approaches for Low-Resource NLP (DeepLo), pages 209–218
Hong Kong, China, November 3, 2019. ©2019 Association for Computational Linguistics
https://doi.org/10.18653/v1/P17

and German datasets: (i) Do neural grammar induction models succeed on languages which are unrelated to English? (ii) Does the required amount of training data vary significantly by language? (iii) Do optimal hyperparameter values differ between languages? Answering those questions provides insight into what to expect when applying a neural grammar induction model to a new, potentially low-resource, language. For instance, we find that the model outperforms trivial baselines for all languages and good hyperparameter values seem to be largely language-independent.

Second, motivated by transfer learning approaches for similar tasks like supervised dependency parsing (de Lhoneux et al., 2018), we propose a multilingual model trained on the related languages English and German, such that information from each language is leveraged for the other one. We find that, for small training corpora, this improves performance and reduces the required number of parameters.

Contributions. To summarize, we make the following contributions: (i) We perform the first thorough study of the PRPN's parsing ability across multiple languages. To facilitate this analysis and interpret the meaning of the experimental results, we compare to baselines and upper bounds for each language. (ii) For each language, we study variations in hyperparameter trends. We further investigate how the PRPN's performance depends on the training set size, and how this differs between languages. (iii) We present a multilingual variant of the model, which has been obtained via parameter sharing across two related languages. We show that this improves the model's performance. Our experiments with sharing parameters between English and German result in up to 4% gain in parsing F1 over training on each language separately.

2 Unsupervised Constituency Parsing

Human language is governed by a set of syntactic rules, which all grammatical or acceptable sentences follow. Unsupervised parsing or *grammar induction* is the task of detecting such structure automatically, i.e., without any human annotation. The underlying research question is: how much of this latent structure of language can be discovered from raw text alone and how much requires an inherent bias towards acquiring a valid grammar or additional (potentially non-linguistic) informa-

tion? From a practical NLP perspective, grammar induction enables us to obtain syntactic information without labeled data, i.e., even in low-resource settings and for resource-poor languages. This information can then be of help for downstream tasks like machine translation (Aharoni and Goldberg, 2017).

In this work, we explore unsupervised *constituency* parsing. The PRPN, which we experiment with, aims at detecting so-called constituents in sentences. Thus, it splits a sentence's tokens into groups, usually based on their meaning. For example, in Figure 1, *The cat* and *on the mat* are constituents, inter alia. Constituency parsing is recursive: sentences are constructed from units which themselves consist of even smaller constituents which, in turn, consist of smaller groups of words, and so on.

This recursive structure of language is represented explicitly in recursive neural networks (Socher et al., 2011), which are also known as Tree-LSTMs. Successful induction of constituents enables us to then process input sentences using such a computational model instead of a sequential one like, e.g., a standard long short-term memory network (LSTM; Hochreiter and Schmidhuber, 1997). Since this can be relevant especially for low-resource languages with limited or zero training examples, we investigate in this work how the PRPN model for grammar induction behaves across languages and different (unlabeled) training set sizes.

3 Model and Setup

In this section, we first introduce the PRPN, which is the object of our investigations. We then present all datasets, baselines, and upper bounds we use in the set of experiments described in the next sections.

3.1 PRPN

The PRPN[2] consists of three principal components: (i) a parsing network, (ii) a reading network, and (iii) a predict network. We will summarize them in this section. A detailed explanation can be found in Shen et al. (2018a).

Parsing network. Given an input sentence $x = (x_0, x_1, \cdots, x_n)$ of length $n + 1$, the parsing net-

---

[2] We use the code from the original paper with minimal modifications: `https://github.com/yikangshen/PRPN.git`

work uses two convolutional layers to predict syntactic distances d_i between x_{i-1} and x_i for all pairs of adjacent words. This syntactic distance represents syntactic relationships between tokens in a sentence. Mathematically, the syntactic distance d_i between x_{i-1} and x_i is predicted by the PRPN as

$$h_i = \text{ReLU}(W_c \begin{bmatrix} x_{i-L} \\ x_{i-L+1} \\ \cdots \\ x_i \end{bmatrix} + b_c) \qquad (1)$$

$$d_i = \text{ReLU}(W_d h_i + b_d), \qquad (2)$$

where L is a a look-back parameter, which defines how many previous token are taken into account to compute the syntactic distance. W_c and b_c are kernel parameters, W_d and b_d represent another convolutional layer with a unit kernel size. Since the PRPN belongs to the family of unsupervised models with regard to parsing, there is no direct supervision on absolute values of the syntactic distance. Instead, these distances are trained via a language modeling downstream task.

For generating a constituency parse tree from the distances computed by the PRPN model, a recursive algorithm is used. Following this algorithm, we first, for a given set of distances $d_0, \ldots, d_n$, find the maximum distance d_i. Then, we split the input sequence $x = (x_0, x_1, \cdots, x_n)$ corresponding to the distances into a left $(0, \ldots, i-1)$ and a right $(i, \ldots, n)$ part or subtree. For each of those, we then again find the maximum value to split the sequence into two parts. This process repeats till the leaf nodes are reached, thus generating the entire tree.

Reading network. The reading network processes a sentence based on gate values g_i^t, which are, at each time step t, computed from the syntactic distances as follows:

$$\alpha_j^t = \frac{\text{hardtanh}((d_t - d_j)\tau) + 1}{2} \qquad (3)$$

and

$$g_i^t = \prod_{j=i+1}^{t-1} \alpha_j^t. \qquad (4)$$

where $\text{hardtanh}(x)$ is defined as

$$\text{hardtanh}(x) = \max(-1, \min(1, x)), \qquad (5)$$

and τ is a temperature parameter controlling the sensitivity to differences between distances.

The reading network then computes the memory state m_t at time step t from the input x_t, previous memory states $(m_{t-N_m}, \cdots, m_{t-1})$, and gate values $(g_0^t, \cdots, g_{t-1}^t)$. The memory consists of two sequences of vectors: a hidden tape $H_{t-1} = \{h_{t-N_m}, \cdots, h_{t-1}\}$, and a memory tape $C_{t-1} = \{c_{t-N_m}, \cdots, c_{t-1}\}$. Thus, the hidden state at time step t is defined as $m_t = (h_t, c_t)$, wherein h_t and c_t constitute the hidden and memory tape respectively. N_m represents the length of the memory span. At each step, the reading network performs an update using a structured attention mechanism, which is a variant of vanilla attention, but considers dependency relationship from the tree structure.

$$k_t = W_h h_{t-1} + W_x x_t \qquad (6)$$

$$q_i^t = \text{softmax} \frac{h_i k_t^T}{\sqrt{(\delta_k)}} \qquad (7)$$

$$s_i^T = \frac{g_i^t q_i^t}{\sum_i g_i^t} \qquad (8)$$

$$\begin{bmatrix} \tilde{h}_t \\ \tilde{c}_t \end{bmatrix} = \sum_{i=1}^{t-1} s_i^t \begin{bmatrix} h_i \\ c_i \end{bmatrix} \qquad (9)$$

Here, δ_k is the dimension of the hidden states. New values for h_t and c_t are then computed from $x_t, \tilde{h}_t$ and $\tilde{c}_t$ via the LSTM recurrent update.

Predict network. The last component of the PRPN predicts the probability of the next token x_{t+1} based on the memory states $m_0, \cdots, m_t$ from the reading network as well as the gates $g_0^{t+1}, \cdots, g_t^{t+1}$ from the parsing network. Since the true x_{t+1} is unknown at time step $t+1$, the predict network computes a temporary value for d_{t+1}:

$$d_{t+1}' = \text{ReLU}(W_d' h_t + b_d'). \qquad (10)$$

Obtaining α^{t+1} and g_i^{t+1} in the same way as before, the probability distribution of the next token x_{t+1} is then computed via a feed-forward network.

3.2 Datasets

We use existing constituency treebanks for Arabic, Chinese, English, and German. Table 1 shows statistics for all languages. For efficiency, we ignore sentences longer than 100 words during both training and evaluation in all our experiments.

	Arabic	Chinese	English	German
vocab size	21,902	23,714	15,617	10,367
train	18,087	57,251	43,738	18,598
dev	2,422	6,736	1,699	1,000
test	2,556	7,075	2,416	1,000

Table 1: Dataset statistics.

English. We perform English constituency parsing experiments for comparison with the original work by Shen et al. (2018a). We use the Wall Street Journal Section of the Penn Treebank (Marcus et al., 1999). We use parts 00-21 for training, 22 for validation and 23 for testing.

Arabic. We use the Arabic Treebank v3.0 (Maamouri et al., 2004). We randomly split the files into training, development and test: 200 files are used for each of test and development, and the remaining 1434 constitute our training set.

Chinese. We use the Chinese Penn Treebank v8.0 (Xue et al., 2005). Again, we randomly separate files into splits: the development and test sets consist of 300 files each, while the training set consists of the remaining 2407.

German. We use the NEGRA corpus (Skut et al., 1997), which consists of approximately $350,000$ words of German newspaper text (20,602 sentences). We divide the dataset into training, development, and test splits as suggested by Dubey and Keller (2003).

3.3 Parsing Baselines and Upper Bounds

We compare to the following baselines and upper bounds to better evaluate the performance of our models:

Best binary tree upper bound (BB). Since our datasets contain n-ary trees, but the PRPN only produces binary trees, obtaining a perfect F1 score is impossible. This upper bound represents the best score which can be obtained with binary trees.

Shen et al. (2018b) upper bound (SUB). Our second upper bound is a supervised parser, differing from the one presented by Shen et al. (2018b) only in that we do not predict or use any tags. It is trained on the gold annotations of the training set. We choose this particular approach since it is, like PRPN, based on the concept of syntactic distances: the parse tree is recovered from predicted distances between words in a sentence. Thus, we

see it as the supervised approach which is most comparable to the PRPN. Since our model does not predict labels which are used to recover n-ary trees in the original work, we compute the F1 score for this approach only with respect to binary gold trees. This is acceptable for our purposes, since we are interested in the supervised parser upper bound only to get an idea of the difficulty of the datasets in our different languages. For the supervised SUB baseline, we use hidden state and embedding dimensions of 100 and 300, respectively, and keep the default settings from Shen et al. (2018b) for all other hyperparameters.

Left/right-branching trees baseline (LBR/RBR). Our next baseline consists of purely left- or right-branching trees. LBR refers to the F1 score strictly left-branching binary trees obtain compared to the gold annotations, and RBR denotes the score of strictly right-branching trees.

Balanced trees baseline (BTB). Finally, this baseline is similar to LBR/RBR, but considering balanced binary trees, which are created by recursively splitting each span into halves. For odd lengths, the middle word becomes a part of the right subtree.

4 Monolingual Experiments

4.1 Language-Dependence of Hyperparameters

It is of practical importance to know whether a set of hyperparameters found for one language transfers to another one without any changes, especially for low-resource language without annotated (development) data. Therefore, we ask the following questions: (i) Do hyperparameters depend on the language when using our datasets? (ii) How to choose good hyperparameters for a new language? We aim at answering these questions with respect to the PRPN.

Setup. We perform an extensive random hyperparameter search, training 45 models for each language, i.e., 180 models in total. The hyperparameters we vary are *embedding size*, *hidden state size*, and *learning rate*. Random combinations of values are selected uniformly from the following parameter ranges: embedding size in $[100, 400]$, hidden state size in $[200, 400]$, and learning rate in $[0.0005, 0.0015]$.

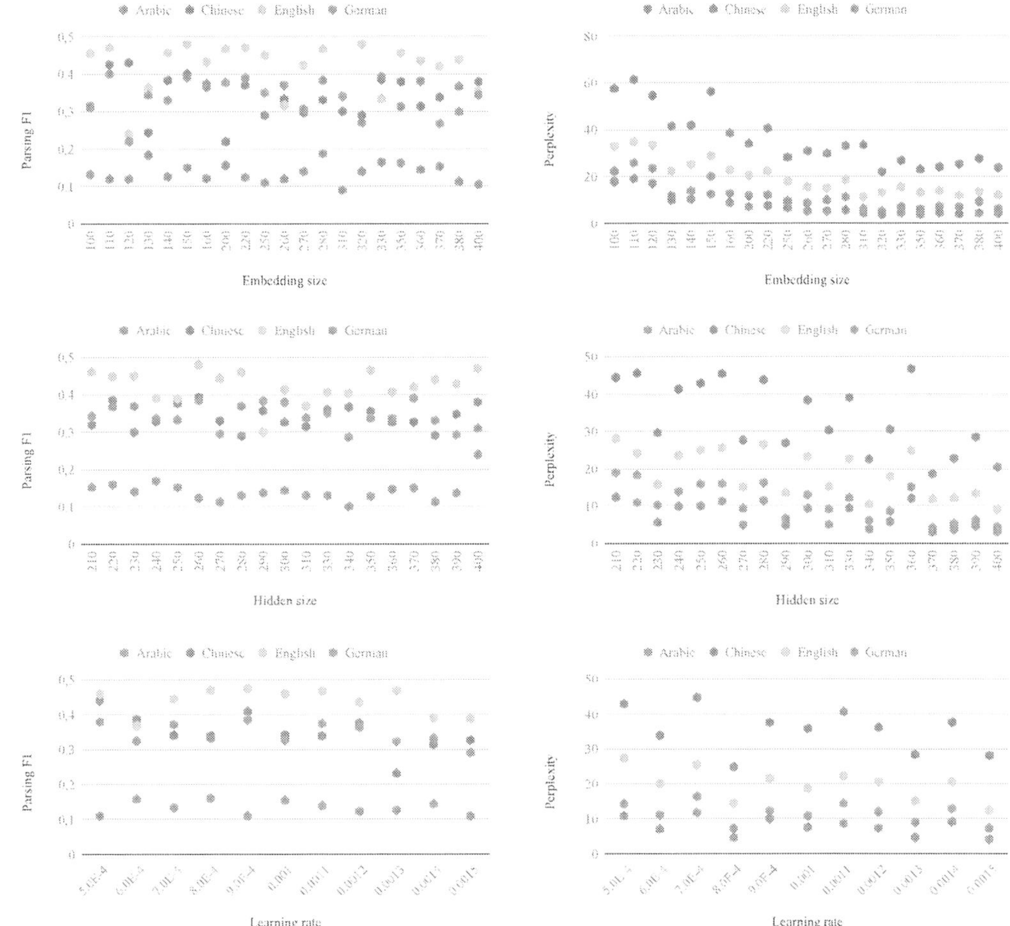

Figure 2: Parsing F1 as a function of different hyperparameters.

Figure 3: Language modeling perplexity as a function of different hyperparameters.

Results. The resulting parsing performances as a function of one hyperparameter at a time are shown in the three plots in Figure 2. The corresponding plots for language modeling perplexity can be found in Figure 3. We observe the following:

- First of all, we find no clear trend regarding which values yield the best parsing performance for either language. This shows that, as far as parsing is concerned, the PRPN is robust to hyperparameter changes. Furthermore, this also indicates that likely any values from within our ranges would be acceptable for a new language.

- Next, we look at the language modeling perplexity of all 180 models. While changes to the hyperparameters seem to not affect parsing performance, perplexity slightly decreases for larger embeddings sizes, as can be seen in Figure 2. This suggests that tuning hyperparameters using a language modeling objective for languages without annotated parsing data might not be helpful.

Because we do not find any substantial language-specific differences regarding the hyperparameter preferences of the model, we keep the default parameters of Shen et al. (2018a) for all following experiments: we use an embedding size of 200, a hidden state size of 400, and a learning rate of 0.001.

	Arabic	Chinese	English	German
PRPN	0.17 (.09)	0.28 (.07)	0.43 (.01)	0.41 (.03)
LBR	0.035	0.018	0.002	0.029
RBR	0.028	0.068	0.056	0.155
BTB	0.126	0.139	0.117	0.127
SUB	0.774	0.822	0.881	0.799
BB	0.914	0.924	0.908	0.878

Table 2: F1 scores for grammar induction. PRPN results are averaged over 5 training runs, with standard deviation in parentheses.

4.2 Unsupervised Parsing

After settling on hyperparameters, we evaluate the PRPN's performance for unsupervised parsing in Arabic, Chinese, English, and German. We train for a maximum of 150 epochs, but stop training anytime after 100 epochs if the training loss does not decrease for 5 consecutive epochs.

Results. All results are shown in Table 2. While unsupervised parsing of English using the PRPN has previously been studied widely (Shen et al., 2018a; Htut et al., 2018), we include the scores on English for comparison. We make the following observations:

- LBR, RBR, and BTB perform poorly for all languages. Since this has been shown to not be the case for English sentences only up to length 10 after filtering of punctuation, we conclude that, for longer sentences and with punctuation, these simple baselines are weak. This might be easily explained by the fact that the diversity of parses increases for longer sentences. The PRPN's F1 score is far higher that that of all trivial baselines for all languages, showing the effectiveness of the model overall.

- The F1 scores obtained by the PRPN differ a lot across languages, ranging from 0.17 for Arabic to 0.43 for English. This is in contrast to the BB and BTB scores, which differ only by 0.046 and 0.022 between extremes, respectively.

- The large difference between the PRPN's performance on one hand and BB as well as SUB, our supervised parsing upper bound, on the other, demonstrates that there is still

room for improvement. Furthermore, the differences between languages for SUB is relatively small. In particular, it is smaller than 5% for all languages. The difference in unsupervised constituency parsing performance across languages could thus be attributed to the PRPN's inherent preference toward English-like languages.

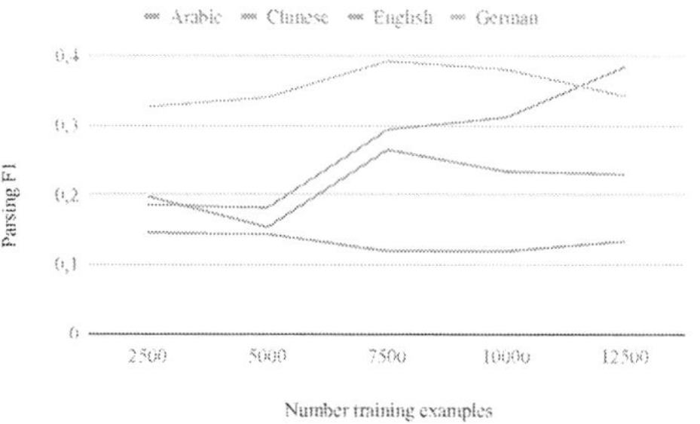

Figure 4: Learning curves for all languages.

4.3 Low-Resource Settings

We now aim to understand how the PRPN's performance for each language depends on the amount of data available. While large unlabeled corpora can be obtained easily for languages which are popular in NLP research, this is not the case for the majority of the world's languages. Thus, this question has practical relevance.

Setup. To simulate different low-resource settings for this experiment, we use the first $n \in \{2500, 5000, 7500, 10000, 12500\}$ sentences from each training set. Since the PRPN has shown to be largely robust to hyperparameter changes and we stop training based on the training loss, development sets are not used. Test sets are kept unmodified. As before, all results are averaged over 5 training runs with different random seeds.

Results. The learning curves in Figure 4 show the F1 scores of all models as a function of the amount of sentences available for training. We observe the following:

- While performance for English strongly increases with more training instances, this is not the case for the remaining languages. The Chinese F1 score increases only slightly for additional examples. The performance for Arabic and German is roughly constant. The fact that the PRPN is better at leveraging additional English data is another indicator that the PRPN might be better suited for English than for the other three languages in our experiments.

- Comparing Figure 4 to Table 2, we see a gap between the PRPN's performances for 12,500 examples and for the entire training sets for all languages. Thus, we conclude that disposing of more than 12,500 examples is generally beneficial.

5 Multilingual Experiment

5.1 Motivation

A multilingual model for unsupervised constituency parsing has desirable benefits. First, since only one model is needed for a set of languages, less memory is required to store all parameters. This facilitates, for instance, the application on mobile devices. Second, neural models which have been trained simultaneously on multiple languages have been shown to leverage knowledge from related languages to improve performance on other languages in the case of limited training data. Such cross-lingual transfer has been successfully employed for a variety of tasks, e.g., for supervised dependency parsing (de Lhoneux et al., 2018), for machine translation (Johnson et al., 2017a), or for paradigm completion (McCarthy et al., 2019).

5.2 Setup

Since transfer learning is mostly needed and also particularly effective in the low-data regime, we combine the training sets of 2,500 examples for English and German—the two of our languages which are related—to form a multilingual training set. We then train PRPN models on this combined training set, sharing all parameters.

The model's hyperparameters remain the same as before, and we again train for a maximum of 150 epochs, or until the training loss has not decreased for 5 consecutive epochs. As for our previous experiments, the reported results are averaged over 5 training runs with different random seeds.

5.3 Results

Results for single-language models as well as the multilingual versions are shown in Table 3. The parsing performance of the multilingual model is

	single language	multilingual
English	0.186 (.08)	0.226 (.03)
German	0.326 (.02)	0.350 (.06)

Table 3: Monolingual and multilingual PRPN test results for 2500 training sentences. Results are averaged over 5 training runs, with standard deviations in parentheses.

4.0% and 2.4% higher than that of the single-language models for English and German, respectively. Thus, the PRPN model indeed benefits from transfer learning, i.e., it can share information across related languages for unsupervised constituency parsing.

6 Related Work

Unsupervised parsing. Previous work on non-neural models for unsupervised parsing includes Clark (2001) and Klein and Manning (2002) for constituency parsing and Carroll and Charniak (1992); Klein and Manning (2004); Cohn et al. (2010); Spitkovsky et al. (2011); and Jiang et al. (2016) for dependency parsing. For Chinese, German, and English, previous work also observed differences in F1 scores; an overview can be found in Bod (2006). We have not included these non-neural baselines as part of our results due to lack of availability of trustworthy implementations.

Following the success of the neural PRPN model in 2018, various other neural unsupervised parsing approaches have been developed and shown promising results. Shen et al. (2018c) enhance the vanilla LSTM network with master forget and input gates to learn the tree structure through soft gating. Drozdov et al. (2019) use a recursive autoencoder-based architecture. Kim et al. (2019b) employ unsupervised recurrent neural network grammars, and Kim et al. (2019a) employ compound probabilistic context free grammars. Shi et al. (2019) show how image captions can be successfully leveraged to identify constituents in sentences. None of these papers performs an explicit analysis of differences between languages.

Jin et al. (2019) extend the PCFG approach to show results on Chinese, English and German. There are certain question that remain unanswered about multilingual grammar induction, especially related to cross-lingual transfer and difference in hyper parameters. In this work, we focus on adapting the PRPN to a multilingual setting, since it is the first neural model which has been shown to obtain robust unsupervised parsing results. Although we have primarily focused on PRPN due to its overall success, it would be interesting to observe whether similar trends in relative performance among languages hold for other models mentioned above. We leave this for future work.

A closely related line of research, which is often referred to as *latent tree learning*, aims to create a parse structure which is well-suited for a particular NLP application. Common choices are sentence classification tasks like natural language inference (Yogatama et al., 2017; Maillard et al., 2017; Choi et al., 2018), machine translation (Bisk and Tran, 2018), or toy datasets where the correct parse can trivially be found by humans (Jacob et al., 2018; Nangia and Bowman, 2018). Latent tree learning models have been shown to outperform sequential models and TreeRNNs on multiple datasets (Maillard et al., 2017; Choi et al., 2018). However, the parses predicted by latent tree models have been shown to mostly be nonsensical (Williams et al., 2018).

Supervised parsing. This research is further related to the line of work on supervised parsing. Two main parsing paradigms exist: dependency parsing, which is concerned with the relationships between words in a sentence, and constituency parsing (or *phrase-structure parsing*), which is what we are interested in here (cf. Figure 1). Neural network models have pushed the state of the art for supervised constituency parsing in the last years. Possible approaches include methods to either build parse trees sequentially by estimating transition probabilities (Zhu et al., 2013; Cross and Huang, 2016), employ a chart-based approach, which performs exact structured inference via dynamic programming (Durrett and Klein, 2015; Stern et al., 2017), or cast the problem as a sequence labeling task (Gómez-Rodríguez and Vilares, 2018). Another, rather new option is to predict syntactic distances between words, which can then be converted into trees (Shen et al., 2018b). This is the same core concept that the PRPN is based on. Thus, we consider Shen et al. (2018b)'s approach one of our upper bounds on the unsupervised parsing performance of the PRPN.

Cross-lingual transfer. Cross-lingual transfer (Wu, 1997; Yarowsky et al., 2001), i.e., us-

ing knowledge gained from one (usually high-resource) language for solving a task in another (usually low-resource) language, is very common when working on resource-poor languages in NLP. There are two very intuitive ways of realizing such a transfer (Liu et al., 2019): One way is to translate the test data into a high-resource language and to solve the task using a system for that second language. Another way is to translate large amount of training data into a low-resource language and train a system in that language. Other methods have been developed as well, many based on parameter sharing—as we do in this work—, e.g., for cross-lingual natural language inference (Conneau et al., 2018), morphological generation (Kann et al., 2017; McCarthy et al., 2019), dialogue systems (Schuster et al., 2019), or machine translation (Johnson et al., 2017b; Aharoni et al., 2019). While we are not aware of any previous work exploring cross-lingual transfer for unsupervised parsing as done in this paper, approaches have been developed which leverage high-resource language data for *supervised* parsing in low-resource languages (Søgaard, 2011; Naseem et al., 2012).

7 Conclusion

We investigated the behavior of the PRPN, a neural unsupervised constituency parsing model, for the languages Arabic, Chinese, English, and German. While, overall, our experiments showed that the model strongly outperformed trivial baselines for all the languages, we made the following additional observations: (i) With regards to its parsing performance, the model is robust to hyperparameter changes for all four languages. (ii) Parsing F1 and language modeling perplexity were not correlated. (iii) The PRPN's unsupervised parsing performance differed a lot between languages, while trivial baselines and upper bounds obtained similar scores. (iv) The model was able to leverage additional training data for English better in low-resource settings, and for no language did the PRPN reach its maximum observed F1 score with 12,500 training instances. Finally, we proposed to train a multilingual PRPN model for the related languages English and German. Besides requiring less parameters, this led to an up to 4% higher F1 score in the low-data regime.

Acknowledgments

This work has benefited from the support of Samsung Research under the project *Improving Deep Learning using Latent Structure* and from the donation of a Titan V GPU by NVIDIA Corporation.

References

Roee Aharoni and Yoav Goldberg. 2017. Towards string-to-tree neural machine translation. In *ACL*.

Roee Aharoni, Melvin Johnson, and Orhan Firat. 2019. Massively multilingual neural machine translation. In *NAACL*.

Yonatan Bisk and Ke Tran. 2018. Inducing grammars with and for neural machine translation. In *WNMT*.

Rens Bod. 2006. An all-subtrees approach to unsupervised parsing. In *ACL*.

Glenn Carroll and Eugene Charniak. 1992. *Two experiments on learning probabilistic dependency grammars from corpora*. AAAI Technical Report.

Jihun Choi, Kang Min Yoo, and Sang-goo Lee. 2018. Learning to compose task-specific tree structures. In *AAAI*.

Alexander Clark. 2001. Unsupervised induction of stochastic context-free grammars using distributional clustering. In *CoNLL*.

Trevor Cohn, Phil Blunsom, and Sharon Goldwater. 2010. Inducing tree-substitution grammars. *JMLR*, 11:3053–3096.

Alexis Conneau, Ruty Rinott, Guillaume Lample, Adina Williams, Samuel Bowman, Holger Schwenk, and Veselin Stoyanov. 2018. XNLI: Evaluating cross-lingual sentence representations. In *EMNLP*.

James Cross and Liang Huang. 2016. Span-based constituency parsing with a structure-label system and provably optimal dynamic oracles. In *EMNLP*.

Andrew Drozdov, Pat Verga, Mohit Yadav, Mohit Iyyer, and Andrew McCallum. 2019. Unsupervised latent tree induction with deep inside-outside recursive autoencoders. *arXiv:1904.02142*.

Amit Dubey and Frank Keller. 2003. Probabilistic parsing for german using sister-head dependencies. In *ACL*.

Greg Durrett and Dan Klein. 2015. Neural CRF parsing. In *ACL–IJCNLP*.

Carlos Gómez-Rodríguez and David Vilares. 2018. Constituent parsing as sequence labeling. In *EMNLP*.

Sepp Hochreiter and Jürgen Schmidhuber. 1997. Long short-term memory. *Neural computation*, 9(8):1735–1780.

Phu Mon Htut, Kyunghyun Cho, and Samuel R Bowman. 2018. Grammar induction with neural language models: An unusual replication. In *EMNLP*.

Athul Paul Jacob, Zhouhan Lin, Alessandro Sordoni, and Yoshua Bengio. 2018. Learning hierarchical structures on-the-fly with a recurrent-recursive model for sequences. In *Repl4NLP*.

Yong Jiang, Wenjuan Han, and Kewei Tu. 2016. Unsupervised neural dependency parsing. In *EMNLP*.

Lifeng Jin, Finale Doshi-Velez, Timothy Miller, Lane Schwartz, and William Schuler. 2019. Unsupervised learning of pcfgs with normalizing flow. In *Proceedings of the 57th Conference of the Association for Computational Linguistics*, pages 2442–2452.

Melvin Johnson, Mike Schuster, Quoc Le, Maxim Krikun, Yonghui Wu, Zhifeng Chen, Nikhil Thorat, Fernand a Vigas, Martin Wattenberg, Greg Corrado, Macduff Hughes, and Jeffrey Dean. 2017a. Google's multilingual neural machine translation system: Enabling zero-shot translation. *TACL*, 5:339–351.

Melvin Johnson, Mike Schuster, Quoc V Le, Maxim Krikun, Yonghui Wu, Zhifeng Chen, Nikhil Thorat, Fernanda Viégas, Martin Wattenberg, Greg Corrado, et al. 2017b. Googles multilingual neural machine translation system: Enabling zero-shot translation. *TACL*, 5:339–351.

Katharina Kann, Ryan Cotterell, and Hinrich Schütze. 2017. One-shot neural cross-lingual transfer for paradigm completion. In *ACL*.

Yoon Kim, Chris Dyer, and Alexander M Rush. 2019a. Compound probabilistic context-free grammars for grammar induction. *arXiv:1906.10225*.

Yoon Kim, Alexander M Rush, Lei Yu, Adhiguna Kuncoro, Chris Dyer, and Gábor Melis. 2019b. Unsupervised recurrent neural network grammars. *arXiv:1904.03746*.

Dan Klein and Christopher D Manning. 2002. A generative constituent-context model for improved grammar induction. In *ACL*.

Dan Klein and Christopher D Manning. 2004. Corpus-based induction of syntactic structure: Models of dependency and constituency. In *ACL*.

Miryam de Lhoneux, Johannes Bjerva, Isabelle Augenstein, and Anders Søgaard. 2018. Parameter sharing between dependency parsers for related languages. In *EMNLP*.

Jiahua Liu, Yankai Lin, Zhiyuan Liu, and Maosong Sun. 2019. XQA: A cross-lingual open-domain question answering dataset. In *ACL*.

Mohamed Maamouri, Ann Bies, Tim Buckwalter, and Wigdan Mekki. 2004. The Penn Arabic treebank: Building a large-scale annotated arabic corpus. In *NEMLAR conference on Arabic language resources and tools*.

Jean Maillard, Stephen Clark, and Dani Yogatama. 2017. Jointly learning sentence embeddings and syntax with unsupervised tree-LSTMs. In *ICLR*.

Mitchell Marcus, Beatrice Santorini, Mary Ann Marcinkiewicz, and Ann Taylor. 1999. Treebank-3 LDC99T42. *CD-ROM. Philadelphia, Penn.: Linguistic Data Consortium*.

Arya D McCarthy, Ekaterina Vylomova, Shijie Wu, Chaitanya Malaviya, Lawrence Wolf-Sonkin, Garrett Nicolai, Miikka Silfverberg, Sebastian J Mielke, Jeffrey Heinz, Ryan Cotterell, et al. 2019. The SIGMORPHON 2019 shared task: Morphological analysis in context and cross-lingual transfer for inflection. In *SIGMORPHON*.

Nikita Nangia and Samuel Bowman. 2018. ListOps: A diagnostic dataset for latent tree learning. In *NAACL-SRW*.

Tahira Naseem, Regina Barzilay, and Amir Globerson. 2012. Selective sharing for multilingual dependency parsing. In *ACL*.

Fernando Pereira and Yves Schabes. 1992. Inside-outside reestimation from partially bracketed corpora. In *ACL*.

Sebastian Schuster, Sonal Gupta, Rushin Shah, and Mike Lewis. 2019. Cross-lingual transfer learning for multilingual task oriented dialog. In *NAACL*.

Yikang Shen, Zhouhan Lin, Chin-Wei Huang, and Aaron Courville. 2018a. Neural language modeling by jointly learning syntax and lexicon. In *ICLR*.

Yikang Shen, Zhouhan Lin, Athul Paul Jacob, Alessandro Sordoni, Aaron Courville, and Yoshua Bengio. 2018b. Straight to the tree: Constituency parsing with neural syntactic distance. In *ACL*.

Yikang Shen, Shawn Tan, Alessandro Sordoni, and Aaron Courville. 2018c. Ordered neurons: Integrating tree structures into recurrent neural networks. *arXiv:1810.09536*.

Haoyue Shi, Jiayuan Mao, Kevin Gimpel, and Karen Livescu. 2019. Visually grounded neural syntax acquisition. *arXiv:1906.02890*.

Wojciech Skut, Brigitte Krenn, Thorsten Brants, and Hans Uszkoreit. 1997. An annotation scheme for free word order languages. In *ANLP*.

Benjamin Snyder, Tahira Naseem, and Regina Barzilay. 2009. Unsupervised multilingual grammar induction. In *ACL–IJCNLP*.

Richard Socher, Cliff C Lin, Chris Manning, and Andrew Y Ng. 2011. Parsing natural scenes and natural language with recursive neural networks. In *ICML*.

Anders Søgaard. 2011. Data point selection for cross-language adaptation of dependency parsers. In *NAACL–HLT*.

Valentin I Spitkovsky, Hiyan Alshawi, Angel X Chang, and Daniel Jurafsky. 2011. Unsupervised dependency parsing without gold part-of-speech tags. In *EMNLP*.

Mitchell Stern, Jacob Andreas, and Dan Klein. 2017. A minimal span-based neural constituency parser. In *ACL*, volume 1, pages 818–827.

Adina Williams, Andrew Drozdov, and Samuel R Bowman. 2018. Do latent tree learning models identify meaningful structure in sentences? *TACL*, 6:253–267.

Dekai Wu. 1997. Stochastic inversion transduction grammars and bilingual parsing of parallel corpora. *Computational linguistics*, 23(3):377–403.

Naiwen Xue, Fei Xia, Fu-Dong Chiou, and Marta Palmer. 2005. The Penn Chinese TreeBank: Phrase structure annotation of a large corpus. *Natural language engineering*, 11(2):207–238.

David Yarowsky, Grace Ngai, and Richard Wicentowski. 2001. Inducing multilingual text analysis tools via robust projection across aligned corpora. In *HLT*.

Dani Yogatama, Phil Blunsom, Chris Dyer, Edward Grefenstette, and Wang Ling. 2017. Learning to compose words into sentences with reinforcement learning. In *ICLR*.

Muhua Zhu, Yue Zhang, Wenliang Chen, Min Zhang, and Jingbo Zhu. 2013. Fast and accurate shift-reduce constituent parsing. In *ACL*.

Reevaluating Argument Component Extraction in Low Resource Settings

Anirudh Joshi[1,2]   **Timothy Baldwin**[1]   **Richard O. Sinnott**[1]

Cecile Paris[2]

[1] The University of Melbourne   [2] CSIRO Data61

anirudhj@student.unimelb.edu.au, tb@ldwin.net

rsinnott@unimelb.edu.au, cecile.paris@data61.csiro.au

Abstract

Argument component extraction is a challenging and complex high-level semantic extraction task. As such, it is both expensive to annotate (meaning training data is limited and low-resource by nature), and hard for current-generation deep learning methods to model. In this paper, we reevaluate the performance of state-of-the-art approaches in both single- and multi-task learning settings using combinations of character-level, GloVe, ELMo, and BERT encodings using standard BiLSTM-CRF encoders. We use evaluation metrics that are more consistent with evaluation practice in named entity recognition to understand how well current baselines address this challenge and compare their performance to lower-level semantic tasks such as CoNLL named entity recognition. We find that performance utilizing various pre-trained representations and training methodologies often leaves a lot to be desired as it currently stands, and suggest future pathways for improvement.

1 Introduction

Argument component (AC) extraction typically involves addressing extremely complex high-level concepts, demanding significant amounts of world knowledge, natural language understanding, and reasoning to address (Moens, 2018). These argument components may come from different datasets, different domains, and have varying tagsets (IOB — inside, outside or at the beginning of an entity), depending on the component and annotation criteria used (Schulz et al., 2018). Originally the field expanded its tagsets across tasks over time; however, due to the inherent difficulty, the field has contracted back to tackling much simpler tasks (Moens, 2018). This difficulty is because performance across domains and tasks with limited resources makes training models extraordinarily difficult.

Recent work such as Schulz et al. (2018) uses single-task learning ("STL") and multi-task learning ("MTL") with character-level encodings and pre-trained GloVe word embeddings as inputs to a BiLSTM-CRF encoder to analyze this issue from a low resource standpoint, while other work approaches the task through the use of graph convolution networks (GCNs) with syntactic dependencies (Morio and Fujita, 2019). However, both evaluate in terms of tag-level F1, including non-target O tags, rather than the more stringent span-based metric conventionally used to evaluate named entity recognition ("NER": Tjong Kim Sang and De Meulder (2003)). In this paper, we compare contemporary embedding approaches in STL and MTL contexts against Schulz et al. (2018) and achieve state-of-the-art results for the dataset, but more importantly, we demonstrate that under span-based evaluation, the current state-of-the-art is woefully low, calling into question whether argument component extraction as currently construed is feasible for current NLP methods.

2 Findings

The focus of the paper is on a rigorous reevaluation of actual low-resource argument component (AC) extraction within argumentation mining (AM); in contrast to previous publications, we find that:

- Tag-based evaluation is inappropriate for evaluating span extraction performance.

- STL improves with embeddings and is better than MTL, in contrast to previously reported results.

- Current state-of-the-art (SOTA) approaches to low-resource AM, when evaluated strictly, do not result in usable systems, with <0.4 F1 in general.

Proceedings of the 2nd Workshop on Deep Learning Approaches for Low-Resource NLP (DeepLo), pages 219–224
Hong Kong, China, November 3, 2019. ©2019 Association for Computational Linguistics
https://doi.org/10.18653/v1/P17

As such, AC extraction in low-resource settings is an unsolved task and will require order of magnitude improvements in pre-training and inclusion of external knowledge to become serviceable.

3 Setup

3.1 Tasks and Evaluation

3.1.1 Task Description

Argument component (AC) extraction is the extraction of ACs such as factual premises and opinion-based claims from text, using a tag-based IOB system to extract the textual components as contiguous sequences of text as NER components (Schulz et al., 2018). The tasks are from a variety of disparate domains, with different IOB tagsets and associated distributions, some with simple claims or premises, others with more complex annotations (Schulz et al., 2018). The tasks are, as per previous work: *var, wiki, news, essays, web* and *hotel* (Schulz et al., 2018). These are NER tagged sentences that contain IOB tagged claims, premises, or more specific argument tags (with respect to the specific dataset annotation guidelines). They are sourced from various editorials/official documents/discussion boards, Wikipedia discussions, news comments, persuasive essays, web discourse, and hotel review domains respectively (Schulz et al., 2018). In each case, we train over training splits of 1k, 6k, 11k, and 21k tagged NER tokens, each of which is within a low-resource range. This NER extraction task is low-resource due to the fact that the number of example tokens is extremely limited, on the order of a few articles or hundreds of sentence examples at the low end, and just over a thousand at the high end (6k vs. 21k tokens). In contrast, other tasks often have examples in the thousands of sentences, and hundreds of thousands of tokens (Tjong Kim Sang and De Meulder, 2003). We also validate our implementation against CoNLL NER, to evaluate the competitiveness of our method over a simpler extraction task as an upper bound. We do this to contextualize how F1 span-based performance operates in low-resource AM vs. low-resource NER, to indicate how SOTA models perform with respect to the simpler NER extraction task.

3.1.2 Evaluation

We evaluate the results based on CoNLL span-based F1, ignoring non-relevant O extraction as it confounds analysis of true extraction performance of components of interest (named entities in the NER case and argumentation components for our task: Tjong Kim Sang and De Meulder (2003); Gardner et al. (2018); Peters et al. (2018)). This span based metric means we do not simply look at the precision and recall of tags in isolation. The span-based evaluation only concerns overlapping contiguous spans whereas tag-based F1 concerns discontinuous spans, meaning it is both looser and less aligned to the key task of contiguous span extraction. This stricter evaluation regime produces more realistic task results, as it is concerned with span extraction, not tag-based classification.

3.2 Framework

We utilize AllenNLP (Gardner et al., 2018) as our base framework, with standard STL training ablations (Peters et al., 2018), and adapt a multi-sampling training approach leveraging Hierarchical Multi-Task Learning (Sanh et al., 2019) for MTL training ablations. In the MTL case, for final test evaluation, we utilize the best epoch weights for each component task from the proportional sampler based on the validation data. We evaluate using the AllenNLP implementation of CoNLL span-based F1 measure, which focuses on the correctness of full-span extraction of components relevant to argumentation (and ignores O components), rather than the isolated tag-based F1 measures previously used.

3.3 Base BiLSTM-CRF Model, Training and Hyper-parameter Configuration

We utilize a variety of pre-trained models to generate word embeddings as input to a standard 2 layer BiLSTM-CRF, with a hidden layer size of 200 and dropout rate of 0.5. This base model is consistent with related task approaches, and SOTA methods (Peters et al., 2018; Schulz et al., 2018; Sanh et al., 2019). In general, previous work has used STL/MTL-trained BiLSTM-CRFs. In addition, as our focus is on the evaluation approach used in current SOTA papers, the point of the paper is not to evaluate every model combination, but simply to demonstrate the "true" performance of current SOTA methods under a rigorous evaluation regime. We improve on previous approaches within AC extraction by using more complex embeddings and cumulative embedding combinations. Specifically, we make use of character-level embeddings using a CNN as a randomly initialized baseline implementation, GloVe (Pennington et al., 2014), ELMo (Peters et al., 2018), and BERT (Devlin et al., 2018), in a monotonically increasing fashion through pre-trained ablations. We based our STL/MTL hyper-parameter configuration on Peters et al. (2018); Sanh et al. (2019), specifically the NER components, with monotonically increasing pre-trained embedding representations following Peters et al. (2018). No hyperparameter tuning is required, as these papers represent NER SOTA baselines in the STL/MTL NER extraction space, and we extend previous papers embedding approaches (Schulz et al., 2018) with more complex embeddings (BERT) and stricter evaluation criteria.

3.4 Monotonically Increasing Pre-trained Embeddings Ablations

We create monotonically increasing ablations of pre-trained embeddings, from least to most complex, as the basis of our SOTA BiLSTM-CRF span extraction model, to analyze their performance under strict evaluation criteria. We jointly train using progressive combinations of embeddings starting with the character-level CNN, and then monotonically adding GloVe, ELMo, and BERT embeddings. We use 16-dimensional character encodings with 128 filters and 3 n-gram filter sizes; pre-trained 50d GloVe vectors; pre-trained ELMo embeddings (with trainable scalar weights); and uncased base BERT (768d) drawing from a variety of previous works (Gardner et al., 2018; Peters et al., 2018; Schulz et al., 2018). For MTL, we utilize the Hierarchical Multi-Task Learning framework (Sanh et al., 2019), taking the best epoch weights from the multi-task sampler for each task based on the validation data. We base our models on the previous papers, to focus on evaluation, extend with BERT, and determine how well SOTA models can really perform on complex AC extraction tasks.

4 Experiments

4.1 Analysis

We find that in general, MTL often underperforms STL for individual tasks, which is in contrast to previous work (Schulz et al., 2018) (see Figure 1). We hypothesize that this is due to the disparate domains, annotations, IOB distributions, and label sets of the various tasks. Therefore even with the extra supervision signal, MTL tends not to aid in the training process, especially with well-

initialized pre-trained embeddings. We hypothesize that focusing training on sampling the core task with the pre-trained embeddings (with suitable regularisation — see Section 3.3) will likely lead to better span extraction performance in low-resource, disparate domains (especially given the disparate label sets for the respective datasets), where the more robust and general performance of MTL is traded for higher performance in specific tasks.

We often find that in the STL/MTL cases there is a minimal improvement over the baseline CNN-based trained character embeddings and that the representational capacity of the pre-trained models is likely not sufficient to provide a significant improvement on these tasks. We find that in general F1 is substantially below much simpler tasks such as CoNLL NER, with the majority of our results well below an F1 of 0.5 (see Figure 2), whereas CoNLL models trained equivalently produce results well in excess of 0.9. In some cases such as the *essays* and *hotel* datasets, we see what we would expect with increasing pre-trained model complexity added to both STL and MTL tasks.

However *news*, *web* and *wiki* all seem to exhibit highly variant baseline performance regardless of training methodology or pre-trained initialisation. In these scenarios, the model is likely fitting annotation artifacts. We find that in general, both in the progress of training and evaluation, test and validation performance is both noisy and unstable. This variance is likely due to the difficult nature of the task, the sparsity of the data, and the disparity between the domains of pre-trained embeddings to the specific task at hand.

4.2 Embedding Ablations

We found that in general as we increase the complexity of pre-trained embeddings, from character-based learned CNN embeddings to pre-trained GloVe, ELMo, and BERT, we see improved performance (see Table 1). However, we still performed much lower when using more advanced pre-trained embeddings than previous systems using span metrics (Schulz et al., 2018) (see Table 1). This difference is due to the focus on tag-based accuracy metrics rather than span-based metrics, and also the disproportionate effect of the O tag. A comparable system to that of Schulz et al. (2018), the glove_stl baseline, performed much worse when using the span-based metric, where

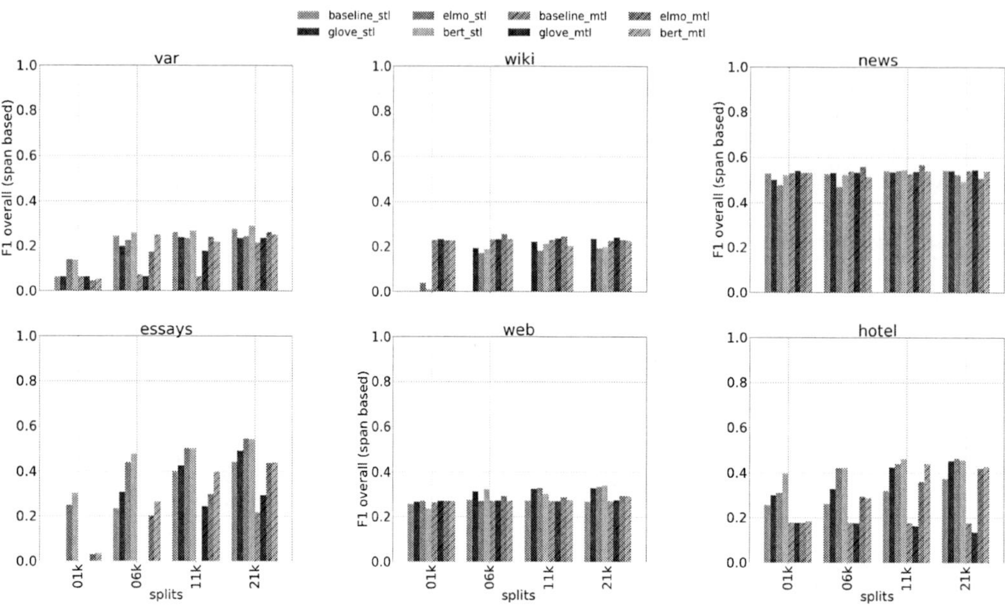

Figure 1: Performance (F1) across splits, tasks, and models. Full F1 range is used to demonstrate performance with full context of upper bound.

task	var_21k	wiki_21k	news_21k	essays_21k	web_21k	hotel_21k
max_stl	0.2863	0.2349	0.5420	0.5439	**0.3404**	0.4632
max_mtl	0.2606	0.2412	0.5445	0.4377	0.2934	0.4267
previous_tag_baseline	(0.3045)	(0.1834)	(0.3263)	(0.4838)	(0.1521)	(0.4569)
previous_tag_stl	(0.4334)	(0.2337)	(0.5649)	(0.6054)	(0.2343)	**(0.4791)**
previous_tag_mtl	**(0.4739)**	**(0.3250)**	**(0.5776)**	**(0.6055)**	(0.2327)	(0.4644)

Table 1: Our best STL/MTL on a more realistic span based evaluation indicates (top) a more realistic but lower performance vs. previous implementations using more simplistic tag based macro F1 evaluation (bottom in brackets).

we found in general that even with the addition of SOTA BERT embeddings, which have produced significant advances in other mid-level NLP tasks (Devlin et al., 2018), we were unable to produce results on par with tag-based evaluation. However span-based extraction provides a more realistic assessment of argument component extraction, with bert_stl generally providing the highest average score.

We also validated our results against the CoNLL NER dataset for all ablations and found performance to be on par with existing SOTA systems (Peters et al., 2018). Thus more pre-trained, more diverse, and more integrated representations do help improve the performance across these tasks on average, but the performance for argumenta-

tion component extraction leaves a lot to be desired under the span-based metric, suggesting that a usable extraction system is still well beyond the reach of current NLP models, based on the existing task formulation.

5 Future Work

It is of crucial importance to improve the representational complexity of pre-trained embeddings for high-level semantic tasks, especially in a low-resource regime. The inclusion of more linguistic and statistical inductive biases is necessary if progress is to be made on problems of extreme complexity, such as natural language argumentation component extraction. Some work has already begun with the introduction of syntactic fea-

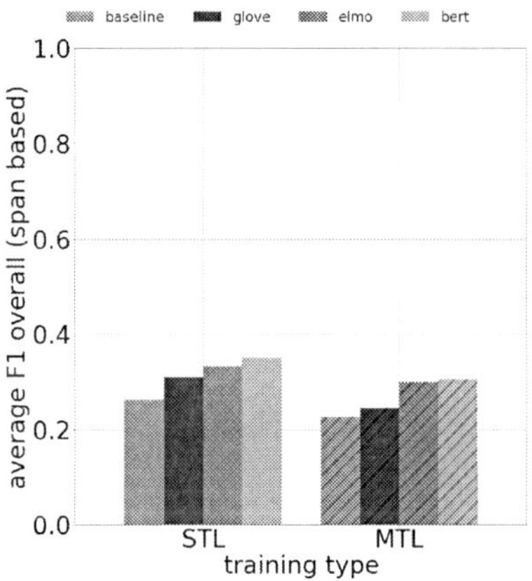

Figure 2: Comparing performance across models on average across all tasks contrasting training type methodologies. Full F1 range is used to demonstrate performance with full context of upper bound.

tures within GCNs for this task, but more integration of inductive biases will be necessary if progress is to be made, both in task performance and representational capability (Morio and Fujita, 2019). Other possible improvements include the use of external knowledge, such as external knowledge graphs and sentence based dependencies.

We find that in general, STL or MTL training over pre-trained embeddings are unlikely to be of significant benefit given the enormous amount of information required for complex semantic extraction tasks. A corollary to this is that it is also likely not sufficient, given the minor improvement of BERT over other pre-trained representations, to solely rely on statistical sequence prediction. To close the gap with human performance a step-order improvement in pre-training for end tasks is required.

6 Conclusion

In this paper, we have reevaluated argumentation component extraction based on STL and MTL approaches across a range of contemporary pre-trained embedding representation models, within a low resource task setting. We found that in general, according to a span-based evaluation metric such as that used for CoNLL NER, the results for the task drop appreciably from published results based on more naive evaluations. We found that MTL across varying domains did not significantly aid the task across domains, and that pre-trained word representations are not substantially better than a character-based word embedding baseline.

The results on average showed that as the pre-trained representations grow in complexity, on average, there was a robust increase in performance, and this was robust in both STL/MTL scenarios. Hence we believe that significant improvements in representational complexity of pre-trained embeddings for low resource tasks are necessary, above and beyond pure statistical inductive biases, if tasks such as argumentation component extraction are to achieve the same level of success as lower-level tasks such as NER.

7 Acknowledgements

This research is based upon work supported in part by CSIRO Data61 and the Office of the Director of National Intelligence (ODNI), Intelligence Advanced Research projects Activity (IARPA), under Contract [2017-16122000002]. The views and conclusions contained herein are those of the authors and should not be interpreted as necessarily representing the official policies, either expressed or implied, of ODNI, IARPA, or the U.S. Government. The U.S. Government is authorized to reproduce and distribute reprints for governmental purposes notwithstanding any copyright annotation therein.

References

Jacob Devlin, Ming-Wei Chang, Kenton Lee, and Kristina Toutanova. 2018. BERT: Pre-training of deep bidirectional transformers for language understanding. In *Proceedings of the 2019 Conference of the North American Chapter of the Association for Computational Linguistics: Human Language Technologies, Volume 1 (Long and Short Papers)*, pages 4171–4186, Minneapolis, USA.

Matt Gardner, Joel Grus, Mark Neumann, Oyvind Tafjord, Pradeep Dasigi, Nelson Liu, Matthew Peters, Michael Schmitz, and Luke Zettlemoyer. 2018. AllenNLP: A deep semantic natural language processing platform. In *Proceedings of the Workshop for Natural Language Processing Open Source Software (NLP-OSS)*, Melbourne, Australia.

Marie-Francine Moens. 2018. Argumentation mining: How can a machine acquire common sense and world knowledge? *AAC*, 9(1):1–14.

Gaku Morio and Katsuhide Fujita. 2019. Syntactic graph convolution in multi-task learning for identifying and classifying the argument component. In *2019 IEEE 13th International Conference on Semantic Computing (ICSC)*, pages 271–278, Newport Beach, USA.

Jeffrey Pennington, Richard Socher, and Christopher Manning. 2014. GloVe: Global vectors for word representation. In *Proceedings of the 2014 Conference on Empirical Methods in Natural Language Processing (EMNLP)*, pages 1532–1543, Doha, Qatar.

Matthew Peters, Mark Neumann, Mohit Iyyer, Matt Gardner, Christopher Clark, Kenton Lee, and Luke Zettlemoyer. 2018. Deep contextualized word representations. In *Proceedings of the 2018 Conference of the North American Chapter of the Association for Computational Linguistics: Human Language Technologies, Volume 1 (Long Papers)*, pages 2227–2237, New Orleans, USA.

Victor Sanh, Thomas Wolf, and Sebastian Ruder. 2019. A hierarchical multi-task approach for learning embeddings from semantic tasks. In *Proceedings of the AAAI Conference on Artificial Intelligence*, volume 33, pages 6949–6956, Honolulu, USA.

Claudia Schulz, Steffen Eger, Johannes Daxenberger, Tobias Kahse, and Iryna Gurevych. 2018. Multi-task learning for argumentation mining in low-resource settings. In *Proceedings of the 2018 Conference of the North American Chapter of the Association for Computational Linguistics: Human Language Technologies, Volume 2 (Short Papers)*, pages 35–41, New Orleans, USA.

Erik F. Tjong Kim Sang and Fien De Meulder. 2003. Introduction to the CoNLL-2003 shared task: Language-independent named entity recognition. In *Proceedings of the Seventh Conference on Natural Language Learning at HLT-NAACL 2003*, pages 142–147, Edmonton, Canada.

Reinforcement-based denoising of distantly supervised NER
with partial annotation

Farhad Nooralahzadeh, Jan Tore Lønning, Lilja Øvrelid
Department of Informatics
University of Oslo, Norway
`{farhadno,jtl,liljao}@ifi.uio.no`

Abstract

Existing named entity recognition (NER) systems rely on large amounts of human-labeled data for supervision. However, obtaining large-scale annotated data is challenging particularly in specific domains like health-care, e-commerce and so on. Given the availability of domain specific knowledge resources, (e.g., ontologies, dictionaries), distant supervision is a solution to generate automatically labeled training data to reduce human effort. The outcome of distant supervision for NER, however, is often noisy. False positive and false negative instances are the main issues that reduce performance on this kind of auto-generated data. In this paper, we explore distant supervision in a supervised setup. We adopt a technique of partial annotation to address false negative cases and implement a reinforcement learning strategy with a neural network policy to identify false positive instances. Our results establish a new state-of-the-art on four benchmark datasets taken from different domains and different languages. We then go on to show that our model reduces the amount of manually annotated data required to perform NER in a new domain.

1 Introduction

Named Entity Recognition (NER) is one of the primary tasks in information extraction pipelines. (Ma and Hovy, 2016; Lample et al., 2016; Peters et al., 2018; Akbik et al., 2018). Traditional studies apply statistical techniques such as Hidden Markov Models (HMM) and Conditional Random Fields (CRF) using large amounts of features and extra resources (Ratinov and Roth, 2009; Passos et al., 2014). In recent years, deep learning approaches achieve state-of-the-art results in the task without any feature engineering (Ma and Hovy, 2016; Lample et al., 2016). Most of these works assume that there is a certain amount of annotated sentences in the training phase. However, avail-

ability of large amounts of labeled data is problematic, particularly in specific domains. Distant supervision is proposed by Mintz et al. (2009) to address the challenge of obtaining training data for new domains using existing knowledge resources (dictionaries, ontologies). It has previously been successfully applied to tasks like relation extraction (Riedel et al., 2010; Augenstein et al., 2014) and entity recognition (Fries et al., 2017; Shang et al., 2018b; Yang et al., 2018). For the task of NER, it identifies entity mentions if it exist in the knowledge base (e.g, domain-specific dictionary, glossary, ontology) and assigns the corresponding type according to the knowledge base.

However, distant supervision approaches encounter two main limitations. First, due to limited coverage of the knowledge resources, unmatched tokens result in False Negatives (FNs). Second, since simple string matching is employed to detect entity mentions, ambiguity in the knowledge resource may lead to False Positives (FPs). For the FN problem, Tsuboi et al. (2008) incorporate partial annotations into CRFs and propose a parameter estimation method for CRFs using partially annotated corpora (here-in after referred to as Partial-CRF). In order to reduce the negative impact of FPs for relation extraction, Qin et al. (2018) propose a deep reinforcement learning (RL) agent where the the agent's goal is to decide whether to remove or keep the distantly supervised instance.

In this paper we make the following contributions:

- We combine the Partial-CRF approach with performance-driven, policy-based reinforcement learning to clean the noisy, distantly supervised data for NER in a pre-processing step.

- We formulate the reward function in RL based on the change in the performance of

Proceedings of the 2nd Workshop on Deep Learning Approaches for Low-Resource NLP (DeepLo), pages 225–233
Hong Kong, China, November 3, 2019. ©2019 Association for Computational Linguistics
https://doi.org/10.18653/v1/P17

the NER module where the policy of RL is trained in an unsupervised manner by interaction with the environment.

- We show that our approach can boost the performance of the neural NER system on four datasets from different domains and for two different languages (English and Chinese).

2   Related work

The task of NER has been widely studied in the last decade and is generally considered as a sequence labeling problem. Using neural techniques, many studies report state-of-the-art results on this type of sequence labeling task (Lample et al., 2016; Ma and Hovy, 2016). These types of studies utilize character and/or word embeddings to encode sentence-level features automatically. Recently, the use of contextualized word representation (Peters et al., 2018; Akbik et al., 2018) significantly improves the state-of-the-art results in many sequence labeling tasks and specifically also in the NER benchmark.

In the supervised NER paradigm, this task suffers from lack of large-scale labeled training data when moving to a new domain or new language. To alleviate the reliance on human annotated data, distant supervision is proposed by Mintz et al. (2009), to generate annotated data by heuristically aligning text to an existing domain-specific knowledge resource. It is widely used for relation extraction (Mintz et al., 2009; Riedel et al., 2010; Augenstein et al., 2014) and lately it has attracted attention also for NER (Ren et al., 2015; Fries et al., 2017; Shang et al., 2018b; Yang et al., 2018). Shang et al. (2018b) present the AutoNER model which employs a new type of tagging scheme (i.e., Tie or Break) rather than common ones (i.e., IOB, IOBES) without any CRF layer and achieves state-of-the-art unsupervised $F1$ scores on several benchmark datasets. Crucially, they employ a set of high-quality phrases in distant supervision, using a phrase mining technique (Shang et al., 2018a) to reduce the false-negative labels. Feng et al. (2018) and Yang et al. (2018) make use of reinforcement learning to tackle false positives in distantly supervised relation classification and NER, respectively. Similar to our work, Yang et al. (2018) address the noisy automatic annotation in NER, by using partial annotation learning and reinforcement learning. However, unlike our approach, they train the NER model and reinforcement learning model jointly, calculating the reward based on the loss of the NER model, whereas we employ the RL module as a pre-processing/filtering step, incorporating the previous state to satisfy a Markov decision process (MDP). Yang et al. (2018) evaluate only on a Chinese dataset, whereas we apply our model also to English datasets. Furthermore, after running their code [1], we observe that to reach the reported results in their paper on e-commerce dataset, the model needs more that 500 epochs and the reinforcement learning component removes all the distantly annotated sentences after some epochs. It means that after some epochs the code performs only the base-line NER model on annotation dataset and ignoring RL module, since there are no distantly annotated sentences. Their two datasets are included in our experiment in order to compare to their results. Qin et al. (2018) explore deep reinforcement learning as a false positive removal tool for distantly supervised relation extraction. Here, we adapt their approach to the NER task. Unlike Qin et al. (2018) however, we learn the policy agent in an unsupervised manner, where the parameters are learnt by interaction with the environment.

3   Model

We implement Partial-CRF together with a performance-driven, policy-based reinforcement learning method to detect FNs and FPs in distantly supervised NER. In contrast to a previous study that has applied RL in NER (Yang et al., 2018), we consider the RL agent as a pre-processing task to clean FPs from the noisy dataset. Furthermore, our RL agent is rewarded based on the change in the performance of the NER module and it is modeled as a Markov decision process (MDP).

Algorithm 1 describes the overall training procedure for our model and in the following, we detail the various components of our model.

3.1   Baseline NER model

The goal of NER is to identify text spans that present named entities and assign them into predefined categories. These categories vary depending on the domain, for example in the general domain, they are categories like organization, person and location names; in bio-medical domain,

---

[1] https://github.com/rainarch/DSNER

B-Disease	B-Disease	B-Disease	B-Disease	B-Disease		
I-Disease	I-Disease	I-Disease	I-Disease	I-Disease		
E-Disease	E-Disease	E-Disease	E-Disease	E-Disease		
S-Disease	S-Disease	S-Disease	S-Disease	S-Disease		
B-Chemical	B-Chemical	B-Chemical	B-Chemical	B-Chemical		
I-Chemical	I-Chemical	I-Chemical	I-Chemical	I-Chemical		
E-Chemical	E-Chemical	E-Chemical	E-Chemical	E-Chemical		
S-Chemical	S-Chemical	S-Chemical	S-Chemical	S-Chemical		
O	O	O	O	O	B-Disease	E-Disease
leprosy	developed	a	Heinz	body	hemolytic	anemia

B-Disease	B-Disease	B-Disease	B-Disease	B-Disease	
I-Disease	I-Disease	I-Disease	I-Disease	I-Disease	
E-Disease	E-Disease	E-Disease	E-Disease	E-Disease	
S-Disease	S-Disease	S-Disease	S-Disease	S-Disease	
B-Chemical	B-Chemical	B-Chemical	B-Chemical	B-Chemical	
I-Chemical	I-Chemical	I-Chemical	I-Chemical	I-Chemical	
E-Chemical	E-Chemical	E-Chemical	E-Chemical	E-Chemical	
S-Chemical	S-Chemical	S-Chemical	S-Chemical	S-Chemical	
O	O	O	O	O	S-Chemical
while	taking	a	dose	of	dapsone

Figure 1: Annotation of distantly labeled example in Partial CRF based on IOBES scheme. The words with green tags are found in dictionary and assigned to the corresponding entity types, and the ones that are not found in dictionary are assigned to all possible tags (yellows).

Algorithm 1: Overall Training Procedure NER+PA+RL

Input: Human Annotated (A) + Distantly Labeled Data (D)

1 Pre-train NER w/ Partial-CRF (NER+PA) on A+D
2 Apply RL on D
3 Train NER+PA using A + cleaned D

---

they are protein, drug, gene, disease names. Intuitively, given a sentence of the words $X = \{x_1, x_2, ..., x_n\}$, NER assigns unique tag for each word like $y = \{y_1, y_2, ..., y_n\}$ from a predefined set of categories $y_i \in \Phi, |\Phi| = k$. Our baseline model is a BiLSTM-CRF architecture (Lample et al., 2016; Habibi et al., 2017). The first layer takes character embeddings for each word sequence and then merge the output vector with the word embedding vector to feed into a second BiLSTM layer. The CRF layer comes on top of the last layer to model the dependencies across output tags and locates the best tag sequence by maximizing the log-probability in following equation:

$$\log(p(y|X)) = \log \frac{e^{s(X,y)}}{\sum_{y' \in Y} e^{s(X,y')}} \quad (1)$$

where

$$s(X, y) = \sum_{i=1}^{n} P_{i,y_i} + \sum_{i=1}^{n} T_{y_i, y_{i+1}} \quad (2)$$

and $\mathbf{P}$ is a $k \times n$ output tensor of a linear encoder applied to the last BiLSTM layer where $P_{i,j}$ corresponds to the score of the jth tag of the ith word in a sentence. T is a $(k + 2) \times (k + 2)$ transition tensor which represents transition probability from i^{th} tag to the jth tag. Two additional tags <BOS> and <EOS> are added at the start and end of a sequence, respectively. In order to infer the final sequence tags the Viterbi algorithm is employed in the CRF model.

3.2 Partial-CRF layer (PA)

As mentioned above, FN instances constitute a common problem in distantly annotated datasets. It is caused by limited coverage of the knowledge base resource, when some of the entity mentions are not found in the resource and followingly labeled as non-entities ('O'). We follow Tsuboi et al. (2008) and treat the result of distant supervision as a partially annotated dataset where non-entity text spans are annotated as any possible tag. Figure 1 illustrates the annotation of distantly supervised examples using the IOBES labeling scheme that we employ.

Let Y_L denote all the possible tag sequences for a distantly supervised sentence X. Then, the conditional probability of the subset Y_L given X is:

$$p(Y_L|X) = \sum_{y \in Y_L} p(y|X). \quad (3)$$

Extending the original equation of the CRF layer (Eq.1) provides the log-probability for the distantly supervised instance:

$$\log(p(Y_L|X)) = \log \frac{\sum_{y' \in Y_L} e^{s(X,y')}}{\sum_{y' \in Y} e^{s(X,y')}}. \quad (4)$$

Using partial annotation, non-entity text spans are annotated as any possible tag. It gives a chance for non-entity text spans to be considered and scored properly in update version of CRF (Partial CRF) and become a part of the most optimal tag sequence.

3.3 Reinforcement Learning for denoising

The RL agent is designed to determine whether the distantly supervised instance is a true positive or not. There are two main components in RL :

Algorithm 2: Reinforcement learning Algorithm to clean FPs in Distantly Labeled Data (D)

Input: Training dataset (A_{train}) + Distantly Labeled Data (D) , Pre-train NER+PA on $A_{train} + D$,
Validation dataset (A_{val})

1   Initialize θ in policy network
2   Initialize s^* as all-zero vector with the same dimension of s_j
3   **for** *epoch* $i = 0 \to N$ **do**
4   **for** *instance* $d_j \in D$ **do**
5   Provide s_j using NER+PA model $\tilde{s}_j =$ concatenation(s_j, s^*)
6   Randomly sample $a_j \sim \pi(a; \theta, \tilde{s}_j)$; compute $p_j = \pi(a; \theta, \tilde{s}_j)$, save (a_j, p_j)
7   **if** $a_j == 0$ **then**
8   save $\tilde{s}_j$ into Ψ_i

9   Recompute the s^* as an average of $\forall \tilde{s}_j \in \Psi_i$
10    $D_i = D - (\forall d_j; j \in \Psi_i)$
11   Train NER+PA on $A_{train} + D_i$
12   Calculate F_1^i on A_{val} and save F_1^i and Ψ_i
13    $r_i = F_1^i - F_1^{i-1}$
14   Find Ω_i, Ω_{i-1} (Eq. 6)
15   Update Policy network (Eq. 5)

16   Update $D = D - (\forall d_j; j \in \Psi_N)$
17   Re-train NER+PA on $A + D$

I) environment II) policy based agent. Following Qin et al. (2018), we model the environment as a Markov Decision Process (MDP), where we add information from the previous state to the current state. The policy based agent is formulated based on the Policy Gradient Algorithm (Sutton et al., 1999), where we update the policy model by computing the reward after finishing the selection process for the whole training set. The algorithm 2 presents additional details of the RL strategy in our NER model. The following subsections describe the elements of the RL agent.

State: The RL agent interacts with the environment to decide about instances at the sentence level. A central component of the environment is the current and previous state in the selection process. The state S_i in step i represents the current instances as well as their label sequences. Following Yang et al. (2018) the state vector S_i includes: I) the vector representation of instances before the Partial-CRF layer, where we concatenate the outputs of the first and last nodes in the BiLSTM layer of the base NER model, and II) the label sequence scores calculated by the linear encoder before the Partial-CRF model. (i.e, $P_{i,j}$ in Eq. 2). If a word is annotated with a certain label, the score will be the corresponding value of the label, otherwise, the score will be the mean of all possible labels of the

word in the linear encoder. These two vectors are concatenated to represent the current state. To satisfy the MDP, the average vector of the removed instances in the earlier step $i - 1$ is concatenated to the current state and represents the state for the RL agent.

Reward: If the RL agent filters out the FP instances from the noisy dataset, the NER model will achieve improved performance. Accordingly, the RL agent will receive a positive reward, otherwise, the agent will received a negative reward. Following Qin et al. (2018), we model the reward as a change of the NER performance; particularly, we adapt the $F1$ score to calculate the reward as the difference between $F1$ scores of the adjacent epochs (i.e., $r_i = F_1^i - F_1^{i-1}$).

Policy Network: The policy network $\pi(a_j; \theta_i, s_j)$ is a feed forward network with two fully-connected hidden layers. It receives the state vector for each distantly supervised instance and then determines whether the instance is a false positive or not. The π as a classifier with parameter θ decides an action $a_j \in \{1, 0\}$ for each $s_j \in S_j$. The loss function for the policy network is formulated based on the policy gradient method (Sutton et al., 1999) and the

REINFORCE algorithm (Williams, 1992). Since we calculate the reward as a difference between $F1$ scores in two contiguous epochs, the agent will be compensated for a set of actions that has direct impact on the performance of the NER model in the current epoch. In other words, the different parts of the removed instances in each epoch are the reason of the change in $F1$ scores. Accordingly, the policy will update using the following gradient:

$$\theta = \theta + \mu[\nabla_\theta \sum_{\Omega_{i-1}}^{\Omega_i} \log \pi(a|S;\theta)r_i + \nabla_\theta \sum \log \pi(a|S;\theta)(-r_i)] \tag{5}$$

According to Qin et al. (2018), assuming Ψ_i is removed in epoch i :

$$\Omega_i = \Psi_i - (\Psi_i \cap \Psi_{i-1})$$
$$\Omega_{i-1} = \Psi_{i-1} - (\Psi_i \cap \Psi_{i-1}) \tag{6}$$

This means that if there is an increase in F_1 at the current epoch i, we will assign a positive reward to the instances that have been removed in epoch i and not in epoch $i-1$ and negative reward to the instances that have been removed in epoch $i-1$ and not in the current epoch.

4 Experiments

We perform experiments on four benchmark datasets to compare our method to similar techniques and investigate the impact of the number of available annotated sentences for our approach.

4.1 Experimental Settings

Datasets: Our approach requires an annotated dataset, a knowledge resource and a corpus of raw text. We rely on the resources used by Shang et al. (2018b) and Yang et al. (2018) for English and Chinese, respectively, as well as their train-test splits. For all datasets, we employ a IOBES labeling scheme. Below we briefly describe the datasets:

- BC5CDR is from BioCreative V Chemical Disease Relation task and contains 12,852 'Disease' and 15,935 'Chemical' entity mentions in 1,500 articles. It is already partitioned into a training, a development and a testing set. The related dictionary comes from the MeSH database[2] and the CTD chemical and Disease[3] vocabularies and contains 322,882 'Disease' and 'Chemical' entities. As a raw text, we use a corpus consisting of 20,217 sentences that is provided in Shang et al. (2018b) and extracted from PubMed papers.

- LaptopReview containing laptop aspect term is taken from the SemEval 2014 Challenge, Task 4 Subtask 1 (Pontiki et al., 2014). The 3,845 review sentences are annotated with 3,012 'AspectTerm' mentions. We extract 15,000 sentences from the Amazon laptop review dataset[4] as a raw text. Wang et al. (2011) design this dataset for the aspect-based sentiment analysis. Thanks to Shang et al. (2018b), they provide the dictionary of 13,457 computer terms crawled from a public website[5].

- EC is a Chinese dataset from the e-commerce domain. We choose this dataset in order to compare our results to the approach by Yang et al. (2018). There are 5 entity types: 'Brand', 'Product', 'Model', 'Material' and 'Specification' on user queries. This corpus contain 1,200 training instances, 400 in development set and 800 in test set. Yang et al. (2018) provide the dictionary of 927 entries and 2,500 sentence as a raw text.

- NEWS is another Chinese dataset in the news domain. It is annotated with PERSON type and provided by Yang et al. (2018). The NEWS dataset contains 3,000 sentences as training, 3,328 as dev data, and 3,186 as testing data. Yang et al. (2018) apply distant supervision to raw data and obtain 3,722 annotated sentences.

Pre-trained Embeddings: We employ pre-trained embeddings as initialization for the embedding layer of the LSTM layers. For the biomedical dataset, we use pre-trained 200-dimensional word vectors trained on PubMed abstracts, all PubMed Central (PMC) articles and English Wikipedia (Pyysalo et al., 2013). Standard pre-trained GloVe 100-dimensional word vectors are employed for the LaptopReview dataset. In

---

[2] https://www.nlm.nih.gov/mesh/download_mesh.html
[3] http://ctdbase.org/downloads/
[4] http://times.cs.uiuc.edu/~wang296/Data/
[5] https://www.computerhope.com/jargon.htm

Model	Data	Pr.	Re.	F1
Liu et al. (2017) *	BC5CDR	88.84	85.16	86.96
Wang et al. (2018)		89.10	**88.47**	88.78
Beltagy et al. (2019)**		-	-	88.94
NER+PA+RL (This work)		**92.05**	87.91	**89.93**
Winner system in Pontiki et al. (2014)	Laptop Review	**84.80**	66.51	74.55
NER+PA+RL (This work)		81.07	**74.01**	**77.38**
Yang et al. (2018)	EC	61.57	61.33	61.45
NER+PA+RL (This work)		**61.86**	**65.36**	**63.56**
Yang et al. (2018)	NEWS	**81.63**	76.95	79.22
NER+PA+RL (This work)		80.20	**79.88**	**80.04**

Table 1: NER models comparison. The results on the Chinese EC and NEWS dataset are without high-quality phrases. *: is the base NER model in our approach and results are reported by Wang et al. (2018). **: is the state-of-the-art result on BC5CDR dataset, where they use Pretrained Contextualized Embeddings for Scientific Text (SciBERT) in Ma and Hovy (2016) for NER.

our experiments on the EC dataset, we use the 100-dimensional Chinese character embeddings provided by Yang et al. (2018) and trained on user-generated text.

Evaluation: We report the performance of the model on the test set as the micro-averaged precision, recall and $F1$ score. A predicted entity is counted as a true positive if both the entity boundary and entity type is the same as the ground-truth (i.e., exact match). To alleviate randomness of the scores, the mean of five different runs are reported.

Model Variants: We use slightly different variants of our model for English and Chinese. For English we follow Liu et al. (2017) in leveraging a language model to extract character-level knowledge. We keep the parameters in the model the same as in the original work. In order to compare to state-of-the-art models, we follow the same approach during training (i.e., by merging the training and development data as a training set in BC5CDR and randomly selecting 20% from the training set as the development set in LaptopReview). For the Chinese EC dataset, we only use character-based LSTM and CRF layers and discard the word-based LSTM and language model. For a fair comparison, the model parameters are set to be the same as in Yang et al. (2018). For RL, the batch size, optimizer and learning rate are equal to the parameters in the related NER model. We use 100 epochs in RL and initialize the average vector of the removed sentences as an all-zero vector.

High-Quality Phrases: Considering all non-entity spans (i.e., 'O' type) as a potential entity provides noise in the Partial-CRF process. To address this issue, we use a set of quality multi-word and single-word phrases, provided by Shang et al. (2018b) and obtained using their AutoPhrase method (Shang et al., 2018a). Note that this resource is available only for the English datasets, therefore, it is not included in the experiments on the Chinese datasets. When using these phrases, we assign all possible tags only for the token spans that are matched with this extended list. In our model, we treat the high-quality phrases as potential entities and we assign all possible entity types in annotation of distantly supervised sentences. For example, in Figure 1, we could only find the word 'leprosy' in this list, therefore, in annotation we assign all possible tags to this token and the other non-entity tokens remain as 'O'.

5 Performance Comparison

The first two rows of Table 1 depicts the comparison of the proposed model to the state-of-the-art NER models on the English datasets. We observe that the NER+PA+RL model achieves higher $F1$ scores on the different datasets compared to the other models. In order to compare to the RL based approach in Yang et al. (2018), we run the model without high-quality phrases on the Chinese EC and NEWS datasets. Our design boosts the reported $F1$ score from 61.45 and 79.22 in the original to 63.56 and 80.04 with our model on EC and NEWS datasets, respectively. The experiments on

Model Variant	Data	Pr.	Re.	F1
NER+PA		85.82	88.58	87.18
NER+PA✪	BC5CDR	91.28	87.07	89.13
NER+PA+RL		87.00	89.04	88.01
NER+PA+RL✪		92.05	87.91	89.93
NER+PA		61.00	70.80	65.53
NER+PA✪	Laptop Review	66.36	66.06	66.21
NER+PA+RL		80.47	73.70	76.94
NER+PA+RL✪		81.07	74.01	77.38

Table 2: Result with different setting of the distantly supervised NER model. ✪ indicates that we use the list of high-quality phrases along with the dictionary to annotate raw text.

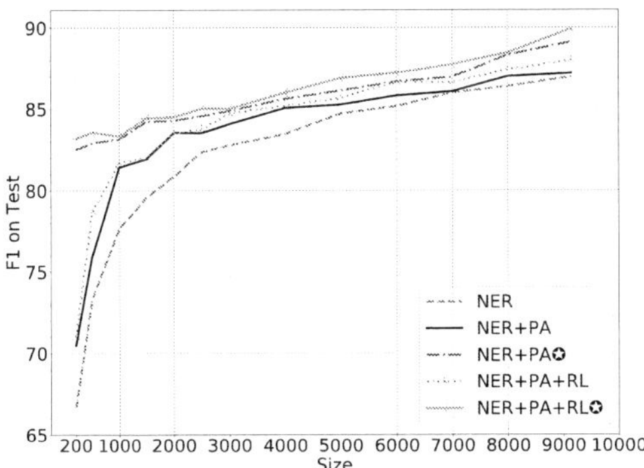

Figure 2: Performance of the different configuration: F1 Score on Test vs, the number of human annotated sentences

Method	Data	Pr.	Re.	F1
Dictionary Match		93.93	58.35	71.98
Fries et al. (2017)	BC5CDR	84.98	83.49	84.23
Shang et al. (2018b)		88.96	81.00	84.80
NER+PA+RL✪		88.73	77.51	82.74
Dictionary Match		90.68	44.65	59.84
Giannakopoulos et al. (2017)	Laptop Review	74.51	31.41	44.37
Shang et al. (2018b)		72.27	59.79	65.44
NER+PA+RL✪		68.63	56.88	62.21

Table 3: Unsupervised NER Performance Comparison. The proposed method is trained only on distantly labeled data.

the proposed model on the BC5CDR corpus by selecting increasing amounts of annotated instances from the gold dataset. As shown in Figure 2, the proposed method achieves a performance of 83.18 only with 2% of the annotated dataset. Whereas the base NER model, requires almost 45% of the ground truth sentences to reach the same performance. This indicates that with a small set of human annotated data, our model can deliver relatively good performance.

We also carry out experiments on the BC5CDR and LaptopReview test sets, where our model is trained exclusively on distantly annotated data. We report the outcome together with the scores of the other state-of-the-art unsupervised methods in Table 3, where we also compare to simple dictionary matching. It is clear that the model of Shang et al. (2018b) (AutoNER) is still the best performing NER method on BC5CDR and LaptopReview datasets in an unsupervised setup. However, as is clear from Figures 3-a and 3-c in Shang et al. (2018b)), if there is at least some manually labeled data available, our method makes better use of the gold supervision compared to the AutoNER system in the similar training scenario. It is also worth noting that the approach proposed by Fries et al. (2017) utilizes extra human effort to design regular expressions and requires specialized hand-tuning.

the Chinese datasets show that the different design of the RL module leads to improved results.

We further investigate the impact of the different components of the model (Table 2) in the two English datasets via ablation experiments, where we contrast the use of partial annotation (PA) and reinforcement-based denoising RL, with and without the high-quality phrases (✪). The experiments confirm the efficiency of the PA and RL modules in resolving FN and FP issues in the distantly labeled dataset. The results also corroborate Shang et al. (2018b) in showing that incorporation of the high-quality phrases always leads to a boost in the precision and subsequently in F1 score.

6 Size Of Gold Dataset

In all the previous experiments, we take advantage of the availability of an annotated dataset. However, one of the challenges in domain specific NER is the availability of a gold supervision data. We here examine the performance of

7 Conclusion and Future work

This work presents an approach to alleviate the problems of auto-generated data in NER. The performance-driven, policy-based reinforcement learning module removes the sentences with FPs, whereas the adapted Partial-CRF layer deals with FNs. We examine the impact of each component in ablation experiments. Combining these in a supervised setting leads to state-of-the-art results on three benchmark datasets from different domains and different languages.

Future work will extend the study to improve the performance of the model in unsupervised fashion and extend our study to additional domains and languages.

References

Alan Akbik, Duncan Blythe, and Roland Vollgraf. 2018. Contextual string embeddings for sequence labeling. In *Proceedings of the 27th International Conference on Computational Linguistics*, pages 1638–1649, Santa Fe, New Mexico, USA. Association for Computational Linguistics.

Isabelle Augenstein, Diana Maynard, and Fabio Ciravegna. 2014. Relation extraction from the web using distant supervision. In *EKAW*, volume 8876 of *Lecture Notes in Computer Science*, pages 26–41. Springer.

Iz Beltagy, Arman Cohan, and Kyle Lo. 2019. Scibert: Pretrained contextualized embeddings for scientific text. *CoRR*, abs/1903.10676.

Jun Feng, Minlie Huang, Li Zhao, Yang Yang, and Xiaoyan Zhu. 2018. Reinforcement learning for relation classification from noisy data. *CoRR*, abs/1808.08013.

Jason A. Fries, Sen Wu, Alexander Ratner, and Christopher Ré. 2017. Swellshark: A generative model for biomedical named entity recognition without labeled data. *CoRR*, abs/1704.06360.

Athanasios Giannakopoulos, Claudiu Musat, Andreea Hossmann, and Michael Baeriswyl. 2017. Unsupervised aspect term extraction with b-LSTM & CRF using automatically labelled datasets. In *Proceedings of the 8th Workshop on Computational Approaches to Subjectivity, Sentiment and Social Media Analysis*, pages 180–188, Copenhagen, Denmark. Association for Computational Linguistics.

Maryam Habibi, Leon Weber, Mariana L. Neves, David Luis Wiegandt, and Ulf Leser. 2017. Deep learning with word embeddings improves biomedical named entity recognition. In *Bioinformatics*.

Guillaume Lample, Miguel Ballesteros, Sandeep Subramanian, Kazuya Kawakami, and Chris Dyer. 2016. Neural architectures for named entity recognition. *CoRR*, abs/1603.01360.

Liyuan Liu, Jingbo Shang, Frank F. Xu, Xiang Ren, Huan Gui, Jian Peng, and Jiawei Han. 2017. Empower sequence labeling with task-aware neural language model. *CoRR*, abs/1709.04109.

Xuezhe Ma and Eduard Hovy. 2016. End-to-end sequence labeling via bi-directional LSTM-CNNs-CRF. In *Proceedings of the 54th Annual Meeting of the Association for Computational Linguistics (Volume 1: Long Papers)*, pages 1064–1074, Berlin, Germany. Association for Computational Linguistics.

Mike Mintz, Steven Bills, Rion Snow, and Dan Jurafsky. 2009. Distant supervision for relation extraction without labeled data. In *Proceedings of the Joint Conference of the 47th Annual Meeting of the ACL and the 4th International Joint Conference on Natural Language Processing of the AFNLP: Volume 2 - Volume 2*, ACL '09, pages 1003–1011, Stroudsburg, PA, USA. Association for Computational Linguistics.

Alexandre Passos, Vineet Kumar, and Andrew McCallum. 2014. Lexicon infused phrase embeddings for named entity resolution. *CoRR*, abs/1404.5367.

Matthew E. Peters, Mark Neumann, Mohit Iyyer, Matt Gardner, Christopher Clark, Kenton Lee, and Luke Zettlemoyer. 2018. Deep contextualized word representations. *CoRR*, abs/1802.05365.

Maria Pontiki, Dimitris Galanis, John Pavlopoulos, Harris Papageorgiou, Ion Androutsopoulos, and Suresh Manandhar. 2014. SemEval-2014 task 4: Aspect based sentiment analysis. In *Proceedings of the 8th International Workshop on Semantic Evaluation (SemEval 2014)*, pages 27–35, Dublin, Ireland. Association for Computational Linguistics.

S. Pyysalo, F. Ginter, H. Moen, T. Salakoski, and S. Ananiadou. 2013. Distributional semantics resources for biomedical text processing. In *Proceedings of LBM 2013*, pages 39–44.

Pengda Qin, Weiran Xu, and William Yang Wang. 2018. Robust distant supervision relation extraction via deep reinforcement learning. *CoRR*, abs/1805.09927.

Lev Ratinov and Dan Roth. 2009. Design challenges and misconceptions in named entity recognition. In *Proceedings of the Thirteenth Conference on Computational Natural Language Learning*, CoNLL '09, pages 147–155, Stroudsburg, PA, USA. Association for Computational Linguistics.

Xiang Ren, Ahmed El-Kishky, Chi Wang, Fangbo Tao, Clare R. Voss, and Jiawei Han. 2015. Clustype: Effective entity recognition and typing by relation phrase-based clustering. In *KDD*, pages 995–1004. ACM.

Sebastian Riedel, Limin Yao, and Andrew McCallum. 2010. Modeling relations and their mentions without labeled text. In *Proceedings of the 2010 European Conference on Machine Learning and Knowledge Discovery in Databases: Part III*, ECML PKDD'10, pages 148–163, Berlin, Heidelberg. Springer-Verlag.

Jingbo Shang, Jialu Liu, Meng Jiang, Xiang Ren, Clare R Voss, and Jiawei Han. 2018a. Automated phrase mining from massive text corpora. *IEEE Transactions on Knowledge and Data Engineering*.

Jingbo Shang, Liyuan Liu, Xiang Ren, Xiaotao Gu, Teng Ren, and Jiawei Han. 2018b. Learning named entity tagger using domain-specific dictionary. In *EMNLP*.

Richard S. Sutton, David McAllester, Satinder Singh, and Yishay Mansour. 1999. Policy gradient methods for reinforcement learning with function approximation. In *Proceedings of the 12th International Conference on Neural Information Processing Systems*, NIPS'99, pages 1057–1063, Cambridge, MA, USA. MIT Press.

Yuta Tsuboi, Hisashi Kashima, Shinsuke Mori, Hiroki Oda, and Yuji Matsumoto. 2008. Training conditional random fields using incomplete annotations. In *Proceedings of the 22nd International Conference on Computational Linguistics (Coling 2008)*, pages 897–904, Manchester, UK. Coling 2008 Organizing Committee.

Hongning Wang, Yue Lu, and ChengXiang Zhai. 2011. Latent aspect rating analysis without aspect keyword supervision. In *Proceedings of the 17th ACM SIGKDD International Conference on Knowledge Discovery and Data Mining*, KDD '11, pages 618–626, New York, NY, USA. ACM.

Xuan Wang, Yu Zhang, Xiang Ren, Yuhao Zhang, Marinka Zitnik, Jingbo Shang, Curtis Langlotz, and Jiawei Han. 2018. Cross-type biomedical named entity recognition with deep multi-task learning. *CoRR*, abs/1801.09851.

Ronald J. Williams. 1992. Simple statistical gradient-following algorithms for connectionist reinforcement learning. *Machine Learning*, 8(3):229–256.

Yaosheng Yang, Wenliang Chen, Zhenghua Li, Zhengqiu He, and Min Zhang. 2018. Distantly supervised NER with partial annotation learning and reinforcement learning. In *Proceedings of the 27th International Conference on Computational Linguistics*, pages 2159–2169, Santa Fe, New Mexico, USA. Association for Computational Linguistics.

Samvaadhana : A Telugu Dialogue System in Hospital Domain

Suma Reddy Duggenpudi
International Institute of
Information Technology,
Hyderabad
`sumareddy.duggenpudi`
`@research.iiit.ac.in`

Subrahamanyam Varma
International Institute of
Information Technology,
Hyderabad
`siva.subrahamanyam`
`@research.iiit.ac.in`

Radhika Mamidi
International Institute of
Information Technology,
Hyderabad
`radhika.mamidi`
`@iiit.ac.in`

Abstract

In this paper, a dialogue system for Hospital domain in Telugu, which is a resource-poor Dravidian language, has been built. It handles various hospital and doctor related queries. The main aim of this paper is to present an approach for modelling a dialogue system in a resource-poor language by combining linguistic and domain knowledge. Focusing on the question answering aspect of the dialogue system, we identified *Question Classification* and *Query Processing* as the two most important parts of the dialogue system. Our method combines deep learning techniques for question classification and computational rule-based analysis for query processing. Human evaluation of the system has been performed as there is no automated evaluation tool for dialogue systems in Telugu. Our system achieves a high overall rating along with a significantly accurate context-capturing method as shown in the results.

1 Introduction

A dialogue system is a computer system which is used for communication with human beings in natural language. It can be used for communication in either written or spoken form. Dialogue systems is a research problem which is being explored very rigorously over the past few years and there are great advancements as well. But despite that, most of the work is limited to English. This might be mainly due to the lack of resources, domain expertise and tools in other languages. Dialogue systems can be broadly classified into two kinds as *Task Oriented Dialogue Systems* and *Non-task Oriented Dialogue Systems* (Chen et al., 2017). Task oriented or domain-specific dialogue systems are systems which handle queries related to a particular task or a fixed domain. The main purpose of such systems is to provide the users with any information or help about that particular chosen domain. On the other hand, Non-task Oriented or Generic Dialogue Systems are modelled to have natural and extended conversations with human beings and can handle multiple domain queries and can act as our assistants.

In this paper, we make an attempt to model a domain-specific dialogue system which answers various queries related to hospitals and their doctors in Telugu. Telugu is an agglutinative South Indian language which belongs to the family of Dravidian languages. It is spoken mainly in Southern India and is also the third most spoken language in India with approximately 93 Million speakers. It is a morphologically rich and highly inflectional language.

Our approach in modelling a domain-specific dialogue system mainly shows that even if there are limited resources like insufficient data, unavailability of linguistic tools etc., still, by taking some suitable measures and creating simple computational tools will lead to the required results. Our dialogue system mainly has two parts namely Question Classification and Query Processing.

Question Classification: In this phase, with the help of a question classifier, the question posed by the user is classified into one of the predefined categories which have been designed using the domain knowledge depending on the aim and intention of the question.

For training the question classifier, the data required was manually created. This is possible when the dialogue system is domain-specific which implies that the questions will only be related to a fixed number of categories. In the hospital domain, questions will majorly be related to the categories like timings and availability of the doctor, specialization of the doctor, location of the hospital and so on. This would result in limited questions classes overall.

Query Processing: Once the category of the

Proceedings of the 2nd Workshop on Deep Learning Approaches for Low-Resource NLP (DeepLo), pages 234–242
Hong Kong, China, November 3, 2019. ©2019 Association for Computational Linguistics
https://doi.org/10.18653/v1/P17

question is known, we process the question using Named Entity Recognition(NER) and extract all the relevant details which are required to answer the question belonging to the particular category. If the information is sufficient to answer the question, then using it, an SQL query is built for retrieving the data which is required to generate a template-answer. But if the information is not sufficient for answering the question belonging to the category, then the user is asked to give the required information following which an SQL query is generated.

Apart from question classification and query processing, context handling is another important task handled by our dialogue system. This serves as the main differentiating factor between a Question Answering system and a Dialogue system. Further, it facilitates the conversation to seem natural.

2   Related Work

Dialogue systems is a field that has rigorous research going on.   There are many novel systems that have been developed already in English. There can be different kinds of dialogue systems based on the purpose that it serves. One of the very first dialogue systems is ELIZA (Weizenbaum, 1966), which was a deterministic rule-based system.   It was one of the first systems to facilitate conversation between man and computer in natural language.   Another such early rule-based dialogue system was PARRY (Colby et al., 1971). It was the first dialogue system to pass the Turing Test.

There are other systems like (Chung, 2004), (Zue et al., 2000) and (Ferguson and Allen, 1998) which are mixed-initiative and domain-specific systems.   They operate and deliver information only related to a particular domain.   In contrast, there are also generic dialogue system architectures which can adapt to domains. (ALLEN et al., 2000) and (Galescu et al., 2018) propose such architectures.

Another kind of dialogue systems is data-driven dialogue systems. They mine conversations from the already available dialogue-corpus.   (Serban et al., 2015a), (Jafarpour and Burges, 2010), (Ritter et al., 2011) and (Leuski and Traum, 2011) are some of the systems which are data-driven. They mainly extract the relevant required response using Information Retrieval techniques.

There is another kind of dialogue systems like (Fujie et al., 2019) which mainly work with the user feedback combined with any other technique. This helps in the evolution and learning of the dialogue system.   There are also some notable dialogue system like (Vinyals and Le, 2015), (Ritter et al., 2010), (Serban et al., 2015b) and (Mutiwokuziva et al., 2017) which are based on neural networks and deep learning.

In Telugu, the first dialogue system is (Nandi Reddy and Bandyopadhyay, 2006) and it uses computational rules and frames for answer generation. Another dialogue system in Telugu is (Ch. Sravanthi et al., 2015). The authors use various complex linguistic properties of the question to understand the meaning of the query and then process it accordingly.

3   Data for the Dialogue System

3.1   About The Database

As this is a domain-specific dialogue system which is about Hospitals and can be used to answer questions related to hospitals and doctors in the area of Gachibowli, the database consists information related to hospitals and is used in the last stage of the architecture to generate template-answer. A database consisting the details of four major hospitals in Gachibowli namely Continental hospital, Sunshine hospital, Himagiri hospital and Care hospital was created. The database created mainly contains the following information:

- Name of the doctor
- Hospital in which the doctor is working
- Qualification of the doctor
- Experience of the doctor
- Specialization of the doctor (multiple fields, also includes the department in which they are working)
- Recommendation Rating of the doctor
- Consultation fees of the doctor
- Days of availability of the doctor
- Timings of availability of the doctor

On the basis of the available information in the database, the following question categories were defined for question classification task based on its aim:

- Information about the hospitals in the localities
    - Number of hospitals
    - List of all the hospitals
    - Address of the hospital

- Timings of availability of the doctor
- Specialization of the doctor
- Qualification of the doctor
- Experience of the doctor
- Consultancy fees of the doctor
- Checking the availability of a doctor
    - At a particular time of the day
    - On a particular day of the week
- Information about which hospital a doctor works in

3.2 Dataset for Question Classification

There is a lack of dialogue conversational data in Telugu. But, any deep learning technique requires some considerable amount of data for training. And due to this, 388 natural language questions were created initially. Since the categories of the questions asked are finite, the questions posed are also limited. But the 388 questions are not sufficient for training a question classifier of 11 classes. Therefore, we performed Data Augmentation which led to a considerable amount of question data that could be used for training the classifier. This idea has been inspired by (Fadaee et al., 2017) and has been modified according to our requirement.

Data augmentation is done by making slight changes in the already present data to create more data. Even when there is a slight change in the sentence, the system always considers it as a different sentence and that is how the dataset grows. The attribute values like doctor name, hospital name, time and day, were replaced with new values and the tenses were changed to generate new questions which finally become a part of the dataset. There are a total of 28837 questions in this dataset after performing data augmentation. Data Augmentation is done for making the system robust.

For training and testing phases of the classifier, the initial manually created data (388 questions) was split in a ratio of 80% (310 questions) for training and 20% (78 questions) for testing. Then the training and testing data were augmented as described above. It is important to note that we first split the manually written data and then we perform data augmentation separately. This is for proper training and evaluation of the question classifier.

4 Question Classification

In this phase, the question posed by the user is classified into one of the already predefined categories depending on the aim of the question. We first get a vector representation of the question with the help of word embeddings[1]. Let the number of words in the question be N. Let the ith word in the question q be q_i. Now each of these words is embedded into a vector with the help of an embedding matrix W. Let the vector representation of the ith word be

$$x_i = W.q_i$$

All the vector representations x_i, i $\in [1, N]$ are concatenated as $[[x_1], [x_2], ..., [x_N]]$ and final representation of 2-dimensional matrix for the question X is obtained.

4.1 Experiments

Multiple experiments using various deep learning models and machine learning approaches were performed for the question classification task. The results are shown in table 1.

4.1.1 Support Vector Machine

SVM(Cortes and Vapnik, 1995) is one of the most popular machine learning classifier. The question representation X is used as the input for SVM. The final question representations are the main features on which SVM is trained.

4.1.2 Naive Bayes

Naive Bayes classifier (Xu, 2018) is used for question classification with the following features:
1. Bag of words of Unigrams
2. Bag of words of Bigrams
3. TFIDF Values of Bigrams
4. TFIDF Values of both Unigrams and Bigrams combined

4.1.3 Logistic Regression

Logistic Regression (Genkin et al., 2007) is used for predicting the question class with the following features:
1. Bag of words of Unigrams
2. Bag of words of Bigrams
3. TFIDF Values of Bigrams
4. TFIDF Values of both Unigrams and Bigrams combined

---

[1] https://drive.google.com/open?id=1fEt7aIzYWGQKto3Nt51M5CdjtzxMqdCz

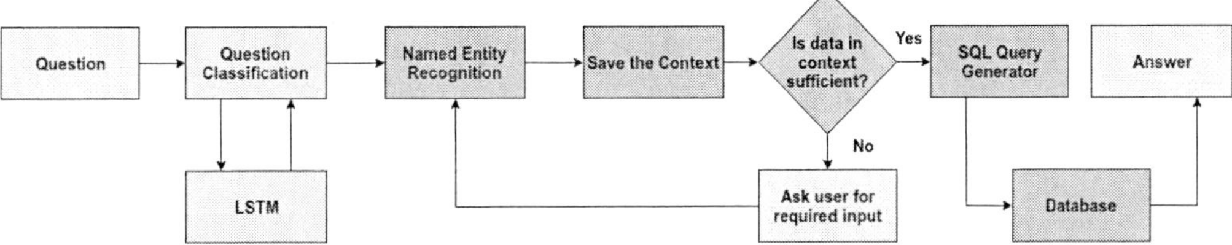

Figure 1: System Flow Diagram

4.1.4 Random Forest

Random Forest(Svetnik et al., 2003) is used for question classification with the following features:

1. Bag of words of Unigrams
2. Bag of words of Bigrams
3. TFIDF Values of Bigrams
4. TFIDF Values of both Unigrams and Bigrams combined

4.1.5 Convolutional Neural Network

Word embedding based model is used for CNN (Kim, 2014), the X matrix is given as input to the CNN model followed by the fully connected layer and finally a softmax layer. The filter of size 4 is used for the convolutions.

4.1.6 Bidirectional LSTM

A single-layer Bidirectional LSTM (Schuster and Paliwal, 1997) is used for question classification. The representation of the question X is given as an input to the Bidirectional LSTM layer. The output of this is then fed into a Dense Layer and then finally softmax is performed. The hidden dimension of Bi-LSTM is 64. The dropout rate is set 0.4 for avoiding overfitting.

4.1.7 Long Short Term Memory

A single-layer LSTM (Hochreiter and Schmidhuber, 1997) model has been implemented for classification. The input to LSTM layer is the concatenated representation of the question X and the output is passed to a dense layer and finally, softmax is performed to predict question category. The hidden dimension of LSTM is 32. A total of 10 epochs were performed and the drop out rate is set to 0.2.

5 Named Entity Recognition

After the classification of the question, the question category designated by the classifier along with the question posed by the user is analyzed to extract the important information from the question which is required for SQL query generation. This information is predominantly named entities and so we use Named Entity Recognition (NER). The named entities which were defined are the following:

1. Name of the Doctor
2. Name of the Hospital
3. Time
4. Date or Day
5. Name of the Locality
6. Hospital domain related Technical Terms

For answering the majority of the questions, the required information is mostly the named entities that belong to the above list. There is no readily available computational tool for Named Entity Recognition in Telugu for our domain. Therefore, as proposed in (Srikanth and Narayana Murthy, 2019), a hybrid model is designed which combines both heuristics and rules, based on the nature of the language and patterns in occurrences for identifying named entities. Here heuristics implies some simple probable cases like, in the context of the question, there is a high probability of finding the Name of the Doctor, as the next two words right after the *doctor* or *Dr.* tag and it is also likely to find the name of the hospital right before the *hospital* tag. Tags like *a.m.* and *p.m.* can be used as a clue to find the time intended in the question right before these tags. It is important to note that there can also be some ambiguities, but since this data is domain-specific, there are less chances of facing such ambiguities.

Apart from such heuristics, some rules were also designed on the basis of nature of the language for identifying the named entities. These are more focused on the language. For example, mostly when the case marker *'ki'* occurs, it is preceded by *time* in the question. In another instance, whenever *'lo'* occurs, it is a case marker which is associated with *location*. We also have some definitive rules like *'gAaru'* is always followed by

User Query	System Response
కాంటినెంటల్ హాస్పిటల్లో పని చేస్తున్న డాక్టర్ అనూషమేక గారు ఎప్పటి నుంచి ఎప్పటి వరకు ఉంటారు? What are availability timings of Dr. Anusha Meka who works in Continental Hospital?	కాంటినెంటల్ లో పని చేస్తున్న డాక్టర్ అనూష మేక 9:00 AM–5:00 PM వరకు అందుబాటులో ఉంటారు. Dr. Anusha Meka, who works at Continental Hospital, is available from 9:00 AM–5:00 PM.
తనకు ఎంత ఎక్స్పీరియన్స్ ఉంది? What is her experience?	కాంటినెంటల్ లో పని చేస్తున్న డాక్టర్ అనూష మేకకి 3 సంవత్సరాల ఎక్స్పీరియన్స్ ఉంది. Dr. Anusha Meka, who works at Continental Hospital, has an experience of 3 years.
క్వాలిఫికేషన్ ఏంటి? What about qualification?	కాంటినెంటల్ లో పని చేస్తున్న డాక్టర్ అనూష మేక క్వాలిఫికేషన్ BDS. Dr. Anusha Meka, who works at Continental Hospital, has a qualification of BDS.
ఫీజు ఎంత? What is the fee?	కాంటినెంటల్ లో పని చేస్తున్న డాక్టర్ అనూష మేక 500 రూపాయలు ఫీజు తీసుకుంటారు. Dr. Anusha Meka, who works at Continental Hospital, charges 500 rupees as fees.
సాయంత్రం ఐదు గంటలప్పుడు అందుబాటులో ఉంటారా? Will she be available at 5 in the evening?	కాంటినెంటల్ లో పని చేస్తున్న డాక్టర్ అనూష మేక ఐదు గంటలప్పుడు అందుబాటులో ఉంటారు. Dr. Anusha Meka, who works at Continental Hospital, will be at 5.

Figure 2: Capturing Linguistic Information from the Context of Chat

User Query	System Response
డాక్టర్ ఎంత ఫీజు తీసుకుంటారు? How much fees does doctor charge?	దయ చేసి హాస్పిటల్ పేరు తెలియచేయండి. Please provide with hospital's name.
కాంటినెంటల్ హాస్పిటల్ గురించి ఆడుగుతున్న. I am asking about Continental Hospital	దయ చేసి డాక్టర్ పేరు తెలియచేయండి. Please provide with doctor's name.
డాక్టర్ పేరు అనూష మేక. Doctor's name is Anusha Meka.	కాంటినెంటల్ లో పని చేస్తున్న డాక్టర్ అనూష మేక 500 రూపాయలు ఫీజు తీసుకుంటారు. Dr. Anusha Meka, who works at Continental Hospital, charges 500 rupees as fees.

Figure 3: System's Response to Missing Data

the doctor's name. It is not necessary that these rules and are also accurate always, but when the previous knowledge of the question category is combined with these rules, it is most likely that the required named entities are found.

6 Check for Answer Retrieval

After performing NER on the input question, the next aim is to generate an SQL query for the given question with the respective attribute values and then to retrieve the answer. But, if there is insufficient data in the context, then the SQL query cannot be generated. It is important to check this first. There are 11 categories of questions that can be handled by the system. For each of those categories, there are a set of attributes which are mandatory for answering the question. If they are not present in the context, then the system reverts back to the user asking for the required information. When the user responds with the information, the context is updated. If this context is sufficient for answering the question, then an SQL query is generated, else the same process is repeated until all the required information is available. The same is conveyed with real-time examples of our system in Figure 3.

From the example in Figure 2, it is understood from the first question that the conversation is about Dr. Anusha Meka. Now as a continuation to the first question, the user asks questions like *How much experience does she have?* or *How much is the consultation fee?*. The basic necessity of the dialogue system is to be able to understand how these questions are related to the first question and to have information as the context while answering these questions. To know that these questions are about Dr. Anusha is the pre-context that is being captured by the system and the further questions are answered accordingly. This is also primarily done by maintaining the context in every level of the dialogue. When a new question comes up without any contextual information, then the system goes back to the context available, looks for the attribute values and fills the missing attributes required for answering the question. When a new question comes up with a different doctor's name from the previous context, then it is assumed that this question is of different context, hence the previous context is flushed and the new context from this question is registered. With this process, context is grabbed and the output also seems more natural and realistic, and this property lets the system and user engage in a normal, natural and complete conversation, which is close to the real-world human-human conversation.

7 SQL Query Generation and Answer Retrieval

There are a total of 11 question categories that are handled. Each question frame has a definite and fixed SQL query. After the question is completely processed and once the required information for answering the question is available, it is put into the attribute blanks of SQL query accordingly. Then this query is given to the SQL database where all the information regarding the hospitals is stored. The attribute values which are required to build the template-answer are retrieved from the database and finally, the template-answer is generated and returned back to the user.

8 Other Simple Handled Issues

Apart from the detailed framework presented above, there is a need to handle some challenging linguistic issues to enhance the dialogue system and make the conversations more natural.

8.1 Anaphora Resolution

In this system, as a part of context handling, it is important for the system to understand various kinds of references. If there is a pronoun in a question, then the system should understand what is the actual reference to that pronoun. In this system, for pronoun handling, simple rule-based anaphora resolution is modelled. For example, if there is a pronoun intended for female, like '*Ame*'(she) then

the system looks for a female doctor in the context available.

8.2 Resolution of ambiguity in names

It is very likely that there are two or more doctors with the same first name and the user also generally addresses the doctor with the first name. In such a case, it is important for the system to understand which of the doctors is being referred to by the user. For this, the system prompts the user to select the doctor from a list of doctors having that same first name.

8.3 Handling Spelling Mistakes

It is possible that users can very easily misspell the name of a doctor or hospital because proper nouns can have many versions of pronunciations and corresponding spellings as well. Therefore, to find out what is exactly being referred to, character level matching is done and the similarity score is calculated with Levenshtein distance(Miller et al., 2009) between the user's spelling and all the names in the database. Based on the similarity score, the one with the highest and which passes the cutoff score is chosen as the correct spelling.

9 Results

9.1 Question Classification

Several models have been used for the task of Question Classification. The accuracies have been reported in Table 1.

Model	Accuracy
Support Vector Machine	68.778%
Naive Bayes+BOW+Unigrams	86.046%
Naive Bayes+TFIDF+Unigrams	83.721%
Naive Bayes+TFIDF+Bigrams	83.721%
Naive Bayes+TFIDF+Both	81.395%
Logistic Regression+BOW+Unigrams	90.697%
Logistic Regression+BOW+Bigrams	93.023%
Logistic Regression+TFIDF+Bigrams	88.372%
Logistic Regression+TFIDF+Both	90.697%
Random Forest+BOW+Unigrams	95.348%
Random Forest+BOW+Bigrams	90.697%
Random Forest+TFIDF+Bigrams	95.348%
Random Forest+TFIDF+Both	95.348%
Convolutional Neural Network	73.423%
Bidirectional LSTM	77.136%
Long Short Term Memory	**99.326%**

Table 1: Experiment Results of Question Classification

We can notice that LSTM outperforms all the other algorithms. It is also important to have such high accuracy because if the question is classified wrong, then the output generated will also be wrong eventually.

9.2 Dialogue System

For evaluating a dialogue system, there is no automated evaluation tool available. Hence the system was manually evaluated by 8 people. The evaluators were native Telugu speakers. A special User Interface was created for easy evaluation of the system. After every answer from the system, the evaluator was expected to mark the response as 'correct', 'not sure' or 'incorrect'. Everyone evaluated the system for about 20-30 dialogues(here dialogue is a conversation between the user and the system until the answer is retrieved). A total of 195 responses were recorded. Table 2 shows the ratings given by the evaluators in various aspects for judging the overall performance of the system. The scaling followed is 0-5, where 0 being Poor and 5 being Excellent. The Table 3 shows the accuracy metrics.

Metric	Percentage
Correct/Total	88.717
Correct/(Correct+Incorrect)	90.769

Table 3: Human-evaluation accuracy metrics

10 Conclusion

This work mainly combines both deep learning techniques as well as rule-based computational techniques. Though this approach is domain-specific, it can be easily extended to any other domain as well. It only requires the creation of some domain-specific data and some domain-specific rules and heuristics. Even if the data is little, using some simple techniques like Data Augmentation and standard classifier gives good results and serves the required purpose. This can really be helpful with resource-poor languages. With such vast applications of the dialogue system, this is definitely one step closer to creating dialogue systems in resource-poor languages.

11 Future Work

Our future work would mainly be focused on working with Telugu-English Code-Mixed Data as more commonly used in Telugu speaking regions.

Another thing that we would focus more on is error handling, that is basically to identify a completely irrelevant question as an irrelevant one and also will try to handle Out-of-Vocabulary(OOV) words. We are also looking forward to design better heuristics for handling spelling mistakes. Also, using the available recommendation ratings in the database, we would try to inculcate the doctor recommendation system also as a part of this Dialogue System. The objective would be to recommend a doctor according to the patient's request or even based on the diseases/symptoms. Apart from that, we would also like to make this a multi-domain dialogue system which would consist of information from multiple domains and switching between the domains in the conversation would also be facilitated.

References

James Allen, Donna Byron, Myroslava Dzikovska, George Ferguson, Lucian Galescu, and Amanda Stent. 2000. An architecture for a generic dialogue shell. *Natural Language Engineering*, 6(3-4):213228.

Mullapudi Ch. Sravanthi, Prathyusha Kuncham, and Radhika Mamidi. 2015. A dialogue system for telugu, a resource-poor language.

Hongshen Chen, Xiaorui Liu, Dawei Yin, and Jiliang Tang. 2017. A survey on dialogue systems: Recent advances and new frontiers. *CoRR*, abs/1711.01731.

Grace Chung. 2004. Developing a flexible spoken dialog system using simulation. In *Proceedings of the 42nd Meeting of the Association for Computational Linguistics (ACL'04), Main Volume*, pages 63–70, Barcelona, Spain.

Kenneth Mark Colby, Sylvia Weber, and Franklin Dennis Hilf. 1971. Artificial paranoia. *Artif. Intell.*, 2:1–25.

Corinna Cortes and Vladimir Vapnik. 1995. Support-vector networks. *Mach. Learn.*, 20(3):273–297.

Marzieh Fadaee, Arianna Bisazza, and Christof Monz. 2017. Data augmentation for low-resource neural machine translation. *CoRR*, abs/1705.00440.

George Ferguson and James F. Allen. 1998. Trips: An integrated intelligent problem-solving assistant. In *AAAI/IAAI*.

Shinya Fujie, Riho Miyake, and Tetsunori Kobayashi. 2019. Spoken dialogue system using recognition of user's feedback for rhythmic dialogue.

Metric	Description	Average Rating
Relevance/Correctness	How relevant/correct is the answer retrieved?	4.375
Robustness	How robust is the system?	4.25
Intention Identification	How well does the system identify the intention of the question posed?	4.625
Context Capturing	How well is the context captured in a full-fledge dialogue conversation?	4.25
System Responsiveness	How responsive is the system?	4.562
Reliability	Is the system helpful in providing all the relevant information?	4.25
Complex Sentences	How well are the complex sentences handled?	3.75
Missing Data	How well are questions with missing data handled? (with respect to the system responses)	4.312
Error Handling	How well are errors handled? (Eg: Absence of data in the database)	4.0
Overall Rating	How much will you rate the system overall?	4.343

Table 2: Human Evaluation Results

Lucian Galescu, Choh Man Teng, James Allen, and Ian Perera. 2018. Cogent: A generic dialogue system shell based on a collaborative problem solving model. In *Proceedings of the 19th Annual SIGdial Meeting on Discourse and Dialogue*, pages 400–409, Melbourne, Australia. Association for Computational Linguistics.

Alexander Genkin, David D Lewis, and David Madigan. 2007. Large-scale bayesian logistic regression for text categorization. *Technometrics*, 49(3):291–304.

Sepp Hochreiter and Jrgen Schmidhuber. 1997. Long short-term memory. *Neural computation*, 9:1735–80.

Sina Jafarpour and Chris J.C. Burges. 2010. Filter, rank, and transfer the knowledge: Learning to chat. Technical Report MSR-TR-2010-93.

Yoon Kim. 2014. Convolutional neural networks for sentence classification. In *Proceedings of the 2014 Conference on Empirical Methods in Natural Language Processing (EMNLP)*, pages 1746–1751, Doha, Qatar. Association for Computational Linguistics.

Anton Leuski and David Traum. 2011. Npceditor: Creating virtual human dialogue using information retrieval techniques. *AI Magazine*, 32:42–56.

Frederic P. Miller, Agnes F. Vandome, and John McBrewster. 2009. *Levenshtein Distance: Information Theory, Computer Science, String (Computer Science), String Metric, Damerau?Levenshtein Distance, Spell Checker, Hamming Distance*. Alpha Press.

Milla T Mutiwokuziva, Melody W Chanda, Prudence Kadebu, Addlight Mukwazvure, and Tatenda Trust Gotora. 2017. A neural-network based chat bot. *2017 2nd International Conference on Communication and Electronics Systems (ICCES)*, pages 212–217.

Rami Reddy Nandi Reddy and Sivaji Bandyopadhyay. 2006. Dialogue based question answering system in telugu. pages 53–60.

Alan Ritter, Colin Cherry, and William B. Dolan. 2011. Data-driven response generation in social media. pages 583–593.

Alan Ritter, Colin Cherry, and Bill Dolan. 2010. Unsupervised modeling of twitter conversations. *Proceedings of HLT-NAACL*.

M. Schuster and K.K. Paliwal. 1997. Bidirectional recurrent neural networks. *Trans. Sig. Proc.*, 45(11):2673–2681.

Iulian Vlad Serban, Ryan Lowe, Peter Henderson, Laurent Charlin, and Joelle Pineau. 2015a. A survey of available corpora for building data-driven dialogue systems. *CoRR*, abs/1512.05742.

Iulian Vlad Serban, Alessandro Sordoni, Yoshua Bengio, Aaron C. Courville, and Joelle Pineau. 2015b. Hierarchical neural network generative models for movie dialogues. *CoRR*, abs/1507.04808.

P Srikanth and Kavi Narayana Murthy. 2019. Named entity recognition for telugu.

Vladimir Svetnik, Andy Liaw, Christopher Tong, John Culberson, Robert P Sheridan, and Bradley Feuston. 2003. Random forest: A classification and regression tool for compound classification and qsar modeling. *Journal of chemical information and computer sciences*, 43:1947–58.

Oriol Vinyals and Quoc V. Le. 2015. A neural conversational model. *CoRR*, abs/1506.05869.

Joseph Weizenbaum. 1966. Eliza—a computer program for the study of natural language communication between man and machine. *Commun. ACM*, 9(1):36–45.

Shuo Xu. 2018. Bayesian nave bayes classifiers to text classification. *Journal of Information Science*, 44(1):48–59.

V. Zue, S. Seneff, J. R. Glass, J. Polifroni, C. Pao, T. J. Hazen, and L. Hetherington. 2000. Juplter: a telephone-based conversational interface for weather information. *IEEE Transactions on Speech and Audio Processing*, 8(1):85–96.

Towards Zero-resource Cross-lingual Entity Linking

Shuyan Zhou, Shruti Rijhwani, Graham Neubig

Language Technologies Institute
Carnegie Mellon University
{shuyanzh,srijhwan,gneubig}@cs.cmu.edu

Abstract

Cross-lingual entity linking (XEL) grounds named entities in a source language to an English Knowledge Base (KB), such as Wikipedia. XEL is challenging for most languages because of limited availability of requisite resources. However, much previous work on XEL has been on simulated settings that actually use significant resources (e.g. source language Wikipedia, bilingual entity maps, multilingual embeddings) that are unavailable in truly low-resource languages. In this work, we first examine the effect of these resource assumptions and quantify how much the availability of these resource affects overall quality of existing XEL systems. Next, we propose three improvements to both entity candidate generation and disambiguation that make better use of the limited data we do have in resource-scarce scenarios. With experiments on four extremely low-resource languages, we show that our model results in gains of 6-23% in end-to-end linking accuracy.[1]

1 Introduction

Entity linking (EL; Bunescu and Paşca (2006); Cucerzan (2007); Dredze et al. (2010); Hoffart et al. (2011)) identifies entity mentions in a document and associates them with their corresponding entries in a structured Knowledge Base (KB) (Shen et al., 2015), such as Wikipedia or Freebase (Bollacker et al., 2008). EL involves two main steps: (1) *candidate generation*, retrieving a list of candidate KB entries for each entity mention, and (2) *disambiguation*, selecting the most likely entry from the candidate list.

In this work, we focus on cross-lingual entity linking (XEL; McNamee et al. (2011), Ji et al. (2015)), where the document is in a (source) language that is different from the (target) language

---

[1]Code is available at https://github.com/shuyanzhou/burn_xel

Figure 1: XEL for two low-resource languages – Oromo and Sinhala, linking source mentions to entity "Netherlands" in English Wikipedia.

of the KB. Following recent work (Sil et al., 2018; Upadhyay et al., 2018), we use English Wikipedia as this KB. Figure 1 shows an example.

XEL to English from major languages such Spanish and Chinese has been carefully studied, and significant progress has been made. Success in these languages can be largely attributed to the availability of rich resources. Specifically, the following is a list of resources required by recent works (Tsai and Roth, 2016; Pan et al., 2017; Sil et al., 2018; Upadhyay et al., 2018):

English Wikipedia ($\mathbb{W}_{eng}$): The target KB and a large corpus of text. Importantly, the text is annotated with anchor text linking between entity mentions (e.g. "Holland" in the body text of an article) and the page for the entity (e.g. "Netherlands"). These annotations can be used to extract mention-entity maps for entity candidate generation, and to directly train entity disambiguation systems.

Source Language Wikipedia ($\mathbb{W}_{src}$): KB and corresponding text in the source language. Similarly to English Wikipedia, this can be used to obtain mention-entity maps or train disambiguation systems, but the size of Wikipedia is relatively small for most low-resource languages.

Bilingual Entity Maps ($\mathbb{M}$): A map between source language entities and English entities. One common source of this map is Wikipedia interlanguage links between the source language and English. These inter-language links can directly

Proceedings of the 2nd Workshop on Deep Learning Approaches for Low-Resource NLP (DeepLo), pages 243–252
Hong Kong, China, November 3, 2019. ©2019 Association for Computational Linguistics
https://doi.org/10.18653/v1/P17

and unambiguously link entities in the source language KB to the English KB.

Multilingual Embeddings ($\mathbb{E}$): These embeddings map words in different languages to the same vector space.

The availability of these resources varies widely among languages. They are available for high-resource languages such as Spanish and Chinese, which have been widely used as test-beds for XEL. For example, there are over 1.5 million articles in Spanish Wikipedia, which provide an abundance of annotations. However, the situation is not as favorable for most other languages: while $\mathbb{W}_{\text{eng}}$ is invariant of the source language to link from, many of the other resources are small or non-existent. In fact, only 300 languages (from ≈ 7000 living languages in the world) have Wikipedia $\mathbb{W}_{\text{src}}$, and among these many have a limited number of pages. For example, Oromo, a Cushitic language with 30 million speakers, has only 776 Wikipedia pages. It is similarly difficult to obtain exhaustive bilingual entity maps, and for many languages even the monolingual/parallel text necessary to train multilingual embeddings is scarce.

This work makes two major contributions regarding XEL for low-resource languages.

The first major contribution is empirical. We extensively evaluate the effect of resource restrictions on existing XEL methods in true low-resource settings instead of simulated ones (Section 4). We compare the performance of both the candidate generation model and the disambiguation model of our baseline XEL system between two high-resource languages and four low-resource languages. We quantify how much the availability of the aforementioned resources affect the overall quality of the existing methods, and find that *with scarce access to these resources, the performance of existing methods drops significantly*. This highlights the effect of resource constraints in realistic settings, and indicates that these constraints should be considered more carefully in future system design.

Our second major contribution is methodological. We propose three methods as first steps towards ameliorating the large degradation in performance we see in low-resource settings. (1) We investigate a *hybrid candidate generation method*, combining existing lookup-based and neural candidate generation methods to improve candidate list recall by 9-24%. (2) We propose a set of *entity disambiguation features that are entirely language-agnostic*, allowing us to train a disambiguation system on English and transfer it directly to low-resource languages. (3) We design a *non-linear feature combination* method, which makes it possible to combine features in a more flexible way. We test these three methodological improvements on four extremely low-resource languages (Oromo, Tigrinya, Kinyarwanda, and Sinhala), and find that the combination of these three techniques leads to consistent performance gains in all four languages, amounting to 6-23% improvement in end-to-end XEL accuracy.

2   Problem Formulation

Given a set of documents $\mathcal{D} = \{D_1, D_2, ..., D_l\}$ in any source language L_s, a set of detected mentions $\mathbf{M}_D = \{m_1, m_2, ..., m_n\}$ for each document D, and the English Wikipedia $\mathbf{E}_{\text{KB}}$, the goal of XEL is to associate each mention with its corresponding entity in the English Wikipedia. We denote an entity in English Wikipedia as e and its parallel entity in the source language Wikipedia as e^{src}.

For each $m_i \in \mathbf{M}_D$, candidate generation first retrieves a list of candidate entities $\mathbf{e}_i = \{e_{i,1}, e_{i,2}, ..., e_{i,n}\}$ from $\mathbf{E}_{\text{KB}}$ based on probabilities $\mathbf{p}_i = \{p_{i,1}, p_{i,2}, ..., p_{i,n}\}$ where $p_{i,j}$ denotes $p(e_{i,j}|m_i)$. Then, the disambiguation model assigns a score $s(e_{i,j}|D)$ to each $e_{i,j}$. These scores are normalized among $\mathbf{e}_i$ and result in the probability $p(e_{i,j}|D)$. The entity with highest score is selected as the prediction. We denote the gold entity as e^*.

Performance of candidate generation is measured by *gold candidate recall*: the proportion of mentions whose top-n candidate list contains the gold entity over all test mentions. This recall upper-bounds performance of an entity disambiguation system. In the consideration of the computational cost of the more complicated downstream disambiguation model, this n is often 30 or smaller (Sil et al., 2018; Upadhyay et al., 2018). The performance of an end-to-end XEL system is measured by *accuracy*: the proportion of mentions whose predictions are correct. We follow Yamada et al. (2017); Ganea and Hofmann (2017) and focus on *in-KB* accuracy; we ignore mentions whose linked entity does not exist in the KB in this work.

3 Baseline Model

This section describes existing methods for candidate generation and disambiguation, and our baseline XEL system, which is heavily inspired by existing works (Ling et al., 2015; Globerson et al., 2016; Pan et al., 2017). We investigate the effect of resource constraints on this system in Section 4. Based on empirical observations, we propose our improved XEL system in Section 5 and present its results in Section 6.

3.1 Candidate Generation

WIKIMENTION: With access to all the resources we list above, there is a straightforward approach to candidate generation used by most state-of-the-art work in XEL (Sil et al., 2018; Upadhyay et al., 2018). Specifically, a monolingual mention-entity map can be extracted from $\mathbb{W}_{src}$ by finding all cross-article links in $\mathbb{W}_{src}$, and using the anchor text as mention m and the linked entity as e^{src}. These entities are then redirected to English Wikipedia with $\mathbb{M}$ to obtain e. For instance, if Oromo mention "Itoophiyaatti" is linked to entity "Itoophiyaa" in some Oromo Wikipedia pages, the corresponding English Wikipedia entity "Ethiopia" will be acquired through $\mathbb{M}$ and used as a candidate entity for the mention. The score $p(e_{i,j}|m_i)$ provided by this model shows the *probability* of linking to $e_{i,j}$ when mentioning m_i. Because of its heavy reliance on $\mathbb{W}_{src}$ and $\mathbb{M}$, WIKIMENTION does not generalize well to real low-resource settings. We discuss this in Section 4.1.

PIVOTING: Recently, Rijhwani et al. (2019) propose a zero-shot transfer learning method for XEL candidate generation, which uses no resources in the source language. A character-level LSTM is trained to encode entities using a bilingual entity map between some high-resource language and English. If the chosen high-resource language is closely related to the low-resource language (same language family, shared orthography etc.), zero-shot transfer will often be successful in generating candidates for the low-resource language. In this case, the model generated score $s(e_{i,j}|m_i)$ indicates the *similarity* which should be further normalized into a *probability* $p(e_{i,j}|m_i)$ (Section 5.1).

Notably, both methods have advantages and disadvantages, with PIVOTING generally being more robust, and WIKIMENTION being more accurate when resources are available. To take advantage of this, we propose a method for calibrated combination of these two methods in Section 5.1.

3.2 Featurization and Linear Scoring

Next, we move to the entity disambiguation step, which we further decompose into (1) the design of features and (2) the choice of inference model that combines these features together.

3.2.1 Featurization

Unfortunately for low-resource settings, many XEL disambiguation models rely on extensive resources such as $\mathbb{E}$ and $\mathbb{W}_{src}$ (Sil et al., 2018; Upadhyay et al., 2018) to obtain features. However, some previous work on XEL does limit its resource usage to $\mathbb{W}_{eng}$, which is available regardless of the source language. Our baseline follows one such method by Pan et al. (2017).

We use two varieties of features: *unary* features that reflect properties of a single entity and *binary* features that quantify coherence between pairs of entities. The top half of Table 1 shows unary feature functions, which take one argument $e_{i,j}$ and return a value that represents some property of this entity. The grayed mention-entity prior $f_l^1(e_{i,j})$ is the main unary feature used by Pan et al. (2017), and we use this in our baseline. Binary features are in the bottom half of Table 1. Each binary feature function $f_g^i(e_{i,j}, e_{k,w})$ takes two entities as arguments, and returns a value that indicates the relatedness between the entities. Similarly, the grayed co-occurrence feature $f_g^1(e_{i,j}, e_{k,w})$ is used in the baseline. We refer to these two features as BASE.

While these features have proven useful in higher-resource XEL, in lower-resource scenarios, we hypothesize that it is more important to design features that make the most use of the language-invariant resource $\mathbb{W}_{eng}$ to make up for the relative lack of other resources in the source language. We discuss more intelligent features in Section 5.2.

3.2.2 Non-iterative Linear Inference Model

While the design of features is resource-sensitive, the choice of an inference model is fortunately resource-agnostic as it only relies on the existence of features. Our baseline follows existing (X)EL works (Ling et al., 2015; Globerson et al., 2016; Pan et al., 2017) to *linearly* aggregate unary features to a *local* score $s_l(e|D)$ and binary features to a *global* score $s_g(e|D)$. The local score reflects the properties of an independent entity, and the global score quantifies the coherence between an entity and other linked entities in the document. The score of each entity is defined as:

$$s(e_{i,j}|D) = s_g(e_{i,j}|D) + s_l(e_{i,j}|D)$$

The local score is the linear combination of unary features $f_l^i(e_{i,j}) \in \mathbf{\Phi}(e_{i,j})$:

$$s_l(e_{i,j}|D) = \mathbf{W}_l^T \mathbf{\Phi}(e_{i,j}) \qquad (1)$$

where $\mathbf{W}_l \in \mathbb{R}^{d_l \times 1}$ and d_l is the number of unary features in the vector.

On the other hand, the global score s_g is an average aggregation of mention evidence s_m across the document. Each $s_m(m_k, e_{i,j})$ indicates how strongly a context mention m_k supports the j-th candidate entity of mention m_i:

$$s_g(e_{i,j}|D) = \frac{1}{|\mathbf{M}_D|} \sum_{k \neq i} s_m(m_k, e_{i,j}) \qquad (2)$$

As a mention is in fact the surface form of other candidate entities, $s_m(m_k, e_{i,j})$ can be measured by the relatedness between the candidate entities e_k of m_k and $e_{i,j}$. Our baseline inference model follows Ling et al. (2015); Globerson et al. (2016) to process this evidence in a GREEDY manner:

$$s_m(m_k, e_{i,j}) = \max_{e_{k,w} \in \mathbf{E}_k} \left(s_e(e_{i,j}, e_{k,w}) \right) \qquad (3)$$

Similarly to s_l, $s_e(e_{i,j}, e_{k,w})$ is the linear combination of binary features $f_g^i(e_{i,j}, e_{k,w}) \in \mathbf{\Psi}(e_{i,j}, e_{k,w})$:

$$s_e(e_{i,j}, e_{k,w}) = \mathbf{W}_g^T \mathbf{\Psi}(e_{i,j}, e_{k,w}) \qquad (4)$$

The greedy strategy often results in a suboptimal assignment, as the confidence of each candidate entity is not taken into consideration. To solve this problem, we propose iteratively updating belief of each candidate entity in Section 5.3.

Following Upadhyay et al. (2018); Sil et al. (2018), we consider WIKIMENTION as the baseline candidate generation model and BASE+GREEDY as the baseline disambiguator. We denote WIKIMENTION+BASE+GREEDY as the end-to-end baseline system.

4 Experiment I: Real Low-resource Constraints in XEL

In this section, we study the effects of resource constraints in truly low-resource settings; we then evaluate how this changes the conclusions we may draw about the efficacy of existing XEL models. We attempt to answer the following research questions: (1) how the does the availability of resources influence the performance of XEL systems, and (2) how do truly low-resource settings diverge from XEL with more resources?

We perform this study within the context of our WIKIMENTION+BASE+GREEDY baseline (which is conceptually similar to previous work). We carry out the study on several languages and datasets:

TAC-KBP: TAC-KBP 2011 for English (*en*) (Ji et al., 2011), TAC-KBP 2015 for Spanish (*es*) and Chinese (*zh*) (Ji et al., 2015). All contain documents from forums and news.

DARPA-LRL: The DARPA LORELEI annotated documents[2] in 4 low-resource languages: Tigrinya (*ti*), Oromo (*om*), Kinyarwanda (*rw*) and Sinhala (*si*). These are news articles, blogs and social media posts about disasters and humanitarian crises.

Detailed experimental settings are in Section 6.1. It is notable that a large number of previous works examine XEL on simulated low-resource settings such as the TAC-KBP datasets for large languages such as Chinese and English (Sil et al., 2018; Upadhyay et al., 2018), while the DARPA-LRL datasets are more reflective of true constraints in low-resource scenarios.

4.1 Results

Table 2 shows various statistics for the baseline system on English, two high-resource, and four low-resource XEL languages. The first row of Table 2 shows the gold candidate recall of WIKIMENTION on 7 languages. The Wikipedia sizes of each language are shown in the last row of the table for reference. In general, the gold candidate recall of WIKIMENTION is positively correlated with the size of available Wikipedia resoruces. We can note that compared to the four low-resource languages, the statistics of the two high-resource languages are closer to those of English.

End-to-end performance of a system that selects the entity with the highest score according to WIKIMENTION is listed in the second row of the table. This trivial context-insensitive disambiguation method results in performance not far from the upper bound in six XEL languages. However, the size of the gap between this method and

---

[2]https://www.darpa.mil/program/low-resource-languages-for-emergent-incidents

Symbol	Feature Name	Equation	Resource
$f_l^1(e_{i,j})$	Mention-entity prior score	$\log(\max(p(e_{i,j}|m_i), \epsilon))$	Variable
$f_l^2(e_{i,j})$	Entity prior	$\log(\max(\frac{c(e_{i,j})}{\sum_{e \in \mathbf{E}_{\mathrm{KB}}} c(e)}, \epsilon))$	$\mathbb{W}_{\mathrm{eng}}$
$f_l^3(e_{i,j})$	Related mention number	$\sum_{m_k \in \mathbf{M}_D \setminus m_i} \mathbb{1}(\mathrm{any}_{e_{k,m} \in \mathbf{E}_k} f_g^1(e_{i,j}, e_{k,m}) > 0)$	-
$f_l^4(e_{i,j})$	Exact match number	$\sum_{m_k \in \mathbf{M}_D \setminus m_i} \mathbb{1}(e \in \mathbf{E}_k)$	-
$f_g^1(e_{i,j}, e_{k,w})$	Co-occurrence probability	$\log(\max(\frac{c(e_{i,j}, e_{k,w})}{c(e_{i,j})}), \epsilon)$	$\mathbb{W}_{\mathrm{eng}}$
$f_g^2(e_{i,j}, e_{k,w})$	Positive Pointwise Mutual Information (PPMI)	$\max(\log_2(\frac{p(e_{i,j}, e_{k,w})}{p'(e_{i,j})p'(e_{k,w})}), 0)$	$\mathbb{W}_{\mathrm{eng}}$
$f_g^3(e_{i,j}, e_{k,w})$	Entity embedding similarity	$\mathrm{cosine}(\mathbf{V}_{e_{i,j}}, \mathbf{V}_{e_{k,w}})$	$\mathbb{W}_{\mathrm{eng}}$
$f_g^4(e_{i,j}, e_{k,w})$	Hyperlink count	$\log(\max(\frac{\sum_{e_k \in \mathbf{H}_{e_{i,j}}} \mathbb{1}(e_{i,j}=e_{k,w})}{|\mathbf{H}_{e_{i,j}}|}, \epsilon)$	$\mathbb{W}_{\mathrm{eng}}$

Table 1: Unary features (top half) and binary features (bottom half). Gray indicates BASE features. "Variable" means this feature comes from the candidate generation model and thus its resource dependency will be decided by that model; ϵ is set to $\mathtt{1e-7}$; $c(e)$ is the frequency of an entity among all anchor links in $\mathbb{W}_{\mathrm{eng}}$; $c(e_i, e_j)$ is the co-occurrence count of two entities in $\mathbb{W}_{\mathrm{eng}}$; $p(e_i, e_j)$ is normalized over all entity pairs and $p'(e_i)$ is normalized over all entities with smoothing parameter $\gamma = 0.75$; $\mathbf{V}_e$ represents the entity embedding of e_i; $\mathbf{H}_{e_i}$ represents a set of entities in e_i's English Wikipedia page.

Model	en	high-resource		low-resource			
		zh	es	ti	om	rw	si
Gold Candidate Recall	92.4	89.2	89.0	21.9	45.3	45.6	66.6
$p(e|m)$	70.1	83.1	78.2	21.5	41.0	45.1	63.1
BASE+GREEDY	77.5	85.5	82.9	21.8	38.4	44.9	64.4
Wikipedia Size	5.0M	1.0M	1.5M	168	775	1.8K	15.1K

Table 2: Gold candidate recall of WIKIMENTION over seven languages, accuracy (%) of selecting the highest score entity, and accuracy after end-to-end EL using the BASE+GREEDY method.

the upper bound is largely different between high- and low-resource settings – this gap is significant for high-resource languages, but quite small for the four low-resource languages. Accordingly, in third row where we apply the disambiguation method BASE+GREEDY, we find gains of 2-7% on the high-resource languages, but little to no gain on the low-resource languages. This shows that when using a standard candidate generation method such as WIKIMENTION, there is *little room for more sophisticated disambiguation models to improve performance*, despite the fact that development of disambiguation methods (rather than candidate generation) has been the focus of much prior work.

5 Proposed Model Improvements

Next, we introduce our proposed methods: (1) calibrated combination of two existing candidate generation models, (2) an XEL disambiguation model that makes best use of resources that *will* be available in extremely low-resource settings.

5.1 Calibrated Candidate List Combination

As the gold candidate recall decides the upper bound of an (X)EL system, candidate lists with close to 100% recall are ideal. However, this is hard to achieve for most low-resource languages where existing candidate generation models only provide candidate lists with low recall (less than 60%, as we show in Section 4.1). Further, combination of candidate lists retrieved by different models is non-trivial as the scores are not comparable among models. For example, scores of WIKIMENTION have probabilistic interpretation while scores of PIVOTING do not.

We propose a simple method to solve this problem: we convert scores without probabilistic interpretation to ones that are scaled to the zero-one simplex. Given mention m_i and its top-n candidate entity list $\mathbf{E}_i$ along with their scores $\mathbf{S}_i$, the re-calibrated scores are identified as:

$$p_{i,j} = \frac{\exp(\gamma \times s_{i,j})}{\sum_{s_{i,k} \in \mathbf{S}_i} \exp(\gamma \times s_{i,k})} \tag{5}$$

where γ is a hyper-parameter that controls the peakiness of the distribution. After calibration, it is safe to combine prior scores with an average.

5.2 Feature Design

Next, we introduce the feature set for our disambiguation model, including features inspired by previous work (Sil and Florian, 2016; Ganea et al., 2016; Pan et al., 2017), as well as novel features specifically designed to tackle the low-resource scenario. We intentionally avoid features that take source language context words into consideration, as these would be heavily reliant on $\mathbb{W}_{\text{eng}}$ and $\mathbb{M}$ and weaken the transferability of the model. The formulation and resource requirements of unary and binary features are shown in the top and bottom halves of Table 1 respectively.

For unary features, we consider the number of mentions an entity is related to as f_l^3, where we consider the entity $e_{i,j}$ related to mention m_k if it co-occurs with any candidate entity of m_k (Moro et al., 2014). We also add the entity prior score f_l^2 among the whole Wikipedia (Yamada et al., 2017) to reflect the entity's overall salience. The exact match number f_l^4 indicates mention coreference.

For binary features, we attempt to deal with the noise and sparsity inherent in the co-occurrence counts of f_g^1. To tackle noise, we calculate the smoothed Positive Pointwise Mutual Information (PPMI) (Church and Hanks, 1990; Ganea et al., 2016) between two entities as f_g^2, which robustly estimates how much more the two entities co-occur than we expect by chance. To tackle sparsity, we incorporate English entity embeddings of Yamada et al. (2017), and calculate embedding similarity between two entities as f_g^3. Similar techniques have also been used by existing works (Ganea and Hofmann, 2017; Kolitsas et al., 2018). We also add the hyperlink count f_g^4 between a pair of entities as, if entity e_i's Wikipedia page mentions e_j, they are likely to be related.

We name our proposed feature set that includes all features listed in Table 1 as FEAT.

5.3 BURN: Feature Combination Model

With the growing number of features, we posit that a linear model with greedy entity pair selection (Section 3.2) is not expressive enough to take advantage of a rich feature set. Yamada et al. (2017) use Gradient Boosted Regression Trees (GBRT; Friedman (2001)) to combine features, but GBRTs do not allow for end-to-end training and thus constrain the flexibility of the model. Ganea et al. (2016); Ganea and Hofmann (2017) propose to use Loopy Belief Propagation (LBP; Murphy et al.

(1999)) to estimate the global score (Equation (2)) and use non-linear functions to combine local and global scores (Equation (1)). However, BP is challenging to implement, and previous work has not attempted to combine more fine-grained features (e.g. unary feature $\Phi(e_{i,j})$) non-linearly.

Instead, we propose a *belief update recurrent network* (BURN) that combines features in a non-linear and iterative fashion. Compared to existing work (Naradowsky and Riedel, 2016; Ganea et al., 2016; Ganea and Hofmann, 2017) as well as our base model, the advantages of BURN are: (1) it is easy to implement with existing neural network toolkits, (2) parameters can be learned end-to-end, (3) it considers non-linear combinations over more fine-grained features and thus has potential to fit more complex combination patterns, (4) it can model (distance) relations between mentions in the document.

Given unary feature vector $\Phi(e_{i,j})$ with d_l features, BURN replaces the linear combination in Equation (1) with two fully connected layers:

$$s_l(e_{i,j}|D) = \mathbf{W}_l^{2^T}(\sigma(\mathbf{W}_l^{1^T}\Phi(e_{i,j}))) + \mathbf{W}_l^{3^T}\Phi(e_{i,j})$$

where $\mathbf{W}_l^1 \in \mathbb{R}^{d_l \times h_l}$, $\mathbf{W}_l^2 \in \mathbb{R}^{h_l \times 1}$ and $\mathbf{W}_l^3 \in \mathbb{R}^{d_l \times 1}$. σ is a non-linear function, for which we use leaky rectified linear units (Leaky ReLu; Maas et al. (2013)). We add a linear addition of the input to alleviate the gradient vanishing problem. Equation (4) is revised in a similar way.

As discussed in Equation (3), our baseline model calculates the mention evidence greedily. However, there may be many candidate entities for each mention, some containing noise. BURN solves this problem by weighting $s_e(e_{i,j}, e_{k,w})$ with the current entity probability $p(e_{k,w}|D)$. An illustration is in the bottom of Figure 2. The evidence from m_k is now defined as:

$$s_m(m_k, e_{i,j}) = \sum_{w=1}^{|C_k|} s_e(e_{i,j}, e_{k,w})p(e_{k,w}|D) \quad (6)$$

Instead of simply averaging mention evidence in Equation (2), we also use a gating function to control the influence of m_k's mention evidence on m_i (top of Figure 2), giving score

$$s_g(e_{i,j}|D) = \sum_{k \neq i} g_m(m_i, m_k)s_m(m_k, e_{i,j})$$

The gating function g is essentially a lookup table that has one scalar for each distance (in words) between two mentions. We train this table along with all other parameters of the model. The motivation for this gating function is that a mention is more likely to be coherent with a nearby mention than a distant one. We assume that this is true for almost all languages, and thus will be useful even without training in the language to be processed.

As shown in Equation (6), there is a circular dependency between entities. To solve this problem, we iteratively update the probability of entities until convergence or reaching a maximum number of iterations T. In iteration t, the calculation of s_m will use entity probabilities from iteration $t - 1$. The revised Equation (6) is as follows:

$$s_m^t(m_k, e_{i,j}) = \sum_{w=1}^{|C_k|} s_e(e_{i,j}, e_{k,w}) p^{t-1}(e_{k,w}|D)$$

Unrolling this network through iterations, we can see that this is in fact a recurrent neural network.

Training BURN: The weights of BURN are learned end-to-end with the objective function:

$$L(\mathcal{D}, \mathcal{E}) = -\sum_{D \in \mathcal{D}} \sum_{m_i \in D} \log(p^T(e_i^*|D)).$$

As discussed above, the disambiguation model is fully language-agnostic and it does not require any annotated EL data or other resources in the source language. The model weights W_l, W_q and the lookup table g_m of gating function are trained on the TAC-KBP 2010 English training set (Ji et al., 2010) *only* and used as-is in another language. We use TAC-KBP 2012 English test set (Mayfield and Javier, 2012) as our development set.

6   Experiment II: Improving Low-resource XEL

Section 4 demonstrated a dramatic performance degradation for XEL in realistic low-resource settings. In this section, we evaluate the utility of our proposed methods that improve low-resource XEL.

6.1   Training Details

All models are implemented in PyTorch (Paszke et al., 2017). The size of the pre-trained entity embeddings (Yamada et al., 2017) is 300, trained with a window size of 15 and 15 negative samples. The hidden size h of both $\mathbf{W}_l^1$ and $\mathbf{W}_g^1$ is set to 128,

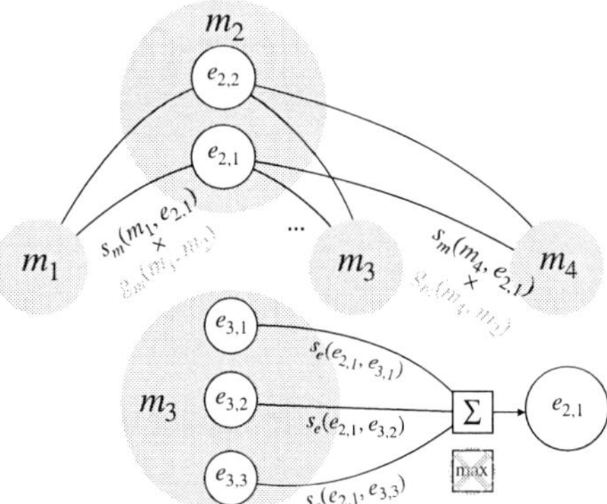

Figure 2: Top: the global score of an entity is a *weighted* aggregation of mention evidence from context mentions, instead of an average. Bottom: each mention evidence is a *weighted* entity-pair score, instead of the max.

the dropout rate is set to 0.5. For the gating function, we set mention distances that are larger than 50 tokens to 50, then bin the distances with a bin size of 4. We only consider the 30 nearest context mentions for each mention. The maximum number of iterations for inference is set to 20. We use the Adam optimizer with the default learning rate (`1e-3`) to train the model. The γ of calibrated candidate combination is set to 1. It takes around two hours to train a GREEDY model and ten hours to train a BURN model with a Titan X GPU, regardless of the feature set.

6.2   Results

Table 3 compares models on the datasets we introduce in Section 4. Given that the critical issue was the degradation of candidate recall of the resource-heavy WIKIMENTION method in low-resource settings (Section 4), we first examine the alternative resource-light PIVOTING model. The first rows of block 1 and 2 of the table show the gold candidate recall of each method. While PIVOTING greatly exceeds WIKIMENTION on *ti*, which only has 168 Wikipedia pages, its performance is much lower on *si*, which has 15k pages. Overall, while these two models could outperform each other in their respective favorable settings (when a similar pivot language exists for the former, and when a large Wikipedia exists for the latter), it is challenging to decide which is more appropriate in the face of the realistic setting of existent, but scarce, resources.

Thus, in the third block of the table we show

Block Index	$\mathbb{W}_{eng}$	$\mathbb{W}_{src}$	$\mathbb{M}$	Candidates	Inference	ti	om	rw	si
1	✓			Pivoting	Gold Candidate Recall	36.2	20.9	59.6	32.1
					$p(e\|m)$	32.9	18.2	54.9	11.8
					Base + Greedy	<u>33.7</u>	<u>18.5</u>	<u>55.9</u>	<u>20.5</u>
					Feat + Greedy	33.7	13.6	46.2	15.5
					Base + Burn	**34.9**	**19.4**	**56.2**	**21.1**
					Feat + Burn	34.5	17.8	50.9	10.6
2	✓	✓	✓	WikiMention	Gold Candidate Recall	21.9	45.3	45.6	66.6
					$p(e\|m)$	21.5	**41.0**	45.1	63.1
					Base + Greedy	<u>21.8</u>	<u>38.4</u>	<u>44.9</u>	<u>64.4</u>
					Feat + Greedy	21.6	38.7	44.6	64.4
					Base + Burn	**21.8**	39.9	44.3	**64.7**
					Feat + Burn	**21.8**	39.9	**45.6**	**64.7**
3	✓	✓	✓	WikiMention + Pivoting	Gold Candidate Recall	38.3	62.0	69.4	75.2
					$p(e\|m)$	33.6	54.0	66.0	66.8
					Base + Greedy	<u>34.4</u>	<u>53.3</u>	<u>67.3</u>	<u>68.1</u>
					Feat + Greedy	34.5	50.3	57.8	67.2
					Base + Burn	**35.6**	**54.5**	65.2	**70.3**
					Feat + Burn	35.2	53.6	**67.5**	68.8

Table 3: Accuracy (%) of different systems. ✓ shows the resource requirements. The performances of the end-to-end baseline system grayed . The performances of baseline disambiguation for each candidate generation model are <u>underlined</u> and numbers in **bold** show the best performance for each setting. $p(e|m)$ refers to the method that chooses the highest prior score provided by corresponding candidate generation method.

results for the hybrid candidate generation model which uses both WikiMention and Pivoting. Compared to WikiMention, this method improves the gold candidate recall between 9 to 24% over all four low-resource languages. The improvement ($> 15\%$) is especially considerable for *om* and *rw*. This reflects the fact that there are a significant number of unique candidate entities retrieved by these two candidate generation methods, and developing a proper way to combine them together results in higher-quality candidate lists. Notably, this method has also increased the headroom for a disambiguation model to contribute – in contrast to the WikiMention setting where the difference between prior $p(e|m)$ and gold accuracy was minimal, now there is a 3-9% accuracy gap between the two settings.

Next, we turn to methods that close this gap. Focusing on this third block of the table, we can see that the proposed disambiguation model can take advantage of better candidate lists and yields significantly better results on all four languages. Notably, we observe that Burn consistently yields the best performance over all languages, improving by 0.2 to 3.3% over Greedy. This result demonstrates the advantage of iterative nonlinear feature combination in low-resource settings. In contrast, there is not a consistent improvement from the proposed feature set Feat compared to the baseline Base. This is interesting as Feat+Burn outperformed Base+Burn by more than 10% on the English development set on which it was validated. We suspect this is because the feature value distribution of the English training data is different from that of low-resource languages, leading to sub-optimal transfer. We leave training algorithms for bridging this gap as an interesting avenue of future work.

In the context of the end-to-end system, the combination of our proposed methods brings 6-23% improvement over the baseline system. For languages (*ti, om, rw*) where resources are relative scarce, the improvement is especially considerable, ranging from 13 to 23%, indicating that our work is a promising first step towards improving XEL in realistic low-resource scenarios.

7 Conclusion

This paper has made two major contributions to the study of low-resource cross-lingual entity linking (XEL). First, we perform an extensive empirical evaluation on the effect of different resource availability assumptions on XEL and demonstrate that (1) the accuracy of existing systems greatly degrades on true low-resource settings, and (2) standard candidate generation systems constrain the performance of end-to-end XEL. This fact has been under-discussed in existing work and we argue that more attention should be paid to candidate generation for low-resource XEL. Second, based on our empirical study, we propose three methodologies for candidate generation and disambiguation that make the best use of limited resources we will have in realistic settings. Experimental results suggest that our proposed methodologies are effective under extremely limited-resource scenarios, giving improvements in 6-23% end-to-end linking accuracy over the baseline system.

An immediate future focus is further improving the performance of candidate generation models in realistic low-resource settings. Further, we could consider more sophisticated strategies for cross-lingual training of entity disambiguation systems that fill the gap between English training data and real world low-resource data.

8   Acknowledgements

We would like to thank the anonymous reviewers for their useful feedback. This material is based upon work supported in part by the Defense Advanced Research Projects Agency Information Innovation Office (I2O) Low Resource Languages for Emergent Incidents (LORELEI) program under Contract No. HR0011-15-C0114. The views and conclusions contained in this document are those of the authors and should not be interpreted as representing the official policies, either expressed or implied, of the U.S. Government. The U.S. Government is authorized to reproduce and distribute reprints for Government purposes notwithstanding any copyright notation here on.

References

Kurt Bollacker, Colin Evans, Praveen Paritosh, Tim Sturge, and Jamie Taylor. 2008. Freebase: a collaboratively created graph database for structuring human knowledge. In *Proceedings of the 2008 ACM SIGMOD international conference on Management of data*, pages 1247–1250. AcM.

Razvan Bunescu and Marius Paşca. 2006. Using encyclopedic knowledge for named entity disambiguation. In *11th conference of the European Chapter of the Association for Computational Linguistics*.

Kenneth Ward Church and Patrick Hanks. 1990. Word association norms, mutual information, and lexicography. *Computational linguistics*, 16(1):22–29.

Silviu Cucerzan. 2007. Large-scale named entity disambiguation based on Wikipedia data. In *Proceedings of the 2007 Joint Conference on Empirical Methods in Natural Language Processing and Computational Natural Language Learning (EMNLP-CoNLL)*.

Mark Dredze, Paul McNamee, Delip Rao, Adam Gerber, and Tim Finin. 2010. Entity disambiguation for knowledge base population. In *Proceedings of the 23rd International Conference on Computational Linguistics*, pages 277–285. Association for Computational Linguistics.

Jerome H Friedman. 2001. Greedy function approximation: a gradient boosting machine. *Annals of statistics*, pages 1189–1232.

Octavian-Eugen Ganea, Marina Ganea, Aurelien Lucchi, Carsten Eickhoff, and Thomas Hofmann. 2016. Probabilistic bag-of-hyperlinks model for entity linking. In *Proceedings of the 25th International Conference on World Wide Web*, pages 927–938. International World Wide Web Conferences Steering Committee.

Octavian-Eugen Ganea and Thomas Hofmann. 2017. Deep joint entity disambiguation with local neural attention. In *Proceedings of the 2017 Conference on Empirical Methods in Natural Language Processing*, pages 2619–2629.

Amir Globerson, Nevena Lazic, Soumen Chakrabarti, Amarnag Subramanya, Michael Ringaard, and Fernando Pereira. 2016. Collective entity resolution with multi-focal attention. In *Proceedings of the 54th Annual Meeting of the Association for Computational Linguistics (Volume 1: Long Papers)*, volume 1, pages 621–631.

Johannes Hoffart, Mohamed Amir Yosef, Ilaria Bordino, Hagen Fürstenau, Manfred Pinkal, Marc Spaniol, Bilyana Taneva, Stefan Thater, and Gerhard Weikum. 2011. Robust disambiguation of named entities in text. In *Proceedings of the Conference on Empirical Methods in Natural Language Processing*, pages 782–792. Association for Computational Linguistics.

Heng Ji, Ralph Grishman, and Hoa Dang. 2011. Overview of the TAC 2011 knowledge base population track. In *TAC 2011 Proceedings Papers*.

Heng Ji, Ralph Grishman, Hoa Trang Dang, Kira Griffitt, and Joe Ellis. 2010. Overview of the TAC 2010 knowledge base population track. In *TAC 2010 Proceedings Papers*, volume 3, pages 3–3.

Heng Ji, Joel Nothman, Ben Hachey, and Radu Florian. 2015. Overview of TAC-KBP 2015 tri-lingual entity discovery and linking. In *TAC 2015 Proceedings Papers*.

Nikolaos Kolitsas, Octavian-Eugen Ganea, and Thomas Hofmann. 2018. End-to-end neural entity linking. In *Proceedings of the 22nd Conference on Computational Natural Language Learning*, pages 519–529, Brussels, Belgium. Association for Computational Linguistics.

Xiao Ling, Sameer Singh, and Daniel S Weld. 2015. Design challenges for entity linking. *Transactions of the Association for Computational Linguistics*, 3:315–328.

Andrew L Maas, Awni Y Hannun, and Andrew Y Ng. 2013. Rectifier nonlinearities improve neural network acoustic models. In *Proc. icml*, volume 30, page 3.

James Mayfield and Artiles Javier. 2012. Overview of the TAC 2012 knowledge base population track. In *TAC 2012 Proceedings Papers*.

Paul McNamee, James Mayfield, Dawn Lawrie, Douglas Oard, and David Doermann. 2011. Cross-language entity linking. In *Proceedings of 5th International Joint Conference on Natural Language Processing*, pages 255–263.

Andrea Moro, Alessandro Raganato, and Roberto Navigli. 2014. Entity linking meets word sense disambiguation: a unified approach. *Transactions of the Association for Computational Linguistics*, 2:231–244.

Kevin P Murphy, Yair Weiss, and Michael I Jordan. 1999. Loopy belief propagation for approximate inference: An empirical study. In *Proceedings of the Fifteenth conference on Uncertainty in artificial intelligence*, pages 467–475. Morgan Kaufmann Publishers Inc.

Jason Naradowsky and Sebastian Riedel. 2016. Represent, aggregate, and constrain: A novel architecture for machine reading from noisy sources. *arXiv preprint arXiv:1610.09722*.

Xiaoman Pan, Boliang Zhang, Jonathan May, Joel Nothman, Kevin Knight, and Heng Ji. 2017. Cross-lingual name tagging and linking for 282 languages. In *Proceedings of the 55th Annual Meeting of the Association for Computational Linguistics (Volume 1: Long Papers)*, volume 1, pages 1946–1958.

Adam Paszke, Sam Gross, Soumith Chintala, Gregory Chanan, Edward Yang, Zachary DeVito, Zeming Lin, Alban Desmaison, Luca Antiga, and Adam Lerer. 2017. Automatic differentiation in PyTorch. In *NIPS Autodiff Workshop*.

Shruti Rijhwani, Jiateng Xie, Graham Neubig, and Jaime Carbonell. 2019. Zero-shot neural transfer for cross-lingual entity linking. In *Thirty-Third AAAI Conference on Artificial Intelligence (AAAI)*, Honolulu, Hawaii.

Wei Shen, Jianyong Wang, and Jiawei Han. 2015. Entity linking with a knowledge base: Issues, techniques, and solutions. *IEEE Transactions on Knowledge and Data Engineering*, 27(2):443–460.

Avirup Sil and Radu Florian. 2016. One for all: Towards language independent named entity linking. In *Proceedings of the 54th Annual Meeting of the Association for Computational Linguistics (Volume 1: Long Papers)*, volume 1, pages 2255–2264.

Avirup Sil, Gourab Kundu, Radu Florian, and Wael Hamza. 2018. Neural cross-lingual entity linking. In *Thirty-Second AAAI Conference on Artificial Intelligence*.

Chen-Tse Tsai and Dan Roth. 2016. Cross-lingual wikification using multilingual embeddings. In *Proceedings of the 2016 Conference of the North American Chapter of the Association for Computational Linguistics: Human Language Technologies*, pages 589–598, San Diego, California. Association for Computational Linguistics.

Shyam Upadhyay, Nitish Gupta, and Dan Roth. 2018. Joint multilingual supervision for cross-lingual entity linking. In *Proceedings of the 2018 Conference on Empirical Methods in Natural Language Processing*, pages 2486–2495.

Ikuya Yamada, Hiroyuki Shindo, Hideaki Takeda, and Yoshiyasu Takefuji. 2017. Learning distributed representations of texts and entities from knowledge base. *Transactions of the Association for Computational Linguistics*, 5:397–411.

Transductive Auxiliary Task Self-Training for Neural Multi-Task Models

Johannes Bjerva[1], Katharina Kann[2], Isabelle Augenstein[1]
[1]Department of Computer Science, University of Copenhagen, Denmark
[2]Center for Data Science, New York University, USA
`bjerva,augenstein@di.ku.dk, kann@nyu.edu`

Abstract

Multi-task learning and self-training are two common ways to improve a machine learning model's performance in settings with limited training data. Drawing heavily on ideas from those two approaches, we suggest transductive auxiliary task self-training: training a multi-task model on (i) a combination of main and auxiliary task training data, and (ii) test instances with auxiliary task labels which a single-task version of the model has previously generated. We perform extensive experiments on 86 combinations of languages and tasks. Our results are that, on average, transductive auxiliary task self-training improves absolute accuracy by up to 9.56% over the pure multi-task model for dependency relation tagging and by up to 13.03% for semantic tagging.

1 Introduction

When data for certain tasks or languages is not readily available, different approaches exist to leverage other resources for the training of machine learning models. Those are commonly either instances from a related task or unlabelled data: During **multi-task training** (Caruana, 1993), a model learns from examples of multiple related tasks at the same time and can therefore benefit from a larger overall number of training instances. **Self-training** (Yarowsky, 1995; Riloff et al., 2003), in contrast, denotes the process of iteratively training a model, using it to label new examples, and adding the most confident ones to the training set before repeating the training. As data without gold standard annotations is used, self-training can be considered a special case of semi-supervised training.

In this work, we propose **transductive auxiliary task self-training**, based on a combination of multi-task training and self-training: We

use the available auxiliary task data to obtain a high-performing single-task model for the auxiliary task, which we then use to label the main task test set with auxiliary task labels. Subsequently, we train a multi-task model on both tasks, while including instances with the newly generated silver standard auxiliary task labels.

Transductive auxiliary task self-training is an extremely cheap procedure, requiring only small amounts of additional computing time, compared to the obvious alternative of manually producing more labels. Our approach is **transductive** since the model generalises from specific training examples to specific test examples. In particular, training on auxiliary task labels for the test set, which have been produced by the single-task model, yields a final multi-task model, which satisfies the defining criterion of transductive inference that predictions depend on the test data (Vapnik, 1998). Note that we do not require gold standard test labels for either task.

In addition to presenting our method, we investigate three research questions (**RQs**):

RQ 1: For which tasks and dataset sizes does transductive auxiliary task self-training help most?

RQ 2: Can a model trained with our cost-free transductive auxiliary task self-training perform similarly to or better than a model trained on additional manual annotations for the auxiliary task?

RQ 3: Even without considering reduced costs, are there scenarios where it is better to perform transductive auxiliary task self-training than adding more main task examples?

In order to find generalisable answers to these research questions, we experiment with several tasks, languages and numbers of training samples. We consider the low-level auxiliary task of part-of-speech tagging and two main tasks: dependency relation (DepRel) tagging and semantic tagging. We furthermore compare with an unsuper-

Proceedings of the 2nd Workshop on Deep Learning Approaches for Low-Resource NLP (DeepLo), pages 253–258
Hong Kong, China, November 3, 2019. ©2019 Association for Computational Linguistics
https://doi.org/10.18653/v1/P17

We	must	draw	attention	to	the	distribution	of	this	form	in	those	dialects	Sentence
PRON	AUX	VERB	NOUN	ADP	DET	NOUN	ADP	DET	NOUN	ADP	DET	NOUN	POS
nsubj	aux	root	obj	case	det	obl	case	det	nmod	case	det	obl	DepRel
PRO	NEC	EXS	CON	REL	DEF	CON	AND	PRX	CON	REL	DST	CON	SemTag

Figure 1: POS tags, DepRel labels and semantic tags for an example sentence.

vised auxiliary task baseline, to show that our results are not simply a result of domain adaptation effects. We experiment on 41 languages, yielding a total of 86 unique language–task combinations. We find that, on average, transductive auxiliary task self-training improves absolute accuracy by up to 9.56% and 13.03% over the pure multi-task model for DepRel tagging and semantic tagging, respectively.

2 Neural Sequence Labelling

2.1 Tasks

Figure 1 shows a sentence with annotations for the three linguistic tasks considered in this paper, which we will describe in the following.[1]

Part-of-speech (POS) tagging is the task of assigning morpho-syntactic tags to each word in a sentence. We use it as an auxiliary task, since respective datasets are available for many languages. It is also a relatively easy task, with state-of-the-art models typically achieving over 95% accuracy (Plank et al., 2016). We use the Universal Dependencies (UD) POS tag set (Nivre et al., 2016).

Dependency relation (DepRel) labelling is the task of assigning dependency labels to each word in a sentence. In our experiments, we use the Universal Dependencies labels (Nivre et al., 2016). We use this task as a main task. Both this task and POS tagging are morpho-syntactic tasks.

Semantic Tagging (SemTag) is the task of assigning a semantic tag to each word in a sentence. We use the labels from the Parallel Meaning Bank (PMB, Abzianidze et al. (2017); Bjerva et al. (2016)). This tag set was designed for multilingual semantic parsing and, therefore, to generalise across languages. As this task is relatively challenging, we use it as a main task. While the UD data is available for 41 languages, the PMB data is only available for four (English, Italian, Dutch, and German).

FreqBin is the task of predicting the binned frequency of a word, as introduced by Plank et al.

---

[1]The example is taken from PMB document 01/3421, which has gold standard SemTags. The UD POS and DepRel tags were obtained using UD-Pipe (Straka et al., 2016).

(2016). We use this task as an unsupervised auxiliary baseline, with frequencies obtained from our training data.

2.2 Model Architecture

We approach sequence labelling by using a variant of a bidirectional recurrent neural network, which uses both preceding and succeeding context when predicting the label of a word. This choice was made as such models at the same time obtain high performance on all three tasks and lend themselves nicely to multi-task training via hard parameter sharing. This system is based on the hierarchical bi-LSTM of Plank et al. (2016) and is implemented using DyNet (Neubig et al., 2017). On the subword-level, the LSTM is bi-directional and operates on characters (Ballesteros et al., 2015; Ling et al., 2015). Second, a context bi-LSTM operates on the word level, from which output is passed on to a classification layer.

Multi-task training is approached using hard parameter sharing (Caruana, 1993). We consider T datasets, each containing pairs of input-output sequences $(w_{1:n}, y_{1:n}^t)$, $w_i \in V$, $y_i^t \in L^t$. The input vocabulary V is shared across tasks, but the outputs (tagsets) L^t are task dependent. At each step in the training process we choose a random task t, followed by a randomly chosen batch of training instance. Each task is associated with an independent classification function, but all tasks share the hidden layers. We train using the Adam optimisation algorithm (Kingma and Ba, 2014) over a maximum of 10 epochs together with early stopping.

3 Transductive Auxiliary Task Self-Training

Manual annotation of data for main or auxiliary tasks is time-consuming and expensive. Instead, we propose to use a preliminary single-task model to label the main task test data with auxiliary task labels which can then be leveraged to train an improved multi-task model.

Transductive auxiliary task self-training is based on two main ideas. First, we assume that the auxiliary task is easier than the main task, such that a high performance can be achieved on it. Hence, the model will be confident about the auxiliary task labels, as is required for self-training. Second, we choose a transductive approach, because we assume that not all auxiliary task examples will lead to equal improvements on the main task. In particular, we expect auxiliary task labels for the test instances to be most useful, since information about those instances is most relevant for the prediction of the main task labels on this data. Similarly to contextualised word representations, this offers an additional signal for the test set instances, as we obtain this through predicted auxiliary labels rather than direct encoding of the context (Devlin et al., 2018; Peters et al., 2018).

3.1 Algorithm

Our proposed algorithm is shown in Algorithm 1. We start by first training a single-task model on the available auxiliary task training data, which then predicts labels for the raw input sentences from the main task test set. Note that we neither observe nor require any labels for this test set, neither for the auxiliary nor for the main task. The labels which the preliminary single-task model predicts are then added to the train set of the auxiliary task for training of the final multi-task model.

Although a transductive approach requires training a new model for each test set, sequence-labelling models such as bi-LSTMs are usually quick to train even on single CPUs, with a full self-training iteration in this paper completing in a matter of hours.

Algorithm 1 Transductive auxiliary task self-training

1: $train_{aux} \leftarrow$ aux. task train data
2: $train_{main} \leftarrow$ main task train data
3: $testinp_{main} \leftarrow$ main task test input
4: $model_{aux} \leftarrow$ **train**$(train_{aux})$
5: **for** $sentence \in testinp_{main}$ **do**
6:     $l \leftarrow$ **label**$(sentence, model_{aux})$
7:     $train_{aux} = train_{aux} + l$
8: $model_{mtl} \leftarrow$ **train**$_{mtl}(train_{aux}, train_{main})$

---

4 Experiments

The experiments described in this section aim at answering the research questions raised in §1, concerned with the best settings for transductive auxiliary task self-training, as well as the theoretical question how it compares to adding additional (expensive) gold-standard annotations for the main and the auxiliary tasks. To ensure that our findings are generalisable, we use a large sample of 56 treebanks, covering 41 languages and several domains. Although this experimental set-up would allow us to run multilingual experiments, we only train monolingual models, and aggregate results across languages and treebanks. We investigate three tasks; two of them being morpho-syntactic (POS tagging and DepRel tagging) and one being semantic (semantic tagging). In all cases, POS is the auxiliary task, and either POS tagging or DepRel tagging is the main task. Experiments are run in several low-resource settings, varying the amount of main task data.

We run experiments under four conditions, in addition to using an MTL baseline. We compare (i) adding gold standard test annotations for the auxiliary task only (**Aux-ST ceiling**), (ii) transductive auxiliary task self-training, as described in Algorithm 1 (**Aux-ST**), (iii) adding gold standard train annotations for the auxiliary task only (**Extra Aux**), or (iv) adding gold standard train annotations for the main task only (**Extra Main**). We expect (iii) and (iv) to constitute challenging conditions to beat, as we are in effect giving our model more annotated data, which is normally expensive to come by.

4.1 Data

We run experiments on the task-combinations DepRel–POS and Semtag–POS for all available languages and datasets. Additionally, we reduce our training sets to 10k, 1k, 0.5k, and 0.1k sentences in order to investigate various low-resource scenarios. For semantic tagging, the 10k setting is omitted as we do not have enough training data.

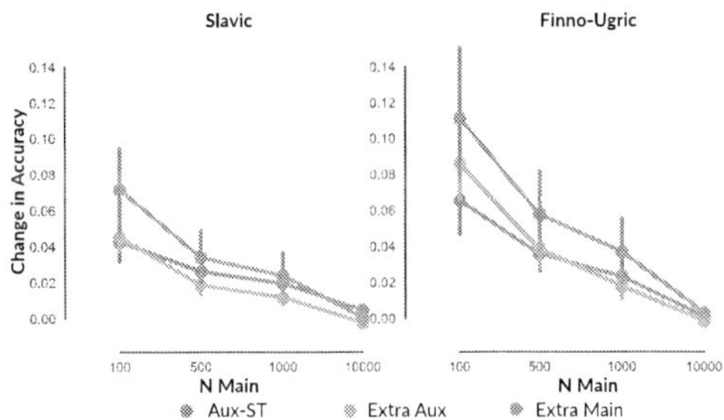

Figure 2: Results for UD treebanks.

N Main	MTL	Aux-ST ceiling	Aux-ST	Extra Aux	Extra Main
10k	86.39	*3.79%	*1.97%	-0.30%	0.19%
1k	79.19	*7.42%	*5.39%	*1.74%	*7.01%
0.5k	75.77	*8.69%	*6.85%	*2.64%	*10.17%
0.1k	66.31	*11.32%	*9.56%	*4.97%	*18.15%
1k	67.82	n/a	*1.74%	0.05%	0.64%
0.5k	63.32	n/a	*4.60%	0.83%	*2.31%
0.1k	50.44	n/a	*13.03%	*4.93%	*11.58%

Table 1: Macro-averaged changes in accuracy from the MTL baseline for DepRel – POS (top), SemTag – POS (bottom). We compare adding gold standard test annotations for the aux task (**Aux-ST ceiling**), transductive aux task self-training (**Aux-ST**), adding gold standard train annotations for the aux task (**Extra Aux**), or for the main task (**Extra Main**) randomly. Significant ($p < 0.05$) differences from the baseline are marked with *.

4.2 Results and Discussion

Table 1 contains results of the experiments macro-averaged across all languages and treebanks in the UD and across all languages in the PMB. Figure 2 contains results for two typologically distinct language families, Slavic and Finno-Ugric.

Across all data sizes, self-training on the auxiliary task is significantly better than the baseline multi-task model without self-training. The results on DepRel tagging show that, when the main task data is sufficiently large, it is more beneficial to do transductive auxiliary task self-training than it is to further increase the size of the main dataset. For semantic tagging, we find this to hold for all of our training data size settings. Our comparison with the FreqBin task does not yield substantial improvements, with mean differences compared to standard MTL at -0.001% (stdev. 0.022).

To rule out that any gains in the self-training conditions are not due to increased vocabulary, we ran experiments with pre-trained word embeddings which included the raw text from the test set and found no significant differences. This can be explained by the fact that, although out-of-vocabulary rate is reduced to zero in this condition, the test set is still relatively small. Thus, the word embeddings do not have much distributional information with which to arrive at good word representations for previously out-of-vocabulary words.

In **RQ1**, we asked for which task and dataset sizes transductive auxiliary task self-training is most beneficial. We found benefits across the board, with larger effects when the main task training set is small.

In **RQ2**, we asked whether using transductive auxiliary task self-training might even be better than the costly process of manually expanding the data with gold standard auxiliary data for random samples. We found that this depends on the main task and the size of its training set. For DepRels, with a low amount of main task data, the largest increase in accuracy is found by adding more main task data. However, given sufficient main task data, adding highly relevant auxiliary task samples, even ones which are potentially erroneous, is more beneficial. In the case of semantic tagging, however, transductive auxiliary task self-training is always more beneficial. As expected, the usefulness of self-training as well as adding extra auxiliary or main task data decreases with increasing dataset size.

In **RQ3**, we asked whether there are cases in which using auxiliary task data is preferable to annotating and adding more main task samples. We found that this is the case when using our proposed method of transductive auxiliary task self-training for all training set sizes for semantic tagging, and in the 10k setting for DepRel tagging.

5 Related Work

Self-training has been shown to be a successful learning approach (Nigam and Ghani, 2000), e.g., for word sense disambiguation (Yarowsky, 1995) or AMR parsing (Konstas et al., 2017). Samples in self-training are typically selected according to confidence (Zhu, 2005) which requires a proxy to measure it. This can be the confidence of the model (Yarowsky, 1995; Riloff et al., 2003) or the agreement of different models, as used in tri-training (Zhou and Li, 2005). Another option is curriculum learning, where selection is based on learning difficulty, increasing the difficulty during learning (Bengio et al., 2009). In contrast, we build upon the assumption that the auxiliary task examples are ones a model can be certain about.

In **multi-task learning**, most research focuses on understanding which auxiliary tasks to select, or on how to share between tasks (Søgaard and Goldberg, 2016a; Lin et al., 2019; Ruder and Plank, 2017; Augenstein et al., 2018; Ruder et al., 2019). For instance, Ruder and Plank (2017) find that similarity as well as diversity measures applied to the main vs. auxiliary task datasets as a whole are useful in selecting auxiliary tasks. In the context of sequence labelling, many combinations of tasks have been explored (Søgaard and Goldberg, 2016b; Martínez Alonso and Plank, 2017; Bjerva, 2017). Ruder et al. (2019) present a flexible architecture, which learns which parameters to share between a main and an auxiliary task. One of the few examples where multi-task learning is combined with other methods is the semi-supervised approach by Chao and Sun (2012), where main task labels are assigned to unlabelled instances which are then added to the main task dataset. However, to the best of our knowledge, no one has applied self-training to label additional instances with auxiliary task labels.

6 Conclusion

We introduced transductive auxiliary task self-training, a straightforward way to improve the performance of multi-task models. Concretely, we applied the idea of self-training to auxiliary tasks, in order to automatically label the main task test data with auxiliary task labels which we subsequently included into the training set for multi-task learning. In experiments on 41 different languages we obtained improvements of up to 9.56% absolute accuracy over the pure multi-task model for DepRel tagging and up to 13.03% absolute accuracy for semantic tagging. We further showed that transductive auxiliary task self-training is more effective than randomly choosing additional gold standard auxiliary task data. In some settings, in addition to not needing additional annotation, it even led to a better performing model than adding a comparable amount of extra gold standard main task data.

References

Lasha Abzianidze, Johannes Bjerva, Kilian Evang, Hessel Haagsma, Rik van Noord, Pierre Ludmann, Duc-Duy Nguyen, and Johan Bos. 2017. The Parallel Meaning Bank: Towards a Multilingual Corpus of Translations Annotated with Compositional Meaning Representations. In *Proceedings of EACL*.

Isabelle Augenstein, Sebastian Ruder, and Anders Søgaard. 2018. Multi-Task Learning of Pairwise Sequence Classification Tasks over Disparate Label Spaces. In *Proceedings of NAACL*.

Miguel Ballesteros, Chris Dyer, and Noah A Smith. 2015. Improved Transition-based Parsing by Modeling Characters instead of Words with LSTMs. In *Proceedings of EMNLP*.

Yoshua Bengio, Jérôme Louradour, Ronan Collobert, and Jason Weston. 2009. Curriculum learning. In *Proceedings of ICML*.

Johannes Bjerva. 2017. *One Model to Rule them all: Multitask and Multilingual Modelling for Lexical Analysis*. Ph.D. thesis, University of Groningen.

Johannes Bjerva, Barbara Plank, and Johan Bos. 2016. Semantic Tagging with Deep Residual Networks. In *COLING*, pages 3531–3541.

Rich Caruana. 1993. Multitask Learning: A Knowledge-Based Source of Inductive Bias. In *Proceedings of ICML*.

Guoqing Chao and Shiliang Sun. 2012. Semi-supervised Multitask Learning via Self-training and Maximum Entropy Discrimination. In *Proceedings of International Conference on Neural Information Processing*.

Jacob Devlin, Ming-Wei Chang, Kenton Lee, and Kristina Toutanova. 2018. Bert: Pre-training of deep bidirectional transformers for language understanding. *arXiv preprint arXiv:1810.04805*.

Diederik Kingma and Jimmy Ba. 2014. Adam: A Method for Stochastic Optimization. *arXiv preprint arXiv:1412.6980*.

Ioannis Konstas, Srinivasan Iyer, Mark Yatskar, Yejin Choi, and Luke Zettlemoyer. 2017. Neural AMR: Sequence-to-Sequence Models for Parsing and Generation. In *Proceedings of ACL*.

Yu-Hsiang Lin, Chian-Yu Chen, Jean Lee, Zirui Li, Yuyan Zhang, Mengzhou Xia, Shruti Rijhwani, Junxian He, Zhisong Zhang, Xuezhe Ma, et al. 2019. Choosing Transfer Languages for Cross-Lingual Learning. *arXiv:1905.12688*.

Wang Ling, Chris Dyer, Alan W. Black, Isabel Trancoso, Ramon Fermandez, Silvio Amir, Luís Marujo, and Tiago Luís. 2015. Finding Function in Form: Compositional Character Models for Open Vocabulary Word Representation. In *Proceedings of EMNLP*.

Héctor Martínez Alonso and Barbara Plank. 2017. When is multitask learning effective? Semantic sequence prediction under varying data conditions. In *EACL*.

Graham Neubig, Chris Dyer, Yoav Goldberg, Austin Matthews, Waleed Ammar, Antonios Anastasopoulos, Miguel Ballesteros, David Chiang, Daniel Clothiaux, Trevor Cohn, et al. 2017. Dynet: The dynamic neural network toolkit. *arXiv preprint arXiv:1701.03980*.

Kamal Nigam and Rayid Ghani. 2000. Analyzing the effectiveness and applicability of co–training. In *Proceedings of Information and Knowledge Management*.

Joakim Nivre, Marie-Catherine de Marneffe, Filip Ginter, Yoav Goldberg, Jan Hajic, Christopher D. Manning, Ryan T. McDonald, Slav Petrov, Sampo Pyysalo, Natalia Silveira, Reut Tsarfaty, and Daniel Zeman. 2016. Universal Dependencies v1: A Multilingual Treebank Collection. In *Proceedings of LREC*.

Matthew Peters, Mark Neumann, Mohit Iyyer, Matt Gardner, Christopher Clark, Kenton Lee, and Luke Zettlemoyer. 2018. Deep Contextualized Word Representations. In *NAACL*, pages 2227–2237. Association for Computational Linguistics.

Barbara Plank, Anders Søgaard, and Yoav Goldberg. 2016. Multilingual Part-of-Speech Tagging with Bidirectional Long Short-Term Memory Models and Auxiliary Loss. In *Proceedings of ACL (Short Papers)*.

Ellen Riloff, Janyce Wiebe, and Theresa Wilson. 2003. Learning Subjective Nouns using Extraction Pattern Bootstrapping. In *Proceedings of CoNLL*.

Sebastian Ruder, Joachim Bingel, Isabelle Augenstein, and Anders Søgaard. 2019. Latent Multi-task Architecture Learning. In *Proceedings of AAAI*.

Sebastian Ruder and Barbara Plank. 2017. Learning to select data for transfer learning with Bayesian Optimization. In *Proceedings of EMNLP*.

Anders Søgaard and Yoav Goldberg. 2016a. Deep multi-task learning with low level tasks supervised at lower layers. In *Proceedings of ACL (Short Papers)*.

Anders Søgaard and Yoav Goldberg. 2016b. Deep multi-task learning with low level tasks supervised at lower layers. In *ACL*.

Milan Straka, Jan Hajic, and Jana Straková. 2016. UDPipe: Trainable pipeline for processing CoNLL-U files performing tokenization, morphological analysis, POS tagging and parsing. In *Proceedings of LREC*.

Vladimir N Vapnik. 1998. *Statistical Learning Theory*. John Wiley.

David Yarowsky. 1995. Unsupervised Word-Sense Disambiguation Rivaling Supervised Methods. In *Proceedings of ACL*.

Zhi-Hua Zhou and Ming Li. 2005. Tri-training: exploiting unlabeled data using three classifiers. *IEEE Transactions on Knowledge and Data Engineering*, 17:1529–1541.

Xiaojin Zhu. 2005. Semi-Supervised Learning Literature Survey. Technical Report 1530, Computer Sciences, University of Wisconsin-Madison.

Weakly Supervised Attentional Model for Low Resource Ad-hoc Cross-lingual Information Retrieval

Lingjun Zhao[†], Rabih Zbib[†], Zhuolin Jiang[†], Damianos Karakos[†], Zhongqiang Huang[‡*]
[†]Raytheon BBN Technologies, Cambridge, MA, USA
[‡]Alibaba Technologies, Hangzhou, China
{lingjun.zhao, rabih.zbib, zhuolin.jiang, damianos.karakos}@raytheon.com,
z.huang@alibaba-inc.com

Abstract

We propose a weakly supervised neural model for Ad-hoc Cross-lingual Information Retrieval (CLIR) from low-resource languages. Low resource languages often lack relevance annotations for CLIR, and when available the training data usually has limited coverage for possible queries. In this paper, we design a model which does not require relevance annotations, instead it is trained on samples extracted from translation corpora as weak supervision. This model relies on an attention mechanism to learn spans in the foreign sentence that are relevant to the query. We report experiments on two low resource languages: Swahili and Tagalog, trained on less than 100k parallel sentences each. The proposed model achieves 19 MAP points improvement compared to using CNNs for feature extraction, 12 points improvement from machine translation-based CLIR, and up to 6 points improvement compared to probabilistic CLIR models.

1 Introduction and Previous Work

Neural models for Information Retrieval (IR) have received a fair amount of attention in recent years (Zhang et al., 2016; Zamani and Croft, 2017; Dehghani et al., 2017; Mitra et al., 2018). This includes Cross-Lingual Information Retrieval (CLIR), where the task is to retrieve documents in a language different from that of the query. Neural models for CLIR can learn relevance ranking without directly relying on translations, but they typically require large amounts of training data annotated for relevance (cross-lingual query-document pairs), which are often not available, especially for low resource languages. When available, the annotated data usually has limited coverage of the large space of possible ad-hoc queries.

In this paper, we propose a novel neural model for Ad-hoc CLIR against short queries using weak

supervision instead of annotated CLIR corpora. The model computes the probability of relevance of each sentence in a foreign document to an input query. These probabilities are then combined to compute a relevance score for a query-document pair. Our model does not rely on relevance-annotated data, but is trained on samples extracted from parallel machine translation data as weak supervision. Compared to CLIR annotated data, sentence translations are often easier to obtain and have better coverage for short queries. The main challenge is designing the model to effectively identify relevant spans in the possibly long foreign sentence. We address that by using an attention mechanism (Bahdanau et al., 2015; Vaswani et al., 2017), thus allowing the model to learn what parts of the sentence to focus on without explicit supervision (e.g. word alignments). To bridge the gap across languages, we pre-train and further optimize bilingual embeddings. We also investigate element-wise interaction between the query and sentence representations to further improve relevance matching.

In contrast, previous methods that directly model CLIR rely on large amounts of relevance-annotated data (Sasaki et al., 2018; Lavrenko et al., 2002; Bai et al., 2009; Sokolov et al., 2013). Other approaches use bilingual embeddings to represent text cross-lingually, but are not specifically optimized for CLIR (Vulic and Moens, 2015; Litschko et al., 2018). (Li and Cheng, 2018) designed a model to learn task-specific text representation using CLIR-annotated data. (Franco-Salvador et al., 2014; Sorg and Cimiano, 2012) crossed the lexical gap using external knowledge sources (Wikipedia), which are limited for low resource languages. An alternative approach translates the queries or documents, and reduces CLIR to monolingual IR (Gupta et al., 2017; Levow et al., 2005; Nie, 2003). But machine translation is not an ideal solution for CLIR either (Zhou et al., 2012), one

---

* Work was done while the author was at Raytheon BBN Technologies.

Proceedings of the 2nd Workshop on Deep Learning Approaches for Low-Resource NLP (DeepLo), pages 259–264
Hong Kong, China, November 3, 2019. ©2019 Association for Computational Linguistics
https://doi.org/10.18653/v1/P17

reason is it often produces hallucinated sentences that has little relevance with the source side for low resource languages. On the other hand, (Zbib et al., 2019; Xu and Weischedel, 2000) model the CLIR problem using generative probabilistic model with lexical translation dictionary, while this assumes independence between query words and ignores the underlying semantic connection.

The main contributions of this paper are:

- We design a weakly supervised neural model for CLIR using parallel machine translation data for training, rather than using annotated CLIR corpora.

- To the best of our knowledge, this is the first application of attention mechanisms to CLIR.

- We further propose and demonstrate the importance of an interaction-based relevance matching layer.

We report experiments on two low-resource languages: Swahili and Tagalog, using data from the MATERIAL (MAT, 2017) program. The proposed model obtains scores 19 MAP points higher than neural models that use CNNs for feature extraction. Compared to the machine translation-based CLIR, this model has about 12 MAP points better performance. The model also has better performance than the probabilistic CLIR models with up to 6 MAP points improvement. Additionally, the proposed interaction-based relevance matching layer is usually effective for the QRANN model.

2 Query Relevance Attentional Neural Network Model (QRANN) for CLIR

Direct modeling of CLIR is not practical for low resource languages, as annotated query-document pairs are usually not available. English queries and foreign sentences extracted from parallel translation corpora can serve as weakly supervised training data to learn a model that estimates relevance between short queries and foreign sentences, which can then be applied to computing the query-document relevance scores.

2.1 QRANN Model

Our goal is to design a model that measures the relevance between an English[1] query and

---

[1]The discussion and experiments are in terms of English queries, but the model is language-independent.

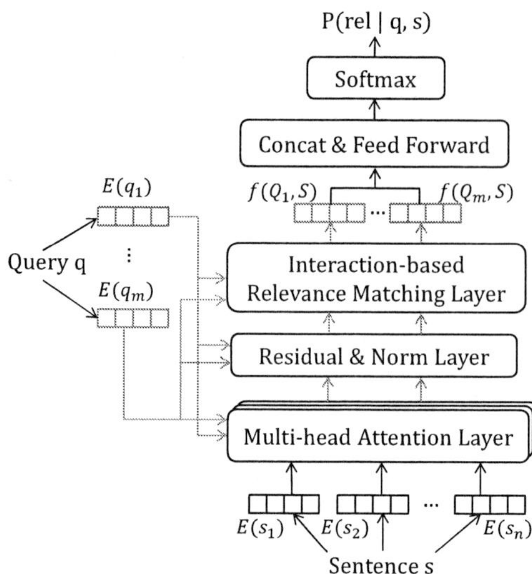

Figure 1: Query relevance attentional neural network (QRANN) model architecture. Each word in the query has an attention mechanism with the sentence to identify relevant spans, followed by a residual connection and layer normalization. After relevance matching, the outputs are fed to a feedforward layer to obtain relevance features of the entire query, which are used for final relevance estimation.

a foreign sentence. Formally, given a query $q = [q_1, q_2, ..., q_m]$ and a foreign sentence $s = [s_1, s_2, ... s_n]$, the model estimates relevance probability $P(rel|q, s) \in [0, 1]$. We first describe the model architecture, shown in Figure 1, and later explain how this model output is used to compute document-level relevance scores. Each word in q and s is represented as a d-dimensional embedding using lookup table $E(\cdot)$:

$$Q = [Q_1, ..., Q_m] = [E(q_1), ..., E(q_m)]$$
$$S = [S_1, .., S_n] = [E(s_1), ..., E(s_n)] \quad (1)$$

Multi-head Attention Layer A key feature of our approach is to avoid an explicit alignment of the query words with the relevant foreign sentence spans. Instead, we use an attention mechanism over S, which allows the model to learn which spans contain relevance evidence, as well as how to weight that evidence. We compute a context vector C_j for word q_j as a weighted sum of S_i:

$$C_j = \sum_{i=1}^{n} \alpha_i^j S_i \quad (2)$$

the attention weight α_i^j for each word s_i in sentence scores how well the sentence word s_i and q_j match: $\alpha_i^j = softmax(e_i^j)$, where $e_i^j = v_\alpha tanh(U_\alpha Q_j + W_\alpha S_i)$. U_α, W_α and v_α are shared across each q_j in q for better generalization. Inspired by recent work in machine translation (Vaswani et al., 2017), we found it beneficial to use a multi-head attention to allow the model to jointly attend to information at different positions. We compute multi-head attention M_j by concatenating k different attention context vectors and applying a linear transformation:

$$M_j = [C_j^1; C_j^2; ...; C_j^k]W_M \qquad (3)$$

Residual & Norm Layer We use a residual connection to the attention outputs, followed by layer normalization: $N_j = LayerNorm(Q_j + M_j))$.

Interaction-based Relevance Matching Layer The essential function of the relevance matching layer is to help the model identify the relatedness or difference between sentence and query. Previous work (Li et al., 2018) shows that element-wise interactions, like difference could capture offset between two words in an embedding space, and inner product could measure their relatedness. Hence, we propose an effective approach for relevance matching by computing both difference and relatedness between Q_j and N_j:

$$e_{N_j,Q_j}^{diff} = N_j - Q_j; e_{N_j,Q_j}^{prod} = N_j \odot Q_j \qquad (4)$$

The interaction-based relevance matching layer is a hidden layer on top of the concatenation of e_{N_j,Q_j}^{diff} and e_{N_j,Q_j}^{prod}:

$$f(Q_j, S) = relu(W_C[e_{N_j,Q_j}^{diff}; e_{N_j,Q_j}^{prod}] + b_C) \qquad (5)$$

W_C, b_C are shared across each q_j in q.

In order to show the effectiveness of interaction-based relevance matching, instead of using (5), we also try simply concat N_j and Q_j as an alternative relevance matching layer:

$$f(Q_j, S) = relu(W_C[N_j; Q_j] + b_C) \qquad (6)$$

Concat & Feed Forward We concatenate the relevance matching outputs and pass them through another hidden layer:

$$g(Q, S) = tanh(W_h[f(Q_1, S); ...; f(Q_m, S)] + b_h) \qquad (7)$$

As shown in Figure 1, the feed forward layer concatenates query-word specific features. Each neuron has connections with all query-specific features, aiming to capture semantic relationships among query words.

Softmax Output Finally, the relevance probability between q and s is computed by:

$$P(rel|q, s) = softmax(W_o g(Q, S) + b_o) \qquad (8)$$

where W_h, b_h, W_o, b_o are trainable parameters.

2.2 Weakly Supervised Learning for CLIR

As mentioned, the QRANN model is not trained on relevance-annotated data. Instead, it is trained with weakly supervised data. Weak supervision has been studied in monolingual IR. For example, (Dehghani et al., 2017) used BM25 to produce weakly supervised query-document labels. Different from monolingual IR, CLIR requires the training data to bridge the language gap, thus we propose a novel weak supervision used in the QRANN model for CLIR: we construct cross-lingual query-sentence pairs from parallel data as weakly supervised labels to learn cross-lingual query-document relevance. Positive samples are constructed from a foreign sentence and a content word or noun phrase from its English translation. We generate negative samples by selecting a foreign sentence and an English word or phrase that does not appear in the sentence translation. We find using larger negative-to-positive ratio improves the model performance as this would provide more negative samples variety, and fix the ratio to 20:1 for both model performance and training speed. We avoid using stop words for both types of samples.

We use bilingual embeddings pre-trained on the same parallel data for both low resource languages, using the method in (Gouws and Søgaard, 2015), and optimize them further during model training.

The CLIR end task requires an estimation of relevance of the whole foreign document to the query, using relevance outputs between query and sentence from the QRANN model. We experimented with different methods for combining sentence relevance scores, including average and maximum, and found the most effective method to be the probability of relevance to at least one sentence in the document:

$$P(rel|q, D) \approx 1 - \prod_{s \in D} \left(1 - P(rel|q, s)\right) \qquad (9)$$

3 Experiments

3.1 Datasets and Experimental Setup

We report experimental results on CLIR datasets provided by the MATERIAL (MAT, 2017) program for two low resource languages: Swahili and Tagalog. Each language has two datasets: Test1 (about 800 documents) and Test2 (about 500 documents). We use two query sets: 83 query phrases in Q1 and 102 query phrases in Q2 for Swahili, 140 query phrases in Q1 and 205 in Q2 for Tagalog. The CLIR performance is reported using Mean Average Precision (MAP).

For training, we use parallel sentences released by the MATERIAL and LORELEI (LOR, 2015) programs (72k for Swahili, 98k for Tagalog), and parallel lexicons dowloaded from Panlex (Kamholz et al., 2014) (190k for Swahili, 65k for Tagalog). We extract 40-50M samples from the parallel corpora for each language to train the QRANN model. We use the Adam optimizer with a learning rate of 0.0005, batch size of 512, and dropout probability of 0.1. We pre-train bilingual word embeddings with size $d = 512$, use 4 attention heads, each with a size of 512. The hidden layer sizes are 512 for W_C and 1024 for W_h.

3.2 Baseline Approaches

Probabilistic CLIR Model with Statistical MT Generative probabilistic models (Miller et al., 1999; Xu and Weischedel, 2000) have been an effective approach to CLIR. We use such a model as baseline, with probabilistic lexical translations estimated from statistical machine translation alignment of the parallel training data. We use the concatenation of GIZA++ (Och and Ney, 2003) and the Berkeley Aligner (Haghighi et al., 2009) to estimate lexical translation probabilities by normalizing the alignment counts.

Occurrence Probability Variant We also use a baseline that computes the document relevance score as the probability of each of the query terms occurring at least once in the document. Using translation probabilities $p(q \mid f)$, the document score is computed as:

$$\prod_{q \in Q} \left[1 - \prod_{f \in Doc} \left(1 - p(q \mid f) \right) \right] \quad (10)$$

Machine Translation (MT) based CLIR We compared our model with a MT-based CLIR, which translates foreign documents into English using Transformer (Vaswani et al., 2017), and then does monolingual information retrieval. This approach is similar to (Nie, 2003).

CNN Feature Extraction Convolutional Neural Networks (CNNs) have been found effective for extracting features from text. Here we use this model for feature extraction for comparison. Instead of using multi-head attention and normalization layers, we build a CNN model to extract features from sentence and query, which includes an embedding layer, a convolutional layer with max-pooling and a dropout layer. We use CNN kernel sizes 1 to 5, each with 100 filters. We then pass the extracted features to an interaction-based relevance matching layer, followed by softmax to obtain relevance probability output. This CNN feature extraction for CLIR is similar to (Sasaki et al., 2018).

3.3 Results and Discussion

We compare the performance of different CLIR models on the two low resource languages in Table 1. Comparing the QRANN models with the CNN baseline model, we note that the MAP scores of QRANN models are significantly higher than CNN model in all cases. While the QRANN models do not use CNNs to extract features, they perform better because of the multi-head attention mechanism, which helps the model identify spans in the foreign sentences that are relevant to the query.

We also note that the QRANN model performs better than two strong baselines: the probabilistic CLIR model as well as the probablistic CLIR occurrence variant using translation dictionary. An important feature of the QRANN model is that it jointly represents the tokens of a multi-word query, while probabilistic CLIR models impose a strong independence assumption between query words. For example, query 'New York Times' is treated as independent words, and the translations for each word are used to rank documents independently, which is problematic. The results in table show the benefit in the QRANN model of dropping the query term independence assumption that the probabilistic CLIR model and its occurrence variant use. The QRANN model is designed to model the dependency between words in a multi-word query, in order to capture compositional semantic relationship.

The MT-based CLIR model does not perform well than the QRANN models or the probablistic

Lang	Model	Test1/Q1+2	Test2/Q2
Swa	Prob. CLIR	0.375	0.376
	Prob. Occ.	0.365	0.443
	MT	0.240	0.373
	CNN	0.228	0.217
	QRANN Con.	**0.408**	0.450
	QRANN Int.	0.402	**0.457**
Tag	Prob. CLIR	0.545	0.486
	Prob. Occ.	0.488	0.510
	MT	0.309	0.424
	CNN	0.384	0.359
	QRANN Con.	0.523	0.475
	QRANN Int.	**0.545**	**0.536**

Table 1: Retrieval performance (MAP scores) of all models on Swahili and Tagalog CLIR evaluation datasets. QRANN Con. corresponds to equation (6), QRANN Int. corresponds to equation (5).

CLIR models, because it does not provide enough variation in lexical translations for matching query words to be effective for CLIR.

The same table also compares two variants of QRANN using different relevance matching layers. The interaction-based relevance matching layer usually has better performance than the simple concatenation.

We run statistical significance testing on our results, and found the difference between the QRANN Int. model and the baseline models is statistically significant with p-value less than 0.05 on more than half of the conditions.

4 Conclusion and Future Work

We propose a weakly supervised model to learn cross-lingual query document relevance for low resource languages. Rather than relying on lexical translations, the model uses a multi-head attention mechanism to learn which foreign sentence spans are important for estimating relevance to the query, and also benefits from an effective interaction-based relevance matching layer. Our future work includes using context-dependent pretrained bilingual embeddings, and using high resource languages to improve the CLIR performance of low resource languages.

References

2015. DARPA LORELEI Program - Broad Agency Announcement (BAA). https://www.darpa.mil/program/low-resource-languages-for-emergent-incidents.

2017. IARPA MATERIAL Program - Broad Agency Announcement (BAA). https://www.iarpa.gov/index.php/research-programs/material.

Dzmitry Bahdanau, Kyunghyun Cho, and Yoshua Bengio. 2015. Neural machine translation by jointly learning to align and translate. *CoRR*, abs/1409.0473.

Bing Bai, Jason Weston, David Grangier, Ronan Collobert, Kunihiko Sadamasa, Yanjun Qi, Olivier Chapelle, and Kilian Q. Weinberger. 2009. Learning to rank with (a lot of) word features. *Information Retrieval*, 13:291–314.

Mostafa Dehghani, Hamed Zamani, Aliaksei Severyn, Jaap Kamps, and W. Bruce Croft. 2017. Neural ranking models with weak supervision. In *SIGIR*.

Marc Franco-Salvador, Paolo Rosso, and Roberto Navigli. 2014. A knowledge-based representation for cross-language document retrieval and categorization. In *EACL*.

Stephan Gouws and Anders Søgaard. 2015. Simple task-specific bilingual word embeddings. In *HLT-NAACL*.

Parth Gupta, Rafael E. Banchs, and Paolo Rosso. 2017. Continuous space models for clir. *Inf. Process. Manage.*, 53(2):359–370.

Aria Haghighi, John Blitzer, John DeNero, and Dan Klein. 2009. Better word alignments with supervised itg models. In *Proceedings of the Joint Conference of the 47th Annual Meeting of the ACL and the 4th International Joint Conference on Natural Language Processing of the AFNLP: Volume 2 - Volume 2*, ACL '09, pages 923–931, Stroudsburg, PA, USA. Association for Computational Linguistics.

David Kamholz, Jonathan Pool, and Susan M. Colowick. 2014. Panlex: Building a resource for panlingual lexical translation. In *LREC*.

Victor Lavrenko, Martin Choquette, and W. Bruce Croft. 2002. Cross-lingual relevance models. In *Proceedings of the 25th Annual International ACM SIGIR Conference on Research and Development in Information Retrieval*, SIGIR '02, pages 175–182, New York, NY, USA. ACM.

Gina-Anne Levow, Douglas W. Oard, and Philip Resnik. 2005. Dictionary-based techniques for cross-language information retrieval. *Inf. Process. Manage.*, 41:523–547.

Bo Li and Ping Cheng. 2018. Learning neural representation for clir with adversarial framework. In *EMNLP*.

Chenliang Li, Wei Zhou, Feng Ji, Yu Duan, and Haiqing Chen. 2018. A deep relevance model for zero-shot document filtering. In *ACL*.

Robert Litschko, Goran Glavas, Simone Paolo Ponzetto, and Ivan Vulic. 2018. Unsupervised cross-lingual information retrieval using monolingual data only. In *SIGIR*.

David R. H. Miller, Tim Leek, and Richard M. Schwartz. 1999. A hidden markov model information retrieval system.

Bhaskar Mitra, Nick Craswell, et al. 2018. An introduction to neural information retrieval. *Foundations and Trends® in Information Retrieval*, 13(1):1–126.

Jian-Yun Nie. 2003. Cross-language information retrieval. In *Cross-Language Information Retrieval*.

Franz Josef Och and Hermann Ney. 2003. A systematic comparison of various statistical alignment models. *Computational Linguistics*, 29(1):19–51.

Shota Sasaki, Shuo Sun, Shigehiko Schamoni, Kevin Duh, and Kentaro Inui. 2018. Cross-lingual learning-to-rank with shared representations. In *Proceedings of the 2018 Conference of the North American Chapter of the Association for Computational Linguistics: Human Language Technologies, Volume 2 (Short Papers)*, pages 458–463. Association for Computational Linguistics.

Artem Sokolov, Laura Jehl, Felix Hieber, and Stefan Riezler. 2013. Boosting cross-language retrieval by learning bilingual phrase associations from relevance rankings. In *EMNLP*.

Philipp Sorg and Philipp Cimiano. 2012. Exploiting wikipedia for cross-lingual and multilingual information retrieval. *Data Knowl. Eng.*, 74:26–45.

Ashish Vaswani, Noam Shazeer, Niki Parmar, Jakob Uszkoreit, Llion Jones, Aidan N Gomez, Ł ukasz Kaiser, and Illia Polosukhin. 2017. Attention is all you need. In I. Guyon, U. V. Luxburg, S. Bengio, H. Wallach, R. Fergus, S. Vishwanathan, and R. Garnett, editors, *Advances in Neural Information Processing Systems 30*, pages 5998–6008. Curran Associates, Inc.

Ivan Vulic and Marie-Francine Moens. 2015. Monolingual and cross-lingual information retrieval models based on (bilingual) word embeddings. In *SIGIR*.

Jinxi Xu and Ralph M. Weischedel. 2000. Cross-lingual information retrieval using hidden markov models. In *EMNLP*.

Hamed Zamani and W. Bruce Croft. 2017. Relevance-based word embedding. In *SIGIR*.

Rabih Zbib, Lingjun Zhao, Damianos Karakos, William Hartmann, Jay DeYoung, Zhongqiang Huang, Zhuolin Jiang, Noah Rivkin, Le Zhang, Richard Schwartz, et al. 2019. Neural-network lexical translation for cross-lingual ir from text and speech. In *Proceedings of the 42nd International ACM SIGIR Conference on Research and Development in Information Retrieval*, pages 645–654. ACM.

Yingjie Zhang, Md. Mustafizur Rahman, Alex Braylan, Brandon Dang, Heng-Lu Chang, Henna Kim, Quinten McNamara, Aaron Angert, Edward Banner, Vivek Khetan, Tyler McDonnell, An Thanh Nguyen, Dan Xu, Byron C. Wallace, and Matthew Lease. 2016. Neural information retrieval: A literature review. *CoRR*, abs/1611.06792.

Dong Zhou, Mark Truran, Tim J. Brailsford, Vincent P. Wade, and Helen Ashman. 2012. Translation techniques in cross-language information retrieval. *ACM Comput. Surv.*, 45:1:1–1:44.

X-WikiRE: A Large, Multilingual Resource for Relation Extraction as Machine Comprehension

Mostafa Abdou, Cezar Sas, Rahul Aralikatte, Isabelle Augenstein and **Anders Søgaard**
{abdou, sas, rahul, augenstein, soegaard} @ di.ku.dk
University of Copenhagen

Abstract

Although the vast majority of knowledge bases (**KBs**) are heavily biased towards English, Wikipedias do cover very different topics in different languages. Exploiting this, we introduce a new multilingual dataset (**X-WikiRE**), framing relation extraction as a multilingual machine reading problem. We show that by leveraging this resource it is possible to robustly transfer models cross-lingually and that multilingual support significantly improves (zero-shot) relation extraction, enabling the population of low-resourced **KBs** from their well-populated counterparts.

1 Introduction

It is a widely lamented fact that linguistic and encyclopedic resources are heavily biased towards English. Even multilingual knowledge bases (KBs) such as Wikidata (Vrandečić and Krötzsch, 2014) are predominantly English-based (Kaffee and Simperl, 2018). This means that coverage is higher for English, and that facts of interest to English-speaking communities are more likely included in a KB. This work introduces a novel multilingual dataset (**X-WikiRE**) and explores techniques for automatically filling such language gaps by learning, from **X-WikiRE**, to add facts in other languages. Finally, we show that multilingual sharing is beneficial for knowledge base completion across all languages, including English.

The task of identifying potential KB entries in running text – i.e., relations that hold between two or more entities, is called *relation extraction* (RE). In the traditional, supervised setting (Bach and Badaskar, 2007), RE models are trained to identify a pre-specified set of relation types, which are observed during training. Models are meant to generalize to new entities, but *not* new *relations*. An alternative flavor is *open* RE (Fader et al.,

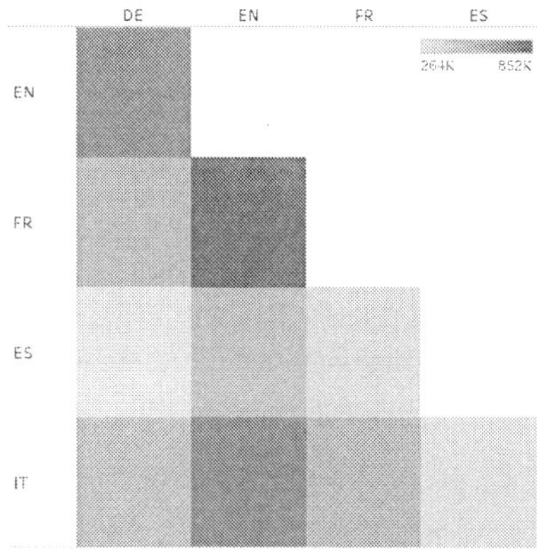

Figure 1: The overlap of triples between languages.

2011; Yates et al., 2007), which detects subject-verb-object triples and clusters semantically related verbs into coarse-grained semantic relations.

In this paper, we consider the middle ground, in which models are trained on a subset of pre-specified relations and applied to both seen and unseen entities, and unseen relations. The latter scenario is known as *zero-shot* RE (Rocktäschel et al., 2015).

Levy et al. (2017) present a reformulation of RE, where the task is framed as reading comprehension. In this formulation, each relation type (e.g. *author*, *occupation*) is mapped to at least one natural language question template (e.g. *"Who is the author of x?"*), where x is filled with an entity (e.g. *"Inferno"*). The model is then tasked with finding an answer (*"Dante Alighieri"*) to this question with respect to a given context. They show that this formulation of the problem both outperforms off-the-shelf RE systems in the typical RE setting and, in addition, enables generalization to unspecified and unseen types of relations. **X-WikiRE** enables exploration of this reformulation of RE in a multilingual setting.

Proceedings of the 2nd Workshop on Deep Learning Approaches for Low-Resource NLP (DeepLo), pages 265–274
Hong Kong, China, November 3, 2019. ©2019 Association for Computational Linguistics
https://doi.org/10.18653/v1/P17

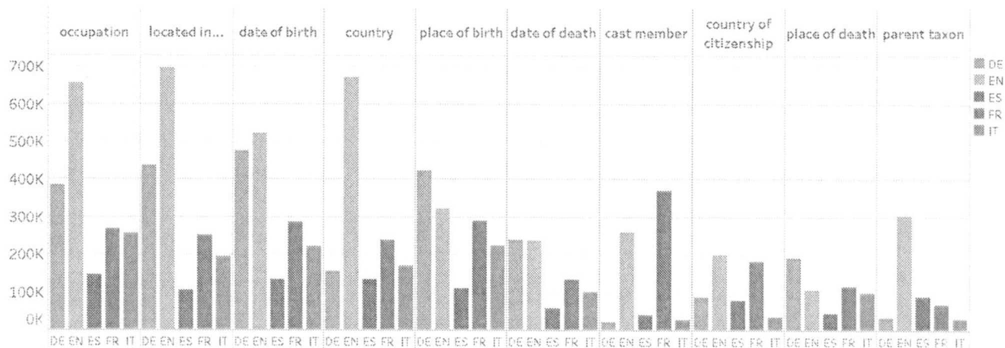

Figure 2: The number of triples for the top 10 properties in each language.

Contributions We introduce a new, large-scale multilingual dataset (**X-WikiRE**) of reading comprehension-based RE for English, German, French, Spanish, and Italian, facilitating research on multilingual methods for RE. Our dataset covers more languages (five) and is at least an order of magnitude larger than existing multilingual RE datasets, e.g., TAC 2016 (Ellis et al., 2015), which covers three languages and consists of $\approx$ 90k examples. We also a) perform cross-lingual RE showing that models pretrained on one language can be effectively transferred to others with minimal in-language finetuning; b) leverage multilingual representations to train a model capable of simultaneously performing (zero-shot) RE in all five languages, rivaling or outperforming its monolingually trained counterparts in many cases while requiring far fewer parameters per language; c) obtain considerable improvements by employing a more carefully designed nil-aware machine comprehension model.

2 Background

Relation extraction We begin with a brief description of our terminology. Given raw text, relation extraction is the task of identifying instances of relations $relation(entity_1, entity_2)$. We refer to these instances of relation and entity pairs as *triples*. Furthermore, throughout this work, we use the term *property* interchangeably with relation.

A large part of previous work on relation extraction has been concerned with extracting relations between unseen entities for a pre-defined set of relations seen during training (Zelenko et al., 2003; Zhou et al., 2005; Miwa and Bansal, 2016). For example, the instances (Barack Obama, Hawaii), (Niels Bohr, Copenhagen),

and (Jacques Brel, Schaerbeek) of the relation $born\_in(x, y)$ would be seen during the training phase, and then the model would be expected to correctly identify other instances of the relation such as (Jean-Paul Sartre, Paris) in running text. This is useful in closed-domain settings where it is possible to pre-select a set of relations of interest. In an open-domain setting, however, we are interested in the far more difficult problem of extracting unseen relation types. Open RE methods (Yates et al., 2007; Banko et al., 2007; Fader et al., 2011) do not require relation-specific data, but treat different phrasings of the same relation as different relations and rely on a combination of syntactic features (e.g. dependency parses) and normalisation rules, and so have limited generalization capacity.

Zero-shot relation extraction Levy et al. (2017) propose a novel approach towards achieving this generalization by transforming relations into natural language question templates. For instance, the relation $born\_in(x, y)$ can be expressed as *"Where was x born?"* or *"In which place was x born?"*. Then, a reading comprehension model (Seo et al., 2016; Chen et al., 2017) can be trained on question, answer, and context examples where the x slot is filled with an entity and the y slot is either an answer if the answer is present in the context, or NIL. The model is then able to extract relation instances (given expressions of the relations as questions) from raw text. To test this *"harsh zero-shot"* setting of relation extraction, they build a dataset for RE as machine comprehension from WikiReading (Hewlett et al., 2016), relying on alignments between Wikipedia pages and Wikidata KB triples. They show that their read-

Lang	Question	Context & Answers
DE	In welchem land befindet man sich, wenn man **Amazonas** besucht?	Der Fluss Amazonas gab seinerseits dem Amazonasbecken sowie mehreren gleichnamigen Verwaltungseinheiten in **Brasilien, Venezuela, Kolumbien** …
EN	What country is **Amazon** located in?	The Amazon proper runs mostly through **Brazil** and **Peru**, and is part of the border between …
ES	¿En qué país se encuentra el **Amazonas**?	El río Amazonas es un río de América del Sur, que atraviesa **Perú, Colombia** y **Brasil**.
FR	Dans quel pays peux-tu trouver **Amazone**?	Le fleuve prend alors le nom d'Amazonas au **Pérou** et en **Colombie**, puis celui de rio Solimões en entrant au **Brésil** au …
IT	Di quale nazione fa parte il **Rio delle Amazzoni**?	Il Rio delle Amazzoni è un fiume dell'America Meridionale che attraversa **Perù, Colombia** e **Brasile** …

Table 1: Examples from our dataset of the same question-context pairs across all the languages with the correct answers highlighted in boldface.

ing comprehension model is able to use linguistic cues to identify relation paraphrases and lexico-syntactic patterns of textual deviation from questions to answers, enabling it to identify instances of new relations. Similar work (Obamuyide and Vlachos, 2018) recently also showed that RE can be framed as natural language inference.

3   X-WikiRE

X-WikiRE is a multilingual reading comprehension-based relation extraction dataset. Each example in the dataset consists of a *question*, a *context*, and an *answer*, where the question is a querified relation and the context may contain the answer or an indication that it is not present (NIL). Questions are obtained by transforming relations into question templates with slots where an entity is inserted. Within the RE framework described in Section 2, $entity_1$ is filled into a slot in the question template and $entity_2$ is the answer. Each triple[1] in the dataset can be identified uniquely across all languages. We construct **X-WikiRE** using the relevant parts of Wikidata and Wikipedia for each language. Wikidata is an open KB where the knowledge contained in each document is expressed as a set of statements, and each statement is a tuple (property_id, value_id) (e.g. statement (P50, Q1067) where P50 refers to $author$ and Q1067 to "*Dante Alighieri*"). We perform data integration on Wikidata, as described by Hewlett et al. (2016): for each entity in Wikipedia

we take the corresponding Wikidata document, add the Wikipedia page text, and denormalize the statements. This consists of replacing the property and value ids of each statement in the document with the text label for values which are entities, and with the human readable form for numeric values (e.g. timestamps are converted to natural forms like "*25 May 1994*") obtaining a tuple $(property, entity)$.[2]

Slot-filling data   To extract the contexts for each triple in our dataset we use the distant supervision method described by Levy et al. (2017). For each Wikidata document belonging to a given $entity_1$ we take all the denormalized tuples $(property, entity_2)$ and extract the first sentence in the text containing both $entity_1$ and $entity_2$. Negatives (contexts without answers) are constructed by finding pairs of triples with common $entity_2$ type (to ensure they contain good distractors), swapping their context if $entity_2$ is not present in the context of the other triple.

Querification   Levy et al. (2017) created 1192 question templates for 120 Wikidata properties. A template contains a placeholder for an entity x (e.g. for property "*author*", some templates are "*Who wrote the novel x?*" and "*Who is the author of x?*"), which can be automatically filled in to create questions so that $question \approx template(property, x)$. For our multilingual dataset, we had these templates translated by human translators. The translators attempted to translate each of the original 1192 templates. If a template was difficult to translate, they were in-

[1]Not to be confused with an example as an example contains an instantiation of a relation in the form of a question. Thus, the different question templates for each relation share the same id.

[2]We make the simplification of referring to all values as entities.

Language	Pos	Neg	Pos*	Neg*
DE	2.5M	545K	11M	2.3M
EN	5.1M	1M	64M	12M
ES	1.2M	211K	5.5M	1.1M
FR	2.3M	867K	18M	6.8M
IT	1.9M	217K	10M	1.2M

Table 2: The number of positive and negative triples for each language with (*) and without templates.

structed to discard it. They were also instructed to create their own templates, paraphrasing the original ones when possible. This resulted in a varying number of templates for each of the properties across languages. In addition to the entity placeholder, some languages with richer morphology (Spanish, Italian, and German) required extra placeholders in the templates because of agreement phenomena (gender). We added a placeholder for definite articles, as well as one for gender-dependent filler words. The gender is automatically inferred from the Wikipedia page statistics and a few heuristics. Table 1 shows the same example across five languages.

Dataset statistics　Table 2 shows the number of positive and negative triples and examples (i.e with and without consideration of the templates).

As expected (due to the size of its Wikidata), English has the highest number of triples for most properties. However, as Figure 2 shows, there are properties where it has fewer triples than other languages (e.g. French has more triples for film related properties such as $cast\_member$ and $nominated\_for$). Figure 1 shows the overlap in the number of triples between different languages. While it can be seen that English, once again, has the highest overall overlap with the other languages, there are interesting deviations from this pattern where for certain properties other languages share a larger intersection.

4　Method

In our framework, a machine comprehension model sees a question-context pair and is tasked with selecting an answer span within the context, or indicating that the context does not contain an answer (returning `NIL`). This 'nil-awareness' goes beyond the traditional reading comprehension setup where it is not required. It has, however, recently been incorporated into newer datasets (Trischler et al., 2017; Rajpurkar et al., 2018; Saha

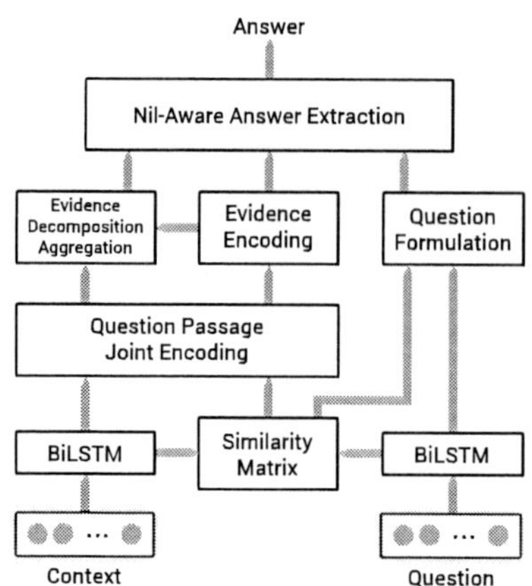

Figure 3: An overview of Namanda's architecture.

et al., 2018). We employ the architecture described in Kundu and Ng (2018) as our standard reading comprehension model for all the experiments. This nil-aware answer extraction framework (NAMANDA) is briefly described below. In a set of initial trials (see Table 3), we found that this model far outperformed the bias-augmented BiDAF model (Seo et al., 2016) used by Levy et al. (2017) on their dataset.

A Nil-aware machine comprehension model
The reading comprehension model we employ, seen in Figure 3, encodes the question and context sequences and computes a similarity matrix between them. A column-wise softmax of the similarity matrix is multiplied with the question encoding to aggregate the most relevant parts of the question with respect to the context. Next, a joint-encoding of the question and context is created and a multi-factor self-attentive encoding is applied to accumulate evidence from the entire context. These representations are called the evidence vectors. Lastly, the evidence vectors are decomposed for every context word with orthogonal decomposition. The parallel components represent the relevant parts of the context and the orthogonal parts represent the irrelevant parts. These decompositions bias the decoder to either output a span or `NIL`.

Multilingual representations　We compare two methods of obtaining multilingual representations. First, we employ fastText embeddings (Bojanowski et al., 2017) mapped to a multilingual space in a supervised fashion (Conneau et al., 2017). Second, we employ the newly released

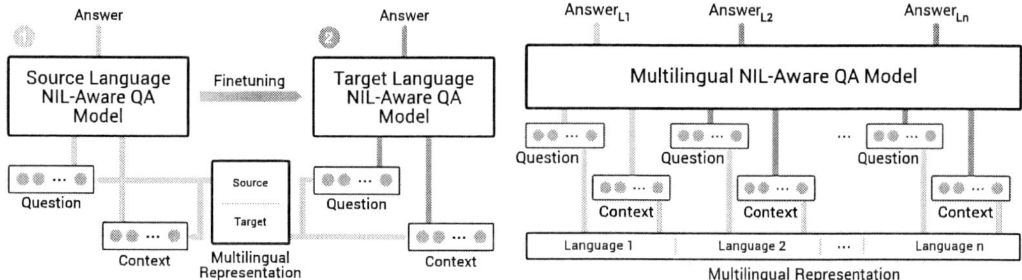

(a) Cross-lingual model transfer. In step (1), a source language model is trained until convergence. In step (2), it is finetuned on a limited amount of target language data.

(b) Joint multilingual training.

Figure 4: Our cross-lingual transfer and multilingual training setups.

multilingual BERT (Devlin et al., 2018) which is trained on the concatenation of the wikipedia corpora of 104 languages.[3] For BERT, we take the contexualized word representations from the final layer as input to our machine comprehension model's question and context Bi-LSTM encoders. We do not fine-tune the pre-trained model.

5 Experiments

Following Levy et al. (2017), we distinguish between the traditional RE setting where the aim is to generalize to unseen entities (**UnENT**) and the zero-shot setting (**UnREL**) where the aim is to do so for unseen relation types (see Section 2). Our goal is to answer these three questions: **A)** how well can RE models be transferred across languages? **B)** in the difficult **UnREL** setting, can the variance between languages in the number of instances of relations (see Figure 2) be exploited to enable more robust RE ? **C)** can one jointly-trained multilingual model which performs RE in multiple languages perform comparably to or outperform its individual monolingual counterparts? For all experiments, we take the *multiple templates* approach where a model sees different paraphrases of the same question during training. This approach was shown by Levy et al. (2017) to have significantly better paraphrasing abilities than when only one question template or simpler relation descriptions are employed.

Evaluation Our evaluation methodology follows Levy et al. (2017). We compute precision, recall and F1 by comparing spans predicted by the models with gold answers. Precision is equal to the true positives divided by total number of non-nil answers predicted by a system. Recall is equal to the true positives divided by the total number of instances that are non-nil in the ground truth answers. Word order and punctuation are not considered.[4]

5.1 Monolingual Baselines

A baseline model is trained on the full monolingual training set (1 million instances) for each of the languages in both the **UnENT** and **UnREL** settings, which serve as a point of comparison for the cross-lingual transfer and multilingual models.

Comparison with Levy et al. (2017) In Table 3, the comparison between the nil-aware machine comprehension framework we employ (Mono) and the results reported by Levy et al. (2017) using the bias-augmented BiDAF model on their dataset (and splits) can be seen. The clear improvements obtained are in line with those reported by Kundu and Ng (2018) of NAMANDA over BiDAF on reading comprehension tasks.

Results Table 3 shows the results of the monolingual baselines. For the cross-lingual transfer experiments, these results can be viewed as a performance ceiling.

Observe that the results on our dataset are in general lower than those reported in Levy et al. (2017). This can be attributed to three factors: a) on average, the context length in our dataset is longer compared to theirs; b) the fastText word embeddings we employ to facilitate multilingual

---

[3]https://github.com/google-research/bert/blob/master/multilingual.md

[4]We do not exclude articles from the evaluation as separating them from entities is not as trivial for other languages as it is for English.

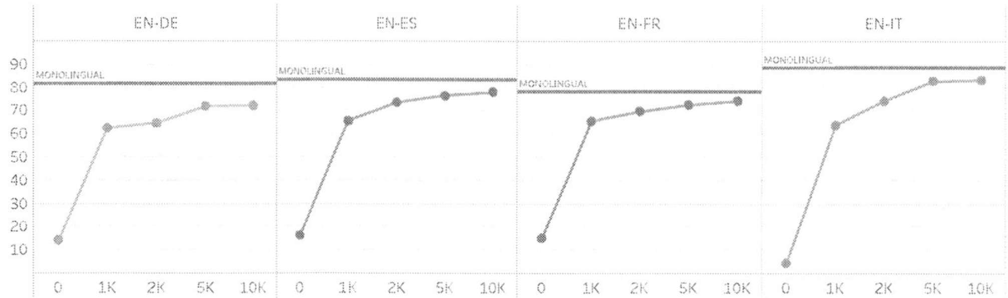

Figure 5: F1-scores for the cross-lingual transfer experiments in the **UnENT** setting. The MONOLINGUAL line shows the corresponding monolingual model's F1-score.

sharing have a lower coverage of the vocabularies of each language than the GloVe word embeddings employed in that work; c) in the **UnREL** setting, we employ a more challenging setup of 5-fold cross-validation (as opposed to 10-fold in their experiments), meaning that a lower number of relations is seen at training time and the test set contains a higher number of unseen relations.

5.2 Cross-Lingual Model Transfer

In this set of experiments, seen in Figure 4a, we test how well RE models can be transferred from a source language with a large number of training examples to target languages with no or minimal training data. In the **UnENT** experiments, we construct pairwise parallel test and development sets between English and each of the languages. An English RE model (built on top of the multilingual representations described in sub-section 4) is trained on a full English training set (1 million instances). We then evaluate how well this model can transfer to each of the four other languages in the following cases: with no finetuning or when 1000, 2000, 5000 or 10000 target language training examples are used for finetuning. Note that entities in the target languages' test and development sets are not seen in the English training data. We compare transfer performance with monolingual performance when a target language's full training set is employed.

A similar approach is followed for **UnREL** experiments. However, since the number of relations is relatively small, cross-validation with five folds is employed instead of fixed splits. Moreover, because this is a substantially more challenging setting we are interested in evaluating along another dimension (Question **B**): when relations are seen in the source language but not in the target lan-

guage. Furthermore, unlike for **UnENT**, we directly use 10k examples for finetuning.

Results Figure 5 shows the results of the cross-lingual transfer experiments for **UnENT**, where transfer is accomplished through multilingually aligned fastText embeddings. In a parallel set of experiments, transfer was performed through the multilingual BERT encoder. The results of this showed a clear advantage for the former over the latter.[5] This is primarily due to the low vocabulary coverage of multilingual BERT which has a total vocabulary size of 100k tokens for 104 languages for coverage statistics). While it is clear that the models suffer from rather low recall when no finetuning is performed, the results show considerable improvements when finetuning with only 1000 target language examples. With 10K target language examples, it is possible to nearly match the performance of a model trained on the full target language monolingual training set.

Similarly, in the **UnREL** experiments, our results (Figure 6) show that it's possible to recover a large part of the fully-supervised monolingual models' performance. It can be seen, however, that with 10k target language examples, a lower proportion of the performance is recovered when compared to the **UnENT** setting. This indicates that it is more difficult to transfer the ability to identify *relation paraphrases* and *entity types* through global cues[6] which Levy et al. (2017) suggested are important for generalizing to new relations in this framework.

---

[5]We therefore continue the rest of our experiments in the paper using the multilingual fastText embeddings.

[6]When context phrasing deviates from the question in a way that is common between relations.

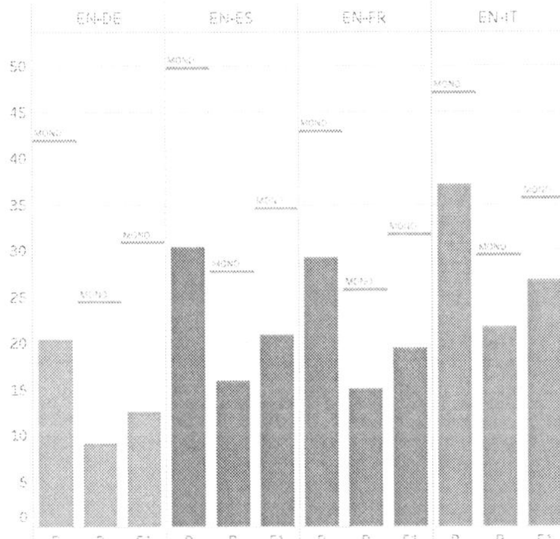

Figure 6: Precision, Recall and F1-scores for the cross-lingual transfer experiments in **UnREL** setting. The results are the mean of 5-fold cross-validation. The MONO line shows the corresponding monolingual model's F1-score.

5.3 One Model, Multiple Languages

We now examine the possibility of training one multilingual model which is able to perform relation extraction across multiple languages, as shown in Figure 4b. We are interested in the case when an entity may be seen in another language's training data, as this is a realistic cross-lingual KB completion scenario where different languages' KBs are better populated for different topics. To control for training set size we include 200k training instances per language, so that the total size of the training set is equal to that of the monolingual baseline. However, an additional benefit of multilingual training is that extra overall training data becomes available. To test the effect of that we also run an experiment where the full training set of each of the languages is employed (adding up to 5 million training examples).

In the **UnREL** experiments, 5-fold cross-validation is performed. We are once again interested in exploiting the fact that KBs are better populated for different properties across different languages. Our setup is therefore as follows: in each of the 5 folds, a test set relation for a particular language is not seen in that language's training set, but may be seen in any of the other languages. This amounts to maintaining the original zero-shot setting (where a relation is not seen) monolingually, but providing supervision by allowing the models to *peek across languages*.

Results In the **UnENT** setting the multilingual models trained on just 200k instances per language perform slightly below the monolingual baselines. This excludes for French where, surprisingly, the baseline performance is actually exceeded. When the full training sets of all languages are combined, the multilingual model outperforms the monolingual baselines for three (English, Spanish, and French) out of five languages and is slightly worse for two (German and Italian). This demonstrates that not only is it possible to utilize a single model to perform RE in multiple languages, but that the multilingual supervision signal will often lead to improvements in performance. These results are shown in the third and fourth columns of Table 3.

The multilingual **UnREL** model outperforms its monolingual counterparts by large margins for all languages reaching a near 100% F1-score improvement for most languages. This is largely in line with our premise that the natural topicality of KBs across languages can be exploited to provide cross-lingual supervision for relation extraction models.

5.4 Hyperparameters

In all experiments, models were trained for five epochs with a learning rate of 0.001 using Adam (Kingma and Ba, 2014). For finetuning in the cross-lingual transfer experiments, the learning rate was lowered to 0.001 to prevent forgetting and a maximum of 30 finetuning iterations over the small target language training set were performed with model selection using the target language development set F1-score. All monolingual models' word embeddings were initialised using fastText embeddings trained on each language's Wikipedia and common crawl corpora,[7] except for the comparison experiments described in sub-section 5.1 where GloVe (Pennington et al., 2014) was used for comparability with Levy et al. (2017).

6 Related Work

Multilingual NLU Advances in natural language understanding tasks have been as impressive as they have been fast-paced. Until recently, however, the multilingual aspect of such tasks has not received as much attention. This is primarily due to the costs associated with annotating data for multiple languages. Recent work such as Conneau et al. (2018); Agic and Schluter

---

[7]https://fasttext.cc/docs/en/crawl-vectors.html

Lang.		UnENT				UnREL		
		Levy et al. (2017)	Mono.	Multi. (S)	Multi. (L)	Levy et al. (2017)	Mono.	Multi.
EN*	P	87.66	**90.49**	n/a	n/a	43.61	**56.53**	n/a
	R	91.32	**94.87**	n/a	n/a	36.45	**44.74**	n/a
	F1	89.44	**92.63**	n/a	n/a	39.61	**49.85**	n/a
EN	P	n/a	74.09	74.33	**77.11**	n/a	46.75	**63.29**
	R	n/a	85.35	83.63	**86.42**	n/a	25.32	**44.40**
	F1	n/a	79.32	78.71	**81.50**	n/a	32.78	**51.99**
ES	P	n/a	81.79	80.60	**83.68**	n/a	49.77	**73.43**
	R	n/a	**85.02**	81.47	83.58	n/a	27.69	**62.82**
	F1	n/a	83.37	81.03	**83.63**	n/a	34.54	**67.64**
IT	P	n/a	**88.69**	86.23	88.43	n/a	47.09	**68.66**
	R	n/a	**88.10**	85.64	86.91	n/a	29.45	**55.24**
	F1	n/a	**88.39**	85.93	87.66	n/a	35.62	**61.13**
FR	P	n/a	82.36	80.82	**82.90**	n/a	42.93	**60.78**
	R	n/a	74.16	76.60	**78.10**	n/a	25.73	**47.09**
	F1	n/a	78.05	78.66	**80.43**	n/a	31.78	**53.06**
DE	P	n/a	**75.85**	69.88	73.67	n/a	41.94	**43.36**
	R	n/a	**88.21**	81.36	84.08	n/a	24.38	**25.32**
	F1	n/a	**81.57**	75.20	78.53	n/a	30.82	**31.97**

Table 3: Precision, Recall, and F1-score results for all languages' monolingual (Mono.) and multilingual (Multi.) models. (S) indicates the small multilingual model which was trained on 200k examples and (L) indicates the large on trained on 5 million examples. * is used to mark the results on Levy et al. (2017)'s English dataset.

(2018) offer important benchmarks for evaluating cross-lingual transfer of natural language inference models. Similarly, Cer et al. (2017) present the Semantic Textual Similarity dataset for four languages.

Multilingual relation extraction Previous investigations of multilingual RE have been few and far between. Faruqui and Kumar (2015) employed a pipeline of machine translation systems to translate to English, then Open RE systems to perform RE on the translated text, followed by cross-lingual projection back to source language. Verga et al. (2016) apply the universal schema framework (Riedel et al., 2013) on top of multilingual embeddings to extract relations from Spanish text without using Spanish training data. This approach, however, only enables generalization to unseen entities and does not have the flexibility to predict unseen relations. Furthermore, both of these works faced a fundamental difficulty with evaluation. The former resort to manual annotation of a small number of examples (1000) in each language and the latter use the 2012 TAC Spanish slot-filling evaluation dataset in which "*the coverage of facts in the available annotation is very small*". With the introduction of **X-WikiRE**, this work provides the first large-scale dataset and benchmark for the evaluation of multilingual RE spanning five languages. While this paves the way for a wide range of research on multilingual relation extraction and knowledge base population, we hope to extend this to a larger variety of languages in future work, particularly as we have been able to show that the amount of training data required for cross-lingual model transfer is minimal, meaning that a small dataset (when only that is available) can go a long way.

7 Conclusion

We introduced **X-WikiRE**, a new, large-scale multilingual relation extraction dataset in which relation extraction is framed as a problem of reading comprehension to allow for generalization to unseen relations. Using this, we demonstrated that a) multilingual training can be employed to exploit the fact that KBs are better populated in different areas for different languages, providing a strong cross-lingual supervision signal which leads to considerably better zero-shot relation extraction; b) models can be transferred cross-lingually with a minimal amount of target language data for fine-tuning; c) better modelling of nil-awareness in reading comprehension models leads to improvements on the task. Our work is a step towards making KBs equally well-resourced across languages. To encourage future work in this direction, we release our code and dataset.

References

Zeljko Agic and Natalie Schluter. 2018. Baselines and Test Data for Cross-Lingual Inference. In *LREC*. European Language Resources Association (ELRA).

Nguyen Bach and Sameer Badaskar. 2007. A Review of Relation Extraction.

Michele Banko, Michael J Cafarella, Stephen Soderland, Matthew Broadhead, and Oren Etzioni. 2007. Open information extraction from the web. In *IJCAI*, volume 7, pages 2670–2676.

Piotr Bojanowski, Edouard Grave, Armand Joulin, and Tomas Mikolov. 2017. Enriching Word Vectors with Subword Information. *Transactions of the Association for Computational Linguistics*, 5:135–146.

Daniel Cer, Mona Diab, Eneko Agirre, Inigo Lopez-Gazpio, and Lucia Specia. 2017. SemEval-2017 Task 1: Semantic Textual Similarity-Multilingual and Cross-lingual Focused Evaluation. *arXiv preprint arXiv:1708.00055*.

Danqi Chen, Adam Fisch, Jason Weston, and Antoine Bordes. 2017. Reading wikipedia to answer open-domain questions. In *Proceedings of the 55th Annual Meeting of the Association for Computational Linguistics (Volume 1: Long Papers)*, pages 1870–1879. Association for Computational Linguistics.

Alexis Conneau, Guillaume Lample, Marc'Aurelio Ranzato, Ludovic Denoyer, and Hervé Jégou. 2017. Word translation without parallel data. *arXiv preprint arXiv:1710.04087*.

Alexis Conneau, Ruty Rinott, Guillaume Lample, Adina Williams, Samuel Bowman, Holger Schwenk, and Veselin Stoyanov. 2018. XNLI: Evaluating Cross-lingual Sentence Representations. In *Proceedings of the 2018 Conference on Empirical Methods in Natural Language Processing*, pages 2475–2485. Association for Computational Linguistics.

Jacob Devlin, Ming-Wei Chang, Kenton Lee, and Kristina Toutanova. 2018. BERT: Pre-training of Deep Bidirectional Transformers for Language Understanding. *arXiv preprint arXiv:1810.04805*.

Joe Ellis, Jeremy Getman, Dana Fore, Neil Kuster, Zhiyi Song, Ann Bies, and Stephanie M Strassel. 2015. Overview of Linguistic Resources for the TAC KBP 2015 Evaluations: Methodologies and Results. In *TAC*.

Anthony Fader, Stephen Soderland, and Oren Etzioni. 2011. Identifying Relations for Open Information Extraction. In *Proceedings of the 2011 Conference on Empirical Methods in Natural Language Processing*, pages 1535–1545. Association for Computational Linguistics.

Manaal Faruqui and Shankar Kumar. 2015. Multilingual Open Relation Extraction Using Cross-lingual Projection. In *Proceedings of the 2015 Conference of the North American Chapter of the Association for Computational Linguistics: Human Language Technologies*, pages 1351–1356. Association for Computational Linguistics.

Daniel Hewlett, Alexandre Lacoste, Llion Jones, Illia Polosukhin, Andrew Fandrianto, Jay Han, Matthew Kelcey, and David Berthelot. 2016. WikiReading: A Novel Large-scale Language Understanding Task over Wikipedia. In *Proceedings of the 54th Annual Meeting of the Association for Computational Linguistics (Volume 1: Long Papers)*, pages 1535–1545. Association for Computational Linguistics.

Lucie-Aimée Kaffee and Elena Simperl. 2018. Analysis of Editors' Languages in Wikidata. In *OpenSym*, pages 21:1–21:5. ACM.

Diederik P Kingma and Jimmy Ba. 2014. Adam: A method for stochastic optimization. *arXiv preprint arXiv:1412.6980*.

Souvik Kundu and Hwee Tou Ng. 2018. A Nil-Aware Answer Extraction Framework for Question Answering. In *Proceedings of the 2018 Conference on Empirical Methods in Natural Language Processing*, pages 4243–4252. Association for Computational Linguistics.

Omer Levy, Minjoon Seo, Eunsol Choi, and Luke Zettlemoyer. 2017. Zero-Shot Relation Extraction via Reading Comprehension. In *Proceedings of the 21st Conference on Computational Natural Language Learning (CoNLL 2017)*, pages 333–342. Association for Computational Linguistics.

Makoto Miwa and Mohit Bansal. 2016. End-to-End Relation Extraction using LSTMs on Sequences and Tree Structures. In *Proceedings of the 54th Annual Meeting of the Association for Computational Linguistics (Volume 1: Long Papers)*, pages 1105–1116. Association for Computational Linguistics.

Abiola Obamuyide and Andreas Vlachos. 2018. Zero-shot relation classification as textual entailment. In *Proceedings of the First Workshop on Fact Extraction and VERification (FEVER)*, pages 72–78.

Jeffrey Pennington, Richard Socher, and Christopher Manning. 2014. Glove: Global Vectors for Word Representation. In *Proceedings of the 2014 Conference on Empirical Methods in Natural Language Processing (EMNLP)*, pages 1532–1543. Association for Computational Linguistics.

Pranav Rajpurkar, Robin Jia, and Percy Liang. 2018. Know What You Don't Know: Unanswerable Questions for SQuAD. In *Proceedings of the 56th Annual Meeting of the Association for Computational Linguistics (Volume 2: Short Papers)*, pages 784–789. Association for Computational Linguistics.

Sebastian Riedel, Limin Yao, Andrew McCallum, and Benjamin M. Marlin. 2013. Relation Extraction with Matrix Factorization and Universal Schemas.

In *Proceedings of the 2013 Conference of the North American Chapter of the Association for Computational Linguistics: Human Language Technologies*, pages 74–84. Association for Computational Linguistics.

Tim Rocktäschel, Sameer Singh, and Sebastian Riedel. 2015. Injecting logical background knowledge into embeddings for relation extraction. In *Proceedings of the 2015 Conference of the North American Chapter of the Association for Computational Linguistics: Human Language Technologies*, pages 1119–1129.

Amrita Saha, Rahul Aralikatte, Mitesh M. Khapra, and Karthik Sankaranarayanan. 2018. DuoRC: Towards Complex Language Understanding with Paraphrased Reading Comprehension. In *Proceedings of the 56th Annual Meeting of the Association for Computational Linguistics (Volume 1: Long Papers)*, pages 1683–1693. Association for Computational Linguistics.

Minjoon Seo, Aniruddha Kembhavi, Ali Farhadi, and Hannaneh Hajishirzi. 2016. Bidirectional attention flow for machine comprehension. *arXiv preprint arXiv:1611.01603*.

Adam Trischler, Tong Wang, Xingdi Yuan, Justin Harris, Alessandro Sordoni, Philip Bachman, and Kaheer Suleman. 2017. NewsQA: A Machine Comprehension Dataset. In *Proceedings of the 2nd Workshop on Representation Learning for NLP*, pages 191–200. Association for Computational Linguistics.

Patrick Verga, David Belanger, Emma Strubell, Benjamin Roth, and Andrew McCallum. 2016. Multilingual Relation Extraction using Compositional Universal Schema. In *Proceedings of the 2016 Conference of the North American Chapter of the Association for Computational Linguistics: Human Language Technologies*, pages 886–896. Association for Computational Linguistics.

Denny Vrandečić and Markus Krötzsch. 2014. Wikidata: a free collaborative knowledge base.

Alexander Yates, Michele Banko, Matthew Broadhead, Michael J Cafarella, Oren Etzioni, and Stephen Soderland. 2007. TextRunner: Open Information Extraction on the Web. In *HLT-NAACL (Demonstrations)*, pages 25–26.

Dmitry Zelenko, Chinatsu Aone, and Anthony Richardella. 2003. Kernel methods for relation extraction. *Journal of Machine Learning Research*, 3:1083–1106.

GuoDong Zhou, Jian Su, Jie Zhang, and Min Zhang. 2005. Exploring Various Knowledge in Relation Extraction. In *Proceedings of the 43rd Annual Meeting of the Association for Computational Linguistics (ACL'05)*, pages 427–434. Association for Computational Linguistics.

Zero-Shot Cross-lingual Name Retrieval for Low-Resource Languages

Kevin Blissett[*], **Heng Ji**[†‡]

[*] Computer Science Department, Rensselaer Polytechnic Institute
blissk@rpi.edu
[†] Department of Computer Science [‡] Department of Electrical and Computer Engineering
University of Illinois at Urbana-Champaign
hengji@illinois.edu

Abstract

In this paper we address a challenging cross-lingual name retrieval task. Given an English named entity query, we aim to find all name mentions in documents in low-resource languages. We present a novel method which relies on zero annotation or resources from the target language. By leveraging freely available, cross-lingual resources and a small amount of training data from another language, we are able to perform name retrieval on a new language without any additional training data. Our method proceeds in a multi-step process: first, we pre-train a language-independent orthographic encoder using Wikipedia inter-lingual links from dozens of languages. Next, we gather user expectations about important entities in an English comparable document and compare those expected entities with actual spans of the target language text in order to perform name finding. Our method shows 11.6% absolute F-score improvement over state-of-the-art methods.

1 Introduction

Disasters happen all over the world, not just in the places where language experts are readily available. During these disasters, governments and aid organizations must be able to rapidly understand what is being said online and reported in the news. Extracting such information requires tools that can perform basic Natural Language Processing (NLP) tasks on all languages without language-specific annotations.

Finding names in documents is a critical part of extracting structured information from unstructured natural language documents. Therefore, it is an essential component for applications including Information Retrieval, Question Answering and Knowledge Base Population. Typical name finding methods rely on supervised learning and re-quire training data from the target language. This makes name finding on languages that do not have annotated data available a useful and challenging problem.

We propose a novel approach for name finding that requires no training data from the language to be tagged. Our approach is based on the observation that the mentions of named entities often "look the same" across languages, even when those languages are not related. This "looks the same" relation is difficult to capture with traditional metrics such as edit distance and soundex. Nevertheless, when combined with user expectations about which entities will likely appear in a particular text, this relation provides enough information to identify named entities across the world's languages. To illustrate, let's consider the sentence, "Bill Gates and Paul Allen founded Microsoft in 1975.", as translated into Hindi and romanized by Google Translate[1]: "bil gets aur pol elan ne 1975 mein maikrosopht kee sthaapana kee." Even without any knowledge of Hindi, an English speaker told to identify the entities "Bill Gates", "Paul Allen", and "Microsoft" can easily match them to the spans "bil gets", "pol elan" and "maikrosopht" respectively by relying on this relation. By leveraging pre-training in a cross-lingual setting with freely available data from Wikipedia, we train a Convolutional Neural Network (CNN) model (Krizhevsky et al., 2012) that captures the orthographic similarity of names across languages. This model is trained to encode name mentions into fixed length vectors such that names which refer to the same entities across a large number of languages are close to one another in the encoding space. Because this cross-lingual encoder model is trained in a highly multilingual setting, it can serve as a metric to compare name

---

[1] https://translate.google.com/

Proceedings of the 2nd Workshop on Deep Learning Approaches for Low-Resource NLP (DeepLo), pages 275–280
Hong Kong, China, November 3, 2019. ©2019 Association for Computational Linguistics
https://doi.org/10.18653/v1/P17

similarity across all of the world's languages, not just those in the training set. We encourage the model to learn more general similarity features across languages by using a large number of training samples and languages relative to the size of the model. After learning these general similarity features, the same encoder model can be applied to new languages without any additional training.

After learning a cross-lingual model of name similarity, we ask a user to provide query names in their native language. We can also extract such queries automatically when comparable corpora are available. Using our language-independent encoder model, these query names can then be compared to spans of text in any language. When those spans of text are similar to the queries provided by the user, we tag them as names. We train a Multilayer Perceptron (MLP) to perform this comparison step using annotations from a language for which we have ground truth name tagging information. Once this comparison model is trained, it can also be applied to find names in new languages without the need for any additional training data.

2 Approach

2.1 Training the Cross-lingual Encoder

The first component of our method is an encoder model that captures name similarity across languages. We first train this model and use it to generate representations of names as fixed length vectors. To train this model, we employ the method proposed by (Blissett and Ji, 2019) which is in turn adapted from (Schroff et al., 2015). In this approach, a neural network is used to encode names into vectors such that names referring to the same entity are close to one another in the vector space. A triplet loss is employed and the negative example in each training instance is sampled dynamically in order to provide consistently challenging and informative samples to the model.

Our encoder model is trained in a cross-linguistic setting using data from Wikipedia inter-lingual links. Wikipedia inter-lingual links are strings of text in various languages which all refer to a single entity's Wikipedia page. Clusters of these strings of text which refer to the same entity in various languages are easily recoverable using Wikipedia metadata. Our model is then trained to minimize the distance between the representations of names which refer to the same entity.

We make a change from the method employed by (Blissett and Ji, 2019) by using a convolutional neural network (CNN) for our encoder rather than a recurrent model. We use a CNN in this case rather than an RNN because we find that CNNs can be trained faster, require fewer parameters, and provide similar overall performance. We apply our encoder network to character embeddings trained jointly with the rest of the encoder. We then use max pooling to derive a fixed length vector from the encoder filter values.

2.2 Applying the Encoder to Name Finding

After the language independent encoder module is trained, we freeze the model and use it as a feature extractor for encoding strings of text both from a source language and from a target unknown language.

To perform name finding, the user is asked for a set of names (queries) the system will search for in the unknown language text. Because we can use our encoder module to derive representations of these queries that are comparable across languages, we can use these encoded queries in order to find their unknown language representation among the rest of the unknown language text.

Typically Recurrent Neural Networks (RNN) are used to perform name tagging. However, recurrent networks become sensitive to the word order of the language or languages that they are used to train them. This makes an RNN unsuitable for our task since we do not know the word order of our unknown target language. Instead, we enumerate the set S of all spans of tokens of a sentence of length l

$$S = \{(i, j) \mid 0 < i < l, i \leq j < l\}$$

These substrings referred to by these spans are then encoded by our cross-lingual encoder and compared to the queries. Their similarities are computed using a simple Multi-layer Perceptron (MLP). We select an MLP since it is well suited to comparing pairs of vectors and requires relatively little training data. This MLP can be trained using labels from a language for which we have ground truth annotations. Since the encoding model providing input vectors to the MLP is language independent, the trained MLP can also be effectively applied to new, previously unseen languages as we show in our results in Table 1.

A problem arises when converting these similarity scores into a sequence of name tags. This

Query: {Nursultan Nazarbayev}

Context: ... rayiys kazakhstan nur sultan nzarbayyf , aldhy qad ...

Spans: [... , rayiys, kazakhstan, nur, ... , rayiys kazakhstan, kazakhstan nur, nur sultan, ... kazakhstan nur sultan, nur sultan nzarbayyf, ...]

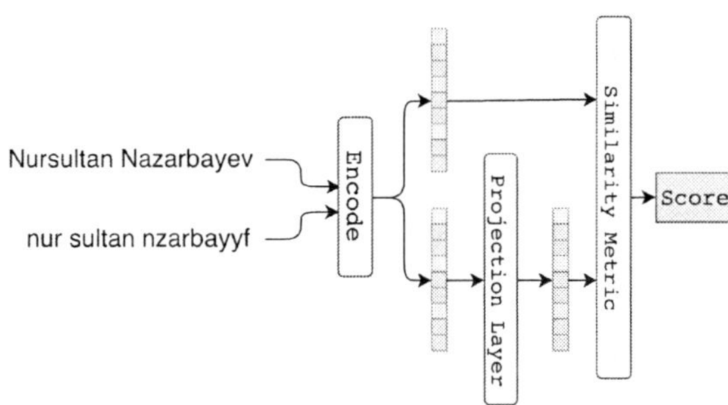

Figure 1: Overview figure for the approach. User provided queries are compared against contexts from the target language. Contexts are broken into individual spans of length 1, 2, etc. for comparison. Both queries and contexts are fed into the pre-trained cross-lingual name encoder and then their similarity is measured using a Multi-layer Perceptron.

Train – Test	Precision	Recall	F-Score
Oromo – Oromo	0.280	0.441	0.343
Oromo – Tigrinya	0.236	0.159	0.190
Tigrinya – Tigrinya	0.745	0.590	0.658
Tigrinya – Oromo	0.360	0.211	0.266

	Precision	Recall	F-Score
Tigrinya	0.429	0.002	0.004
Oromo	0.133	0.008	0.015

(a) string match baseline

	Precision	Recall	F-Score
Tigrinya	0.438	0.040	0.074
Oromo	0.190	0.232	0.209

(b) soundex-based baseline

Table 1: Performance statistics for our model (top) and baseline approaches (bottom).

problem is best illustrated with an example. Suppose our query is *nur sultan nzarbayyf* and our context sentence is *Kazakhstan's President Nursultan Nazarbayev has led the country since independence from the Soviet Union in 1991.* Our expectation is that the spans *Nursultan, Nazarbayev,* and *Nursultan Nazarbayev* will all have a high similarity to the query, but our model must select which of the spans is the best match with the query since each will lead to a different final sequence of tags (e.g. if we select the first span we will assign ['B', 'O'] to this subsequence of tags while selecting the last will lead to the subsequence ['B', 'I'], where 'B' indicates the beginning of a name, 'I' indicates inside a name and 'O' indicates outside of a name).

When faced with a situation where multiple overlapping spans have a high similarity to the query (as calculated by our MLP) we need a tiebreaker which will tell us which of the spans we ought to ultimately select. We train our model to select the correct span automatically by linking this selection directly to our model's loss function

during training.

For each token t_n in the sentence, we assign a score representing the probability that t_n should be assigned the tag 'B' and a score for the probability that the token should be tagged 'I'. To assign a score for the probability that t_n should be assigned the tag 'B', we first collect a subset of spans B_n from the set of all spans S such that the first word in the span is t_n. That is,

$$B_n = \{s_i | s_i \in S \wedge s_i[0] = n\}$$

The score assigned for the probability that t_n should be tagged 'B' is the highest score among the all the scores calculated by comparing the spans in B_n with each query in Q. That is,

$$BScore_n = \max_{s_i \in B_n, q_i \in Q} f(tokens(s_i), q_i)$$

where f represents our trainable similarity function and *tokens* retrieves the tokens referred to by the span s_i.

Likewise, the score assigned for 'I' is the highest score among spans which include this token, but in which it is not the first token. We turn these scores into probabilities using a sigmoid function and then compute the Binary Cross-Entropy Loss for the 'B' tags and the 'I' tags separately. For example,

$$l_B = -w_n(y_n \cdot \log BScore_n$$
$$+ (1 - y_n) \cdot \log (1 - BScore_n))$$

where y_n is a label indicating if t_n should be assigned the tag 'B' and w_n is a weight such that

$$w_n = \begin{cases} 1 & \text{where } y_n = 0 \\ r \cdot \frac{\text{\# 'O' labels}}{\text{\# non-'O' labels}} & \text{where } y_n = 1 \end{cases}$$

where r is a parameter of the model which can be selected to trade off between precision and recall. The number of non-'O' labels is either the number of 'B' or 'I' tags depending on which score we are currently computing. Typical values for r in our models were 0.3 to 0.5. This weighting factor allows us to compensate for the fact that positive labels are rare in the data compared to negative labels.

These two losses are then averaged together to provide our final loss for this sentence.

$$l = \frac{(l_B + l_I)}{2}$$

3 Experiments

We use for our datasets an Oromo and Tigrinya news corpus from the DARPA LORELEI[2] program. Both are low-resource languages spoken primarily in Africa for which we have human annotated ground truth annotations for evaluation. Although the languages are both members of the Afro-Asiatic language family, they differ significantly in phonology, morphology, and vocabulary and are not mutually intelligible. We will use these languages as examples of unrelated languages in order to show that our model transfers well even without training data in languages closely related to the target language.

Our dataset includes annotations for the following types of entities: person, location, and geopolitical entities. We exclude organizations since the names of organizations are commonly translated based on meaning rather than transliterated. We use the top 30 most common names in the dataset as queries to simulate a user who only

knows about the most important entities involved in some event. The model is trained on one language using several hundred sentences from that language with the top 30 entities of that language's dataset as the queries. Since the CNN calculating cross-lingual encodings is pre-trained separately and frozen, model training at this point consists only of training our MLP to calculate span similarity scores. We then test by running the model using context sentences from a separate language and the top 30 entities from that language's dataset. For this experiment, the model is scored only on how many of the query entities identified in the context sentences, ignoring other entities. We only assign credit when the tag perfectly matches the correct spans including boundaries. We use simple "BIO" tags in which the first token of a name is tagged 'B', other tokens in the name are tagged 'I', and all other tokens are tagged 'O'. Our scores show that the model can transfer across languages.

We also compare our performance to two baselines. The first baseline tags names that are exact string matches with the query entities. The second applies the New York State Identification and Intelligence System (NYSIIS) phonetic code algorithm to both queries and target language text and then tags spans of target language text that match the queries. The NYSIIS approach performs significantly better than exact string matching, but our own method outperforms both. Results are summarized in Table 1.

4 Related Work

The problem of name tagging in low-resource languages has had real attention within the last few years. For example, (Zhang et al., 2016) use a variety of non-traditional linguistic resources in order to train a name tagger for use in low-resource languages. (Pan et al., 2017) and (Tsai et al., 2016) both rely on Wikipedia to provide data for training name tagging models for all Wikipedia languages. Much work has also been pursued for systems that rely on very limited silver-standard training data annotated from the target language by non-speakers (e.g., (Ji et al., 2017)). Our method differs from the above in that we do not require our target language to be present in Wikipedia or any other additional resources.

Cross-linguistic name tagging systems have also been pursued. For example, (Curran and

---

[2]LDC2017E57 and LDC2017E58 in the LDC Catalog

Clark, 2003) develop a feature-based model using a maximum entropy tagger to achieve good results in English, Dutch and German. Because we do not assume access to capitalization which does not exist in many languages, many of their most valuable features are not suitable for our setting. (Bharadwaj et al., 2016) demonstrates cross-lingual transfer for name tagging using phonologically grounded word representations. In particular, the authors demonstrate 0-shot transfer for their name tagging system between Uzbek and Turkish. While this approach requires monolingual word embeddings in the target language and benefits greatly from capitalization information, our method makes no such assumptions.

(Ji et al., 2008) used a phonetically based method to match English person names in Mandarin audio segments. This method uses an English-to-pinyin transliteration model and then applies fuzzy matching to the transliterated output. This is similar to our work in that it also exploits the phonetics underlying the spelling of names in order to produce matches, but differs in that we use the underlying learned representation directly rather than string matching.

Our approach differs primarily from all those outlined above in that we require no resources or information about the target unknown language. We also require no additional time for training our method in order to tag new languages.

5   Conclusions and Future Work

We propose a method to perform name tagging on an unknown languages using a pre-trained cross-lingual name encoder and user expectations about what names may appear in a given dataset. Our method requires no resources from the new language to be tagged. Future work may include performing graph-based query expansion on the target entities provided by the user. This could provide coverage of additional names not specifically searched for by the user.

Acknowledgments

This research is based upon work supported in part by U.S. DARPA LORELEI Program HR0011-15-C-0115, the Office of the Director of National Intelligence (ODNI), and Intelligence Advanced Research Projects Activity (IARPA), via contract FA8650-17-C-9116. The views and conclusions contained herein are those of the authors and should not be interpreted as necessarily representing the official policies, either expressed or implied, of DARPA, ODNI, IARPA, or the U.S. Government. The U.S. Government is authorized to reproduce and distribute reprints for governmental purposes notwithstanding any copyright annotation therein.

References

Akash Bharadwaj, David Mortensen, Chris Dyer, and Jaime Carbonell. 2016. Phonologically aware neural model for named entity recognition in low resource transfer settings. In *Proceedings of the 2016 Conference on Empirical Methods in Natural Language Processing*, pages 1462–1472.

Kevin Blissett and Heng Ji. 2019. Cross-lingual NIL entity clustering for low-resource languages. In *Proceedings of the Second Workshop on Computational Models of Reference, Anaphora and Coreference*, pages 20–25.

James Curran and Stephen Clark. 2003. Language independent NER using a maximum entropy tagger. In *NAACL-HLT*.

Heng Ji, Ralph Grishman, and Wen Wang. 2008. Phonetic name matching for cross-lingual spoken sentence retrieval. In *2008 IEEE Spoken Language Technology Workshop*, pages 281–284. IEEE.

Heng Ji, Xiaoman Pan, Boliang Zhang, Joel Nothman, James Mayfield, Paul McNamee, Cash Costello, and Sydney Informatics Hub. 2017. Overview of TAC-KBP2017 13 languages entity discovery and linking. In *TAC*.

Alex Krizhevsky, Ilya Sutskever, and Geoffrey E. Hinton. 2012. Imagenet classification with deep convolutional neural networks. *Advances in Neural Information Processing Systems 25 (NIPS 2012)*.

Xiaoman Pan, Boliang Zhang, Jonathan May, Joel Nothman, Kevin Knight, and Heng Ji. 2017. Cross-lingual name tagging and linking for 282 languages. In *Proceedings of the 55th Annual Meeting of the Association for Computational Linguistics (Volume 1: Long Papers)*, volume 1, pages 1946–1958.

Florian Schroff, Dmitry Kalenichenko, and James Philbin. 2015. FaceNet: A unified embedding for face recognition and clustering. In *Proceedings of the IEEE conference on computer vision and pattern recognition*, pages 815–823.

Chen-Tse Tsai, Stephen Mayhew, and Dan Roth. 2016. Cross-lingual named entity recognition via wikification. In *Proceedings of The 20th SIGNLL Conference on Computational Natural Language Learning*, pages 219–228.

Boliang Zhang, Xiaoman Pan, Tianlu Wang, Ashish
Vaswani, Heng Ji, Kevin Knight, and Daniel Marcu.
2016. Name tagging for low-resource incident languages based on expectation-driven learning. In
NAACL-HLT, pages 249–259.

Zero-shot Dependency Parsing with Pre-trained Multilingual Sentence Representations

Ke Tran[*]
Amazon Alexa AI
trnke@amazon.com

Arianna Bisazza[†]
University of Groningen
a.bisazza@rug.nl

Abstract

We investigate whether off-the-shelf deep bidirectional sentence representations (Devlin et al., 2018) trained on a massively multilingual corpus (multilingual BERT) enable the development of an unsupervised universal dependency parser. This approach only leverages a mix of monolingual corpora in many languages and does not require any translation data making it applicable to low-resource languages. In our experiments we outperform the best CoNLL 2018 language-specific systems in all of the shared task's six truly low-resource languages while using a single system. However, we also find that (i) parsing accuracy still varies dramatically when changing the training languages and (ii) in some target languages zero-shot transfer fails under all tested conditions, raising concerns on the 'universality' of the whole approach.

1 Introduction

Pretrained sentence representations (Howard and Ruder, 2018; Radford et al., 2018; Peters et al., 2018; Devlin et al., 2018) have recently set the new state of the art in many language understanding tasks (Wang et al., 2018). An appealing avenue for this line of work is to use a mix of training data in several languages and a shared subword vocabulary leading to general-purpose multilingual representations. In turn, this opens the way to a number of promising cross-lingual transfer techniques that can address the lack of annotated data in the large majority of world languages.

In this paper, we investigate whether deep bidirectional sentence representations (Devlin et al., 2018) trained on a massively multilingual corpus

(m-BERT) allow for the development of a universal dependency parser that is able to parse sentences in a diverse range of languages without receiving *any supervision* in those language. Our parser is fully lexicalized, in contrast to a successful approach based on delexicalized parsers (Zeman and Resnik, 2008; McDonald et al., 2011). Building on the delexicalized approach, previous work employed additional features such as typological properties (Naseem et al., 2012), syntactic embeddings (Duong et al., 2015), and cross-lingual word clusters (Täckström et al., 2012) to boost parsing performance. More recent work by Ammar et al. (2016); Guo et al. (2016) requires translation data for projecting word embeddings into a shared multilingual space.

Among lexicalized systems in CoNLL18, the top system (Che et al., 2018) utilizes contextualized vectors from ELMo. However, they train each ELMo for each language in the shared task. While their approach achieves the best LAS score on average, for low resource languages, the performance of their parser lags behind other systems that do not use pre-trained models (Zeman et al., 2018). By contrast, we build our dependency parser on top of general-purpose context-dependent word representations pretrained on a multilingual corpus. This approach does not require any translation data making it applicable to truly low-resource languages (§3.3). While m-BERT's training objective is inherently monolingual (predict a word in language ℓ given its sentence context, also in language ℓ), we hypothesize that cross-lingual syntactic transfer occurs via the shared subword vocabulary and hidden layer parameters. Indeed, on the challenging task of universal dependency parsing from raw text, we outperform by a large margin the best CoNLL18 language-specific systems (Zeman et al., 2018) on the shared task's truly low-resource

---

[*] Work done prior to joining Amazon.
[†] Work done while at Leiden University. Both authors contributed equally.

Proceedings of the 2nd Workshop on Deep Learning Approaches for Low-Resource NLP (DeepLo), pages 281–288
Hong Kong, China, November 3, 2019. ©2019 Association for Computational Linguistics
https://doi.org/10.18653/v1/P17

languages while using a single system.

The effectiveness of m-BERT for cross-lingual transfer of UD parsers has also been demonstrated in concurrent work by Wu and Dredze (2019) and Kondratyuk (2019). While the former utilizes only English as the training language, the latter trains on a concatenation of all available UD treebanks. We additionally experiment with three different sets of training languages beyond English-only and make interesting observations on the resulting large, and sometimes unexplicable, variation of performance among test languages.

2 Model

We use the representations produced by BERT (Devlin et al., 2018) which is a self-attentive deep bidirectional network (Vaswani et al., 2017) trained with a masked language model objective. Specifically we use BERT's multilingual cased version[1] which was trained on the 100 languages with the largest available Wikipedias. Exponentially smoothed weighting was applied to prevent high-resource languages from dominating the training data, and a shared vocabulary of 110k shared WordPieces (Wu et al., 2016) was used. For parsing we employ a modification of the graph-based dependency parser of Dozat and Manning (2016). We use deep biaffine attention to score arcs and their label from the head to its dependent. While our label prediction model is similar to that of Dozat and Manning (2016), our arc prediction model is a globally normalized model which computes partition functions of non-projective dependency structures using Kirchhoff's Matrix-Tree Theorem (Koo et al., 2007).

Let $\mathbf{x} = w_1, w_2, \ldots, w_n$ be an input sentence of n tokens, which are given by the gold segmentation in training or by an automatic tokenizer in testing (§3.1). To obtain the m-BERT representation of $\mathbf{x}$, we first obtain a sequence $\mathbf{t} = t_1, \ldots, t_m$ of $m \geq n$ subwords from $\mathbf{x}$ using the WordPiece algorithm. Then we feed $\mathbf{t}$ to m-BERT and extract the representations $\mathbf{e}_1, \ldots, \mathbf{e}_m$ from the last layer. If word w_i is tokenized into $(t_j, \ldots, t_k)$ then the representation $\mathbf{h}_i$ of w_i is computed as the mean of $(\mathbf{e}_j, \ldots, \mathbf{e}_k)$.

The arc score is computed similar to Dozat and Manning (2016):

$$\mathbf{s}^{(\mathrm{arc})} = \mathtt{DeepBiaffine}(\mathbf{H}^{(\mathrm{arc\text{-}head})}, \mathbf{H}^{(\mathrm{arc\text{-}dep})}) \quad (1)$$

The log probability of the dependency tree $\mathbf{y}$ of $\mathbf{x}$ is given by

$$\log p(\mathbf{y} \mid \mathbf{x}) = \sum_{(h,c)\in\mathbf{y}} \mathbf{s}^{(\mathrm{arc})}[h, c] - \log Z(\mathbf{x}) \quad (2)$$

where $Z(\mathbf{x})$ is the partition function. Our objective function for predicting dependency arcs therefore is globally normalized. We compute $Z(\mathbf{x})$ via matrix determinant (Koo et al., 2007). In our experiments, we find that training with a global objective is more stable if the score $\mathbf{s}^{(\mathrm{arc})}[h, c]$ is locally normalized[2] such that $\sum_h \exp(\mathbf{s}^{(\mathrm{arc})}[h, c]) = 1$. During training, we update both m-BERT and parsing layer parameters.

3 Experiments

While most previous work on parser transfer, including the closely related (Duong et al., 2015) relies on gold tokenization and POS tags, we adopt the more realistic scenario of parsing from *raw text* (Zeman et al., 2018) and adopt the automatic sentence segmenter and tokenizer provided as baselines by the shared task organizers.

3.1 Data

We use the UDpipe-tokenized test data[3] (Straka and Straková, 2017) and the CoNLL18 official script for evaluation. Gold tokenization is only used for the training data, while POS information is never used. All of our experiments are carried out on the Universal Dependencies (UD) corpus version 2.2 (Nivre et al., 2018) for a fair comparison with previous work.

While our sentence representations are always initialized from m-BERT, we experiment with four sets of parser training (i.e. fine-tuning) languages, namely: *expEn* only English (200K words); *expLatin* a mix of four Latin-script European languages: English, Italian, Norwegian, Czech (50K each, 200K in total); *expSOV* a mix of two

---

[1] https://github.com/google-research/bert/blob/master/multilingual.md

[2] We use $\mathtt{log\_softmax}(\mathbf{s}^{(\mathrm{arc})})$ in place of $\mathbf{s}^{(\mathrm{arc})}$ in equation 2.

[3] Preprocessed data available at http://hdl.handle.net/11234/1-2899

SOV languages: Hindi and Korean (100K each, 200K in total); *expMix* a larger mix of eight languages including different language families and scripts: English, Italian, Norwegian, Czech, Russian, Hindi, Korean, Arabic (50K each, 400K in total). For high resource languages that have more than one treebank, we choose the treebank that has the best LAS score in ConLL18 for training and the lowest LAS score for zero-shot evaluation.

3.2 Training details

Similar to Dozat et al. (2017), we use a neural network output size of 400 for arc prediction and 100 for label prediction. We use the Adam optimizer with learning rate $5e^{-6}$ to update the parameters of our models. The model is evaluated every 500 updates and we stop training if the score LAS does not increase in ten consecutive validations.

3.3 Results

To put our results into perspective, we report the accuracy of the best CoNLL18 system for each language and that of the Stanford system submitted at the same evaluation (Qi et al., 2018). The latter is also based on the deep biaffine parser of Dozat and Manning (2016), it does not use ensembles and was ranked 2nd on official evaluation metric LAS[4]. Both these parsers receive supervision in most of the languages, therefore comparison to our parser is only fair for the low-resource languages where training data is not available (or negligible, i.e. less than 1K tokens).

Results for a subset of UD languages are presented in Table 1. Beside common European languages, we choose languages with different writing scripts than those presented in the parser training data. We also include SOV (*e.g.*, Korean, Persian) and VSO (*e.g.*, Arabic, Breton) languages. Parser training languages for each experiment are highlighted in grey in Table 1.

In the high resource setting, there is a considerable gap between zero-shot and supervised parsers with Swedish as an exception (slightly better than Stanford's parser and 2 points below CoNLL18). By contrast, the benefit of multilingual transfer becomes evident in the low resource setting. Here,

most CoNLL18 systems including Stanford's use knowledge of each target language to customize the parser, *e.g.*, to choose the optimal training language(s). Nevertheless, our single parser trained on the largest mix of languages (*expMix*) beats the best CoNLL18 language-specific systems on all six languages, even though three of these languages are not represented in m-BERT's training data[5]. This result highlights the advantage of multilingual pre-trained model in the truly low resource scenario.

We notice the poor performance of our parser on spoken French in comparison to other European languages. While there is sufficient amount of Wikipedia text for French, it seems that zero-shot parsing on a different domain remains a challenge even with a large pre-trained model.

4 Analysis

By varying the set of parser training languages we analyze our results with respect to two factors: parser training language diversity and word order similarity.

4.1 Training language diversity

Increasing language diversity (*expEn→expLatin* and *expLatin→expMix*) leads to improvements in most test languages, even when the total amount of training data is fixed (*expEn→expLatin*). The only exceptions are the languages for which training data is reduced (English in *expLatin*) or becomes a smaller proportion of the total training data (Czech, Italian, Norwegian in *expMix*), which confirms previous findings (Ammar et al., 2016). Swedish and Upper Sorbian being related to Norwegian and Czech respectively also lose some accuracy in *expMix*. On the other hand, newly included languages (Czech, Italian, Norwegian in *expLatin* and Arabic, Hindi, Korean, Russian in *expMix*) show the biggest improvements, which was also expected.

More interestingly, some large gains are reported for languages that are unrelated from all training languages of *expLatin*. We hypothesize that such languages (Arabic, Armenian, Hungarian) may benefit from an exposure of the parser to a

---

[4]Updated results at `https://stanfordnlp.github.io/stanfordnlp/performance.html` March, 2018

[5]This is possible because their sub-words are in BERT's vocabulary due other similar languages in training data.

target	tbk-code	m-BERT based				State of the art		#TrWrds
		expEn	*expLatin*	*expSOV*	*expMix*	Stanford	CoNLL18	
Russian	ru_syntagrus	59.53	73.13	34.44	81.91	91.20	92.48	872 K
Hindi	hi_hdtb	32.94	33.75	88.51	85.66	91.65	92.41	281 K
Italian	it_isdt	75.45	89.59	25.95	89.44	90.51	92.00	276 K
Norwegian	no_nynorsk	72.09	86.01	33.93	85.11	89.58	90.99	245 K
Czech	cs_pdt	59.97	84.91	34.31	84.36	89.63	89.63	1,173 K
Finnish	fi_tdt	50.65	61.13	40.12	62.29	86.33	88.73	163 K
Persian	fa_seraji	44.34	56.39	24.77	56.92	86.55	88.11	121 K
Korean	ko_kaist	33.67	38.87	84.39	81.73	86.58	86.91	296 K
English	en_ewt	84.64	82.38	30.03	81.65	83.80	84.57	205 K
Urdu	ur_udtb	23.46	23.94	65.21	63.06	82.58	83.39	109 K
Japanese	ja_gsd	12.92	12.65	19.25	24.10	78.48	83.11	162 K
Hungarian	hu_szeged	52.72	61.11	39.65	61.11	78.58	82.66	20 K
German	de_gsd	68.30	70.93	36.30	70.93	79.17	80.36	264 K
Swedish	sv_pud	76.02	78.71	37.58	78.70	78.39	80.35	– K
Arabic	ar_padt	34.55	50.20	12.26	68.20	76.99	77.06	224 K
French	fr_spoken	54.12	59.70	16.06	59.54	69.56	75.78	15 K
Vietnamese	vi_vtb	29.72	30.09	14.13	29.71	47.56	55.22	20 K
Tamil	ta_ttb	18.09	25.79	29.64	32.78	–	–	5 K
Telugu	te_mtg	54.47	63.06	61.68	64.03	–	–	5 K
Faroese*	fo_oft	58.28	61.71	36.27	**61.98**	41.54	49.43	0 K
Upper Sorbian*	hsb_ufal	36.66	**49.90**	23.90	49.74	23.61	46.42	0 K
Breton	br_keb	45.16	51.85	22.49	**52.62**	11.25	38.64	0 K
Armenian	hy_armtdp	40.20	55.44	41.91	**58.95**	31.47	37.01	1 K
Kazakh	kk_ktb	33.56	40.18	40.18	**44.56**	26.25	31.93	1 K
Buryat*	bxr_bdt	19.19	20.90	22.94	**23.11**	12.47	19.53	0 K
avg(lowRes)		39.41	47.26	31.28	48.45	24.43	37.16	

Table 1: LAS scores of our parser in the raw text setup. Languages not in m-BERT's training corpus are marked with *. SVO and SOV languages are indicated by purple and green respectively. Stanford and CoNLL18's best submitted systems are provided as representative state-of-the-art supervised systems. #TrWrds = Total training data made available at CoNLL18. The amount of training used in each experiment is specified in §3.1. Training languages for each experiment are highlighted in grey.

more diverse set of word orders (§4.2). For instance, Arabic being head initial is closer to Italian than to English in terms of word order.

Actual language relatedness does not always play a clear role: For instance, Upper Sorbian seems to benefit largely from its closeness to Czech in *expLatin* and *expMix*, while Faroese (related to Norwegian) does not improve as much.

In summary, language diversity in training is clearly a great asset. However, there is a large variation in gains among test languages, for which language family relatedness can only offer a partial explanation.

4.2 Training language typology

Training on languages with similar typological features has been shown beneficial for parsing target languages in the delexicalized setup. In particular, word order similarities have been proved beneficial to select source languages for parsing model transfer (Naseem et al., 2012; Duong et al., 2015).

Indeed, when Hindi and Korean are presented in *expSOV*, we report better LAS scores in various SOV languages (Japanese, Tamil, Urdu, Buryat) however some other SOV languages (Persian and Armenian) perform much worse than in *expLatin* showing that word order is not a reliable criterion for training language selection.

Given these observations, we construct our largest training data (*expMix*) by merging all the languages of *expEn*, *expLatin*, and *expSOV* and adding two more languages with diverse word order profiles for which large treebanks exist, namely Russian and Arabic.

Concurrently to this work, Lin et al. (2019) have proposed an automatic method to choose the optimal transfer languages in various tasks including parsing, based on a variety of typological but also data-dependent features. We leave adoption of their method to future work.[6]

---

[6]Unfortunately at the time of writing we have not yet managed to use their released implementation.

4.3 Towards explaining transfer performance

Even when keeping the training languages fixed, for instance in *expMix*, we observe a large variation of zero-shot parsing transfer accuracy among test languages which does not often correlate with supervised parsing accuracy. As an attempt to explain this variation we look at the overlap of test vocabulary with (i) parser's training data vocabulary τ and (ii) m-BERT's training data vocabulary. Because m-BERT uses a subword vocabulary that also includes characters we resort to measuring the unsegmented word score η:

$$\tau = 100 \times |\text{type\_w}(D_\text{test}) \cap \text{type\_w}(D_\text{train})|/|\text{type\_w}(D_\text{test})|$$

$$\eta = 100 \times |\text{token\_g}(D_\text{test})|/|\text{token\_w}(D_\text{test})|$$

where $\text{type\_w}(D)$ and $\text{token\_w}(D)$ are sets of WordPieces types and tokens in dataset D respectively, and $\text{token\_g}(D)$ is the set of gold tokens in D before applying WordPieces. A higher η indicates a less segmented text.

To account for typological features, we also plot the average syntactic similarity $\bar{\sigma}$ of each test language to the eight *expSOV* training languages as computed by the URIEL database[7] (Littell et al., 2017).

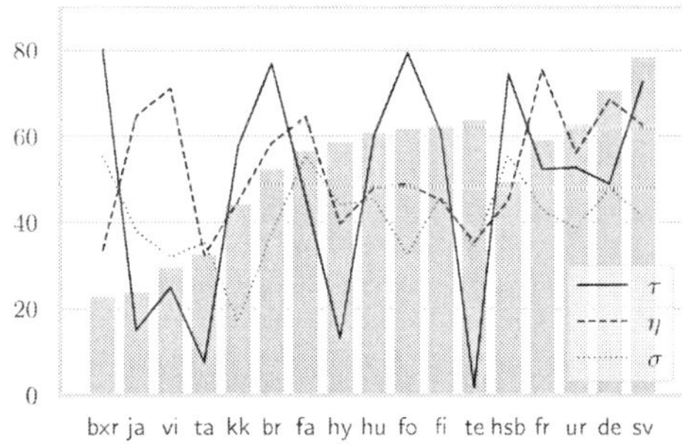

Figure 1: Relationship between parsing accuracy (*expMix*), parser training-test vocabulary overlap τ, m-BERT unsegmented word score η, and average typological syntactic similarity $\bar{\sigma}$. Purple bar indicates there is no language that belongs to the same family presented in training data. Languages in the training set of *expMix* are not shown.

We observe a correlation between LAS, η and τ for test languages that have a relative in the training data, like Urdu and Hindi. For test languages

that belong to a different family than all training languages, no correlation appears. A similar observation is also reported by Pires et al. (2019): namely, they find that the performance of cross-lingual named entity recognition with m-BERT is largely independent of vocabulary overlap.

Although typological features have been shown to be useful when incorporated into the parser (Naseem et al., 2012; Ammar et al., 2016), we do not find a clear correlation between $\bar{\sigma}$ and LAS in our setup. Thus none of our investigated factors can explain transfer performance in a systematic way.

4.4 Language outliers

While massively pre-trained language models promise a more inclusive future for NLP, we find it important to note that cross-lingual transfer performs very badly for some languages.

For instance, in our experiments, Japanese and Vietnamese stand out as strikingly negative outliers. Wu and Dredze (2019) also report a very low performance on Japanese in their zero-shot dependency parsing experiments.[8] In (Lin et al., 2019) Japanese is completely excluded from the parsing experiments because of unstable results. Japanese and Vietnamese are *language isolates* in an NLP sense, meaning that they do not enjoy the presence of a closely related language among the high-resourced training languages.[9] For this class of languages, transfer performance is overall very inconsistent and hard to explain.

	UDpipe	Gold
ko→ja	14.96	20.04
ja→ko	37.44	37.45

Table 2: LAS scores when transferring between Korean and Japanese in two tokenization conditions.

The case of Japanese is particularly interesting for its relation to Korean. Family relatedness between these two languages is very controversial but their syntactic features are extremely similar. To put our

---

[7]Specifically, we compute $1 - d$ where d is the precomputed *syntactic* distance in lang2vec.

[8]They do not report parsing results for Vietnamese.

[9]The original definition of language isolate in linguistics is actually stronger: "a language that has no known relatives, that is, that has no demonstrable phylogenetic relationship with any other language" (Campbell, 2017)

parser in optimal transfer conditions, we perform one last experiment by training only on Korean (all available data) and testing on Japanese, and vice versa. As shown in Table 2, Japanese performance becomes even lower in this setup. We can also see that transferring in the opposite direction leads to a much better result, despite the fact that state-of-the-art supervised systems in these two languages achieve similar results (Japanese: 83.11, Korean: 86.92 by the best CoNLL18 systems). To rule out the impact of unsupervised sentence and token segmentation, which may be performing particularly poorly on some languages, we retrain the parser with gold segmentation and find that it explains only a small part of the gap.

While Pires et al. (2019) hypothesize word order is the main culprit for the poor zero-shot performance for Japanese when transferring a POS-tagger from English, our experiments with Korean and Japanese show a different picture.

5 Conclusions

We have built a Universal Dependency parser on top of deep bidirectional sentence representations pre-trained on a massively multilingual corpus (m-BERT) without any need for parallel data, tree-banks or other linguistic resources in the test languages.

Evaluated in the challenging scenario of parsing from raw text, our best parser trained on a mix of languages representing both language family and word order diversity outperforms the best CoNLL18 language-specific systems on the six truly low-resource languages presented at the shared task.

Our experiments show that language diversity in the training treebank is a great asset for transfer to low-resource languages. Moreover, the massively multilingual nature of m-BERT does not neutralize the impact of transfer languages on parsing accuracy, which is only partially explained by language relatedness and word order similarity.

Finally we have raised the issue of language outliers that perform very poorly in all our tested conditions and that, given our analysis, are unlikely to benefit even from automatic methods of transfer language selection (Lin et al., 2019).

Acknowledgements

Arianna Bisazza was funded by the the Netherlands Organization for Scientific Research (NWO) under project number 639.021.646.

References

Joakim Nivre et al. 2018. Universal dependencies 2.2. LINDAT/CLARIN digital library at the Institute of Formal and Applied Linguistics (ÚFAL), Faculty of Mathematics and Physics, Charles University.

Waleed Ammar, George Mulcaire, Miguel Ballesteros, Chris Dyer, and Noah Smith. 2016. Many languages, one parser. *Transactions of the Association for Computational Linguistics*, 4:431–444.

Lyle Campbell. 2017. *"Language Isolates"*. Routledge.

Wanxiang Che, Yijia Liu, Yuxuan Wang, Bo Zheng, and Ting Liu. 2018. Towards better UD parsing: Deep contextualized word embeddings, ensemble, and treebank concatenation. In *Proceedings of the CoNLL 2018 Shared Task: Multilingual Parsing from Raw Text to Universal Dependencies*, pages 55–64, Brussels, Belgium. Association for Computational Linguistics.

Jacob Devlin, Ming-Wei Chang, Kenton Lee, and Kristina Toutanova. 2018. BERT: Pre-training of Deep Bidirectional Transformers for Language Understanding. *arXiv e-prints*, page arXiv:1810.04805.

Timothy Dozat and Christopher D. Manning. 2016. Deep biaffine attention for neural dependency parsing. *CoRR*, abs/1611.01734.

Timothy Dozat, Peng Qi, and Christopher D. Manning. 2017. Stanford's graph-based neural dependency parser at the conll 2017 shared task. In *Proceedings of the CoNLL 2017 Shared Task: Multilingual Parsing from Raw Text to Universal Dependencies*, pages 20–30. Association for Computational Linguistics.

Long Duong, Trevor Cohn, Steven Bird, and Paul Cook. 2015. Cross-lingual transfer for unsupervised dependency parsing without parallel data. In *Proceedings of the Nineteenth Conference on Computational Natural Language Learning*, pages 113–122, Beijing, China. Association for Computational Linguistics.

Jiang Guo, Wanxiang Che, David Yarowsky, Haifeng Wang, and Ting Liu. 2016. A representation learning framework for multi-source transfer parsing. In *Proceedings of the Thirtieth AAAI Conference on Artificial Intelligence*, AAAI'16, pages 2734–2740. AAAI Press.

Jeremy Howard and Sebastian Ruder. 2018. Universal language model fine-tuning for text classification. In *Proceedings of the 56th Annual Meeting of the Association for Computational Linguistics (Volume 1: Long Papers)*, pages 328–339, Melbourne, Australia. Association for Computational Linguistics.

Daniel Kondratyuk. 2019. 75 languages, 1 model: Parsing universal dependencies universally. *CoRR*, abs/1904.02099.

Terry Koo, Amir Globerson, Xavier Carreras, and Michael Collins. 2007. Structured prediction models via the matrix-tree theorem. In *Proceedings of the 2007 Joint Conference on Empirical Methods in Natural Language Processing and Computational Natural Language Learning (EMNLP-CoNLL)*, pages 141–150, Prague, Czech Republic. Association for Computational Linguistics.

Yu-Hsiang Lin, Chian-Yu Chen, Jean Lee, Zirui Li, Yuyan Zhang, Mengzhou Xia, Shruti Rijhwani, Junxian He, Zhisong Zhang, Xuezhe Ma, Antonios Anastasopoulos, Patrick Littell, and Graham Neubig. 2019. Choosing transfer languages for cross-lingual learning. In *Proceedings of the 57th Annual Meeting of the Association for Computational Linguistics*, pages 3125–3135, Florence, Italy. Association for Computational Linguistics.

Patrick Littell, David R Mortensen, Ke Lin, Katherine Kairis, Carlisle Turner, and Lori Levin. 2017. Uriel and lang2vec: Representing languages as typological, geographical, and phylogenetic vectors. In *Proceedings of the 15th Conference of the European Chapter of the Association for Computational Linguistics: Volume 2, Short Papers*, volume 2, pages 8–14.

Ryan McDonald, Slav Petrov, and Keith Hall. 2011. Multi-source transfer of delexicalized dependency parsers. In *Proceedings of the 2011 Conference on Empirical Methods in Natural Language Processing*, pages 62–72, Edinburgh, Scotland, UK. Association for Computational Linguistics.

Tahira Naseem, Regina Barzilay, and Amir Globerson. 2012. Selective sharing for multilingual dependency parsing. In *Proceedings of the 50th Annual Meeting of the Association for Computational Linguistics (Volume 1: Long Papers)*, pages 629–637, Jeju Island, Korea. Association for Computational Linguistics.

Matthew Peters, Mark Neumann, Mohit Iyyer, Matt Gardner, Christopher Clark, Kenton Lee, and Luke Zettlemoyer. 2018. Deep contextualized word representations. In *Proceedings of the 2018 Conference of the North American Chapter of the Association for Computational Linguistics: Human Language Technologies, Volume 1 (Long Papers)*, pages 2227–2237, New Orleans, Louisiana. Association for Computational Linguistics.

Telmo Pires, Eva Schlinger, and Dan Garrette. 2019. How multilingual is multilingual BERT? In *Proceedings of the 57th Annual Meeting of the Association for Computational Linguistics*, pages 4996–5001, Florence, Italy. Association for Computational Linguistics.

Peng Qi, Timothy Dozat, Yuhao Zhang, and Christopher D. Manning. 2018. Universal dependency parsing from scratch. In *Proceedings of the CoNLL 2018 Shared Task: Multilingual Parsing from Raw Text to Universal Dependencies*, pages 160–170, Brussels, Belgium. Association for Computational Linguistics.

Alec Radford, Karthik Narasimhan, Tim Salimans, and Ilya Sutskever. 2018. Improving language understanding with unsupervised learning. Technical report, OpenAI.

Milan Straka and Jana Straková. 2017. Tokenizing, pos tagging, lemmatizing and parsing ud 2.0 with udpipe. In *Proceedings of the CoNLL 2017 Shared Task: Multilingual Parsing from Raw Text to Universal Dependencies*, pages 88–99, Vancouver, Canada. Association for Computational Linguistics.

Oscar Täckström, Ryan McDonald, and Jakob Uszkoreit. 2012. Cross-lingual word clusters for direct transfer of linguistic structure. In *Proceedings of the 2012 Conference of the North American Chapter of the Association for Computational Linguistics: Human Language Technologies*, pages 477–487. Association for Computational Linguistics.

Ashish Vaswani, Noam Shazeer, Niki Parmar, Jakob Uszkoreit, Llion Jones, Aidan N Gomez, Ł ukasz Kaiser, and Illia Polosukhin. 2017. Attention is all you need. In I. Guyon, U. V. Luxburg, S. Bengio, H. Wallach, R. Fergus, S. Vishwanathan, and R. Garnett, editors, *Advances in Neural Information Processing Systems 30*, pages 5998–6008. Curran Associates, Inc.

Alex Wang, Amanpreet Singh, Julian Michael, Felix Hill, Omer Levy, and Samuel Bowman. 2018. Glue: A multi-task benchmark and analysis platform for natural language understanding. In *Proceedings of the 2018 EMNLP Workshop BlackboxNLP: Analyzing and Interpreting Neural Networks for NLP*, pages 353–355, Brussels, Belgium. Association for Computational Linguistics.

Shijie Wu and Mark Dredze. 2019. Beto, bentz, becas: The surprising cross-lingual effectiveness of BERT. *CoRR*, abs/1904.09077.

Yonghui Wu, Mike Schuster, Zhifeng Chen, Quoc V. Le, Mohammad Norouzi, Wolfgang Macherey, Maxim Krikun, Yuan Cao, Qin Gao, Klaus Macherey, Jeff Klingner, Apurva Shah, Melvin Johnson, Xiaobing Liu, Lukasz Kaiser, Stephan Gouws, Yoshikiyo Kato, Taku Kudo, Hideto Kazawa, Keith Stevens, George Kurian, Nishant Patil, Wei Wang, Cliff Young, Jason Smith, Jason Riesa, Alex Rudnick, Oriol Vinyals, Greg Corrado, Macduff Hughes, and Jeffrey Dean. 2016. Google's neural machine translation system: Bridging the gap between human and machine translation. *CoRR*, abs/1609.08144.

Daniel Zeman, Hajič Jan, Martin Popel, Martin Potthast, Milan Straka, Filip Ginter, Joakim Nivre, and Slav Petrov. 2018. Conll 2018 shared task: Multilingual parsing from raw text to universal dependencies. In *Proceedings of the CoNLL 2018 Shared Task: Multilingual Parsing from Raw Text to Universal Dependencies*, pages 1–21. Association for Computational Linguistics.

Daniel Zeman and Philip Resnik. 2008. Cross-language

parser adaptation between related languages. In *Proceedings of the IJCNLP-08 Workshop on NLP for Less Privileged Languages*.

Author Index

Association for Computational Linguistics
209 N. Eighth Street
Stroudsburg, Pennsylvania 18360

ISBN 978-1-7138-0077-4